Prehistoric Humans
in Film and Television

ALSO BY MICHAEL KLOSSNER

*The Europe of 1500–1815 on Film and Television:
A Worldwide Filmography of Over
2550 Works, 1895 through 2000*
(McFarland, 2002)

Prehistoric Humans in Film and Television

581 Dramas, Comedies and Documentaries, 1905–2004

Michael Klossner

McFarland & Company, Inc., Publishers
Jefferson, North Carolina, and London

LIBRARY OF CONGRESS CATALOGUING-IN-PUBLICATION DATA

Klossner, Michael.
Prehistoric humans in film and television : 581 dramas,
comedies and documentaries, 1905–2004 /
Michael Klossner.
p. cm.
Includes bibliographical references and index.

ISBN 0-7864-2215-7 (softcover : 50# alkaline paper)

1. Prehistoric peoples in motion pictures.
2. Prehistoric peoples on television.
3. Motion pictures — Catalogs.
4. Television programs — Catalogs.
I. Title.
PN1995.9.P675K55   2006   791.43'652 — dc22   2005013990

British Library cataloguing data are available

©2006 Michael Klossner. All rights reserved

*No part of this book may be reproduced or transmitted in any form
or by any means, electronic or mechanical, including photocopying
or recording, or by any information storage and retrieval system,
without permission in writing from the publisher.*

Cover photograph from *Dawn of Man: The Story of Human Evolution* (2000)

Manufactured in the United States of America

*McFarland & Company, Inc., Publishers
Box 611, Jefferson, North Carolina 28640
www.mcfarlandpub.com*

To caveladies Mae Marsh, Carole Landis,
Raquel Welch, Martine Beswick and Rae Dawn Chong,
and to Greg Martell, "one terrific caveman."

Contents

Preface 1

I. Fictional Works in Prehistorical Settings 7
II. Documentaries 167
III. Fictional Works in Historical, Modern and Extraterrestrial Settings 211

Appendix A: Misleading Titles, Unknown Contents, Aborted and Proposed Projects 279

Appendix B: Post-Apocalypse Primitives in Film and Television 285

Appendix C: Outstanding Performances as Prehistoric Characters 287

Appendix D: The Creationist Challenge: Productions That Question the Existence of Prehistoric Humans 288

Bibliography 291

Index 293

Preface

"We wouldn't last ten minutes in their world."
— Jean-Jacques Annaud, director of *Quest for Fire*

Joss Whedon, producer of *Buffy the Vampire Slayer*, once said, "I think it's important for academics to study popular culture, even if the thing being studied is ridiculous." So far no academic has taken up his challenge by producing a book about caveman movies. This book is by a fan.

Part I of this volume covers fictional works (both film and television) set in human prehistory. (This part includes stories in which modern people dream about prehistory, such as *Journey to the Beginning of Time* (1955), even though such stories are technically set entirely in modern times.) Part II covers documentaries about prehistoric humans. Part III covers fictional works in which prehistoric people, or creatures described as "ape men" or "missing links," somehow exist in historical periods—from the advent of civilization up to the present—or in extraterrestrial settings.

Several categories of films and television programs are omitted. Those about biblical prehistory—telling, for instance, the stories of Adam and Eve, Noah, or the Tower of Babel—are excluded. *Blue Paradise* (1982), which places Adam and Eve in a setting similar to other prehistoric films, is the one exception. However, documentaries which examine the possible historical facts behind the biblical stories are included in Part II. Creationist documentaries which claim that the biblical stories are literally true are briefly noted under in Appendix D.

Sword-and-sorcery films, such as *Conan the Barbarian* (1982), are often set in a mythical period prior to the rise of the civilizations known to history. These films are omitted from this list, except for a few works in Part III, such as *Conan the Destroyer* and *Ator the Blade Master* (both 1984), which include prehistoric people. The few films that place fictitious prehistoric civilizations such as Atlantis and Mu in prehistory are included. The more numerous films showing either a functioning Atlantis or the ruins of Atlantis in historical or modern periods are noted briefly in the entry for *The Giant of Metropolis* (1962), one of the films about a prehistoric Atlantis. Documentaries on Atlantis are briefly noted in Part II under *Calypso's Search for Atlantis* (1978). The many Hindu mythological films made by the enormous Indian film industry are excluded even when they are set in the earliest ages.

Films and television programs about the Abominable Snowman (or Yeti) and Bigfoot (or Sasquatch) are omitted, even though both creatures are supposed to date back to prehistory. Films in which scientists revive prehistoric people in the modern world, such as *Iceman* (1984), are included; films in which scientists create animalistic humans who may resemble prehistoric people but who never lived in prehistory, such as *Island of Lost Souls* (1932) and *The Island of Dr. Moreau* (1977, 1996), are not.

Excluded from Part III are works about primitive peoples of modern times. Some stories have been filmed several times, sometimes including prehistoric characters, sometimes present-day primitives. Thus, 1925 and 1998 films of Arthur Conan Doyle's *The Lost World*, as well as a 1999 TV film, a 1999–2002 TV series and a 2001 miniseries of the same story, are included because they involve either prehistoric humans or "ape men," but two other films of the story, made in 1960 and 1992, are omitted because they feature only modern "natives." The dozens of Tarzan films and TV series are excluded, as is the *Survivor* TV series, in which modern people play at being primitive and act out what John Powers, in his 2004 book *Sore Winners*, called "faux Darwinian games of selection, extinction, survival and victory."

Films set after the fall of modern civilization are excluded altogether if the characters live in the wreckage of the destroyed civilization. Post-Apocalypse films in which people live like prehistoric humans are briefly noted in Appendix B. For instance, the first two *Mad Max* films (*Mad Max*, 1979, and *The Road Warrior*, 1981) are omitted, but the third film in the series, *Mad Max Beyond Thunderdome* (1985), is in Appendix B because of the desert children who form a new society not dependent on the remnants of the old world. A complicated case is Roger Corman's *Teenage Caveman* (1958), which is set among primitive people after a nuclear war; the film's narrator says that the story is set in the past after an advanced prehistoric civilization destroyed itself, so the film is in Part I, not the appendix.

The film industry was launched only a few decades after scientists began to study prehistoric humans and the newly emerging popular press began to popularize scientific ideas about prehistory. Ever since, four tendencies have jostled each other in the history of filmed prehistory: attempts at realism, comedy, fantasy-adventure and erotica. Often these tendencies are mixed in the same film.

Most attempts at realism in prehistoric films are not really accurate. "Realism" in this case means a style and an intention, not true realism. The filmmakers wish to present some facts about prehistory as they understand them. Ignorance and errors by filmmakers and conscious compromises they make to tell a story mean that the result is often far from a true picture of the distant past. The realistic impulse began in 1912 when D.W. Griffith, then perhaps the most important director in the world, made *Man's Genesis*. Significantly, when Griffith made a sequel, *Brute Force* (1914), he felt compelled to add not only comedy but also a grossly unrealistic dinosaur threatening the cave people. Subsequent projects which attempted a degree of realism are *One Million B.C.* (1940), which mixed realistic details with dinosaurs; *Prehistoric Women* (1950); Roger Corman's surprisingly serious *Teenage Caveman* (1958); *Colossus of the Stone Age* (1962), a prehistoric peplum from Italy; the *Dawn of Man* sequence in *2001: A Space Odyssey*; Hammer Film's final caveman movie *Creatures the World Forgot* (1971); *The Tribe*, a 1974 U.S. TV film; and the children's TV series *Korg: 70,000 B.C.* (1974-75).

The 1980s saw the first attempts at a high degree of scientific realism, first in *Quest for Fire* (1981), then *Iceman* (1984) and *Clan of the Cave Bear* (1986). However, *Quest for Fire* was seriously inaccurate in several respects, especially its depiction of Neanderthals, while *Iceman* presented a realistic prehistoric man but revived him in the modern world. *Altered States* (1980) had a convincing primal man, even though he roamed the streets of Cambridge, Mass. *Clan of the Cave Bear*, the most accurate movie ever made about prehistoric people, was a critical and box office flop. *Missing Link* (1988), a realistic depiction of early hominids, was little noted by critics or audiences. The Italians contributed a semirealistic film, *Ironmaster* (1982). Since the 1980s, only a few relatively realistic films about prehistory have appeared: the first segment of *Being Human* (1993); Japan's *Peking Man* (1997), which adopted the *Iceman* strategy by showing convincing prehistoric humans in the modern world; and the human-centered scenes of two animated talking-animal fantasies, *Ice Age* (2002) and *Brother Bear* (2003).

Filmmakers have often felt compelled to add either dinosaurs or tribal wars to prehistoric movies. Dinosaurs of course never coexisted with humans, and prehistoric wars were rare because early human groups usually avoided each other. The abundant violence in even the relatively realistic caveman movies is perhaps the most common blunder in those films. Another error is the assumption that cavemen existed in the Western Hemisphere. Four of the films about revived cavemen in the modern world are set in the West Indies (*Dinosaurus!*, 1960), Alaska (*Iceman*), California (*Encino Man*, 1992), and the desert Southwest (*Eegah!*, 1962). In fact only anatomically modern humans with excellent Arctic survival skills could reach the Western Hemisphere.

In the early twentieth century, as soon as ordinary people learned about scientists' concepts of prehistoric man, they decided that cavemen were funny. Comedy dominated early films about prehistory. In 1914, the year Griffith released his second serious caveman film, *Brute Force*, Charlie Chaplin made *His Prehistoric Past*, which directly lampooned Griffith's films. This was followed by six stop-motion comedies by Willis O'Brien, all released in 1917; many other short caveman cartoons of the 1920s and 1930s; Buster Keaton's *The Three Ages* (1923); Laurel and Hardy's *Flying Elephants* (1928); and the Three Stooges' *I'm a Monkey's Uncle* (1948). After a mirthless spell in the 1950s came the animated television series *The Flintstones* (1960–66) and its many follow-up series and specials; *Carry on Cleo* (1964); TV's *It's About Time* (1966–67); an Italian series of three caveman sex comedies beginning with *When Women Had Tails* (1970); *The 2,000 Year Old Man* (1975); *B.C. Rock* (1979); *Caveman* (1981); *Cavegirl* (1985); *The Flintstones* live action film (1994) and a sequel (2000); *Gogs* (1996–98) and *Cavegirl* (2002), both on British TV; and the animated comedies *Ice Age* and *Brother Bear*, both with humans playing second fiddle to talking animals.

The prehistoric adventure-fantasy film got off to a strong start in 1940 with *One Million B.C.*, a film which owed much to *King Kong* and *The Most Dangerous Game* from the early 1930s. *One Million Years B.C.* (1966), a remake of the 1940 movie, was so splendidly done that it seems other filmmakers hesitated to emulate it. Hammer made only one other film of the same type, *When Dinosaurs Ruled the Earth* (1970), before turning to realism with *Creatures the World Forgot*. Hammer's rival Amicus made three middle-budget Lost World adventures: *The Land That Time Forgot*, *At the Earth's Core* and *The People That Time Forgot* (1975–77). Ray Harryhausen included a troglodyte in *Sinbad and the Eye of the Tiger* (1977), and *Fire and Ice* (1983) presented an animated fantasy influenced by the art of Frank Frazetta.

Brief notes on a few pornographic films are found in this list. More prehistoric pornography no doubt exists, but I am not sorry that I failed to find it. The mainstream caveman film has always provided filmmakers with an excuse to showcase women's bodies. In 1912, brief glimpses of Mae Marsh's 16-year-old legs through her long grass skirt in *Man's Genesis* were considered mildly controversial. Hardly more than a decade later, a bevy of bare-legged prehistoric flappers graced *Flying Elephants*. Cavegirls' costumes proceeded through the miniskirt in 1940 (*One Million B.C.*) to the bikini in 1966 (*One Million Years B.C.*) and the absolutely minimal bikini in 1970 (*When Dinosaurs Ruled the Earth*). By the time of the latter film, men's costumes had become about as minimal as women's and reached the point of obvious homoerotic display. The brief trend toward realism in the 1980s did not reverse this tendency. In *Quest for Fire* Rae Dawn Chong wore only bodypaint.

The many films and TV programs placing prehistoric people in historic, modern or extraterrestrial settings (see Part III) reflect the producers' fears that audiences would be bored by cavemen shown in their own world. In Appendix C's list of outstanding performances in prehistoric films and TV, five of eleven listed performances were in modern settings. This "fish out of water" strategy has produced some of the best depictions of primitive humans. The best children's TV series on prehistoric humans, *Valley of the Dinosaurs* (1974), also mixed prehistoric and modern people.

Most prehistoric people in films have been anatomically modern; the second most popular option has been the Neanderthals. With the exceptions of *2001: A Space Odyssey* and *Missing Link* (1988) and the appearance of "ape-men" in modern settings in several low-budget films, the movies have ignored the many species of hominids who preceded the Neanderthals and modern man. Filmmakers have also neglected the Neolithic Period, the last age before civilization. During the Neolithic, people settled in villages, began raising crops and domesticating animals and developed many new crafts and skills. These developments have been of no interest to filmmakers, who also neglect the heroic story of how humans spread out all over the world, from Africa to Asia and Europe, then Australia and the Americas. The prehistory of the Western Hemisphere has been almost entirely ignored, except for the fantasy *Brother Bear* (2003) and the Mexican comedy film *El Bello Durmiente* (1952).

Movie cave people have been not only anatomically modern but also white, even though white people with modern bodies and minds may not have existed until about 40,000 years ago. Films credit these white, anatomically modern, pre–Neolithic humans with advances and skills, many of which were innovations of either premodern species, anatomically modern black people or Neolithic people.

Most historical films do not really provide a sense of how people lived in the past. Many tell us more about ourselves than about our ancestors. So it is with prehistoric films. In this book I have pointed out some of the errors in films and TV programs, but my chief concern has been to appraise the works as entertainment. I feel that realism is not the only permissible approach for filmmakers. If the ancient and medieval film epic can have Cecil B. DeMille, if the Western can have John Wayne, if the modern political film can have Oliver Stone and Michael Moore, why shouldn't the prehistoric film have Raquel Welch and her doeskin bikini?

Documentaries about prehistoric humans began with the superficial and quickly outdated *Evolution* (1923) and the obscure *Mystery of Life* (1931). Mark F. Berry, author of *The Dinosaur Filmography*, reports that *The Animal World* (1955) was poor. Aside from Roberto Rossellini's controversial *Man's Struggle for Survival* (1970-71), the first excellent documentary was *Primal Man* (1973-74). The 1990s and the first years of the new century have seen a torrent of good documentaries, fed by the insatiable needs of PBS and cable TV (A&E, Discovery Channel, History Channel and The Learning Channel) for quality programming. These included *Iceman* (1992) and several other documentaries on Ötzi, the Neolithic ice mummy found in 1991; *Ape Man* (1994); *In Search of Human Origins* (1994); *Paleoworld: Tracing Human Origins* (1995); *The Cavemen* (1997); *The First Americans* (1998); *The Fate of Neanderthal Man* (1999); *The Human Journey* (1999); *Dawn of Man* (2000); *Mystery of the First Americans* (2000); *Early Man* (2001); *Neanderthal* (2001); *Neanderthals on Trial* (2001); *Our Earliest Ancestors* (2001); *The Real Eve* (2002); *What Killed the Mega-Beasts?* (2002); *Before We Ruled the Earth* (2003); *Ice World* (2003); *Journey of Man* (2003); *Prehistoric America* (2003); *Walking with Cavemen* (2003); and *Land of Lost Monsters* (2004). For the first time, interested audiences could learn a great deal of accurate information on prehistory by watching TV. Two of these programs presented dramatized stories, performed by actors. *Before We Ruled the Earth* was a series of short vignettes set in several different periods, while *Ice World* told one story, which amounted to a highly accurate feature film on the Ice Age.

Although the genre of prehistoric film has generally been both commercially unsuccessful and critically despised, it has produced a surprising number of good movies. *2001: A Space Odyssey* is one of the most prestigious films ever made. In this book I make big claims for the excellence of *One Million Years B.C.* and *Missing Link*, and I assert that several other films were above average: *Man's Genesis*, *Brute Force*, Willis O'Brien's caveman shorts, *The Three Ages*, *Flying Elephants*, *The Lost World* (1925 and 2001 versions), *One Million B.C.*, *Toot, Whistle, Plunk and Boom*, *Journey to the Beginning of Time*, *Teenage Caveman*, *When Dinosaurs Ruled the Earth*, *B.C. Rock*, *Caveman*, *Quest for Fire*, *Fire and Ice*, *The Flintstones* (both the TV series and the 1994 film), British TV's *Gogs* and *Cavegirl*, *Ice Age* and *Brother Bear*, not to mention the ambitious, honorable failure *Clan of the Cave Bear*. Several of the films which place prehistoric characters in non-prehistoric settings are also highly acceptable, including *Rocketship X-M*, *Creature from the Black Lagoon*, *Dinosaurus!*, *Carry On Cleo*, *The Tale of Tsar Saltan*, *Quatermass and the Pit*, *Themroc*, *Schlock!*, *Frankenstein and the Monster from Hell*, *The Ugly Little Boy*, *Altered States*, *Peking Man*, *The 13th Warrior*, and on TV, *Valley of the Dinosaurs* and *Land of the Lost*. Directors who made caveman films include Griffith, Chaplin, Keaton, DeMille, Corman, Kubrick and Jean-Jacques Annaud. Actors who played cave people include Chaplin, Keaton, Laurel and Hardy, Victor Mature, Carol Landis, Red Skelton, Raquel Welch, Sid Caesar, Ringo Starr, Robin Williams, Elizabeth Taylor, Gerard Depardieu, and even Alec Guinness! This is not a bad record for any subgenre.

Caveman movies matter because what they say about prehistoric people implies lessons about modern mankind. Directors have used the subgenre to express their social and political ideas. Griffith was optimistic about human progress—but only if the right people had the best weapons and defeated the lesser races. Chaplin, Keaton, Laurel and Hardy and the makers of *Caveman* considered the human race a bit ridiculous but redeemable. The makers of *One Million B.C.* and *Prehistoric Women* had a very sunny, optimistic view of man, while Hammer Films' caveman movies were much more pessimistic and cynical. The trivial B-film *Neanderthal Man* (1953) goes farther than any other film to endorse the horror and disgust many people feel about prehistoric humans, while *Altered*

Preface

States (1980) does not blame its hero for enjoying the experience of reverting to a primitive state. *Dinosaurus!*, *Iceman* and *Peking Man* present heroic images of prehistoric man. *The Flintstones* offers mild satire of suburban America while *Themroc* presents the case for the abolition of civilization. *2001: A Space Odyssey* and *Planet of the Apes* are thoroughly misanthropic while *Quest for Fire* sees mankind as schlemiels who make progress by faltering steps. *Clan of the Cave Bear* was based on a novel which paid tribute to the vanished Neanderthals but the film failed to put this viewpoint on the screen effectively.

Ratings ("MK") are to be found at the end of many entries. The scoring ranges from a low of 1 to a high of 10; only those film and television programs that have been viewed are rated. Fiction films and programs are scored for entertainment value, documentaries for the importance and accuracy of the information they present.

My thanks go especially to Mark F. Berry, who helped me obtain hard-to-find videos and illustrations. I also wish to thank Roger Carpenter, Kevin J. Harty, Peter Elliott, Walter Albert, Janet Berry, Darrell Fitts and Mark Zimmer.

I

FICTIONAL WORKS IN PREHISTORICAL SETTINGS

A Spasso nel Tempo (1996) *see* **Adrift in Time** (1996)

Adam and Eve, the First Story of Love (1982) *see* **Blue Paradise** (1982)

Adam Raises Cain (1921) U.S.; dir. Tony Sarg; Sarg-Dawley/Rialto. Animated short film; silent; b&w. (In series *Tony Sarg's Almanac*).

In this silhouette animated film, caveman Adam's infant son Cain and his friends use the neck of a dinosaur skeleton as a playground slide. It is unusual for films to use Biblical names for cavemen. *Tony Sarg's Almanac* (1921–1923) included several other caveman comedies; see index. Ref: Berry. *Dinosaur Filmography*; Jones. *Illustrated Dinosaur Movie Guide*; Webb. *Animated Film Encyclopedia*; not viewed.

Adamo ed Eva, la Prima Storia d'Amore (1982) *see* **Blue Paradise** (1982)

Adam's Rib (1923) U.S., dir. Cecil B. DeMille; Lasky/Famous Players/Paramount. 10 reels (ca. 100 min.); silent; b&w with color sequence. Screenplay, Jeannie MacPherson; photography, L. Guy Wilky, Alvin Wyckoff. *CAST:* Milton Sills (*Michael Ramsay*); Elliott Dexter (*Prof. Reade*); Theodore Kosloff (*Monsieur Jaromir*); Anna Q. Nilsson (*Mrs. Ramsay*); Pauline Garon (*Matilda Ramsay*); Clarence Burton (*Cave Man*).

The restless, 40ish wife of a millionaire is compromised by a foreign adventurer, but her daughter takes the blame. Most of the characters (Sills, Dexter, Kosloff, Goran) are seen in a prehistoric two-color fantasy sequence. *Variety* (March 1, 1923) dismissed the film as a "silly, piffling" romance and ignored the caveman sequence. Neil Sinyard, in his *Silent Movies*, notes that DeMille used flashbacks to earlier periods in three films, including *Male and Female* (1919) and *Manslaughter* (1922), but says the sequence in *Adam's Rib* was the most "thematically relevant" of the three. DeMille, Sills and screenwriter MacPherson were major figures in Hollywood at the time. Burton, who played a caveman here, had supporting parts in more than 100 silent films. Ref: Ringgold/Bodeen. *Complete Films of Cecil B. DeMille*; Blum. *Pictorial History of the Silent Screen*; Jones. *Illustrated Dinosaur Movie Guide*; Connelly. *Motion Picture Guide: Silent Film*; not viewed.

Adrift in Time (1996) [alt. *A Spasso nel Tempo*] Italy; dir. Carlo Vanzini; Filmauro. 94 min.; color. Screenplay, Enrico Vanzini, Carlo Vanzini; photography, Gianlorenzo Battaglia;

Milton Sills gets tough with Pauline Garon and Theodore Kosloff in *Adam's Rib*.

music, Manuel de Sica. CAST: Christian de Sica (*Ascanio*); Massimo Boldi (*Walter*).

An Italian aristocrat and a film executive are accidentally transported first to the Stone Age, then to other periods. In prehistory, a tribe of "beautiful monokini-clad cannibals" try to eat them, according to *Variety* (Jan. 6, 1997), which found the whole film full of clichés and vulgarity. It was nevertheless the most popular film of the 1996 Christmas season in Italy. (Information on the contents of a sequel, *A Spasso nel Tempo: L'Avventura Continua* (1997) is elusive.) Ref: *Internet Movie Database*; not viewed.

The Adventures of Superman (1953–57) Episode *Through the Time Barrier* (1955). U.S.; dir. Harry Gerstad; Lippert. Episode of TV series; 25 min.; color. Screenplay, David Chantler. CAST: George Reeves (*Clark Kent/Superman*); Noel Neill (*Lois Lane*); Jack Larson (*Jimmy Olson*); John Hamilton (*Perry White*); Sterling Holloway (*Professor Twiddle*); Jim Hyland (*Turk Jackson*); Florence Lake (*Cave Woman*); Ed Hinton (*Cave Man*).

A professor's time machine accidentally transports everyone in an elevator — the professor, a gangster and the *Daily Planet* staff — to the Stone Age. Clark Kent must deal with the gangster and get everyone back to the present without revealing his secret identity as Superman. Hamilton is very funny as pompous editor Perry White, arrayed in caveman's furs. This episode of the long-lived, fondly-remembered series was produced, but not broadcast, in color. Ref: Morton. *Complete Directory of Science Fiction, Fantasy and Horror Television Series*; *Internet Movie Database*; Lucanio/Coville. *American Science Fiction Television Series of the 1950s*; MK 6.

After School (1989) [alt. *Return to Eden*] U.S.; dir. William Olsen; Moviestore Entertainment. 89 min.; color. Screenplay, Hugh Parks, Joseph Tankersley, John Linde, Rob McBride; photography, Austin McKinney; music, David C. Williams. CAST: Sam Bottoms (*Father Michael McCarren*); Renée Coleman (*September Lane*); Edward Binns (*Monsignor Frank Barrett*); Dick Cavett (*Himself*); Page Hannah (*Annie*); Robert Lansing (*C.A. Thomas*); James Farkas (*First Leader*); Catherine Williams (*Leader's Mate*); Jacqueline Rodriguez (*Berry Girl*); Alison Woodward (*Beautiful Woman*); Tony Cucci (*Second Leader*); Leo Besstette (*Apeman*); Sherrie Rose (*Tribeswoman*).

A doubting priest (Bottoms) prepares to debate an atheistic ex-priest (Lansing) on the *Dick Cavett Show*. The film includes flashbacks to the time of primitive man. *Variety* (March 22, 1989) called the film "intriguing but disappointing" and complained it "drags on repetitively rather than developing its religious ideas." The *Variety* reviewer said the primitive footage was "a bit suspect, since it includes lots of topless scenes of beautiful cavewomen ... that are extraneous to the main action." Ref: *Internet Movie Database*; *Encyclopedia of Fantastic Film and Television* [website]; not viewed.

Age of the Great Dinosaurs (1979) Japan; dir. Shotaro Ishinomori, Hideki Takayama; Ishinomori Productions/Toei/Nippon TV. Animated TV special; 73 min. Screenplay, Shotaro Ishinomori, Makato Naito.

Three modern children are transported back to the Cretaceous Period, where they find Cro-Magnons interacting with dinosaurs! The TV special goes on to suggest that aliens wiped out the dinosaurs when their population became too great. Clements' and McCarty's *Anime Encyclopedia* says this was meant as a warning about human overpopulation, "a typical touch for the dour Ishinomori." Aliens also destroyed the dinosaurs, to the advantage of early man, in a Japanese animated film, *The Laws of the Sun* (2000, q.v.). Ref: Clements/McCarthy. *Anime Encyclopedia*; not viewed.

Alley Oop (1971–73) *see* **Archie's TV Funnies** (1971–73) and **The Fabulous Funnies** (1978–79)

The Anals of History (1992) U.S.; dir. Milton Ingley; Midnight Video. Feature film; color. CAST: Saki; Cassidy; Trixie; Tracey Wynn; Ted Wilson.

A pornographic film involving cavemen, according to the online *Encyclopedia of Fantastic Film and Television*, which cites a book, *The X-Rated Videotape Guide, Volume III* by Patrick Riley. Ref: *Encyclopedia of Fantastic Film and Television* [website]; not viewed.

The Anals of History 2 (1992) U.S.; dir. Scotty Fox; Midnight Video. 73 min.; color.

CAST: Meekah; Alicia Rio; Mona Lisa; Christine Appleigh; Ted Wilson.

A pornographic film involving cavemen, according to the online *Encyclopedia of Fantastic Film and Television*, which cites a book, *The X-Rated Videotape Guide, Volume III* by Patrick Riley. Ref: *Encyclopedia of Fantastic Film and Television* [website]; not viewed.

Archie's TV Funnies (1971–73) Segment, *Alley Oop*. U.S; Filmation/CBS. Segment of animated TV series; 30-min. episodes; color. VOICES: Bob Holt (*Alley Oop*); June Foray (*Oola*); Alan Oppenheimer (*King Guzzle*). Based on comic books, the animated adventures of teenaged Archie and his friends appeared on TV in several series from 1968–1978. In the *TV Funnies* series the Archie gang produces a TV show featuring their own favorite comic strip characters. Nine non-Archie segments were shown, from *Dick Tracy* to *The Katzenjammer Kids*; probably only four segments were shown each week, so each strip was usually shown every other week. Lenburg notes that "no studio records exist of the episode titles ... for these segments."

V.T. Hamlin's *Alley Oop* had been a popular comic strip since 1934. In the comics, Oop was a barrel-chested, courageous and far-from-stupid caveman who dealt with problems in the Kingdom of Moo. *Alley Oop* was revived as a segment of another animated anthology series, *The Fabulous Funnies* (1978–79). June Foray was one of the busiest voice artists in cartoons and one of the few who became famous; she also voiced Rocky and Natasha in *Rocky and Bullwinkle*. Ref: Lenburg. *Encyclopedia of Animated Cartoons* (1991); Erickson. *Television Cartoon Shows*; Woolery. *Children's Television. Part I: Animated Cartoon Series*; not viewed.

The Art of Self Defense (1941) U.S.; dir. Jack Kinney; Disney. Animated short film; 7 min.; color. Screenplay, Ralph Wright, Rex Cox, Leo Thiele. VOICE: John McLeish (*Narrator*).

Disney made several Goofy sports shorts. In each, bumbling Goofy remains silent while a pompous narrator instructs him in his path to inevitable catastrophe. *The Art of Self Defense* surveys fighting from the Stone Age to modern boxing. In the prehistoric scene two fur-clad cavemen (both of them played by Goofy) duke it out on a narrow rock shelf high up a cliff. They hit each other with club and stone ax until both men are driven deep into the ground with their heads buried and their legs sticking out the bottom of the rock shelf. They continue to fight by kicking each other in the shins with bare feet as the narrator passes languidly on to the next scene. This short is in the DVD anthology *The Complete Goofy*. Ref: Webb. *Animated Film Encyclopedia*; Smith. *Disney A to Z*; MK 7.

As in Days of Yore (1917) U.K.; dir. Maurice Sandground; Gaiety. Short film; 2000 feet (ca. 30 min.); b&w; silent. CAST: Bob Reed (*Caveman*).

This short comedy was a "prehistoric fantasy" according to a contemporary source quoted by Gifford. Ref: Gifford. *British Film Catalogue*; not viewed.

Battle of the Giants (1940) *see* **One Million B.C.** (1940)

B.C. (1971–73) *see* **Curiosity Shop** (1971–73)

B.C.: A Special Christmas (1971) U.S.; dir. Jim Miko; Cinera Productions. Animated TV special; ca. 25 min.; color. Screenplay, Johnny Hart; music, Sam Dari. VOICES: Bob Elliott (*Peter*); Ray Goulding (*Wiley*); Barbara Hamilton (*Fat Broad*); Melleny Brown (*Cute Chick*); Henry Ramer (*Thor*); Keith Hampshire (*Clumsy*); John Stocker (*Curls*). [B.C. and Santa Claus non-speaking] Johnny Hart's comic strip *B.C.* (1958–) has been popular but has failed to produce a media franchise like the *Peanuts* strip. Only two TV specials, including *B.C.: The First Thanksgiving* (1973, q.v.), and segments of *Curiosity Shop* (1971–73, q.v.) were made from the strip. In *A Special Christmas* Peter and Wiley invent gift-giving and a character they call Santa Claus in an attempt to swindle their friends; they are surprised when the real Santa Claus shows up and gives everyone real gifts. The gifts are all actual inventions of prehistoric people — a wheel, a sundial, footwear and a necklace. Ref: Woolery. *Animated TV Specials*; Lenburg. *Encyclopedia of Animated Cartoons*; not viewed.

B.C. Rock (1979) [alt. *Le Chaînon Manquant*; *The Missing Link*] France/Belgium; dir. Picha [Jean-Paul Walravens]; Pils Films/SND. Animated film. 95 or 80 min.; color. Screenplay,

(I) B.C. Rock

Picha; English language version, Tony Hendra; U.S. version written by Joseph Plewa, Jonathan Schmock, James Vallely, Christine Neubaur; musical arrangements, Roy Budd; U.S. version music direction, Alan Brewer. VOICES: U.S. version: James Vallely (*Stewie*); Jonathan Schmock (*Slick*); Joseph Plewa (*Bone*); U.K. version: Ron Venable; John Graham; Bob Kaliban; Christopher Guest; Warren Clarke; French version: Richard Darbois (*O.*); Georges Aminel (*Igua*); Roger Carel (*Croak*); Jacques Dacqmine (*Narrator*).

The voice of Stewie Babcock, caveman, tells us that while some people believe in evolution and some in the Adam and Eve story, he is going to tell us the true story of the beginnings of man. Since Stewie is both cute and intelligent, he is rejected at birth by his parents and his whole tribe of really primitive, cannibalistic cave people. Among this crowd, "you either found food or you became food." Stewie's father is a particularly rough character. "Evolution meant nothing to him." Cast out from the tribe, baby Stewie is saved by kindly brontosaurus Bone and befriended by smart-talking pterodactyl Slick.

Both as a child and an adult, Stewie has innumerable episodic, picaresque adventures. He learns about fire from a dragon, is captured and tied up Gulliver-like by an army of ants and even meets the Serpent of the Garden of Eden. Stewie quarrels with Bone but repeatedly has to be rescued by him. As Stewie proudly recounts, he invents "fire and the wheel and casual sex and eggs over easy." The sex is with Cadi, an insatiable, long-tailed, red-skinned catwoman who has to save Stewie from her Amazon tribe. Most of the inventions backfire; for instance, the smell of the first cooked breakfast only attracts a big predator.

In addition to his own horrid tribe, Stewie meets the No-Lobes, humans who cheerfully work together and never complain, and really dumb Arctic humans who burn their own clothes and freeze to death as soon as Stewie introduces them to fire. After being swallowed by a whale like Jonah, Stewie lights a fire inside the whale, who fills with smoke and floats high in the air. Stewie escapes from the flying whale's anus and drops into the midst of his old tribe, just as his incorrigible father dies.

Stewie gives the tribe basic lessons in language ("Leg! Arm! Mouth!") and walking upright, then introduces them to fire, the wheel, sex and his other inventions. This backfires completely, as the tribe gets a new, especially brutal leader, who throws Stewie out again. The tribe then embarks on a new life of burning and ravaging the environment, killing animals and waging war with other tribes. ("We kill everybody who isn't like us.") The peaceful No-Lobes are wiped out. Doomed dinosaurs commit mass suicide by jumping off cliffs. Stewie, Bone and Slick flee to Easter Island, where they build the famous giant stone faces.

COMMENTARY. *B.C. Rock* is visually imaginative from beginning to end. Both humans and animals are unforgettably bizarre. Humans walk on their hands or on all fours, or crawl, hop or somersault to get around. Some of the animals are anthropomorphic versions of real species, others are

The appropriately surreal poster for B.C. Rock.

indescribably strange. The backgrounds are often quite beautiful.

Picha's film has more sex, violence, nudity and rough language than most R-rated live-action movies. The animals play deadly, ingenious tricks on each other, like characters in an Italian Western. Each killing is marked by abundant on-screen gore. Stewie and all the other humans, including the catwomen, are naked. Stewie's crude tribe tries out all sorts of absurd sexual positions before finding one that will actually produce children. The characters, both humans and animals, often use foul language, at least in the English version. All this, plus the downbeat ending and misanthropic outlook, make *B.C. Rock* just about the last film anyone would show to children.

The point of *B.C. Rock* is that mankind is nasty, so advances only make people more dangerous. Humans should have stayed primitive. A handful of idealistic, intellectual individuals lead to man's progress, but their efforts are always used for bad ends by vile leaders.

The version I have seen is the 1984 U.S. release, which was only 80 minutes. The original European version was 15 minutes longer. The American version doesn't seem rushed or incomplete, so perhaps the original benefited from some cutting. The hero was called "O" in the original film, which was better than the overly-cute "Stewie Babcock." (Stewie says that the tribe wanted to call him Ugh, which was "a really popular name in those days" but he preferred Stewie Babcock because it had "more class.") In the European version, Bone the dinosaur was Igua and Slick the pterodactyl was Croak. The original version had a narrator; in the U.S. version Stewie tells his own story. The music in the European version by Roy Budd, which was eliminated from the U.S. version, quotes and spoofs the familiar scores of *2001*, *Jaws* and *Star Wars*.

Reviewing the 1980 European version, *Variety* (May 14, 1980) praised Belgian cartoonist Picha's "exuberant imagination, with its Rabelaisian verve and bracing disdain for good taste" and the film's "marvelously naïve graphic delirium." In his book *Cartoons* Giannalberto Bendazzi says that in *Le Chaînon Manquant* Picha's "vitality somehow counterbalanced the heavy comicality and sophomoric sexual jokes, gaining an unconditional acceptance by audiences." Picha made only four animated features during his short career (1972–84). *Le Chaînon Manquant* was nominated for the Golden Palm Prize at the 1980 Cannes Film Festival. Only three feature-length cartoons have been set among cavemen: Picha's *Chaînon Manquant*, Ralph Bakshi's *Fire and Ice* (1983) and the minor *The Man Called Flintstone* (1966). Ref: *Internet Movie Database*; Bendazzi. *Cartoons*; MK 7.

B.C., the First Thanksgiving (1973) U.S.; dir. Abe Levitow; Levitow-Hanson Films. Animated TV special; 25 min.; color. Screenplay, Johnny Hart, Jack Caprio; music, Mario Darpino. VOICES: Daws Butler (*Clumsy*); Don Messick (*Turkey/Peter/Thor*); Bob Holt (*Grog/Wiley*); Joannie Sommers (*Fat Broad/Cute Chick*). [B.C. non-speaking]

After B.C. accidentally invents fire, the Fat Broad invents stone soup, which must be flavored with turkey. She sends her friends out to hunt turkey, undeterred by the fact that no one knows what a turkey looks like. The second of two animated specials based on Hart's comic strip, following *B.C.: A Special Christmas* (1971, q.v.). Ref: Woolery. *Animated TV Specials*; Lenburg. *Encyclopedia of Animated Cartoons*; not viewed.

Beauties of the Night (1952) *see* **Les Belles de Nuit** (1952)

The Bedrock Cops (1980–82) *see* **The Flintstones Comedy Show** (1980–82)

Before a Book Was Written (1912) *see* **The Caveman, or, Before a Book Was Written** (1912)

Being Human (1993) U.S.; dir. Bill Forsyth; Warner Bros./Enigma Productions. 122 min.; color. Screenplay, Bill Forsyth; photography, Michael Coulter; music, Michael Gibbs. CAST: Robin Williams (*Caveman Father, Hector*); Kelly Hunter (*Cave Mother, Deirdre*); Robert Carlyle (*Shaman*); Eoin McCarthy (*Leader*); Maudie Johnson (*Girl Child*); Max Johnson (*Boy Child*); Theresa Russell (*Narrator*).

The first of the film's five segments is set in prehistory and opens with a man on a beach urinating into the sea. The man lives in a cave with a woman and their small son and daughter. They wear trousers made from skins; the father's are badly torn at the knees. They make fire. Their few words are spoken in English. In the cave at night the father slightly hurts his daughter while playing with her and looks abashed.

The next day, without warning, about a dozen men approach the beach in two small rowboats and come ashore. They speak a different language and carry only a few weapons. The father, who has no weapons at all, flees with his woman and children. He and the woman argue over where to go. The woman is caught by the raiders while the father escapes with his children. Later, while the father searches for food, the children are caught and taken to the beach.

As the raiders prepare to row away with their captives, the father watches. He finally runs down to the beach and throws rocks at the men. They capture him and tie his hands. The leader of the raiders is interested in a small tower of stones on a hill overlooking the beach. Accompanied by a few men and the captive father, the leader studies the tower. The father says he knows nothing of who built the tower; the raiders don't understand him. The men return to the boats and start to row away with the woman and children. The father watches helplessly. A man cuts his hands free and gives him a bone necklace, in trade for his family. They row away as the father stares disconsolately.

COMMENTARY. The film passes on to its second story, with Williams as a Roman slave called Hector. This is followed by three more segments, set in the Middle Ages, the Renaissance and the modern world. No names are used in the prehistoric tale, but the cave mother is called "Deirdre" in the credits and Williams' character is called "Hector" in all the other stories. Most sources say that Williams is "Hector" in the prehistory segment.

The prehistoric story has an admirable air of realism. The costumes are convincing. The raiders do not kill the father because they don't have to. They simply take what they want. They appear to treat the captive woman and children well. The captives are calm and stoical. There is no violence in the story but the absence of law and security is total. The tragic 15 minute episode is an effective opening for the film.

The narrator has too much to say throughout *Being Human*. She opens each story with the words "Every day they awoke in the only world they would ever know." The repetition of this line in the modern story makes the audience realize that we modern people are as trapped in our big cities as the prehistoric people were in their world. The narrator has an especially effective line during the caveman story. "Of course he had heard the stories about the wandering men, who came and took — everything." Since the family lives by itself and must have little contact with other people, and since news can hardly travel at all in their world, the simple fact that the father has heard of the wanderers is chillingly significant.

The second, Roman story is the best segment in the film. The last three parts are unmemorable and *Being Human* was a rare flop for Robin Williams. Writer-director Bill Forsyth had become famous for *Gregory's Girl* (1981) and *Local Hero* (1983) but by 1993, when this film was made, his star had waned; *Being Human* was almost his last film. While several well-known stars (John Turturro, Vincent D'Onofrio, Lindsay Crouse) appear with Williams in the other segments, the prehistoric story has no stars except Williams. Robert Carlyle, who played the raiders' shaman, went on to become a busy tough-guy star of British action films and of James Bond's *The World Is Not Enough* (1999).

Critics in general and *Variety* (May 9, 1994) in particular were scathing about *Being Human*. The *Variety* reviewer found it "so flat and ill-conceived that it could convince the uninitiated that neither Robin William nor the highly idiosyncratic Scottish writer-director Bill Forsyth had any talent." Ref: *Internet Movie Database*; MK 6.

Les Belles de Nuit (1952) [alt. *Beauties of the Night*; *Night Beauties*] France/Italy; dir. René Clair; Franco-London/Film Rizzoli. 89 min.; b&w. Screenplay, René Clair; photography, Armand Thiraud; music, Georges van Parys. CAST: Gerard Philipe (*Claude*); Martine Carol; Gina Lollobrigida. A romantic composer who dislikes modern noise and bureaucracy dreams he is in many former ages, but the 19th, 18th and 17th centuries don't please him either. He shouts "I would have liked to live in the Golden Age" and finds himself in prehistory, where an old caveman laments, "What a sad time!" as two cardboard dinosaurs lumber by. Three cavemen with huge clubs chase the hero, who escapes back to the present in a jeep.

The dream sequence is in keeping with the light, witty, high-spirited comedy. *Variety* (Oct. 15, 1952) reported that Clair "has done this complicated tale with consummate filmic skill." Ref: Jones. *Illustrated Dinosaur Movie Guide*; Bergan/Karney. *Holt Foreign Film Guide*; MK 6.

El Bello Durmiente (1952) [trans. *The Handsome Sleeper*] Mexico; dir. Gilberto Martinez Solares; Cinematografica Valdés/Mier y Brooks. 76 min.; b&w. Screenplay, Juan Garcia, Gilberto Martinez Solares; photography, Raul Martinez Solares; music, Manuel Esperón. CAST: Germán Valdés, alt. Tin-Tan (*Tricitan*); Lilia del Valle (*Kali/Yolande*); Wolf Ruvinskis (*Tracatá/Heinrich*).

Ten thousand years ago easy-going Tricitan outsmarts the brutish Tracatá to win a girl and prevent a tribal war. Enraged, Tracatá feeds Tricitan a herb which makes him sleep for a hundred centuries. A volcanic eruption buries Tricitan and scatters the cave people.

In the modern world Tricitan awakens and finds Yolande, a lady archeologist who looks just like his prehistoric love but who is about to marry a nasty financier who is the spitting image of Tracatá. With the help of the ancient gods (who provide a timely earthquake), Tricitan revives the girl's latent memories of her past life and again wins her from his old rival.

COMMENTARY. *El Bello Durmiente* is a light romantic musical comedy with goofy dinosaurs, a good deal of physical slapstick worthy of the Three Stooges and a lively score by Esperón, including the "Mambo Prehistorico." Everyone, including the girls, repeatedly get hit in the head with clubs. In one scene the burly villain hits the hero with a huge club, driving him into the ground up to his neck. Everyone has long, thick hair which is so dirty that dust flies when they get hit in the head. The hero drags the heroine by her hair. Cavemen try to cook a belligerent dwarf in a cooking pot; he escapes during one of the frequent brawls. The cave people rub noses instead of kissing. There is a big dance scene with dozens of extras.

Rubber-faced comic Tin-Tan (Valdés) was a major star in Mexican films of the time. His manic performance, especially as the confused Tricitan in the modern world, is the film's biggest asset. The dinosaurs are crudely animated but funny. A Brontosaurus kibitzes on a love scene and a Tyrannosaurus Rex dances to mambo music. Mark F. Berry (*Dinosaur Filmography*) was amused by *El Bello Durmiente*. Brief excerpts from the film were included in Mexico's *Aventura al Centro de la Tierra* (1964; see Part III.) Ref: Jones. *Illustrated Dinosaur Movie Guide*; Berry. *Dinosaur Filmography*; viewed in Spanish; MK 6.

Big Wars (1993) Japan; Toshifumi Takizawa; Takuma/Magic Bus. Animated made-for-video film; 70 min.; color. Screenplay, Kazumi Koide.

Aliens land on ancient Earth and are hailed as gods by primitive people. After they leave, the remnants of their technology help humans to reach civilization. In the 25th century the aliens return and expect mankind to serve them. Clements/McCarthy called the anime "carefully detailed." Ref: Clements/McCarthy. *Anime Encyclopedia*; not viewed.

Bill and Ted's Excellent Adventure (1989) U.S.; dir. Stephen Herek; Orion. 90 min.; color. Screenplay, Chris Matheson, Ed Solomon; photography, Timothy Suhrstedt; music, David Newman. CAST: Keanu Reeves (*Ted Logan*); Alex Winter (*Bill S. Preston*); George Carlin (*Rufus*); Bernie Casey (*Mr. Ryan*); Mark Ogden (*Neanderthal #1*); Tom Dugan (*Neanderthal #2*).

Two air-headed high school boys about to flunk history (which would ruin their plans for a rock video) are helped by Rufus, a cosmic benefactor who leads them through time, where they meet Napoleon, Billy the Kid, Socrates, Freud, Genghis Khan, Joan of Arc, Lincoln, Beethoven and two Neanderthals. The boys introduce the Neanderthals to bubble gum.

The two loveable idiots became immensely popular; a new, young audience had discovered their own version of The Three Stooges and Laurel and Hardy. Bill and Ted's stops in several historical periods are very short and of course not very informative. *Variety* (Feb. 22, 1989) enjoyed the stars' "inspired chemistry" but nothing else in the "overcrowded, dismally shallow adventure." Ref: *Internet Movie Database*; Jones. *Illustrated Dinosaur Movie Guide*; MK 6.

The Birth of a Flivver (1917) U.S.; dir. Willis O'Brien; Conquest/Edison. Short stop-motion animation short film; b&w; silent.

Two cavemen invent the wheel, build a cart and try to get a stubborn brontosaurus to pull it, with "disastrous consequences" (according to Stephen Jones' *Illustrated Dinosaur Movie Guide*). The cavemen decide the wheel has no future.

One of six stop-motion animated shorts about cavemen made by O'Brien, *Birth of a Flivver* is apparently a lost film. See *The Dinosaur and the Missing Link* (1917) for information on O'Brien's films. Ref: Jones. *Illustrated*

Dinosaur Movie Guide; Berry. *Dinosaur Filmography*; not viewed.

Blue Paradise (1982) [alt. *Adamo ed Eva, la Prima Storia d'Amore*; *Adam and Eve, The First Love Story*] Italy/Spain; dir. Enzo Doria, Luigi Russo; Alex Film International/Argo Film. 91 min.; color. Screenplay, Jaime Comas Gil, Enzo Doria, Domenico Rafele, Luigi Russo, Lidia Ravera; photography, Fernando Espiga; music, Guido de Angelis, Maurizio de Angelis. CAST: Mark Gregory (*Adam*); Andrea Goldman (*Eve*); Angel Alcazar; Constantino Rossi; Pierangelo Pozzato; Vito Fornari; Liliana Gerace; Andrea Aureli.

After Eve eats the Forbidden Fruit, she and Adam are expelled from Eden by a volcano (footage from *One Million Years B.C.*, 1966) and a rolling boulder (a la *Raiders of the Lost Ark*). In a prehistoric world they are attacked by a pterodactyl (also lifted from *One Million Years B.C.*) and mingle with primitive tribes at various levels of development. After the quarrelsome couple splits up, Eve has an affair with an advanced humanoid, until Adam shows up and drives his rival away. The Ice Age comes and goes. Eve gives birth.

Films about Biblical prehistory, including Adam and Eve, Noah's Flood, and the Tower of Babel, are omitted from this list, but this Italian-Spanish production places Adam and Eve in a prehistoric world little different from that seen in other caveman films. Gary A. Smith (*Epic Films*) calls *Blue Paradise* "surely the strangest version of Adam and Eve on film," a "hodgepodge of fundamentalism, Darwinism and pure idiocy." Ref: Smith. *Epic Films*; *Internet Movie Database*; not viewed.

The Bonehead Age (1925) U.S.; dir. Paul Terry; Fables Pictures/Pathé, Animated short film. 10 min.; b&w; silent. (In the series *Aesop's Film Fables*).

"Farmer Al Falfa and his girl appear as cavemen," according to Webb. Farmer Al Falfa survived as a character into the talking cartoons of the early Thirties. Ref: Webb. *Animated Film Encyclopedia*; not viewed.

Bothered by a Beard (1946) Great Britain; dir. E.V.H. Emmett; Instructional. 36 min.; b&w. Screenplay, E.V.H. Emmett. CAST: Jerry Verno; Tod Slaughter.

A comic history of man's efforts to shave, from the Bronze Age to modern times. Ref: Gifford. *British Film Catalogue*; not viewed.

Brother Bear (2003) U.S.; dir. Aaron Blaise, Robert Walker; Disney. Animated film; 85 min.; color. Screenplay, Steve Bencich, Lorne Cameron, Ron J. Friedman, David Hoselton; music, Phil Collins, Mark Mancina, Tab Murphy. VOICES: Joaquin Phoenix (*Kenai*); Jeremy Suarez (*Koda*); Jason Raize (*Denahi*); Rick Moranis (*Rutt*); Dave Thomas (*Tuke*); D.B. Sweeney (*Sitka*); Joan Copeland (*Tanana*); Tina Turner (*Singer of "Great Spirits"*).

Among the Inuit of ancient coastal Alaska, three brothers must follow the totems assigned to them by wise woman shaman Tanana, who communes with the spirits of dead people and animals who live in the Northern Lights. Sitka, the eldest, lives up to his Eagle totem, signifying leadership, principally by keeping his brothers Denahi and Kenai from fighting all the time. Denahi does not always manage to live up to his totem, the Wolf for wisdom. Irresponsible, fun-loving Kenai, the youngest, is disgusted with his Bear totem, indicative of love. He wants to be a mighty hunter, not a lover, and he considers bears to be stupid brutes.

Kenai foolishly chases and picks a fight with a female bear who stole some fish Kenai had carelessly left unsecured. Brave Sitka saves Kenai but is killed in a fall as the bear escapes. In denial over his own guilt, Kenai hunts the bear and with difficulty kills her. The Northern Lights descend and envelope Kenai. An eagle, who is the spirit of Sitka, puts Kenai's spirit into the bear's corpse which comes alive (and apparently turns into a male). Denahi assumes the bear killed Kenai and pursues the creature (actually his own brother) for revenge.

Tanana, the only human who understands what has happened, gives terrified Kenai minimal information about his predicament. To be restored to human form, he must go to the mountain where the Northern Lights touch the Earth, seek Sitka's spirit and learn to live in accordance with his totem. Kenai cannot be understood by humans but finds he can talk with animals. He meets Koda, a friendly, mischievous, talkative bear cub who has been separated from his mother. Selfish and self-pitying Kenai is annoyed by Koda but accompanies him since Koda knows where the Lights meet the Earth.

On their quest they meet some mute but helpful mammoths and many talking animals, including two amusingly stupid moose, Rutt and Tuke. Kenai gradually becomes more fond of Koda. They finally arrive at the Great Salmon Run, where many jovial bears have gathered to feast and tell stories. As Koda tells the story of his mother's disappearance, Kenai realizes with horror that he had killed Koda's mother. In his first unselfish act, Kenai confesses what he did.

Kenai climbs the great mountain to find the Northern Lights. Denahi catches him at the top and is about to kill Kenai when the Eagle spirit of Sitka appears and changes Kenai back into a human. Kenai realizes that he must take care of Koda, who has forgiven him for the death of his mother. At Kenai's request, the Eagle spirit turns Kenai once more into a bear. The tribe celebrates "the boy who became a man by becoming a bear."

COMMENTARY. A few films depict pre-Columbian Indians, including several versions of *Hiawatha*, the excellent silent film *The Silent Enemy* (1930), and the magnificent *Fast Runner* (2001). A few more, including *Kings of the Sun* (1963) and the animated comedy *The Emperor's New Groove* (2000), depict the civilized Indians of Mexico and Peru. Other than Mexico's *El Bello Durmiente* (1952), *Brother Bear* is the only fiction film I know of that portrays the earliest inhabitants of the Western Hemisphere.

The characters' names suggest the story is set in coastal Alaska, the first area of the Americas inhabited by humans. Denali (not "Denahi") National Park, the town of Sitka and the Kenai Peninsula are all in Southern Alaska. The setting is a glorious mix of mountains, rivers, forests, geysers and glaciers. Mammoths died out early in the human penetration of the Western Hemisphere; their presence establishes the early date of the story. The first part of the film presents a modestly detailed but convincing picture of Inuit life in the far North, complete with kayaks, heavy clothes, hunting spears, nose rubbing and shamanism. Denahi mentions it took him two weeks to make a fish basket — one of the film's few realistic details on ancient life.

After Kenai is transformed, the film becomes a typical Disney funny talking-animal cartoon. There is a difference in tone between the relatively realistic first half and the mythical second half, but they are connected satisfactorily by the story of Kenai's selfishness and his growing maturity. His quest for self-discovery and salvation make *Brother Bear* one children's film

Stika (left) and Denahi laugh at Kenai's dismay as he receives the undesirable bear totem from shamaness Tanana in *Brother Bear*.

which adults and youngsters can both enjoy.

A key moment in Kenai's reformation occurs when Kenai (in bear form) and Koda find human cliff paintings depicting a fight between a hunter and a bear. The primitive stick figures give Kenai (and the audience watching the film) the impression of a human with a fragile spear bravely facing a monstrous bear. Kenai and the audience have a revelation when Koda says, "Those monsters are scary — especially with those big sticks."

The animation is handsome and often magnificent but the dialogue is sometimes gratingly modern. Almost the first words out of Sitka's mouth are "Knock it off, you two!" Since the second half of the film is fantasy, the slangy dialogue is less annoying, coming from the mouths of animals. We expect the speech of animals to be non-realistic. Rutt and Tuke, the two dimwitted moose, do a Laurel and Hardy routine. Like Laurel, Tuke knows he's dumb while Rutt, like Hardy, is at least as dumb as Tuke, but thinks he's smart and should be in charge. For some reason the mammoths, the only species shown that did not survive, are the only animals who do not speak.

H. Clark Wakabayashi's book, *Brother Bear: A Transformation Tale* (2003), is a detailed account of the film's script development, written with the cooperation of the filmmakers and published by Disney. Disney Chairman Michael Eisner had long wanted to make an animated film about North American bears, hoping to repeat the enormous success of *The Lion King* (1994). At first the film, like *The Lion King*, was to have only animal characters. Even after the human characters were added, the script went through many changes.

Aaron Blaise and Robert Walker were both first-time directors who had previously worked as animators and layout artists. Under their leadership artists from Disney's Florida Animation Studio visited the American West and Alaska and produced a body of beautifully impressionistic rather than slavishly realistic development art. While the film's artistic style was blossoming, relations between the directors and the "story team" were marked by "anger" and "lack of respect," according to Wakabayashi. The evolving story was considered "humorless and melodramatic." After several crises and interventions by Disney higher-ups, a breakthrough occurred with the introduction of Koda, the bear cub, who rescued the film from its didactic tendencies and provided much-needed humor and audience identification. (*Paths of Discovery: The Making of Brother Bear* is a 45-minute bonus featurette on the DVD. The directors and other participants describe the production process with a more sanitized tone than Wakabayashi's book. There is some information on the music score in the DVD featurette that is not in the book.)

The script was not based on a specific existing story but on traditional tales from several Indian cultures about humans who learn wisdom by becoming animals. We know nothing of prehistoric religion, but it is tempting to assume that the first religions resembled the beliefs of traditional cultures of our time, who often see a close connection between the animal and human worlds. In a tactic reminiscent of the change from b&w to color when Dorothy arrives in Oz in *The Wizard of Oz* (1939), when Kenai becomes a bear the screen widens from a 1.85:1 ratio to 2.35:1, and the color palette brightens, visually establishing that Kenai is seeing the world with new eyes.

Joaquin Phoenix (Kenai) was the best known voice actor in the film, having played Commodus in *Gladiator* (2000). The best performance was by child star Jeremy Suarez as mischievous, funny Koda. As Rutt and Tuke, Rick Moranis and Dave Thomas reprised the McKenzie Brothers, a pair of dim-witted Canadians they had first played in TV sketches in the 1980s. Moranis had previously played caveman Barney Rubble in *The Flintstones* (1994).

Brother Bear broke with the traditions of Disney animated features by featuring neither a villain nor a young female character. Even *The Lion King* had an attractive young lioness. Wakabayashi reports that directors Blaise and Williams insisted "the cast of characters would not fall into traditional parodies of good and evil. Rather, their conflicts would be more internal, demanding far subtler shades of mind, and reflecting more honest and relatable emotions."

Eschewing both villains and girls, the film relies for success on beautiful artwork, spectacular scenery, the story of Kenai's growth from selfishness to responsibility, the growing friendship between Kenai and Koda, and the humorous talking animals. (The two dim-witted moose are often very funny.) These assets combine to make a satisfying, often moving, film but critics were unimpressed. The Metacritic website, which assigns numeric ratings to film critics' opinions, reported that *Brother Bear* received only a modest 49 average rating on a scale of 1 to 100. In a typical jibe, *Variety* (Oct. 20, 2003) called *Brother Bear* "a very mild animated entry from Disney with a distinctly recycled feel" which "mixes the indigenous warrior format of the likes of *Mulan* and *Pocahontas* with the coming-of-age and quasi-mystical elements of *The Lion King* to underwhelming effect." Nevertheless, the *Variety* critic noted "the animation is handsome, detailed and occasionally dramatic."

Other major critics were more favorable. Roger Ebert said *Brother Bear* was "ambitious in its artistry" and predicted "Children and their parents are likely to relate on completely different levels, the adults connecting with the transfer of souls from man to beast, while the kids are excited by the adventure stuff." Online critic James Berardinelli wrote that the film "will not go down in the annals of traditional animation as a classic, but it is proof that Disney remains capable of producing enjoyable, family-oriented animated movies ... It is a strong enough effort that we may find ourselves looking back on it with a certain nostalgic wistfulness years from now, when this kind of motion picture has passed into the realm of 'things filmmakers used to do.'"

Despite critical brickbats, *Brother Bear* had modest success at the box office, taking $85 million in the U.S. and Canada. The film did better overseas than in North America; *Variety* reported (April 12, 2004, p. 15) that *Brother Bear* film had taken an additional $141 million in foreign markets. In April 2004 *Brother Bear* was released on DVD and sold 5,500,000 copies in its first month.

Brother Bear was the last film made by Disney's Florida Animation Studio, which was closed in 2004, and was the second-to-the-last hand-drawn animated feature released by Disney (the last was *Home on the Range*, 2004). Significantly, *Brother Bear* was better received among animators than by film critics. The Disney film was one of three nominated for the Oscar for best animated feature, losing to *Finding Nemo*. At the 2004 Annie Awards, given by animators, *Brother Bear* was nominated for best feature, writing, effects animation (Jason Wolbert), music, voice acting (Jeremy Suarez), character design (Rune Brandt Bennicke), character animation (Byron Howard) and production design (Robh Ruppel). It lost in all these categories, mostly to *Finding Nemo*.

Brother Bear may have been perceived by critics as too serious for children, without holding much interest for adults. One thing it was not perceived as was a prehistoric film. Not a single critic I know of compared it to any other movie about prehistory. Caveman films have been so unrealistic and formulaic that when a different and more serious picture of prehistory came along, people didn't even connect it with the prehistoric subgenre.

Judged as a prehistoric film, *Brother Bear* is welcome as an unusual and relatively realistic entry. However, it concentrates more on the mythological, fantasy story than on a detailed depiction of real ancient humans. For all we know, the beliefs of ancient man may have been completely different from the myths of traditional peoples of the modern world, on which *Brother Bear* is based. Once again, a film is most interested in an aspect of prehistoric life about which we know nothing. Ref: *Internet Movie Database*; Wakabayashi. *Brother Bear: A Transformation Tale*; MK 7.

Una Bruja sin Escoba (1967) *see* **Witch Without a Broom** (1967)

Brute Force (1914) [alt. *Wars of the Primal Tribes*; *In Prehistoric Days*; included in *The Primitive Man*] U.S.; dir. D.W. Griffith; Biograph. 2 reels (ca. 22 min.); silent; b&w. Photography, G.W. (Billy) Bitzer. CAST: Robert Harron (*Harry Faulkner/Weakhands*); Mae Marsh (*Priscilla Mayhew/Lilywhite*); Alfred Paget (*Tribesman*); Harry Carey (*Man in Womanless Tribe*); Jennie Lee (*Rejected Woman*); Elmo Lincoln (*Tribesman*); Charles H. Mailes (*Tribesman*); Lionel Barrymore; Edwin August; Blanche Sweet (*unconfirmed*).

In a modern club, Harry is annoyed when his fiancée Priscilla flirts with another man. He drinks a cocktail and falls asleep over a book telling the tale of Weakhands and Lilywhite.

The new story begins after Weakhand's victory over Brute Force (seen in Griffith's *Man's Genesis*, 1912). An intertitle informs us, "Weakhands, through his superior intelligence, [is] now leader of the Stone Club Men, who inhabit the upper caves of the mountain." We see many primitive people in a large, well-lit cave. A big animal's skull is stuck on a tree trunk incongruously inside the cave. Lilywhite tries to control two small boys, who wear bodypaint and play at fighting with clubs.

Intertitle: "After a devastating war, Monkeywalk, leader of the Low Cave Men, seeks another dwelling-place." Monkeywalk's men, who walk hunched over, emerge from the rocks in large numbers.

Intertitle: "Primeval domesticity." After constant interruptions, Weakhands and Lilywhite leave the cave to find a little privacy. "Man, ever the protector." As Weakhands and Lilywhite share a tender moment, a giant snake approaches them; they flee. The snake also chases off two of Weakhand's men. Weakhands and Lilywhite find another place to try to make love. This time they are driven off by a giant lizard with a horn and four fins. The lovers flee back to the cave.

"The choice of husbands. With their only surviving wife, the Low Cave Men settle in the Stone Club land." Presumably as a result of the war mentioned in the previous intertitle, Monkeywalk's men have only one heavy-built and homely old woman in their new cave. She clearly enjoys her privileged position.

"Interrupted domestic harmony." A large

(I) Brute Force

but fortunately sluggish Tyrannosaurus Rex drives Weakhand's men into their cave, then abruptly disappears.

"The inventive brain." In the cave, Weakhands experiments with a piece of wood and a flexible thong. He almost creates a bow with a bowstring but he finally gives up and goes back to playing with his club.

"Monkeywalk covets the wives of Weakhand's men." Monkeywalk's unarmed men attack the cave and are driven off by Weakhand's men, who are all armed with clubs. Even Lilywhite and other girls grab clubs and join the fight. Weakhand's forces are outnumbered but due to their superior weapons they are victorious and drive the enemy downhill. A rather unnecessary intertitle announces "Thus the stone club first invented by Weakhands brings victory over mere brute force." The Stone Club Men and their women celebrate with much waving of clubs and return triumphantly to their cave.

"The secret of the enemy's power." In Monkeywalk's cave, a big man shows the others a club he captured in the battle.

"The descent into the valley for food." Weakhand's men leave the women and children and a few men in the cave and march downhill.

"Now armed with the stone club, Monkeywalk and his men go forth to meet the enemy." Monkeywalk's forces have quickly produced enough clubs to arm every man. The film cuts back and forth between unsuspecting Weakhands and his men going downhill and Monkeywalk and his group swarming uphill.

"The vanquished Monkeywalk a most unexpected suitor." The Low Cave Men attack the Stone Club Men's cave, killing the few male defenders. Monkeywalk also kills a boy (who appears to be Weakhand's and Lilywhite's son). The women are taken away.

"The one woman's power eclipsed." The old woman is surprised when Monkeywalk's men arrive back with many captive girls. In one of the most shocking scenes in any prehistoric film, the men turn on the now superfluous and undesirable old woman and brutally club her to the ground. Meanwhile, Weakhands returns to

The Old Woman (Jennie Lee), the only woman in Monkeywalk's band, has suitors competing for her favor in *Brute Force*.

his cave and finds the dead men and boys. Weakhands cradles the dead boy who is apparently his son and vows revenge. Monkeywalk's simian followers menace Lilywhite in their cave. Weakhands leads his men downhill to attack the enemy.

"The call of love." Lilywhite tries to escape from the cave. As she is recaptured, Weakhands hears her call for help. He and his men attack. In a wild fight both sides have clubs but the numerically-superior Lower Cave Men drive Weakhands' men back. "Monkeywalk's superior strength wins the battle." Several of the Stone Club Men are killed. The survivors retreat to their cave.

"Annihilation faces Weakhand's band." Monkeywalk lays siege to Weakhands' cave. A man who tries to break out is killed. If the Stone Club Men stay inside the cave, they will starve.

"The eternal law of progress." Driven by necessity, Weakhands fashions a bow, then quickly makes arrows and arrowheads. He experiments inside the cave, as Monkeywalk's men celebrate outside.

At the lower cave, Lilywhite again tries to escape and again fails. Weakhands shoots arrows from his cave, killing two men. The besiegers flee. As Weakhands and his men chase them downhill, Lilywhite and the other girls escape for the third time and are caught up in the final battle. The Stone Club Men have only one bow, wielded by Weakhands, but he dominates the enemy. Monkeywalk grabs Lilywhite. Weakhands shoots him, then finishes him off with his trusty old club. "Hero worship in every age." Monkeywalk's surviving men hail Weakhands and accept his leadership.

In the modern scene, Harry almost fights a man who wakes him up. After he calms down, Priscilla returns to him. They are reconciled and Harry quickly makes friends with the man she had been flirting with.

COMMENTARY. I have seen *Brute Force* only as the last two-thirds of *The Primitive Man*, which combined *Man's Genesis* (1912) and *Brute Force*. The modern frame story seen in *Man's Genesis*, involving two children and an old man, was the only footage from the 1912 film jettisoned from *Primitive Man*. No doubt Robert Harron and especially Mae Marsh were glad to do the modern frame scenes for *Brute Force*, in which they could wear normal clothes and look like the movie stars they were, instead of running around in skins for the whole film.

Griffith was on the cusp of greatness when he made *Brute Force*, the last short he ever directed. He preceded *Brute Force* with an exceptional two-reeler *The Battle at Elderbrush Gulch* and the important four-reeler *Judith of Bethulia* (both 1914), then went on to the immense *Birth of a Nation* (1915) and *Intolerance* (1916). In the midst of this incredible record of achievement, this caveman mini-epic "seems something of a regression" according to Richard Schickel (*D.W. Griffith: An American Life*), who found it "neither worse or better than its thematic predecessor." Wagenknecht and Slide (*Films of D.W. Griffith*) felt the sequel was "less appealing" than *Man's Genesis*, "though done on a considerably larger scale" with a tribal war instead of the personal conflict between Weakhands and Brute Force depicted in the earlier film.

While there are only a few cave people in *Man's Genesis*, there are crowds of them in *Brute Force*. There are only two girls in the first film. Several girls are seen in the sequel, all wearing the same kind of grass dress worn by Lilywhite. While there were no animals at all in *Man's Genesis*, three monstrous animals appear in *Brute Force*. Mark F. Berry (*Dinosaur Filmography*) credits *Brute Force* with "likely cinema's first full-scale dinosaur mock-up" as well as the "cosmetically-altered" snake and alligator.

With his big plans for the future, Griffith may not have had much interest in *Brute Force*, which was the last of four shorts he made in 1914. This was a major change from 1911–1913 when Griffith directed dozens of films every year. It is significant that even Griffith, who tried earnestly to be as accurate as he knew how in *Man's Genesis*, felt he had to jettison accuracy and throw humans and dinosaurs together only two years later. *Brute Force* was the first of a long line of dinosaurs-versus-cavemen movies. If even Griffith couldn't make two films about early man without compromising his attempts at realism, it's no surprise that almost all subsequent caveman movies have been ridiculously inaccurate.

The first scenes in *Brute Force* have cave people milling around, apparently with nothing to do. Indeed, there is no indication in the film that cave dwellers ever did anything except make love, take care of children, invent weapons, flee from monsters and fight each other. Once the story starts, Griffith provides abundant action. First, there are the comic scenes in which Weakhands and Lilywhite, seeking privacy for love-making, are driven from place to place by kibitzing cave people and monstrous animals. As the tribal war gets going, we have a succession of escalating fight scenes, involving dozens of men. The fighting sweeps up and down the hill as the tide of battle shifts. First it's clubs against unarmed men, then clubs against clubs, then a bow against clubs. Griffith ends the film without asking the obvious question of what happens when the bad guys graduate from clubs to bows.

The story is not much different from the tale of *Man's Genesis*. The villain wants to seize and ravish Lilywhite; Weakhands defeats him the only way he can, by using his active brain to invent a new weapon. There are far more people on both sides in the second film, but the biggest change is the suggestion of a major difference in the level of humanity of the heroes and villains. In *Man's Genesis* Brute Force was a stupid thug, but he seemed to be of the same species as Weakhands and Lilywhite. In *Brute Force* Monkeywalk's men are well described by their leader's name. They walk hunched over and leap about in simian excitement. When one of the Low Cave Men becomes romantically interested in the group's lone, elderly woman, he embraces her and they jump up and down in unison, apparently a form of primitive foreplay. At the end, the simian Low Cave Men bow and grovel before Weakhands, as he strikes a heroic pose above them, brandishing club and bow. The racism which would infect *Birth of a Nation* is all too obvious.

Nevertheless, the idealism Griffith would display in *Intolerance* is also in evidence. Man marches forward, making progress through intelligence, courage and determination. The comic scenes of the hero and heroine seeking privacy, followed by the fight to save Lilywhite from sexual slavery, make *Brute Force* a tale about the invention of domesticity, a theme dear to Griffith's late Victorian heart. This old-fashioned idealism did not prevent Griffith from presenting some scenes of shocking brutality, including the murders of children and the murder of the old woman by Monkeywalk's band.

Several of the actors in the two-reeler had major careers. Jennie Lee, who played the Low Cave old woman, was born in 1848 and played in dozens of silent films. Alfred Paget had made almost 200 short films when he appeared in *Brute Force*. Lionel Barrymore went on to become a distinguished star. Harry Carey worked constantly as a character actor until his death in 1947. Elmo Lincoln was one of the first screen Tarzans. See *Man's Genesis* for information on Harron and Marsh.

Brute Force exists but is not easy to find. Excerpts pop up in documentaries, including *The Cavemen* (1997), where it is used to support the claim that the movies made cave people look brutish and violent. This is not Griffith's intention, but it may have been the main impression that audiences got from the film. *Brute Force* is in an anthology tape *D.W. Griffith 1913–14*, now out-of-print, from Grapevine Video. *The Primitive Man*, which includes both *Man's Genesis* and *Brute Force*, is available from Glenn Video Vistas, 6924 Canby Ave., Suite 103, Reseda, CA 91335 (web site *http://emgee.free yellow.com*). Ref: Wagenknecht/Slide. *Films of D.W. Griffith*; Schickel. *D.W. Griffith: An American Life*; Berry. *Dinosaur Filmography*; MK 8.

The Bullwinkle Show (1959–61) *see* **Rocky and Bullwinkle** (1959–61)

Captain Caveman *see* **The Flintstone Kids** (1986–88) and **The Flintstones Comedy Show** (1980–82) in Part I; and **Captain Caveman and the Teen Angels** (1980) and **Scooby's All-Star Laff-a-Lympics** (1978–80) in Part III

Carry on Christmas (1973) U.K.; Thames TV. TV special; color. CAST: Sid James (*Seed Pod*); Joan Sims (*Senna Pod*); Bernard Bresslaw (*Beepod*); Kenneth Connor (*Anthropod*); Barbara Windsor (*Crompet*); Peter Butterworth (*Carol Singer*); Jack Douglas (*Carol Singer*).

"2001 B.C. The Pods, a caveman family, are preparing Christmas dinner. Things aren't going too well until Seedpod brings home a present for his son — Crompet. When the Angles invade, Seed hatches a plan to be alone with his son's new toy."

The *Carry On Laughing* website gives this synopsis for the prehistoric section of a 1973 Christmas TV special celebrating Britain's defiantly vulgar *Carry On* comedy films. Other sections of the special were set at Christmas in 1172, 1759 and 1917. James, Sims, Bresslaw, Connor, Windsor and Butterworth all appeared in several *Carry On* films. The Angles actually invaded England about 2500 years after 2001 B.C. Ref: *Carry On Laughing* website (*www.carry-online.com*); not viewed.

Cave Dwellers (1913) [alt. *The Cave Dweller's Romance*] U.S.; Bison Films. Short film. 2 reels; b&w; silent.

A caveman story without dinosaurs, according to Jones. Lee says that in addition to cavemen the film features a scene in which a "man is turned into a pony." Ref: Jones. *Illustrated Dinosaur Movie Guide*; Lee. *Reference Guide to Fantastic Films*; not viewed.

The Cave Dwellers (1940) *see* **One Million B.C.** (1940)

The Cave Dweller's Romance (1913) *see* **Cave Dwellers** (1913)

Cave Girls (1981) U.S.; dir. Kiki Smith, Ellen Cooper; Collaborative Projects/Media Bureau/Potato Wolf/Monday-Wednesday-Friday Video Club. 28 min.; color. Producer, Cara Brownell.

Jones reports the "critically acclaimed experimental" short film "depicts how a society of Stone Age women interact with each other and relate to their surroundings." Ref: *OCLC World Cat*; Jones. *Illustrated Dinosaur Movie Guide*; not viewed.

Cave Kids Adventures (2000) U.S.; Hanna-Barbera. Animated TV series; 25-min. episodes; color. VOICES: Aria Noelle Curzon

(*Pebbles*); Christine Cavanaugh (*Bamm-Bamm Rubble*); Frank Welker (*Dino*).

Yet another spin-off series from *The Flintstones*. The children of the Flintstones and the Rubbles were featured as teenagers in *Pebbles and Bamm-Bamm* (1971-72). Here they are preschoolers; Dino the dinosaur is their babysitter. Ref: *Internet Movie Database*; Lenburg. *Encyclopedia of Animated Cartoons* (1999); not viewed.

The Cave-Man (1914) *see* **His Prehistoric Past** (1914)

The Cave Man (1933) U.S.; dir. Ub Iwerks; Celebrity/MGM. Animated short film; 6 min.; b&w. Music, Art Turkisher.

Willie Whopper, a cartoon character notorious for tall tales, tells how he was once a caveman who saved his girlfriend from an amorous dinosaur. The remarkably-named Ub Iwerks was an Oscar-winning cartoonist and effects artist who worked for Disney and other studios. Ref: Webb. *Animated Film Encyclopedia*; Jones. *Illustrated Dinosaur Movie Guide*; not viewed.

Cavegirl (1985) [alt. *Cave Girl*] U.S.; dir. David Oliver; Crown International. 82 min.; color. Screenplay, Phil Groves, David Oliver; photographer, David Oliver; music, Jon St. James. CAST: Daniel Roebuck (*Rex*); Cindy Ann Thompson (*Eba*); Darren Young (*Dar*); Saba More (*Saba*); Jeff Chayette (*Argh*); Charles Mitchell (*Char*); Cynthia Rullo (*Aka*);Valerie Graybe (*Attila*); Michelle Bauer (*Student*).

Studious high school geek Rex's classmates tease him mercilessly. On a field trip to a cave in the California desert, Rex touches a glowing crystal and is taken back in time 25,000 years where he finds grunting cave people and makes friends with Eba, a sexy, cheerful cavegirl in a bikini. Rex tries to interest Eba in sex while fending off their loutish neighbors.

When Eba and her people are captured by cannibals, Rex scares the cannibals off by disguising himself as a monster. He and Eba finally make love. Rex returns to modern times, where his teacher and classmates believe his story only because a caveman accidentally accompanies him. Rex decides to return to the Stone Age and live with Eba.

COMMENTARY. This depressingly un-

Cindy Ann Thompson is cheerful Eba in *Cavegirl* (1985).

funny, episodic low comedy has some nudity but no onscreen sex. The film claims that Homo Erectus lived 25,000 years ago, which is much too recent. Eba is a modern human but the other cave people are more simian and simple-minded than she is. They grunt while she speaks a real language. This is one of the most insulting and stereotyped films about prehistoric man. The cavemen and women grunt, pick noses, fart, eat leaves, insects and each other's lice, fall off cliffs and have other misadventures. They try to eat a flashlight, then smash it. When they discover Rex's shaving cream they instantly have a shaving cream fight. Rex can feel superior to everyone. Like Eba, the cannibals are more advanced than the comic cavemen. They have better weapons and shoes and an impressive woman leader.

Eba and the briefly-seen cannibal woman are the only assets in the film. Cindy Ann Thompson is delightfully enthusiastic, with an infectious grin and giggle. When Rex thinks he's about to score with her and shows her a condom, she blows it up like a balloon and delightedly lets it go. The film is of course a teenage boy's wish fulfillment fantasy (though pudgy Roebuck was far too old to play a teenager). The undesirable hero can make it with a great girl because he is the only male in her world who isn't either an idiot or a cannibal.

Cavegirl's producer-director-writer-cinematographer Oliver had previously earned a living shooting credit sequences; he never worked in a major capacity in any other film. Roebuck has been in dozens of films. Surprisingly, Cindy Ann Thompson was in only a few films.

Variety (May 8, 1985) denounced this "dreck" as "excruciatingly dull, raunchy [and] tacky." If not for the presence of Cindy Ann Thompson, this would have been as bad as *Wild Women of Wongo* (1958). Ref: Jones. *Illustrated Dinosaur Movie Guide*; Senn/Johnson. *Fantastic Cinema Subject Guide*; MK 3.

Cavegirl (2002) Great Britain; dir. Daniel Peacock; BBC/Two Hats Productions. TV series; 12-min. episodes; color. Screenplays, Daniel Peacock. CAST: Stacey Cadman (*Cavegirl*); Stephen Marcus (*Dad*); Harry Capehorn (*Roast the Rugged*); Jennifer Guy (*Mum*); Gabrielle Downey (*Gran*); Lucinda Rhodes-Flaherty (*Big Sis*); T.J. Sorrell (*Stiks*); Tanya Baleson (*Netal*); Paul Leyshon (*Trunk the Tasty*).

Cavegirl is the smartest, cutest, sexiest, most athletic (and certainly the most self-adoring) girl in her tribe. She routinely outsmarts both adults and her peers, but her ego and her fascination with boys repeatedly get her into trouble. In spite of her extreme self-regard she learns lessons about friendship, relationships and responsibility and that even her parents aren't always wrong.

The opening episode "Second Kiss, First Love" was typical of Cavegirl's escapades. She cuts up the tribe's "warning drum," a large hide on a frame which is hit with a club to sound an alarm in case of attack, and uses the pieces to make herself a new outfit for a date. When raiders attack (while Cavegirl, who is supposed to be on guard duty, is fooling around with a boy) no one can sound the alarm. Fortunately Cavegirl is just as good at getting out of trouble as she is getting into it. She knocks down and captures the leader of the raiders and scares the others off with a bluff. Then she notices that her prisoner, far from being the hideous monster her parents had warned her about, is actually quite attractive and worth kissing.

The situation comedy series was filmed in South Africa, amid gorgeous wild mountain scenery. Everyone seems to spend all their time outdoors in glorious weather; no cave is ever seen. Cavegirl looks about 15; she and her girlfriends are younger than the Hammer cavegirls and wear miniskirts and tops which are more modest than the Hammer girls' bikinis. Cavegirl is mad about boys, but she never goes beyond kissing in the tall grass. Like its heroine, the series is frivolous and a little silly, but far from stupid. *Cavegirl* is an above-average sitcom, suitable for small children, amusing for adults and catnip for teenagers. Most episodes are only 12 minutes long; anything longer would risk stretching the material too thin.

Cavegirl's father, known only as Dad, is a big, dumb, ineffective authority figure, rather like Fred Flintstone, who protests feebly at being told what to do by his wife as well as his brilliant daughter. He does give Cavegirl good advice from time to time, especially urging her not to make it too obvious that she is cleverer than everyone else, but of course she ignores him. As she sings in her theme song, "I'm wild in the country! I'm absolutely free!"

The show usually ignores the adults and con-

Cavegirl (Stacey Cadman) muses on her vast evolutionary superiority over her parents and all possible boyfriends in the BBC's *Cavegirl* (2002).

centrates on Cavegirl and her teenage friends. Episodes feature teen politics, crushes, a rock band (no, they don't use real rocks) and "pigball," a prehistoric form of football. Cavegirl occasionally does something useful like inventing the stone ax or leading a girls' revolt against male dominance, but rather little is made of these advances. Mainly the show comes down to beautiful, tanned young people in skimpy costumes arguing, kissing and performing stunts. Stacey Cadman is the perfect Cavegirl—independent, spunky and totally self-confident but easily embarrassed when she messes up. She is the kind of teenager who is likeable on TV but could be a little hard to take in person.

Since the series is liveaction and modestly budgeted it does not have the ingenious prehistoric technology of *The Flintstones*, and the seven episodes I have seen did not have any dinosaurs. It resembles *The Flintstones* by giving the characters completely modern dialogue and attitudes, unlike the very primitive characters in the BBC's claymation series *Gogs* (1996).

The BBC's DVD *Cavegirl Rocks!* includes seven episodes from the first season: Second Kiss, First Love; The Prisoner; Runaway; The Chosen One; Proud to Be Purple; New Bands; and Pigball, a 24-min. episode. The DVD also promises there will be a second season. Ref: *Internet Movie Database*; 7 episodes viewed; MK 7.

Caveman (1981) U.S.; dir. Carl Gottlieb; United Artists. 91 min.; color. Screenplay, Rudy de Luca, Carl Gottlieb; photography, Alan Hume; music, Lalo Schifrin. CAST: Ringo Starr (*Atouk*); Barbara Bach (*Lana*); Dennis Quaid (*Lar*); Shelley Long (*Tala*); John Matuszak (*Tonda*); Avery Schreiber (*Ock*); Jack Gilford (*Gog*); Richard Moll (*Abominable Snowman*); Evan Kim (*Nook*); Carl Lumbly (*Bork*).

A title tells us it is "One Zillion B.C.—October 9th." Among a tribe of cavemen, who walk stooped over, the big men get all the food and bully little schlemiel Atouk. When a Big Horned Lizard (a small dinosaur) rampages through the tribe's camp, Lar, who is more brave than smart, attacks the monster and is injured. Tonda, the tribe's massive bully, immediately throws Lar out. Atouk is in lust for sexy, scheming Lana, who prefers to remain Tonda's girl. The tribe uses Atouk as a guinea pig to test unfamiliar fruit. Atouk falls asleep after eating some red berries. That night he sneaks the red berries into Tonda's and Lana's food and tries to make love with Lana while she and Tonda are both asleep. He fails; Tonda catches him and drives him out of the tribe.

Atouk meets Lar in the wilderness. As they embrace, they accidentally straighten each other's backs with a loud cracking sound and discover the joys of walking erect. They meet cute Tala and her blind father Gog and straighten them up too. Gradually they gather other outcasts into a new tribe, the multicultural Misfits Tribe, which includes a black, an Asian, two gays and a dwarf. This group proves to be the greatest center of creativity prior to classical Athens. In addition to walking erect, in short order they discover fire, cooking, several musical instruments and campfire singing.

Tonda figures out how to straighten the backs of his tribe. He attacks Atouk's tribe and steals their fire. Atouk steals it back. The tribes also fight over a giant egg. While fishing, Lana is swept down a river and rescued by Atouk, but Lar is swept away and apparently killed. Ever the opportunist, Lana claims to love Atouk. Tala is shocked that Atouk has forgotten her and wants only Lana. Atouk and his men go looking for Lar. In order to get rid of Lana, Tala goes to Tonda's cave and tells him that Lana, whom Tonda believed was drowned, is still alive and is with Atouk. Tonda and his men attack Atouk's camp and, to Tala's horror, kidnap not only Lana but all the women, including Tala.

Atouk and his band return with Lar, whom they rescued from an ice cave and an Abominable Snowman. Discovering the women gone, Atouk has another flurry of creativity, inventing maces made of stone and bone, flails, slings, a catapult, a smoke bomb, body armor, shields and turtle-shell helmets. Thus formidably armed, Atouk and his men attack Tonda's lair. After a big fight Atouk gets the upper hand when he appears mounted on the back of the Big Horned Lizard which he has tamed. He knocks Tonda out with a stone from his sling.

Lana, who had hit Atouk when he was down, instantly transfers her allegiance to him. Atouk takes Lana as his prize and Tala goes off to pout. As the cavemen cheer, Atouk lifts Lana in his arms. Suddenly Atouk (Mr. Ringo Starr) hurls Lana (soon to be Mrs. Ringo Starr) into a huge pit of dinosaur droppings. As the hapless villainess flounders in the muck, the cave people make noisy expressions of disgust. Tala

Atouk (Ringo Starr) finds one of the perils of prehistory attached to his friend Lar (Dennis Quaid) in *Caveman*.

perks up immediately and rushes into Atouk's arms for the happy finale.

COMMENTARY. *Caveman* is the only feature-length caveman comedy which does not star the Flintstones, with the exception of three Italian comedies of the early 1970s (*When Women Had Tails*, 1970; *When Women Lost Their Tails*, 1971; and *When Men Carried Clubs and Women Played Ding Dong*, 1971). The Flintstones inhabit their own special world, which has its own rules and conventions and is essentially a mild satire of our world. *Caveman* and the Italian comedies are the only comedy features which satirize not only stereotypes about prehistory but also the conventions of caveman movies. Of the silent caveman comedies, Chaplin's *His Prehistoric Past* (1914) is minor. Keaton's *The Three Ages* (1923) and Laurel and Hardy's *Flying Elephants* (1928) may have more good jokes per minute than Carl Gottlieb's *Caveman* but *Flying Elephants* is a short and the caveman scenes are only about a third of *The Three Ages*. *Caveman* is funnier than the three Italian films and is the greatest collection of caveman belly laughs ever filmed.

The film is a mix of physical slapstick, outrageous situations and broad, exaggerated acting, expressing fear, lust, joy, anger or dumbfounded amazement with minimal dialogue. The fun starts when the Big Horned Lizard attacks the cavemen's camp. Lar is a typical good-looking young leading man, who would be the hero in most films, but here he doesn't show much sense. He leaps heroically on the tail of the dinosaur, then he doesn't know what to do. He ends up biting the dinosaur's tail, which only irritates the animal, who throws Lar and injures him. Meanwhile enormous Tonda climbs the biggest tree to get away from the dinosaur, hurling cavemen out of the tree. The cavemen rush to a much smaller tree and crowd into a panicked ball at the top as the dinosaur rampages below.

Gigantic Tonda twice tries to crush Atouk with a big rock. The first time his backswing topples him over backwards. The next time he throws a rock down from a cliff but he forgets to let go and follows the rock over the cliff. Tonda's method of fishing is to hold Lana under water until she catches a fish. When Lana apparently drowns Tonda calmly lines up the remaining girls and considers their physical assets before picking a new favorite. When Tonda decides that everyone in his band should walk upright, he straightens everyone's back with his immense strength, then realizes that no one is strong enough to straighten his back. The scene builds to a crazy but logical solution; Tonda lies down on the floor of the cave and everyone piles on top of him until his back cracks and straightens.

The two women are a study in contrasts. Lana is tall and arrogant, with a huge mane of dark hair and a spectacular body in a striped bikini. She could stop traffic if there were any traffic. She is totally confident of her ability to fascinate any man, even one she has just betrayed. By contrast, Tala is short, cute and unconfident, with short blonde hair behind a fur sweatband and a less than sensational body in a modest miniskirt.

Animals provide many of the best laughs. An amorous snake wraps itself around Atouk and gives him a kiss with its huge mouth before he escapes. In a spoof of *Alien* (1979), a giant insect attaches itself to Lar's face and won't let go. Atouk finally smashes the big bug, leaving poor Lar plastered with insect goo. Best of all are the dinosaurs. The Big Horned Lizard is squat, pop-eyed and a rather ineffectual hunter. Another dinosaur howls at the moon like a coyote and, in the most audacious joke in the film,

Tonda (John Matuszak) leads the dumber faction of cavemen in *Caveman*.

greets the dawn with a cock-a-doodle-doo. *Cavemen*'s Tyrannosaurus Rex is perhaps the funniest dinosaur ever filmed. He's clearly a great hunter, since he's become obese. Whenever he thinks he's about to eat somebody, he smacks his lips and rubs his little hands together. When the Tyrannosaurus steps into a fire, it takes several seconds for the pain signal to reach his tiny brain. When the Tyrannosaurus chases Atouk's people, Tala falls and, like so many other movie heroines in a tight spot, is unaccountably unable to get up. Desperate, Atouk grabs a bush full of the powerful red berries and thrusts it into the dinosaur's mouth. The Tyrannosaurus immediately gets high, staggers around with a goofy look on his face and falls over a cliff.

Lar has a hard time of it. He looks like a hero but he's dumber than Atouk and therefore comes off second-best in a film in which brains always win over brawn. Lar doesn't even get a girl. He spends part of the film hopping around on one foot. After his foot recovers, he is swept down an underground river and emerges in an ice cave, where he is so cold he urinates ice cubes. He is chased by an Abominable Snowman with long arms and big teeth; then he's frozen alive. The Misfit Tribe thaws him out, all but one leg. When the Abominable Snowman attacks again, Lars has to flee with one leg still encased in ice. The Misfits and the Abominable Snowman have a wild fight in the ice cave, with everyone slipping and sliding on the ice.

The film is constructed largely around sight gags, such as cavemen struggling across the landscape, trying to carry an enormous egg, or fur-clad cavemen with torches sliding down an ice tunnel. The cavemen's language consists of fifteen words, some with multiple meanings. "Bobo" means either "person" or "friend." "Pooka" means "injured" or "useless." "Fech" is "bad" or "ugly." "Macha" means "dinosaur." "Alunda" is "love" while "zug zug" is "sex." "Ool" is "food." "Aiiee" means "help me!" and "Kooda" is "let's go." "Nya" is either "no" or "dead." As soon as Atouk discovers fire he names it "araka." Midway through the film Nook, a character who unaccountably speaks English, is introduced. Nook speaking English while everyone else speaks Caveman is supposed to be funny but comes off as one of the lamest jokes in the picture.

Caveman displays good knowledge of earlier caveman films. Atouk's name resembles Tumak, the hero of *One Million B.C.* and *One Million Years B.C.* Lana's name resembles Loana in the same two films, just as her bikini and giant mass of hair recall Raquel Welch in the 1966 film. In *Caveman*, as in the two straight action films, there is a violent tribe with a bad leader and a good tribe with a smart leader. In the two older films an injured old man is abandoned to die by the brutal tribe; in *Caveman* Lar is thrown out after he is injured and Atouk's whole Misfit Tribe consists of people discarded by other tribes. In both the two *Million Years* films and *Caveman* dialogue is minimal but audiences can figure out a lot of the few words spoken. The convention of cave people making epochal discoveries is burlesqued by the string of ingenious inventions Atouk comes up with. At one point Atouk plays with a wheel, then throws it away.

Besides the face-hugger scene from *Alien*, *Caveman* also quotes from some other non-caveman films. When Atouk and Lar meet they run toward each other joyfully in slow motion, recalling a famous scene in *10* (1979). Giant Tonda and sexy Lana, who bully the Misfits, remind me of circus strongman Hercules and beautiful Cleopatra, who bully the circus freaks in Tod Browning's horror film *Freaks* (1932). The conflict between Atouk and Tonda is of course the David and Goliath story — including the sling.

In addition to his clever, percussive caveman score, Lalo Schifrin wittily quotes famous music from other sources. The cavemen march off with the giant egg to the *Col. Bogey March*, well-known from *The Bridge on the River Kwai* (1957). When the Misfits discover fire, mock-heroic music echoes the familiar Richard Strauss music from the *Dawn of Man* in *2001: A Space Odyssey*. We hear the *William Tell Overture*, best known as the *Lone Ranger* theme on TV, as the Misfits rally to save Lar. When Tonda faces off against Atouk astride the Big Horned Lizard, we hear bullfight music. And when Lana smugly thinks she has defeated Tala again and won back Atouk's affection, we get the *Wedding March*.

Writer-director Gottlieb wrote or co-wrote the first three *Jaws* films. His co-writer Rudy De Luca co-wrote many of Mel Brooks' comedies. Barbara Bach was famous for playing one of the most striking Bond girls in *The Spy Who Loved Me* (1977), one of the better Bond films. She and Ringo Starr fell in love while making *Caveman* and have been married ever since. *Caveman* was one of the first films for Shelley Long, who had a modest film career but became a TV star on *Cheers*. Special effects artist Jim Danforth, who had created the dinosaurs in *When Dinosaurs Ruled the Earth* (1970), worked on *Caveman* for a year before departing the troubled production to work with Harryhausen on *Clash of the Titans*. Danforth designed the comic dinosaurs and directed some of the live-action scenes needed for the animated dinosaurs. The effects work for *Caveman* was completed by David Allen, Peter Kleinow and Jim Aupperle.

Variety (April 15, 1981) was appreciative, noting the "film aims for belly laughs and gets them. ... Pic's very unpretentiousness gives it a certain appeal." The *Variety* reviewer and Mark F. Berry (*Dinosaur Filmography*) comment on the abundance of jokes about flatulence and bodily functions. I hope I have established that there are plenty of jokes in *Caveman* which do not depend on these elements. *Variety* compared *Caveman* to *Animal House* (1978) while Berry compares it to *Airplane* (1980). *Caveman* was much less popular than those two comedies, but I feel that the public and critics have always been cool to caveman films. *Caveman* is underrated, just as *One Million B.C.* and *One Million Years B.C.* have been. It took in $11,800,000 at the box office, not bad for 1981, but far below *Airplane*'s $83,400,000 or the $141,600,000 taken by *Animal House*. *Caveman* is now rated 2½ by Leonard Maltin's *Guide*, midway between *Animal House* (two stars) and *Airplane* (three stars).

Pauline Kael in *The New Yorker* (May 18, 1981) warmly defended *Caveman* for its "funky buoyancy. Its humor is the sort of indecorous silliness that still delights people when they see the casual Paramount comedies of the thirties." She praised Gottlieb who "gets crack timing from the whole cast and never lets a routine go on too long." Ref: Jones. *Illustrated Dinosaur Movie Guide*; Berry. *Dinosaur Filmography*; Senn/Johnson. *Fantastic Cinema Subject Guide*; Smith. *Epic Films*; MK 8.

Caveman Inki (1950) U.S.; dir. Chuck Jones; Warner Bros. Animated short film; 7 min.;

color. Screenplay, Charles Maltese; music, Carl Stalling, Milt Franklyn.

In this *Looney Tunes* cartoon short, Inki the caveman, his pet dinosaur, a saber-tooth lion (not tiger) and the Minah Bird, a mischievous creature which emerges from the earth after a volcanic eruption, chase each other and harass another caveman who is trying to prepare stew. A note in the program for the 2003 Cinefest film convention says, "It features one of the great star entrances in cartoon history as the Minah Bird enters the short." The last of four Warner Bros. cartoons by Jones about Inki and the Minah Bird. Ref: Webb. *Animated Film Encyclopedia*; Beck/Friedwald. *Looney Tunes and Merrie Melodies*; not viewed.

The Caveman, or, Before a Book Was Written (1912) U.S.; dir. Ralph Ince, Charles L. Gaskill; Vitagraph. Short film; 1000 feet; b&w; silent. CAST: Ralph Ince (*Eric*); Edith Storey (*Chloe*); Harry Northrup (*Dagban*); Rose Tapley (*Else*); Tefft Johnson (*Aleric*).

A prehistoric tribe (with some modern-sounding names) struggles to survive. Jones says this early short was based on Darwinism. Ref: Jones. *Illustrated Dinosaur Movie Guide*; Lee. *Reference Guide to Fantastic Films*; *Internet Movie Database*; not viewed.

The Caveman's War (1913) U.S.; Kalem. Short film; 2 reels; b&w; silent.

A war between the Cave Dwellers and the Shell People is decided when the Shell leader, Strong Arm, invents the bow and arrow. Ref: Jones. *Illustrated Dinosaur Movie Guide*; Lee. *Reference Guide to Fantastic Films*; not viewed.

Cesta do Praveku (1955, 1966)
  see **Journey to the Beginning of Time** (1955, 1966)

Le Chaînon Manquant (1979)
  see **B.C. Rock** (1979)

The Clan of the Cave Bear (1986) U.S.; dir. Michael Chapman; Warner Bros. 98 min.; color. Screenplay, John Sayles, based on novel by Jean M. Auel; photography, Jon de Bont; music, Alan Silvestri. CAST: Daryl Hannah (*Ayla*); Pamela Reed (*Iza*); James Remar (*Creb*); Thomas G. Waites (*Broud*); John Doolittle (*Brun*); Curtis Armstrong (*Goov*); Martin Doyle (*Grod*); Tony Montanaro (*Zoug*); Mike Muscat (*Dorv*); Lycia Naff (*Uba*); Paul Carafotes (*Brug*); Emma Floria (*Young Ayla*); Mary Reid (*Ayla's Mother*); Nicole Eggert (*Middle Ayla*); Rory L. Crowley (*Durc*); Salome Jens (*Narrator*); Bart the Bear (*Cave Bear*).

A title tells us that 35,000 years ago "for a brief time" Neanderthals and Cro-Magnons shared prehistoric Europe but only the Cro-Magnons went on to become our ancestors. The narrator is a Cro-Magnon woman who tells the story of a girl called Ayla. "The legends still speak of her." Ayla is a small Cro-Magnon child when her mother is killed by an earthquake. She wanders away, is chased by a lion and runs into a cave. The lion slashes her leg but she escapes.

The same earthquake that killed Ayla's mother also destroyed the cave occupied by a Neanderthal group, the Clan of the Cave Bear. They search for another cave, without which they will not survive the winter. They find Ayla but Brun, the leader, decides to leave the little girl to die, since she is one of "the Others" (the Cro-Magnons). Iza the Medicine Woman and Creb the Clan's one-eyed Mog-ur (holy man) are amazed that Ayla's leg shows the mark of the cave lion's claws. Pregnant Iza takes Ayla with her but she knows the Clan will not allow Ayla to stay with them for long. Fortunately,

Ayla (Daryl Hannah) and a Neanderthal in *Clan of the Bear*.

Ayla by chance finds a cave which contains the skull of a cave bear. This is taken as a sign from the Spirits and Ayla is accepted.

The Clan is ruled by the Memories (strict traditional rules of conduct), and by the omnipresent Spirits. Women must kneel to men and must never touch weapons. As she grows up, Ayla is disliked by most Clan people, who find the tall, blonde girl ugly and (as the narrator says) "a threat to the Clan's unchanging ways." Brun's son Broud, who expects to be the next leader when his father grows too old, especially detests Ayla. Creb and Iza protect Ayla, whose only other friend is Iza's daughter Uba. When Creb shows Ayla how to count to 5, as high as anyone in the Clan can count, Ayla happily counts up to 20. Creb warns her, "Don't show this to the Clan" since a talent foreign to the Clan would make her even more unpopular.

As she grows up, Ayla must have a totem to protect her, like all Clan people. Seeking guidance from the Spirits about Ayla, Creb has a vision of a cave lion. Meanwhile, Broud kills a musk ox, attaining status as a hunter and future leader of the Clan. This status gives him rights which permit him to bully Ayla. Creb announces that Ayla has the totem of the cave lion. The Clan is outraged since the cave lion is a "strong totem," indisputably a male hunter's totem. Iza teaches Ayla her healing skills in order to give her a place in the Clan. They work together pulling teeth, delivering babies and treating burns.

Iza warns Ayla that the Spirits will never give her a baby because her totem is too strong. Ayla watches men practicing throwing stones with a sling. Ayla steals a sling the men cast aside and teaches herself how to use it. She invents an overhead, horizontal windup instead of the men's unsuccessful vertical windup. Later, Broud hits Ayla for showing disrespect; Brun rebukes Broud for hitting one of his people. In the forest Broud rapes Ayla, who only briefly resists, since Broud has a right to take her. Ayla finds a small cave and often hides there to avoid Broud. Broud begins having sex with Ayla in the cave, in front of everyone, to show his power. (Mothers cover their children's eyes.) Ayla is happy when she becomes pregnant. The next time Broud assaults her sexually, she feigns indifference, causing him to fail and thus embarrassing him in front of the Clan.

Later a wolf grabs a small boy. Ayla fires a stone from her sling, scaring off the wolf and saving the boy. The penalty for a woman touching a hunter's weapon is death, but after Ayla shows the men her accurate overhead windup, the Clan agrees that since she saved the child and showed them her superior technique, they will exile her "for one turning of the moon." Since it is winter and she is pregnant, she is not expected to survive even this short exile. Ayla goes to her private cave, where her baby is born. She survives and returns to the Clan with her son Durc.

Many in the Clan want to kill Ayla's child but Ayla says she will die too if they kill her son. When Creb asks for her life, Ayla and Durc are spared and she is even permitted to hunt. By the time Durc is four years old, he is accepted as a Clan member. He resembles Clan people and accepts their teachings about the Memories.

The Clan goes to an infrequent Gathering of many Neanderthal clans. Iza says she is too old to go and gives Ayla her sacred medicine bowl. She tells Ayla she must find a mate if she is to survive with one of the clans. At the Gathering, however, the other clans refuse to recognize Ayla as a medicine woman and the bowl is taken from her. Ayla meets Brug, a young man with blue eyes like Ayla's, who lives with another Neanderthal clan. Brug is clearly one of the Others and seems to be a possible mate for Ayla, but he is killed in a sacred ceremony in which several young hunters prove their prowess by attacking a cave bear. During another ceremony, Ayla is drugged. She has a vision of a lion (her totem) walking away from Durc, which she takes as a message from the Spirits that she must leave her son.

Iza tells Ayla that she will never be a woman of the Clan. Instead she must search for the Others. Soon after, Iza dies and Brun retires, making Broud the new leader. Brun also replaces Creb with another man as Mog-ur. Broud takes immediate, drastic revenge on his enemies. He announces that he is taking Ayla to his hearth (making her available to him for sexual purposes). He also revokes her permission to hunt, gives her son Durc to another man's hearth and exiles Creb. Ayla accepts all this except the exile of Creb, which would mean the death of the man who has been her father. When Broud threatens Creb with a spear, Ayla breaks his spear with a stone from her sling, then knocks him down. Broud moves to kill

Ayla, but Brun stops him. Brun resumes the leadership and tells Broud that "You are fighting a Spirit. Ayla has won." Humiliated, Broud can never be a candidate for the leadership. Creb can stay with the Clan. Ayla believes that her vision means that Durc will someday be the Clan's leader. She sadly says goodbye to Durc and leaves. She has "felt the strength of her own Spirit."

COMMENTARY. The 1986 film of *Clan of the Cave Bear* was a major disappointment to anyone who had hopes for the prehistoric film subgenre. The novel by Jean M. Auel came out in 1980 and was a surprise best-seller. 1981 saw the release of *Quest for Fire*, the most realistic film about prehistoric man to date and a surprise hit. In 1982 the second novel in Auel's *Earth's Children* series, *The Valley of Horses*, was published and became another major bestseller. In 1985, the year the film was made, Auel's third novel, *The Mammoth Hunters*, was published in the first ever million-copy first printing.

It seemed that the public was ready for serious films about prehistoric humans. Auel planned to write more novels about her Cro-Magnon heroine Ayla. If the film of *Clan of the Cave Bear* were a success, there could be a series of films about Ayla and her Neanderthal and Cro-Magnon contemporaries. The film seemed to be in good hands. It was Michael Chapman's second film as director, but he was already famous as cinematographer of several major films, including Martin Scorsese's *Taxi Driver* (1976) and *Raging Bull* (1980). The script was by respected screenwriter-director John Sayles. Cinematographer Jan de Bont and composer Alan Silvestri were veterans. Daryl Hannah had just become a popular star after appearing in *Blade Runner* (1982) and *Splash* (1984).

In spite of these assets, *Clan of the Cave Bear* was a critical and commercial fiasco. Auel demanded that her name be removed from the film and sued Warner Bros., claiming that the movie was so shoddy that it injured her reputation. Her displeasure was well-known to both her fans and film critics before the film was released in January 1986. January is a month when studios dump films for which they have little hope of success. Auel's name remained on the film but critics were highly dismissive and the U.S. box-office was (according to *Internet Movie Database*) a disastrous $1,950,000. Of course there would be no more films about Ayla, although fans of the novels continue to hope for a miniseries someday. (Stephen Jones' *Illustrated Dinosaur Movie Guide* and an October 1985 *Cinefantastique* article both say that *Clan of the Cave Bear* was originally planned as a miniseries before it was finally made as a feature film.)

Auel's novels were based on extensive research and crammed with fascinating details about the realities of prehistoric life. The film leaves out most of this information and rushes through Ayla's story. Fans of Auel's novel felt cheated while people who had not read the book felt no connection to the story.

In the novel, the Neanderthals talk mainly with their hands and only occasionally add a few simple vocalizations. In the film, they speak much more and sign less than in the book. The filmmakers may have felt that showing the Neanderthals speaking with their hands would make them appear dim-witted and primitive to audiences. That might have happened, even though it takes about as much intelligence to talk with the hands as to speak orally. The moviemakers may also have feared that audiences would find a lot of hand-talking silly, or that it would distract viewers. There is much more dialogue in *Clan of the Cave Bear* than in the film to which it is most often (and unfavorably) compared, *Quest for Fire* (1981), the other realistic caveman film of the 1980s. The dialogue all had to be translated by subtitles, as in a foreign film. The abundant subtitles, as well as the film's dependence on the loquacious narrator, no doubt contributed to the movie's unpopularity.

The film's failure to make audiences understand the Neanderthal lifestyle probably led viewers who had not read the book to consider the film's Neanderthals as brutish and evil. Auel created a detailed picture of Neanderthal society which made their actions understandable. For instance, they placed little importance on sex and felt that it was a woman's job to "serve a man's needs." Audiences who did not know the book must have been shocked that the Clan permitted Broud to rape Ayla. Daryl Hannah's popularity probably made the rape scene even more unacceptable.

Audiences must also have been appalled at Ayla's happiness when she became pregnant by Broud. The film failed to establish the fact (explained in the novel) that the Neanderthals (and therefore Ayla, who knew only their beliefs) did not think that sex had anything to do with pregnancy. They thought that any man could get any woman pregnant, with or without sex, if his spirit was stronger than hers. Ayla therefore does not associate her pregnancy with Broud, whom she detests. She is glad when she becomes pregnant because she has been told that her unusually strong, masculine lion totem would prevent her from ever having a child.

In each of four films in which prehistoric men find themselves in the modern world (*Dinosaurus!* (1960), *Eegah!* (1962), *Iceman* (1984) and *Peking Man* (1997)), the prehistoric male assumes as a matter of course that a modern woman would be glad to have sex with him because he is a strong, competent male and such man are very valuable and desirable in his world. In all four films modern women reject the prehistoric man. Ayla, however, was brought up in the Neanderthal's world and understands their beliefs. She knows that Broud, a fine hunter who kills a musk ox and a bear in difficult hunts, would be considered by the Clan an excellent mate for any woman. She doesn't like him but she knows that everyone would agree that she has no right to reject him, especially since the clan considers her to be inferior.

In the book Ayla is about 12 when Broud begins his sexual assaults on her. Of course the film would have attracted virulent criticism if it had shown sexual abuse of a child. Instead of establishing that sexual activity began very early for prehistoric people, the movie simply has Broud keep his hands off Ayla until she is an older teenager. The sex scenes begin after Daryl Hannah, who was then 24, took over the role from 13-year-old Nicole Eggert.

Some critics have even claimed that the film flirted with racism, since the Neanderthals are short and dark and have lesser intelligence, while Ayla is tall, blonde and smart. The fact that Ayla is raped by Broud the Neanderthal bully seemed to confirm this suspicion. However, Neanderthals really were short, stocky and dark, while Cro-Magnons were taller and probably included some blondes. Ayla and her mother are blonde but Brug, the other Cro-Magnon in the film, has blue eyes but dark hair. Neanderthal intelligence really was more limited and less capable of innovation than the intelligence of Cro-Magnons, who had exactly the same intellectual capacities as modern humans.

These facts are in Auel's novels. Critics did not venture to accuse Auel of racism but the film was criticized for presenting the same concepts.

As for the rape, the unpleasant Clan custom of allowing men to demand sexual favors from any woman was postulated by Auel, not invented by the filmmakers. It seems certain that girls in prehistoric societies did not remain virgins long. People died fairly young and therefore had to hurry to produce children. Ayla disliked Broud and his treatment of her but she accepted Clan customs on sexuality. She did not react to the rape with the horror a modern woman would feel. She certainly did not feel superior to the Clan. She had a hard enough time convincing the Clan she wasn't inferior to them. She loved her foster parents Iza and Creb and her foster sister Uba. The film is not racist but it leaves itself open to charges of bigotry because it fails to show the Neanderthals in the favorable light in which they appeared in Auel's novel.

Many critics jeered at the film for its supposedly excessively modern "feminism." The conflict between Ayla and the clan over the position of women is in Auel's book. Apparently some critics are quicker to criticize unsuccessful films than they are best-selling novels. But they have a point about the film. Sayles' script reduces the complex story in the novel to a simple struggle by a brave heroine against hidebound misogynists.

Some of the critics displayed their own ignorance of prehistory. For instance, Roger Ebert wrote that "Instead of people who are scarred, wind-burned, thin and toothless, it gives us graduates of the Los Angeles health club scene." He did not know that although ancient people did not live long lives, they were strong and healthy for most of their lives. They had to be. Nor did he realize that prehistoric people generally had excellent dental health, since they never ate processed foods or sugars.

Ebert also complained that "it needs the muddy, exhausted desperation of the characters in *Quest for Fire*." The difference between the two films is that *Clan of the Cave Bear* shows a small society which is in long-term crisis but not in immediate danger, a society which has survived successfully for thousands of years. *Quest for Fire* presents people in an immediate crisis which threatens their survival now. *Quest* covers a few weeks; *Clan* covers fifteen years. *Quest* is an action film while *Clan* tries to be a social drama. Audiences expect action in cavemen films, but in fact prehistoric people rarely fought each other. Audiences expect crises and emergencies but prehistoric societies had to be stable to survive for long periods in difficult conditions. As online critic Richard Scheib notes, the film "is encumbered by having to tell a complex story while relying only on narration, subtitled dialogue and sign language to relay the narrative." If *Clan of the Cave Bear* was a failure, it was an ambitious failure because it tried to do something difficult, while most movies take the easy road.

Audiences laughed when Ayla easily counts up to 20 while Creb cannot count beyond 5; this scene made many viewers think that the Neanderthals are quite stupid. The film does not explain that Neanderthals had brains about as large as ours and were very smart about hunting and other activities vital to their lives. Some parts of their brains were bigger than ours while other parts were smaller, so that Neanderthals had excellent memories but were incapable of understanding abstract concepts, such as large numbers. Auel explained this in her book, and one of the reasons her novel was so exciting was that she portrayed humans with a different kind of intelligence than ours. The movie makes no attempt to describe Neanderthal intelligence and allows most of its cast to look dumber than real Neanderthals were.

We are certainly told often enough by the film's talkative narrator about the Clan's impenetrable conservatism and the vast importance of the Spirits. We see religious ceremonies and spiritual visions. But without the rich details about Neanderthal life found in Auel's novel, the Clan appears to casual audiences to be sexist, arbitrary, backward and brutal. (We also do not learn in the film that Neanderthals had about three times the upper body strength of modern humans. No wonder they considered themselves superior.) Except for Iza, Creb and Uba, the Clan people come off as standard villains. In the key scene in which pregnant Ayla is exiled she looks to Iza and Creb for help and they turn away. The narrator tells us that for the Clan Ayla "was now a Spirit. Even to look at her would bring evil among them." If the audience does not accept the importance of that belief even Iza and Creb seem to have abandoned Ayla. Even the people who love her appear heartless.

Sayles changed the ending of Auel's story to give Ayla a more clear-cut victory over Broud before she leaves the Clan. In the novel, Creb dies and Broud and Ayla never come to blows. Brun does not take the leadership away from Broud. Ayla's only victory comes when Brun rebukes Broud for taking revenge on Ayla and promises to protect Durc from Broud. In the movie Ayla hurls Broud to the ground when he attacks her. (Sayles never explains in his screenplay how Ayla acquired skill at hand-to-hand fighting.) In the film when Brun calls Ayla a Spirit it sounds like a compliment. In the book, calling her a Spirit would mean she's dead.

The film does include some good material. The scene in which the child Ayla is slashed by the lion is certainly scary. Several accurate or plausible details are presented for alert audiences to spot. We see that Ayla's mother wears a well-sewn tunic and trousers, establishing that Cro-Magnons could make better clothes than the Neanderthals. (Later the film errs by showing Ayla in trousers among the non-sewing Neanderthals.) The hunt in which Broud kills a musk ox is frightening and shows how difficult and dangerous prehistoric hunting was. We see three examples of prehistoric medicine (tooth-pulling, delivering a baby and treating a burn). Men paint their bodies and faces as camouflage in the hunt and both men and women paint their faces to help them communicate with Spirits. A man whirls a noisemaker to get in touch with the Spirits. When Iza dies, flowers are laid on her grave.

We also see men of the Clan spear-fishing, while girls take fish from the fishermen and run to deposit them on the bank and go back for more. I like this scene because it shows the Neanderthal division of labor between the sexes, with men handling weapons and women doing the other work, and because the Neanderthals are very serious about the fishing, while Ayla is laughing and having fun. The Clan people are annoyed at Ayla's frivolity. Humor is a Cro-Magnon trait which the Neanderthals were not able to train out of Ayla. The Neanderthals rarely laugh. The only real Neanderthal humor we see in the film comes when Broud tries to copulate with Ayla in the cave, Ayla pretends boredom and indifference, causing Broud to fail, and Iza significantly holds a bone erect and lets it topple over. Even then, nobody chuckles.

There were many specific problems with the film. The opening title says that Neanderthals and Cro-Magnons co-existed "for a brief time."

(I) The Clan of the Cave Bear

Actually they lived near each other in the same areas of Europe and the Middle East for thousands of years. The opening credits are shown in front of a wall of cave art, which is correct for Cro-Magnons but not for Neanderthals. Since the film is set among Neanderthals and we never see anything of Cro-Magnon culture, this must have confused and misled audiences. Also, in some scenes during her winter exile, Ayla is shown wearing trousers. We believe that the Neanderthals did not have bone needles and therefore could not make weatherproof clothes.

Clan of the Clave Bear was nominated for only one Oscar, for Best Makeup. *Clan* was the third prehistoric assignment for makeup artist Michael Michelle Burke and the second for Michael Westmore. Both previously worked on *Iceman* (1984). Burke won a Oscar for her makeup for *Quest for Fire* (1981). In spite of the Oscar nomination, the Neanderthals in *Clan* look too modern. Except for deformed Creb, their faces are only a little rougher than Ayla's. It would have been better if the film had made the physical differences between Cro-Magnons and Neanderthals more obvious, but perhaps the filmmakers feared they would lose all audience sympathy with the Neanderthals if they did that. As it is, there is not enough difference between Ayla and the Clan to make it credible when the Neanderthals (in a nod to the classic *Twilight Zone* episode "Eye of the Beholder") deride Ayla as "so ugly" and even Ayla dislikes her own reflection in a pond. (Ironically, Michelle Burke's Neanderthals were too primitive in *Quest for Fire* and too modern in *Clan of the Cave Bear*. This was no doubt the result of decisions by the films' producers and directors, not due to any lack of skill by Burke, who has been nominated for six Oscars and won two.)

The makeup work on *Clan of the Cave Bear* is described in an article by Martin Perlman in *Cinefantastique* (Oct. 1985). Perlman also discusses the difficulties costume designer Kelly Kimball had. "The biggest problem was that the hides and furs tended to look awfully good and terribly sexy," Kimball said. "We'd take a couple of goat hides and throw them over the top of somebody to see what they looked like." The loose hides "hung beautifully and looked very contemporary. We were really stuck. We didn't know what to do to make it look more primitive." Kimball had the additional problem of a producer who asked her to make Daryl Hannah's costume more revealing. With the support of the director, Kimball refused.

I like to compare the Auel's novel and Chapman's film to Margaret Mitchell's *Gone with the Wind* and the 1939 film made from it. Both stories are about a rebellious girl in a profoundly conservative society which is under severe stress. Both novels were extremely popular. The difference between the two films is that the 1939 movie took the time to establish not only the heroine's feelings but also the opinions of people who disapprove of her (notably Mammy). In the film of *Clan of the Cave Bear* audience sympathy lies wholly with Ayla while most of the others look like bullies.

Hannah did not appear until one-third of the way through the film. Nicole Eggert, who played the younger teenage Ayla, later became a TV star on *Baywatch*. The whole cast does decent work; Pamela Reed and James Remar are especially good. I have no problems with Chapman's direction. Jan de Bont (who later became a director, making *Speed* (1994) and *Twister* (1996)) photographed the British Columbia and Yukon locations beautifully. Alan Silvestri's score is stirring.

The only person who let the film down badly was the film's most prestigious contributor, screenwriter John Sayles. His was the hardest task of all. The failure of *Clan of the Cave Bear* is particularly galling because it was based on a recent novel written by an expert on prehistory while the successful 1981 realistic prehistoric film, *Quest for Fire*, was based on a 1911 novel which of course was much less accurate. J.H. Rosny's simple tale of human progress translated well to the screen, while Auel's much more complex story of cultural conflict may have been unfilmable.

Finally, it is worthwhile to compare *Clan of the Cave Bear* to the embarrassing 1950 antiquity *Prehistoric Women*. Both were earnest attempts to showcase some real facts about human prehistory. Both centered on women and on their defiance of a misogynous male-led society. Both films enjoy dire reputations. The 1950 film failed because of its cheapness and the filmmakers' inaccurate understanding of prehistory. The much bigger 1986 film was unsuccessful because it did not take the time to explore the richly-detailed world presented in its source novel.

Variety (Jan. 15, 1986) denounced *Clan* as a "dull, overly genteel" effort despite de Bont's "splendidly colorful location lensing." The reviewer complained that the film "displays little of the anthropological ambition of *Quest for Fire*" and that "nothing in the customs, habits or attitudes of the people proves very interesting." He also felt that most of the film wasn't "harsh" enough, while the R rating, and the rape scenes which necessitated it, would keep away teenage girls, whom he saw as the film's main audience. Ref: Jones. *Illustrated Dinosaur Movie Guide*; Senn/Johnson. *Fantastic Cinema Subject Guide*; Smith. *Epic Films*; MK 6.

Club Life in the Stone Age (1940) U.S.; dir. Mannie Davis; Terry-Toon. Animated short film; 6 min.; b&w. Screenplay, John Foster; music, Philip A. Scheib.

"The Cave-woman gets her man," according to Webb. Ref: Webb. *Animated Film Encyclopedia*; not viewed.

Col. Heeza Liar, Cave Man (1924) U.S.; dir. Vernon Stallings; Bray Company/Selznick Pictures. Animated short film; b&w; silent.

Several dozen *Col. Heeza Liar* cartoons were made 1913–24. The Colonel, a character based on both Baron Munchausen and Theodore Roosevelt, told tall tales about his prowess. Lenburg says that the cartoons were cheaply made and the "animation was quite limited." Ref: Lenburg. *Encyclopedia of Animated Cartoons*; Webb. *Animated Film Encyclopedia*; not viewed.

Colossus of the Stone Age (1962) [alt. *Maciste Contro I Mostri*; *Land of The Monsters*; *Fire Monsters Against the Son of Hercules*] Italy; dir. Guido Malatesta; E.U.R. Cinematografica/Embassy Pictures. 82 min.; color. Screenplay, Arpad DeRiso, Guido Malatesta; photography, Giuseppe La Torre; music, Guido Robuschi, Gian Stellari. CAST: Reg Lewis (*Maciste, or Maxus*); Margaret Lee (*Moa*); Luciano Marin (*Eikar or Idar*); Andrea Aureli (*Fuwan*); Birgit Bergen (*Rya*); Nello Pazzafini; Rocco Spataro (*Dorak*); Ivan Pengow (*Gamel the Fire Keeper*).

According to the narrator, "thousands of years ago" during the Ice Age humans flee glacial conditions. "Great numbers died in the wanderings, but small bands did survive" including the Dora Tribe (also called the Sun People) who worship the sun. Led by statesmanlike Dorak they settle in a peaceful valley. When a dinosaur-like lake monster threatens Dorak's son Eikar and his girlfriend Rya, they are saved by Maxus (or Maciste) a giant wanderer who kills the creature with a mighty spear throw. Maxus declines to join the tribe, saying "As I live alone, I am a free man."

As Eikar and Rya are joined (in a ceremony *not* called a marriage) the village is attacked by the warlike Droods (also called the "People of the Cave"), who worship the moon. Dorak and many others are killed and all the women kidnapped; worst of all, the villagers' fire is extinguished. The Droods live in an enormous cave with a stone door controlled by a turnstile. The cavemen and their brutal leader Fuwan hope to enjoy the girls, but Fuwan's fierce old father insists on sacrificing the girls to "the pale goddess" of the moon. Fuwan already has a female prisoner, Moa, whose family he killed and who hates him and refuses to submit to him. "I'll tame you yet, you can be sure—and a lot sooner than you think," Fuwan assures her.

Summoned by Eikar, Maxus restores the fire ("Two stones solve the problem!") and leads the villagers to the Droods' cave. Maxus swims an underground river into the cave, encountering and (quite easily) killing a three-headed, dragon-like underwater monster. The mass sacrifice of the girls is fortunately delayed by a lunar eclipse. Guided by Moa, Maxus opens the stone door and lets Eikar and his men in. The audience gets to see one girl sacrificed before the heroes save the other girls and escape.

Maxus is captured. The Droods bury him and Moa up to their necks but an earthquake opens the earth, freeing Maxus and Moa and killing many of the Droods. As he and Moa flee, Maxus polishes off yet another giant monster. Fuwan makes a quick alliance with the primitive cannibal Ulma tribe (in spite of his men's rather comic protest, "But they're a barbarian people!"), promising to teach the Ulma fire-making and even "how we divert the course of water." The Droods and Ulma attack the Sun Tribe but Maxus arrives and saves the day, though it is Eikar who gets the honor of killing Fuwan. Maxus and Moa depart together, leaving Eikar and Rya the leaders of "the first free people in the world."

COMMENTARY. The "pepla" were the Italian muscleman movies of the late 1950s and early 1960s, beginning with Steve Reeves' *Hercules* (1959). *Colossus of the Stone Age* was one the few pepla set among prehistoric people.

(I) Colossus of the Stone Age   36

The villainous Drood Tribe kidnaps women of the Dora Tribe in Italy's prehistoric peplum *Colossus of the Stone Age*.

Others were the science fiction-Atlantean peplum *The Giant of Metropolis* (1962), *Taur the Mighty* (1962) and *Thor and the Amazon Women* (1963). So many pepla were made that by 1962 the producers of *Colossus* and the other prehistory films decided to at least change the setting if not the increasingly familiar conventions of their subgenre. *Colossus* seems to be the only film to mix dinosaurs and the Ice Age, except for Ralph Bakshi's cartoon feature *Fire and Ice* (1983).

In spite of the American title *Fire Monsters Against the Son of Hercules* none of the monsters have anything to do with fire. In addition to changing the title, the Americans changed the name of the hero from Maciste to Maxus and made it part of the "Sons of Hercules" series on U.S. TV. The U.S. version opens with the familiar series theme song, beginning "The mighty sons of Hercules once thundered through the years!"

We see cave drawings behind the opening credits, followed by a long, impressive line of people marching through the snow. A few scenes present some reasonably convincing prehistoric huts, boats, tools and weapons. The costumes, other than Maxus' standard peplum loincloth, are the normal movie caveman attire. The people look pretty silly walking through the snow with bare legs. The good Dora tribe wears white furs while the evil Drood tribe wears dark furs, so the audience can tell them apart in the big fight scenes. (This may even make sense, since the Dora come from the glacial region and would have killed animals with white fur for camouflage.) Later the Ulma wear horns in their hair (looking a little like Vikings) so viewers can identify them easily.

When Rya is annoyed that Eikar is slow to woo her, she complains "I'm 18 and I'll be old soon." This may have been intended as a joke but it is all too true of the short, hard lives of prehistoric people. Eikar and Rya (and later Maxus and Moa) join their lives by cutting their hands and mixing their blood. Even among the virtuous sun-worshipping people, the mating ceremony for Rya and Eikar includes the words, "May you protect her, Eikar. Watch over her always. Rya will obey you humbly. She will obey you humbly. She will skin the animals which you have killed and she will prepare for you their hides. And should she not obey you, then you have the right to put her to death." The mating is not described as a wedding or marriage. Dorak tells the couple, "You are her man, and you are his woman for as long as our great sun god shall bring light to your days."

The Sun Tribe takes its religion seriously. As Dorak lies dying, he is terrified by the loss of the holy fire and says "They put out the fire. Now we're in darkness. Darkness forever." Eikar curses the god of the sun, asking "Why do you let all our shelters be demolished, all our works go to ruin?" Gamel the wise Fire Keeper rebukes him for impiety. "What would become of our lives, Eikar, if there were no sun? Everything comes from him. Would you offend him and have him terrify the world once more with rivers of fire? Would you have him crumble mountains, throw great rocks into the sky, and make the earth heave and tremble?" Idar asks "But tell me in what way we have offended the sun god. Why has he taken away the gift of fire? How will we live without it? Who will defend us from the wild beasts and from the cold?"

After these half-hearted attempts at anthropological realism, the film becomes more fanciful as the action story unfolds. There are two dances, by the Dora and Drood girls. The good tribe's dance is meant to be primitive but seems merely silly. The bad girls do a sexier dance in skimpier costumes. In pepla, women are starkly divided into the innocent and the wicked. The Drood women have little to do after their dance, except for one memorable scene in which a girl sadistically dangles grapes in front of Maxus, who is buried up to his neck, and laughs at him spitefully.

The Drood tribe has no redeeming qualities, but it does seem more advanced than the virtuous Dora. The Droods have cave art while the Dora seem to have no art. The Droods know how to make fire while the Dora and the Ulma don't. Perhaps the film's worst error is giving the Dora good tools and weapons but making them unable to produce fire. The Dora live in huts while the Droods live in a cave, but this does not mean the Dora are more advanced. The Droods could have built huts but prefer their cave, which is spacious and easy to defend. In both *Colossus* and *Thor and the Amazon Women* an advanced group bullies more primitive people and in both cases the advanced group lives in caves and the primitive people live aboveground.

The monsters are very poor special effects creatures, almost incapable of movement. Their immobility makes the scenes in which Maxus kills them far from exciting. One giant lizard, which looks like it may have been lifted from the 1940 *One Million B.C.*, is seen briefly. The scenes of Drood tribesmen falling into crevices during the earthquake are certainly inspired by the 1940 film. The three tribal fights are perhaps the biggest such scenes in any prehistoric film, with several dozen men on each side, all swinging away with clubs, axes and spears, amid noisy sound effects, music and cries of battle. These battle scenes are certainly entertaining but too prolonged.

Gary A. Smith (*Epic Films*) rightly calls *Colossus of the Stone Age* "one of the silliest films" in the whole pepla cycle, which is saying a lot. Everything except the prehistoric setting is all too typical of the worst pepla — the story, the absurd dialogue and crazed English dubbing, the cut-rate special effects and the ridiculous wigs sported by the leading players.

Award-winning body-builder Lewis certainly looks like a pepla hero, but he only made three films, of which this was his only peplum. Margaret Lee went on to a long career in a variety of Italian films, despite being type-cast in a couple pepla. (She is not to be confused with Belinda Lee, who was in several pepla.) Andrea Aureli was one of the busiest Italian B-film actors (Internet Movie Database wrongly credits Aureli, a male actor, for playing Rya, the well-endowed young heroine!). Director Malatesta made about 20 low-budget Italian films, including six pepla. Ref: Jones. *Illustrated Dinosaur Movie Guide*; Smith. *Epic Films*; *Internet Movie Database*; Lucanio. *With Fire and Sword*; MK 4.

Conqueror of the World (1983) *see* **Master of the World** (1983)

Conquest (1983) [alt. *La Conquista; La Conquista de la Tierra Perdida*] Italy/Spain/Mexico; dir. Lucio Fulci; Clemi Cinematografica/Golden Sun/Esme. 89 or 93 min.; color. Screenplay, Gino Capone, José Antonio de la Loma, Carlos Vasallo; photography, Alejandro Ulloa (working as Alonso Garcia); music, Claudio

(I) Conquest

Simonetti. *CAST:* Jorge Rivero (*Mace*); Andrea Occhipinti (*Ilias*); Sabrina Siani (as Sabrina Sellers) (*Ocron*); Conrado San Martín (*Zora*); Violeta Cela (*Girl*); Maria Escola; José Gras Palau.

A tribe of relatively advanced people send Ilias, the son of their chief, on a rather vague mission to fight evil. His father tells Ilias, "You have chosen the path of courage and sacrifice, the path to manhood." The chief gives Ilias the bow of Cronos, a distant ancestor who once ran out of arrows as he fought many enemies. The sun entered into his bow and shot forth "a hail of flaming arrows." Ilias departs by boat with the magic bow.

Ilias, in a brief leather costume, finds a land of hairy people who wear only shaggy furs. The women paint their faces and bodies. These primitives watch in awe at dawn as Ocron, an evil sorceress who wears only bodypaint, a G-string and a golden mask, ceremoniously calls on the sun to rise. Ocron's minions, who include both men and wolfmen and are armed with stone axes and spears, raid a cave and tell the terrified people that Ocron will make the sun go away if they do not obey her. They scalp an old man and seize a naked woman, whom they split in two lengthwise while she is alive and screaming. The wolfmen take the victim's head to Ocron, who eats the brain, which she calls the "temple of secrets." Ocron communes with a snake, which crawls over her almost-naked body, and a large wolf. Her beast-men blow drugs through straws into each other's noses, then into Ocron's nose. She has a vision of a man in Ilias's costume but with no face, who shoots her with an arrow.

Ilias saves a girl by shooting a snake which almost bit her. She flees, unwilling to trust even someone who helped her. Suddenly several of Ocron's men and beasts attack Ilias. He kills or wounds many of them until he runs out of arrows. They catch him and are about to kill him when they are attacked by Mace, a mighty, long-haired man who fights with a pair of nunchucks. Mace kills many villains and drives off the others.

The bow is a new weapon for both Mace and Ocron. Ilias asks, "Who are you?" "My enemies call me Mace." "What about your friends?" "I don't have any friends." Mace has a symbol on his forehead which marks him as an enemy of all men. He prefers animals to people. Mace says he did not care about saving Ilias but only wanted to get the bow. He promises to guide Ilias if the stranger will teach him how to use the bow. Mace tends a wounded bird and cures it, possibly by magic. Ocron's defeated men tell her of an enemy whose "weapons fly like the wind." She realizes this is the archer she saw in her vision. Alarmed, she orders her men and beasts to find Ilias. "I want him — and his weapon."

Mace does not kill animals but he steals and eats animals killed by other men. After learning to use the bow, Mace ruthlessly shoots a hunter and asks with satisfaction "I learn fast, don't I?" Ilias is shocked but Mace explains, "When a man meets a man, you never know who is going to die first." Ocron's army traps Ilias and Mace in a cave by setting fires at the entrances. A snake, one of Mace's animal friends, shows them a way out. Although he wars with all men, Mace likes women and children. He and Ilias visit Iza, who lives in a cave with her sister and children. "Is she your woman?" Ilias asks. "She is when I pass by. You can have her too if you want." "Oh, that's all right," says the virtuous youth. "Have her sister then."

The sister is the girl Ilias saved from the snake. After a messy meal of a sheep Mace stole from a herdsman who had killed it, the girl leads Ilias into the cave for sex. Suddenly she is killed gorily by Ocron's men, who capture Ilias and knock Mace out. When he wakes up, even the ruthless Mace is shocked to find Iza and her family killed. His friends the birds help him track Ilias. The leader of the wolfmen tells Ilias, "Ocron rule the sun and make day and night." Mace kills many of the wolfmen and frees Ilias.

When the defeated wolfmen's leader returns to Ocron she remarks "Ocron does not forgive those who fail" and burns him to death.

Ocron calls on her wolf companion to take his true form as Zora, a masked, heavily-armored killer who commands "the most dreadful creatures of the earth." If he destroys Ilias, "In return I will give you my body and soul forever." Meanwhile, Mace declines to join Ilias in a crusade against Ocron. When Ilias points out how many people Ocron has killed, Mace remarks imperturbably "Everyone dies sooner or later." He considers Ocron too powerful to attack and has no particular sympathy for her victims. He urges Ilias to go home, but the young would-be hero says "No, I can't. I would be a coward." As they travel the two friends are suddenly attacked by swarms of small arrows; apparently Ocron's creatures figured out quickly how to produce their own version of Ilias's "flying weapons." Mace and Ilias flee but Ilias is wounded by a poisoned arrow; his body, then his face break out in swelling, bleeding sores.

Mace goes to a secret valley to get a "magic plant" which can save his dying friend. On his way back he is attacked by swamp zombies, whom he finds can be killed only by a stake through the body. Then he has to fight the powerful Zora. When Mace gets the better of him, Zora vanishes. Mace saves Ilias, who finally agrees to go home. Ilias tries to give Mace his bow, since "I won't need it where I'm going" but Mace refuses the gift, saying "This weapon is still too dangerous for this land."

After Ilias leaves in his boat, Mace is captured by spiderweb-clad cave zombies who seem smarter than the swamp zombies and easily defeat the formidable Mace by entangling him in nets. At sea, Ilias remembers the words of his father and turns back to face his destiny. He arrives at a cliff overlooking the sea to find Mace spreadeagled and tied to a cross by the zombies, who are trying to make him tell them where Ilias is. Ilias announces, "I've come back. I'm not afraid." His bow suddenly begins to glow with light and he fires arrows made of light; each light arrow breaks into several arrows, each of which unerringly finds a target. After many of the zombies are killed, one of the last of them vindictively pushes Mace, still tied to the cross, over the cliff into the sea.

Mace almost drowns on the bottom of the sea but he is saved by two dolphins who chew away the ropes tying his wrists to the cross, then bring him to the surface. Ilias insists on going after Ocron and Mace reluctantly agrees. At night, as the two friends sleep a hand emerges from the earth and pulls Ilias and his bow into a deep cave. When Mace follows he is attacked in the dark cave by creatures he can scarcely see (probably more zombies), then by hordes of subterranean bats. He drives them off and finds an exit, but as he is happily climbing toward the surface, in a great shock to him and the audience, he finds Ilias's headless body hanging upside-down from the ceiling.

Zora takes Ilias's head and his bow to Ocron, who is delighted. As Ocron is about to eat Ilias's brain, the severed head opens its eyes and looks at the witch, terrifying her. Meanwhile, Mace burns Ilias's body and hears Ilias say from the dead that Ocron must be punished. Convinced of this at last, Mace anoints himself with Ilias's ashes and goes to Ocron's lair. At dawn the people gather to see Ocron once more make the sun rise. Mace announces, "Today the sun will rise without you." Ilias's bow flies of its own accord through the air from Ocron to Mace. Mace fires several light arrows, each of which splits apart and kills several men and wolfmen. The cave people scatter. Zora vanishes, leaving Ocron to face Mace alone.

Ocron retreats into her cave but Mace fires a light arrow through solid rock; the arrow smashes Ocron's mask, revealing her hideous, deformed face. Mace shoots her in the chest. She vanishes, then reappears in the form of a wolf. She and the large wolf who is actually Zora run off together. Mace wanders off into the distance as the credits begin with a comically unnecessary "Any reference to persons or events is purely coincidental."

COMMENTARY. Lucio Fulci was a prolific director in all popular Italian genres, from costume films to "*gialli*" crime films and spaghetti Westerns. He is best known for extremely gory but stylish horror films such as *Zombie* (1979). After 1981, Hollywood's year of sword-and-sorcery films (*Conan the Barbarian, Excalibur, Clash of the Titans, Dragonslayer*), the Italian industry churned out a string of derivative sword-swinging fantasy films, and Fulci made his only film in this subgenre.

Fulci wouldn't be Fulci if the film weren't weird, horrific and sexual. This imagined prehistoric world is a nightmarish land of dog-eat-dog conflict, rather like the violent landscape of the Italian Westerns. Mace is not a gentle animal-lover but a murderer, who kills an innocent hunter and sees no reason to risk his life fighting Ocron. Ocron speaks outrageous lines ("I want him—and his weapon") and spends the entire film almost naked. The camera lingers over bloody, spurting wounds and the poisonous swellings that almost kill Ilias. Women and children are killed. The death of the woman who is pulled in two is the most hideous scene in any prehistoric film. In the end, has anything been gained? Ilias accomplishes little before he dies. Ocron is defeated but not destroyed. She ate a few people's brains but Mace is also a killer and ends up with the only bow in the land. Will he continue to murder?

Fulci's film is exceptionally atmospheric. Much of *Conquest* is set in gloomy swamps and caves, drenched in fog or shot with a camera filter which throws a haze over everything. The wolfmen (who are wrongly called werewolves in some sources; they never turn into humans) look a bit silly but the zombies, especially the ones covered with cobwebs, are frightening monsters. Ilias is surprisingly effeminate and his brief, bare-midriff costume resembles the classic costume of the movie cavegirl. The messy meal before sex recalls a famous scene in *Tom Jones* (1963), while the girl being killed as she seeks privacy for sex is a convention of the slasher films. Animal-lover Mace may have been suggested by the Hollywood sword-and-sorcery film *Beastmaster* (1982). Except for Ocron's mask, the topless, bodypainted women in *Conquest* recall Rae Dawn Chong's getup in *Quest for Fire*. The film is somewhat repetitious, with the heroes constantly fighting monstrous foes and taking turns saving each other, but *Conquest* is sufficiently eerie, surreal, imaginative and well-detailed to maintain interest. This is a sword-and-sorcery film like no other (for one thing, there are no swords) and a prehistoric film like no other.

Jorge Rivero and Conrado San Martín were each in dozens of European films and a few U.S. productions. Rivero is convincingly tough and cynical. San Martín and Sabrina Siani (who for some reason uses the pseudonym Sabrina Sellers in this film) both perform without ever showing their faces. Siani had a much shorter career than Rivero and San Martín but she was a familiar figure in many of the Italian sword films of the early 1980s. With her face first in a gold mask, then in a deformed monster mask, she performs solely with her almost nude body and urgent, vicious voice.

The gross horrors and deliberately hazy visuals in *Conquest* will certainly repulse most audiences. On the other hand fan comments attached to the film's *Internet Movie Database* page indicate that Fulci's fans find it fairly tame compared to his horror films. *Variety* (May 2, 1984) noted that Fulci's "only trademark on display here is extraneous gore" and complained that the "visuals offer a nonstop array of smoke, sunlight and filtered distortion, creating a general sort of soft blur."

Video Watchdog's John Charles was more favorable. In *VW* 40 (1997), reviewing the videocassette, Charles called *Conquest* "one of Lucio Fulci's strangest (and most strangely satisfying) films" and admired Claudio Simonetti's "wonderfully gritty electronic score." (Simonetti was a member of Goblin, an Italian rock group who scored *Suspiria* (1977) and other notable horror films.) Charles reported the film "gets more than a little silly at times" but boasted "one of the most surreal and otherworldly settings since Mario Bava's *Hercules in the Haunted World* (1961)" and a storyline which included not only cannibalism but also "Stone Age drug rituals ... laser arrows, web-shrouded reptoids, and a subterranean bat attack" as well as "a few moldy zombies." In his review of the DVD in *VW* 113 (2004) Charles noted the "heavily filtered visuals" but still enjoyed "this agreeably unusual" entry which "remains the most interesting and novel production undertaken during the brief peplum revival of the early '80s." Ref: *Internet Movie Database*. MK 7.

Creatures the World Forgot (1971) U.K.; dir. Don Chaffey; Hammer/Columbia. 92 min.; color. Screenplay, Michael Carreras; photography, Vincent Cox; music, Mario Nascimbene. CAST: Julie Ege (*The Girl [Nala]*); Tony Bonner (*The Fair One [Toomak]*); Robert John (*The Dark One [Rool]*); Brian O'Shaughnessy (*The Father [Mak]*); Marcia Fox (*Dumb Girl*); Rosalie Crutchley (*Old Crone*); Don Leonard (*Old Leader*); Sue Wilson (*The Mother [Noo]*); Frank Hayden (*The Murderer [Zen]*); Ken Hare (*Leader of the Fair Tribe*); Beverley Blake (*Young Lover*); Doon Baide (*Young Lover*); Rosita Moulin (*Tribal Dancer*); Fred Swart (*Marauder Leader*); Gerard Bonthuys (*Young Fair One [Toomak]*); Hans Kiesouw (*Young Dark One [Rool]*); Josje Kiesouw (*Young Dumb Girl*).

[The film's credits list characters only with descriptive words, such as "The Girl" and "The Fair One." Names for many of the characters were given in printed sources, including the 1971 *Variety* review. Since the characters do not have a language, presumably they have no names. Hammer probably decided that asking audiences and film critics to refer to characters by terms such as "the Young Fair One" was inviting ridicule, so they assigned names after filming was completed. They called the hero Toomak, the same name as the hero of *One Million Years B.C.* In the credits above the personal names are given in brackets after the descriptive terms. After making the film without any names for the groups depicted, Hammer found it necessary to invent names for three tribes for the film's publicity. The main tribe is called the Rock Tribe, the same name used in *One Million Years B.C.* The two villainous tribes are the Marauders and the Mud Tribe.]

There are no opening titles or narration. In a desolate land of deserts and mountains, we see paintings depicting animals and people on a cliff-face (not in a cave). Men wearing only loin clothes and necklaces of animal teeth and armed with stone-tipped spears and stone knives hunt a herd of large horned ruminants. They kill an animal and hurriedly carve it up, eating raw meat. One of the horned animals suddenly attacks and gores a man to death. The others remove his necklace and quickly bury him in a fetal position (using rocks as shovels). They bury his spear with him and cover him with rocks. The men carry away their kill; a hyena immediately approaches the grave and begins digging up the corpse.

After carrying the kill a long way across the desert, the men reach their people's camp. Almost naked people crawl out of tiny cave openings. Men quarrel over the kill. No one speaks; they vocalize only grunts and brief, threatening ejaculations. A hunter unceremoniously gives the dead man's necklace to his mate, a woman with three children. The men divide up the meat and hide as women and children watch hungrily. The Old Crone, the tribe's medicine woman, makes a big entrance, wearing so many necklaces she rattles. She paints a mark on the face of the man who made the kill.

Suddenly two twin volcanoes erupt, showering rocks on the people. An earthquake opens the ground and people fall into fissures. (This scene includes footage from *One Million Years B.C.*) After the quake stops, an ambitious survivor finds the tribe's leader still alive but pinned under rocks. The man takes the leader's elaborate necklace of very big animal teeth and surreptitiously crushes the leader's head with a rock. The murderer fights another strong man

The Old Crone (Rosalie Crutchley) leads the Fair One (Tony Bonner) and the Dark One (Robert John) in mourning their father in *Creatures the World Forgot*.

for the leadership and comes off worse. First his ear is bitten off, then he is killed with a spear. The Old Crone endorses the winner as leader and gives him the dead leader's necklace.

Fearful of staying near the volcanoes, the tribe migrates through the desert. They eat scorpions and field mice and carry water in large ostrich eggs. As they pass along a ridge among sand dunes, a girl who has no water collapses. Another girl, with water in an egg, refuses to give her any. Desperate, the waterless girl attacks the girl with the egg. They roll down a sandy slope. The water pours from the egg into the sand. The girl who had the water buries the other woman's head in the sand and kills her. Then she finds she has no water and cannot climb up the steep sand slope. The tribe leaves her to die.

The leader drills in the sand under a small bush with a hollow tube, sucks water from the ground into his mouth, then passes it out through another tube into a small bowl, gradually providing a tiny amount of water. The dark-haired migrating tribe finally finds a rocky oasis, inhabited by a tribe of blonde people. The two tribal leaders almost come to blows, but they notice the children of the two tribes beginning to play together and exchange small objects. The tribes make peace and merge into one. The blonde tribe must have come from the seacoast; they have seashells and pearls and the leader has a spear with a long spearhead which looks like a narwhale's tusk. They even carve a log into the shape of a shark. The blonde people also paint on hides, which is a novelty to the dark people.

The merged tribes celebrate with a wild dance. Music is provided by a man beating on a log. The blonde leader gives a blonde woman to the leader of the dark people as his mate. The Old Crone discovers a girl and a young man together; the girl is promised as the mate of another man. The guilty young man is tied up. The guilty girl and the blonde woman who was given to the leader of the dark-haired tribe are both flogged on their breasts by an old woman with a branch from a bush, apparently as a mating ritual. At night the young man breaks free. He and the girl flee together but her mate catches them. In the morning the two young lovers are found dead, hanging from opposite sides of a giant rock, their arms bound together across the top of the rock.

The passage of time is marked by scenes of people working hides, making various small objects and making fire with a drill twirled between their hands. In time the blonde mate of the leader gives birth to two boys, then dies. The Old Crone cuts the first-born, a blonde boy, on his chest to make a permanent scar. She is about to cut the second, dark-haired boy when lightning hits a tree and sets it on fire. At that moment another pregnant woman collapses and gives birth to a girl. The superstitious people want to kill the baby girl but the Old Crone will not permit this. She takes the girl away herself. She leaves the second-born boy unscarred, believing that is how the gods want it.

When the three children are about 15, the Fair One (the first-born, with the scar on his chest) plays with a porcupine he has caught, then lets it go. The Dark One, the second-born brother, kills the porcupine and uses its quills to torture the blonde Mute Girl (called the Dumb Girl in the British credits), the girl who was born the same day as the twins and who has been brought up by the Old Crone. The boys fight. The Dark One beats up the Fair One. The Old Crone teaches the Mute Girl magic.

As adults, the brothers are still enemies. The Dark One spits on meat that the Fair One is carving. The Mute Girl is of interest to the young men of the tribe since she has no mate. When the Mute Girl is out getting water the Dark One tries to rape her. She clobbers him with a rock, but as she flees she is captured by long-haired men of another tribe (called the Marauders in the film's publicity). The Fair One leads the tribe against the kidnappers, who have prepared an ambush with weighted spears which they drop in a hail from tree branches. These weapons kill two of the pursuers, but the Fair One leads his men into the enemy's enormous cave.

The rescuers quickly gain the upper hand and kill most of the long-haired men. The leader of the kidnappers carries the Mute Girl deep into the cave, where he is attacked by a giant cave bear. The Mute Girl escapes but is waylaid by a young woman of the big-cave tribe, who is referred to only as The Girl. The two women have a wild fight, tumbling down the steep passages of the inner cave. The big-cave leader incredibly manages to kill the bear, but he is wounded and the Dark One finishes him off. The Fair One breaks up the girl fight and captures the Girl. She is shocked when she sees the men of her tribe have all been killed; she mourns one man in particular. Nonetheless, the Fair One looks on her with great interest, to the frustration of the Mute Girl, who secretly loves the Fair One.

The tribe celebrates with another wild dance. The Fair One and the captured Girl quickly become lovers. While hunting, the tribe's aging leader, the brothers' father, is gored by a wildebeest. Dying, he indicates that the Fair One will succeed him. The Dark One challenges the Fair One and the tribe divides into factions. The rivals have a duel in which each is unarmed and their arms are tied together by a long rope. After a long fight the Fair One defeats his brother and is handed a spear to finish him off. Instead he stabs the Dark One in the leg, to the disgust of everyone, especially the Old Crone, who spits on both brothers.

Disgraced by his act of mercy, the Fair One gives up his necklace of leadership, burns his hut and goes into exile, accompanied by the Girl and a few men who support him. They find a very nice oasis. As soon as his leg has recovered enough for him to walk with a limp, the Dark One leads his larger force in pursuit of the exiles. The Mute Girl follows them, having psychic premonitions of danger. A man in the Fair One's faction abruptly tries to rape the Girl. The Fair One drives him away. The would-be rapist tries to defect to the Dark One, but as soon as he reveals where to find the Fair One, the Dark One kills him. The Dark One and his followers are ambushed by a new enemy, men who wear giant clay helmets and paint their bodies white, except for their leader who wears a helmet and whose body is painted black with white stripes. (These are called the Mud Tribe in the film's publicity.) In a horrifying scene, the helmeted men begin to blind their captives. The Fair One hears the screams and leads his men to the rescue.

During the fight the Dark One frees his men who have not been killed or mutilated. Instead of helping the Fair One and his men they flee, leaving their rivals to fight the horrendous enemy alone. The Fair One finally smashes the helmet of the leader of the helmeted man, revealing an albino who appears to be light-sensitive. The albino and his men flee. The Dark One and his gang kidnap the Girl. Led by the Mute Girl's psychic visions, the Fair One catches up with them.

As his men fight a rear guard left by the Dark One, the Fair One goes after the Dark One and his last two men, who lead the Girl up a steep slope by a waterfall. The plucky Girl grabs a knife and kills one of her captors. The Fair One kills the other man and catches up with the Dark One on a hilltop surrounded by cliffs. As they fight, the Girl, who is tied up, is menaced by a giant snake. The Fair One kills the snake but the Dark One gets an advantage and is about to kill the Fair One when the Mute Girl suddenly appears and stabs him, sending him over a cliff. The Fair One departs with the Girl, leaving the Mute Girl to a lifetime of magic-making and (apparently) celibacy.

COMMENTARY. Hammer made two films featuring dinosaurs and cave people. After each of them, the studio made a much less expensive film involving prehistoric people but no dinosaurs. After *One Million Years B.C.* (1966) they made *Slave Girls* (1967). One year after *When Dinosaurs Ruled the Earth* (1970) came *Creatures the World Forgot. Creatures* is more serious and realistic than *Slave Girls* (and the only Hammer attempt at a realistic prehistoric film), but it is mediocre at best and exploitative at worst. (And it doesn't have Martine Beswick, the one great asset of *Slave Girls*.)

Creatures reminds me a good deal of *Prehistoric Women* (1950). Both films attempted to mix a little education and a little exploitation, to present a relatively realistic picture of prehistory while entertaining the masses. *Prehistoric Women* wasn't very realistic because the filmmakers showed their ignorance and made many mistakes about prehistory. The 1950 film also wasn't very exploitative because they wanted a child audience and there were plenty of things they were not allowed to do in 1950. By 1971 audiences were more sophisticated and expected more when it came to both realism and exploitation.

Creatures has a grubby, gritty look which is considerably different from the fantasy worlds of *One Million Years B.C.* and *When Dinosaurs Ruled*. You can feel the dirt and sweat. The two scenes in which men are killed by animals are alarmingly realistic. Only real African animals were used. The stark, beautiful but frightening locations, shot in Namibia, add considerably to the atmosphere. People eat insects and rodents and fight over food and water.

Creatures is modestly ambitious. It tells a story that covered two generations and about 20 years, all without a word of dialogue and with characters who had no names. In the previous Hammer prehistory films and the comedy *Caveman* (1981) the audience could decipher several words of the invented languages, but in *Creatures* the characters use no words at all. The hero, heroine and villain do not even appear as adults until halfway through the film.

There were several realistic details. The people live in huts as well as caves. We see fire-making, working of hides, drawing water from beneath the sand and a variety of weapons. The tribes use spears, knives, bows and arrows, axes and nets for hunting. They set ambushes with nets and weighted drop-spears. We see how dangerous ancient hunting was. They keep domestic goats. People decorate themselves with animal teeth, bones, paint and pearls. The prominence of the Old Crone was a concession to realism. No old woman had such a prominent part in *One Million Years B.C.* or *When Dinosaurs Ruled*. Her constant magic-making (she even waves her tufted wand angrily at the exploding volcanoes!) shows how important it was for ancient people to have someone who could deal with the spirit world.

Some other details are much less realistic. People who practice long-distance hunting, keep domestic animals, make a variety of weapons and have elaborate systems of magic and personal decoration would probably have had speech. Why would an aggressive tribe blind prisoners? To use them as slaves? As a particularly sadistic way to remove them as a threat? Wouldn't the Dark One be afraid to attack the Mute Girl, since she and her protector the Old Crone practice magic and could presumably put a curse on him? Everyone wears necklaces that rattle noisily, yet the necklaces make no noise when the men are hunting. Why call the Old Crone's protégé the Mute Girl when no one speaks? Would the tribe allow the Fair One to burn an entire hut made of valuable hides when he went into exile? And what is the source of light in the scenes deep in the Marauders' big cave?

On the exploitation side, one problem for Hammer was what to do about the girls' costumes. Bikinis had been done to death in *One Million Years B.C.* and *When Dinosaurs Ruled*. Critics and even audiences knew that prehistoric bikinis were unrealistic and the costumes certainly couldn't get any smaller than they were in *When Dinosaurs Ruled*. Some of the older women in *Creatures*, including the Old Crone, wear short dresses. Some younger girls wear bikinis, but others are topless. They were filmed from behind, at a distance, in semi-darkness or with hair over their breasts. Hammer also for once used women with smaller breasts for some of the parts. (One can imagine the shock among British starlets and stuntwomen when Hammer put out a call for small-breasted women.) An ingenious solution was used for the two female leads, the Girl and the Mute Girl, which permitted them to go topless and avoid the bikini look while not showing more than was wanted. They both wear heavy necklaces which cover their breasts. The Girl's fur necklace stays firmly in place no matter what trouble she gets into.

Over the years prehistoric films have seen a steady escalation in fights between women. *One Million B.C.* (1940) had no such fights. *Prehistoric Women* (1950) had one cat fight between girls wearing modest miniskirts. *One Million Years B.C.* had one between two women in bikinis. *When Dinosaurs Ruled the Earth* had a fight with three women in bikinis in water. *Creatures* has two cat fights, both between topless girls. The costumes and the fights are the fun part of the film's exploitation. The scene in which a woman is murdered in the sand pit and the murderess cannot escape from the pit is effectively shocking, as is the blinding of the prisoners in the big battle. Four scenes are distastefully exploitative without being either fun or shocking. Perhaps the least offensive of these are the attempted rapes of the Mute Girl and the Girl. Worse is the torture of the Mute Girl with porcupine quills when she is 15, by a 15-year-old boy. Worst of all is the flogging of the bare breasts of two women. Their breasts are not shown and the flogging is done by a woman, not a man, but there are prolonged shots of the victims' agonized faces. *Creatures* was rated PG at a time when PG–13 did not exist and almost every film was either PG or R. This rating shows Hammer's expertise at manipulating the rating system while getting away with as much as possible.

Creatures is the first Hammer prehistoric film in which the heroine kills someone. The characters played by Raquel Welch and Victoria Vetri in *One Million Years B.C.* and *When Dinosaurs Ruled the Earth* never hurt anyone. Hammer seems to have been obsessed with snakes when it made its last two caveman movies. Both Victoria Vetri in *When Dinosaurs Ruled* and Julie Ege in *Creatures* have deadly snakes crawl over their almost naked bodies.

Several details make *Creatures* more optimistic and less misanthropic than *One Million Years B.C.* and *When Dinosaurs Ruled*. In the opening scene the hunters bury their dead comrade even though they fear more dangerous animals will show up. They bury his spear with him even though spears are valuable and difficult to make. This contrasts with the callous abandonment of the injured old man in the opening scene of *One Million Years B.C.* Two murders are committed in the first half of the film but both the killer of the tribe's first leader and the woman who drowns another girl in the sand pit are killed in circumstances which produce a rough kind of justice.

The twin's father is tough but reasonable and even sensitive. When his mate dies in childbirth he shakes the dead woman's head angrily, then breaks down and weeps. The dark and fair tribes merge peacefully, exchange mates and never have any problems with each other. The twins' father seems to be an excellent leader and there appears to be peace for about 20 years after the birth of the twins. Later the tribe kills the men who kidnapped the Mute Girl, but they permit the marauders' women to join their tribe. The tribe does pretty well until it is split by the disastrous civil war between the Fair One and the Dark One, which accounts for most of the killings in the film. Even when the tribe splits into factions, it isn't along old tribal lines; both the Fair One and the Dark One have both blonde and dark-haired supporters.

Johnson and Del Vecchio (*Hammer Films*) say that the old leader, who was injured in the earthquake, was killed by his son and that the new leader, who killed the murderer, was also the old leader's son and had to kill his own brother. Those facts are not obvious to me in the film but Johnson and Del Vecchio must have got the story from Hammer's publicity. It means that the tribe was torn by deadly conflict between two brothers in two successive generations. Since the killing of the murderer in the first generation was followed by 20 years of peace while the Fair One's refusal to kill his brother led to a bloody civil war, the film seems to be arguing in favor of capitol punishment, at least in primitive societies.

Three of the principals in *Creatures* had worked in previous Hammer prehistoric epics. Don Chaffey directed *One Million Years B.C.*, as well as the magnificent *Jason and the Argonauts* (1963). Producer-writer Michael Carreras wrote and produced *One Million Years B.C.* and *Slave Girls* and directed *Slave Girls*. Mario Nascimbene had written ground-breaking scores for *One Million Years B.C.* and *When Dinosaurs Ruled*. Randall Larson (*Music from the House of Hammer*) writes that Nascimbene's score for *Creatures* "seemed little more than a reworking of the previous two compositions."

Julie Ege, once Miss Norway, was 27 years old when she made *Creatures*. Hammer gave maximum publicity to their search for a "new sex symbol" to follow in the footsteps of Raquel Welch and Victoria Vetri. Her grubby cavegirl in *Creatures* was much less glamorous than the leads in *One Million Years B.C.* and *When Dinosaurs Ruled* but the likeable Ege shrewdly managed to parlay the publicity into a short but busy career (16 films in six years), outdoing Victoria Vetri. The most dignified performances are by Rosalie Crutchley, who played the almost androgynous Old Crone, and Brian O'Shaughnessy as the Leader. Crutchley was in over 100 films and TV shows, from *Quo Vadis* (1951) to *Four Weddings and a Funeral* (1994). South African O'Shaughnessy was in about 30 films, including *The Gods Must Be Crazy* (1980). Australian Tony Bonner worked in about 30 minor films from the 1960s to the 90s.

Variety (April 7, 1971) was cautious about this "bizarre and violent Stone Age horror film which, though the most incredible twaddle, has sufficient good production values, direction, scraps [fights] and nubile damsels to amuse undemanding audiences." The reviewer praised Chaffey who "has directed with gusto though tongue in cheek" and noted the "remarkably-planned and lensed earthquake sequence," without recognizing that much of the scene was lifted from *One Million Years B.C.* Johnson and Del Vecchio (*Hammer Films*) considered *Creatures* "one of Hammer's worst pictures." Jones (*Illustrated Dinosaur Movie Guide*) gives *Creatures* a fairly good rating of 2½ out of four points and writes "despite the lack of monsters, the mystical elements work quite well."

Creatures That Time Forgot has many plausible details but reviewers have generally been distracted from its modest virtues by the overwrought exploitation elements—too many killings, abundant near-nudity and an atmosphere of brutality. I would say *Creatures*, the last of Hammer's four prehistoric films, is mediocre rather than dreadful and has points of interest as one of the more realistic prehistoric films of its time. Ref: Smith. *Epic Films*; Johnson/Del Vecchio. *Hammer Films*; Larson. *Music from the House of Hammer*; Jones. *Illustrated Dinosaur Movie Guide*; Senn/Johnson. *Fantastic Cinema Subject Guide*; MK 5.

Cro (1993) U.S.; producer, Bob Richardson; Film Roman/Children's Television Workshop/ABC. Animated TV series; 21 23-min. episodes; color. Based on book *The Way Things Work* by David Macaulay. VOICES: Max Casella (*Cro*); Charlie Adler (*Mojo, a mammoth*); Ruth Buzzi (*Nandy, a Neanderthal*); Jim Cummings (*Phil/Ogg, a Neanderthal*); Tress MacNeille (*Esmeralda, a mammoth*); Candy Milo (*Paka, a mammoth*); Laurie O'Brien (*Ivana, a mammoth*); April Ortiz (*Dr. C*); Jane Singer (*Selene, a sabre-tooth tiger*); Jussie

Smollett (*Mike*); Frank Welker (*Gogg, a Neanderthal/Bob, a monkey/Earle, a mammoth*).

Phil, a hip-talking woolly mammoth revived in modern times after being frozen during the Ice Age, tells his new friends Mike and Dr. C. stories of his adventures with clever Cro-Magnon orphan boy Cro. Cro is raised by a Neanderthal foster family. Phil is Cro's mentor as the boy discovers levers, pulleys, wheels, screws, springs, the buoyancy of water, the phases of the moon and how to construct musical instruments.

All these were real discoveries of early man, as documented in David Macaulay's book *The Way Things Work*, on which *Cro* was based. Unfortunately the series also includes a glider among Cro's inventions. Hal Erickson (*Television Cartoon Shows*) found *Cro* "trivial, patronizing and misleading," with the characters speaking in "pop-culture patois, the Neanderthals swapping 1990s slang in an Early Tonto dialect."

The worst aspect of *Cro* was its contemptuous depiction of Cro's Neanderthal friends Ogg and Gogg. They hang out with Bob the Monkey and are clearly no brighter than he is. They constantly fall down holes, or rocks falls on their heads, or some other calamity proves their pathetic stupidity. Ogg admits disconsolately, "Ogg just dumb." Not only Cro the Cro-Magnon but also all the talking mammoths are smarter than the Neanderthals. A collector's card in a *Cro* video container tells children, "With their low, thick brows, Ogg and Gogg may look like half-wits, but they're more like quarter-wits."

Cro was supposed to be educational because it presented simple facts about basic inventions, but it also promoted ignorance and prejudice about early humans. Since Cro is a child and his Neanderthal friends are adults, the series panders to children's delight in seeing themselves portrayed as smarter than grown-ups. Of course Neanderthals were probably less intelligent than modern humans, but films like *Dinosaurus!* (1960) have treated Neanderthals with respect. Long before *Cro*, *Valley of the Dinosaurs* (1974) was an animated TV series for children which portrayed primitive people as intelligent and eager to learn.

Cro is especially disappointing coming from Children's Television Workshop which was responsible for prestigious children's series such as *Sesame Street* and *The Electric Company* on PBS. *Cro* was CTW's first animated series and its first project with a commercial network. The National Science Foundation also supported *Cro*.

The video collection *Cro: Adventures in Woollyville* includes the episodes "Pulley For You" and "A Bridge Too Short." The video *Cro: Have Mammoth, Will Travel* has the episodes "No Way Up" and "Escape from Mung Island." Information on the titles and contents of other episodes is elusive. Ref: Erickson. *Television Cartoon Shows*; Lenburg. *Encyclopedia of Animated Cartoons* (1999); viewed 4 episodes; MK 3.

Cro-Magnon (1974) *see* **The Tribe** (1974)

Curiosity Shop (1971–73) Segment, *B.C.* U.S.; Sandler-Burns-Marmer/ABC. Animated segment of liveaction & animated TV series; 17 50-min. episodes; color.

Woolery calls this educational children's series "puzzling ... off-beat." Besides liveaction scenes, *Curiosity Shop* offered several animated segments based on popular comic strips, including Johnny Hart's *B.C.* strip about amiable cavemen. According to Woolery, the *B.C.* characters "participated in such ancient discoveries as 'The Invention of the Sundial.'" Ref: Woolery. *Children's Television.*; not viewed.

Curious Pets of Our Ancestors (1917) U.S.; dir. Willis O'Brien; Conquest Pictures/Edison. Short puppet film; 1 reel; b&w; silent.

One of six prehistoric films made by stop-motion animator O'Brien 1915–1917, *Curious Pets* is a lost film. See *The Dinosaur and the Missing Link* (1917) for information on O'Brien's films. Ref: Jones. *Illustrated Dinosaur Movie Guide*; Berry. *Dinosaur Filmography*; not viewed.

Daffy Duck and the Dinosaur (1939) U.S.; dir, Chuck Jones; Warner Bros. Animated short film; 7 min.; color. Screenplay, Dave Monahan; music, Carl W. Stalling. *VOICES:* Mel Blanc; Jack Lescoulie.

Casper Caveman (a parody of Jack Benny) and his dopey pet dinosaur Fido try to capture Daffy Duck for breakfast. They stand no chance at all; for instance, when Casper tries to dive into the lake, Daffy's "Positively No Swimming!"

sign stops him dead. Casper shoots a rock at Daffy with a slingshot; the rock reacts anthropomorphically to Daffy's efforts to avoid it. At this time in the late 1930s Daffy was at his most lunatic and anarchic, but this short depends too much on the gag of Jack Benny as a caveman and has fewer laughs than Chuck Jones's best cartoons. Ref: Webb. *Animated Film Encyclopedia*; Beck/Friedwald. *Looney Tunes and Merrie Melodies*; Jones. *Illustrated Dinosaur Movie Guide*; MK 6.

Darling, Get Me a Crocodile (1960s?) U.S.; dir. E. Husiatowicz; EM Films/Fleetwood Films. Animated short film; 6 min.; color.

Two cavemen live carefree lives among colorful animals until two cavewomen become jealous of a stylish woman who wears a beautiful bird in her hair. The two women demand that the men get them a bird for their hair. After a many difficulties, including falling from a high rock, the men present a bird to the women, who fight over it. The stylish woman then appears wearing a tiger skin stole around her neck. The jealous women send the cavemen after a tiger. The tiger chases the nervous hunters, who manage to get the tiger's skin by dumb luck; the skinned tiger departs in a huff. The women fight over the tiger skin.

The stylish woman next appears riding on a tame crocodile, which resembles a big, finned automobile. The two women try to make the very reluctant cavemen dive into a pool to get a crocodile. When the men won't do it, the women throw them in. The men race from the pool, pursued by the crocodile, who becomes alarmed by the predatory women and dives back in the pool. The two cavemen then hop on the stylish woman's crocodile and ride off with her, leaving the two women alone.

This delightful short cartoon appeared in the supplementary material of the Something Weird DVD of *When Men Carried Clubs and Women Played Ding Dong* (1971) and *50,000 B.C. (Before Clothing)* (1963). It is much better than the two low-brow features. MK 7.

The Dawn of Man (1968), segment of **2001: A Space Odyssey** (1968)

Dino and the Cavemouse (1980–82) *see* **The Flintstones Comedy Show** (1980–82)

The Dinosaur and the Baboon (1915/1917) *see* **The Dinosaur and the Missing Link** (1915/1917)

The Dinosaur and the Missing Link (made 1915, released 1917) [alt. *The Dinosaur and the Baboon*] U.S.; dir. Willis O'Brien; Conquest Pictures/Edison. Short stop-motion film; 5 or 7 min.; b&w; silent.

Intertitle: "Having procured a modest bouquet of cactus, the Duke prepares to call on Miss Araminta Rockface." The Duke, a tall caveman, is so dumb he walks into a tree branch. We see "Mr. Rockface and his daughter Araminta in the drawing room of their country home." Araminta is sweeping the cave floor while her father sits on a comfortable rock. The walls are covered with cave art. When he arrives at the cave "the Duke discovers his hated rival, Steve Stonejaw, has also come to call on Miss Rockface." Steve, who seems smarter than the Duke, knocks his rival into the stone food bucket the Rockfaces keep in front of their cave.

"In the midst of the argument, our unassuming hero, Theophilus Ivoryhead, arrives." Theophilus is much smaller than Steve and the Duke. Araminta invites all three suitors into the cave but quickly puts them to work. "If you young gentlemen want any dinner, you'll have to go out and get it. Duke, we shall depend on you and Stonejaw for the meat course. Theophilus, you may catch some fish." An intertitle announces "Wild Willie, the Missing Link, is the terror of the countryside." Willie looks entirely like an ape rather than a man; he is slightly larger than the cavemen and climbs trees with agility. Willie steals snakes from the Rockface food store and eats them greedily.

On his hunting expedition, Stonejaw aims an arrow at a big bird. The bird ducks and the arrow flies on to hit Mr. Rockface in the behind, knocking him into the food bucket. Meanwhile, Theophilus is fishing from a small boat in a stream as a large dinosaur stalks him from the shore. The little caveman fails to notice the danger but "Wild Willie decides to go down to the stream and catch a few snakes for his dinner." Willie stupidly mistakes the dinosaur's tail for a snake and hits it with a rock. After a fight, the dinosaur throws Willie to the ground, killing him. The dinosaur departs and Theophilus takes the credit for killing Willie when his rivals and the Rockfaces arrive. Araminta is impressed and embraces Theophilus.

(1) Dinosaur Babes

COMMENTARY. Willis O'Brien was the principal pioneer in the development of stop-motion animation. From 1915 to 1917 he made six short caveman comedies by this time-consuming method. *The Dinosaur and Missing Link* was the second longest of the series (after *R.F.D, 10,000 B.C.*) and probably the best, full of humorous bits of business and clever details like the cave art on the walls of the Rockfaces' "country home."

In addition to *The Dinosaur and the Missing Link*, O'Brien's cavemen films were *Morpheus Mike, Prehistoric Poultry, Curious Pets of Our Ancestors, The Birth of a Flivver* and *R.F.D. 10,0000 B.C.* All were released by Conquest and Edison in 1917. *Curious Pets* and *Birth of a Flivver* are apparently lost films. Giannalberto Bendazzi, in his book *Cartoons*, says that O'Brien's early short films "are excellent for their believable animation of prehistoric animals. As works of art, however, they lack substance and display corny, simplistic humour, clumsy rhythm and uninteresting plots." Robert K. Klepper (*Silent Films*) on the other hand gives *The Dinosaur and the Missing Link*, *R.F.D. 10,000 B.C.* and *Prehistoric Poultry* each three stars in his four-star rating system.

Webb (*Animated Film Encyclopedia*) says *The Dinosaur and the Missing Link* was 7 min. long. The version I have seen was 5 min. A shorter version, about 4 min., is included in the Slingshot DVD of *The Lost World* (1925). O'Brien's *The Ghost of Slumber Mountain* (1918) had dinosaurs but no cavemen. O'Brien went on to work on *The Lost World, King Kong* (1931), *Mighty Joe Young* (1949) and the documentary *The Animal World* (1956). Ref: Jones. *Illustrated Dinosaur Movie Guide*; Webb. *Animated Film Encyclopedia*; Berry. *Dinosaur Filmography*; Bendazzi. *Cartoons*; Klepper. *Silent Films*; MK 7.

Dinosaur Babes (1996) U.S.; dir. Brett Piper; Take 2 Productions. 93 min,; color. Screenplay, Brett Piper. CAST: Rick Bureau (*Zach*); Mike Whitehead (*Shifty*); Jeff Cornello (*Bruno*); Melissa Ann (*Lona*); Kathi Trotter (*Leela*); Iris Lynne (*Monga*); Kelly Lynn (*Greta*); Dianne Thorne (*Mook*).

Cavemen Zach, Shifty and Bruno discover their tribe has been massacred, except for Leela, Gretta and Mook, who have been captured by an all-female tribe. The Amazons' tyrannical leader Monga sacrifices Mook to a Tyrannosaurus Rex. The three cavemen search for the women, dodging dinosaurs and easily defeating three "genetically altered sub-humans" who have something to do with a wrecked spaceship!

Monga punishes Amazon Lona for making friends with Leela. Zach and his friends lure a dinosaur into the Amazons' camp as a diversion. Zach and Lona escape, find a ray gun in the wrecked spaceship and use it to save Leela just as she is about to be sacrificed.

COMMENTARY. Mark F. Berry (*Dinosaur Filmography*) found the direct-to-video film "slow and schizophrenic," lurching from low slapstick comedy to "mean-spirited and misogynistic" scenes of torture of women. Some of the dinosaurs are surprisingly good, but the backgrounds behind them are poor. The film announces "Four million years

Wild Willie, the Missing Link from Willis O'Brien's *The Dinosaur and the Missing Link.*

ago, the first true humans and the last of the dinosaurs briefly coexisted." This misdates modern humans by 3.9 million years and the dinosaurs by about 60 million years. Director Brett Piper repudiated the film, which was finished by the producers. Ref: *Internet Movie Database*; Berry. *Dinosaur Filmography*; not viewed.

Dinosaur Valley Girls (1996) U.S.; dir. Donald F. Glut; Frontline Entertainment. 94 min.; color. Screenplay, Donald F. Glut; music, Thomas Morse. CAST: Jeff Rector (*Tony Markham*); Denise Ames (*Hea-Thor*); William Marshall (*Dr. Michaels*); Karen Black (*Ro-Kell*); Ed Fury (*Ur-So*); Harrison Ray (*Beeg-Mak*); Griffen Drew (*Daphne Adrian*); Arkeni (*Tam-Mee*); Caree (*Bar-Bee*); S.G. Ellison (*Tor-Ree*); Staci Flood (*Deb-Bee*); Nina Keliiliki (*Bran-Dee*); Donna Spangler (*Mee-Shell*); Michelle Stanger (*Buf-Fee*); Lauren Bea (*Bam-Bee*); William Blair (*Bro-Mo*); Giovanni Cuarez (*Kar-Bo*); Gilbert George (*Sly-Dor*); Just Matt (*Slur-Pee*); Jason Peters (*Korn-Dang*); John-Michael Williams (*Wa-Por*); Jerry Warren; Forrest Ackerman.

While making *Feet of Fury IV* action film star Tony Markham is disturbed by visions of dinosaurs and a beautiful cavegirl. At a paleontology museum, pompous scientist Dr. Michaels shows Tony a prehistoric talisman which grants wishes. Using the icon, Tony finds himself in Dinosaur Valley, where he is chased by brutish cavemen led by Beeg-Mak (groan!) and rescued by Hea-Thor, the girl of his visions.

The women, led by Ro-Kell, have all left the crude men. Tony and Hea-Thor fall in love, though Tony has to fight off the other cavegirls, except for standoffish Ro-Kell. Tony teaches the girls martial arts. When Beeg-Mak and his men try to kidnap women, the women beat them up. Ro-Kell is reconciled with her former mate Ur-So and all the men and women pair off in couples, although Tony has to defeat Beeg-Mak. After briefly returning to the modern world, Tony decides to go back and stay with Hea-Thor in Dinosaur Valley.

COMMENTARY. Donald F. Glut is the author of serious reference books on both old horror films (*The Dracula Book*, 1975; *The Frankenstein Catalog*, 1984) and dinosaurs (*Dinosaurs: The Encyclopedia*, 1997). However, when he combined his two interests and wrote and directed his first film, he set his sights pretty low. *Dinosaur Valley Girls* is intended simply as a spoof and a celebration of the conventions of the dinosaur-and-cavegirl B movie. The girls are busty, man-hungry and frequently topless. The cavemen are almost all dumb. There's a fight between two dinosaurs, a fight between two girls, fights between men and women and even a hair-dragging scene. Even with all this going on, the film drags at only 94 minutes.

One thing Glut did insist on was good dinosaurs. Noted special effects artist Jim Danforth dropped out of the project. After several other changes in personnel Thomas Dickens and a small crew created several species of admirably realistic predators. As for the script, there are a few good lines mocking Hollywood, such as Tony's "Where's a stuntman when you need one?" as a dinosaur bears down on him. Ur-So uses a dinosaur's arm bone as a backscratcher. When two girls have the inevitable catfight, they hiss like real cats. The Three Stooges are heard briefly on TV in the modern world; in Dinosaur Valley the men fight like the Stooges and even snore like them. The men also belch and fart loudly, making this one battle-of-the-sexes caveman movie in which the women are clearly superior.

There is a great deal of dialogue in the invented cavemen language. No doubt viewers who concentrate and decipher the language would be repaid by a string of jokes, but probably few of the film's intended audience bothered. Glut's *Dinosaur Valley Girls: The Book* (1998) has a caveman–English dictionary.

Besides cameos by low-budget director Jerry Warren and super-fan Forrest Ackerman, the only well-known actors are Ed Fury, who played Ursus in a few Italian pepla films (and is therefore called Ur-So here); William Marshall, the mellifluous-voiced Shakespearean actor who became a cult star in *Blacula* (1972) and who reads the "Brave new world" line from *The Tempest*, which Glut audaciously inserted in *Dinosaur Valley Girls*; and Oscar-nominee Karen Black, who was 56 when she worked on the film. While all the younger actresses play pouting stereotypes, Black saw her role as an acting challenge and plays a real primitive, almost simian character. She grunts, glowers and chomps on a bone. Her costume is less revealing than the other women's and she is the only actress not to go topless. All the girls are given cave language versions of modern Valley Girl names such as "Hea-Thor" and "Tam-Mee"; Karen Black's "Ro-Kell" is a homage to Raquel Welch of *One Million Years B.C.*

Glut's book on the making of the movie is considered one of the most entertaining accounts of the travails of low-budget filmmaking. Ref: Glut. *Dinosaur Valley Girls: The Book*; Berry. *Dinosaur Filmography*; MK 4.

Dinosaurs (1991–94) U.S.; producers, Brian Henson, Michael Jacobs, Jeff McCracken; Disney/Jim Henson Productions/Jacobs Productions/ABC. Puppet animation TV series. 58 or 65 25-min. episodes; color. *VOICES:* Stuart Pankin (*Earl Sinclair*); Jessica Walter (*Fran Sinclair*); Jason Willinger (*Robbie Sinclair*); Sally Struthers (*Charlene Sinclair*); Kevin Clash (*Baby Sinclair*).

Like *The Honeymooners* (1952–57) and *The Flintstones* (1960–66), *Dinosaurs* was a satiric comedy about a blowhard husband and father. In *Dinosaurs* the klutzy patriarch and his family are talking dinosaurs with modern amenities, including clothes and TVs. The messages were ecological and anti-business. Audiences were intended to draw "parallels between the bone-headed dinosaur civilization of 60,000,003 B.C. and modern America," as Russell Wodell notes on the epguides.com site.

Humans were introduced to the series in the tenth episode *Endangered Species* (dir. Jay Dubin; screenplay, David A. Caplan and Brian Lapan). Greedy Earl wants to eat the last "grapdelites" in the world for dinner, but his idealistic son Robbie Sinclair saves them. The grapdelites look like humanoid apes and are clearly intended to represent primitive humans. Thus humans are saved from early extinction by dinosaurs with ecological consciousness. One of the grapdelites was voiced by Kevin Clash, who also played Baby Sinclair, the tiniest dinosaur. The other grapdelite voice was provided by Dave Goelz.

In episode 33, *The Discovery* (dir. Tom Trbovich; screenplay, Andy Goodman), the Sinclairs are taken hostage by newly-discovered cavemen who object to the dinosaur corporation's development plans. Michelan Sisti voiced "Elder Caveman."

In the 34th episode, *Little Boy Boo* (dir. Tom Trbovich; screenplay, Kirk R. Thatcher), Baby Sinclair is alarmed by scary legends about the Wereman, who is half-dinosaur and half human. The Wereman's voice was provided by Kirk Thatcher; the voice of "Rabid Caveman" by Bill Barretta.

In episode 46, *Swamp Music* (dir. Tom Trbovich; screenplay, Mark Drop), Robbie tries to get his swamp-dwelling human friends a record contract despite the dinosaur prejudice against "mammal music."

In *Charlene and Her Amazing Humans* (episode 50; dir. Bruce Bilson; screenplay, Dava Savel), Charlene Sinclair puts on a stage act exploiting cave children. Ben Ganger, Alyssa McGraw and Tiffany Taubman voiced the "Cavelings."

The 58th episode, *Changing Nature*, brought the series to a literally chilling conclusion as a corporate blunder leads to an Ice Age and the extinction of the dinosaurs. Baby Sinclair delivers the last line "But I don't want to be extinct!" (Seven more episodes, nos. 59–65, were seen only in syndication and were of course set before the grim finale.) Ref: Jones. *Illustrated Dinosaur Movie Guide*; Internet Movie Database; EpGuides.com (http://www.epguides.com); one episode ("Endangered Species") viewed; MK 6.

The Divine Gift (1918) U.K.; dir. Thomas Bentley; British Actors/Philips. Feature film; 5300 feet (ca. 65 min.); b&w; silent. Screenplay, Kenelm Foss. *CAST:* Joyce Dearsley (*Shopgirl*); Jack Livesey (*Bank Clerk*); F. Pope-Stamper (*Tristan*); Wanda Redford (*Iseult*); Micheline Poteus (*Prehistoric Woman*).

"Stories illustrate discussion on whether God's greatest gift is humanity, piety, love, intellect or self-sacrifice." Information on the story involving a "Prehistoric Woman" is elusive. Ref: Gifford. *British Film Catalogue*; not viewed.

Doctor Who (1963–1989) story *An Unearthly Child* (1963) [alt. *100,000 B.C.*; *The Tribe of Gum*] U.K.; dir. Waris Hussein; BBC. 4-episode story in TV series; 97 min.; b&w. Screenplay, Anthony Coburn; music, Ron Grainer. *CAST:* William Hartnell (*The Doctor*); William Russell (*Ian Chesterton*); Jacqueline Hill (*Barbara Wright*); Carole Ann Ford (*Susan Foreman*); Derek Newark (*Za*); Alethea Charlton (*Hur*); Jeremy Young (*Kal*); Howard Young (*Horg*); Eileen Way (*Old Mother*).

In modern England, teachers Ian and Barbara are puzzled by their new student Susan, who has an encyclopedic knowledge of science and history but is ignorant about everyday life. They discover that she lives in what appears to be a phone booth. The booth is much larger on the inside than the outside and contains ultra-advanced scientific equipment and Susan's irascible grandfather, the Doctor. He is a Time Lord from a distant planet and the phone booth is his TARDIS (Time and Relative Dimensions in Space), a machine for traveling to any place and time in the universe! By accident the TARDIS takes them to 100,000 B.C. The first episode ends as the alarming shadow of a primitive man approaches the TARDIS.

The tribe of Gum has been torn apart by the death of the Firemaker, who kept the means of making fire a secret so that he could control the tribe. The Firemaker's son Za does not know the secret but he nevertheless demands the leadership of the tribe. The Old Mother, a true reactionary, wants to do without fire. When Za says "My father made fire," the Mother replies "They killed him for it. It is better that we live as we have always lived." She accuses Za of wanting to make fire "so everyone will bow down to you as they did to him.... Fire will destroy us all." Kal, a cocky outsider, says that he has seen fire made and that he should be the leader. Everyone agrees that Orb the sun god will give the power to make fire to the tribe's true leader.

Za captures the Doctor. When Ian, Barbara and Susan try to find him the tribe captures all of them. The Doctor announces that he can make fire, but he has lost his matches and fails to do it. The tribe imprisons the time travelers in the Cave of Skulls (which, of course, is full of skulls). The Old Mother sets them free so that they will leave and not make fire. As the Doctor and his friends flee through the forest, trying to find the TARDIS, they are pursued by Za and Hur, a woman who will be given to the new leader and who prefers Za over Kal.

Za is injured (off-camera) by a beast which he kills with his stone ax. The Doctor wants to leave him, but Ian and Barbara insist on helping him. Meanwhile, Kal discovers that the Old Mother has let the strangers go. He kills her and blames the murder on Za and Hur. The tribe catches the four strangers with Za and Hur. The Doctor cleverly points out that there is blood on Kal's knife but none on Za's knife. The tribe realizes that Kal killed the Old Mother and drives him out.

Za recovers. He is grateful that the strangers helped him and exposed Kal but he still keeps them imprisoned in the cave, demanding that they show him how to make fire. Science teacher Ian finally manages to make a bow-drill and start a fire. Kal returns, kills a man and attacks Za. They fight, Za armed with a club and Kal with an ax and a knife. Za kills Kal and, with his new knowledge of firemaking, takes over the tribe. Nevertheless, Za still isn't ready to let the strangers go; now he wants them to arrange an alliance between his tribe and theirs, which he imagines lives over the mountain.

Fed up, the time travelers rub fat on four skulls, put them on sticks and set them alight. While the tribe is overawed by this apparition, the Doctor and his friends make their escape. The tribe soon sees through the trick and pursues them. Just as the time travelers enter the TARDIS, the tribesmen arrive and bombard the TARDIS with spears. The TARDIS vanishes, taking its four passengers to an unknown time and place.

Episodes: An Unearthly Child; The Cave of Skulls; The Forest of Fear; The Firemaker.

COMMENTARY. *An Unearthly Child* was the first story in the *Doctor Who* series, which survived until 1989, becoming one of the longest-lasting TV series in any genre and one of the most beloved science fiction series. The initial episode was the first regular programming shown by the BBC on Nov. 23, 1963 after they ended special coverage of the assassination of President Kennedy. The first episode, set in modern London and with only four actors, is a suspenseful classic. The other three episodes, set among the cave people, are simple, padded and talky.

The Doctor was played by seven actors over 26 years, with the explanation that Time Lords who die can revive in a new body. William Hartnell played the First Doctor as an arrogant, irritating, selfish old tyrant, not an easy man to like. Later Doctors would be younger, more attractive and more likeable, though still eccentric.

The prehistoric people in *An Unearthly Child* are anatomically-modern, played without special makeup. They wear ill-fitting, shaggy fur costumes with bare arms and legs—and bare feet, which is ridiculous for people who are afraid of freezing to death if they do not regain the secret of firemaking. They have the usual weapons—clubs, axes, spears and small stone knives without handles. Children put a skin over a small frame and play at killing this "animal." The cave people are unsophisticated, simple-minded and rather nasty. One fellow nostalgically recalls cooking with the words, "I remember how the meat and the fire joined together." These cave people are always threatening to kill someone. Za muses, "I will have to spill some blood, make people bow to me." Three people are killed in the story, about one-tenth of the small band. Before the story starts, the cave people killed the Firemaker, Za's father, even though he was the only one who knew how to make fire. That wasn't very smart.

Hur, the young woman, seems to be the smartest of the cave people. She is constantly giving Za advice, usually good advice. But even clever Hur is needlessly suspicious of the strangers. When Ian and Barbara try to help injured Za, Hur rejects them. "She doesn't understand kindness, friendship," says Ian. When Ian tells Za "I'm a friend—friend," Za thinks that "Friend" is Ian's name, which indicates that the cave people have no word for friend. The Doctor says scornfully, "Do you think these people have any capacity for reason or logic? Their minds change as easily as day and night."

Za is violent, suspicious and ungrateful but he is preferable to the sneaky Kal and he does seem to learn during the story. When Ian says to him "The whole tribe is stronger than Kal," Za finds a great deal of meaning in this statement. He tells Hur that the whole tribe acting together can solve problems better than if each man acts alone and they quarrel among themselves. He begins to get a glimmering of Ian's idea of friendship and says "They are of a new tribe, not like ours, not like Kal." At the end, Za is likely to be a good leader of the tribe. And he has the secret of fire; the night forest no longer holds terrors for the humans. Za proclaims triumphantly, "With fire the night is day."

The cave people all speak English, or at least they are understood by the time travelers and the audience as if they were speaking English. Much later in the series, the Fourth Doctor explains to one of his companions that the ability to understand any language instantly is "a gift of the Time Lords," a gift which he can apparently bestow on his companions without their even knowing it. Most of the companions aren't smart enough to question the miracle.

Waris Hussein was only 25 when he directed *An Unearthly Child.* He went on to be a busy director of both TV and film in Britain, including some *Masterpiece Theatre* productions. Derek Newark and Eileen Way were useful character actors with long careers. William Russell was an occasional leading man, including in the TV series *The Adventures of Sir Lancelot* (1956–57).

Doctor Who was planned as an educational program about both history and science and it was assumed that many stories would take place in the past. In fact, historical stories were much less popular than tales set on futuristic alien planets or in the modern world under alien invasion. (The second story, *The Daleks,* introduced the series' popular robot villains.) Only a couple dozen of the series' 159 multi-episode stories were set in the human past. *An Unearthly Child* was the only story set among prehistoric humans, but it would not be *Doctor Who*'s last word on prehistory.

Doctor Who also featured several "prehistoric menace" tales, about non-human species from prehistoric Earth or aliens who arrived on Earth during prehistory, both of which menace modern Earth. The Silurians were intelligent man-like reptiles who hibernated for millions of years and now claim to be the rightful masters of Earth in *The Silurians* (1970). The Sea Devils were underwater versions of the Silurians in *The Sea Devils* (1972). Both Silurians and Sea Devils returned in *Warriors of the Deep* (1984). The alien Zygons have plotted and planned in their spaceship on the bottom of Loch Ness since 50,000 B.C. in *Terror of the Zygons* (1975); they created the Loch's Monster. Twice aliens have been credited with influencing the development of early man: the Daemons in *The Daemons* (1971) and Scaroth, an alien Jagorath who exists at several different periods of history, in *City of Death* (1979). In *Ghost Light* (1989), one of the last *Doctor Who* stories, the Seventh Doctor discovers a Neanderthal butler (a brilliant concept!) in a Victorian household. Finally, there were nine stories (1977–78) featuring Leela, a primitive warrior girl from another planet, who became the Doctor's companion. Leela was a far more attractive and intelligent representative of primitive humans than the grunting savages of *An Unearthly Child.* Ref: Jones. *Illustrated Dinosaur Movie Guide*; Lofficier. *Doctor Who: The Programme Guide*; MK 6.

Donald and the Wheel (1961) U.S.; dir. Hamilton S. Luske; Disney. 18 min.; color. Screenplay, Bill Berg; music, Buddy Baker.

VOICES: Clarence Nash (*Donald Duck*); Thurl Ravenscroft (*Spirit of Progress*).

The Spirit of Progress introduces us to caveman Donald Duck, the inventor of the wheel. The two-reel educational film then traces the history of the wheel to the present. One of the last Donald Duck cartoons. An updated version was released in 1990. Ref: Smith. *Disney A to Z*; Webb. *Animated Film Encyclopedia*; not viewed.

Dorf Goes Fishing (1993) U.S.; dir. Berry Landen; MVP Home Entertainment. Direct-to-video film; 45 min.; color. Screenplay, Tim Conway. CAST: Tim Conway (*Dorf/Grunt the Caveman*).

Conway was a comedian on *McHale's Navy* (1962–66) and had his own TV show in 1970. In the 1990s he did a series of sports comedy videos. Here he plays a caveman learning to fish. Ref: *Internet Movie Database*; not viewed.

A Dream (1914) *see* **His Prehistoric Past** (1914)

La Edad de Piedra (1962) [trans. *The Stone Age*] Mexico; dir. René Cardona. 84 min.; b&w. Photography, Raul Martinez Solares; music, Manuel Esperón. CAST: Marco Antonio Campos (*Viruta*); Gaspar Henaine (*Capulina*); Jorge Beirute (*King of the Cave People*); Lorena Velasquez; Sonia Infante; Eduardo Silvestre.

Two zanies are sent back in time when they deliver flowers to a mad scientist. They make friends with Dino, a baby dinosaur, and are captured by two club-wielding cavegirls. The boys successfully introduce the cave people to Mexican music, sombreros, arithmetic, chess and the two favorite sports of modern Mexico, football and wrestling. They start a barber shop and beauty salon. (For once there is a reason why the cavegirls' hair looks so nice.) After finding the rare metal which permits time travel, the boys briefly return to the modern world, then decide to go back to their girlfriends in the Stone Age.

La Edad de Piedra comes off like *The Three Stooges Meet the Flintstones*, with nonstop knockabout comedy. The filmmakers must have been inspired by *The Flintstones*; the boys have a small pet dinosaur they call Dino and invent a wooden, human-powered car. The prehistoric tribe is unusually large, with about 100 people. They already have cave art when the modern duo arrive. The cave children prove to be better at arithmetic than their time-traveling teachers. Dino is played by a child in a suit and is far too cute. The bigger dinosaurs are cheaply-made and seen only briefly. About 55 minutes of the feature are set among the cave people.

Campos and Henaine played Viruta and Capulina in dozens of Mexican comedies. Cardona directed more than 100 films. Ref: Jones. *Illustrated Dinosaur Movie Guide*; *Internet Movie Database*; *Encyclopedia of Fantastic Film and Television* [website]; viewed in Spanish; MK 5.

Eek! and the Terrible Thunderlizards (1993) U.S.; Nelvana/Fox Network; creator, Savage Steve Holland. Animated TV series; 25-min. episodes; color. VOICES: Bill Kopp (*Eek/Scooter*); Curtis Armstrong (*Scooter*); Dan Castellaneta (*Bill*); Kurtwood Smith (*Dinosaur Commander*).

Eek was introduced in the series *Eek! The Cat* on Fox in 1992. The 1993 series replayed *Eek!* episodes from the 1992 series, together with new episodes involving the Thunderlizards, anthropomorphic "commando dinosaurs" who constantly try to destroy cavemen Bill and Scooter and always fail. Scooter is an inventor. A third series, *Eek! Stravaganza* (1995–97) included new episodes of *Thunderlizards*. Ref: *Internet Movie Database*; Lenburg. *Encyclopedia of Animated Cartoons* (1999 ed.); Erickson. *Television Cartoon Shows*; not viewed.

The Eternal Feminine (1915) U.S.; dir. George O. Nicholls; Selig. Short film; b&w; silent.

A woman dreams of the Stone Age, where she is the leader of the all-woman Feminine Tribe, which is attacked by male cavemen whose leader is called Strongarm. A 1915 comment on the women's suffrage issue. Ref: Jones. *Illustrated Dinosaur Movie Guide*; *Internet Movie Database*; not viewed.

Extinct Pink (1969) U.S.; dir. Hawley Pratt; Mirisch Corp./DePatie-Freleng. Animated short film; 6 min.; color. Screenplay, John W. Dunn; music, Doug Goodwin, Henry Mancini.

The Pink Panther, a short, pointy-nosed caveman, a dinosaur and a speedy lizard all compete for a single bone in prehistoric times. Ref: Webb. *Animated Film Encyclopedia*; not viewed.

The Fable of a Stoneage Romeo (1922) U.S.; dir. Paul Terry; Fable Pictures/Pathé. Animated short film; 5 min.; b&w; silent. (In the series *Aesop's Film Fables*).

Information on the story is unavailable. Ref: Webb. *Animated Film Encyclopedia*; *Internet Movie Database*; not viewed.

The Fabulous Funnies (1978–79) Segment, *Alley Oop*. U.S.; Filmation. Segment of animated TV series; 13 25-min. episodes; color. Based on comic strip by V.T. Hamlin. VOICES: Bob Holt (*Alley Oop*); June Foray (*Oola*); Alan Oppenheimer (*King Guzzle*).

Alley Oop shared this anthology series with *Nancy and Sluggo*, *Broom Hilda*, *Emmy Lou* and *The Captain and the Kids*. Lenburg says that some of the stories in *The Fabulous Funnies* were first shown on *Archie's TV Funnies* (1971–73); Erickson claims that all the *Fabulous Funnies* material was new.

Lenburg notes that the *Los Angeles Times* was unenthusiastic about the show's "heavy-handed ... pro-social messages." For instance, in an episode about tolerance Alley Oop taught his Stone Age friends not to fear a strange tribe but to share their hunting grounds. TV's Oop was much less belligerent than the original in V.T. Hamlin's comic strip. Erickson finds the series "actually pretty funny" with "surprisingly good animation" but deplores the fact that "such marvelously uninhibited, havoc-wreaking characters like Alley Oop and the Katzenjammer Kids were required to warn the kids at home to behave like responsible ladies and gentlemen."

Erickson says that each character had a seven-minute segment within a series episode, but I have seen a videocassette of a 25-min. *Alley Oop* story, dated 1978 and titled "That's Life," a title not in Lenburg's list of *Fabulous Funnies* episodes. When Oop's girlfriend Oola falls dangerously ill, Oop and his friend Foozy have to help the Grand Wizer, Moo's medicine man, recover his confidence, which was broken when Yum-Yum, a magical bird, died despite Wizer's medicines. Oop and his dinosaur steed Dinny have to climb a dangerous mountain to find a root that Wizer needs to make medicine for Oola. Oop uses a giant leaf as a matador's cape to fight a stegosaurus. The simply-drawn but fast-moving story tells children that they have to get on with life after someone dies. Oop shows a little of the belligerence of his original comic strip self when he chews out lazy King Guzzle. "Some king you are. You're good for nothing. You're stupid, ornery, pushy. Not only that, you're ugly."

June Foray was one of the busiest and most popular voice artists working in cartoons. According to Lenburg the episodes were: "Animal Crack-Ups," "School Daze," "Comic-ition," "Bods and Clods," "Save Our World," "But Would You Want Your Sister to Marry an Artist," "Money Madness," "Fear," "Different Jokes for Different Folks," "Death," "Safety Second," "Drinking," and "Shot in the Light." Ref: Lenburg. *The Encyclopedia of Animated Cartoons*; Erickson. *Television Cartoon Shows*; Woolery. *Children's Television*; 1 episode viewed; MK 5.

Alley Oop moved from comic strip to television as a segment of *The Fabulous Funnies.*

Felix in the Bone Age (1923) *see* **Felix the Cat in the Bone Age** (1923) **Felix in the Stone Age** (1923) *see* **Felix the Cat in the Bone Age** (1923)

Felix the Cat in the Bone Age (1923) [alt. *Felix in the Bone Age*; *Felix in the Stone Age*] U.S.; dir. Otto Messmer; Sullivan Studio/Winkler. Based on comic strip by Pat Sullivan. Animated short film; three or 6 min.; b&w; silent.

Felix the Cat sees a caveman offer his girl a skin. She tells him "I don't want that old-fashioned thing." She wants "a short model" and points out Felix as a good candidate. The caveman chases Felix, waving a stone ax. Felix is saved when a gang of monkeys put their tails together to make a fireman's pole he slides down, leaving the baffled caveman on top of a cliff. Felix then throws a rock which hits a giant gorilla. The gorilla chases Felix for the rest of the film, which ends abruptly with Felix hiding.

Felix was the hero of more than 100 silent cartoons and was the biggest star of silent animation before Mickey Mouse. His forte was silent slapstick with few subtitles. Webb's *Animated Film Encyclopedia* says the film was titled *The Bone Age* and was 6 minutes long and that Felix dreamed he was in the Stone Age. The version on the Bosco Video-Image Entertainment DVD *Felix the Cat: The Otto Messmer Classics, 1919–1924* is titled *Felix in the Stone Age*, is only three minutes long and starts with Felix in prehistory, without any indication that he is dreaming. Ref: Webb. *Animated Film Encyclopedia*; *Internet Movie Database*; MK 6.

Le Feu? Pas pour les Hommes! (1971) *see* **Hot Stuff** (1971)

50,000 B.C. (Before Clothing) (1963) [alt. *Nudes on the Rocks*] U.S.; dir. Warner Rose, Arnold Drake; Biolane. 75 min.; color. Screenplay, Warner Rose; photography, Warner Rose; music, Martin Roman. CAST: Charlie Robinson (*Charlie Wishnick*); Gigi Darlene (*Zelda*); Audrey Campbell; Eddie Carmel.

Short, homely, middle-aged ex-burlesque comic Charlie flees his shrilly complaining wife and accidentally rides in a crazy inventor's time machine (which looks like a taxi) to the Stone Age. Here almost all the women are nude; the men are not. The really ugly caveman king cracks burlesque jokes with Charlie. The cavemen's problem is Gorax the Giant, who kidnaps women and threatens to eat anyone who gets in his way. Diminutive Charlie manages to kill Gorax with a trick and is awarded a nude woman as a mate. He returns to modern times, gets another taste of his nagging wife and decides to go back to the old days, when men had everything their way.

50,000 B.C. (Before Clothing) is an old-fashioned "nudie." Production values are rock-bottom. There is abundant nudity, all female, all breasts and butts, with no full frontal nudity. The men don't have to get naked and don't have to be handsome or desirable. Any schlemiel can score. Anyone tempted to regard the film as innocent, nostalgic fun should note a nasty scene in which a girl in a bikini dances with a snake in front of the ugly men, until the snake strangles her; the men don't try to help her. The film bills Eddie Carmel, who played Gorax the giant cannibal, as the tallest man in the world. In a trailer, Gigi Darlene announces "I want posterity to know all about my posterior." Reviewing *50,000 B.C.* in *Video Watchdog* 112, John Charles called it "proof positive that the demise of vaudeville did not come one second too soon."

This repellant blast from the past was released on a DVD with the somewhat less distasteful Italian caveman sex comedy *When Men Carried Clubs and Women Played Ding Dong* (1971). The disc also includes four undated shorts. In the color short *Prehistoric Strip*, the narrator announces, "Ladies and gentlemen, you are about to watch the first striptease in history." A cavewoman figures out how to arouse her mate, but the big lug falls asleep anyway. *Cavewoman* is a series of b&w romps by two nude women, made for a peepshow, with no narration but several cards demanding "Put in another coin." *The Battery* is a short by Union Oil Company, dir. by Marvin Bryan, presenting a humorous history of the battery. Prehistoric people have oil but don't know what to do with it until a clever cavewoman invents the battery. The fourth short, and the only amusing one, is a cartoon, *Darling, Get Me a Crocodile*; see separate entry. Ref: *Internet Movie Database*; MK 1.

Fig Leaves (1926) U.S.; dir. Howard Hawks; Fox. 7 reels; b&w and color; silent. Screenplay, Howard Hawks, Louis D. Lighton, Hope Loring; photography, Joseph H. August. CAST: George O'Brien (*Adam Smith*); Olive Borden (*Eve Smith*).

A modern (1926) suburban couple, Adam and Eve Smith, bicker over her obsession with clothes and her work as a model. In a prehistoric prologue, Adam and Eve argue over much the same problems.

Biblical Adam and Eve stories are omitted from this list, but *Fig Leaves* merely uses the names of the Biblical couple in a far different prehistoric story. As described in the July 7, 1926

(I) Fire and Ice

Variety review, "story starts off jazzily" at the end of Adam and Eve's honeymoon. When a prehistoric alarm clock fills with sand it tilts and drops a coconut on Adam's head. He has a breakfast of grapefruit, which he eats with a clamshell.

The newsboy throws in a stone newspaper. He reads the sports page, she the fashion news. She declares she "hasn't a thing to wear." At this point comes an amazingly bold, pre–Code intertitle, "Ever since you ate the apple you've had the gimmies.

First it was twin beds and now it's clothes." Adam departs for work on the local commuter transport, a "sort of flatboat on land drawn by a dinosaur, with a ridge pole down the middle for the straphangers." Eve is annoyed when Adam flirts with a blonde. Soon Eve is deep in conversation with the Serpent, as the story switches to modern times.

COMMENTARY. A knowledgeable fan commentator on *Internet Movie Database* notes "the Garden of Eden bookends resemble a silent-era *Flintstones*, with rocks and dinosaurs ingeniously serving modern bourgeois purposes. The contemporary section is a sophisticated comedy of manners.... This delightful comedy already presages many of the thematic concerns of [Hawks'] late masterpieces." *Variety* found *Fig Leaves* "full of quick comedy surprises. It is expensively and beautifully mounted. It has subdued horse-play for those who like their laughs rough, and it has certain subtleties that the discriminating will appreciate." The *Variety* reviewer noted "there is a laughable prolog in the Garden of Eden which is a giggle from start to finish." Ref: Jones. *Illustrated Dinosaur Movie Guide*; Berry. *Dinosaur Filmography*; *Internet Movie Database*; not viewed.

Fire and Ice (1983) U.S.; dir. Ralph Bakshi; Twentieth Century–Fox/Producer Sales. Animated film; 81 min.; color. Screenplay, Roy Thomas, Gerry Conway based on characters created by Ralph Bakshi and Frank Frazetta; music, William Kraft. CAST: Randy Norton (*Larn*); Cynthia Leake (*Teegra*); Steve Sandor (*Darkwolf*); Sean Hannon (*Nekron*); Leo Gordon (*Jarol*); William Ostrander (*Taro*); Eileen O'Neill (*Juliana*); Elizabeth Lloyd Shaw (*Roleil*); Holly Frazetta (*Subhuman Priestess*); Jimmy Bridges (*Subhuman*); Shane Callan (*Subhuman*); Archie Hamilton (*Subhuman*); VOICES: Susan Tyrell (*Juliana*); Maggie Roswell (*Teegra*); William Ostrander (*Larn*); Stephen Mendel (*Nekron*).

"Long ago at the end of the last Ice Age" (according to the narrator) powerful sorceress Juliana rules the region of ice from Ice Peak. She trains her son Nekron in the dark arts and together they send glaciers south to destroy all peoples who resist their rule. A village is destroyed by the advancing glaciers and the ice rulers' troops, apemen called "Subhumans" or "Nekron's dogs." The only survivor is lone hero Larn. Nekron demands the surrender of King Jarol of Fire Keep. When Jarol refuses, Nekron's Subhumans kidnap his beautiful daughter Teegra, who seems to have a positive phobia for clothing.

Teegra and Larn are saved repeatedly by Darkwolf, a mighty, solitary warrior. Nekron, whose powers are so great he can force men to kill each other or kill themselves, treacherously slays Jarol's son Taro. After many changes in fortune, Teegra is once more Nekron's prisoner when Larn and Jarol's warriors attack Ice Peak riding Dragonhawks (pterodactyls). Many are killed but Darkwolf appears again, overcomes Nekron's powers and kills him. Jarol releases lava from a mountain, melting the glaciers and then Ice Peak itself and killing Juliana. Gentle Teegra stops Larn from killing a surviving Subhuman, telling him that peace has finally come.

COMMENTARY. Ralph Bakshi produced and directed *Fire and Ice* after winning a reputation as one of the most innovative directors of animated features. His *Fritz the Cat* (1972), *Heavy Traffic* (1973) and *Wizards* (1977) were bizarre, sexy, violent and far removed from the Disney cartoons Americans were used to. Bakshi's feature-length animated *Lord of the Rings* (1978) and the liveaction sword-and-sorcery wave which began with *Conan the Barbarian* (1982) were the inspiration for *Fire and Ice*, one of the few animated sword-and-sorcery movies. Fantasy artist Frank Frazetta co-produced *Fire and Ice*, painted the poster and contributed eight stills of characters and landscapes which were shown at the beginning of the film. The hero and heroine wear minimal clothing, which is silly since they are supposed to be in a cold climate. Teegra is in a bikini as skimpy as any in Hammer's *When Dinosaurs Ruled the Earth* (1970). The weapons, costumes and paraphernalia are typical of sword fantasies set in mythical ancient settings rather than prehistory. The heroes and villains use a large variety

Darkwolf (left) fights Nekron in Ralph Bakshi's *Fire and Ice*.

of weapons, including maces, spears, swords, knives, bolas, axes and bows and arrows. We see fortresses and cities built of wood and stone. Besides the Ice Age, the film's prehistoric elements are a giant lizard resembling a dinosaur which kills several Subhumans, giant wolves, a giant squid in a shallow lake, the pterodactyls and of course the Subhumans themselves.

Bakshi's career faded after *Fire and Ice*. One reason was that he left himself open to charges of racism. The villains' troops are called Subhumans in the film's credits. They are much darker than the heroes or their masters Juliana and Nekron; most filmgoers would assume they are black. They speak their own guttural language while everyone else speaks English; they can understand orders and reply in their bosses' language. Sometimes they walk stooped over; at other times they walk erect. They climb agilely. They have normal human bodies but brutish, apelike faces. They eye Teegra lustfully and are presumably prevented from raping her only by their orders. Many reviews of the film refer to them as "apemen." On the other hand they seem no less intelligent than villain's henchmen usually are in such films (which isn't much). There is a white character, the henchman of the witch Roleil, who is as brutish as the Subhumans. Three intelligent Subhumans are employed as diplomats by Nekron and speak the heroes' language fluently.

In addition to the film's racial problem, two of the three principal villains are obviously homosexual. Roleil, a witch, makes clear lesbian advances to Teegra, while Nekron is disgusted by his mother's plan that he should "mate" with Teegra, but he is very interested in the muscular male hero. 1983 was rather late for a film to insult both blacks and gays and reviewers came down hard on Bakshi's political blunders.

Fire and Ice was filmed using the rotoscoping method. Live actors performed all the action and artists traced the film's animated characters over this footage. Different actors performed and voiced the same character. One actor, William Ostrander, performed one character (Taro) but did the voice of another (Larn). This technique yielded excellent character movement, but it was unpopular with many animation buffs. In his vast book *Cartoons*, Giannalberto Bendazzi writes that Bakshi "demonstrated little imagination in handling his themes, and a culture and taste which did not go beyond the interests and passions of teenagers. Stylistically, his over-use of the rotoscope often led to unpleasant technical results."

Unlike Bendazzi, I found *Fire and Ice* visually impressive. Besides the excellent rotoscoped movements, the film has a dark, forest setting reminiscent of *King Kong*. Landscapes, fog, ruined buildings, animals and nearly naked people all combine to produce an intoxicating, often beautiful pulp fantasy atmosphere. The story is simple, with clearly defined good and evil characters, providing opportunity for imaginative chases, fights and crises. Kraft contributes a resounding score. The visual spectacle is better than the script. There is usually little need for dialogue. There certainly isn't any real character development but the most serious fault of the script is that the hero Larn doesn't get to do much. He kills many Subhumans, but the most impressive fighting is done by the mysterious Darkwolf, who resembles the Death Dealer, a famous character created by illustrator Frazetta, the film's co-producer. Larn fails to kill any of the main villains. Subhumans kill Roleil, the lava flood kills Juliana and Darkwolf kills Nekron. Finally, King Jarol could release the lava flood from his mountain and destroy the enemy any time he wanted, which makes the whole film rather pointless.

Variety (Aug. 31, 1983) wrote "the production represents a clear design on Bakshi's part to capture an wider and younger audience than any of his previous films" and that "in an effort to backoff former narrow band demographics, narrative is almost fairy-tale simplistic in its war between good and evil." Bakshi was no doubt trying to make *Fire and Ice* his most accessible film and to corral the teenage audience, but the film is too scary, gory and sexy for children, too mild for teenagers and too simple for adults. *Fire and Ice* is a simple fairy tale but it has a practically naked heroine who constantly dodges rape by apemen. These problems have caused critics and audiences to overlook the film's visual splendors. Ref: Lenburg. *Encyclopedia of Animated Cartoons*; Jones. *Illustrated Dinosaur Movie Guide*; *Internet Movie Database*; Bendazzi. *Cartoons*; MK 7.

Fire Monsters Against the Son of Hercules (1962) *see* Colossus of the Stone Age (1962)

The First Bad Man (1955) U.S.; dir. Tex Avery; MGM. Animated short film; 7 min.; color. Screenplay, Heck Allen; music, Scott Bradley. *VOICE:* Tex Ritter (*Narrator*).

In 1,000,000 B.C., Dinosaur Dan, the first outlaw, terrorizes Stone Age Texas. Like the posses who pursue him, Dan has a modern six-shooter but rides a brontosaurus instead of a horse. He rustles honest folks' dinosaurs and robs the town bank.

Avery is known as the craziest of the classic American animators. This prehistoric cowboy comedy is not one of his most imaginative efforts but has some fine moments. The cavemen's town satirizes postwar GI housing projects. The sight of tiny cowboys on huge dinosaurs racing across the plains, shooting at each other, is irresistibly funny. A highlight comes during the big chase scene, when Dan rides his brontosaurus into a maze of canyons, followed by the posse on their brontosauri. When they emerge the necks of posse's brontos' are tied hopelessly in a knot. Ref: Webb. *The Animated Film Encyclopedia*; Jones. *The Illustrated Dinosaur Movie Guide*; *Internet Movie Database*; MK 7.

The First Circus (1921) U.S.; Sarg-Dawley/Rialto. Animated short film; b&w; silent. Animator, Tony Sarg. (in the *Tony Sarg's Almanac* series).

In this silhouette animation short, cavemen acrobats use a tame dinosaur in their act, balancing and vaulting on the beast and walking a snake stretched as a tightrope between the dinosaur's head and tail. Ref: Berry. *Dinosaur Encyclopedia*; Webb. *Animated Film Encyclopedia*; not viewed.

The First Dentist (1921) U.S.; Sarg-Dawley/Rialto. Animated short film; b&w; silent. Animator, Tony Sarg. (In the *Tony Sarg's Almanac* series).

In this silhouette animation short, primitive people will do anything to cure toothache. Ref: Webb. *Animated Film Encyclopedia*; not viewed.

The First Flivver (1922) U.S.; Sarg-Dawley/Rialto. Animated short film; b&w; silent. Animator, Tony Sarg. (In the *Tony Sarg's Almanac* series).

In this silhouette animation short, a caveman bests his romantic rivals with a goat-powered "flivver" (a term for an early auto).

Ref: Webb. *Animated Film Encyclopedia*; not viewed.

The First Thanksgiving (1973) *see* **B.C., the First Thanksgiving** (1973)

The Five Ages: From Stone Age to Modern (1920) U.S.; producer, Joe Rock. Short film; b&w; silent. Joe Rock was a prolific producer of silent short films. Information on the contents of this short is elusive. Ref: *Internet Movie Database*; not viewed.

A Flintstone Christmas (1977) U.S.; dir. Charles A. Nichols; Hanna-Barbera. Animated TV special; 25 min.; color. Screenplay, Duane Poole, Dick Robbins; music, Hoyt Curtin, Paul DeKorte. VOICES: Henry Corden (*Fred Flintstone*); Mel Blanc (*Barney Rubble*); Gay Hartwig (*Betty Rubble/Pebbles Flintstone*); Jean Vander-Pyl (*Wilma Flintstone*); Lucille Bliss (*Bamm Bamm Rubble*); Virginia Gregg (*Mrs. Santa*); Hal Smith (*Santa*); Don Messick (*Ed/Otis*); John Stephenson (*Mr. Slate*).

Fred and Barney take over for injured Santa and deliver presents to a poor children's party, but get in trouble with their wives and boss. The first of several *Flintstones* specials 1977–1981. Ref: Woolery. *Animated TV Specials*; Lenburg. *Encyclopedia of Animated Cartoons*; not viewed.

The Flintstone Family Adventures (1980–82) *see* **The Flintstones Comedy Show** (1980–82)

A Flintstone Family Christmas (1993) U.S.; Hanna-Barbera/ABC. Animated TV special; 25 min.; color. VOICES: Henry Corden (*Fred Flintstone*); Jean VanderPyl (*Wilma*); Frank Welker (*Barney Rubble*); B.J. Ward (*Betty Rubble/Dino*).

The Flintstones take in Stony, a "caveless" urchin "from the wrong side of the tar pits" and have a hard time domesticating him. Ref: Lenburg. *Encyclopedia of Animated Cartoons* (1999); not viewed.

The Flintstone Kids (1986–88) U.S.; Hanna-Barbera. Animated TV series; 50-min. episodes; color. VOICES: Lennie Weinrib (*Freddy*); Scott Menville (*Freddie*); Hamilton Camp (*Barney*); Julie Dees (*Wilma*); Elizabeth Lyn Fraser (*Wilma*); B.J. Ward (*Betty*); Mel Blanc (*Dino/Captain Caveman/Robert Rubble*); Henry Corden (*Ed Flintstone*); Charles Adler (*Cavey Jr.*); Ken Mars (*Narrator*).

The series consisted of four segments. *The Flintstone Kids* told the adventures of Fred, Barney, Betty and Wilma as 10-year-olds in Bedrock. Among the gadgets were PCs (prehistoric calculators), consisting of a monkey with an abacus in the monitor. *Captain Caveman and Son* were the exploits of the first superhero and his son. *Dino's Dilemmas* focused on Dino the dog-like dinosaur. *Flintstone Funnies* (1986–87 only) was a series of fantasy adventures.

Segments: *Flintstone Kids*. "The Great Freddini," "Heroes for Hire," "The Bad News Brontos," "Dusty Disappears," "Poor Little Rich Girl," "Born in the U.S. Cave," "Curse of the Gemstone Diamond," "I Think That I Shall Never See Barney Rubble As a Tree," "The Fugitives," "Freddy's Rocky Road to Karate," "Barney's Moving Experience," "The Little Visitor," "Grandpa for Loan," "Freddy's New Crush," "The Flintstone Fake Ache," "Better Buddy Blues," "Anything You Can Do, I Can Do Betty," "Camper Scamper," "A Tiny Egg," "Haircutastrophe," "Freddy the 13th," "Little Rubble, Big Trouble," "Philo's D-Feat," "Rocky's Rocky Road." *Captain Caveman and Son*: "Freezy Does it," "Invasion of the Mommy Snatchers," "The Ditto Masters," "I Was a Teenage Grown-Up," "Grime and Punishment," "A Tale of Too Silly," "To Baby or Not to Baby," "Day of the Villains," "Hero Today, Gone Tomorrow," "Curse of the Reverse," "Captain Caveman's First Adventure," "Leave It to Mother," "Greed It and Weep"; "Captain Knaveman," "Attack of the Fifty Foot Teenage Lizard," "The Cream-Pier Strikes Back," "Captain Caveman's Super Cold," "The Big Bedrock Bully Bash," "Captain Cavedog." *Dino's Dilemmas*: "Yard Wars," "Dreamchip's Cur Wash," "Dressed Up Dino," "Fred's Mechanical Dog," "The Butcher Shoppe," "The Vet," "The Dino Diet," "What Price Fleadom," "The Terror Within," "Revenge of the Bullied," "The Chocolate Chip Catastrophe," "Watchdog Blues," "Captain Cavepuppy," "Killer Kitty," "Who's Falutin' Who?," "Bone Voyage," "World War Flea," "A Midnite Pet Peeve," "The Birthday Shuffle."

Flintstone Funnies: "Bedrock P.I.s," "Princess Wilma," "Frankenstone," "Rubble Without a

Cause," "Indiana Flintstone," "Freddy in the Big House," "Sugar and Spies," "Monster from the Tar Pits," "Betty's Big Break," "Dino Goes Hollyrock," "Bedrock 'n Roll," "The Twilight Stone," "Philo's Invention." Ref: Lenburg. *Encyclopedia of Animated Cartoons*; Adams. *The Flintstones*; not viewed.

The Flintstone Kids' "Just Say No" Special (1988) U.S.; Hanna-Barbera/Just Say no Foundation/ABC. Animated TV special; 25 min.; color. Screenplay, Laren Bright, Lane Raichert. VOICES: Elisabeth Fraser (*Wilma*); Scott Menville (*Freddy*); Hamilton Camp (*Barney*); B.J. Ward (*Betty*); Bumper Robinson (*Philo*); Frank Welker (*Dino*); Kip Lennon (*Michael Jackstone*); with Nancy Reagan.

In this spinoff of *The Flintstone Kids* series (1986–88), the pre-teen denizens of Bedrock joined First Lady Nancy Reagan's campaign against drug use by children. In the thin story, the kids, together with their black friend Philo, try to get tickets to a "Michael Jackstone" (a play on Michael Jackson) concert. The special was shown both in primetime and on Saturday morning as an *ABC Weekend Special*, with Mrs. Reagan appearing in a commercial plugging her Just Say No clubs.

Variety (Sept. 21, 1988) moaned, "What ever happened to the clever and witty Hanna-Barbera TV series *The Flintstones* of yore? Apparently, the creators of the animated the *Flintstone Kids' Just Say No Special* were so wrapped up in the show's hard-hitting anti-drug message, that all the fun of the original was lost." Ref: Lenburg. *Encyclopedia of Animated Cartoons*; not viewed.

The Flintstones (1960–66) U.S.; Hanna-Barbera. Animated TV series; 166 24-min. episodes; b&w and color. Producers, William Hanna, Joseph Barbera; music, Hoyt Curtin. VOICES: Alan Reed (*Fred Flintstone*); Mel Blanc (*Barney Rubble*); Daws Butler (*Barney Rubble*); Jean VanderPyl (*Wilma Flintstone/Pebbles*); Bea Benadaret (*Betty Rubble*); Gerry Johnson (*Betty Rubble*); Chips Spam (*Dino*); Don Messick (*Bamm-Bamm*); John Stephenson (*George Slate*); notable guest stars include Ann-Margret (*Ann Margrock*); Tony Curtis (*Stoney Curtis*); Hoagy Carmichael (*Hoagy*); Elizabeth Montgomery (*Samantha*).

Loud-mouthed caveman Fred Flintstone lives in "the modern Stone Age town" of Bedrock with his smart wife Wilma, an expert in "husband management," and their pet dinosaur Dino. Fred works down at the quarry for irascible Mr. Slate, operating Mildred the Bronto-crane. Fred's cheerful friend Barney is wary of Fred's hare-brained get-rich-quick schemes but he usually goes along out of friendship; the schemes always fail. Fred is often disconsolate but he is always forgiven and cheered up by Wilma and quickly returns to his ebullient, overbearing self, frequently shouting his trademark cry, "Yabba-Dabba-Doo!" In time, Fred and Wilma have an adorable baby daughter, Pebbles, while the Rubbles adopt super-strong little boy Bamm-Bamm. (For what it's worth, Pebble's birth establishes the date of *The Flintstones*. She was born February 22, 10,000 B.C.)

COMMENTARY. You can't get much farther from the anthropology books than this. The Flintstones inhabit a fantasy Bedrock in which speech, attitudes and situations are all completely modern, while everything physical is made of stone, wood, bone or skins and powered by animals or human-power. The clever use of prehistoric gadgets and animals is one of the chief glories of *The Flintstones*. In addition to Dino the house pet and Mildred the Bronto-crane, a dinosaur is used as a stairway in Macyrock Department Store. A bird with a long beak plays a stone record on a stone phonograph. A mammoth's trunk is used to wash the car, water the lawn or vacuum a room. There are birds' beaks for clothespins, a stone piano (a Stoneway, of course), a ram's horn telephone, a crab on wheels used as a lawnmower and a bird who serves as an alarm clock. The Flintstones' automobile is a skin-topped convertible with wooden rollers instead of wheels; it is propelled by the Flintstones' feet. Fred shaves with a bee-powered razor and is regularly decked by the paperboy throwing a stone newspaper.

The Flintstones are in the tradition of anachronistic caveman humor begun by Chaplin, Keaton and Laurel and Hardy in the silents *His Prehistoric Past* (1914), *The Three Ages* (1923) and *Flying Elephants* (1925) and continued by many animated shorts, two Three Stooges shorts and the liveaction comedy feature *Caveman* (1981). Of all of these, *The Flintstones* is by far the most famous. The prehistoric subgenre in film and TV has been notably unsuccessful and characterized by critical contempt and audience indifference. In contrast, *The Flintstones* has been incredibly popular and has been shown in 80 countries, in 22 languages. The 1960–66 series, plus spin-off TV series and specials, as well as three feature films, *A Man Called Flintstone* (1966), *The Flintstones* (1994) and *The Flintstones in Viva Rock Vegas* (2000), add up to more than 100 hours of *Flintstones* material (probably almost as much as all the other films and TV in this list put together) and have given rise to books, toys and an enormous variety of other products. Mills Laboratories, one of the original sponsors of the show in 1960, still makes Flintstones Vitamins, which remains the number one selling children's vitamin.

The *Flintstones* franchise has been quiet since the poorly-received 2000 film, but after more than forty years no one should bet against its revival.

The gadgets and animals were funny but the human characters were the series' chief asset. Fred, as T.R. Adams says in his book *The Flintstones: A Modern Stone Age Phenomenon*, is a "boisterous and brash ... prehistoric Everyman." He is constantly boasting and scheming, he always gets into trouble and he always admits to his mistakes. In spite of his bluster, "Fred is obviously a loving man. He's upfront with everything, he has the sweetness and the ability to say, 'Hey, I'm sorry. I goofed,'" according to Henry Corden, who voiced Fred in several spinoff series after the retirement of Alan Reed. Fred is enthusiastic and always bounces back after each failure. He is a loving, even ardent, husband and a doting father.

Wilma is the model for many subsequent situation comedy wives. She is smarter than her husband, but careful not to make that fact too obvious unless absolutely necessary. Wilma's attitude toward Fred is highly irreverent. In an early episode, she tells Betty Rubble she can go shopping "as soon as I serve His Majesty's lunch." When Fred calls her at the top of his voice, she asks coldly, "You bellowed?" She will take only so much nonsense from Fred but she always forgives Fred when he realizes his

Wilma, Barney, Betty, Fred, Bamm-Bamm and Pebbles in *The Flintstones.*

mistakes. As for Barney, he is essentially the same as Art Carney's Ed Norton on *The Honeymooners*; what other character had the luck to be played by two such masters as Carney and Mel Blanc?

In spite of all the trouble Fred gets into, Bedrock is a paradise, a Garden of Eden, reflecting the optimism of America in the early 1960s. Of course, Bedrock *is* suburban America, with mild satire of some of laughable aspects of suburban life. (For instance, Fred and Barney belong to The Royal Order of Water Buffaloes.) It is no doubt significant that the most popular prehistoric media product is totally inaccurate but very happy, cheerful and optimistic. *The Flintstones* is so non-realistic that it is harmless; even the most ignorant viewer knows that it has nothing to do with real prehistory.

The series grew out of a crisis which seemed likely to destroy the American animation industry. In the late 1950s Hollywood studios were abandoning animated short films and laying off artists and writers who had created thousands

(I) The Flintstones (1960–66)

of high-quality films. William Hanna and Joseph Barbera were laid off by MGM after 20 years of producing *Tom and Jerry* shorts. They formed their own production company and were able to hire many of the country's best animators and gag-writers to create TV cartoons. At first they made children's shows such as *Ruff and Reddy* and *Huckleberry Hound*, but they discovered that about 60 percent of their audience were adults. Hanna and Barbera proposed making the first prime-time animated series, which would also be the first adult-oriented TV cartoon, the first TV cartoon with human characters instead of anthropomorphic animals and the first half-hour cartoon series.

The idea of a caveman comedy based loosely on *The Honeymooners* quickly took shape. Veteran animators Dan Gordon and Ed Benedict were the concept artists and developed the main characters' appearance and the series' ingenious prehistoric gadgets. In *The Flintstones: A Modern Stone Age Phenomenon*, T.R. Adams credits Gordon and Benedict as the main inspirations behind *The Flintstones*, although most of the first season's episodes were written by Warren Foster. Gordon and Benedict had both worked on prehistoric cartoons before. Benedict was a layout artist on Tex Avery's *The First Bad Man* (1955) while Gordon contributed to Max Fleischer's *Stone Age Comedies* series (1940). During the development process, the male characters became less primitive and the women less seductive until they emerged as the characters who became famous. The studio developed a catalog an inch-and-a-half thick full of character details and Stone Age gadgets.

The series was so innovative that networks and advertisers were skeptical but after much anguish ABC, Mills Laboratories and Reynolds Tobacco finally picked up the show. Budgets were small; the series had to produce a 25-minute episode for about the same money that studios used to spend on a seven-minute theatrical short. Hanna and Barbera had to invent yet another innovation, "limited animation." Animators used every trick possible to simplify characters and backgrounds and re-use art. *Flintstones* characters have four fingers per hand and three toes per foot, to save drawing time.

In addition to several of the best writers and artists, Hanna-Barbera obtained the services of many of the most expert voice actors, veterans of years in radio and animation. Mel Blanc was already the most famous voice in cartoons when he began to voice Barney Rubble. Alan Reed, the first voice of Fred, had 30 years experience in radio. It was Reed who invented Fred's joyous cry, "Yabba-Dabba-Doo!" Hoyt Curtin worked in *Mr. Magoo* before writing the music for *The Flintstones*. (The famous *Flintstones* theme song was not used until the third season, when the series changed from b&w to color.) The show was made by enthusiastic, experienced professionals who, in spite of their long careers, were innovators able to change their work to meet new challenges.

The connection between *The Flintstones* and *The Honeymooners* is obvious. Fred, like Ralph Kramden, is a blowhard husband with a smart wife and a dumb friend. He's full of schemes, which always fail and get him into trouble. Hanna admired *The Honeymooners* and went so far as to admit that the Jackie Gleason show was "a kind of basis for the concept" of his series. According to Adams, Gleason wanted to sue Hanna-Barbera but was persuaded that he would do his reputation no good by driving one of the most popular shows on TV off the air.

Harry Castleman and Walter Podrazik (*Harry and Wally's Favorite TV Shows*) consider *The Flintstones* far inferior to *The Honeymooners*. Certainly *The Flintstones* was lighter and less realistic than *The Honeymooners*. There were about 80 hours of the original *Flintstones*, followed by dozens of hours of spinoffs, while *The Honeymooners* added up to about 50 hours. Quantity does tend to be the enemy of quality. However, there is no reason to use one fine program as a weapon with which to attack another good show, even if one is less excellent than the other. We should be glad that we have both of them and recognize the achievements of the professionals who made them. (It is noteworthy that, although *The Flintstones* began only three years after *The Honeymooners* left the air, Fred never threatens Wilma with violence, as Ralph often threatened Alice Kramden.)

ABC felt the need to censure even *The Flintstones*. They forbade the word "pregnant"; before Pebbles was born Wilma was "expecting." The series was not permitted to show a stone toilet. On the other hand, Adams reports that Fred and Wilma were the first couple in prime-time TV to share a double bed (with crossed mammoth tusks at the head of the bed).

Daily Variety (Oct. 3, 1960) and *Variety* (Oct. 5, 1960) were "disappointed" by the first *Flint-*

stones episode and worried that Fred was too unlikeable. *Daily Variety* (Nov. 3, 1990) found it "a skilled amalgam of character, dialog and story line. The drawings are uproarious, the voices expertly fitted and a story to tell that doesn't just ramble from one violent episode to another." By Sept. 20, 1961 *Variety* considered the show "worthy of an adult as well as a juve [juvenile] following." At the beginning of the third season (Sept. 19, 1962) *Variety* grumbled that "the storylines are beginning to repeat themselves." For the fourth season opener (Sept. 25, 1963) *Variety* announced that the show had "become almost as much a part of TV watching as the news and weather report." As the fifth season began (Sept. 30, 1964) *Variety* hailed the "zesty pace" and noted the "show is a regular with most moppet viewers and is luring lotsa adults." For the start of the final season (Sept. 29, 1965), *Variety* reported "the novelty may well be wearing off this Neolithic fantasy, but the quality of the show remains high" especially "sharply-honed characterizations" and "usually deft dialog."

Leslie Halliwell (*Halliwell's Television Companion*) wrote "Semi-animation was of a higher standard than we have seen since, and there always seemed to be something inventive going on." Hal Erickson (*Television Cartoon Shows*) notes a tendency in the latter days of *The Flintstones*' six seasons to "repetition and laziness" and reliance on tired gags, such as "mother-in-law and rolling pin jokes," but notes "Overall, however, *The Flintstones* was a remarkable achievement.... Though its animation was cut to the bone and the draftsmanship only fair, audiences accepted the *Flintstones* characters as real, living beings worth caring about. And as its best, the series was one of the most consistently entertaining and succinctly written programs on TV."

For episode synopses, see T.R. Adams' book *The Flintstones: A Modern Stone Age Phenomenon*. Episodes: "The Swimming Pool," "The Flintstone Flyer," "The Prowler," "The Baby Sitters," "The Engagement Ring," "No Help Wanted," "At the Race," "The Drive-In," "Hot Lips Hannigan," "The Split Personality," "The Snorkasaurus Incident," "Hollyrock Here I Come," "The Girls' Night Out," "The Monster from the Tar Pits," "The Gold Champion," "The Sweepstakes Ticket," "The Hypnotist," "The Hot Piano," "The Big Bank Robbery," "Arthur Quarry's Dance Class," "Love Letters on the Rocks," "The Tycoon," "The Astronuts," "The Long Long Weekend," "In the Dough," "The Good Scout," "Rooms for Rent," "Fred Flintstone—Before or After," "Droop Along Flintstone," "Fred Flintstone Woos Again," "The Hit Song Writer," "The Rock Quarry Story," "The Little White Lie," "The Soft Touchables," "Flintstone of Prinstone," "The Beauty Contest," "The Missing Bus," "Social Climbers," "The House Guest," "Alvin Brickrock Presents," "The Picnic," "The Masquerade Ball," "The X-Ray Story," "The Entertainer," "The Gambler," "Wilma's Vanishing Money," "A Star Is Almost Born," "Operation Barney," "Impractical Joker," "Feudin' and Fussin,'" "The Happy Household," "This Is Your Lifesaver," "Fred Strikes Out," "The Rock Vegas Caper," "The Mailman Cometh," "Trouble-In-Law," "Divided We Sail," "Kleptomaniac Caper," "Latin Lover," "Take Me Out of the Ball Game," "Fred's New Boss," Dino Goes Hollyrock," "The Twitch," "Barney the Invisible," "The Bowling Ballet," "Baby Barney," "The Buffalo Convention," "Here's Snow in Your Eyes," "The Little Stranger," "Ladies' Day," "Hawaiian Escapade," "Nothing But the Tooth," "High School Fred," "Dial S for Suspicion," "Flashgun Freddie," "The Kissing Burglar," "The Birthday Party," "Wilma the Maid," "The Hero," "Foxy Grandma," "The Surprise," "Mother-In-Law's Visit," "Fred's New Job," "The Blessed Event," "Carry On, Nurse Fred," "Ventriloquist Barney," "The Big Move," "Swedish Visitors," "Divided We Sail," "Dino Disappears," "Groom Gloom," "Fred's Monkeyshiners," "The Flintstone Canaries," "Glue for Two," "Big League Freddy," "Sleep On, Sweet Fred," "Old Lady Betty," "Kleptomaniac Pebbles," "Daddies Anonymous," "Daddy's Little Beauty," "Bedrock Hillbillies," "Little Bamm-Bamm," "Peek-a-Boo Camera," "Ann Margrock Presents," "Ten Little Flintstones," "Once Upon a Coward," "Fred El Terrifico," "Flintstone and the Lion," "Cave Scout Jamboree," "Ladies' Night at the Lodge," "Room for Two," "Reel Trouble," "Bachelor Daze," "Son of Rockzilla," "Operation Switchover," "Pebbles' Birthday Party," "Hop Happy," "Cinderellastone," "Monster Fred," "Itty Bitty Fred," "Bedrock Rodeo Round-Up," "A Haunted House Is Not a Home," "Dr. Sinister," "The Gruesomes," "Most Beautiful Baby in Bedrock," "Dino and Juliet," "King for a Night," "Indianrockolis 500," "Adobe Dick,"

(I) The Flintstones (1994)

"Fred's Flying Lesson," "Fred's Second Car," "Christmas Flintstone," "The Hatrocks and the Gruesomes," "Time Machine," "Moonlight Maintenance," "Sheriff for a Day," "Deep In the Heart of Texarock," "Superstone," "The Rolls Rock Caper," "Fred Meets Hercurock," "Surfin' Fred," "House That Fred Built," "No Biz Like Show Biz," "Disorder in the Court," "Return to Stoney Curtis," "The Great Gazoo," "Circus Business," "Rip van Flintstone," "Samantha," "The Gravelberry Pie King," "The Stonefinger Caper," "Masquerade Party," "Shinrock-A-Go-Go," "Royal Rubble," "Seeing Doubles," "How to Pick a Fight With Your Wife Without Really Trying," "Two Men on a Dinosaur," "Feds Goes Ape," "The Long, Long, Long Weekend," "The Treasure of Sierra Madrock," "Curtain Call at Bedrock," "Boss for a Day," "Fred's Island," "Jealousy," "Dripper," "The Story of Rocky's Raiders," "My Fair Freddy."

During initial development, the series was called *The Flagstones*. A brief scene from a *Flagstones* pilot is included in the DVD *The Flintstones: The Complete First Season*, which colored the b&w first season episodes. The scene appears unchanged in the first *Flintstones* episode, "The Swimming Pool."

Specials, films and series in the *Flintstones* franchise with titles which do not begin with *Flintstone* or *Flintstones* can be found in the index under "Flintstones franchise." Fred and Barney also appeared with many other cartoon stars in the TV specials *Yabba Dabba 2* (1979), *Yogi Bear's All-Star Comedy Christmas Caper* (1984) and *Hanna-Barbera's 50th: A Yabba Dabba Doo Celebration* (1989). In 1984, Joe Piscopo and Danny DeVito did a Fred and Barney skit on *The Joe Piscopo Show*. Ref: Lenburg. *Encyclopedia of Animated Cartoons*; Adams. *The Flintstones*; Erickson. *Television Cartoon Shows*; many episodes viewed; MK 8.

The Flintstones (1994) U.S.; dir. Brian Levant; Universal/Amblin/Hanna-Barbera. 91 min.; color. Screenplay, Tom S. Parker, Jim Jennewein, Steven E. De Souza; photography, Dean Cundey; music, David Newman. CAST: John Goodman (*Fred Flintstones*); Elizabeth Perkins (*Wilma Flintstone*); Rick Moranis (*Barney Rubble*); Rosie O'Donnell (*Betty Rubble*); Kyle MacLachlan (*Cliff Vandercave*); Halle Berry (*Sharon Stone*); Elizabeth Taylor (*Pearl Slaghoople*); Dann Florek (*Mr. Slate*); Richard Moll (*Hoagie*); Jonathan Winters (*Grizzled Man*); Harvey Korman (*Dictabird voice*); Elaine Silver (*Pebbles*); Melanie Silver (*Pebbles*); Hlynur Sigurdsson (*Bamm-Bamm*); Jean VanderPyl (*Mrs. Feldspar*); Jay Leno (*Bedrock's Most Wanted Host*); Sam Raimi; Joseph Barbera; William Hanna; Mel Blanc (*Archive recording of Dino voice*).

In Bedrock, Fred Flintstone works cheerfully at the quarry for Mr. Slate's construction company. At home he is happy with wife Wilma, daughter Pebbles and pet dinosaur Dino. Fred generously lends his friend and co-employee Barney Rubble his savings so childless Barney and his wife Betty can adopt super-strong orphan boy Bamm-Bamm. The only cloud in Fred's horizon is his visiting mother-in-law Pearl Slaghoople, who loudly expresses her opinion that Fred isn't good enough for her daughter. "You could have married the man who invented the wheel!"

Stung, Fred vows to make a success of himself. Slate & Co.'s scheming vice-president Cliff Vandercave announces an aptitude test for an executive training program. Barney sees that Fred is hopelessly confused by the test and, grateful for Fred's loan, substitutes his test form for Fred's. Cliff, who wants a brainless patsy for his embezzlement scheme, discusses the test results with his co-conspirator Sharon Stone. "Who came in first?" "Flintstone." "That big ape?" "No, the big ape got a 65." Cliff makes Fred a Vice-President and makes seductive, sarong-clad Sharon his secretary. They easily get Fred to sign orders for funds they embezzle, despite the warnings of Fred's only ally in the executive suite, his Dictabird.

Cliff orders Fred to fire Barney, who got the lowest score in the test (actually Fred's score). Reluctantly, Fred does so. Later Cliff fools Fred into signing an order firing dozens of men. With the employees rioting, Cliff "exposes" Fred as an embezzler and Fred goes into hiding. Cliff plans to flee with the stolen money to Rockapulco. Sharon, who has come to respect Fred's meat-headed integrity, realizes that Cliff intends to betray her as well. Wilma and the Rubbles get hold of the Dictabird, who can expose Cliff and Sharon as the real thieves.

Cliff kidnaps Pebbles and Bamm-Bamm and demands that Flintstone give him the Dictabird. Fred and Barney hand over the bird to Cliff at the quarry. Cliff flees, leaving the children in danger of being pulled into a rock-pounding machine. While Fred and Barney

Fred Flintstone (John Goodman) loses his temper with his mother-in-law Pearl Slaghoople (Elizabeth Taylor, right) to the consternation of Wilma (Elizabeth Perkins, center) in *The Flintstones*.

save the kids, Sharon attacks Cliff. The Dictabird is rescued and Cliff is buried under wet gravel, becoming a concrete statue. Mr. Slate is delighted and gives Fred credit for inventing concrete. "It's the end of the Stone Age!" He offers Fred an executive job, but Fred modestly asks for his old job back, working on the Bronto-crane.

COMMENTARY. The script (allegedly by 33 contributors, including the director; three screenwriters are credited) is more serviceable than inspired but *The Flintstones* scores as a film and is worthy of the wildly popular animated TV series because of two assets: the ebullient John Goodman and a witty, stunningly detailed liveaction reconstruction of the fantasy world of Bedrock. Goodman's expressions are priceless; his rubber face conveys enthusiasm, imbecility, confusion, remorse, greed and pure contentment with equal facility. Steven Spielberg supposedly chose Goodman to play Fred early in the planning for the film, and Goodman, a popular but somewhat hard-to-cast TV star, clearly understood that for him Fred Flintstone was the role of a lifetime.

Director Levant was a big fan of *The Flintstones*, with a big personal collection of memorabilia from the show. Spielberg's Amblin, George Lucas's Industrial Light & Magic and Jim Henson's Creature Shop all contributed to the creation of a Bedrock suburban neighborhood among the giant rocks and cliffs of frequently-filmed Vasquez Rocks. Besides the Bronto-crane, the Dictabird and Dino, we get Kitty the sabretooth tiger, a mammoth whose trunk is used as a shower, a lobster lawnmower, lobster pin-setters at the bowling alley, a pterodactyl airplane and an assortment of giant vegetables and eggs. The interiors are decorated with an obsessive attention to detail and the costumes are almost exactly the same as the cartoon version. Fred uses his twinkle-toes run while bowling. The Royal Order of Water Buffaloes wear horned helmets. The film was allowed to show what the TV show could not — a stone toilet, with birch bark for toilet paper. (Dino drinks from the toilet.) The Flintstones go to the drive-in and watch *Tar Wars*. A restaurant set resembles Stonehenge. There are even a couple of Loch Ness monsters.

The workers include some hairy Neanderthals, although Fred announces, "For your information, the Lodge no longer accepts Neanderthal members." There is some bright dialogue, besides the lines quoted above. Barney, "Can you do it, Fred?" Fred, "Is the Earth flat?" Fred, "My father ate this everyday and he lived to the ripe old age of 38." Fred on his secretary, "Did I mention she chisels 18 words a minute." Fred again, "We'll make new friends. After all, there are 4000 people in the world." In a clever visual joke, during the test a dumb-looking caveman tries to crib answers from a chimp.

Despite Levant's devotion to the old series, he made some significant changes to the characters. Fred is less abrasive and more immediately likeable than on TV. Barney is a lot smarter. Wilma is less acerbic. And Betty Rubble gets more personality from Rosie O'Donnell (like the director, a dedicated fan of the show) than I remember her having on television. Not much is done with the two children. The two little girls who play Pebbles are less adorable than the original (but who wouldn't be?). An implausible but necessary plot device requires slimy but not physically formidable Cliff to kidnap husky Bamm-Bamm, who routinely throws large rocks around.

Elizabeth Taylor had not done a feature film in 14 years when she worked on *The Flintstones* at age 71. Taylor said she was a big fan of the series and she attacked her part with gusto. She exchanges insults with John Goodman. She dances in a conga line with Dino and several grubby cavemen. She gets tied up on the floor. Fred smirks happily while dreaming of his mother-in-law struggling in the jaws of a dinosaur. At this writing, Taylor has not yet done another film. In the narrow category of prehistoric final films for great ladies of Hollywood, *The Flintstones* was certainly better than *Trog* (1970), the last film of Taylor's old rival Joan Crawford.

The presence of Taylor and Halle Berry makes *The Flintstones* the only prehistoric film with two Oscar-winning actors in its cast. (Berry's Oscar came several years after *The Flintstones*.) The studio reportedly asked the real Sharon Stone to play the film's Sharon Stone but she declined. Jean VanderPyl, who has a small part in the film, voiced Wilma and Pebbles in the original series.

Levant, a comedy specialist, has been a busy director, despite having made the lamentable sequel *The Flintstones in Viva Rock Vegas* (2000). Effects supervisor Michael Lantieri has been nominated for five Oscars and won once, for *Jurassic Park*. After working on three *Jurassic Park* films and *The Flintstones*, he is perhaps Hollywood's premier maker of dinosaurs. In addition to Lantieri, photographer Dean Cundey, art director Jim Teegarden and visual effects supervisor Mark Dippé worked on both *Jurassic Park* and *The Flintstones*.

The Flintstones is brief and fast-moving, only about 84 minutes without the lengthy end credits. It was made for $45,000,000 and took in $130,000,000 in the U.S. and $228,000,000 in other markets. It is the second most popular prehistoric feature ever made, after *Ice Age* (2002), which took $176,000,000 in domestic box office.

Variety (May 23, 1994) was cool to the picture, calling it "a fine popcorn picture for small fry, and perfectly inoffensive for adults.... There is little to compel great interest, but the slew of filmmakers have come up with enough contempo [contemporary] references, little jokes and bits of business to keep things busy." *The Flintstones* deserves a better appraisal than that. It is lighthearted, giddy and marvelously detailed with a classic lead performance. It looks especially good next to the sequel. As Mark Berry (*Dinosaur Filmography*) put it, "*The Flintstones* is silly and lightweight and even a little corny and it's also a boulder-size good time." Ref: Berry. *Dinosaur Filmography*; MK 7.

A Flintstones Christmas Carol (1994) U.S.; dir. Joanna Romersa; Hanna-Barbera. Animated TV special; 25 min.; color. Screenplay based on *A Christmas Carol* by Charles Dickens. VOICES: Henry Corden (*Fred Flintstone*); Jean VanderPyl (*Wilma*); Frank Welker (*Barney Rubble/Spirit of Christmas Past*); B.J. Ward (*Betty Rubble/Dino*); Don Messick (*Joe Rockhead*); John Stephenson (*Bamm-Bamm/Slate*); Russi Taylor (*Pebbles/Spirit of Christmas Present*); Brian Cummings (*Santa Claus*).

Fred plays Ebenezer Scrooge in a Bedrock amateur production of *A Christmas Carol*, then almost ruins Christmas by becoming a Scrooge himself. Lenburg. *Encyclopedia of Animated Cartoons* (1999); *Internet Movie Database*; not viewed.

The Flintstones Comedy Hour (1972–73) [alt. *The Flintstones Show*] U.S.; Hanna-Barbera. Animated TV series; 50-min. episodes; color.

This series recycled episodes from *The Flintstones* (1960–66) and *Pebbles and Bamm-Bamm*

(1971–72), together with "brief vignettes, comedy gag and dance" segments and only four new episodes, all *Pebbles and Bamm-Bamm*, according to Lenburg. New episodes: "Squawkie Talkies," "The Suitor Computer," "Bedlam in Bedrock," "Beauty and the Beast." Ref: Lenburg. *Encyclopedia of Animated Cartoons*; Adams. *The Flintstones*; not viewed.

The Flintstones Comedy Show (1980–82) U.S; Hanna-Barbera. Animated TV series; 75-min. episodes; color. VOICES: Henry Corden (*Fred Flintstone*); Jean VanderPyl (*Wilma*); Mel Blanc (*Barney Rubble/Dino*); Gay Autterson (*Betty*); Russi Taylor (*Pebbles/Cavemouse*); Michael Sheehan (*Bamm-Bamm*); John Stephenson (*George Slate*); Frank Welker (*Shmoo/Rockjaw*); Charles Nelson Reilly (*Frank Frankenstone*); Ruta Lee (*Hidea*); Zelda Rubinstein (*Atrocia*).

The Flintstones Comedy Show consisted of six component series: *The Flintstone Family Adventures*, with the characters from the original series; *Pebbles, Dino and Bamm-Bamm*, with the two teenagers and their dinosaur solving spooky mysteries; *Captain Caveman*, in which a zany superhero is helped by Wilma and Betty; *The Bedrock Cops*, with Fred and Barney as part-time police aided by the supernatural Shmoo; *Dino and the Cavemouse*, with zany watchdog-vs.-mouse stories; and *The Frankenstones*, about the Flintstones' ghoulish neighbors. *Variety*, reviewing the show as *The Flintstone Funnies* (Sept. 29, 1982), said the *Captain Caveman* segment "managed to lose much of the show's original humor."

Episodes: *The Flintstone Family Adventures*: "R.V. Fever," "Sands of Saharastone," "Gold Fever," "Bogged Down," "Be Patient, Fred," "Country Club Clods," "The Rockdale Diet," "Dino's Girl," "The Gourmet Dinner," "The Stand-In," "Go Take a Hike," "The Great Bedrock Air Race," "Fred's Last Resort," "The Not-Such-a-Pleasure Cruise," "Fred's Big Top Flop," "In a Stew," "Fred vs. the Energy Crisis," "Fred's Friend in Need." *Pebbles, Dino and Bamm-Bamm*: "Ghost Sitters," "The Secret of Scary Valley," "The Witch of the Wardrobe," "Monster Madness," "The Show Must Go On," "The Beast of Muscle Rock Beach," "In Tune with Terror," "The Curse of Tutrockamen," "The Hideous Hiss of the Lizard Monsters," "The Legend of Haunted Forest," "Double Trouble with Long John Silverrock," "A Night of Fright," "The Dust Devil of Palm Rock Springs," "Dino and the Zombies," "The Ghost of the Neanderthal Giant," "Creature from the Rock Lagoon," "Dino and the Giant Spiders," "The Ghastly Gatosaurus."

Captain Caveman: "Clownfoot," "The Masquerader," "The Animal Master," "The Mole," "Rollerman," "Vulcan," "Punk Rock," "Braino," "The Incredible Hunk," "The Ice Man," "The Mummy's Worse," "Pinkbeard," "The Blimp," "Futuro," "Mister Big," "Stormfront and Weathergirl," "Crypto," "Presto."

The Bedrock Cops: "Fred Goes Ape," "Off the Beaten Track," "A Bad Case of Rock Jaw," "Follow That Dogosaurus," "Mountain Frustration," "Bedlam on the Bedrock Express," "Hot Air to Spare," "Rockjaw Rides Again," "Pretty Kitty," "The Roller Robber," "Put Up Your Duke," "Undercover Shmoo," "On the Ball," "Shop Treatment," "Country Clubbed," "Barney and the Bandit," "Shore Thing," "Rotten Actors."

Dino and the Cavemouse: "Quiet Please," "Mouse Cleaning," "Camp Out Mouse," "Piece o' Cake," "Ghost Mouse," "Beach Party," "Disco Dino," "Going Ape," "Wet Paint," "Finger Lick 'n Bad," "Rocko Socko," "Flying Mouse," "Arcade Antics," "Aloha Mouse," "Robin Mouse," "Dino Comes Home," "L'il Orphan Alphie," "A Fool for Pool," "The Bedrock 500," "Abra-Ca-Dino," "Pow Pow the Dino-Mite," "Double Trouble," "Sleepy Time Trouble," "Goofed Up Golf," "S'No Place Like Home," "Super-Dupes," "Dinner for Two," "Invasion of the Cheese Snatchers," "Handle with Scare," "The World's Strongest Mouse," "Trick or Treat," "Bats All," "Do or Diet," "Mouse for Sale," "The Invisible Mouse," "Maltcheese Falcon."

The Frankenstones: "Birthday Boy," "Potion Problems," " A Night on the Town," "Out of Their League," "Clone for a Day," "A Stone Is Born," "A Rocks-Pox on You," "The Luck Stops Here," "The Monster of Invention," "Rock and Rolling Frankenstone," "Sand Doom," "Pet Peeves," "The Charity Bizarre," "Getting the Business," "Ugly Is Only Skin Deep," "Three Days of the Mastodon," "First Family Fiasco," "House Wars."

Ref: Lenburg. *Encyclopedia of Animated Cartoons*; Adams. *The Flintstones*; not viewed.

The Flintstones: Fred's Final Fling (1981) U.S.; dir. Oscar Dufau, Ray Patterson; Hanna-Barbera. Animated TV special; 25 min.; color.

Screenplay, Bob Ogle; music, Hoyt Curtin, Paul DeKorte. VOICES: Henry Corden (*Fred

(I) Flintstones in Viva Rock Vegas

Flintstone); Jean VanderPyl (*Wilma/Pebbles*); Mel Blanc (*Barney Rubble/Dino*); Gay Autterson (*Betty Rubble*); John Stephenson (*Frank Frankenstone*); Don Messick (*Doctor*).

Fred believes he has only 24 hours to live. Ref: Lenburg. *Encyclopedia of Animated Cartoons*; Woolery. *Animated TV Specials*; not viewed.

The Flintstones in Viva Rock Vegas (2000)

U.S.; dir. Brian Levant; Amblin/Hanna-Barbera/Universal. 90 min.; color. Screenplay, Deborah Kaplan, Harry Elfont, Jim Cash, Jack Epps, Jr.; photography, Jamie Anderson; music, David Newman. CAST: Mark Addy (*Fred Flintstone*); Stephen Baldwin (*Barney Rubble*); Kristen Johnson (*Wilma Slaghoople*); Jane Krakowski (*Betty Shale*); Joan Collins (*Pearl Slaghoople*); Thomas Gibson (*Chip Rockefeller*); Alan Cumming (*Gazoo/Mike Jagged*); Harvey Korman (*Col. Slaghoople*); Alex Meneses (*Roxy*); Rosie O'Donnell (*Octopus Masseuse*); John Stephenson (*Announcer*); Mel Blanc (*Puppy Dino, archival voice*); William Hanna; Joseph Barbera.

Unhappy rich girl Wilma Slaghoople runs away from her arrogant family and hides out in working-class Bedrock, where she makes friends with waitress Betty Shale. Meanwhile, young Fred Flintstone and Barney Rubble, new workers at the rock quarry, meet Gazoo, a space alien sent to Earth to study primitive mating customs. Although Gazoo jeers at Fred's dating techniques, Wilma likes Fred as a regular guy; she and Fred fall in love, as do Barney and Betty.

Wilma unwisely takes Fred, Barney and Betty to Slaghoople Mansion to visit her family, who make fun of her lower-class friends. Her snobbish mother, Pearl Slaghoople, wants her to marry the equally wealthy and arrogant Chip Rockefeller.

When Wilma stays loyal to Fred, Chip, with deceptive generosity, invites Wilma and her three friends to his casino in Rock Vegas. There Chip, who is in debt to mobsters and must marry Wilma for her money, rigs a table to allow Fred to win big. Soon Fred is obsessed by winning and Wilma becomes disenchanted with him. Chip also sets Barney up with Roxy, a showgirl. Broken-hearted Betty falls for lascivious rock singer Mick Jagged.

Chuck rigs some more games and takes back all of Fred's newly-won money, then frames Fred for stealing Wilma's pearl necklace. With Gazoo's help Fred breaks out of jail and rather effortlessly wins Wilma back. (Presumably Wilma's mother cut her off from the Slaghoople fortune, since she and Fred are not rich in the TV series.) Barney and Betty are also reunited.

COMMENTARY. Director Levant had to wait six years to make this dreary prequel to his very popular 1994 film *The Flintstones*. He lost all his cast except for Harvey Korman, who voiced the Dictabird in the first film and plays Wilma's father in the prequel; Rosie O'Donnell, who played Betty in the 1994 film and voices an Octopus Masseuse here; and Mel Blanc, whose voice was reused 11 years after his death.

Stephen Baldwin was a cult actor for *The Usual Suspects* (1995), but his career of mostly B-ish films meant nothing to the general public. Mark Addy was in *The Full Monty* (1997). The fact that the studio made a major effort to find a new Fred Flintstone and came up with a British actor who proved inadequate is more evidence that Fred is a challenging character to play. Although the film is supposed to be about the Flintstones and Rubbles as young people, all four of the leads were in their '30s. John Stephenson, who has a small part in the prequel, was the voice of Mr. Slate in the TV series.

The only famous star in the prequel is acid-tongued Joan Collins, who ably replaced Elizabeth Taylor as Pearl Slaghoople. Ann-Margret, who guest-starred as Ann-Margrock in the original series, sings a new version of the title song from *Viva Los Vegas*, her 1964 film with Elvis Presley.

There are some acceptable gags, such as dinosaur roller-coasters and a huge dinosaur used as a highway bridge over a canyon, but there is also an unfunny dinosaur fart joke. Collins amusingly plays one of her patented arrogant bitches. When Fred announces humbly, "I'd like to propose a toast," Pearl hisses "Must you?" The few funny lines include Fred's "Barney, tonight we shower!" when he and Barney finally get dates, and a carnival barker's "See the 40 year old man — a miracle of Nature!"

Addy's voice and hair style recall Moe Howard of the Three Stooges, as do the two huge stocking caps Fred and Barney wear. The story about roughneck but good-hearted working class guys invading snobbish high society is reminiscent of innumerable Three Stooges shorts as well as *The Beverly Hillbillies*, but the Stooges and the Hillbillies wisely never tried to stretch that theme to feature length. Barney is a lot dumber than in the 1994 film; this at least makes him closer to the animated original.

Addy lacks the ebullience John Goodman showed in the first film. Gazoo speaks with a stereotyped upper-class English accent. Production values are good but lack the freshness and imagination of the first film. *Viva Rock Vegas* is a thin comedy with little for either children or adults.

The prequel had a slightly larger budget ($58,000,000) than the 1994 film and took only $35,000,000 at the box office. *Variety* (May 1, 2000) called the film "excruciatingly lame" with a "silly script, broad slapstick and overstated lead perfs [performances] by B-team cast." Mark F. Berry (*Dinosaur Filmography*) deemed the film a resounding failure. (On a trivia note, *The Flintstones in Viva Rock Vegas* may be the last film to use the word "gay" in its traditional sense, in the song lyrics "We'll have a gay old time!") In the four years since *Viva Rock Vegas* there has been only one new entry in the *Flintstones* franchise, the perhaps too-aptly named *The Flintstones: On the Rocks* (2001), an animated film made for the Cartoon Network. Ref: Berry. *Dinosaur Filmography*; *Internet Movie Database*; MK 3.

The Flintstones: Jogging Fever (1981) U.S.; dir. Ray Patterson; Hanna-Barbera. Animated TV special; 25 min.; color. Screenplay, Bob Ogle; music, Hoyt Curtin, Paul DeKorte. VOICES: Henry Corden (*Fred Flintstone*); Jean VanderPyl (*Wilma/Pebbles*); Mel Blanc (*Barney Rubble/Dino*); Gay Autterson (*Betty Rubble*); John Stephenson (*Frank Frankenstone/Mr. Slate*).

Stung by everyone's remarks about his weight, Fred enters the Rockston Marathon, training to music Rocky Balboa-style and billing himself "The Stoneage Stallion."

Ref: Lenburg. *Encyclopedia of Animated Cartoons*; Woolery. *Animated TV Specials*; not viewed.

The Flintstones' Little Big League (1978) U.S.; dir. Chris Cuddington; Hanna-Barbera. Animated TV special; 25 min.; color. Screenplay, Jameson Brewer; music, Hoyt Curtin, Paul DeKorte. VOICES: Henry Corden (*Fred Flintstone*); Jean VanderPyl (*Wilma*); Mel Blanc (*Barney Rubble/Dino*); Gay Hartwig (*Betty Rubble*); Pamela Anderson (*Pebbles*); Frank Welker (*Bamm Bamm Rubbles*); John Stephenson; Don Messick.

Fred coaches a hopeless Little League team which seems doomed to lose to Barney's ace team. Ref: Lenburg. *Encyclopedia of Animated Cartoons*; Woolery. *Animated TV Specials*; not viewed.

The Flintstones Meet Rockula and Frankenstone (1980) U.S.; dir. Ray Patterson, Chris Cuddington; Hanna-Barbera. Animated TV special; 25 min.; color. Screenplay, Willie Gilbert; music, Hoyt Curtin, Paul DeKorte. VOICES: Henry Corden (*Fred Flintstone*); Jean VanderPyl (*Wilma*); Mel Blanc (*Barney Rubble*); Gay Autterson (*Betty Rubble*); John Stephenson (*Count Rockula*); Ted Cassidy (*Frankenstone*); Don Messick (*Igor*).

The Flintstones and Rubbles are stranded at Rockula's castle in Rocksylvania. To make matters worse, they also manage to wake up Frankenstone. Ref: Lenburg. *Encyclopedia of Animated Cartoons*; Woolery. *Animated TV Specials*; not viewed.

The Flintstones' New Neighbors (1980) U.S.; dir. Carl Urbano; Hanna-Barbera. Animated TV special; 25 min.; color. Screenplay, Willie Gilbert; music, Hoyt Curtin, Paul DeKorte. VOICES: Henry Corden (*Fred Flintstone*); Jean VanderPyl (*Wilma/Pebbles*); Mel Blanc (*Barney Rubble/Dino*); Gay Autterson (*Betty Rubble*); John Stephenson (*Frank Frankenstone*); Don Messick; Frank Welker.

Fred is prejudiced against his new neighbors, the ghoulish Frankenstones (who eat scorpions and whose daughters are called Oblivia and Hidea), until they help rescue Pebbles, who has fallen into a pterodactyl's nest. Ref: Lenburg. *Encyclopedia of Animated Cartoons*; Woolery. *Animated TV Specials*; not viewed.

The Flintstones on Ice (1973) U.S.; dir. Walter C. Miller; CBS. TV special; 50 min.; color. Screenplay, Eli Bass. CAST: Lothar Dobberstein; Teri Tucker; Malcolm Smith; Mitsuko Funakoshi.

The only live-action *Flintstones* show before the 1994 film, and probably the only caveman iceshow ever. *Variety* (Feb. 14, 1973) was mildly favorable, despite the special's "slight, comedy-of-errors script" and heavy headdresses which restricted the dancers' movements. Not viewed.

The Flintstones: On the Rocks (2001) U.S.; dir. Chris Savino, David Smith; Cartoon Network/Hanna-Barbera. Animated TV film; 85 min.; color. Screenplay, Cindy Morrow, Clay Morrow, Chris Savino, David Smith; music, Hoyt Curtin. CAST: Jeff Bergman (*Fred Flintstone*); Tress MacNeille (*Wilma Flintstone*); Kevin Richardson (*Barney Rubble*); Grey DeLisle (*Betty Rubble*); Frank Welker (*Dino*); George Stephenson (*Mr. Slate*).

Fred and Wilma go on a vacation at the advice of a marriage counselor. Their frayed nerves are not helped when Barney and Betty accompany them.

This animated TV film was one of the few *Flintstones* projects without Pebbles and Bamm Bamm and the only *Flintstones* since the poorly-received 2000 film *The Flintstones in Viva Rock Vegas*. It has attracted a low users' rating (5.1) and few users' comments on Internet Movie Database. Ref: *Internet Movie Database*; not viewed.

The Flintstones Show (1972–73) *see* **The Flintstones Comedy Hour** (1972–73)

The Flintstones' 25th Anniversary Celebration (1986) U.S.; dir. Robert Guenette; Hanna-Barbera. Animated TV special; 50 min.; color. CAST: Tim Conway; Harvey Korman; Vanna White. VOICES: Alan Reed (*Fred Flintstone*); Henry Corden (*Fred Flintstone*); Jean VanderPyl (*Wilma*); Mel Blanc (*Barney Rubble*); Bea Benadaret (*Betty Rubble*).

Liveaction stars Conway, Korman and White introduce clips from old *Flintstones* cartoons and some new animation created for this special.

Variety (June 4, 1986) said the "puff piece" was "n.s.g." (not so good). Ref: Woolery. *Animated TV Specials*; Lenburg. *Encyclopedia of Animated Cartoons*; not viewed.

The Flintstones: Wind Up Wilma (1981) U.S.; dir. Carl Urbano, Geoffrey Collins; Hanna-Barbera. Animated TV special; 25 min.; color. Screenplay, Len Jenson; music, Hoyt Curtin, Paul DeKorte. VOICES: Henry Corden (*Fred Flintstone*); Jean VanderPyl (*Wilma/Pebbles*); Mel Blanc (*Barney Rubble/Dino*); Gay Autterson (*Betty Rubble*); Julie McWhirter (*Frank Frankenstone*); Don Messick; Frank Welker.

Chauvinistic Fred feels mortified when Wilma wins a big contract as a baseball pitcher. Ref: Woolery. *Animated TV Specials*; Lenburg. *Encyclopedia of Animated Cartoons*; not viewed.

Flying Elephants (1928) U.S.; dir. Frank Butler; Hal Roach/Pathé. Short film; 20 min.; b&w; silent. Screenplay, Hal Roach, H.M. Walker. CAST: Stan Laurel (*Little Twinkle Star*); Oliver Hardy (*Mighty Giant*); James Finlayson (*Saxophonus*); Viola Richard (*Blushing Rose*); Edna Marion (*Cavewoman*); Dorothy Coburn (*Gorgeous Wrestler*); Bud Fine (*Hulking Caveman*); Tiny Sandford (*Hulking Caveman*).

"Six thousand years ago all men were forced to marry or work on the rock pile—that's why it was called the Stone Age," according to the intertitle immediately after the credits. Hieroglyphics on a stone wall announce (in subtitled translation) that "King Ferdinand proclaims: All males over 13 and under 99 years of age must marry within 24 hours, under penalty of banishment or death or both." Mighty Giant (Hardy with a wild hairstyle) and Little Twinkle Star (a very effeminate Laurel) both decide to wed Blushing Rose, daughter of short-tempered Saxophonus, who suffers from toothache.

Mighty Giant cures Saxophonus' toothache by drastic means and wins his blessing to marry Blushing Rose, but she runs and hides. Little Twinkle Star tries to kill Mighty Giant and fails, but a goat butts Giant over a cliff. Blushing Rose and Twinkle Star are happily united, but a bear chases everyone in the finale.

COMMENTARY. *Flying Elephants* is one of the silliest and craziest of the hundreds of short comedies made during the silent era. It was the third silent caveman film made by major comedians (after Chaplin's *His Prehistoric Past* (1914) and Keaton's *The Three Ages* (1923)) and may be the funniest. Almost every imaginable joke involving lunk-headed cavemen and knowing cavegirls is crammed into 20 minutes. There's even a brief scene with a dinosaur. Everyone talks in pseudo-medieval dialogue, such as "Read yon script. 'Tis the king's voice!" As Mighty Giant woos a girl he mentions conversationally "Beautiful weather we're having. The elephants are flying South" and we see the animated silhouettes of three elephants in flight—one male, one female and one baby.

As usual, Hardy is boastful but inept, while Laurel is humble and inept. When told he has to marry, Hardy brags "I can get five women in five minutes. And you should see me when I'm working fast!" When effete Laurel is told of the marriage edict he simpers "I'm too young. My mother hasn't told me everything." Laurel and Hardy did effete characters in other films. Laurel wore a kilt in *Putting the Pants on Philip* (1927) and appeared in drag in *That's My Wife* (1929), while Hardy wore an apron and carried a baby in *Their First Mistake* (1932). None of these scenes was as excessive as Laurel's effeminacy in *Flying Elephants*, which may have been intended as a parody of scenes in Douglas Fairbanks' *Robin Hood* (1922), in which the all-too–Merry Men prance around the forest. Saxophonus' toothache is not very accurate; prehistoric people usually had excellent dental health.

The women, who can only be described as prehistoric flappers, seem much smarter than the men and completely in control. All the cavegirls wear naughty 1920s costumes revealing bare legs and midriffs. In two scenes a girl watches excitedly as two men bash each other with clubs over her. Women flirt freely with Mighty Giant even though they already have husbands; the annoyed men clobber Mighty Giant, not their straying wives. When Twinkle Star tries to kidnap a girl, she resists; when he complains "I'm going to carry you to my cave. Don't you know the rules?" she easily outwrestles him.

It is Blushing Rose who figures out how to cure her father's toothache, although Mighty Giant gets the credit. When her father gives her as a reward to Mighty Giant even though she prefers Twinkle Star, she simply runs away and hides until Giant is eliminated.

Flying Elephants came fairy early in Laurel and Hardy's collaboration, which began in 1927. Sour-pussed James Finlayson, giant Tiny Sandford and Edna Marion were each in dozens of

Mighty Giant (Oliver Hardy) temporarily bests effete Little Twinkle Star (Stan Laurel, complete with drooping phallic symbol) for the affections of Stone Age flapper Blushing Rose (Viola Richard) in *Flying Elephants*.

silent comedies, but enchanting Viola Richard had only a brief career. Ref: Jones. *Illustrated Dinosaur Movie Guide*; Berry. *Dinosaur Filmography*; *Internet Movie Database*; MK 7.

The Foul Ball Player (1940) U.S.; dir. Dave Fleischer; Fleischer/Paramount. Animated short film; 6 min.; b&w. (*Stone Age* series). Screenplay, Jack Ward; music, Sammy Timberg.

"Hay fever upsets the cavemen's baseball game," according to Webb. One of 12 films in Fleischer/Paramount *Stone Age* series. Ref: Webb. *Animated Film Encyclopedia*; not viewed.

The Frankenstones (1980–82) *see* **The Flintstones Comedy Show** (1980–82)

Fred and Barney Meet the Shmoo (1979–80) U.S.; Hanna-Barbera/NBC. 75-min. episodes; color.

Included repeats of 17 episodes originally shown in *The New Fred and Barney Show* (1979, q.v.) and repeated in *Fred and Barney Meet the Thing* (1979), as well as episodes of *The Thing* and *The Shmoo*. Ref: Lenburg. *Encyclopedia of Animated Cartoons*; not viewed.

Fred and Barney Meet the Thing (1979) U.S.; Hanna-Barbera. Animated TV series; 50-min. episodes; color. VOICES: Henry Corden (*Fred Flintstone*); Jean VanderPyl (*Wilma/Pebbles*); Mel Blanc (*Barney Rubble/Dino*); Gay Autterson (*Betty Rubble*); Don Messick (*Bamm-Bamm*); John Stephenson (*Slate*).

One *Fred and Barney* episode and two episodes of *The Thing*, about a high school student with superpowers, were shown in each hour of this animated series. The 17 *Fred and Barney* episodes were repeated from *The New Fred and Barney Show* (1979). All the *Fred and Barney* and *The Thing* episodes from this series were again repeated, together with new episodes, in *Fred and Barney Meet the Shmoo* (1979–80). Ref: Lenburg. *Encyclopedia of Animated Cartoons*; not viewed.

Fred Flintstone and Friends (1977) US.; Hanna-Barbera. Animated TV series; 25-min. episodes; color. VOICE: Henry Corden (*Fred Flintstone/Host*). Fred Flintstone introduces old cartoons from *The Flintstones* (1960–66) and *Pebbles and Bamm-Bamm* (1971–72) and several other animated series. Ref: Lenburg. *Encyclopedia of Animated Cartoons*.; not viewed.

Fred's Final Fling (1981) *see* **The Flintstones: Fred's Final Fling** (1981)

The Fulla Bluff Man (1940) U.S.; U.S.; dir. Dave Fleischer; Fleischer/Paramount. Animated short film; 6 min.; b&w. (*Stone Age* series). Screenplay, Ted Pierce; music, Sammy Timberg.

"A prehistoric salesman fails at selling carpet sweepers. He incites a street brawl, then sells clubs to the brawlers," according to Webb. The title is a play on the Fuller Brush Men, well-known salesmen in the 1930s. One of 12 films in Fleischer/Paramount's *Stone Age* series. Ref: Webb. *Animated Film Encyclopedia*.; not viewed.

The Funtastic World of Hanna-Barbera (1985–?) U.S.; Hanna-Barbera. Animated TV series; 75-min. episodes; color.

Each episode of this anthology series showed segments from several old animated TV series. The 1988–89 season included repeats of *The Flintstone Kids* (1986–88). Ref: Lenburg. *Encyclopedia of Animated Cartoons*; not viewed.

G Spots? (2001) U.S.; dir. Daniel Scott Fine; Bagel Fish Productions. Short film; 13 min.; color. Screenplay, Daniel Scott Fine, Carla Stockton. CAST: Michael Chaban (*The Knight*); Sandy Duncan (*The Queen*); Markanthony Izzo (*Caveman*).

A knight "travels across time to answer his Queen's question, 'What do women really want?'" Ref: *Internet Movie Database*; not viewed.

The Gardles (1974) Japan. Animated film. Based on manga (comic book) by Shunji Sonoyama.

The Gardles is a caveman "anime" (a Japanese animated film), according to a note under *Gon the First Man* (1996, an animated TV series, also created by Sonoyama) in Clements' and McCarthy's *Anime Encyclopedia*. Ref: Clements/McCarthy. *The Anime Encyclopedia*; not viewed.

Garfield: His Nine Lives (1988) Segment, *Cave Cat*. U.S.; dir. Phil Roman; Roman Productions/United Media. Animated TV special; 50 min.; color. Screenplay, Jim Davis. VOICES: Lorenzo Music (*Garfield*); Gregg Berger (*Narrator*).

This special shows Jim Davis's popular anthropomorphic cat in nine segments, set in different periods. The *Variety* (Dec. 7, 1988) review said the special had both "more or less standard Garfield" and "more experimental bits" and that of the first group "best of this lot is the "Cave Cat" seg that comes up with lots of clever prehistoric humor." *His Nine Lives* also has an Adam and Eve segment, making it perhaps the only film or TV program to present both the anthropological and Biblical versions of human origins. Interestingly, Garfield's version of Genesis was placed after both prehistory and a segment set in ancient Egypt. Ref: Lenburg. *Encyclopedia of Animated Cartoons*; MK 6.

Genius Man (1966) U.S.; dir.-screenplay, Nicholas Spargo; ACI Films. Animated short film; 2 min.; color.

Writer-animator Spargo's film tells of a prehistoric inventor whose friends reject all his useful inventions, except one which can be used as a weapon. Ref: *OCLC WorldCat*; not viewed.

The Giant of Metropolis (1962) [orig. *Il Gigante di Metropolis*] Italy; dir. Umberto Scarpelli; Centroproduzione/seven Arts. 92 min.; color. Screenplay, Sabatino Ciuffino, Oreste Palella, Ambrodio Molteni, Gino Stafford, Umberto Scarpelli, Emimmo Salvi; photography, Mario Sensi; music, Armando Trovajoli. CAST: Gordon Mitchell (*Obro*); Bella Cortez (*Princess Mecede*); Roldano Lupi (*King Yotar*); Liana Orfei (*Queen Texen*); Furio Meniconi (*Egon*); Marietto (*Elmos*).

In 20,000 B.C. (or A.D. 10,000; see below) a dying old man entrusts muscular hero Obro with the mission of journeying to Metropolis (or Atlantis), a "terrifying civilization" with advanced science, to convince King Yotar that the Metropolitans "should never use their knowledge of science to defeat the ends of Nature." Proud Yotar ("No one is more powerful than me. I have enslaved all the people of the world") refuses to mend his ways and sentences Obro to ordeal by combat, in which he must fight first a giant, then five cannibal "dwarfs of death" (great name!) who fight only with their teeth. Yotar also plans to replace his son Elmos' brain with that of his father Egon and thus give Elmos immortality. (Huh?) Egon and Elmos' unhappy mother Queen Texen aid Obro, but both die, Texen by her own hand. Princess Mecede, Yotar's daughter by a previous wife, and Obro fall in love; he tells her that he and his people recognize "a superior being" who is more powerful than Yotar's science. Yotar's experiments get out of control and unleash a flood which destroys Metropolis. Yotar repents, announces that "Nature has humbled me in the dust" and permits Obro, Mecede and Elmos to escape to the hills.

COMMENTARY. As with Roger Corman's *Teenage Caveman* (1958), there is controversy over whether this film is set in the prehistoric past or the distant future.

According to Lucanio's *With Fire and Sword* all American advertising art said the film took place in A.D. 10,000, but a synopsis by the Italian producers said it was set in 20,000 B.C. The Italian synopsis called the city Atlantis but the characters refer to it as Metropolis. The English language DVD I viewed gave the date 20,000 B.C. and said that the city of Metropolis was part of the continent of Atlantis.

Hardy's *Science Fiction* doesn't specify the period but does call the city Atlantis. Maltin's *Movie and Video Guide* claims the film is set in 20,000 B.C. in Atlantis.

Walt Lee's *Reference Guide to Fantastic Films* gives the period as 10,000 B.C.

On the other hand, Gary Allen Smith's *Epic Films* omits *Giant of Metropolis*, presumably on the assumption that it is not set in the ancient world. Probably the Italians intended the story to take place in a prehistoric Atlantis but the American distributors felt that a futuristic story would be more popular than a prehistoric tale.

Most of *Giant* takes places among the futuristic sets and costumes of Metropolis and owes more to *Flash Gordon* and other SF serial films than to any peplum film.

There seems to be three levels of human existence — primitive, ancient and advanced. The giant and the five dwarfs whom the villains send to kill Obro all look primitive; the giant wears a typical caveman costume. Obro wears the conventional short, shirtless costume of the peplum hero and his short-lived companions are dressed like the oppressed peasants of any ancient epic. The sophisticated Metropolitan scientists' dialogue is pompous and formal, though they do enjoy an occasional dancing girl. They sacrifice humans for their experiments and can kill at a distance with death rays. Texen says that despite the Metropolitans' advanced science Obro is of "a race superior to ours" because of his great strength and courage. By contrast, the ordinary people of Metropolis have no free will and do not revolt against Yotar until it is too late.

Hardy says "script and direction are cheerfully tongue-in-cheek." Maltin's *Movie and Video Guide* calls the film a "blah sci-fi throwaway." *Giant*'s simplistic Nature-over-science script is silly but it has splendidly bizarre sets, a really fit hero and an impressive climatic flood scene.

Assuming that *Giant of Metropolis* is set in the past, it is one of only two prehistoric pepla;

the other is *Colossus of the Stone Age* (1962). *Giant* is also the only Western film to place Atlantis in prehistory. *Atlantis, the Lost Continent* (1961), directed by George Pal, and *Atlantis: The Lost Empire* (2001), a Disney animated feature, are the two best known films on the Atlantean legend. Pal sets his story after the rise of Greek civilization, while the heroes of the Disney film find a functioning Atlantis in the late 19th century. With the exception of *Giant of Metropolis* and two Japanese animated (anime) films, *The Weathering Continent* (1992) and *The Laws of the Sun* (2000), I know of no other films that have depicted Atlantis or the less famous legendary civilization of Mu (or Murania) in prehistoric settings.

Atlantis has appeared in the ancient world in *Atlantis, the Lost Continent* and in the pepla *Conqueror of Atlantis* (1965, Italy, dir. Alfonso Brescia) and *Hercules at the Conquest of Atlantis* (alt. *Hercules and the Captive Women*, 1961, Italy, dir. Vittorio Cottafavi), the sex film *Les Exploits Erotique de Maciste dans l'Atlantide* (1973, France, dir. Jesus Franco) and in an episode called "Atlantis" (1998) in the TV series *Hercules: the Legendary Journeys* (1995–2000). In the sword-and-sorcery *Kull the Conqueror* (1997, U.S., dir. John Nicoletta) a refugee from the fall of Atlantis conquers a new kingdom.

Pierre Benoit's novel *L'Atlantide*, which places Atlantis in the modern world, has been filmed at least six times, as *L'Atlantide* (1921, France, dir. Jacques Feyder); *The Mistress of Atlantis* (alt. *Die Herrin von Atlantis*, 1932, Germany, dir. G.W. Pabst, with Brigitte Helm); *Siren of Atlantis* (1949, U.S., dir. Gregg C. Tallas, with Maria Montez); *Journey Beneath the Desert* (France/Italy, 1961, dir. Edgar G. Ulmer); *L'Atlantide* (1972, France) and *L'Atlantide* (1992, France), all featuring evil Atlantean Queen Antinea. The maddest entry of all in this category is *Phantom Empire* (1935, U.S.), a serial film in which singing cowboy Gene Autry finds Murania, an underground kingdom complete with evil queen, under the Texas plains. (A B-film remake, *Phantom Empire* (1986), is in Part III because it includes a cavewoman.)

Other modern-set Atlantis stories have included *Undersea Kingdom* (1936, U.S.), a serial film, later edited to the feature-length *Sharad of Atlantis* (1966); *The Sub-Mariner* (1966), an animated TV series; a *Doctor Who* story *The Underwater Menace* (1967); the *Aquaman* segment of *The Superman/Aquaman Hour of Adventure* (1967–68), followed by *Aquaman* (1968–69), both animated TV series; *Santo Contra Blue Demon en la Atlantida* (1968, Mexico); another *Doctor Who* story *The Time Monster* (1972); *Beyond Atlantis* (1973, U.S.); *The Man from Atlantis* (1977, U.S.), a short-lived TV series; the episode "Atlantium" in the TV series *Fantastic Journey* (1977); *Warlords of Atlantis* (1978, Great Britain); *I Predatori di Atlantide* (1983, Italy); the British TV series *Neptune's Children* (1985); *Alien from L.A.* (1988, U.S.); *Journey to the Center of the Earth* (1989, U.S.); *MacGuyver: Lost Treasure of Atlantis* (1994, U.S., TV film); *Escape from Atlantis* (1997, U.S., TV film); and *Atlantis: Milo's Return* (2003, U.S.), a direct-to-video animated sequel by Disney to *Atlantis, the Lost Empire*. The ruins of Atlantis are found in *Journey to the Center of the Earth* (1959, U.S.), in which the heroes splendidly ride an Atlantean altar-stone up the shaft of an exploding volcano, and in *Mysterious Island* (1961, U.S./U.K.) and *Screamers* (1979, U.S.). The lost kingdom of Mu rises again in the modern world in Japan's *Atragon* (1964, dir. Inoshira Honda). (See *The Laws of the Sun* (2000) for a survey of Japanese animated films on prehistory.) Descendants of Atlanteans are discovered on a moon of Saturn in *Fire Maidens from Outer Space* (1963, U.S.)! Atlantis once existed in Antarctica and is now to be found in another galaxy in the Sci-Fi Channel series *Stargate Atlantis* (2004–).

With the exception of the delirious *Phantom Empire* and the delightful *Journey to the Center of the Earth*, filmmakers have certainly not covered themselves with glory in retelling the legends of Atlantis and Mu. Even worse was *Veritas: The Quest* (2003), a very short-lived U.S. TV series about heroes and villains hunting the secrets of an unidentified prehistoric super-civilization. (On a trivial note, early in the new millennium film and TV makers seemed to be obsessed with the idea of a pyramid built by an ancient civilization under the ice of Antarctica. Such a structure was featured on TV in *Veritas* and *Stargate Atlantis* and in the film *Alien vs. Predator* (2004).)

Film and TV makers have occasionally invented prehistoric civilizations other than Atlantis. Two animated TV series, *The Inhumanoids* (1986) and *Spartakus and the Sun Beneath the Sea* (1986), both featured revived underground prehistoric civilizations which threaten the modern world. Three films about

Mole People, *Superman and the Mole Men* (U.S., 1952, a good film), *The Mole People* (U.S., 1956) and *Mole Men Against the Son of Hercules* (Italy, 1960) all involved underground prehistoric civilizations found in the ancient or modern worlds. Ref: *Internet Movie Database*; Senn/Johnson. *Fantastic Cinema Subject Guide*; Hardy. *Overland Film Encyclopedia: Science Fiction*; Lucanio. *With Fire and Sword*; MK 4.

Il Gigante di Metropolis (1962) *see* **The Giant of Metropolis** (1962)

Gilligan's Island (1964–67) episode *The Secret of Gilligan's Island* (1967). U.S.; dir. Gary Nelson; CBS/Gladasaya/United Artists. Episode of TV series; 25 min.; color. Screenplay, Bruce Howard, Arne Sultan. *CAST:* Bob Denver (*Gilligan*); Alan Hale, Jr. (*The Skipper*); Jim Backus (*Thurston Howell III*); Natalie Schafer (*Mrs. Howell*); Tina Louise (*Ginger*); Dawn Wells (*Mary Ann*); Russell Johnson (*The Professor*).

Gilligan dreams about the castaways as prehistoric people. Everyone acts just as they usually do. Gilligan and the Skipper fight; the girls seek husbands; Mr. Howell bullies everyone; and the Professor struggles to invent the wheel. A dinosaur appears briefly.

The series, like its hero, was dumb but likeable. According to its famous theme song, the denizens of *Gilligan's Island* were "as primitive as can be." The show resembled a caveman film in several ways, not only the primitive lifestyle but also the bumbling comedy, the scantily-clad girls and the Professor's stream of inventions. *The Secret of Gilligan's Island*, the 93rd of 98 episodes, was as amusing as most of the popular series. Producer Sherwood Schwarz used sets made for his much less successful CBS comedy series *It's About Time* (1966–67), which was set in prehistory, on this *Gilligan's* episode. Ref: Berry. *Dinosaur Filmography*; MK 6.

Le Gladiatrici (1963) *see* **Thor and the Amazon Women** (1963)

Gogs (1996–98) U.K.; dir. Deiniol Morris, Michael Mort; Aaargh (sic) Animation; Harlech TV/Channel 4 Wales (S4C)/BBC. Claymation TV series; seven, six-to-10-min. and one 26-min. episodes; color. Music, Arwyn Davies. *VOICES:* Marie Clifford, Gillian Elisa, Dafydd Emyr, Rob Rackstraw, Nick Upton.

The embattled Gog Family (with dinosaur) in the BBC's claymation *Gogs*.

The Gog family consists of a Mother who rules with a fist of iron; a belligerent Father; a fierce old Grandfather who objects to newfangled inventions (such as clothing); a Young Woman who is smarter than the other Gogs (not that it usually does her much good); a Young Man who is (if possible) even stupider than the rest; and a Baby who enjoys crying very loud and making messes. They get into all kinds of trouble with the local wildlife, which includes not only the inevitable dinosaurs but also bears, apes, a gopher which is definitely smarter than the humans, a huge carnivorous tree and a fire-breathing frog. A story in which the Gogs try to remove a sleeping bear from their cave is a sort of classic of the imbecilic versus the immovable.

The Gogs, who do not seem to have names, speak in indecipherable but expressive shouts. They laugh heartily when one of them gets into a mess and they lose their tempers and hit each other a lot but they have no real malice. They are full of curiosity and ingenuity born of desperation. Their reactions, whether of joy, annoyance or terror, are always oversized. The show features flatulence, snot, vomit and excrement, especially the Baby's. (The British DVD has a PG rating.)

While *The Flintstones* depended on anachronistic humor, with the characters aping modern Americans, the Gogs are very primitive. The Flintstones have to speak to get their stories across; the Gogs never speak but rely on silent slapstick. The gags come breathlessly fast, such as using leaves as playing cards or sticking rocks in their ears when the baby is crying or building a Stonehenge-style megalith as a support for the baby's swing. The models for the show are the silent caveman films (Keaton's *The Three Ages* and Laurel and Hardy's *Flying Elephants*) as well as the mayhem of the Three Stooges.

In the longest episode, *Gogwana*, the Gogs survive an earthquake and a desert migration before being captured by pygmy cannibals who are more advanced than they are. The cannibals have masks, nets and dungeons but a woman captive who used to be the old Gog's sweetheart helps the Gogs escape. They flee in a hot air balloon invented very quickly by the Gog Young Woman, but are pursued by the cannibals riding on pterodactyls! (How often do you get to see cavemen in a hot air balloon fighting pygmy cannibals on pterodactyls?) After an aerial dogfight the Gogs land in an Eden, complete with a nice cave, an apple tree and a serpent, but an approaching meteorite suggests that the Gogs will have to survive the cataclysm that destroyed the dinosaurs.

The claymation is wonderfully done, especially the almost realistic dinosaurs. The humans are more exaggerated. Some of *Gogs* directly satirizes the conventions of Hollywood and Hammer prehistory, including portentous music and dinosaurs falling into crevices. *Gogs* won the 1996 BAFTA (British Film and TV Award) for animation. Ref: *Internet Movie Database*; MK 8.

Gon the First Man (1996) [alt. *Hajime Ningen Gon*] Japan; dir. Yutaka Kagawa, Takashi Yamazaki, Hiroyuki Yokoyama; KSS/NHK2. Animated TV series; 39 25-min. episodes; color. Screenplay, Yoshio Urasawa, Megumi Sugiwara, based on manga comic book by Shunji Sonoyama.

Gon, a little caveman, and his friends begin this "wacky" comedy series by "trying to hunt mammoths, running from sabre-tooth tigers and cowering from thunder," according to Clements' and McCarthy's *Anime Encyclopedia*. Later the series moved to satire, with Gon at the prehistoric equivalent of summer camp; then science fiction, as aliens arrive in a flying saucer. Shunji Sonoyama, author of the "manga" (comic book) on which *Gon* was based, also created a much earlier caveman "anime" (animated film), *The Gardles* (1974). Ref: Clements/McCarthy. *The Anime Encyclopedia*; not viewed.

Granite Hotel (1940) U.S.; U.S.; dir. Dave Fleischer; Fleischer/Paramount. Animated short film; 6 min.; b&w. Screenplay, George Manuell; music, Sammy Timberg. VOICES: Jack Mercer; Margie Hines. (In the *Stone Age* series).

Prehistoric firemen use a brontosaurus as a fire engine. Amid chaos, a telephone operator insists "Nothing ever happens at the Granite Hotel." One of 12 films in Fleischer/Paramount's *Stone Age* series. Ref: Webb. *Animated Film Encyclopedia*; not viewed.

La Guerra del Ferro (1982) see **Ironmaster** (1982)

La Guerre du Feu (1981) see **Quest for Fire** (1981)

Hajime Ningen Gon (1966) see **Gon the First Man** (1996)

The Handsome Sleeper (1952) see **El Bello Durmiente** (1952)

His Prehistoric Past (1914) [alt. *The Cave-Man*; *A Dream*; *The Hula-Hula Dance*; *King Charlie*] U.S.; dir. Charlie Chaplin; Keystone. 11 min.; b&w; silent. Screenplay, Charlie Chaplin; photography, Frank D. Williams. CAST: Charlie Chaplin (*Mr. Weakchin*); Mack Swain (*King Low-Brow*); Gene Marsh (*Sum-Babee*); Fritz Schade (*Ku-Ku the Medicine Man*); Cecile Arnold (*Cave Woman*); Al St. John (*Cave Man*).

Ku-Ku, an effeminate jester, is performing a mincing dance for hulking caveman King Low-Brow and his harem when "a castaway" arrives. The newcomer is Weakchin — Chaplin in furs, bowler hat and cane. He lights a pipe by striking a flint stone on his backside. When he meets Sum-Babee, the king's favorite wife, who is wearing a grass dress, the debonair Weakchin assures her "Shredded wheat is very becoming to you." As he flirts with her, Weakchin plays with the animal tail that hangs down the back of his costume. Back at the cave, the king hits a girl in the backside with his club as she walks past.

The king tells Weakchin, "You are now in the Solomon Islands, where every man has a thousand wives." "A thousand wives? I wish I had brought a bigger club." "Don't worry. We catch 'em young, treat 'em rough and tell 'em nothing." "You look healthy for a guy with a thousand mothers-in-law." Weakchin and the king play practical jokes on each other; Weakchin always gets the upper hand. The king tells him, "Nothing is prohibited here except work." The harem girls, who must prostrate themselves before the king, clearly prefer Weakchin.

The king discovers Weakchin kissing Sum-Babee and tries to attack her. Weakchin defends her ("I like you, King, because I had a dog called Prince once") and cleverly knocks the king over a cliff. Weakchin announces to Sum-Babee "Now I'm the King, and you're going to be Mrs. King." The harem girls are thrilled and prostrate themselves before Weakchin, who daintily walks across their backs. Ku-Ku rescues Low-Brow, who sneaks into the cave to find Weakchin enjoying the company of a harem girl. As Low-Brow hits Weakchin in the head with a rock, Charlie wakes up in the modern world, on a park bench with a cop hitting him.

COMMENTARY. All the harem girls are pretty (although only one dared to reveal bare legs in 1914) except Sum-Babee, whose main asset is her hefty body, not her plain face. The film has quite a lot to say about mistreatment of women. Unfortunately, it was also one of Chaplin's weakest efforts. The short, which seems padded even at only 11 minutes, has some bright lines in the intertitles, but no good sight gags, except for the spectacle of Chaplin twirling a club like his cane.

The name Weakchin and the crack "Shredded wheat is very becoming to you" are of course takeoffs on Weakhands and Mae Marsh's grass dress in Griffith's *Man's Genesis* (1912) and prove that Griffith's film was famous enough to attract spoofs.

Ku-Ku the jester is almost as effeminate as

Weakchin (Charlie Chaplin) with hat, cane and caveman costume, enjoys the attentions of King Lowbrow's harem in *His Prehistoric Past*.

Stan Laurel's Little Twinkle Star in *Flying Elephants* (1928). What was it about effete cavemen in silent comedy?

A line refers to the Solomon Islands and one of the alternate titles is *The Hula-Hula Dance*, but everything about the film is prehistoric. Chaplin may have wanted to be able to pass it off as either a caveman film or a South Seas movie, depending on what the public seemed to prefer.

His Prehistoric Past was the last film Chaplin made for Keystone, before moving to Broncho Billy Anderson's studio. In those circumstances, he was probably not very interested in the film and may have rushed through it. Exhaustion may have also played a part. Chaplin worked in 35 films in 1914.

Hulking, homely Mack Swain and dour Al St. John were frequent co-stars for Chaplin; both went on to long careers as character actors. Ref: *Internet Movie Database*; Jones. *Illustrated Dinosaur Movie Guide*; MK 6.

Histeria! (1998–99) U.S.; Warner Bros. TV. TV animated series; 47 25-min. episodes; color.

The relevant episode of this animated children's series, which mocked history, was *The Dawn of Man*, the 39th of 52 episodes. Ref: *Internet Movie Database*; not viewed.

History of the World, Part I (1981) U.S.; dir. Mel Brooks; Brooksfilms/20th Century Fox. 92 min.; color. Screenplay, Mel Brooks; photography, Woody Omens; music, John Morris. CAST: Sid Caesar (*Chief Caveman, Goonga*); Orson Welles (*Narrator*); Leigh French,

The Chief Caveman (Sid Caesar) experiments with his newly invented spear in Mel Brooks' *History of the World, Part I*.

Richard Karron, Susette Carroll, Sammy Shore, J.J. Barry, Earl Finn, Suzanne Kent, Michael Champion (*Prehistoric People*).

Portentous narration by Orson Welles leads us through several skits.

First we see The Dawn of Man, "20,000,000 years ago," a parody of *2001: A Space Odyssey*. As the narrator announces "the apes stood and became man" several big apes rise from the ground, reach up to the sky, then begin masturbating and fall to the ground again, all to the *Zarathushtra* music from the Kubrick film.

In the Stone Age, the narrator informs us that "if he could not light a fire, he and his would surely die." The Chief Caveman tries desperately to light a fire by striking two rocks together over kindling. As a cave full of anxious people look on, he repeatedly fails. Another caveman helpfully holds a lighted torch closer so the firemaker can see better. Still no luck. Finally, he heats one of the rocks in the torch and throws it into the kindling. This fails too and the whole cave gives way to despair. No one is smart enough to figure out how to light one fire from another. (This is of course a spoof of the entire premise of *Quest for Fire* (1982).

2,000,000 years ago in North America, the first artist paints a bison in profile on a cave wall. Immediately, the first critic appears—and urinates on the art. 1,000,000 years ago the "first homo sapiens marriage" takes place, as a man bashes a girl with his club and drags her off, followed by "the first homosexual marriage," in which a man treats another man in exactly the same way.

The Chief Caveman invents the first spear, throws it out the entrance of his cave and hits his neighbor, who was just coming for a friendly visit. Everyone is delighted except the victim, who dies. The narrator then tells us that "death was greeted with a certain awe" and the whole crowd of cave people go "awww" in chorus as they stand around the body. "Funeral services were often brief." The cave people heave the body out of the cave and spit after it.

"The need to laugh was vital for emotional survival." The first comic performs some unfunny capers in the entrance to the cave and gets no laughs until a dinosaur reaches down and grabs him. The audience dissolves in laughter. Music is discovered when a caveman named Goonga drops a rock on the foot of a man called Gali and likes the sound Gali makes. When Gali can't reproduce the sound, Goonga drops more rocks on his foot, with excellent results. The Stone Age segment ends as Goonga, bone in hand, conducts a chorus of cavemen singing the Hallelujah Chorus, with rocks dropped on everyone's feet for the high notes.

COMMENTARY. The prehistoric segment of *History of the World Part I* lasts 6 minutes, after which the film goes on to longer farces about the Romans, the Inquisition and the French Revolution. Mel Brooks played several parts in the other segments of the film, but none in the caveman skits, where the Chief Caveman is ably portrayed by Sid Caesar (aged 59 but looking good in a fur costume). Brooks wrote the film alone, in contrast to most of his other comedies, which each had several writers.

The humor in the caveman sequence in *History of the World* is cynical and obviously harks back to the much funnier Carl Reiner-Mel Brooks TV short *The 2,000 Year Old Man* (1975). The death of the first comic especially recalls the death of Murray the Nut in *2,000 Year Old Man*. None of the caveman jokes are worth more than a brief smile. *Variety* (June 10, 1981) liked only the Roman segment of the "uneven" film. Ref: *Internet Movie Database*; MK 4.

The Hitch-Hiker's Guide to the Galaxy (1981) U.K.; dir. Alan J.W. Bell; BBC. TV miniseries; six 35-min. episodes; color. Screenplay, Douglas Adams; music, Paddie Kingsland. *CAST:* Simon Jones (*Arthur Dent*); David Dixon (*Ford Prefect*).

Everyman Arthur Dent escapes in a spaceship as the Earth is destroyed by aliens. After many zany adventures, he arrives on prehistoric Earth with his friend Ford on a spaceship carrying nobody except advertising account executives, documentary filmmakers, bureaucrats and other utterly useless people exiled from another planet. While the exiles hold endless meetings considering reports on how to invent fire and the wheel, Arthur tries to educate cavemen, so that mankind may avoid its grim fate. He fails and complains "They only know one word. 'Uhn.' And they don't know how to spell it." The cavemen go about their simple lives as Arthur and Ford exchange witty dialogue and realize they can't change anything.

The cavemen are dull-witted and unteachable, but they at least are competent doing everything necessary for their own survival, in contrast with the useless, chattering modern bureaucrats. Adams' SF comedy began as a 1978 radio series. On both radio and TV it became an international hit. Ref: Fulton/Betancourt. *Sci-Fi Channel Encyclopedia of TV Science Fiction*; MK 7.

Hollyrock-a-Bye-Baby (1993) U.S.; dir. William Hanna; Hanna-Barbera. Animated TV special; ca. 100 min.; color. *CAST:* Henry Corden (*Fred Flintstone*); Frank Welker (*Barney Rubble/Dino*); Jean VanderPyl (*Wilma*); Kath Soucie (*Pebbles Flintstone-Rubble*); Jerry Houser (*Bamm-Bamm Rubble*); Raquel Welch (*Shelley Millstone*); Mark Hamill (*Slick*); Ruth Buzzi; Don Messick.

In glamorous Hollyrock, the Flintstones and the Rubbles await the birth of Pebble's baby (she has twins), while Fred tangles with jewel thieves and a starlet while helping his son-in-law Bamm-Bamm sell a screenplay. This feature-length special features prehistoric high-rises instead of the traditional suburban Bedrock stone dwellings. *Hollyrock-a-Bye-Baby* also features Raquel Welch's second performance as a cave person. Amusingly, in *One Million Years B.C.* Welch was (memorably) seen but had little dialogue; in this cartoon she is heard but not seen. Ref: *Internet Movie Database*; Lenburg. *Encyclopedia of Animated Cartoons*; Adams. *The Flintstones*; not viewed.

Hot Stuff (1971) [alt. *Le Feu? Pas pour les Hommes!*] Canada; dir. Zlatko Grgic; National Film Board of Canada. Animated short films; nine min.; color. Screenplay, Don Arioli; music, Bill Brooks. *VOICES:* Don Arioli; Gerald Budner; John Howe.

Prehistoric man is freezing; the gods take pity and give him fire, with a warning to use it with care. The cartoon goes on to show advances in the use of fire and its continuing danger. Ref: *Internet Movie Database*; not viewed.

The Hula-Hula Dance (1914) *see* **His Prehistoric Past** (1914)

I Yabba-Dabba-Do! (1993) U.S.; dir. William Hanna, Ray Patterson; Hanna-Barbera/ABC. Animated TV film; 100 min; color. Screenplay,

Mark Seidenberg, Rich Fogel; music, John Debney, Hoyt Curtin. VOICES: Henry Corden (*Fred Flintstone*); Megan Mullahy (*Pebbles*); Jerry Houser (*Bamm-Bamm*); Frank Welker (*Barney Rubble/Dino*); Jean VanderPyl (*Wilma*); B.J. Ward (*Betty Rubble*); John Stephenson (*Mr. Slate*); Don Messick; June Foray.

Pebbles and Bamm-Bamm are getting married and Fred is getting deeper and deeper in debt to pay for wedding expenses. *Variety* (Feb. 1, 1993) reported that despite "some nicely-handled, even touching moments" direction was "generally lethargic" and "the script is the key weak link." Followed by a sequel, *Hollyrock-a-Bye Baby* (1993). Ref: *Internet Movie Database*; Lenburg. *Encyclopedia of Animated Cartoons*; not viewed.

Ice Age (2002) U.S.; dir. Chris Wedge, Carlos Saldanha; Blue Sky Studios/Fox Animation. 81 min.; color. Screenplay, Michael Berg, Michael J. Wilson, Peter Ackerman; music, David Newman. VOICES: Ray Romano (*Manfred*); John Leguizamo (*Sid*); Denis Leary (*Diego*); Goran Visnjic (*Soto*); Jack Black (*Zeke*); Cedric the Entertainer (*Rhino*); Chris Wedge (*Dodo/Scrat*); Tara Strong (*Roshan*).

During the Ice Age, as most animals are migrating south, Sid, an irritating, zany, talkative tree sloth, finds that his herd has migrated without telling him. He attaches himself to Manfred, a solitary, grumpy mammoth. Soto, leader of a pack of sabre-tooth cats, wants revenge against a settlement of Neanderthals who have killed many of the big cats. He orders his smartest cat, Diego, to grab the infant son of the human leader while Soto leads the other cats in a raid on the village.

While the men and dogs are fighting the cats, Diego enters the leader's hut, but the baby's mother flees with Roshan, the infant. Trapped by Diego on top of a cliff, she jumps into a river.

Soto orders Diego to find the baby and bring him to the pack or face death himself. Sid and Manfred watch as the exhausted mother pushes Roshan ashore; she is then carried away by the river. Sid insists on returning the baby to its "herd" and Manfred reluctantly agrees. Diego joins them and claims to want to help them return the baby, while watching his chance to grab the child. After many adventures, during which Manfred risks his life to save Diego from a lava flood, the trio reach a pass the humans must cross. Diego admits he has led Sid and Manfred into an ambush by the cats. Together, the three new friends defeat the cats, kill Soto and return Roshan to his father.

COMMENTARY. The first years of the new century saw two expensive animated features with prehistoric humans playing secondary parts to anthropomorphic talking animals. *Ice Age* came out a year before *Brother Bear* and was more successful at the box office, taking $176,000,000 in the U.S. market plus $202,000,000 in foreign markets. As of mid-2004, *Ice Age* was the 78th most popular film ever in the U.S., surpassing all other prehistoric films.

The animal scenes in *Ice Age* feature zany slapstick and funny dialogue, such as Sid's "I thought you were going to eat me!" and Diego's reply "I don't eat junk food."

The show is almost stolen by Scrat, a manic saber-tooth squirrel (!) who obsessively guards a single acorn. Although no one would call the movie realistic, the backgrounds and the design and movements of some of the animals, especially Manfred, are convincing. The background scenery is often quite beautiful. Generally, the larger the animal, the better he and his movements look; the smaller the beast the more he dashes around zanily. Manfred and the other big animals lumber along realistically, more so than Diego, who is more convincing than Sid, who is a little less manic than Scrat. The modern, slangy dialogue works better than in *Dinosaur* (2000), a Disney talking-dinosaur animated feature, possibly because most of the animals in *Ice Age* are more cartoonish than in *Dinosaur*, so *Ice Age* avoided the stark contrast between realistic animals and unrealistic dialogue which marred the Disney film.

While the animals in *Ice Age* are funny, the humans are not. The baby is the most-seen human in the film. He gets into babyish mischief and hugs the animals lovingly but he is not really a character. He is identified by name only in the DVD extras. Other humans are seen only briefly. The death of the brave mother is similar to the death of Ayla's mother in *Clan of the Cave Bear* (1986). The two women wear similar costumes; each drowns while trying to save her child.

The humans are not identified in the film but an extra feature in the DVD identifies them as Neanderthals. They have big noses like

Neanderthals, but they are tall and slender, while Neanderthals were short and stocky. In their village they have guard dogs, fire, large huts made from animal skins, baskets, pottery, necklaces, a crib for the baby and what appears to be a line for drying fish. They have spears and wear well-made animal skin clothes. They mourn their dead. Except for a few monosyllabic shouts, they do not speak. (This is a running joke in the film. The animals speak, but the humans don't. At the end Diego says to Sid, "Don't waste your time. You know humans can't talk.")

A lot of the humans' paraphernalia is fairly advanced, but except for the baby the people have sloped foreheads which gives them a half-witted appearance. The depiction of humans is somewhat realistic but inconsistent. Neanderthals had fire and may or may not have talked, but they probably didn't have needles with which to make well-fitting clothes and they relied on caves rather than building huts. The humans in the film throw spears; the documentary *Before We Ruled the Earth* (2003) claims that Neanderthals probably had only heavy spears which could not be thrown far and only Cro-Magnons had light throwing spears. The humans in the film have everything they need to live through tough conditions, but they look dull-witted and don't talk. They have Cro-Magnon body shape and gear, big Neanderthal noses, no ability to speak and cranium size much smaller than either group. Their lack of speech and dumb appearance are inconsistent with their evident competence and skill. It's commendable that the film presented advanced and capable prehistoric humans, but deplorable that the filmmakers contradicted themselves by making them look too primitive.

While taking Roshan, the human baby, back to his "herd" the animals discuss the fact that if the baby lives he will probably become a hunter and hunt them. As they pass through a big cave, they see cave art made by humans. (Neanderthals did not produce cave art; only modern humans did that.) Manfred looks at a cave painting of a mammoth family and envisions the killing of his parents by humans. Nevertheless he picks up the human baby gently and carries him out of the cave, nobly refusing to hold a grudge. (There is a brilliant gag in the cave sequence. Sid rushes past a frozen gallery and sees the alien space ship from *The*

A prehistoric mother with her baby flees a sabre-tooth cat in *Ice Age*.

Thing from Another World (1951) suspended in the ice. He shrugs and races on.) At another point, Sid passes a small structure suggestive of Stonehenge and remarks "Modern architecture. It'll never last." (Neanderthals did not build stone structures.)

There is another annoying and unnecessary error in the film. Diego and the other sabre-tooth cats are called "tigers." There never was such a thing as a sabre-tooth tiger. The several species of huge cats with long, curved teeth are properly called sabre-tooth cats.

Chris Wedge was already an Oscar winner for *Bunny*, a 1998 short animated film when he co-directed *Ice Age*. *Variety* (March 18, 2002) praised the film for "setting new standards for computer-generated anthropomorphism" and noted "better still, the eye-popping technique is employed in support of an entertaining story that, while not terribly original, is sufficiently arresting and often laugh-out-loud funny."

Most critics were as pleased as the audiences. *Ice Age* was nominated for an Oscar for Best Animated Feature (losing to *Spirited Away*) and for several Annies (animation awards) including Best Picture, Direction and Writing. Ref: *Internet Movie Database*; MK 7.

Il Etait une Fois l'Homme (1978) *see* **Once Upon a Time: Man** (1978)

I'm a Monkey's Uncle (1948) U.S.; dir. Jules White; Columbia. Short film; 16 min.; b&w. Screenplay, Zion Myers; photography, George F. Kelley. CAST: Shemp Howard (*Shemp*); Larry Fine (*Larry*); Moe Howard (*Moe*); Dee Green (*Aggie*); Virginia Hunter (*Baggie*); Nancy Saunders (*Maggie*); Cy Schindell (*Caveman*); Joe Palma (*Caveman*); Bill Wallace (*Caveman*).

As cavemen the Three Stooges have trouble hunting and gathering, but more luck wooing cavewomen Aggie, Baggie and Maggie. When the girls' three hulking boyfriends turn up the boys drive them off, using a tree branch as a catapult to launch rocks, mudballs and eggs.

Somehow it seems inevitable and fitting that The Three Stooges did a caveman film. This short was made a year after Curly Howard's illness forced his retirement as the third Stooge and his replacement by his brother Shemp. As a result it is Moe who does a duck hunting scene in which the humor depends on his frustration at repeated defeats; Curly would have done this scene in earlier shorts.

The Stooges play the same characters as in all their films. Their dialogue is completely modern and the gags come thick and fast. Moe catches a fish that barks and exclaims "Oh, a dogfish!" "I hope it doesn't have fleas," Larry remarks. They make butter by having Larry tickle Shemp who shakes with laughter while holding a stone churn full of milk. Moe combs his hair with a fish skeleton.

When the boys hit the three girls in the head with their clubs, the assault has no effect. One girl smilingly advises the others, "Let's just ignore them, girls." The boys launch a skunk at their opponents after donning "gas masks" (wishbones to pinch their noses).

Footage from *I'm a Monkey's Uncle* was reused in *Stone Age Romeos* (1955), a short set in modern times and found in Part III of this list. Ref: Jones. *Illustrated Dinosaur Movie Guide*; Lenburg/Maurer/Lenburg. *Three Stooges Scrapbook*; MK 6.

The Improbable History of Mr. Peabody (1959–61) *see* **Rocky and Bullwinkle** (1959–61)

In Prehistoric Days (1914) *see* **Brute Force** (1914)

Ironmaster (1982) [alt. *La Guerra del Ferro*] France/Italy; dir. Umberto Lenzi; Films Leitienne/Nuova Dania Cinematografica/Société Imp.Ex.Ci. 98 min.; color. Screenplay, Alberto Cavallone, Lea Martino; photography, Giancarlo Ferrando; music, Guido de Angelis, Maurizio de Angelis. CAST: Sam Pasco (*Ela*); Elvire Audray (*Isa*); George Eastman (*Vood*); Pamela Prati (as Pamela Field) (*Lith*); Jacques Herlin (*Rag*); Brian Redford (*Tog*); Benito Stefanelli (*Iksay*); William Berger (*Mogo*).

The narrator speaks his only words at the beginning of the film: "Many thousands of years ago, a tribe of men discovered a terrifying weapon and learned how to wage war." Iksay, aging leader of the Children of Zod, is concerned because an earthquake has driven away the small animals the tribe can kill. The large animals that remain in the area, the mammoths and buffalo, cannot be killed with the tribe's stone axes and sticks with fire-hardened points. Young Vood is ambitious to rule the tribe and jealous of Ela, whom Iksay favors. As the hunters return from a hunt, they are attacked by painted men throwing bolas. Iksay's men drive the attackers away, killing many, but as Iksay kills an enemy Vood clubs him from behind and kills him. Ela arrives a few seconds later and realizes Vood is the killer.

The Three Stooges (from left, Moe Howard, Shemp Howard, and Larry Fine) in *I'm a Monkey's Uncle.*

Ironmaster (I)

At Iksay's funeral, in a large cave with a great stone column through which the tribe talks to its gods, Ela accuses Vood of the murder and Vood attacks him. When the tribe's elderly shaman tries to stop the fight Vood kills him. Vood flees across the "mountain of fire" and is almost killed when the volcano erupts. The eruption topples the stone column in the sacred cave, profoundly shocking the tribesmen. After the eruption and a rainstorm, Vood finds an iron rod which has been formed by the action of lava on iron ore and cooled by the rain. He finds the rod can shatter stones and instantly realizes its significance.

Lith, a woman of a tribe from "beyond the fire mountain," tells Vood that Epheron the fire god sent her a vision that Vood would become the "master of this land" and she would be his woman. Vood and Lith return to the cave of the Zod tribe where Vood easily defeats Ela, smashing his wood-handled stone ax and his wooden staff. After Vood wounds Ela, Lith announces Vood's new law: only those who submit to him will live. "Honor and obedience to Vood is the will of the god Epheron. Otherwise his anger will be great. The ground will shake again and all will be burned." The whole tribe submits except Ela. Vood has Ela tied to a wooden cross in the land of the Ursus, apemen who walk erect but use only rocks for weapons.

Mighty Ela breaks his bonds, uses the cross as a weapon, kills two Ursus and flees. He is found and his wound is healed by Isa, a girl of the Lake Tribe. Meanwhile Vood, egged on by Lith, tells the Zod men that "We will be a race of conquerors." Vood and his men find more "black rocks" (iron ore) on the volcano and learn how to melt iron in fire, form it in a stone mold, cool it and pound it into shape. They mass-produce long, hiltless iron swords. Lith announces, "Tomorrow a new age will dawn." Vood and his men attack a nearby village, easily kill many men and force the survivors to submit. When the defeated tribe's leader refuses to agree to give up the game he takes in the hunt to Vood ("The hunt is sacred!"), Vood kills him.

Ela and Isa observe Vood's men killing apemen and realize the power of Vood's new weapon. When the surviving Ursus take refuge in their cave, Vood builds a fire across the entrance. As the Ursus try to escape the fire, Vood's men kill them (in a scene reminiscent of Kurosawa's *Yojimbo* and Leone's *Fistful of Dollars*). Vood conquers one village after another. Ela and Isa take news of Vood's conquests to the Lake People, whose leader Mogo is Isa's father. The Lake People are somewhat more advanced than other tribes and have huts built on stilts in the lake, but they have no weapons. Despite Ela's urgent warnings, Mogo refuses to fight under any circumstances, because "weapons are evil and life to us is holy."

While Ela, Mogo and a few others are out tracking a dangerous lion, Vood's army attacks and takes the Lake Village and enslaves its people. Ela begins to make weapons and gather men to fight back. Mogo continues to reject war, warning Ela that "though weapons may give you back your freedom, they may take it away again." Mogo walks off completely alone. Men of Vood's army catch Mogo who tells them he is "of the tribe of rabbits." When he refuses to kiss an iron sword in submission to Vood, the Zod men kill the saintly leader.

Ela respects Mogo's decision to remain true to his principles until death, but he is determined to fight. Vood and Lith plan to rule the world, but Vood is still obsessed with finding and killing Ela. Tog, one of Vood's men, suggest they stop their wars but Vood tells him "We are happy only in battle. War is our reason for living. What's the use of having invincible weapons, if you can't use them?"

Ela with a few men infiltrates the Lake Village and kills Vood's small garrison, capturing their iron swords and Lith, who has gotten into the habit of threatening to put women's eyes out if they do not work hard enough to suit her. Ela sends Lith to Vood with a challenge to meet him alone and settle the war in a personal duel. Isa asks Ela, "You will kill also, and then what difference will there be between you and Vood?" Fed up, Ela asks her "Why don't you just go away?" But soon they are reconciled and become mates. Meanwhile, Ela develops the longbow and arrows (which he calls "small spears"). Refugees from defeated tribes rally to Ela. He makes many bows and teaches Isa and his growing army of men and women to use them.

Vood arrives, of course not alone as he agreed but with many men. Isa begins the battle by shooting Lith with an arrow. Ela's army shoots down several of Vood's men; the rest flee. Ela and Vood meet in history's first swordfight. After killing Vood, Ela remembers Mogo's warning and pleases Isa by throwing all the iron weapons into the lake, hoping they will never be needed again. (We know how that turned out.)

COMMENTARY. *Ironmaster* has received few and very bad notices. This is a mistake. Umberto Lenzi was a prolific director of all sorts of Italian B films, from the pepla and spaghetti Westerns to the gialli (grim thrillers) and Italy's gory cannibal films of the 1980s. Stephen R. Bissette, in his self-published manuscript on the cannibal movies *We Are Going to Eat You!*, says Lenzi's films are characterized by "misanthropy, nihilism and an eye for scatological detail." However, Lenzi does have his fans. An erudite fan comment on the *Internet Movie Database* page for *Ironmaster* calls Lenzi "one of Italy's better B-movie directors, delivering consistently entertaining films throughout his career."

Alberto Cavallone wrote and directed *Master of the World*, another caveman film, one year after he wrote *Ironmaster*. *Master of the World* enjoys an even worse reputation than *Ironmaster*. I have never seen it but I have no reason to think it deserves better. *Ironmaster* was clearly intended to appeal to a wider audience than Lenzi's most extreme horror films. Much of it functions like a typical B Western, in which simple but not stupid characters wrestle with moral choices. The villain gets worse and worse while the hero must decide whether to indulge in excessive violence.

Vood is a smart, formidable villain. Starting as a lone exile, he discovers iron, figures out how to make it, takes over his tribe, builds up an army and conquers an empire. He could be considered a ruthless agent of progress. He is strong and brave and kills a lion single-handed. Lith is another ambitious and domineering villain, who gets big ideas even quicker than Vood. She presumably has some supernatural powers, since she knew before she met Vood that he was going to become a conqueror. One of the problems with *Ironmaster* is that the two villains are more memorable than the hero and heroine. Ela and Isa fail to make an impression except when Ela is tempted to turn villainous himself.

The film makes admirable attempts at physical realism. The cavemen are skinny and lithe and look very strong. It's no surprise they quickly master new weapons and tactics. Most of the women look convincing too, though no women except Isa and Lith have much to do. Isa and some of the other women have too much of the Hammer bikini look. Isa's hair is especially modern-looking. Ela is the only unconvincing man. He has bulging muscles and a huge chest, like a pepla hero, unlike the other, much more compact cavemen. Ela and Isa are too pretty, less interesting than Vood and Lith and less realistic than the rank-and-file cavemen and look like they belong in another film.

We briefly see cave art and firemaking. Different aspects of primitive religion are shown: first the shaman's humane suggestions and the simple funeral for Iksay; then people's terror at the earthquake and eruption, which must mean that a god is angry at them; then enthusiasm for the bloody worship of Epheron; and finally Mogo's saintly pacifism. The scenes in which men work iron and forge swords are convincing, though they probably understate the difficulty of making iron weapons. We see two sides of ancient medicine. Men afflicted with "the evil sickness," perhaps leprosy, live in a cave by themselves; even the bravest warriors flee at the sight of them. The only way to escape infection is to avoid the sick. On the other hand, Isa is skilled at healing wounds and saves Ela.

The film is set among mountains, meadows and lakes. The caves look real, not like sets. Mammoths are seen only once and at a distance, but there are many scenes with buffalo. (The film was shot partly in South Dakota.) There are no anachronistic dinosaurs or monsters, but the apemen would not have existed at the same time as modern humans. The volcanic eruption is achieved by a brief, poor special effect, together with stock footage.

Ironmaster takes a pessimistic view of man. Except for Ela, the whole Zod tribe agrees to follow Vood. They quickly become adept killers of anyone in their path. The men of Zod are clearly corrupted by their success. The invention of new weapons leads only to horrors. Only Tog questions their war policy and he backs down when Vood insists on continuing. When Ela begins fighting back, he kills men who were formerly his friends in large numbers and without apparent regret.

However, these cavemen are not dim-witted. As the dialogue quoted above shows, they have sophisticated speech. Both good and evil people are quick to learn. A nice touch happens when Ela arrives at the Lake Village and glances around. He stares for a couple seconds at objects the advanced Lake People have that his people don't have, then walks on without comment. He recognizes that the Lake People have superior techniques but he's not going to let the Lake People tell him what to do. He doesn't hesitate to disagree with the Lake People's leader Mogo.

Ironmaster is of course an antiwar film and Vood, a demagogue who comes out of nowhere and tries to conquer the world, could represent Hitler. Lith is a perfect totalitarian bully. She even announces a policy of free love, in order to produce more children to be Vood's soldiers. "Any man will have any woman, and any woman any man, so long as they both serve Vood."

George Eastman (Vood) and William Berger (Mogo) had long careers in dozens of European B films. Elvire Audray (Isa) and the alarming Pamela Prati (here credited as Pamela Field, playing Lith) had more modest careers. Sam Pasco (Ela) never worked in another film.

Lenzi's *Ironmaster* is simple, only modestly ambitious and has its share of flaws. However, it's hard not to like a film which shows intelligent, articulate prehistoric people making discoveries, facing moral issues and showing capacity for great evil and finally for good. Ref: Senn/Johnson. *Fantastic Cinema Subject Guide*; Jones. *Illustrated Dinosaur Movie Guide*; Bissette. *We Are Going to Eat You*; MK 6.

It's About Time (1966–67) U.S.; producer, Sherwood Schwartz; United Artists TV/CBS. TV series; 26 25-min. episodes; color. Music, Gerald Fried, Sherwood Schwartz, George Wyle. CAST: Jack Mullaney (*Hector*); Frank Aletter (*Mac*); Imogene Coca (*Shad*); Joe E. Ross (*Gronk*); Cliff Norton (*Boss*); Kathleen Freeman (*Mrs. Boss*); Pat Cardi (*Breer, Gronk's Son*); Mary Grace [i.e. Mary Grace Canfield] (*Mlor, Gronk's Daughter*); Mike Mazurki (*Clon*).

Accidentally traveling back in time to prehistory, astronauts Hector and Mac are taken in by cave-dwelling couple Gronk and Shad, their smart son Breer and miniskirted daughter Mlor. The local heavies are dumb bully Clon and irascible tyrant Boss. Later the astronauts repair their ship and return to the modern world, but the cave family accompany them.

The cave people speak English, but only of the Tarzan variety. "Shad make mastodon soup," Shad announces. "I've never had that!" Mac replies. Joe E. Ross repeats far too often his

Gronk (Joe E. Ross) and Shad (Imogene Coca) in *It's About Time.*

trademark exclamation "Ooh! Ooh! Ooh!," familiar to fans of his previous series *Sgt. Bilko* (1955–59) and *Car 54, Where Are You?* (1961–63). In the modern world, Hector shows Gronk a chair and calls it "Soft rock!" The completely unambitious humor and insistent laugh track make the sit-com painful to watch.

Astronaut Hector is foolish and timid, while Mac is smarter but bland. The cave people are all more or less stupid except little Breer. Most of the prehistoric conventions are trotted out, from shapeless fur costumes and massive clubs, to prowling dinosaurs, a girl being dragged by her hair and an enemy tribe called the Painted People.

Imogene Coca was one of America's most popular comediennes after four years on the clever skit series *Your Show of Shows* (1950–54). Joe E. Ross was almost equally famous for his work on *Bilko* and *Car 54*. *It's About Time* did neither of the stars any favors. Leslie Halliwell (*Halliwell's Television Companion*) calls it "woeful" and Castleman and Podrazik (*Harry and Wally's Favorite TV Shows*) consider it one of the worst sitcoms in TV history, with a "moronic level of humor," but feel that the last eight episodes, set in the 20th Century, are a little better than the prehistoric episodes. Having seen two prehistoric and two modern episodes, I would agree that the latter were preferable. In one, the cave people learn to say "Charge it" and quickly buy vast amounts of consumer goods. In another, Gronk joins the Army but quickly gets fed up and clobbers the officers.

Variety reviewed the series in the same issue (Sept. 14, 1966) it reviewed the first episodes of two more serious science fiction series, *Star Trek* and *The Time Tunnel*. Not at their most brilliant, *Variety*'s reviewers felt *Star Trek* was hopeless, but thought *It's About Time* showed promise and "affords a good range of made-to-order situations for an able cast of sight comics who get the latitude here to play in funny-paper style" while "the production (on a nifty set) is of high order for such a knockabout show." In a follow-up review (Jan. 25, 1967, at the time of the switch to modern stories), *Variety* had given up on the series, noting "the humor was broad without being funny" and moaning "What a waste for Imogene Coca!"

The only fondly-remembered element of the short-lived series was the catchy theme song. The lyrics were written by the show's producer, Sherwood Schwartz, also the creator of *Gilligan's Island* and *The Brady Bunch*. The first episode was directed by Richard Donner, later director of the film version of *Superman* (1978). Three episodes were directed by Jack Arnold, director of some of the most important SF films of the 1950s, including *Creature from the Black Lagoon* (1954) and *The Incredible Shrinking Man* (1957).

Episodes: "And Then I Wrote Happy Birthday to You," "The Copper Caper," "The Initiation," "Tailor Made Man," "The Rainmakers," "Me Caveman, You Woman," "The Champ," "Mark Your Bullets," "Have I Got a Girl For You," "Cave Movies," "Androcles and Clon," "Love Me, Love My Gnook," "The Broken Idol," "The Sacrifice," "King Hec," "The Mother-In-Law," "Which Doctor's Witch," "To Catch a Thief," "20th Century, Here We Come" (including the trip back to the modern world), "Shad Rack and Other Tortures," "The Cave Family Swingers," "To Sign or Not To Sign," "School Days, School Days," "Our Brother's Keeper," "The Stone Age Diplomats," "The Stowaway." For episode synopses, see Morton's *Complete Directory to Science Fiction, Fantasy and Horror Television Series*. Ref: Jones. *Illustrated Dinosaur Movie Guide*; viewed 4 episodes; MK 3.

It's Tough to Be a Bird (1969) U.S.; dir. Ward Kimball; Disney. Animated and liveaction short film; 22 min.; color. Screenplay, Ted Berman, Ward Kimball; music, George Bruns, Mel Leven. VOICES: Richard Bakalyan (*M.C. Bird, Narrator*); Ruth Buzzi. A humorous pseudo-documentary about the bird's struggle for survival from prehistoric times to the present. Winner of an Oscar for Best Animated Short. Ref: Jones. *Illustrated Dinosaur Movie Guide*; Smith. *Disney A to Z*; not viewed.

The Jetsons Meet the Flintstones (1987) U.S.; dir. Don Lusk, Ray Patterson; Hanna-Barbera. Animated TV film; 100 min.; color. Screenplay, Don Nelson, Arthur Alsberg; VOICES: Henry Corden (*Fred Flintstone*); Jean VanderPyl (*Wilma/Rosie*); Mel Blanc (*Barney Rubble/Dino/Mr. Spacely*); Julie Dees (*Betty Rubble*); George O'Hanlon (*George Jetson*); John Stephenson (*Mr. Slate*).

As part of a school science project, the Jetson family travel by time machine from the far future to the prehistoric past where they meet the Flintstones. Ref: Lenburg. *Encyclopedia of Animated Cartoons*; not viewed.

Jogging Fever (1981) *see* **The Flintstones: Jogging Fever** (1981)

Journey to Prehistory (1955, 1966) *see* **Journey to the Beginning of Time** (1955, 1966)

Journey to the Beginning of Time (1955, 1966) [alt. *Cesta do Praveku*; *Journey to Prehistory*] Czech/U.S.; dir. Karel Zeman, Fred Ladd; New Trend. 83 min.; color. Screenplay, Karel Zeman, J.A. Novotny, William Cayton; photography, Antonin Horák, Vaclav Pazdernik; music, E.F. Burian, Frantisek Strangmüller. CAST: Josef Lukas (*Petr/Doc*); Vladimir Bejval (*Jirka/Jo-Jo*); Zdenek Hustak (*Jenda/Ben*); Petr Herrman (*Tonik/Tony*).

Four boys visit the American Museum of Natural History in New York, then go on a boat ride which takes them back in time. They see a live mammoth, then find the cave home of a prehistoric man (who is not seen). In the cave are a fireplace, the antlers of a big animal killed by the caveman, the tusks of several mammoths, a large stone-ax and cave art. Outside,

The time-traveling boys (from left, Josef Lukas, Petr Herrmann, Vladimir Bejval) examine a caveman's ax in *Journey to the Beginning of Time*.

Tony finds the caveman's spear and an animal trap.

The boys are impressed by the absent caveman, remarking "He must have been really strong!" Doc, the erudite science student who explains everything they see to the other boys, praises the cave paintings. "Whoever painted these was no beginner. He had talent." Strangely, Doc insists that one caveman lived alone in the cave. It would have been more realistic to show evidence of a prehistoric family. Later, Doc drives off menacing crocodiles with a lantern and exclaims "What a moment it must have been when man first discovered fire!" (All dialogue in the English version is by Cayton, not Zeman.)

The boys continue down the magic river through time, observe the dinosaurs, arrive at the beginnings of life, then find themselves back in the present.

COMMENTARY. Zeman specialized in stop-motion animation films. Eleven years after he made *Cesta do Praveku*, which has more live-action scenes than most of Zeman's work, it was purchased by American producer William Cayton, who added the New York scenes using boys who resembled the Czech child actors. The resulting *Journey to the Beginning of Time* was syndicated on U.S. TV and became extremely popular for its charming story and convincing, mostly accurate dinosaurs. Ref: Berry. *Dinosaur Encyclopedia*; Jones. *Illustrated Dinosaur Movie Guide*; Lee. *Reference Guide to Fantastic Films*; MK 7.

Kablam! (1996–2000) Segment *Prometheus and Bob*. U.S.; Viacom/Nickelodeon. Segment of animated TV series; 25-min. episodes; color.

The *Prometheus and Bob* segments of the *Kablam!* series were supposed to be 900,000-year-old video tapes, made by extraterrestrial Prometheus to record his effects to educate Bob, a slow-witted but willing caveman. A third character, Monkey, seems to be smarter than either Bob or the alien. *Prometheus and Bob* segments each focused on a different invention including: "Bridge," "Music," "Cooking,"

"Clothing," "Wheel," "Shelter," "Fishing," "Kite," "Art," "Bowling," "Trapping," "Spear," "Breakfast," "Farming," "Construction," "Milking," "Boxing," "Ice Skating," "Canoe," "Pottery," "Hammock," "Ball." Ref: Lenburg. *Encyclopedia of Animated Cartoons*; Internet Movie Database; Kablam! website, *http://www.echoes.com/kablam*; not viewed.

King Charlie (1914) *see* **His Prehistoric Past** (1914)

Korg: 70,000 B.C. (1974–75) U.S.; producers, Richard L. O'Connor, Fred Freiberger; Hanna-Barbera/ABC. TV series; 24 25-min. episodes; color. Music, Hoyt Curtin. CAST: Jim Malinda (*Korg*); Bill Ewing (*Bok*); Naomi Pollack (*Mara*); Christopher Man (*Tane*); Charles Morteo (*Tor*); Janelle Pransky (*Ree*); Burgess Meredith (*Narrator*).

Neanderthal Korg, his mate Mara, their teenage son Bok, younger sons Tane and Tor and daughter Ree struggle to survive in ancient Europe.

A decade after giving the world the zany *Flintstones*, a gentle satire on modern foibles, Hanna-Barbera attempted a serious, accurate, liveaction children's drama about prehistory. Researchers at the American Museum of Natural History in New York and the Los Angeles County Museum of Natural History advised the series on ancient life, customs and costumes. Oscar winner Burgess Meredith narrated. The little-known actors were well-chosen for rugged looks. Stories dealt with the search for food, dangers from wild animals and other tribes and (inevitably) epochal discoveries. In one story, a piece of meat is dropped in the sea, then recovered; the cave people thereby discover that salt makes meat taste much better.

In a Sept. 11, 1974 article on children's TV programming, *Variety* called *Korg* "slow-moving and ludicrously funny." George Woolery reports that the series "was a trifle heavy on educational and scientific themes, containing few entertainment features. It was a colossal ratings failure." The series was shown on Saturday mornings opposite less ambitious fare — *Shazam!* and *Sigmund and the Sea Monster*. There was a series of comic books (9 issues, 1975–76, by Charlton Publications) and a simple board game, in which players were to collect food, water, clothing and weapons while avoiding ambushes. Ref: Jones. *Illustrated Dinosaur Movie Guide*; Woolery. *Children's Television*; Terrace. *Encyclopedia of Television Series, Pilots and Specials*; not viewed.

Kum-Kum (1975) [alt. *Kum-Kum the Caveman*; *Naughty Ancient Kum-Kum*; *Wanpaku Omukashi Kum-Kum*] Japan; dir. Rintaro (pseud. for Shigeyuki Hayashi), Noburo Ishiguro, Wataru Mizusawa; ITC Japan. Animated TV series; 26 25-min. episodes. Screenplay, Eiichi Tachi, Keisuke Fujikawa, Yoshiaki Yoshida.

Caveboy Kum-Kum lives in the mountains of prehistoric Japan, with his sister Furufuru and friends Chilchil, Mochi-Mochi and Aron. Clements and McCarthy (*Anime Encyclopedia*) say the children's adventures involve "mammoth rides, troublesome dinosaurs, and the opportunity to throw rocks at each other." *Kum-Kum* was popular on British children's TV in the early 1980s. Ref: Clements/McCarthy. *The Anime Encyclopedia*; not viewed.

(From left) Tor (Charles Morteo), Mara (Naomi Pollack), Ree (Janelle Pransky), Korg (Jim Malinda), Bok (Bill Ewing) and Tane (Christopher Man) in *Korg: 70,000 B.C.* Note that all the males carry weapons while the mother and daughter carry bundles.

Lacets (2004) Spain; D'Ocon. TV animated series; 26 26-min. episodes; color. "A prehistoric tribe discovers a brand-new world that will open up the doors to the future" in this children's animated series, according to a note in *Variety*'s MIP Market report (March 29, 2004, p. A25). The production company's website (*www.docon.es*) says that the tribe's children are "fighting against murky mystification, old beliefs and superstitions of the witch doctor, who does not want to expand their horizons." Not viewed.

Land of the Monsters (1962) *see* **Colossus of the Stone Age** (1962)

The Laws of the Sun (2000) Japan; dir. Takaaki Ishiyama; Tac. Animated film; 101 min.; color. Screenplay, Laws of the Sun Scenario Project, based on book by Ryuho Okawa.

Forty billion years ago (sic!) the Cosmic Consciousness creates mankind on Venus, but that planet is so idyllic that people fail to strive for perfection. They are therefore moved to the less hospitable environment of Earth, where they are expected to seek enlightenment though repeated reincarnations. Early human civilization is destroyed by dinosaurs, who are wiped out by aliens. Further human development occurs amid repeated alien invasions and the schemes of Satan. Mu and Atlantis rise and fall in the age before the Greeks and Incas.

Clements and McCarthy (*Anime Encyclopedia*) say this religious propaganda film, based on the writings of the leader of the Buddhist Institute for Research in Human Happiness, is "risibly incoherent, mixing myths and pulp sci-fi." However, *Laws of the Sun* and another Japanese feature *The Weathering Continent* (1992) are among the few films to portray Atlantis as a prehistoric civilization. See *The Giant of Metropolis* (1962) for an overview of the Western films which set Atlantis in various periods.

The Japanese have made several anime (animated) films presenting unorthodox pictures of prehistory. The most famous is *Princess Mononoke* (1997), a masterwork of the most important anime director, Hayao Miyazaki. Clements and McCarthy write that the film is "purportedly set in medieval Japan but depicting a symbolic neverwhen clash of three proto–Japanese races (the Jomon, Yamato and Emishi)."

The Jomon Culture was Neolithic and lasted from 4500 to 250 B.C. The Iron Age Yamato culture existed from A.D. 200 to 600. The Emishi are the Ainu, the indigenous people of Japan. The film, which was the most popular made in Japan to that date, is concerned with ecological issues. A woodland god opposes humans who are destroying the forest and its creatures. Whatever Miyazaki's intentions, *Princess Mononoke* certainly looks medieval rather than prehistoric.

Less celebrated but equally unorthodox anime views of prehistory include *Babel II* (1973), a TV series in which a race of aliens in the Euphrates basin in the distant past build the "Three Servants," mighty beings which survive long after the alien civilization has disappeared. In *Brave Raideen* (1975), a TV series, the Demon Empire awakes after sleeping for 12,000 years in a base hidden in a volcano and plots to conquer Earth. A giant robot built by the ancient human civilization of Mu and a boy who is descended from the Muranians are mankind's only defenses. In another TV series, *The White Whale of Mu* (1980), the last remnant of Muranian civilization, the White Whale, causes disasters in the modern world, but Atlantean survivors help humans to defend themselves. The ancient Mu civilization revives in modern times in *Atragon*, a 1964 live-action film, in *Fight! Opsa*, a 1965 anime TV series, and in *Super Atragon*, a 1995 made-for-video anime.

Birth of Japan (1970), an animated TV series, proposes that a Kappa, an amphibious humanoid in South China, brought iron weapons and rice culture to early Japan during his thousand-year long lifetime. Clements and McCarthy say *Birth of Japan* suffers from "typical Japanese vagueness about historical origins," which permits the mixture of fantasy and history. More serious was the anime TV series *Japanese History* (1976) which told the whole story of the country from prehistory to modern times in 52 episodes.

In *Dark Myth* (1990), a made-for-video anime, ancient clans from Japanese prehistory are active today. The film also claims that before humans lived in Japan, an ancient race of Indian gods fought over the land. Clements and McCarthy note that *Dark Myth* director Takashi Anno made other films (*Maddomen*, 1989; *Confucius's Dark Myth*, 1977; *Phantom Monkey's Journey to the West*, 1983) inspired by the mixture of Ainu, Jomon, Yamato, Chinese, Korean, Manchurian and Southeast Asian elements in early Japan.

Exploding Campus Guardress (1994), an anime TV series, told the story of three heroes who saved the world from invaders from the Dark World 30,000 years ago and who return once more to rescue mankind in modern Tokyo.

In a made-for-video anime, *Psychic Wars* (1991), a doctor discovers that a war between demons and ninja took place in prehistoric Japan and is about to resume in modern times. Clements and McCarthy called the film "disappointingly trite." In *Golden Bat* (1967), an anime TV series, Atlanteans send a warrior in the form of a golden statue to protect the modern world against monsters.

Guyver (1989) was a made-for-video episodic anime series. In prehistory an alien race tampered with human DNA, creating the zoanoids, unbeatable warriors who interbred with humans. In modern Japan, humans, zoanoids and "Zoalords" fight for possession of powerful zoanoid armor.

In *Three-Eyed Prince* (1985), an anime TV series, a naïve modern schoolboy is actually "the last descendant of a three-eyed race who once ruled the world with advanced technology and vast intelligence." The 1991 TV series *3 × 3 Eyes* was a sequel about the three-eyed supermen.

According to *Twilight of the Dark Master* (1997), a made-for-video anime, in the earliest times the Great Mother created the Demon Master to test humans; she then had to create the Guardian to save mankind when the Demon Master proved too powerful. As usual, the ancient fight continues in modern times.

Relatively realistic Japanese animes about cavemen are *Big Wars* (1993, made-for-video), *Gon the First Man* (TV series, 1996) and *Kum-Kum* (TV series, 1975); see separate entries in this section. *Flint the Time Detective* (1998), an anime TV series about a caveman in modern times, is found in Part III. Ref: Clements/McCarthy. *Anime Encyclopedia*; not viewed, except *Princess Mononoke*.

The Link (1988) *see* **Missing Link** (1988)

Maciste Contro I Mostri (1962) *see* **Colossus of the Stone Age** (1962)

Man and His Mate (1940) *see* **One Million B.C.** (1940)

A Man Called Flintstone (1965) U.S.; dir. Joseph Barbera, William Hanna; Hanna-Barbera/Columbia. Animated film; 90 min.; color. Screenplay, Harvey Bullock, R.S. Allen; music, Marty Paich, Ted Nicholls. VOICES: Alan Reed (*Fred Flintstone*); Mel Blanc (*Barney Rubble*); Jean VanderPyl (*Wilma*); Gerry Johnson (*Betty Rubble*); Paul Frees (*Rock Slag*); June Foray (*Tanya*); Don Messick; Harvey Korman; John Stephenson; Janet Waldo.

While visiting Paris, Fred Flintstone is mistaken for secret agent Rock Slag by the agents of mastermind villain The Green Goose.

Variety (Aug. 10, 1966) was impressed by the film's "pleasant, cleancut sense of humor," the seven "lively" songs and the clever spoofs of spy film clichés, in addition to Stone Age satire such as a stone Eiffel Tower and fourth class air passengers seated on an airliner's wings. This was the first *Flintstones* spinoff from the 1960–66 series and the only *Flintstones* theatrical film until the 1994 liveaction John Goodman film. Ref: Jones. *Illustrated Dinosaur Movie Guide*; Lenburg. *Encyclopedia of Animated Cartoons*; Adams. *The Flintstones*; not viewed.

Man's Genesis: A Psychological Comedy Founded on the Darwinian Theory of the Evolution of Man (1912) [included in 1914 film *The Primitive Man*] U.S.; dir. D.W. Griffith; Biograph Company. 10 min.; silent; b&w. Screenplay, D.W. Griffith, Frank E. Woods; cinematography, G.W. (Billy) Bitzer. CAST: Robert Harron (*Weakhands*); Mae Marsh (*Lilywhite*); Wilfred Lucas (*Bruteforce*); W. Christy Miller (*Old Man*); Charles H. Mailes (*Caveman*); W.C. Robinson (*Caveman*).

An intertitle: "The old man asks the quarrelling child to lay down the stick as that belongs to the old days when might was right and tells them the story of Weakhands and Bruteforce in the primeval village." On a modern hillside above a bucolic scene, a boy threatens a girl with a stick. An old man calms him and tells the children a story from a book he conveniently has with him.

In prehistoric times, we see a hillside full of large boulders. Two hairy men emerge from the rocks, eating and looking around fearfully.

An intertitle announces: "Weakhands." The weakling hero exits the small entrance to his cave very cautiously. Intertitle: "When the bare fist was the only weapon, Weakhands was not popular as a suitor." Weakhands courts a rough-looking girl who rejects him; two men emerge from the rocks and order Weakhands off.

Intertitle: "Lilywhite, after her mother's death, is forced to go out from the cave to where danger lurks on every side." In a long grass costume, the young heroine emerges timorously from her cave.

Intertitle: "Weakhands meets Bruteforce." Weakhands is trying his luck with the rough girl again when big, hulking Bruteforce drives him off. Lilywhite approaches the discouraged Weakhands. He puts his hand on her head and leads her to his cave. They enter and embrace.

Intertitle: "The primeval bridal breakfast." The new couple share a frugal meal. Weakhands exits the cave with his usual nervousness. Lilywhite follows him and kisses him before he leaves.

Intertitle: "When Might was Right, Bruteforce would wreck the home." When Lilywhite returns to Weakhands' cave she finds Bruteforce blocking the entrance. She flees; Bruteforce chases and catches her and carries her away to his lair. Maddened, Weakhands attacks the brute, who easily throws him downhill.

Intertitle: "Helpless Weakhands." Despairing, Weakhands again attacks Bruteforce, who this time drives him all the way back to his own cave. Bruteforce does not venture to enter the cave, since crawling through the tiny entrance would put him at a disadvantage.

Intertitle: "The Dawn of an Idea. Brains produce a new force." In his cave, Weakhands finds a rock with a hole in the middle, shaped like a doughnut. He discovers the rock just fits on the end of a stick. Weakhands tests the new weapon by hitting himself in the head with it!

Cut to despairing Lilywhite. Armed with his superweapon, Weakhands emerges confidently from his cave and attacks Bruteforce in his lair. First he hits Bruteforce in the arm. The big man is confused but attacks his opponent. Weakhands hits him in the head. Dazed, Bruteforce chases his tormenter. Weakhands hits

The terrifying Bruteforce (Wilfred Lucas) kidnaps Lilywhite (Mae Marsh) in *Man's Genesis.*

Bruteforce again and again. The giant finally falls dead. The victor holds the club aloft in triumph.

Lilywhite happily joins Weakhands. Two cavemen approach them. Weakhands hits each of them in the arm, awing them into submission. He and Lilywhite walk off together, masters of their world.

In the modern frame story, the old man closes his book. The boy throws away his stick. He and the girl walk off arm in arm.

COMMENTARY. Griffith's *Man's Genesis* is not one of the great director's masterpieces but it is an unusually ambitious short and an example of eloquent, economical storytelling. The modern frame story takes less than a minute at the beginning of the film and only a few seconds at the end. Parallels are swiftly drawn between the civilized hillside and the primeval hillside at the beginning, and between the prehistoric lovers and the modern children at the end.

According to Wagenknecht's and Slide's *The Films of D.W. Griffith*, Griffith directed 64 films in 1912, all of them one-reelers like *Man's Genesis* except for one two-reeler. *Man's Genesis* was one of six Griffith shorts released in July of that year. Despite this breakneck production pace, *Man's Genesis* was clearly something special. The director who later mused on the whole history of civilization in *Intolerance* (1916) wanted to make a serious comment on the origins of man.

Richard Schickel (*D.W. Griffith: An American Life*) writes that Griffith intended the film to be "a parable about reason and unreason, the pacifistic impulse opposed to the aggressive instinct." Schickel considers the film to be only "a pioneering example of the camp spirit" but admits that in its time it was "considered a formidable art film, a major experiment."

Griffith's colleagues, especially his business associate Lee Dougherty, told him that cavemen could be used only for comic purposes. The film's subtitle says that *Man's Genesis* is a "comedy" but there are only two real jokes. One occurs when Lilywhite first enters Weakhands' cave, looks around approvingly, nods and smiles, as if saying "Nice cave!" The other comes when Weakhands bonks himself in the head to test his new club. By "comedy" Griffith simply meant that the film had a happy ending for the hero and heroine and for mankind.

The prehistoric people repeatedly emerge from caves or from behind rocks, as if they were growing from the earth. Entrances to the caves are tiny, forcing people to crawl when they enter or leave. Everyone walks with an apelike shuffle except for Lilywhite, who walks almost normally. This suggests that Griffith saw women as a civilizing influence. The moment when Weakhands puts his hand on the top of Lilywhite's head, taking her as his mate, is both moving and convincingly apelike.

The male characters wear animal skin costumes; Weakhand's costume consists of both skins and grass. Lilywhite wears a long grass skirt which leaves her legs visible when she walks. The actors all took their parts seriously despite the odd costumes. As far as I know, no other film about prehistoric humans has used grass costumes except *Man's Genesis*, its sequel *Brute Force* (1914) and Chaplin's farce *His Prehistoric Life* (1914). Surprisingly, Griffith was correct about the costume; when the ice mummy dubbed the Iceman was found in the Alps in 1991, he was wearing a grass and bark cloak.

The characters communicate more by gestures than speech. Surprisingly, the brutish Bruteforce seems to talk more than the more civilized characters. No doubt Griffith, who regretted the arrival of sound 15 years after this film, was excited by the idea of making a film about people who hardly spoke at all.

The film must have been strong stuff in its time. The virginal Lilywhite (played by 16-year-old Marsh) enters Weakhands' cave and embraces him, followed by the intertitle "The primeval bridal breakfast." Then she is kidnapped by Bruteforce, who will certainly molest her. The fight with the club, in which Weakhands repeatedly hits the unarmed and uncomprehending Bruteforce, can still cause viewers to wince. Griffith softened the violence by filming most of the fight scene at a distance, with only the start and finish in medium shot.

Just as the film's subtitle claims *Man's Genesis* is "founded on the Darwinian theory," the intertitle "When the bare fist was the only weapon, Weakhands was not popular as a suitor" makes it clear that Griffith accepted Darwin's theory of natural selection, which in this case means that a weakling would have difficulty finding a mate and would not be likely to produce children. I suspect that Griffith saw Social Darwinism as a justification for his racism, that he used a new scientific theory to defend an old prejudice.

It seems fair to assume that Griffith saw Bruteforce as a primitive character like the blacks in *Birth of a Nation*, a threat to white womanhood. The name "Lilywhite" strongly suggests

Weakhands (Robert Harron) kills Bruteforce (Wilfred Lucas) and saves Lilywhite (Mae Marsh) in D.W. Griffith's ***Man's Genesis.***

both virginity and racial purity, though Lilywhite is not a virgin after her encounter with Weakhands, and Bruteforce is apparently of the same race as his victims.

Like Stanley Kubrick in the *Dawn of Man* sequence of *2001: A Space Odyssey* (1968), Griffith makes the point that early creatures became human only when they learned to kill. Kubrick dates that discovery to Africa 4,000,000 years ago; Griffith to a past with anatomically-modern white cavemen. Kubrick of course was far more accurate. Tools and weapons go back to very early man — before anatomically-modern people.

What has the boy in the modern scene learned at the end when he throws away his stick? After all, Weakhands won by inventing a weapon. Presumably Griffith means that the boy's aggressiveness is more reminiscent of Bruteforce's arbitrary violence than Weakhand's cleverness. The justification for Weakhand's action is found in natural selection. Griffith is saying that if intelligent people had not invented weapons they would never have been able to win mates from big, stupid men like Bruteforce. They would never have reproduced and mankind would have all become like Bruteforce.

Robert Harron and Mae Marsh gave Griffith what he needed but the outstanding performance was by Wilfred Lucas as Bruteforce, a believable, grimacing human monster. He is truly frightening when he menaces tiny Lilywhite. When Weakhands hits him in the arm with the club, Bruteforce looks incredulously at his injured arm, hesitates, then charges blindly at his opponent.

Robert Harron, Wilfred Lucas and elderly W. Christy Miller were veterans who had worked in dozens of shorts. Harron was a busy actor in many Griffith films, including *Birth of a Nation* and *Intolerance*, until his death in 1920 from a self-inflicted gunshot, which was ruled an accident, not suicide. Lucas directed several films and worked at often uncredited supporting parts until his death in 1940.

Griffith had difficulty casting Lilywhite. All his established actresses, including Mary Pickford and Blanche Sweet, turned down the part because it required bare legs at a time when women always wore stockings. Inexperienced, 16-year-old Mae Marsh cheerfully agreed to take the role. At the time Griffith was also casting his next major literary adaptation, *The Sands of Dee* (1912), which all the Biograph actresses wanted. He called his actresses together and announced "for the benefit of those who may be interested, as a result of her graciousness Miss Marsh will also receive the role of the heroine in *The Sands of Dee*."

Marsh worked for years with Griffith, including major parts in *Birth of a Nation* and *Intolerance*, followed by decades of roles in talkies until shortly before her death in 1968. She was the first of three actresses who became stars as a result of their work in prehistoric films, followed by Carole Landis in *One Million B.C.* (1940) and Raquel Welch in *One Million Years B.C.* (1966).

Griffith kept returning to prehistory. In 1914 he made a new film with the same characters, *Brute Force*. *Man's Genesis* and *Brute Force* were combined to make *The Primitive Man* (1914). And in 1940, while trying to revive his defunct career, he was briefly employed on Hal Roach's *One Million B.C.*

Man's Genesis was released on two video anthologies: *D.W. Griffith, 1912* from Grapevine Video and *The Short Films of D.W. Griffith, Volume Two* from Matinee Classics. Both are out-of-print. *The Primitive Man*, which includes both *Man's Genesis* (except for the frame story with the modern children and the old man) and *Brute Force*, is available from Glenn Video Vistas, 6924 Canby Ave., Suite 103, Reseda, CA 91335 (web site http://emgee.freeyellow.com). Ref: Wagenknecht/Slide. *Films of D.W. Griffith*; Schickel. *D.W. Griffith: An American Life*; *Internet Movie Database*; MK 8.

Master of the World (1983) [alt. *Conqueror of the World*; *I Padroni del Mondo*] Italy; dir. Alberto Cavallone [under pseudonym Dick Morris]; Falco Film. 80 min.; color. Screenplay, Alberto Cavallone. CAST: Sven Kruger; Viviana Maria Rispoli; Sasha D'Arc; Maria Vittoria Garlanda.

This Italian caveman B-film is apparently even more obscure than *Ironmaster* (1982), which was written but not directed by Cavallone. According to one of only two viewers' comments on *Internet Movie Database*, a blond Cro-Magnon hunter (Kruger) is left for dead by a barbarian band, then saved by Neanderthals, including a "very simian" woman (Rispoli) who heals him with herbs. The hero joins her band and helps them fight the villains, who behead their victims and eat their brains.

The fan commentator who provides this synopsis calls the film "crude, shocking and repulsive." The other fan reviewer writes that the movie has "an amusing (and very out of place) Goblin-style synth [synthesizer] score and the opening narration is pretty funny" before the film becomes deadly dull. Jones calls it a "*Quest for Fire* rip-off." Stephen R. Bissette (*We Are Going to Eat You!*) also considers the film "a threadbare ripoff" with graphic cannibal sequences "to negligible effect." *Master of the World* was made during the thankfully short-lived Italian cannibal ultra-horror movie wave of the early 1980s, which Bissette chronicles and which began with *Cannibal Holocaust* (1980). Ref: Jones. *Illustrated Dinosaur Movie Guide*; Bissette. *We are Going to Eat You!*; *Internet Movie Database*; not viewed.

The Mighty Mightor *see* **Moby Dick and the Mighty Mightor** (1967–69)

Mighty Mouse in Prehistoric Peril (1952) *see* **Prehistoric Perils** (1952)

The Miser's Reversion (1914) U.S.; Thanhouser. Short film; b&w; silent.

A miser insists his daughter marry a rich man. He dreams himself into prehistory as an ape-like creature, "with humorous and meaningful results," according to Jones. He wakes and allows his daughter to marry the man she prefers. Ref: Jones. *Illustrated Dinosaur Movie Guide*; *Internet Movie Database*; not viewed.

The Missing Link (1979) *see* **B.C. Rock** (1979)

Missing Link (1988) [alt. *The Link*] U.S./Namibia; dir. David Hughes, Carol Hughes; Universal/Kane International. 91 min.; color. Screenplay, David Hughes, Carol Hughes; photography, David Hughes, Carol Hughes; music, Mike Trim, Sammy Hurden. CAST: Peter Elliott (Man-Ape); Michael Gambon (Narrator).

In an African plain 1,000,000 years ago "there exists a race with whom man will not share," the narrator tells us. Man with his tools, weapons and fire surrounds the man-ape's "shrinking world." The man-ape has a massive head with long hair and a beard, an apelike face with prominent eyebrow ridges and a jutting lower face. His body is hairy and naked; even his hands are hairy. He walks erect. Of course he is barefoot. He has no speech except brief cries. We see him drink water with his hand from a tiny pool. He looks around constantly, checking for predators.

Suddenly the man-ape becomes agitated. He runs a long distance and finds his small clan slaughtered. (We are not told whether it is acute hearing, smell or some instinct which tells him of the disaster.) He looks at his dead mate and baby with shock and grief. He picks up a broken, bloody stone-ax which was abandoned by the killers. As he examines the ax uncomprehendingly, he is suddenly hit in the back of the head by a stone-ax. We see only the arm of the man who strikes him.

The man-ape survives and wakes up at night. He takes shelter in a tree as lions and then hyenas eat his family. He weeps. The fires of man are nearby. The narrator tells us, "He is the last of his race." In the morning he wanders off, carrying the stone-ax with "the scent of his enemy and the blood of his mate" on it "but what it is he cannot know."

In his ignorance, he carries the ax by the stone ax-head, not by the handle. He finds a small fire left by men and walks on the coals, burning his feet. He hears human voices and flees.

A lioness turns a turtle over on its back and tries to kill it but the turtle pulls his head and legs inside his shell until the lioness gives up and leaves. The turtle is still helplessly on his back when the man-ape comes along and gently turns him over and lets him walk away. The man-ape is constantly using his keen sense of smell. He travels with herbivorous animals; if they are alarmed he knows a predator is nearby.

As he watches animals mating, he weeps, remembering his mate. He washes his wounded head with water. He sees a human footprint and flees again. The narrator explains that if he remains where he is he will certainly be killed.

The man-ape gathers ostrich eggs. He cracks one with the handle of the ax, not the stone ax-head, spraying egg all over himself. Later he throws a rock at a wild dog to prevent it from killing a baby antelope. "He has the gentle nature of a race that has no defense against the violence of man. Now he is more alone than he knows," says the narrator. He chuckles at the antics of big frogs. He tries to give a beetle to a lizard; when the lizard doesn't eat the insect, he eats it himself. He continues to examine the ax and begins to carry it by the handle. After crossing a desert area, he finds refuge at an oasis but soon he sees men in the distance and must move on again. He crosses a large desert in a sandstorm, constantly calling out for others of his kind.

Arriving at a rocky area where he finds water, the man-ape eats some mushrooms which give him a hallucinogenic vision. He again sees his dead family; he repeatedly sees a zebra kicking a lioness, suggestive of a victim striking back at an aggressor. He figures out how to use the stone ax and smashes a sand formation with the weapon. He feels his injured head and contemplates the ax. He arrives at the sea, which is an unimaginable surprise to him. He finds he cannot drink the sea water and realizes that he can go no further. He is at the end of his journey.

The man-ape begins to hit the sand with the ax. He finds human footprints and hits them. He hits his own hand with the ax. He goes in the direction the footprints lead, obviously intending to find humans and take revenge. Then he stops and feels his head injury again. He throws the ax into the sea, smiles and sits down.

The narrator announces the end of "the gentle race that shared the world with man for nearly two million years. Rooted in their own primordial past, they could not survive into the violent future that belongs to mankind." A subtitle tells us that the man-ape was Australopithecus Robustus, who died out 1,000,000 years ago, "probably the first of many species pushed into oblivion by man."

COMMENTARY. *Missing Link* is the most realistic non-documentary film I know of about prehistoric man, although it may sentimentalize its subject more than is reasonable. There are no dinosaurs, no bikini-clad beauties, no cavemen revived in the modern world. This is the only film about early hominids except for the *Dawn of Man* sequence in *2001:A Space Odyssey* (1968). *Missing Link* is far longer than the brief *2001* sequence and is the only extended film treatment of proto-humans more primitive than the Neanderthals and anatomically-modern humans. *2001* speculated on the very beginning of the first hominids; *Missing Link* shows us the end of a hominid species.

It is one of the few films with only one char-

The gentle Man-Ape (Peter Elliott) in *Missing Link*.

acter—and no intelligible dialogue. The narrator says very little (much less than the loquacious narrator in a much earlier and less sophisticated attempt at a realistic approach to prehistory, *Prehistoric Women* (1950)). The African locations and animals give the film an impression of realism unique in prehistoric fiction films. We see the same sights and the same animals (zebras, lions, giraffes, antelopes, elephants) we are used to seeing in documentaries and in fiction films set in modern Africa. No extinct animals are presented, except the man-ape himself. Directors-screenwriters-photographers David and Carol Hughes had previously made wildlife documentaries in Africa. Many people will feel that the movie has too many shots of scenery and animals. Almost a third of the film consists of this footage, as if the Hugheses could not make their simple story into a feature film without padding. But the nature footage emphasizes the affinity between the man-ape and the natural world that surrounds him. He is an animal, not a human.

The advanced African humans who wiped

out Robustus were Homo Ergaster. We see three of them at a distance and hear their voices. They are tall and slender and were probably played by African actors without makeup. We see them from so far away that we can't make out details of their appearance, but the impression of their bodies and especially their voices is of modern Africans. Their speech sounds like a modern African language. It would have been more accurate if the film had shown that the humans who destroyed Robustus were themselves far different from us, but perhaps this would have confused audiences.

Missing Link is a fiction film, but it is almost the same as a documentary film with extensive reenactments, such as *Ice World* (2003, in the documentary section of this list). In both films, the facts about ancient life are presented as accurately as possible, while telling a simple story. In each case, the story is a journey for survival. There is no intelligible dialogue in either film and the narrator explains what is happening.

The film is, of course, terribly sad. The narrator tells us immediately that the man-ape is the last of his kind, so all during the film, as he struggles to find others like himself, we know that he is doomed. The major problem with *Missing Link* is that its hero becomes tiresomely saintly, as he goes about setting overturned turtles right-side-up, saving baby antelopes from wild dogs and even feeding lizards. At the end, he figures out how to use a weapon but he decides not to use it, even though he will die leaving his family unavenged. The point, which may be the most speculative part of the film, is that Robustus was too gentle to survive. In *2001*, the alien monolith suggests to Moonwatcher the concept of changing the world; the ape becomes a man by learning to kill. In *Missing Link*, the stone-ax finally suggests the same thing, but the man-ape nobly refuses to kill and remains an ape.

Missing Link was the last film by Carol and David Hughes and their only fiction film. Previously they had co-directed the nature documentaries *Rain Forest* (1983, set in the Amazon) and *Lions of the African Night* (1987). David Hughes co-directed *The Living Sands of Namib* (1978), with David Saxon. The man-ape makeup and costume was by Rick Baker, who was nominated for the Oscar for Best Makeup ten times and won six times. Baker and Peter Elliott worked together in *Greystoke: The Legend of Tarzan* (1984), *Harry and the Hendersons* (1987) and *Gorillas in the Mist* (1988), as well as *Missing Link*.

Peter Elliott is an English actor and athlete who has specialized in playing primates. After playing a caveman in *Quest for Fire* (1981) he played King Kong in *King Kong Lives* (1986), the gorilla in *Congo* (1995; a character in the film is named Peter Elliott after him) and Assassimon in *Island of Dr. Moreau* (1996). He was "animal coordinator" for *Harry and the Hendersons* (1987, about Bigfoot) and "primate choreographer" for *Greystoke: the Legend of Tarzan* and *Gorillas in the Mist*. Elliott's and Baker's work in *Missing Link* is impeccable. The makeup is worthy of any of Baker's more famous, Oscar-nominated films. The man-ape is Elliott's masterpiece, a fully developed, realistic character who is on camera for most of a feature film. Elliott's man-ape in *Missing Link* is one of the best performances by an actor playing a prehistoric character. See Appendix C for other outstanding performances.

Universal, the distributors of *Missing Link*, was apparently afraid that the man-ape looked too gentle and dim-witted to be interesting to audiences. Their poster showed the film's hero as a dark, sinister silhouette, holding the stone-ax by its handle as a weapon. Unfortunately, this is the only picture I have found from the film. I greatly regret not being able to reproduce a picture showing Baker's makeup. A good picture of the man-ape can be found in the gallery of Peter Elliott's website (www.mrlink.net).

Missing Link did not attract the audience it deserves. It is not in Maltin's current *Movie & Video Guide*. Only a few dozen users have rated it on *Internet Movie Database* and they gave it a modest 5.3 rating. In one of the few reviews, Rita Kempley of the *Washington Post* (Nov. 4, 1988) wrote that *Missing Link* was "at once sobering, boring, simplistic and slow" although also "beautifully photographed." *Variety* (July 19, 1989) noted that the film had had a "brief theatrical run" in November 1988. The reviewer felt the film's ecological message was delivered with "agreeable understatement" and praised the "handsome visuals" but deplored the "absence of a strong narrative."

Filmed in Namibia, *Missing Link* can be recommended to fans of African wildlife films; to anthropologists, as the only highly accurate prehistory film; and of course to fans of caveman movies. Ref: Jones. *Illustrated Dinosaur Movie Guide*; MK 9.

Moby Dick and the Mighty Mightor (1967–69) U.S.; Hanna-Barbera. Animated TV series; 25-min. episodes; color. *VOICES:* Bobby Diamond (*Tor*); Paul Stewart (*Mightor*); Patsy Garrett (*Sheera*); John Stephenson (*Tog//Pondo*); Norma MacMillan (*Li'l Rok*).

Each episode included one segment of *Moby Dick* and two of *Mighty Mightor*, which took place in a world in which humans and dinosaurs co-exist. The opening narration explains "While on a hunting trip, Tor and his faithful companion Tog rescue an ancient hermit from a Tyrannosaurus Rex. Grateful, the old man gives Tor a club which possesses great powers. Tor raises the club and he becomes Mightor, and Tog is transformed into a fire-breathing dragon. Together they become champions of good and the nemesis of evil!"

When not transformed into superbeings, Tor is a weakling and Tog is his pet dinosaur. The show is something like a prehistoric *Superman*. Tor has a secret identity and even a Lois Lane character, Sheera, who scorns Tor as a wimp. Pondo is the cave people's leader; Li'l Rok is a boy who tries to emulate Mightor. Several of the series' villains are named in the episode titles below.

Mightor segments: "The Monster Keeper," "The Tiger Men," "The Bird People," "The Serpent Queen," "Mightor Meets Tyrannor," "The Giant Hunters," "Return of Korg," "Brutor, the Barbarian," "The Tusk People," "Krager and the Cave Creatures," "The Snow Trapper," "The People Keepers," "The Tree Pygmies," "The Vulture Men," "Charr and the Fire People," "The Stone Men," "Vampire Island," "Cult of the Cavebearers," "Attack of the Ice Creatures," "Revenge of the Serpent Queen," "Rok and His Gang," "The Scorpion Men," "The Sea Slavers," "A Big Day for Little Rok," "The Plant People," "Tribe of the Witchmen," "The Return of the Vulture Men," "Battle of the Mountain Monsters," "Vengeance of the Storm King," "The Mightiest Warrior," "Dinosaur Island," "Rok to the Rescue," "The Missing Village," "The Greatest Escape," "Rok and the Golden Rok," "Battle of the Mightors." Ref: Lenburg. *Encyclopedia of Animated Cartoons*; Erickson. *Television Cartoon Shows*; Woolery. *Children's Television*; *Internet Movie Database*; not viewed.

Morpheus Mike (1917) U.S.; dir. Willis O'Brien; Conquest/Edison. Animated short film; 3 min.; b&w; silent.

After a dog steals his dinner a disappointed hobo lights his pipe and an intertitle announces "Mike has a pipe dream." (The name Morpheus Mike and the term "pipe dream" probably mean he is smoking opium.) He dreams he is a bare-chested caveman in a cave restaurant. A caveman waiter with a dapper Italian-looking mustache proffers a menu written on a stone tablet in animal symbols, which are translated as "Snake soup, Ostrich eggs, Hot dogs." (The symbol suggests that the last item is made from a real dog.)

The customer places an order and the waiter shouts out the window "One order of tiger stew!" A tame mammoth outside scoops up the food in a ladle with his trunk and passes it through the window. Mike eats and orders "Ostrich egg! Well done!" The mammoth picks up an ostrich, which drops an egg. The mammoth passes the egg through the window but as Mike cracks the egg a tiny ostrich emerges and flies away. Annoyed, Mike orders "One trunk of soup!" The mammoth sprays the soup over the caveman, and Mike wakes up in the modern world to find a housewife pouring water on him from a window.

COMMENTARY. For information on O'Brien's stop-motion caveman shorts, see *The Dinosaur and the Missing Link* (1917). *Morpheus Mike* is simple but funny fare which still charms. Ref: Jones. *Illustrated Dinosaur Movie Guide*; MK 7.

Na Veliké Rece (1978) Czechoslovakia; dir. Jan Schmidt; Filmové Studio Barrandov. Feature film. Screenplay, Milan Pavlik, based on novel by Eduard Storch; photography, Jirí Macák; music, Zdenek Liska. *CAST:* Ludvik Hradilek; Jirí Bartoska; Vilém Besser; Ivan Lutansky; Borivoj Navrátil; Gabriela Osvaldová; Beta Ponicanová; Marie Sykorová; Bohumil Vávra.

One of three Czech films made by the same director and largely the same cast in 1978, all based on Storch's prehistoric novels. See also *Settlement of Crows* (1978) and *Voláni Rodu* (1978). Ref: *Internet Movie Database*; not viewed.

Naughty Ancient Kum-Kum (1975) *see* Kum-Kum (1975)

The New Fred and Barney Show (1979) U.S.; Hanna-Barbera/NBC. Animated TV series; 17 25-min. episodes; color. *VOICES:* Henry

Corden (*Fred Flintstone*); Jean VanderPyl (*Wilma/Pebbles*); Mel Blanc (*Barney Rubble/Dino*); Gay Autterson (*Betty Rubble*); Don Messick (*Bamm-Bamm*); John Stephenson (*Slate*).

Of the 17 episodes in this Saturday morning series, thirteen were repeats of original *Flintstones* episodes under new titles and with Corden and Autterson redubbing the original voices. The episodes were again repeated in *Fred and Barney Meet the Thing* (1979) and *Fred and Barney Meet the Shmoo* (1979–80).

Episodes: "Sand-Witch," "Haunted Inheritance," "Roughin' It," "C.B. Buddies," "Bedrock Rocks," "Blood Brothers," "Barney's Chickens," "The Butler Did It — And Did It Better," "It's Not their Bag," "Barney's Luck," "The Bad Luck Genie," "Fred and Barney Meet the Frankenstones," "Physical Fitness Fred," "Fred Goes to the Houndasaurs," "Moonlighters," "Dinosaur Country Safari," "Stone Age Werewolf." Ref: Lenburg. *Encyclopedia of Animated Cartoons*; Adams. *The Flintstones*; not viewed.

Night Beauties (1952) *see* **Les Belles de Nuit** (1952)

The Nine Ages of Nakedness (1969) U.K.; dir. George Harrison Marks; Token. 95 min.; color. Screenplay, George Harrison Marks. CAST: George Harrison Marks (*Harrison Marks*); Charles Gray (*Narrator*); Big Bruno Elrington (*Caveman*); June Palmer (*Cavegirl*).

"Photographer recounts ancestors' problems with naked ladies," according to Gifford. Several nudist skits were set in various periods, beginning with prehistory. The British Film Institute's *Monthly Film Bulletin* (Oct. 1969) called the film "a series of excruciatingly corny sketches." Ref: Jones. *Illustrated Dinosaur Movie Guide*; Gifford. *British Film Catalogue*; not viewed.

Not Tonite, Henry (1961) U.S.; dir. W. Merle Connell; Foremost Films. 75 min.; color. Screenplay, Bob Heiderich, Harold Lime; photography, W. Merle Connell; music, Hal Borne. CAST: Hank Henry (*Henry, Caveman/Other Lovers*); Babe McDonnell (*Cave Girl*).

In this ultra-cheap nudie, a modern man neglected by his wife dreams of being several great lovers in the past, including Samson, Marc Antony and Napoleon. In a prehistoric skit, a caveman's wife orders him to go out and bring home a dinosaur for dinner. He spends most of his expedition ogling skinny-dipping girls.

An 11-min. segment from *Not Tonite, Henry*, titled *Prehistoric Daze*, was included in a DVD of the features *The Mighty Gorga* (1968) and *One Million AC/DC* (1969, q.v.). Ref: DVD review by John Charles, *Video Watchdog*, no. 96; Jones. *Illustrated Dinosaur Movie Guide*; Internet Movie Database; not viewed.

Nudes on the Rocks (1963) *see* **50,000 B.C. (Before Clothing)** (1963)

The Oldest Profession (1967) Segment *The Prehistoric Era.* [alt. *La Plus Vieux Métier du Monde. L'Ere Préhistorique*] France/West Germany/Italy; dir. Franco Indovina; Athos Films/Francoriz/Les Films Gibé/Rialto Film/Rizzoli Film. Segment of 115 min. anthology film; color. Screenplay, Ennio Flaiano; photography, Pierre Lhomme; music, Michel Legrand. CAST: Michelle Mercier (*Brit*); Enrico Maria Salerno (*Older Man*); Gabriel Tinti (*Younger Man*).

This anthology of six sketches by six directors presents a farcical history of prostitution from the cave period to the science fiction future. *Variety* (May 24, 1967) said the film was "gamey" but "avoids vulgarity," beginning with "an anachronistic prehistoric bit about a girl who finds that inventing makeup and making men give her things to be with her is a worthwhile new trend." Mercier was a busy French star, aged 28 in 1967; *Variety* found her "lacking in needed comedic wit and timing." Indovina directed only six films in his career. (Raquel Welch was featured in one of the other sketches, only a few months after completing *One Million Years B.C.* (1966). She was probably grateful she had nothing to do with the prehistoric sketch.) Ref: *Internet Movie Database*; not viewed.

Once Upon a Time: Man (1978) [alt. *Il Etait une Fois l'Homme*] France; dir. Albert Barillé; Procidis. Animated TV series; 26 25-min. episodes; color. Screenplay, Albert Barillé.

This audacious and opinionated animated series, a one-man show for producer-writer-director Barillé, attempted to popularize the whole of human history for children. Barillé presented a good deal of real history, dates and all, but the dramatization was often silly.

I have never seen the prehistoric episode.

The series was a hit in Europe and came to America in the 1990s, on the History Channel. Barillé produced four other educational animated series, of which *Once Upon a Time: The Americas* (1991) dealt with the Western Hemisphere before the arrival of Europeans and may have included one or more episodes on the prehistoric Paleo-Indians. Ref: *Internet Movie Database*; only non-prehistoric episodes viewed.

One Million AC/DC (1969) U.S.; dir. Ed de Priest; Canyon Films. 80 min.; color. Screenplay, Ed Wood (as "Akdon Telmig"); photography, Ed de Priest, Eric Torgesson, Michael Weldon. *CAST:* Gary Kent, Susan Berkely, Sharon Wells, Tod Bodker; Maria Lease.

This is the only prehistoric feature which is available on video which I refused to acquire and watch for this book. I will take the word of Mark F. Berry (*Dinosaur Filmography*) and John Charles (in his review of the DVD containing this film and *The Mighty Gorga* (1968) in *Video Watchdog* 96) that the film is unspeakable. Notoriously inept amateur director Ed Wood wrote the screenplay under the pseudonym "Akdon Telmig," (a misspelled reversal of "vodka gimlet"). Wood intended it to be a humorous, nudist romp, but Charles damns it as "unerotic, unfunny, unbearable."

When cave people are trapped in their cave by a dinosaur, "boredom leads to sex, and, amazingly, sex leads to boredom for the audience as the groping is so badly staged, photographed, and edited, the turn-on factor is virtually nil," according to Charles. Besides the "orgy," we see borrowed footage from *One Million B.C.* (1940), *The Mighty Gorga* and other films; a topless cave girl sexually assaulted by a gorilla; another girl eaten by a dinosaur (both are pathetically unconvincing models); and the hero (Kent) saying "I'm off to see the lizard." A DVD of the features *One Million AC/DC* and *Mighty Gorga* also included *Prehistoric Daze*, an 11-min. excerpt from the 1961 nudie-cheapie *Not Tonite Henry* (1961, q.v.). Ref: Jones. *Illustrated Dinosaur Movie Guide*; Berry. *Dinosaur Filmography*; *Internet Movie Database*; not viewed.

One Million B.C. (1940) [alt. *Battle of the Giants*; *The Cave Dwellers*; *Man and His Mate*] U.S.; dir. Hal Roach, Hal Roach, Jr.; Hal Roach Studios. 80 min.; b&w. Screenplay, Mickell Novak, George Baker, Joseph Frickert, Grover Jones; cinematography, Norbert Brodine; music, Werner R. Heymann. *CAST:* Victor Mature (*Tumak/Modern Young Man*); Carole Landis (*Loana/Modern Young Girl*); Lon Chaney Jr. (*Akhoba*); John Hubbard (*Ohtao*); Nigel de Brulier (*Peytow*); Mamo Clark (*Nupondi*); Inez Palange (*Tohana*); Edgar Edwards (*Skakana*); Jacqueline Dalya (*Ataf*); Mary Gale Fisher (*Wandi*); Conrad Nagel (*Archeologist/Narrator*); Creighton Hale (*Shell Person*).

Loana (Carole Landis) and "the best legs in Hollywood" in *One Million B.C.* (1940).

In a mountainous area of Europe in the present day, a party of hikers takes shelter from a storm in a rather spacious cave. There they find a lone, elderly archeologist, who tells them a story written in prehistoric cave carvings on the walls.

(I) One Million B.C.

In primeval times, the Rock Tribe are a brutal people. Their only weapons are staffs and the strongest man is always the leader. Tumak, son of the brutish leader Akhoba, kills a giant tusked boar and hopes for praise from his father, but Akhoba brushes him aside. An old man is hurt in a fall; the hunting party casually leaves him to die. Among the Rock People the useless deserve no consideration.

At the cave, Akhoba eats first and throws some meat to his dogs, then permits other men to eat in order of their prowess; women and children eat last of all. Each member of the tribe takes food to his or her own private corner and guards it against the others. Tumak quarrels with Akhoba, who unhesitatingly attacks his son and drives him from the cave and over a cliff.

Tumak is immediately chased by a mammoth. He takes refuge in a tree but the mammoth pushes part of the tree into a river. Tumak clings to a limb as it floats downstream, past giant lizards and steaming hot springs. Unconscious, he is found by Loana, a girl of the gentle Shell People.

As he recovers, Tumak is astonished to observe the Shell People cooperate with each other, while the Shell People are appalled by Tumak's crudity. Their leader is the wise Peytow, who is too old to survive, let alone rule, among the Rock People. At their meals, the Shell People pass food to one another, while Tumak takes his food to a corner and threatens anyone who comes near him. Gradually Loana wins his trust. Meanwhile, Akhoba is injured hunting a giant ox. In keeping with his own harsh rules, his hunters abandon him. Skakana takes over leadership of the tribe, threatening the other men and winning their submission. When Akhoba, crippled, drags himself to the cave, Skakana wants to kill him but is prevented by Akhoba's mate and (apparently) by popular opinion.

The Shell People have better clothing than the Rock People and superior weapons, including stone axes and stone-tipped spears. Tumak grows frustrated when he cannot master new skills such as tying a stone tip to a wooden shaft, or fishing with a light fish-spear. His stock goes up when he grabs a spear and kills a predatory dinosaur, about eight feet tall, which was about to kill a small girl.

Tumak learns music and laughter from the Shell People but he remains truculent. He steals a spear and an ax from Ohtao, then attacks Ohtao when he objects. Peytow orders Tumak to leave the Shell People. Loana, who has come to love Tumak, goes with him.

On their way to Tumak's people in the mountains, Tumak and Loana are threatened by a lizard, a snake and an armadillo, all giants. They escape death when two immense reptiles fight each other instead of gobbling the diminutive humans.

When they arrive at the Rock People, Skakana threatens Loana. Tumak defeats him and wins the Rock men's submission. At first it seems that Tumak may revert to Rock Tribe habits. He moves to kill his crippled father, but Loana stops him. Loana then begins to civilize the Rock Tribe, beginning with the women. In a funny scene, the Rock men stand flabbergasted as Loana feeds the women and children and makes the men wait.

At first Loana's reforms are enforced by Tumak's spear, but soon even the habitually suspicious Rock folk accept her. She teaches them which fruits are edible and they become gatherers as well as hunters.

A sudden volcanic eruption unleashes an earthquake, rockslides and a flood of lava. Giant lizards fall into the crevices opened by the cataclysm. In a shocking scene, a woman is buried by lava while trying to rescue her small daughter Wandi. Loana rescues Wandi but becomes separated from the tribe.

Next, Loana, Wandi and most of the Shell People are besieged in their cave by an enormous reptile. A Shell man summons the Rock People to help. Armed with their new spears, the Rock men attack the monster, without success until Akhoba has a bright idea. Tumak lures the creature to the bottom of a cliff and the men set off a rockslide to bury it. The two tribes happily unite while Tumak and Loana adopt Wandi and face a bright future as a family.

COMMENTARY. Besides mixing dinosaurs and humans, the biggest inaccuracy in the film was its depiction of the savage Rock People. Any group that quarrelsome and self-destructive could not have survived. We can assume that ancient people were usually cooperative within their small groups. Despite these errors, the film was intended as a presentation of rather simple but serious ideas about prehistoric humans. Man must overcome his savage habits to become civilized and march toward the future.

Tumak (Victor Mature) defends Loana (Carole Landis) in *One Million B.C.* (1940).

The filmmakers did not think they could assume that audiences had any knowledge of or sympathy with prehistoric people. They even felt the need to introduce the concept of prehistory carefully, through repetition. When the archeologist in the modern prologue says "Welcome to the hospitality offered by the home of an ancient people" the hikers' guide replies "Say, do you mean that at some time a primitive people made this cave their home?" When the scientist points out "these markings, hidden for many centuries, which I've been able to uncover" the slow-on-the-uptake guide demands "Am I to understand that there's a meaning to these markings that you've been able to decipher?" "Not only a meaning, but a complete story as well. On this wall, a learned man left a saga."

Having explained to the audience the existence of prehistoric people and the possibility of learning about them from their relics, the filmmakers go on to argue against stereotypes about ancient humans. The scientist announces that the cave markings "paint the message of an intelligent man." The stubbornly-ignorant guide asks, "You mean there were people of intelligence that long ago?" "Intelligence, my friend, is inherent. Education and culture are acquired. Civilization has of course brought complications. But here are the same thoughts, the same emotions, the same struggles with the problems of life and death, that we of today experience." "I've always thought of those ancient people as animals rather than humans," the guide admits.

The guide then wants to know what prehistoric people looked like. The archeologist replies "I don't know. I never thought of it. It never seemed important to me what they looked like. Suppose we assume that they were just human beings, like you people sitting here." Here the writers are openly discussing a problem which they and all other makers of films about prehistory face — the fact that details which are necessary for a dramatic film are the very information we may not have about the distant past. Audiences expect films to answer such questions as what people looked like, whether they called each other by name or what relations existed between men and women, but science often cannot provide the answers.

Having assured the audience that the film will be about real, intelligent people, the film then has to introduce and explain the nasty Rock People. The archeologist, now the narrator, calls them "a cruel tribe. Pity and compassion played little part in the existence of those people, who ate only what they could kill. They depended solely on their ability to kill for subsistence. They despised weakness, worshipped strength.... The strongest was their leader."

The film suggests a technological reason for the Rock Tribe's brutality; they had "no weapons except a crude staff, which responded only to brute strength." Later the film associates the eating of plants instead of solely meat with a more advanced way of life. (This is wrong. Gathering and eating plants date back even earlier than hunting.)

In the first hunting scene Akhoba has two large dogs. It is not made clear whether the animals are hunting dogs but they must be since the Rock People would not tolerate useless pets. By contrast the more advanced Shell People have a small bear as a pet, even though he provides only amusement. Also in the first scene the Rock hunting party is accompanied by girls with sticks. At first the audience may think that the girls are carrying staffs and are hunters themselves, but when Tumak kills the prey the girls hoist it on their sticks. It is the women's job, not the hunters', to carry the meat back to the cave!

Both tribes have speech. The narrator falls mercifully silent and their short, simple words in their own language are not translated by either voice-over narration or subtitles.

The Shell People predictably seem to have a bigger vocabulary than the Rock People, but both have many more words than the tribes in the remake *One Million Years B.C.* (1966). The word "akita" is heard a few times, once when the old man is left behind to die at the end of the hunting scene; the word apparently simply means "help." In the remake "akita" would become notorious for endless repetitions and multiple meanings.

The differences between the two tribes are unrealistically stark but they illustrate the steps which the filmmakers believe man had to take to reach civilization. The Shell People are peaceable and have better clothes and better weapons. They have a warning system for danger and a plan to defend their cave. They smile, laugh, hum music and carve cave art. They have pets and respect old people. They have a wise leader rather than a thug. The Rock Tribe is defined as people who have and do none of these things.

In the end the Rock People are thoroughly rehabilitated. Even fierce old Akhoba is smart enough to change. After his initial astonishment he approves of Loana's reforms. He is credited with the clever idea for finishing off the last and biggest dinosaur. Akhoba, who ruthlessly left the injured old man to die in the first hunting scene, apparently saw the light when he himself was helpless and terrified that either Skakana or Tumak would kill him.

Tumak and Akhoba both start out as brutes but both turn out to be intelligent and malleable. Like many outlaws in old-fashioned Westerns, they overcome bad circumstances and bad habits and are reformed through the example of a good woman. *One Million B.C.* offers a subtle clue that the reformation was successful. In the modern prologue the cave art telling the story of Tumak and Loana is found in the Rock People's mountain cave, not the Shell People's valley cave. Therefore the Rock People must have learned to make art.

The film errs by having the art carved on the cave wall. Most prehistoric art was painted, not carved. The dignified Peytow looks pretty silly banging away at the cave wall with a hammer and chisel. Roach probably introduced the tools to show another way in which the Shell People were more advanced than the tool-less Rock People.

Few prehistoric films have received Oscar nominations. *One Million B.C.* was nominated twice, for Werner H. Heymann's music and for both Roy Seawright's "photographic effects" and Elmer Raguse's "sound effects," which were lumped together in one category for "best effects." Norbert Brodine's cinematography was also admirable. Tumak's and Loana's flight through the dark, foggy, monster-filled forest is reminiscent of *King Kong* (1933) and *The Most Dangerous Game* (1932). Indeed, *One Million B.C.* owes much to those two films and to the numerous Tarzan films made before 1940, including Johnny Weissmuller's first four *Tarzans*. The confrontations with dangerous jungle animals and the cast's brief costumes would be familiar to 1930s fans of the Weissmuller films while Tumak's uncomprehending reactions to Loana's customs and his growing devotion to Loana recall Weissmuller's Tarzan and Maureen O'Sullivan's Jane. Like Tarzan Tumak is crude and ignorant but good-hearted, brave and capable of learning new ways.

Unlike the creatures in *King Kong*, the monsters in *One Million B.C.* were not created by stop-motion animation. Real animals were used; elephants were turned into mammoths, a bull into the giant musk ox that cripples Akhoba. The giant lizards were real reptiles enhanced by fins and other attachments. Some modern viewers complain about the unrealistic monsters but they were effective and frightening at the time. Berry (*Dinosaur Filmography*) notes that the creature footage from *One Million B.C.* was re-used in at least eleven other films from 1943 to 1970.

Unhappily, the reptiles used in *One Million B.C.* were mistreated, as animals often were in Hollywood films of that time. A fight between a lizard and a dwarf alligator is especially gory. In his *Dinosaur Scrapbook* (1980), Donald Glut recalls that special effects technician Roy Seawright told him "the reptiles were starved for a few days, then brought on to the miniature sets. With a quick and mild shock from an electric prod, the animals would leap out at the nearest creature — such as another equally hungry and shocked reptile."

The script by four writers moves along briskly and has only one major problem. There are two endings, which are poorly connected to each other. The volcanic eruption, rockslides and lava flood, together with the rescue of Wandi, would have been a fine ending (and were a good climax in the 1966 remake), but immediately after the eruption Loana mysteriously ends up back in the Shell People's cave in time for the siege by the giant lizard. The final fight with the dinosaur is an anticlimax, although enhanced by very fast cutting of men stabbing the monster and throwing rocks, and by the big lizard's bizarre cry, almost like a dog's barking.

The cast, especially the three leads, rise to the challenge of telling a complicated story without comprehensible dialogue. Victor Mature and Lon Chaney Jr. are equally convincing as brutes and as reformed heroes. Mature was 25, only nine years younger than Chaney, who played his father.

Young Carole Landis perhaps has the most difficult role. She has to teach first Tumak, and then the whole Rock Tribe, civility without coming off as a tiresome schoolteacher and she has to seem able to survive in her dangerous world without sporting the tough look of the Rock women. Landis in *One Million B.C.* is the perfect tomboy — beautiful, charming, funny, spunky and athletic. Her brief costume shows off what Hollywood (according to Ephraim Katz's *Film Encyclopedia*) called "the best legs in town."

Lon Chaney Sr. had virtually invented the art of film makeup and his son wanted to do the makeup for Akhoba, but union rules prevented this. Chaney Jr. had been doing mostly small parts in films since the death of his father in 1930. Akhoba was one of his best parts, but neither *One Million B.C.* nor *Of Mice and Men* (also 1940; his best performance) saved him from a string of B-movies which made up most of his long career until his death in 1973.

Both Victor Mature and Carole Landis had been supporting players before *One Million B.C.*, which made them both stars. Mature worked steadily until the 1970s, often underrated by critics because of his athletic body and his presence in many unsophisticated historical and Biblical epics. Landis was busy either in films or in the wartime USO for eight years after *One Million B.C.* In 1948, aged 29 and after three divorces, Carole Landis killed herself.

Nigel de Brulier, who played Peytow, the wise leader of the Shell People, was a veteran of over 100 films, best known for dignified parts such as Cardinal Richelieu in silent and talkie versions of *The Three Musketeers* and *The Man in the Iron Mask*. Other actors with over 100 films to their credit were Conrad Nagel, the archeologist-narrator, and Creighton Hale, a Shell Tribesman.

Hal Roach, Mack Sennett's chief rival in silent comedy, produced over 700 films beginning in 1915, including the films of Harold Lloyd, Laurel and Hardy, Charley Chase and the Little Rascals. He directed a few dozen films, mostly early silents and short talkies. In 1940, his studio was small and devoted to B films. Richard Schickel, biographer of D.W. Griffith, describes it as "somewhat raffish." In 1943, the Roach Studio ceased production. Hal Roach was associate producer of *One Million Years B.C.*, the 1966 remake. He lived to the fabulous age of 100.

His son Hal Roach Jr. was 22 when he assisted his father as co-director of *One Million B.C.* He never directed another feature.

The most controversial aspect of the production of *One Million B.C.* was the participation of D.W. Griffith. The pioneering director had not made a film since 1931. As late as 2003, he was still listed as an "uncredited" co-director of *One Million B.C.* by the *Internet Movie Database*. He did not co-direct the film but he was on Roach's payroll for several weeks. Richard Schickel (*D.W. Griffith*) believes Griffith probably supervised special effects shots. Griffith also cast Landis and Mature. Griffith showed Landis off to Roach by having her take off her shoes and run across the back lot. Roach was impressed by Landis' graceful athleticism and hired her.

Griffith was doubtless grateful for any employment at that point in his life. Probably he was especially pleased to work in a film which told its story without words, as he had done in the silents. Nonetheless, when Roach and Griffith gave a joint interview on the project, Roach opined "It's a screwy idea" and Griffith replied "I concur in the sentiment."

Variety (May 1, 1940) dismissed *One Million B.C.* for its "corny ... pretty thin" story and "phoney-looking monsters." Berry reports that it was a "solid success" at the box-office, but even today, voters on the *Internet Movie Database* give the film only a modest 5.4 rating. This is a mistake. *One Million B.C.* was made with craft and dedication by skilled workers who took their jobs and the film seriously. It tells a simple, idealistic story efficiently and benefits from a crisp script; attractive, sincere actors; frightening monsters; stark scenery; excellent photography and Oscar-nominated effects and music. It remains one of the classics of the prehistoric subgenre. Ref: Schickel. *D.W. Griffith: An American Life*; Jones. *Illustrated Dinosaur Movie Guide*; Berry. *Dinosaur Filmography*; *Internet Movie Database*; Nash. *Motion Picture Guide*; Smith. *Epic Films*; MK 8.

One Million Years B.C. (1966) U.K.; dir. Don Chaffey; Hammer/20th Century–Fox. 100 or 91 min.; color. Screenplay, Michael Carreras, based on 1940 screenplay by George Baker; photography, Wilkie Cooper; music, Mario Nascimbene. CAST: Raquel Welch (*Loana*); John Richardson (*Tumak*); Percy Herbert (*Sakana*); Robert Brown (*Akhoba*); Martine Beswick (*Nupondi*); Jean Wladon (*Ahot*); Lisa Thomas (*Sura*); Malya Tappi (*Tohana*); William Lyon Brown (*Payto*); Yvonne Horner (*Ullah*); Richard James (*Young Rock Man*); Frank Hayden (*Rock Man*).

"This is a story of long, long ago, when the world was just beginning." After the narrator speaks that one sentence, the camera slowly and silently swoops in from Outer Space through banks of clouds, to the surface of a tormented Earth torn by fiery explosions, as the opening credits unfold to resounding music. We come in on a stark mountainous landscape as the narrator resumes. "A young world. A world early in the morning of time. A hard, unfriendly world." Eerie winds are heard as the camera pans across a barren land. "Creatures who sit and wait. Creatures who must kill to live." We see a vulture and a large snake in a tree.

Then a man's eyes peer out from a rocky hiding place. "And man — superior to the creatures only in his cunning." The man, Tumak, leaps from hiding and runs past a warthog which chases him. Tumak jumps over a small patch of greenery. The warthog runs across the same patch and drops into a hidden pit dug by the hunters. Tumak cries in triumph and other men appear. "There are not many men yet. Just a few tribes scattered across the wilderness. Never venturing far, unaware that other tribes exist even. Too busy with their own lives to be curious, too frightened of the unknown to wander. Their laws are simple. The strong take everything." The narrator introduces Akhoba, leader of the Rock Tribe, and his sons Tumak and Sakana. "There is no love lost between them. And that is our story." Here the narrator falls silent and no more English is heard for the rest of the film.

The two brothers quarrel over which of them will kill the trapped animal. Akhoba justly gives Tumak the honor. The young caveman dives into the pit, wrestles the beast and kills it, as the hunters shriek with satisfaction and Sakana scowls jealously. Akhoba tears off the warthog's tusk (with his bare hands) and gives it to Tumak. As the hunters prepare to carry the kill back to their cave, an old man falls into the pit and is injured. He cannot get out and pleads for help. The men ignore him and walk off with the kill as vultures gather. The hunters do not stop when the old man screams.

At the cave, Tumak's wild-haired mate Nupondi greets him happily. Akhoba carefully maintains discipline as his mate Tohana cooks

Loana (Raquel Welch) and other Shell Tribe women spearfishing in *One Million Years B.C.* (1966).

the hog. When an old man tries to grab a piece of meat, Tohana hits him in the face with a rock. Akhoba steps on the hand of a boy who tries the same thing, burning the hand on a hot rock near the cooking fire. Akhoba takes all he wants, then Sakana and Tumak, then the other hunters. The women, children and old men take what's left. Fierce Nupondi gets a piece of meat away from another woman. Two old men struggle over a piece Akhoba throws away. Everyone eats hurriedly by himself.

Perhaps to show his power, Akhoba takes some meat from Tumak. Tumak fights back and Akhoba immediately attacks him. As they fight with staffs, the tribe's weaklings grab as much food as they can. To Sakana's satisfaction and Nupondi's dismay, Akhoba drives Tumak out of the cave and knocks him over a cliff. Sakana loses no time in grabbing Nupondi and making her his unwilling mate.

In the morning, Tumak wakes up in a bush at the bottom of the cliff. He limps off, incredibly alone in an apparently empty world. As he wanders, Tumak is attacked by an enormous lizard. When the creature wraps his long tongue around Tumak's leg the caveman saves himself by hitting the tongue with a rock. Tumak escapes into a vast cave with a hole in the high roof, making a skylight, and a big tree growing in the center of the cave. When an erect ape enters the grotto, Tumak has to flee out the back way.

Meanwhile back at the cave (I always wanted to write that), Akhoba and Sakana almost come to blows over Nupondi. As Tumak flees across the landscape he avoids a Brontosaurus and a giant tarantula. He staggers across a waterless area under a blazing sun until he comes to the sea, which he never knew existed. He collapses at the top of a sand dune and does not see several laughing girls of the Shell Tribe who have come to spear fish at the edge of the sea. Loana, the boldest of the girls, approaches Tumak, who wakes up, sees Loana and probably thinks he's died and gone to heaven.

Suddenly an Archelon, a giant turtle, appears

just above Loana and Tumak. The other girls flee but Loana blows a warning on her conch shell and bravely drags Tumak out of the way of the creature. Ahot and other men of the Shell Tribe come running and fight the turtle with spears and rocks. The turtle makes his way to the sea and the Shell People take Tumak to their cave.

During a hunt, Akhoba climbs to a craggy height to catch a goat. He slips and hangs from a cliff. While the other men kill the goat, Sakana coolly steps on Akhoba's hands; the old leader falls from the cliff. Akhoba demands and wins the submission of the other hunters.

In the Shell Tribe's cave Tumak is surprised to see the tribesmen working quietly together without violence. Payto the elderly leader shows children how he paints figures of animals on the cave wall. Shell children laugh when Tumak grabs at food Loana was giving him freely. Despite his bad manners Loana finds Tumak attractive, to the dismay of Ahot who wants Loana himself.

In the Rock Tribe's cave Nupondi does a wild dance at a ceremony recognizing Sakana as leader and awarding him Nupondi as his mate. Suddenly Akhoba, wounded and crippled, appears at the entrance to the cave, terrifying everyone.

Tumak examines uncomprehendingly the Shell People's wall art and advanced artifacts, such as a bone needle and a necklace. He sees that the Shell men have better spears than the Rock People. Loana tries to teach Tumak spear fishing in a shallow pool but he can't get the hang of it. He begins to understand laughter, which is unknown among the Rock Tribe.

A juvenile Allosaurus, about eight feet high, suddenly attacks the Shell People, killing a man. The people retreat to their cave, but when the monster threatens a little girl in a tree, Tumak grabs Ahot's spear and fights the beast. Ahot and other men join him; the dinosaur kills another man. The beast is finally killed when it runs onto a thick pole which Tumak grabs from a drying platform and uses as a giant spear. Tumak gives Ahot's spear back to him only when Loana asks him to. The Shell People bury one of their dead with more respect than the Rock People ever dreamed of. Tumak steals Ahot's spear and fights Ahot when the Shell man tries to get it back. The men break up the fight and Payto orders Tumak to leave. Loana goes with him. To help protect Loana, Ahot gives Tumak the spear. Tumak heads back to the Rock Tribe's territory for his revenge.

Tumak leads Loana to the cave where he met the erect ape, apparently because it is the only place with water in the desert they must traverse. Suddenly not one but five apes appear. The humans hide in the tree inside the cave. Two apes fight; as soon as one gains an advantage the others finish off the loser. The victim's head is mounted on a stake. Tumak and Loana manage to climb out through the hole in the roof. Tumak is as surprised when Loana cries as he was when she laughed. Up to now Tumak has treated Loana brusquely; now he begins to be gentle with her.

The two lovers flee from a Triceratops, only to run into a Ceratosaurus. Fortunately the two big dinosaurs fight each other, as the humans cower in a shallow cave. The Triceratops finally wins. The humans flee but are separated. Sakana finds Loana and of course instantly assaults her. Tumak arrives, knocks down three of Sakana's men and defeats and injures Sakana. He is prevented from killing Sakana only by Loana's pleas.

Everyone at the Rock cave is amazed when Tumak appears and takes control of the tribe. Tumak seriously considers killing crippled Akhoba but he relents. Nupondi is delighted to see Tumak, whom she hopes will liberate her from Sakana, but she is horrified to see that Tumak has brought his own mate. Nupondi wastes no time in starting a fight with Loana. Rather surprisingly, Loana wins and knocks Nupondi to the ground. The Rock People helpfully give Loana a rock with which to finish Nupondi off, but the Shell girl refuses to kill her opponent.

The rough Rock women examine Loana's blonde hair and necklace curiously. In the morning Loana begins teaching the Rock People a better way to scrap hides. Tumak and Sakana snarl at each other. Everyone goes fishing and Loana teaches the Rock folk to enjoy swimming. Suddenly a pteranodon attacks the people, grabs Loana and carries her off; Nupondi smiles with evil satisfaction. Tumak and another man go after Loana, who is saved when a second pterosaur attacks the first and she is dropped into the sea.

Tumak arrives to find the second pterosaur eating the young of the first and mistakenly believes Loana is dead.

In Tumak's absence Sakana and his supporters

stage a coup and take command of the Tribe's hunters. The pteranodon had taken Loana all the way back to the sea and she runs to the Shell People and asks them to help Tumak. Ahot, several other Shell men and even Sura (a Shell woman who likes Ahot and worries about losing him to Loana) go with her to the Rock Tribe area. Tumak meets Loana and the Shell party in the desert. A young hunter from the Rock Tribe who supports Tumak brings them news of Sakana's takeover.

As Tumak, Loana and their Shell allies arrive at the Rock Tribe's cave, Sakana is laying siege to the cave and demanding that Akhoba come out to be killed. Rather embarrassingly, Tumak is knocked cold at the very beginning of the battle. Fortunately, the Rock People who support Akhoba, including Nupondi, make a snap decision to support the strangers who are attacking Sakana and his men (although fierce old Akhoba seems to be throwing rocks at both sides without distinction). The two forces battle with clubs, rocks and fists as Loana revives Tumak. Sakana grabs Loana and Tumak tackles him. Just as Tumak is about to finish Sakana off with a rock, the nearby volcano erupts.

The eruption sets off rockslides and an earthquake. Akhoba and Tohana stay in the cave and are killed when the whole place collapses. Sakana tries to flees but Tumak kills him with a spear. Many people, including Nupondi, are killed as great chasms open in the earth. Even a giant lizard falls into one of the chasms. As the earthquake subsides, the shocked, dust-covered survivors, led by Tumak and Loana, trek off through a cloud of smoke into an uncertain future.

COMMENTARY. When I came of out the theater after seeing the disappointing *Clan of the Cave Bear* in 1986, I had to take a cab home. The driver asked me what movie I had seen. I told him and mentioned that it was about prehistoric people. He laughed and said, "The last time I saw a caveman movie was that one with Raquel Welch."

Many people could still say the same thing

Hammer turned one of the greatest publicity shots in film history into the centerpiece of their poster for *One Million Years B.C.* (1966).

today. Of all the film and TV projects in this book, only three have made a lasting impression on the public: *The Flintstones*, *2001: A Space Odyssey* and *One Million Years B.C.* Nevertheless the film has been harshly treated. Critics were standoffish or hostile when the remake of *One Million B.C.* (1940) came out in 1966. The American version had only 91 of the 100 minutes in the British film. Hammer's three attempts to make another successful prehistoric film (*Slave Girls*, 1967; *When Dinosaurs Ruled the Earth*, 1970; *Creatures the World Forgot*, 1971) all failed. *One Million Years B.C.* was not released on video in the U.S. until a videocassette appeared in 1994, a laserdisc in 1996 and a DVD in 2003. Of these, only the laserdisc had the 100-minute U.K. version of the film; the VHS cassette and even the DVD contained the 91-minute U.S. version. The only extra features on the U.S. DVD are trailers and notes on the restoration, which revealed that the original negative has been lost. In spite of this comparative neglect, audiences still remember the film, and in this case, audiences were wiser than the critics. If *2001: A Space Odyssey* is the *Citizen Kane* of prehistoric films, *One Million Years B.C.* is the subgenre's *Gone with the Wind*, a popular masterpiece which simply defies criticism.

The most common explanation for the film's popularity is Raquel Welch. The U.S. DVD carries only one quote from a critic, the *Los Angeles Herald Tribune*'s opinion that "The movie has one delightful asset. A vision of Amazon-like beauty known as Raquel Welch." This of course implies that Welch was the film's only asset. All video versions, from the laserdisc to the U.S. and U.K. VHS and DVD releases, feature on their covers the famous shot of Welch in her doeskin bikini (often incorrectly called a "fur bikini"), which was also the dominant image of Hammer's 1966 poster. Welch went on to become the biggest star ever to have a major role in a prehistoric feature. She was the fourth actor to gain stardom as a result of an appearance in a caveman film, after Mae Marsh in *Man's Genesis* (1912) and Victor Mature and Carole Landis in *One Million B.C.*

Wiser critics realized that the film had many assets besides its leading lady. The stop-motion dinosaurs created by Ray Harryhausen, Mario Nascimbene's resounding score and the stark Canary Island locations have all come in for praise. Beyond the undoubted success of Welch, Harryhausen, Nascimbene and the locations, *One Million Years B.C.* is a fabulous adventure fantasy. There are quiet interludes between action sequences, as in all successful adventure films, but the movie features every possible confrontation which could happen in its imagined world: man versus man, man versus dinosaur, dinosaur versus dinosaur, pterosaur versus girl, pterosaur versus pterosaur, man versus girl, girl versus girl, tribe versus tribe. All that before the volcanic eruption and the earthquake. Of all the top action-adventure films (*King Kong*, 1933; *Tarzan and His Mate*, 1934; *The Adventures of Robin Hood*, 1938; *The Seven Samurai*, 1954; *From Russia With Love*, 1963; *Jason and the Argonauts*, another Chaffey-Harryhausen collaboration, 1963; *The Dirty Dozen*, 1967; *The Man Who Would Be King*, 1975; *Jaws*, 1975; *Raiders of the Lost Ark*, 1981; *Aliens*, 1986; *The Princess Bride*, 1987; *Die Hard*, 1988; *Crouching Tiger, Hidden Dragon*, 2000), *One Million Years B.C.* is the least realistic, the most dreamlike and fantastic. It should be noted that of the action films listed above, only *Seven Samurai* offers a realistic depiction of its world. All the others are more or less non-realistic. *One Million Years B.C.* is simply a little more so.

Hammer's four prehistoric films have all presented pessimistic views of prehistoric man and by implication of mankind in general, in keeping with the grim outlook of the studio's Gothic horror films. In *One Million Years B.C.* tribes and individuals fight each other almost routinely. At the end, it is hard to tell which of the dust-covered survivors is of which tribe and everyone seems prepared to forget their differences— but for how long? Some critics have suggested that the cloud of smoke through which the people struggle in the finale is meant to suggest a nuclear cloud, a warning about mankind's present dilemma. This idea seems fanciful but it would not contradict Hammer's gloomy outlook.

In the 1940 *One Million B.C.* when Akhoba returns to the cave crippled, Skakana (whose name is Sakana in the remake) wants to kill him but is prevented by the pleas of Akhoba's mate, backed up by tribal opinion. In the remake Akhoba appears at the cave and the film immediately cuts away. We do not see why Sakana did not kill his father. In the older film the Rock Tribe is merciful for once, which foreshadows their reformation under Loana's influence; the remake could have shown the same scene but did not. Hammer evaded an opportunity to show the Rock Tribe being merciful, since that would contradict the film's misanthropic attitude. (In the remake when Tumak is tempted to kill his father, Akhoba's mate begs for his life and Tumak relents, but since Tumak is not evil like Sakana, changing Tumak's mind is less significant than stopping Sakana.)

As the Hammer prehistoric series progressed, the two cheaper, dinosaur-less films were even darker in tone than the two more expensive, dinosaur-infested movies. In *Slave Girls* a primitive white tribe invades prehistoric Africa and drives away black tribes— and then the whites begin to enslave each other and practice human sacrifice! The tale is bizarre and convoluted but as gloomy as most Hammer films.

In *When Dinosaurs Ruled the Earth* two tribes get along well but almost everyone agrees that girls ought to be sacrificed to the sun god. The two tribes are punished for this violence when both are almost wiped out by exactly the same kind of cataclysm they sought to avoid through human sacrifice. In the final film, *Creatures the World Forgot* (1971), two tribes unite but they have to fight two other violent tribes; the protagonists' tribe is in the habit of torturing and raping women and is torn apart by civil war.

Since its release, *One Million Years B.C.* has acquired many defenders who have dissented from the original unfavorable critical reaction. Leonard Maltin's *Movie & Video Guide* gives the film only a modest rating of 2½ out of 4, but Senn and Johnson's *Fantastic Cinema Subject Guide* gives it an eight out of 10. (Senn and Johnson are often quite harsh in their ratings; they give *Quest for Fire* (1981) only a six; *One Million B.C.* (1940) and *Iceman* (1984) only 5 and *Caveman* (1981) only 2.) George MacDonald Fraser, author of the *Flashman* novels, in his *The Hollywood History of the World* (1988), notes "*One Million Years B.C.* was the kind of film which was commonly greeted with derision. It happened to be good in every respect.... The sets were excellent, Ray Harryhausen's dinosaurs were unusually realistic ... the players behaved like savage children with discernable characters, and the final eruption was first-rate."

Stephen R. Bissette offered a definitive defense of *One Million Years B.C.* in a review of the 1996 laserdisc in elite fan magazine *Video Watchdog* 40 (1997). "It was the *Dr. Zhivago* of monster movies: expansive in scope, unabashedly romantic, and genuinely entertaining. Its absurd science and archaic dramaturgy were integral to its sweep and charm.... Hammer embraced the story with the same sobriety and integrity it brought to Dracula, Frankenstein and the Gothics: the earnestness of the performances, Don Chaffey's dead-serious direction and Wilkie Cooper's lavish cinematography brought weight, dignity and grandeur to material that invited derision.... *One Million Years B.C.* remains the contemporary classic of its peculiar genre and has yet to be bettered."

By 1966 Hammer was expert at remaking the fantasy classics of the Golden Age of Hollywood for new audiences. The British studio had already become famous for remaking Universal's classic *Dracula* and *Frankenstein*. The script of the Hammer version improves on Hal Roach's 1940 *One Million B.C.* (which was 20 minutes shorter than the remake) in several ways. First it removes the modern introduction and mercifully shortens the remarks of the narrator. When Tumak has to get from the mountainous Rock Tribe area to the Shell Tribe by the sea, instead of the implausible sequence in the 1940 version in which Tumak floats downstream (unconscious but clinging to a floating tree, menaced by monsters but never attacked), the hero has to walk the whole distance. Besides being much more sensible, this gives him a chance to get into trouble with dinosaurs and ape-men. I have always found the scene in which Tumak strides off, utterly alone in a world he cannot fathom, extremely moving. The narrator has already told us that the tribes know nothing of each other's existence, so we know that Tumak believes that there may be no one in the world except the Tribe from which he has been exiled.

Nupondi is a minor character in the 1940 film but is promoted to a major villain and a personal enemy of Loana in the remake. The Roach film suffers from a clumsy double ending, first the earthquake, then the dinosaur siege. The Hammer version wisely has all the dinosaur scenes before the earthquake, which is a satisfying finale.

In keeping with the harsher, more pessimistic outlook of the remake, Loana has almost no time to reform and improve the Rock Tribe. While Carole Landis's Loana teaches the Rock People many innovations, Raquel Welch's Loana barely manages to show one woman a better way to scrap hides and to teach people to bathe before the next crisis erupts. There is much less in the 1966 remake than in the 1940 original about the Shell People's superior technology. I think this minimizing of the Shell People's superiority is a mistake by the remake. In the fight between Loana and Nupondi it would have been a good idea to have Loana know some wrestling moves or do something clever to show she was from a more advanced people, rather than just battling it out.

The dinosaur effects are much improved in the remake. The Roach film used enlarged lizards for its dinosaurs. Harryhausen has been criticized for using an enlarged lizard for the first dinosaur in the Hammer film, but that can be seen as a graceful homage to the 1940 film. After the lizard comes one masterpiece after another. The Archelon (the giant turtle), the

Allosaurus in the Shell camp, the battle between the Triceratops and the Ceratosaurus and the Pteranodon attack on Loana are all among the greatest dinosaur sequences in films prior to Spielberg. The Archelon scene is so realistic that some critics thought a real turtle was used. (An actor actually cries "Archelon" during the scene; the screenwriter felt that the correct term sounded like a plausible ancient word.) In the Pteranodon attack, the sight of the flying creature swooping over the alarmed cave people, carrying Raquel Welch in her doeskin bikini to an uncertain fate, is a fabulous moment of film kitsch. The animation work in *One Million Years B.C.* took nine months to complete.

Werner Heymann's music for *One Million B.C.* was Oscar-nominated in 1940 and Mario Nascimbene's score for the Hammer remake was not nominated, but Nascimbene's is the more memorable achievement. In *Music From the House of Hammer* Randall Larson writes that the score "nicely suggests the immensity of the newly created world and retains a sense of tremendous primitivity through an orchestra consisting mostly of percussion and brass. The use of choir added a dramatic, profound sense of historical importance." Stephen Bissette notes that the *One Million Years B.C.* score "would anticipate the impending [Sergio] Leone universe: amplified grunts, groans, roars and battle cries were inseparable from Mario Nascimbene's evocative score, wedding soaring arias with bone-dry percussive effects and orchestrative earthquakes." In the script, special effects and music for *One Million Years B.C.* Hammer accomplished what they did best: they updated and improved on an old classic.

For the U.S. release 20th Century–Fox trimmed nine minutes from the 100-minute British film. They cut the shot of the old man being hit in the face with a rock when he tries to steal a piece of meat in the cave banquet; a shot of an old man scrambling after meat thrown away by Akhoba; Nupondi's erotic dance as she is given to Sakana; some shots of Tumak's uncomprehending exploration of the Shell people's cave; much of the second scene in the ape-men's cave, including shots suggestive of cannibalism and the shot of the severed head being put on the stake; and several shots from the climactic tribal battle. Remarkably, most of Harryhausen's dinosaur scenes also suffered cuts. Stephen Bissette writes that the fight between the Triceratops and the Ceratosaurus is "the only animation sequence in the entire film which was not trimmed for U.S. release."

Of course realism is beside the point in such films as this, but one specific inaccuracy should be mentioned. (That is, besides the dinosaurs, Raquel Welch, her bikini, and the fact that ancient people were not as quarrelsome and self-destructive as the Rock Tribe.) Prehistoric hunters were not in the habit of jumping into pits and wrestling large wild animals. In a world without doctors, why would they do that? If they trapped a wild animal in a pit, they would kill it safely from above, with spears or rocks. Tumak leaps into the pit to impress his father and the

Cave people scatter as a Ray Harryhausen pteranodon swoops against the stark backdrop of the Canary Islands in Hammer's *One Million Years B.C.* (1966).

other older hunters of the tribe, but the custom only makes the tribe look a bit stupid.

There are a few minor errors in the film. When Loana saves Tumak from the Archelon on the beach, she is barefoot in most shots but she is wearing boots in one shot, as she leans over the unconscious Tumak. The geography is all messed up. It takes Tumak and then Tumak and Loana a long time to cross the desert between the Rock Tribe and the Shell Tribe, but the pteranodon takes Loana by air all the way from the Rock Tribe area to the sea. Tumak chases her on foot and gets there almost as fast as the flying reptile. When Loana gets back to the Shell Tribe she asks them to come help Tumak even though she has no way of knowing that Sakana has taken the Rock Tribe back from Tumak.

On the much-discussed topic of bikinis in *One Million Years B.C.* it should be noted that few of the young women in the film wear them except for Loana and Nupondi. Most other women wear short but modest costumes. There are also some older, less attractive women, such as Akhoba's mate Tohana. In *When Dinosaurs Ruled the Earth* and in such tripe as *Wild Women of Wongo* we have what can only be described as a bevy of beauties, but in *One Million Years B.C.* Hammer wisely had a layer of reality to keep the fantasy from becoming too unreal. The costume designer, who designed for Welch the most famous costume in any prehistoric film, was Carl Toms.

The erect apes in the desert cave are photographed at a distance or from above and we never see their faces clearly, except for the severed head which is stuck on a stake. The head looks fairly human. We know they are ape-men, not real apes, since they walk erect and since they behead the loser of the fight. Hammer's publicity referred to them as "gorilla men," whatever that may be. They are tall and slimmer than the usual movie gorilla suit. I would say they are midway between an old-fashioned gorilla suit and the carefully-designed suits of *2001* two years later. The Hammer ape-men's movements are convincing.

Raquel Welch was reluctant to take the lead in *One Million Years B.C.* Her career was just getting started and she feared being ridiculed for appearing in a "dinosaur movie." She was especially unhappy that she had almost no dialogue. However, she agreed to take the job, assuming that the film would be ignored and little-seen. She flew to the Canary Islands, made the film, flew back to London and was amazed to find the airport crowded with journalists eager to interview and photograph her. While on location, she had become one of the most famous actresses in the world thanks to a single photograph. In his autobiography, Ray Harryhausen recalls "Although Michael [Carreras of Hammer] had flown in professional photographers to take publicity stills, with an emphasis on getting the right Raquel Welch shot, in the end the one that everyone remembers was shot by our local unit photographer [Pierre Luigi]. I should think that this picture created more publicity for the film than any other still picture in the history of motion pictures."

The photo has just the right mix of wildness and innocence, the glamorous and the primitive, an unreal vision of perfection in front of a stark, harsh landscape. It encapsulated the successful contradictions of the film itself. Hammer of course made the photo the centerpiece of the film's poster, which is one of the greatest posters ever. The photo was also one of the top-selling pinup pictures of its day. Welch and the photo helped make *One Million Years B.C.* a hit and the film helped make Welch a star. In a short interview on the 2002 British DVD, Welch laughingly recalls her assumption that no one would ever see the film. She has clearly come to terms with the facts that the despised "dinosaur movie" ignited her career and is now one of her most-remembered films, though I am sure that she is confident that she would have become a star even if she had never made *One Million Years B.C.*

In spite of Welch's reservations about the movie, Harryhausen recalls in his autobiography that she "took her acting and the film very seriously." Stephen Bissette writes "Raquel never again radiated such a primal fusion of strength and vulnerability" as she did in her "dinosaur movie." I have called many performers in this book "likeable." None have been more so than Raquel Welch. She was the major sex symbol of her day, but she never did a nude scene. She didn't have to. (Berry notes reports that Welch's voice was dubbed in *One Million Years B.C.* by minor actress Nicolette McKenzie. George MacDonald Fraser claims this was done because Welch's voice "lacked the true prehistoric timbre.")

Despite his approval of Hammer's film, Fraser feels that the casting of Raquel Welch was "sacrificing authenticity to aesthetics with a

(I) One Million Years B.C.

vengeance" and also objects to John Richardson whose "classic features were not to be disguised beneath any amount of hair and prehistoric dirt." In contrast he approves heartily of Robert Brown and Percy Herbert "who, clad in skins and glaring madly as they tore carcasses apart, made splendid cavemen." I think Fraser makes too much of the undoubted fact that Welch and Richardson look much less primitive than Brown and Herbert. The film is a fantasy, so certain unrealistic elements should not be an issue. It is necessary to have audience identification with the heroes, which usually means the heroes have to be more like us than the villains. And the modern good looks of the hero and heroine, contrasted with the crude villains, establish that the film's conflict is between those who have the capacity to become civilized and those who never will.

Mark F. Berry (*Dinosaur Filmography*) dismisses Robert Brown's "generic and unremarkable presence" and notes "the thought of the corpulent Brown beating the athletic 6 ft. 3 in. Richardson in hand-to-hand combat is hard to swallow." Like Fraser, I felt that Brown was admirable. He grimaces with sadistic glee as Tumak kills the warthog. He tears the tusk from the dead animal's head with his bare hands. In his staff fight with Tumak, Brown's Akhoba is ferociously aggressive. I believed he could kill Tumak. He is suspicious, touchy and rules with a hand of iron. That's how he has always run the Rock Tribe and he is not about to change. Nobody gets the better of Akhoba until he is crippled.

Akhoba knows that he is getting old. He fears that Tumak or Sakana will overthrow and kill him. He steals Tumak's food in order to force his son to either submit or fight. As for Brown being overweight, that makes sense for Akhoba, who not only grabs as much food as he wants for himself, he also made his mate the tribe's cook! His paunch is a sign of power and prestige. Berry rightly points out that Lon Chaney Jr.'s Akhoba in the 1940 film was much more "sympathetic." Of course he was. The 1940 film was an optimistic view of prehistory in which ever the roughhewn Rock People reform and almost everyone survives. The Hammer version was more pessimistic; the bad characters stay bad and die and there is no reason to be sure that tribal reformation will succeed.

Hammer advertised *One Million Years B.C.* as its 100th film. Most sources on Hammer, including Berry's *Dinosaur Filmography*, say the claim was untrue and was made arbitrarily to support one of the studio's most expensive films (costing about 500,000 pounds). *Variety* (Dec. 28, 1966), reviewing the 100-minute British version, called it "a likely click [success] for unsophisticated situations.... The whole thing is good-humored full-of-action commercial nonsense but the moppets [children] will love it and older male moppets will probably love Miss Welch." *One Million Years B.C.* was Hammer's most profitable film, earning about $9,000,000 in worldwide release.

Don Chaffey had a long but unremarkable career, including a lot of TV and work for both Disney and Hammer. His best film is *Jason and the Argonauts*, in which he collaborated with Harryhausen for the first time. He went on to direct Hammer's final prehistoric film *Creatures the World Forgot*. In 1966 Ray Harryhausen had done several of his most acclaimed films and his work was already well-known to discerning fans. Their eager anticipation of his dinosaur film may have done as much as Raquel Welch to make *One Million Years B.C.* a hit. (Well, almost as much.) Mario Nascimbene had scored about 100 films by 1966, including large-scale epics such as *Alexander the Great* (1956), *The Vikings* (1958) and *Solomon and Sheba* (1959). He went on to score *When Dinosaurs Ruled the Earth* and *Creatures the World Forgot*, making him perhaps the outstanding prehistoric composer in films. Cinematographer Wilkie Cooper had a long career in minor British films, as well as all of Harryhausen's films from 1958–1966: *The Seventh Voyage of Sinbad, The Three Worlds of Gulliver, Mysterious Island, Jason and the Argonauts, First Men in the Moon* and *One Million Years B.C.*

When she did her caveman movie in 1966, Raquel Welch had had a good part in only one film, *Fantastic Voyage*, which very unwisely encased her legs in trousers during the entire film. After *One Million Years B.C.* she starred in 24 films from 1967 to 1978. She played a cavewoman one more time, in a voice performance in *Hollyrock-a-bye Baby* (1993), a *Flintstones* animated TV special. (If Welch's voice was indeed dubbed for her cave lingo in *One Million Years B.C.*, she was seen but not heard in her Hammer film and heard but not seen in her *Flintstones* TV special.) Welch usually played modern women until 1982 when she was the leading lady in *The Legend of Walks Far Woman*, a TV film about Blackfoot Indians in the Old West. Welch fought to have *Walks Far Woman* made. Perhaps, after her experiences in *One Million Years B.C.*, she got some satisfaction in finally playing a woman in a realistically-depicted tribal society.

John Richardson was in Hammer's *She* (1965) and *The Vengeance of She* (1968). Thereafter he worked mostly in Italian B films. Martine Beswick made such a strong impression in *One Million Years B.C.* that she was cast in the lead in *Slave Girls*, Hammer's follow-up prehistoric film. After *Slave Girls*, Beswick was briefly busy in B films, as a female Hyde in Hammer's *Dr. Jekyll and Sister Hyde* (1971) and as the Queen of Evil in *Seizure* (1974), Oliver Stone's first feature. By 1980 Beswick was down to playing the lead in *The Happy Hooker Goes Hollywood*. Robert Brown and Percy Herbert had supporting parts in dozens of films. Frank Hayden was in three of Hammer's four caveman films, following *One Million Years B.C.* with *Slave Girls* and *Creatures the World Forgot*. He had small parts in all three, but a good primitive face was too valuable to waste. Yvonne Horner worked in both *One Million Years B.C.* and *Slave Girls* in small parts. Jean Wladon, who played Ahot, was in only one film besides *One Million Years B.C.*

This is as good a place as any to consider the surprising number of actors who have worked in both caveman movies and the suave James Bond films. Before she played memorable villainesses in *One Million Years B.C.* and *Slave Girls*, Jamaican actress Martine Beswick was an uncredited dancing girl in *Dr. No* (1962), one of the wrestling gypsy girls in *From Russia with Love* (1963) and Paula, the British agent who kills herself under torture, in *Thunderball* (1965). Robert Brown, who played Akhoba in *One Million Years B.C.*, played M in four Bond films (the last two Roger Moore films, *Octopussy* (1983) and *A View to a Kill* (1985), and the two Timothy Dalton outings, *The Living Daylights* (1987) and *Licence to Kill* (1989)). Brown's films as M were sandwiched between those of impeccable Bernard Lee and prestigious Dame Judi Dench.

Towering Richard Kiel was Jaws, perhaps the most famous Bond villain, in *The Spy Who Loved Me* (1977), one of Roger Moore's best Bonds, and in *Moonraker* (1979), one of the worst films in the series. Earlier Kiel was Eegah in *Eegah!* (1962) and a caveman on the *Land of the Lost* TV series (1974–77). Barbara Bach was one of the most dynamic Bond women in *The Spy Who Loved Me* and the villainess in *Caveman* (1981).

Harryhausen went on to make *Valley of Gwangi* (1969) with dinosaurs but no cavemen, and then to do his only stop-motion prehistoric hominid character, Trog in *Sinbad and the Eye of the Tiger* (1977). In his autobiography Harryhausen lists several film projects about prehistory or primitive humans which he planned but never realized, including an *Abominable Snowman* project. He also considered using a Yeti in *Sinbad and the Eye of the Tiger*. He planned an *Atlantis* feature; an *Island of Dr. Moreau*; *The People of the Mist*, with a Lost World where "mankind began its evolution"; and *Ugala*, with a 13-foot tall missing link found in Mexico. *When the Earth Cracked Open* was to be set in prehistory; the hero's tribe was to confront giant animals (though not dinosaurs), a volcano and a villainous tribe which kidnaps the good tribe's women.

One Million Years B.C. has become a favorite cult film and was recently the subject of a homage. Joe Dante's part-animated *Looney Tunes Back in Action* (2003) is filled with erudite references to popular culture, liveaction as well as animated. The *Video Watchdog* 113 review mentioned that the DVD includes a scene cut from the film, in which Jenna Elfman, the funniest of the human cast, briefly reverts to a cavewoman, wearing a bikini reminiscent of Welch's in *One Million Years B.C.* Ref: Jones. *Illustrated Dinosaur Movie Guide*; Senn/Johnson. *Fantastic Cinema Subject; Guide*; Berry. *Dinosaur Filmography*; Harryhausen/Dalton. *Ray Harryhausen: An Animated Life*; Smith. *Epic Films*; Lucanio. *With Fire and Sword*; Bissette. "One Million Years B.C." review in *Video Watchdog* 40; Fraser. *Hollywood History of the World*; Webber. *Dinosaur Films of Ray Harryhausen*; MK 9.

Osada Havranu (1978) *see* **Settlement of Crows** (1978)

Out of the Darkness (1958) *see* **Teenage Caveman** (1958)

I Padroni del Mondo (1983) *see* **Master of the World** (1983)

Pancho Talero en la Prehistoria (1930) Argentina; dir. Arturo Lanteri. Feature film. CAST: Pepito Petray.

This minimal information is found in the *Internet Movie Database*. Not viewed.

The Pebbles and Bamm Bamm Show (1971–72) U.S.; Hanna-Barbera. Animated TV series; 25-min. episodes; color. VOICES: Sally Struthers (*Pebbles*); Jay North (*Bamm-Bamm*); Mickey Stevens (*Pebbles*); Russi Taylor (*Pebbles*); Lennie Weinrib (*Moonrock*); Mitzi McCall (*Penny*); Gay Hartwig (*Wiggy/Cindy*); Carl Esser (*Fabian*).

Barney Rubble's husky son Bamm-Bamm and Fred Flintstone's cute daughter Pebbles face the problems of teenagers in prehistoric Bedrock. (They call each other "Pebbs" and "Bammer.") Sally Struthers voiced Pebbles just before gaining fame on *All in the Family*; two other actresses played Pebbles after Struthers left.

Jay North was the star of the *Dennis the Menace* series. Episodes were repeated in the two later series, *The Flintstones Comedy Hour* (1972–73) and *Fred Flintstone and Friends* (1977). Episodes: "Gridiron Girl Trouble," "Putty in Her Hands," "Frog for a Day," "The Golden Voice," "Pebbles Bib Boat," "Focus Foolery," "The Grand Prix Pebbles," "The Terrible Snorkosaurus," "Schleprock's New Image," "Daddy's Little Helper," "Coach Pebbles," "No Cash and Carry," "Woolly the Great," "Mayor May Not," "They Went That Away," "The Birthday Present." Ref: Lenburg. *Encyclopedia of Animated Cartoons*; Adams. *The Flintstones*; not viewed.

Pebbles, Dino and Bamm-Bamm (1980–82) *see* **The Flintstones Comedy Show** (1980–82)

La Plus Vieux Métier du Monde (1967) *see* **The Oldest Profession** (1967)

The Popeye and Olive Show (1981–82) Segment *Prehistoric Popeye*. U.S.; Hanna-Barbera. Animated TV series; 25-min. episodes; color. VOICES: Jack Mercer (*Popeye*); Marilyn Schreffler (*Olive Oyl*); Allan Melvin (*Blutto*).

The *Popeye and Olive Show* consisted of three segments— *Prehistoric Popeye, The Popeye Show* and *Private Olive Oyl*. Some of the episode titles seem quite modern; others certainly sound prehistoric.

Prehistoric Popeye episodes: "Olive's Moving Experience," "The Incredible Shrinking Popeye," "So Who's Watching the Bird Watchers," "Winner Window Washers," "Reptile Ranch," "Olive's Devastating Decorators," "The Midnight Ride of Popeye Revere," "Hogwash at the Car Wash," "Up a Lizard River," "Would He Come Back, Little Fluffasaurus," "Neanderthal Nuisance," "Vegetable Stew," "Cheap Skate Date," "Bronto Beach," "The First Resort," "Chilly Con Caveman." Ref: Lenburg. *Encyclopedia of Animated Cartoons*; not viewed.

Prehistoric Daze (1961), an excerpt from **Not Tonite, Henry** (1961)

A Prehistoric Love Story (1915) U.K.; dir. Leedham Bantock; Zenith. Short film; 2600 feet; b&w; silent. Screenplay, Seymour Hicks. CAST: Seymour Hicks (*The Man*); Isabel Elsom (*The Girl*).

A "burlesque romance set in cave-man days," according to Gifford. Seymour Hicks had a long career in British films and is best known for playing the miser in *Scrooge* (1935, alt. *A Christmas Carol*). Ref: Gifford. *British Film Catalogue*; Jones. *Illustrated Dinosaur Movie Guide*; Lee. *Reference Guide to Fantastic Films*; not viewed.

The Prehistoric Man (1924/British) Great Britain; dir. A.E. Coleby; Stoll. 3858 feet (ca. 30 min.); b&w; silent. Screenplay, Sinclair Hall, George Robey. CAST: George Robey (*He-of-the-Beetle-Brows*); Marie Blanche (*She-of-the–Permanent-Wave*); H. Agar Lyons (*He-of-the–Clutching-Hand*); W.G. Saunders (*He-of-the–Knotty-Joints*); Johnny Butt (*He-of-the–Cedar-Mop*); Elsie Marriott-Wilson (*She-of-the–Tireless-Tongue*); Laurie Leslie (*He-of-the–Matted-Beaver*).

In prehistoric Britain "He-of-the-Beetle-Brows rescues his sweetheart She-of-the–Permanent-Wave, from an auction, where she is being sold by her father, He-of-the–Clutching-Hands. They elope in a prehistoric car. After Beetle-Brows has helped the Stonehenge Wanderers win back the football cup, her father is reconciled and gives his consent to their marriage" according to the British Film Institute.

Music hall comedian George Robey was 55 when he co-wrote and starred in this anachronistic caveman farce. The minor film may be the only non-documentary prehistoric film to mention Stonehenge, which has been featured in many films and TV shows set in later times. A *Xena: Warrior Princess* episode, "The Deliverer" (1997), facetiously claimed that Stonehenge was created when Xena demolished the temple of a villainous cult during Caesar's invasion of Britain in the first century B.C. King Arthur's knights tore down Stonehenge in *The Black Knight* (1954), with no explanation of who put it up again. Stonehenge was also associated with the Arthur story in *Knights of the Round Table* (1953), *Merlin and the Sword* (1983) and *Quest for Camelot* (1998) and with Robin Hood in the TV series *Robin of Sherwood* (1984–86). The monument has also shown up in films set in modern times, such as *Shanghai Knights* (2003). Ref: Gifford. *British Film Catalogue, 1895–1985*; Jones. *Illustrated Dinosaur Movie Guide*; *British Film Institute Catalog* website *(http://www.bfi.org.uk/collections/catalogues)*; not viewed.

Pre-Historic Man (1924/U.S.) U.S.; dir. Bryan Foy; Universal. Short film; silent; b&w. Screenplay, Bryan Foy. (In the series *Hysterical History*).

One in a series of farcical historical shorts by Universal. Others in the 1924–25 series were on such topics as *Rembrandt* (1924) and *Sir Walter Raleigh* (1925). Most of the films in the series were directed by Foy. Ref: *Internet Movie Database*; not viewed.

Prehistoric Peeps (1905) Great Britain; dir. Lewin Fitzhamon; Hepworth. 375 feet (ca. 6 min.); silent; b&w. Screenplay, Lewin Fitzhamon. CAST: Sebastian Smith (*Prof. Chump*); W. Young (*Giant*); Wordsworth Harrison (*Apeman*).

A professor dreams himself into prehistory, where he meets dinosaurs (played by men in suits), a giant and an apeman. Berry credits this comedy short, based on a cartoon series in *Punch* magazine, as "the earliest known film to include dinosaurs." It is probably also the earliest with a prehistoric human. Hepworth was the most important British silent studio. Ref: Berry. *Dinosaur Filmography*; Gifford, *British Film Catalogue, 1895–1985*; *British Film Institute Catalog (http://www.bfi.org.uk/colletions/catalogues)*; not viewed.

Prehistoric Perils (1952) [alt. *Mighty Mouse in Prehistoric Peril*] U.S.; dir. Connie Rasinski; Terrytoons/Fox. Animated short; 6 min.; color. Screenplay, Tom Morrison; music, Philip A. Scheib. In this Mighty Mouse cartoon, "Oil Can Harry abducts Pearl Pureheart into a time machine, transporting them back to Stone Age times." Ref: Webb. *Animated Film Encyclopedia*; not viewed.

Prehistoric Pink (1968) U.S.; dir. Hawley Pratt; DePatie-Freleng/Mirisch/United Artists. Animated short; 6 min.; color. Screenplay, John W. Dunn; music, Walter Greene, Henry Mancini.

The Pink Panther (complete with club and spotted caveman's costume) and a caveman push a large slab of rock across the landscape. They chisel the slab into a sphere to make it easier to move but the sphere repeatedly flattens the caveman. They put the stone on log rollers with similar disastrous results. They finally refine their invention into a wheeled

The Pink Panther strikes a heroic pose in *Prehistoric Pink*.

cart. After imagining the future of the wheel, including automobiles and congested highways, they destroy the wheels and go back to pushing the slab.

The story also involves a dinosaur, a pterodactyl and the caveman's bow and arrow. The progression from sphere to rollers to wheel is historically correct. In the 1960s and 70s the dialogue-free *Panther* cartoons with their simple designs and jazzy Henry Mancini theme music seemed the height of sophistication. This short and its anti-technology theme hold up well. Ref: Webb. *Animated Film Encyclopedia*; *Internet Movie Database*; MK 7.

Prehistoric Popeye (1981–82) *see* **The Popeye and Olive Show** (1981–82)

Prehistoric Porky (1940) U.S.; dir. Robert Clampett; Schlesinger/Warner Bros. Animated short; 7 min.; b&w. Screenplay, Melvin Millar; music, Carl W. Stalling. *VOICES:* Mel Blanc; Sara Berner; The Sportsmen Quartet.

"One Billion Trillion B.C. (a long time ago)" caveman Porky Pig sees an ad in "Expire, the magazine for cavemen" (a gag on *Esquire*) and sallies forth from his cave in pursuit of a fashionable spotted leopard suit. A fierce black panther (after checking his watch and finding it's dinner time) corners Porky, who vainly tries to fight him off with his club. The panther eats the club and spits out clothespins! Porky explains he was just looking for a new suit. The panther asks, "Why didn't you say so? I can get it for you wholesale!"

The short also features a vulture who sings like Jerry Colonna, a dinosaur who greets the audience with "Hello, everybody!" like Kate Smith, and Porky's pet dinosaur Rover, who wags his tail so violently he sets off landslides. Ref: Jones. *Illustrated Dinosaur Movie Guide*; Webb. *Animated Film Encyclopedia*; Beck/Friedwald. *Looney Tunes and Merrie Melodies*; not viewed.

Prehistoric Poultry: The Dinornis, or Great Roaring Whiffenpoof (1917) U.S., dir. Willis O'Brien; Edison/Conquest Pictures. Animated short film; 4 min.; b&w; silent.

An intertitle opens the film, telling us "The Dinornis was the ancestor of our modern chicken. It had long legs and a kind face." The foolish-looking bird, as tall as a man, is eating rocks. A caveman pulls his pet brontosaurus out of his cave by a rope around its neck. The Dinornis snuggles up to the caveman as an intertitle notes "Its heart was tender and affectionate." The caveman drives the bird away, while the brontosaurus eats a whole tree.

Trying to impress a cavegirl, the caveman blows on an animal horn. "The horn of the huntsman is heard on the hill." A hunter hears the horn and spots the Dinornis. The first caveman sits down, rubs two sticks together to make fire and lights his pipe. The hunter launches a rock with a large catapult; the missile misses the Dinornis and hits the pipe-smoking caveman in the head. He exclaims to the girl, "It's that pesky Dinornis again — drat his hide!"

The caveman attacks the Dinornis, who kicks him all the way back to his cave. An intertitle announces, "Although the mildest of creatures, the Dinornis was a most ferocious beast when aroused." The Dinornis then attacks the hunter and launches him with his own catapult. As the hunter flies high above them, the caveman tells the girl, "Look, a shooting star in the daytime! Make a wish!" The hunter hits the ground without being much hurt. The Dinornis flies in on tiny wings, kicks the hunter and poses for a triumphant final shot.

COMMENTARY. Robert F. Klepper (*Silent Films*) said this humorous short cartoon "remains an entertaining conversation piece today" and gave it a rating of three stars. Mark F. Berry (*Dinosaur Filmography*) gave it two and a half stars. *Prehistoric Poultry* is as amusing as O'Brien's other early short cavemen cartoons; see *The Dinosaur and the Missing Link* (1916) for information on the O'Brien series. A shortened version of *Prehistoric Poultry* is included in the Slingshot DVD of *The Lost World* (1925). Ref: Jones. *Illustrated Dinosaur Movie Guide*; Webb. *Animated Film Encyclopedia*; Berry. *Dinosaur Filmography*; Klepper. *Silent Films*; MK 7.

Prehistoric Super Salesman (1969) U.S.; dir. Paul J. Smith; Walter Lantz/Universal. Animated short film; 6 min.; color. Screenplay, Homer Brightman; music, Walter Greene. *VOICES:* Daws Butler; Grace Stafford.

A mad inventor tricks salesman Woody Woodpecker into a "Time Tunnel" and transports him to the Stone Age. Ref: Webb. *Animated Film Encyclopedia*; Lee. *Reference Guide to Fantastic Films*; not viewed.

Prehistoric Women (1950) [alt. *The Virgin Goddess*] U.S.; dir. Gregg C. Tallas; Alliance-/Eagle-Lion. 74 min.; color. Screenplay, Sam X. Abarbanel, Gregg C. Tallas; photography, Lionel Lindon; music, Raoul Kraushaar. CAST: Laurette Luez (*Tigri*); Allan Nixon (*Engor*); Joan Shawlee (*Lotee*); Judy Landon (*Eras*); Mara Lynn (*Arva*); Jo Carroll Dennison (*Nika*); Kerry Vaughn (*Tulee*); Tony Devlin (*Ruig*); James Summers (*Adh*); Dennis Dengate (*Kama*); Jeanne Sorel (*Tana*); Johann Petursson (*Guadi the Giant*); John Merrick (*Tribe Leader*); Janet Scott (*Wise One*); David Vaille (*Commentator*).

"The story of romance when the world was young" in a "wild tropic jungle" is told by a loquacious narrator, who claims the tale is based on the findings of archeologists. The six women of a rather small Amazon tribe, led by Tigri, "dance restlessly, savagely, impelled by a feeling of frustration, of a promise unfulfilled." After they "dance to exhaustion" the Wise One, an old woman, retells the story of Tana, Tigri's mother, who led a women's revolt against the male tyrants who enslaved them. In flashback we see Tana strike a man who works women to exhaustion. She then flees with three other women and six small girls into the jungle.

Soon after, Tana was killed and two other women captured by Guadi the Giant, nine feet tall (according to the narrator) and "the most feared thing in the prehistoric world," a wanderer who kills everyone he meets. The only woman left is the oldest, who is later known as the Wise One. She takes the six girls deeper into the jungle, where they grow to adulthood. The Wise One tells the girls not to hate men, but they must capture men to produce children.

As the six young women, accompanied by one of their tame panthers, seek captive mates, Engor and his three friends from a male-dominated tribe kill a tiger by luring it into a covered trap. The women's panther attacks and wounds Engor, who with difficulty kills it. The women attack with slings and light clubs designed to stun, not kill. The men, armed only with stone axes, are astounded at being attacked by women. Engor gets away but the other three men are captured.

At the women's jungle camp, the old Wise One examines the young men's muscles and teeth with relish. (It's been awhile for her.) The women order the men into their treehouses (for purposes to which the film averts its gaze). The men are kept in line by the women's remaining tame panther, which sounds an alarm if anyone tries to escape. When Ruig tries to attack Tigri, he is quickly subdued with clubs and slung stones.

Meanwhile, Engor returns to his people, who live in caves in the mountains. In his tribe, men rule but treat women reasonably well. After recovering from his wounds, Engor swears to capture the wild women as slaves. His father and mother urge him to relent, but he departs on his mission of vengeance. On the journey, he is chased by a mammoth and loses his stone ax. As he makes a new ax, he accidentally discovers how to make fire.

Meanwhile Guadi, still powerful after all these years, captures two more women (from an unidentified tribe). The huge man even kills a tiger. Engor is ambushed and captured by the women and taken to their camp, where he is disgusted to see the other men slaving away at women's commands. One poor fellow is forced to help a woman fix her hair. Soon Tigri and Arva get into a fight over Engor, which Tigri wins. Tigri takes Engor to her treehouse but when he touches her she slaps him away. She will decide when they make love.

Tigri and Engor become friends but Engor still wants to get the upper hand. Tigri orders Engor to move a big rock and laughs "scornfully at the stupidity of men" when he cannot. She then moves the rock easily with a lever, a tool which Engor had never seen before. The men watch "with mixed emotions" as the women prepare for a mass, forced marriage. Engor quietly makes some fire. Just as he is about to make his move, "Corax the flying dragon" (a small, poorly-designed pterodactyl) attacks the camp. Engor saves a girl by killing the flying menace with a torch. He then drives off the women's tame panther and takes over, terrifying the women with his undreamed-of control of fire. The men now make the women work for them. When a man vindictively throws some meat in the fire instead of giving it to hungry women, everyone learns that meat tastes better cooked.

Engor and the men head back to their mountain home, taking the six captive girls and the old Wise One with them. On the way they are all chased by Guadi and flee into a cave with an entrance too small for the giant. With his vast strength Guadi tries to rip the roof off the pile of rocks which forms the natural cave. Engor orders all the men to light torches. They attack Guadi, burn his legs with their torches and set a ring of fire around him. Guadi dies as Engor does a Tarzan swing on a vine to safety.

Engor and Tigri are now reconciled. Everyone returns to the women's camp to found a new tribe. Four couples pair off (leaving two women with faint prospects). The Wise One marries the couples by cutting their hands and mixing their blood. The narrator notes, "So in those distant days as in today the eternal battle for supremacy between women and men was solved not by the clout and the club but through romance."

COMMENTARY. The makers of this humble B film had two goals: a little mild exploitation and some lessons about prehistory. The film earnestly presents a few basic facts about the ancient world, including a technique for hunting dangerous animals (the covered trap in which the tiger dies), several weapons (clubs, axes and slings), the use of tamed animals (the women's two panthers), the use of tree sap to treat wounds, a man shaving with a sharp-edged stone, the discovery of firemaking, cooking and the lever, and the use of fire as a weapon.

The people talk in their own language, which is not translated by dubbing or subtitles. Everything is made clear by one of the most voluble narrators in film history. All of the quotes above are from the loquacious narrator. As soon as anyone does anything the narrator pipes up and tells us what just happened. When Engor loses his ax while being chased by the mammoth, the narrator feels obliged to announce, "Engor stumbles and loses his weapon but cannot stop to retrieve it."

The story is about reconciliation between good people; villains are seen only briefly. Fortunately the only two villains, Guadi the Giant and the male tyrant who bullies the women in the flashback, are quite nasty. The buildup to Tana's revolt against the male bully is one of the few effective scenes in the flat-footed film. Guadi is not only huge but looks tough enough to live alone in the wild and kill anything he meets. He has an intense, insane hate-filled stare. In his first appearance he has a club, but in his last scene he is completely unarmed but still terrifies a crowd of 11 men and women, ten of them young and accustomed to using weapons. Throughout the film men with stone axes and women with slings, clubs and tame panthers all fear Guadi. The giant villain may even be realistic. In a time when people lived in tiny, isolated groups and followed their own laws, an outlaw who obeyed no rules could terrify people for years.

There are of course many inaccuracies. All of the actors are white and are certainly intended to represent anatomically-modern humans, but white modern humans would rarely have lived in "tropic jungles" in prehistory. People probably mastered fire before they learned to speak, not after. As usual, the women's hair is too modern.

Director Tallas and all his stars had minor, undistinguished careers, though Joan Shawlee was in no fewer than 60 films. Allan Nixon looks like he could handle himself in a jungle. Of the women, only Laurette Luez looks primitive and able to survive in the wild. Only she dances with real abandon. The fight between Tigri and Arva is prolonged and half-hearted, but it is no surprise that Luez's Tigri wins it.

Although it is good to see the women using

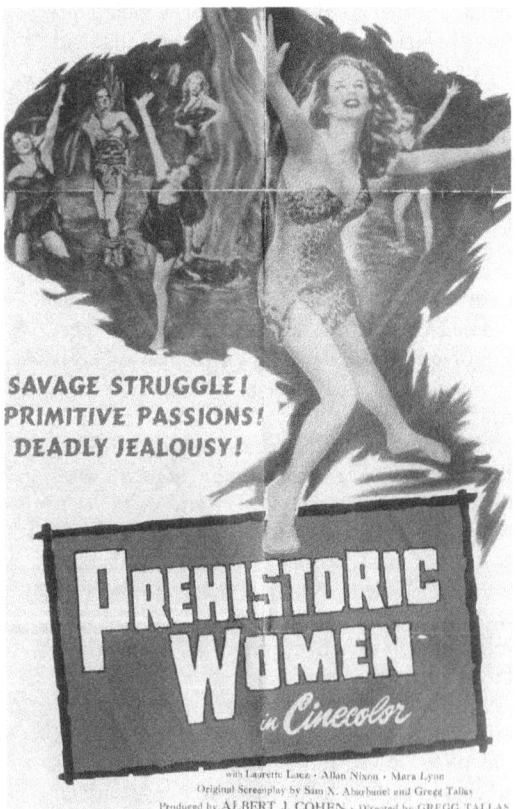

Tigri (Laurette Luez) leads the "savage" dancing girls of *Prehistoric Women*.

sling-shots successfully and wearing modest miniskirts instead of the bikinis of later prehistoric fantasies, the film's attempt at a little feminism is very weak. Except for Tigri the women don't really look formidable. The men are more afraid of the women's pet panther than of the women. Tigri and Arva come to blows over Engor. Women are ahead of men at developing the lever, but a man first tames fire. At the end, they still haven't settled the question of who's going to be in charge — but we all know how that turned out. Nevertheless the film did live up to its title and must have given 1950 audiences some idea of how tough prehistoric women had to be.

Acting is minimal. All the animals are unaltered modern creatures except the mammoth (an elephant with tusks attached) and the ill-made, very briefly-seen and tiny pterodactyl. The "primitive" dances are darkly-lit and prolonged. *Variety* (Jan. 3, 1951) cautiously called *Prehistoric Women* "somewhat ludicrous" with "good exploitation values" but "too elementary to be taken seriously on any count." Leonard Maltin's book calls the film "incredibly boring" and rates it a "bomb." Jones (*Illustrated Dinosaur Movie Guide*), who also gives *Prehistoric Women* his lowest rating, notes with incredulity that Alain Resnais, director of such art film classics as *Hiroshima Mon Amour* (1959) and *Last Year at Marienbad* (1961), "apparently chose this 'Adults-Only' mock-documentary as one of the 10 best films released in France in 1955!" Resnais must have been impressed by the film's honest attempt to mix accuracy and fantasy. Jones is certainly wrong to call *Prehistoric Women* "adults-only," even for 1950. Gary Smith (*Epic Films*) notes that "the generally inferior Cinecolor process is actually quite effective in *Prehistoric Women* with its emphasis on muted brown and green colors." This modest little jungle movie was one of the few prehistoric feature films released between *One Million B.C.* (1940) and its 1966 remake *One Million Years B.C.* It certainly beats *Wild Women of Wongo* (1958) by a mile. Ref: Smith. *Epic Films*; Jones. *Illustrated Dinosaur Movie Guide*; Warren. *Keep Watching the Skies*; MK 5.

Prehistoric Women (1967) *see* **Slave Girls** (1967)

Prehistoric World (1958) *see* **Teenage Caveman** (1958)

Pre-Hysterical Hare (1958) U.S.; dir. Robert McKimson; Warner Bros. Animated short film; 7 min.; color. Screenplay, Tedd Pierce; music, John Brown. *VOICES:* Mel Blanc; Dave Barry.

Hiding in a cave from hunter Elmer Fudd, Bugs Bunny finds a very old film reel — "A Micronesian Film Documentary in Cromagnoscope, Color by Neanderthal Color." It shows prehistoric Bugs (a sabretooth rabbit) outwitting hairy caveman Elmer Fuddstone — even after Elmer invents gunpowder. Ref: Webb. *Animated Film Encyclopedia*; Beck/Friedwald. *Looney Tunes and Merrie Melodies*; not viewed.

Primal Desires (1993) U.S.; dir. Nancy Nemo; Executive Video. Direct-to-video film; color. Screenplay, Monroe Stahr. *CAST:* P.J. Sparxx (*Joey*); Teri Driver (*Mimi*); Mike Horner (*Dirk*); Mickey Ray (*Caveman Leader*); Diane O'Daine (*Cavegirl*); Jaylin (*Cavegirl*); Rick Masters (*Caveman*); Michael J. Cox (*Caveman*).

A hardcore pornographic video, according to *Internet Movie Database*. The credits include character names for both modern and prehistoric people. Whether the story is set in prehistory or the present or both is not clear. Ref: *Internet Movie Database*; not viewed.

Primitive Instinct (1914) U.S.; dir. George Melford; Kalem. Short film; b&w; silent. *CAST:* Marin Sais.

"A woman dreams about prehistoric times" according to Jones. Melford directed dozens of films in the silent period and the 1930s and is best known for Universal's Spanish-language *Dracula* (1931). Actress Marin Sais also worked steadily from the silents through the 1940s, usually in serials and Westerns. Ref: Jones. *Illustrated Dinosaur Movie Guide*; Lee. *Reference Guide to Fantastic Films*; not viewed.

The Primitive Man (1914) was a compilation film which included Brute Force (1914) and most of *Man's Genesis* (1912).

Prometheus and Bob *see* **Kablam!** (1996–2000)

Quando Gli Uomini Armarono la Clava e con le Donne Fecero Din-Don (1971) *see* **When Men Carried Clubs and Women Played Ding Dong** (1971)

Quando le Donne Avevano la Coda (1970) see **When Women Had Tails** (1970)

Quando le Donne Persero la Coda (1971) see **When Women Lost Their Tails** (1971)

Quest for Fire (1981) [alt. *La Guerre du Feu*] France/Canada; dir. Jean-Jacques Annaud; AMLF/ICC/Belstar/Stephan Films/20th Century Fox. 100 min.; color. Screenplay, Gérard Brach, based on novel by J.H. Rosny; special languages by Anthony Burgess; body language and gestures by Desmond Morris; photography, Claude Agostini; music, Phillipe Sarde. CAST: Everett McGill (*Naoh*); Rae Dawn Chong (*Ika*); Ron Perlman (*Amoukar*); Nameer El Kadi (*Gaw*); Gary Schwartz (*Rouka*); Kurt Schiegl (*Faum*); Franck-Olivier Bonnet (*Aghoo*); Jean-Michel Kindt (*Lakar*); Brian Gill (*Modoc*); Terry Fitt (*Hourk*); Bibi Caspari (*Gammla*); Peter Elliott (*Mikr*); Naseer El Kadi (*Nam*); Michelle Leduc (*Matr*); Robert Lavoie (*Tsor*); Matt Berman (*Morah*); Christian Benard (*Umbre*); Mohammad Siad Cokei (*Ota Otarok*); Tarlok Sing Seva (*Tavawa*); Lalomal Kapisisi (alt. Walter Masai) (*Ivaka Firemaker*).

The opening title tells us that 80,000 years ago humans had fire but did not know how to make it. We hear wolves howling as the camera pans over a vast night landscape until it shows a tiny flame in the distance. The flame is a fire burning in front of the cave of the Ulam People, a tribe of anatomically-modern but very primitive humans. The fire is tended all night by Amoukar. As wolves approach the cave, Amoukar throws a firebrand among them, putting them to flight. Inside the cave another, smaller fire is kept burning constantly by Rouka the firetender in a fire-cage, a frame which contains a small amount of fuel, is somewhat protected from the weather and can be carried from place to place. The people sleep in close quarters in the cave.

In the morning the Ulam are uneasy and sniff the air for smells which warn of danger. At a water hole a man casually copulates with a woman from behind. Suddenly, a band of large, hairy, apelike Neanderthals of the Wagabou tribe attacks. They are armed with huge clubs and open the attack by dropping rocks from above the cave opening. The Ulam fight back with rocks and fire-hardened staves but the Wagabou kill many Ulam, take over the cave and drive the Ulam survivors away.

As the survivors flee through the forest, wolves kill a man. The Ulam gather on a small island in a swamp. Rouka the firetender arrives with the fire-cage but the fire is almost out. There is no dry fuel to feed the flame and despite frantic efforts, the fire dies. The Ulam huddle hopelessly in the rain, facing extermination from wild animals, starvation and cold.

Faum, the Ulam leader, decides to send three young men to find fire. Three vicious brothers, Aghoo, Modoc and Hourk, try to take the fire-cage but Faum insists on giving the mission to his three choices: Naoh, the leader; big, tough Amoukar; and little Gaw. They depart with the fire-cage and no plan whatever. After walking through forests and uplands, they are chased by two sabre-tooth lions, which trap them up a small tree. The men eat every leaf on the tree while waiting for the patient lions to leave. The three Ulam fall asleep, until Amoukar falls out of the tree and discovers that the lions have departed.

The starving men eat birds' eggs; Gaw and Amoukar get into a fight over the eggs. They see a fire in the distance but when they reach the site they find the fire is out and the camp is deserted. They eat some burned meat until they find a human skull in the ashes. The men who had the fire were cannibals. The Ulam spit out the meat and follow the cannibals, who are the Kzamm tribe. The Kzamm have two captives, a man and a woman, tied up in the branches of a tree. Both are naked except for blue body paint. The male captive is dying after his arm was chopped off by the Kzamm, who are eating it. Amoukar and Gaw divert most of the Kzamm into chasing them while Naoh attacks the two man left in the camp. He kills one, but the other man bites Naoh's genitals before Naoh bashes his head in with a rock. In great pain, Naoh steals a firebrand and throws the other burning brands into a pond, leaving the Kzamm without fire. The surviving girl, Ika, escapes but Naoh ignores her.

As the three Ulam journey to return to their people with fire in the fire-cage, Ika follows them, talking volubly in a language much more complex than the Ulam's. The men try to dump her, until she mixes a poultice of herbs and mud, which relieves Naoh's suffering. The Kzamm catch up with the Ulam, following the fire which they can see at a great distance. As

The Ulam Tribe try to defend their cave from (inaccurate) Neanderthals in *Quest for Fire*.

the Kzamm attack, a large herd of mammoths appears.

The Kzamm back off but the Ulam and Ika are caught between the cannibals and the enormous animals. Naoh offers a handful of grass to the lead mammoth. The animal takes the grass in his trunk and the four humans are able to get away through the mammoth herd as the Kzamm watch in astonishment.

At night Naoh has intercourse with Ika from behind. She objects noisily. In the morning she wants to go in a different direction but the Ulam insist on going back to their tribe. As they rest, a rock falls on Amoukar's head. Ika laughs uproariously, startling the three Ulam, whose people never laugh. Soon after, Ika runs off. After some indecision, Naoh follows her and the other two follow him. The three Ulam find an abandoned hut. Having never seen a structure made by humans, Naoh throws a spear at the hut to see what it will do. They finally enter the hut and find a gourd which was used as a water container, an object which is as new to them as the hut.

Naoh pursues Ika to a village of huts. As he approaches, he is caught in quicksand, which is the natural defense of the village. The Ivaka people, who are Ika's tribe, shoot javelins from atlatls (spear throwers) at Naoh's head as he sinks. Ika persuades them to save Naoh. The Ivaka women all wear facial and body paint; the men wear frightening wicker masks. They laugh at frightened Naoh, who seems a simpleton to them, but (after their religious leader Ota Otarok examines his genitalia) they offer him a lineup of big, voluptuous women for sexual purposes. They clearly want him to impregnate their women. Ika tries to join the happy party but the Ivaka leaders shoo her away.

Later an Ivaka man takes Naoh aside and shows him his fire-kit. He puts one end of a drill into a hole in a board, expertly twirls the drill between his hands and produces a fire. Naoh actually weeps, utterly stupefied by the unimaginable miracle of firemaking. Amoukar and Gaw arrive and are promptly caught in the quicksand. They are rescued and treated to a good deal of Ivaka laughter but they are not offered any of Naoh's harem. They are astonished to see Naoh painted with Ivaka makeup. At night Amoukar and Gaw club two Ivaka men, then club Naoh and carry him away. They

(I) Quest for Fire

From left, Ika (Rae Dawn Chong), Naoh (Everett McGill) and Amoukar (Ron Perlman) protect wounded Gaw (Nameer El-Kadi) in *Quest for Fire*.

also take light Ivaka javelins and atlatls, a fire-kit and of course fire in the fire-cage. Having decided to leave her people and stay with Naoh, Ika guides them through the quicksand. As they rest, Amoukar drops a rock on Gaw's head; this is the first practical joke among the Ulam. All four laugh happily. As Naoh tries to make love with Ika from behind, she shows him another innovation—the missionary position.

Nearing the Ulam territory, the party meets Aghoo, Modoc and Hourk. The three brutes decide to kill Naoh and his companions and take the fire for themselves. Gaw and Ika hide in a cave where Gaw is injured by a bear. Forced to fight, Naoh, Amoukar and Ika kill the three renegade Ulam with Ivaka javelins fired from atlatls at a much greater range than the villains can hand-throw their heavier spears.

The heroes reach the Ulam on the island in the swamp. As they wade out to the island there is a mob scene as the starving people pass the fire-cage from man to man. Rouka the fire-tender (of all people) falls into the water and extinguishes the fire, causing universal dismay. Naoh makes his longest speech of the film, end-

ing with the momentous words, "Naoh nak atra." "I will make fire."

Noah takes the Ivaka fire kit and tries clumsily to do what he saw the Ivaka firemaker do. He fails. Ika takes the fire kit and quickly and dexterously produces a fire. The people are astounded. Soon they are cooking eels. Next we see that they have taken their old cave back from the Wagabou, no doubt using the Ivaka javelins and atlatls. At night Naoh and pregnant Ika sit contemplating the moon. The film ends as it began, with a shot of a tiny, distant fire in a vast, dark wilderness.

COMMENTARY. When I saw *Quest for Fire* in 1981 I thought it was the best and most accurate film imaginable about prehistoric humans. Now I still think it is a wonderful movie but I know there are serious inaccuracies in *Quest for Fire*'s presentation of early man.

If paleoanthropologists were in the habit of picketing movies, they would probably have marched outside theaters in 1981 carrying signs reading "*Quest for Fire* unfair to Neanderthals!" Annaud's Neanderthals, called the Wagabou, are enormous and hairy and look like gorillas with semi-human faces. Real Neanderthals were short and stocky and probably not covered with hair. The Wagabou look about as primitive as Homo Erectus. However, Annaud somewhat contradicts this picture by giving his Neanderthals credit for brains. They show cunning in their well-planned attack on the Ulam's cave. One group is positioned above the cave opening and is ready to rain rocks down on the Ulam when the other group attacks from the front.

The Ulam are supposed to be anatomically-modern humans, but most of them except Naoh look primitive, with jutting lower faces. If Annaud's Neanderthals look like Homo Erectus his anatomically-modern humans act sometimes like Neanderthals and sometimes more like apes. They use few words and make many animalistic sounds. When they find the ashes of a spent fire at the cannibals' abandoned camp, the three heroes are so distraught they roll over in the ashes, lamenting their failure. The Ulam are often shown sniffing the air for signs of danger. This is inaccurate; we believe early man did not have a more acute sense of smell than we do today.

Firemaking is believed to date back much further than anatomically-modern humans. The earliest anatomically-moderns probably could make fire, having inherited the skill from their predecessors. The Neanderthals also made fire, but the film says they didn't. The movie's opening title says explicitly that the story is set 80,000 years ago. In his commentary on the DVD, Annaud says of this date, "That is what we believed when we made the movie. Now we could add a zero." That suggestion does not really solve the problem. 800,000 years ago there were no modern humans at all. 80,000 years ago the only anatomically-modern humans in the world were probably black. They lived in Africa or may have begun moving into the Middle East. By the time white anatomically-modern people, such as the Ulam and Ivaka in this film, came along much later and moved North into areas like those shown in the film, they probably already were much more advanced than the Ulam. (Rosny's book and Brach's script do not specify where the story takes place, but Annaud said on the DVD that he thought the tale was set in the Pyrenees and Spain.)

The problems with the film's claim to be a realistic picture of prehistory are its depiction of too many highly diverse groups all living at the same time and in the same area and the fact that it got two groups, the supposedly Neanderthal Wagabou and the presumably modern Ulam, wrong. Annaud presents four different human groups. The Ulam and Ivaka are both anatomically-modern but vastly different in their level of civilization. (We know that the Ulam are the same species as the Ivaka because Naoh makes Ika pregnant.) The Wagabou are Neanderthals, though they look and act much more primitive than real Neanderthals. The cannibalistic Kzamm are very stocky and broad-faced and covered with red hair and seem to be midway between the Wagabou and the Ulam. The Ivaka resemble primitive people living in remote areas of the modern world, such as the Yanomana of the Amazon. According to an article in *Cinefantastique* (Feb. 1982), based no doubt on hints from the filmmakers, the Wagabou and the Kzamm represent "early and late Neanderthals" while the Ulam and Ivaka are "early and late Homo Sapiens." But the Wagabou are too apelike in appearance to be any kind of Neanderthal and the Ulam are too apelike in their behavior to represent any anatomically-modern people. The DVD commentary and the *Cinefantastique* article agree that the actors were trained to "chimp out," to emulate chimpanzee behavior, which is not correct for early anatomically-modern humans.

Perhaps the best solution would have been to date the story around 60,000 years ago, call the Wagabou a remnant of very early hominids such as Homo Erectus and make the Kzamm Neanderthals, but in 1982 both Brach's screenplay and the film's publicity called the Wagabou Neanderthals. It would have been highly unusual to have four such disparate groups living in close contact with each other. Since the Neanderthals are completely inaccurate, the Kzamms are just plain bizarre and Ulam are more apelike in their behavior than anatomically-modern people actually were, it is fair to say that the situation depicted in *Quest for Fire* could never have existed.

Frank Sanello's book *Reel v. Real* (2003) comments on the accuracy of many historical films. As the most accurate prehistoric film (except for *Clan of the Cave Bear*), *Quest* is the only caveman film examined by Sanello. He notes that fire was made by humans at least 500,000 years ago, but also notes Annaud's theory that firemaking was lost and rediscovered many times in prehistory. For instance, 19th century Tasmanians (before they were wiped out by British convicts and colonists) could not make fire, although their Australian aboriginal ancestors could. Sanello also quotes anthropologists who deplored Annaud's inaccurate view of the Neanderthals and the fact that tribes in the film invariably fight each other instead of practicing the more accurate tactics of avoidance or cooperation. Another anthropologist points out that face-to-face sex is probably as old as bipedalism and has been around for more than a million years old.

In spite of these inaccuracies *Quest for Fire* was accepted by critics and audiences as the most realistic caveman film to date. Rain, mud, the characters' heavy, dirty costumes, the many dangerous animals and people, the stark, frightening landscapes, scary and horrific scenes of murder and cannibalism, and brave but not too formidable heroes all gave the impression of greater realism than the film actually had.

While in the novel by J.H. Rosny Naoh is a muscular hero who can outfight anyone, in the movie he and his companions are vulnerable, nervous and hesitant — a pack of schlemiels. There are several very funny scenes, all at the expense of the heroes. The Ulam men spend hours or days up a tree eating leaves and waiting for hungry lions to go away. Naoh throws a spear at a hut which he suspects is some kind of big animal. Naoh charges bravely into the cannibals' camp, grabs a brand from the fire, runs away with it and then notices that it has already gone out. Amoukar and Gaw end up in the same quicksand that caught Naoh at the Ivaka village. Amoukar tries to carry so many fruit that he drops one piece every time he tries to add another one. When the heroes get the fire back to the Ulam after enormous efforts, it is immediately extinguished by accident. The fact that the heroes are not very clever or formidable makes them even more likeable. They risk their lives for their people even though they're not very smart and, by the standards of the film's other characters, not very dangerous. We can root for them as the plucky underdogs.

They are certainly nicer than the other people in the film. Even though they are starving, when they realize they are eating human flesh they spit it out. On the other hand, the Ulam heroes seem surprisingly irresponsible at times, especially since they are on a mission to save their people from extinction. Naoh makes a detour to find Ika even though he has the fire which can save the Ulam. Amoukar and Gaw then chase after Naoh instead of taking the fire to the Ulam. All of them manage to get caught by the Ivaka. Naoh is happy servicing the many voluptuous women given to him by the Ivaka and is too dim-witted to figure out that he'll probably be killed when he's done impregnating them. Amoukar and Gaw actually have to knock Naoh out to get him away from the Ivaka and he might not have stayed away if Ika hadn't volunteered to come with him. This irresponsible behavior may be another indicator of the Ulam's primitive nature. Sometimes the Ulam seem childish in everything except their sexuality.

According to *Internet Movie Database*, *Quest for Fire* was made for $12,500,000 and took in $67,400,000 at the U.S.-Canadian box office, while *Clan of the Cave Bear* (budget not given) took in only $1,950,000. This one-sided popular preference for *Quest* is frustrating since *Clan* was much more accurate than Annaud's film. *Quest* was based on a novel written in 1911, when knowledge of early man was very sketchy, while *Clan of the Cave Bear* was based on the 1980 novel by Jean M. Auel, an authority on prehistory.

J.H. Rosny's 1911 novel *La Guerre du Feu* was not translated into English until 1967, and then the translation *Quest for Fire* by Harold Talbott was much shorter than the original. According to the 1982 *Cinefantastique* article on *Quest for Fire* Rosny's book had sold 20,000,000 copies in the seven decades before the film's release. In the novel (or at least in Talbott's translation) Naoh is a mighty warrior of "great courage and impressive musculature" who slays a bear, a tigress and many Kzamm and other enemies before polishing off Aghoo and his brothers. Naoh is as invincible and confident a fighter as Tarzan, and Rosny wrote *Guerre de Feu* only one year before Edgar Rice Burroughs's *Tarzan of the Apes* first appeared in a U.S. magazine in 1912. In Rosny's book Naoh makes friends with mammoths and uses them to literally crush a band of Kzamm, just as Tarzan later used elephants to flatten his enemies. Annaud has a less gory scene in which Naoh briefly befriends the mammoths and uses them to get away from the Kzamm.

In his novel Rosny does not specify the date his story takes place or whether any of the groups depicted are either anatomically-modern or Neanderthal. He writes that the Oulhamr People (the Ulam in the film) have "heavy faces, low craniums, fierce jaws" and a keen sense of smell. The novel, like the film, presents a world in which many human or semi-human species co-exist and usually fight each other fiercely. However, in the film different groups try to deprive each other of fire, while in the novel Naoh is a little more reasonable. Annaud's Naoh throws the Kzamm's fire in the water to leave them completely without fire, instead of merely stealing a firebrand. In the book Naoh offers to let the Kzamm alone if they give him some fire. On the other hand, at the end of the novel when Naoh triumphantly gives fire to the Oulhamr and becomes their new leader he keeps the secret of firemaking to himself "out of distrust and guile."

In the novel, in addition to the cannibalistic Kzamm Naoh and his friends meet the Little Men, the Thin Men and the Blue Men. The Thin Men, also called the Wah, are an advanced people who can make fire, like the Ivaka in the movie. Very surprisingly they have a woman leader, who is mentioned only briefly and given no name. There is no Ika, no girl from the advanced tribe who joins Naoh and the Ulam. Instead, Naoh's love interest is Gammla, an Ulam woman who is a minor character in the film.

In the DVD commentary, Annaud says that he and screenwriter Gérard Brach disliked Rosny's novel "except for the fear." So they changed the heroes from mighty warriors to hardy but vulnerable prehistoric schlemiels. Brach's script says the Ulam have "heavy features" and "low foreheads" while Naoh is "finer-featured and more slender than most of his race" even though all the Ulam are supposed to be anatomically-modern. Describing the Neanderthals Brach writes wrongly "now and then they ran on their arms and legs, much like rhesus monkeys." The Ivaka have bows and arrows in the script. In the film they have atl-atls but not bows. Annaud viewed several previous prehistoric films, of which he admired only *2001: A Space Odyssey*. Annaud's DVD commentary says that he viewed and firmly rejected the Hammer prehistoric films.

There are several good reasons why *Quest for Fire* is many people's favorite caveman movie. It has a colorful, exciting adventure story, humor, horror, pathos, likeable heroes, a convincing setting, sex scenes, mammoths, sabre-tooth cats and a nearly-naked girl who is smarter than the men and at least as brave as they are. If you don't worry too much about accuracy, it's almost perfect. Two scenes are classics: the confrontation with the mammoths and Naoh's incredulous reaction the first time he sees firemaking.

Despite Annaud's claim to be making the first realistic caveman film and despite his dislike for Rosny's novel and for the Hammer movies, *Quest for Fire* maintains several of the conventions of previous prehistoric films. It continues the tradition of *One Million B.C.* and most of the Hammer films by telling its story without intelligible dialogue. Like the older films, *Quest* deals with conflict between tribes of vastly different habits and levels of culture, with the transfer of technology and culture between tribes and with women as the agents of transfer. Just as the older films have a parade of innovations either invented or transferred between groups, in *Quest for Fire* the Ulam learn laughter, the atlatl, lovemaking face-to-face and of course firemaking. The final scene, in which Naoh and Ika gaze at the moon, may be a homage to Moonwatcher in *2001: A Space Odyssey*.

Ika's role in transferring knowledge from the Ivaka to the Ulam of course recalls Loana's role in civilizing the Rock People in both *One Million B.C.* and *One Million Years B.C.* This tradition of women as transmitters of new knowledge may be accurate. It is easy to suppose that women, as runaways, captives, hostages or simply as mates exchanged between groups, really did help spread knowledge. It is Ika rather than Naoh who makes fire for the Ulam. Naoh's failure shows the audience how difficult firemaking actually was in the distant past.

Probably few people who saw *Quest for Fire* understood more than a few words of Anthony Burgess's invented languages, besides "atra" for fire and the names of characters and groups. Nevertheless the languages add much to the film's verisimilitude. Burgess's Ulam language, based on Indo-European root words, had 350 words. Burgess discussed how he invented the *Quest for Fire* languages in "Firetalk," an essay in his collection *But Do Blondes Prefer Gentlemen?* (1986), noting "People usually expect what is called a primitive language to be simple, but the farther back you go in the study of language the more complications you find. Simplicity is the fruit of the ability to generalize, and primitive man found it hard to generalize." Thus Ika's nonstop, birdlike chatter is monosyllabic while the Ulam's few words are often polysyllabic. In Brach's script, Naoh's speech to the Ulam as he promises to make fire begins with "Veda nak a paur. Nao kras remargion ss Ulam. Ulam kas ss Nao!" Ika's Ivaka tongue includes this speech (when she wants to treat Naoh's genital wound), "Tho na me giz nos a tha tho na. Tho na me giz pau na bri lu pau na." An appendix to C.J. Henderson's *Encyclopedia of Science Fiction Movies* (2001) contains a five-page appendix listing the Ulam words and body language for 40 concepts. The DVD extras include a section on the film's languages.

Quest for Fire was made entirely on location in Canada, Scotland and Kenya. A real cave was used for the cave scenes. Locations were remote and often very cold, hot or wet. The actors were actually barefoot and wore nothing under their genuine (and genuinely filthy) wolf and bear skins. Rae Dawn Chong was actually naked under her bodypaint. The stars ate real leaves. In their DVD commentaries Chong and Ron Perlman recall how cold they were and that when they are seen shivering in the film, they weren't acting. Chong says, "We were suffering and it shows.... It was the toughest thing I ever did." Annaud recalls that Chong once became so fed up she refused to work.

Makeup for the principle actors took five hours a day, including the application of artificial dentures and enlarged eyebrow ridges, nostrils and lips. A new latex process was used for the makeup, which won the film's only Oscar. The Ivakas' bodypaint was inspired by Leni Riefensthal's photographs of Africa's Nuba tribe and by New Guinea tribal people. The Wagabou and Kzamm wore full masks, not makeup. The elephants used as mammoths were trained for a year to wear their "costumes" of yak hair and plastic tusks; even after all that training they stampeded and destroyed equipment.

Annaud had a hard time finding the actors he needed for both big and small parts. He spent two years looking for his Ika. He finally used dancers and mimes as well as actors. Gary Schwartz, who played Rouka, and Nameer El Kadi, who played Gaw, were mimes and helped train the actors. The stars underwent six months of preparation, learning the spoken languages and body language and toughening their feet. Wrestlers were used for the massive Kzamm. Masai warriors in Kenya played many of the Ivaka.

Quest for Fire was the first film for Perlman and the second for Chong. Perlman has had a busy career of mostly B work, in addition to the lead in the TV series *Beauty and the Beast* (1987–90), in which he played another kind of caveman) and in *Hellboy* (2004).

He worked again for Annaud, who expresses his admiration for Perlman in the *Quest for Fire* DVD commentary, in *The Name of the Rose* (1986) and *Enemy at the Gate* (2001). Chong, the daughter of comic Tommy Chong, was only 19 when she did *Quest*. She has worked regularly in mostly small films. At one time she had such "street credibility" with young people that she was used in a safe-sex ad. Everett McGill has done only a few films since *Quest for Fire* and has often been cast as a villain. In the DVD commentary Chong and Perlman say that McGill never cared much for a film career. Iraqi-born Nameer El Kadi (who played Gaw) and Naseer El Kadi (who played Nam, a character killed early in the film) are twin brothers. Peter Elliott, who played an Ulam, was already an expert on portraying primates and later starred in *Missing Link* (1988).

Annaud says on the DVD that he had great difficulty getting finance and studio support for his plan to make the first realistic caveman movie. He doubts he would have succeeded if not for the fact that his first film, *Black and White in Color* (1976), had won the Oscar for Best Foreign Film. Annaud has made only ten films as of 2004, but most have been ambitious, including *The Bear* (1988), one of the best-received wildlife films ever made. Gérard Brach is one of Europe's most prolific screenwriters, with more than 50 films to his credit. He wrote three more films for Annaud, besides *Quest for Fire*: *The Name of the Rose* (1986), *The Bear* and *The Lover* (1992). He has written several films for Roman Polanski, including *Repulsion* (1965), *The Fearless Vampire Killers* (1967) and *Tess* (1979).

Michael Gruskoff, the most important of several producers of *Quest for Fire*, had previously produced *Silent Running* (1972), *Young Frankenstein* (1974) and Werner Herzog's *Nosferatu* (1979) and went on to produce *My Favorite Year* (1982). Michelle Burke and Sarah Manzoni shared the Oscar for Best Makeup for *Quest for Fire*. Burke went on to do prehistoric makeup for *Iceman* (1984) and *Clan of the Cave*

Bear (1986). She has been nominated for six Oscars and won twice.

Anthony Burgess of course wrote *A Clockwork Orange*, a tale about another kind of savage. Desmond Morris, designer of the film's body language, wrote *The Naked Ape*, an influential book on human evolution. Another big name associated with *Quest for Fire* was Orson Welles, who narrated a 24-minute making-of featurette *The Quest for Fire Adventure*, which is on the DVD. Welles also presented *Quest for Fire*'s Cesar Award (the French Oscar) for Best Film. Welles narrated a comic firemaking scene in Mel Brooks' *History of the World, Part I* (1981) which directly spoofed the premise of *Quest for Fire*.

In addition to the Makeup Oscar, *Quest for Fire* won Césars for Best Film and Director and was nominated for Césars for Best Writing, Production Design, Cinematography and Music. It was nominated for a Golden Globe for Best Foreign Film. Critics have mostly applauded *Quest for Fire*, but there have been dissenters. Leonard Maltin gives it his second-highest rating and calls it "funny, tense, touching and fascinating" while Leslie Halliwell (*Halliwell's Film & Video Guide*) gives it his lowest rating and deems it a "sometimes unintentionally funny attempt to make us care about the problems of prehistoric man. Lively sequences are separated by longeurs."

When *Quest for Fire* was released, two of the nation's most prestigious film critics disagreed starkly about its merits. Pauline Kael of *The New Yorker* (March 8, 1982), jeered at the film's "overblown solemnity" and compared it unfavorably to the 1981 comedy *Caveman*. Kael often liked to stand up for well-done low-brow films and make fun of pretentious movies. In this case she was right to recommend *Caveman* but wrong to attack *Quest for Fire*. Kael even calls *Quest* "a new wrinkle on racism" and objects that it shows early men (whom she says are "potentially Caucasian") progressing toward civilization through violence. She adds that while the film equates violence with progress this "is something of a fake, since the relatively peaceful, giggly Ivaka" are the most advanced tribe. Kael ignores the fact that the reason the Ivaka do not fight much is that they have such advanced weapons that nobody dares go near them. And in some scenes there is a decidedly sadistic ring to the Ivaka's "giggly" laughter.

Another top critic, John Simon in *National Review* (April 30, 1982) was much more favorable. "The film is to be enjoyed principally not for the scientific or quasi-scientific baggage it caries, but for its scope and gusto.... There are faintly preposterous things here that are nevertheless droll, such as Ika teaching Naoh, who hitherto had sex only in the Ulam doggy fashion, the joys of the missionary position.... On the whole, Annaud strikes a fine balance between ferocity — prehistory red in tooth and claw — and comic, romantic and just visually spectacular episodes." At the time Simon was the toughest critic in America. He didn't like many films. When Simon said a film was bad, it might not be very bad, but when he said a movie was good, that settled it. It really was good.

Another hard-to-please critic who enjoyed *Quest for Fire* was *Video Watchdog* editor Tim Lucas, in his review of the laserdisc in *VW* 19 (1993). *Variety* (Dec. 30, 1981) hailed this "engaging prehistoric yarn ... a polished entertainment that is just right in scope, texture and length.... Claude Agostini's fine lensing achieves a raw epic splendor." However, the reviewer worried that "an episodic screenplay that contains no real dramatic buildup and few spectacular setpieces" could make *Quest for Fire* "an iffy commercial prospect." He also noted that Hollywood's previous prehistoric films were "today all but forgotten."

I cannot remember where I saw this quotation: "Knowledge has a peculiar quality. When you give it away, you still have it." Fire has the same quality and fire is a metaphor for knowledge and power in *Quest for Fire*. Pauline Kael does make an valid point when she claims that the film overstated the importance of fighting in the world of early man. In *Surviving in Africa*, the second part of his PBS documentary *In Search of Human Origins*, Don Johanson shows the big fight scene from *Quest for Fire* (and the Moonwatcher bone-crushing scene from *2001*) as examples of films that exaggerated early man's aggressiveness. However, in the film the Ulam get only the Ivaka javelins and atlatls by theft. They get the other important innovations (laughter, lovemaking face-to-face, firemaking) because the girl chose to join them. As the accidental extinguishing of the stolen fire shows, the Ulam wouldn't have got far by simply stealing other people's fire. To gain a real advancement in their precarious existence, they had to learn to make fire. And love rather than fighting brought them the secret of firemaking. Ref: Henderson. *Encyclopedia of Science Fiction Movies*; *Internet Movie Database*; Rosny, J.H. *Quest for Fire*; Brach. *Quest for Fire* (screenplay); Jones. *Illustrated Dinosaur Movie Guide*; Smith. *Epic Films*; Sanello. *Reel vs. Real*; Fox. "Quest for Fire" article in *Cinefantastique*, Feb. 1982; MK 9.

Race Memories (1913) U.S.; Pathé. Short film; two reels; b&w; silent. CAST: Lillian Wiggins; M.O. Penn; Charles Arling.

"In a dream, two lovers are united in prehistoric and modern times," according to Jones. Ref: Lee. *Illustrated Dinosaur Movie Guide*; Lee. *Reference Guide to Fantastic Films*; *Internet Movie Database*; not viewed.

Race Suicide (1916) U.S.; dir. George W. Terwilliger, Raymond Dittmars; Lubin. six reels; b&w; silent. Screenplay, George W. Terwilliger. CAST: Ormi Hawley; Earl Metcalfe; Kempton Greene; Octavia Handworth; Herbert Fortier; Hazel Hubbard.

After a prologue showing that animals often desert their young, a prehistoric story shows a rejected suitor murder the child of the woman he loves. Three other stories follow, set in ancient Rome, the Elizabethan era and the modern period. Each shows men who fail to have or protect children. This anthology film with stories set in four periods, all presenting a common theme, was released nine months before Griffith's *Intolerance* but attracted little notice. Each of the principal cast members appeared in all the segments. Ref: *American Film Institute Catalog, Feature Films 1911–1920*; Jones. *Illustrated Dinosaur Movie Guide*; not viewed.

Das Rad (2001) *see* **Rocks (2001)**

Rahan Fils des Ages Farouches (1987) France,; France Animation/Canal+. Animated TV series; 26 24-min. episodes; color. Producer, Nina Wolmark; based on comic books by André Chéret, Roger Lecureux. VOICE: Edgar Givry (*Rahan*). When a volcanic eruption kills everyone else in his tribe, young Rahan becomes a wanderer, discovering new peoples, dangers and adventures.

This animated TV show was based on a popular series of French comic books. A user on *Internet Movie Database* recalls a favorite episode. Rahan finds a people who worship a Tyrannosaurus Rex and offer it human sacrifices. The hero convinces them that the Tyrannosaurus is just a big animal and not a god by finding the skeleton of a Tyrannosaurus. The superstitious villagers also think that a nearby hill is haunted because lightning always strikes its peak. Rahan finds a metal spear, which acts as a lightning rod, stuck in the ground on the peak. He fights the Tyrannosaurus and stabs it in the head with the metal spear; lightning strikes and kills the dinosaur. The *IMDB* user compares the *Rahan* series favorably with Ralph Bakshi's animated prehistoric adventure feature *Fire and Ice* (1983). Ref: *Internet Movie Database*.

Relic Hunter (1999–2002) U.S.; dir. John Bell; Fireworks Entertainment/Rysher/ Paramount TV. Episode *The Legend of the Lost* (2000) Episode of TV series; 44 min.; color. Screenplay, Leonard Dick. CAST: Tia Carrere (*Sydney Fox*).

Each episode of this series about an adventurous lady archeologist (inspired by the *Indiana Jones* films) opened with a brief (usually about 1 min.) segment set in the past, anywhere from ancient times to World War II. The only story with a prologue set in prehistory was the 26th episode, *The Legend of the Lost*. The opening segment takes place in the Vanuata Islands in the Pacific in 4800 B.C., showing the destruction of an ancient civilization by a volcano. In the modern scenes Sydney seeks to rediscover the lost world.

The series' main asset was the immensely likeable Carrere. Scripts were mediocre at best and implied that the only reason to study the past was to find treasure or supernatural objects. As a series about people passionate about the artifacts of the past, *Relic Hunter* was insignificant next to the marvelous U.K. series *Lovejoy* (1986–94).

In the 35th episode, *Out of the Past*, Sydney recovers an object which permits people to recall their past incarnations. Her nerdy assistant Nigel sees himself and Sydney as cave people. Grinning lasciviously, she drags him off by the hair for obvious carnal purposes, a gender reversal of an old caveman stereotype. Ref: *Internet Movie Database*; Epguides.com (*http:// www.epguides.com*); MK 5.

Return to Eden (1989) *see* **After School (1989)**

R.F.D. 10,000 B.C.: A Mannikin Comedy (made 1915, released 1917) U.S.; dir. Willis O'Brien; Conquest/Edison. Stop-motion animated short film; 8 min.; b&w; silent.

An intertitle: "Winnie Warclub tries out a new recipe for custard pie." Winnie, a tall cavewoman, is busy in her kitchen when the mailman arrives. The mail cart is drawn by a brontosaurus. The mailman wears a caveman's bearskin and a modern mailman's hat with "R.F.D." (for Rural Free Delivery) on the front. He delivers heavy stone letters, then tries to kiss Winnie, who knocks him down. "Johnny Bearskin, the favored suitor, arrives at an unlucky moment." Johnny walks in just in time to receive a pie, thrown by Winnie at the mailman. (This is the only pie in the face in caveman films that I know of, other than one in *Dinosaurus* [1960]). The mailman flees as Winnie and Johnny cuddle.

"On St. Valentine's Day, Bearskin writes a tender missive." Johnny writes his valentine on stone with hammer and chisel. We see the symbols on the stone and the translation: "I know you and you know me. How'd you like my wife to be?" Johnny leaves the valentine for the mailman, who is seen "Reading the neighbors' mail." The mailman chisels his own vindictive valentine for Winnie, with a picture of an ugly woman and the words "Old maid!" "This fiend in human form exchanges the two valentines!" The mailman chisels his name on Johnny's valentine and Johnny's name on his nasty one.

"Bearskin plans to follow his valentine with a call." Johnny goes to visit Winnie with a bouquet of flowers. The mailman delivers so many stone valentines to Winnie that he collapses under them and Winnie finds a pile of stones outside her cave door. She reads the nasty valentine and exclaims "Old Maid! And from Johnny Valentine too!" She unburies the mailman from the bottom of the pile of stone letters and accepts Johnny's card as his. He kisses her hand. She accepts his offer of marriage and calls her father from the cave. The mailman shakes her father's hand so enthusiastically the father looks ruefully at his hand as the delighted mailman leaves.

Johnny arrives with his bouquet. Winnie promptly bashes him with the nasty stone valentine. Johnny denies sending the "Old Maid" valentine and exclaims, "Ah! I see it all! He shall pay for this!" The brontosaurus, who is apparently disgusted with the mailman's antics, overturns the mail cart. Johnny arrives and attacks the mailman, armed with a rock. The mailman knocks Johnny down and probably would have done worse had not the brontosaurus grabbed him. The bronto tears off the top half of the mailman and throws him a long distance, into a tree where the mailman's head and his body above the waist hang from a branch. His legs, clad in his bearskin, run to catch up. The two halves join together and the defeated mailman flees.

Johnny appropriates the dinosaur and cart and drives to Winnie's cave. Winnie is ready to get married, but her father asks "But, my boy, how can you support a wife?" Johnny points out, "I have just acquired a flourishing business." The film ends with a kiss between Johnny and Winnie.

COMMENTARY: *R.F.D. 10,000 B.C.* is the longest and one of the most amusing of the four stop-motion caveman films released by O'Brien in 1917. See *The Dinosaur and the Missing Link* (1917) for information on the series. O'Brien created three strong-willed cavewomen, in *R.F.D. 10,000 B.C.*, *The Dinosaur and the Missing Link* and *Prehistoric Poultry*. All three wear short fur costumes, revealing their legs, and all display confident, even belligerent attitudes much different from the sweet, helpless Lilywhite in Griffith's *Man's Genesis* (1912) and *Brute Force* (1914). *R.F.D. 10,000 B.C.* is included in the Slingshot DVD of *The Lost World* (1925). Ref: Jones. *Illustrated Dinosaur Movie Guide*; Berry. *Dinosaur Filmography*; Webb. *Animated Film Encyclopedia*; Klepper. *Silent Films*; MK 7.

Rhythm 'n' Greens (1964) U.K.; dir. Christopher Miles; Interstate/AB Pathe. 32 min.; color. Screenplay, Christopher Miles. CAST: Robert Morley (*Narrator*); Hank B. Marvin; Brian Bennett; Bruce Welch; John Rostill; Joan Palethrope.

A musical comedy short in which the rock group The Shadows present British history from the Stone Age to the present. Ref: Gifford. *British Film Catalogue*; Jones. *Illustrated Dinosaur Movie Guide*; not viewed.

Rocks (2001) [orig. *Das Rad*; trans. *The Wheel*] Germany; dir. Chris Stenner, Arvid Uibel, Heidi Wittlinger; Filmakademie Baden-Württemberg. Animated short film; 8 min.; color. Screenplay, Chris Stenner, Arvid Uibel,

Heidi Wittlinger; music, Roland Hackl. *VOICES:* Rainer Basedow; Michael Habeck.

On top of a mountain two animated rockpiles, Hew and Kew, observe and comment on mankind "just as the ice age is over." Everything appears to happen fast, from the unmoving, long-term view of the rocks. First trees grow instantly, then humans speedily build wooden houses. The film changes to fast, human speed; the rocks by contrast stop speaking and moving. A caveman cuts down a tree. An intelligent-looking caveman closely examines a round rock Kew had been playing with, but is distracted before he can invent the wheel. The film changes back to the rocks' point of view, with everything speeded up. They see bigger buildings appear, then a road and carts. Finally they see a modern city of tall buildings coming closer and closer. Just as the rocks are about to be destroyed, the city suddenly stops, then disappears. To the rocks' relief, green spreads back over the land.

The film draws a contrast between the long-term view of the rocks and the short-term outlook of man. Nominated for an Oscar as Best Animated Short. Ref: *Internet Movie Database*; MK 8.

Rocky and Bullwinkle (1959–61) [alt. *The Bullwinkle Show*] Segment *The Improbable History of Mr. Peabody.* Episode *The First Caveman.* Segment of animated TV series. 30 min. episodes; b&w. U.S.; Jay Ward Productions. Producer, Jay Ward. *VOICES:* Bill Scott (*Peabody; Caveman no. 2*); Walter Tetley (*Sherman*); Paul Frees (*First Caveman*).

The *Bullwinkle* series was crudely-drawn but a feast of wit. Each *Mr. Peabody* segment was about five minutes long. Peabody, a clever talking dog, and his dimwitted boy Sherman travel through time in Peabody's "Way-Back Machine." At each stop Peabody finds a famous historical character doing everything wrong and masterfully sets him straight. For instance, Peabody finds Shakespeare rehearsing *Romeo and Zelda* and suggests a title change. In *The First Caveman*, the 58th *Peabody* segment, cavemen are terrified of a sabre-tooth tiger. Presumably Peabody persuades the humans that they are supposed to be masters of the animals. Ref: Scott. *The Moose That Roared*; Lenburg. *Encyclopedia of Animated Cartoons*; prehistoric episode not viewed.

RRRrrrr!!! (2004) France; dir. Alain Chabat; Studio Canal/Chez Wam. 99 min; color. Screenplay, Jean-Paul Rouve, Maurice Barthélémy, Marina Foïs, Pef Martin-Laval, Alain Chabat (Les Robins des Bois); photography, Laurent Dailland; music, Frederic Talgorn. *CAST:* Maurice Barthélémy (*Pierre, Chief of the Clean Hairs*); Pef Martin-Laval (*Pierre with a Tuft*); Jean-Paul Rouve (*Blond Pierre*); Marina Foïs (*Guy*); Elise Larnicol (*Pierre, the Chief's Woman*); Pascal Vincent (*Pierre*); Sebastian Thiery (*Pierre*); Edith Lemerdy (*Pierre, the Mother of Blond Pierre*); Gérard Depardieu (*Chief of the Dirty Hair Tribe*); Jean Rochefort (*Lucie*); Juliette Poissonnier (*Pierre the Herdswoman*); Gilles David (*Too Big Pierre 1*); Jean-Paul Bonnaire (*Too Big Pierre 2*); Alain Chabat (*Pierre the Healer*).

In 35,000 B.C. the Clean Hair Tribe and the Dirty Hair Tribe live in uneasy coexistence. Lucie, an old Dirty Hair man, is determined to steal the secret of shampoo from the Clean Hairs. Lucie's son, the chief of the Dirty Hairs (Depardieu), sends his daughter Guy to seduce a Clean Hair and get the shampoo. At the same time, the first murder leads to the first investigation.

RRRrrrr!!! was the first film written by popular French comedy troupe Les Robins des Bois ("the Robin Hoods"). Director Chabat had previously made the historical farce *Asterix et Obelix: Mission Cleopatra*, the most popular French film of 2002. Chabat and the members of Les Robins des Bois all took major acting parts in the film. Depardieu is the most important French star and played Obelix in *Asterix et Obelix.*

Two running gags in *RRRrrrr!!!* suggest the film's zany humor. Since the French term for the Stone Age is "L'Age de Pierre," every member of the Clean Hair Tribe is called Pierre — a total of 119 Pierre's, including 26 speaking parts. And every creature, including geese, rabbits and even worms, is decked out with mammoth-style tusks.

The *Variety* (Feb. 2, 2004) review said that *RRRrrrr!!!* "gets off to a roaring start but only manages to survive by the skin of its prehistoric teeth." The reviewer concluded that the film had "quite a few pleasingly silly gags, and deadpan tone is nicely sustained, but overall pic is only mildly entertaining." *Variety* approved the "nifty" production design, the "playfully majestic score" and the film's "vivid sense of place"

Zany cavemen in *RRRrrrr!!!* from France.

and praised the cast's depiction of "persistent dopiness."

A week later *Variety* (Feb. 9, 2004, p. 21) reported that in its first week at the box-office the comedy "was tops in France, but exhibs [exhibitors] were disappointed and feared a fast fade-out after it got dire reviews and lousy word of mouth." The next *Variety* (Feb. 16, p. 17) noted that *RRRrrrr!!!* had dropped off 58 percent in its second week and had taken only $7,797,000 in two weeks in France. Ref: *Internet Movie Database*; not viewed.

The Serpents (1912) U.S.; dir. Ralph Ince, Charles L. Gaskill; Vitagraph. Short film; b&w; color. Screenplay, Ralph Ince. CAST: Edith Storey (*Chloe*); Ralph Ince (*Eric*); Tefft Johnson (*Haakon*); Helen Gardner (*Linda*); James Morrison (*Gregg*); William V. Ranous (*Idiot*).

In spite of the modern-sounding character names, Jones says that this film was a prehistoric story in which jealous caveman Haakon enlists an evil priest against Eric, his rival for Chloe. *The Serpents* had the same director and largely the same cast as *The Caveman* (also 1912) and, according to Jones, included two scenes from *The Caveman*. Ref: Jones. *Illustrated Dinosaur Movie Guide*; *Internet Movie Guide*; not viewed.

Settlement of Crows (1978) [alt. *Osada Havranu*] Czechoslovakia; dir. Jan Schmidt; Filmové Studio Barrandov. Feature film. Screenplay, Milan Pavlik, based on novel by Eduard

Storch; photography, Jirí Macák; music, Zdenek Liska. CAST: Ludvik Hradilek (*Havrapirko*); Jirí Bartoska (*Sokol*); Vilém Besser; Milada Janderová; Ivan Lutansky; Miroslav Moravec; Borivoj Navrátil; Gabriela Osvaldová; Marie Sykorová; Bohumil Vávra; Vaclav Tvaroh (*Child Havranpirko*).

One of three Czech films made by the same director and largely the same cast in 1978, all based on Storch's prehistoric novels. See also *Na Veliké Rece* (1978) and *Voláni Rodu* (1978). Storch is listed in the *Prehistoric Fiction* website (*http://www.trussel.com/f_prehis.htm*) as the author of *Les Chasseurs des Mammouths* (*The Mammoth Hunters*, 1957). Ref: *Internet Movie Database*; not viewed.

Sexy Proibitissimo (1963) Italy; dir. Marcello Martinelli; Mordini. 63 min.; color. Photography, Adalberto Albertini; music, Coriolano Gori.

A series of burlesque striptease dances set in periods from the cavemen to the modern world. Ref: Jones. *Illustrated Dinosaur Movie Guide*; *American Film Institute Catalog, Feature Films, 1961–1970*; not viewed.

Slave Girls (1967) [alt. *Prehistoric Women*] U.K.; dir. Michael Carreras; Hammer. 74, 90 or 95 min.; color. Screenplay, Michael Carreras (as Henry Younger); photography, Michael Reed; music, Carlo Martelli. CAST: Martine Beswick (*Kari*); Edina Ronay (*Saria/Sarah*); Michael Latimer (*David*); Stephanie Randall (*Amyak*); Carol White (*Gido*); Alexandra Stevenson (*Luri*); Yvonne Horner (*First Amazon*); Sydney Bromley (*Ullo*); Frank Hayden (*Arja*).

In early 20th century Africa, big game hunter David has to enter a dangerous forest to finish off a wounded tiger. He finds a picture of a white rhino carved on a rock. His African assistant tells him that the "spirits of the past protect their shrine from desecration of unworthy eyes" and refuses to go any further. David kills the tiger but is captured by black tribesmen who worship the rhino. Suddenly the moon vanishes from the sky!

The leader of the tribesmen tells David that "your fate was sealed in the dark of the past" when, in prehistory, primitive whites from the north invaded their land and slaughtered the sacred white rhinos, then made a "false idol," a stone statue of the rhino. The tribesmen's ancestors impiously made an alliance with the invaders, for which the gods still punish them. They will not be free until the rhino idol, which still stands in the shrine, shatters. They are about to kill David when suddenly they all freeze, the stone wall of their shrine magically opens and David finds himself in the distant past.

He meets Saria, a blonde girl who immediately bites him, then tries to stab him. She is fleeing from grim, dark-haired Amazons who capture both David and Saria and whose leader casually punches David. The Amazons take him to their town, where he sees the same stone statue of the rhino. Here dark-haired (white) Amazons in dark costumes with whips and spears rule over blond woman slaves in brown costumes—and no men are to be seen. The Amazons' Queen Kari is bathing when David arrives. She approaches him nude, smiling contemptuously, with complete confidence. David and Saria are imprisoned in a cave together. Saria tells him that Kari's power is backed by "devils." Frequently a blonde slave girl is sacrificed as a "bride" of the "devils." Kari takes David away from Saria and tells him, "I did not save you for others, strange one. You are mine and mine alone." Kari presides over a ceremony in a bikini, a lion-tooth crown, a long, white fur cape and an array of gold (a necklace, two armlets and a bracelet), while the slave girls dance before her. When a slave girl complains of hunger, Kari has the Amazons throw the slaves' food on the ground. Most of the slave women grovel for the food. When the complaining girl still defies Kari, the queen personally kills her, after contemptuously throwing aside her knife. She then commands blandly, "Let the dancing continue." The slaves show a little rebellious spirit by doing a mourning dance.

Kari has David brought to her bed chamber where she demands that he become her lover. He refuses, telling her that men and women should be equal and that he will join her only if she rules mercifully. She points out that his making this demand on her contradicts his alleged belief in their equality and she assures him that he will be hers "on my terms." She tells him that the dark-haired women, including herself, were once slaves to the blonde women and now they will take their revenge forever.

At night, David sees Kari bow first to the

rhino statue, then to dimly-seen figures in the forest, who are the "devils." When David again refuses her, Kari puts him in a cave prison with the other men. A male overseer with a whip presides in the work cave; he vindictively spits on an old man. (David asks the old man, "Why does he hate you?" The old man answers with the only memorable line in the film not spoken by Kari, "The man he used to hate died last week. He needs someone new.") The old man tells David more of the strange history of this place, making the confusing story a little more clear. After the whites invaded the area, killed the rhinos and erected the rhino statue, blondes enslaved dark-haired (but white) people; Kari, one of the dark slaves, escaped into the jungle and came back with "devils" who put her and the dark Amazons in charge.

Kari chooses Amyak to be the next sacrificial "bride" of the "devils," probably because Amyak is the leader of the slave girls. After a ceremony, Amyak is left alone astride the stone rhino. A hairy, masked "devil" comes from the forest and takes her. Saria succeeds Amyak as leader of the oppressed women. She asks David to submit to Kari, then use his inside status to help the slave girls revolt. Although he and Saria are in love, David agrees to this. He becomes Kari's lover and her personal servant. They make love for the first time — with two Amazon guards watching.

Later Kari performs a wild erotic dance for David in front of everyone. Unable to bear David's humiliation, Saria blurts out that she told David to submit to Kari. Enraged, Kari sentences David to perpetual imprisonment in the men's cave and selects Saria as the next sacrificial bride. The men escape, attack the Amazons, free the slave girls and save Saria. Kari's comment: "They dare to rebel against me? Kill them all!" After defeating the Amazons the men and the slave girls fight a battle with the "devils" who are really black men (the ancestors of the tribesmen enslaved to the rhino statue in the modern world) wearing fright masks. As the battle hangs in the balance, a living white rhino appears. Kari kneels and worships it, but the beast kills her, sending the black men fleeing in terror.

Merciless Queen Kari (Martine Beswick), with bikini, fur cloak, whip and lion-tooth crown, in *Slave Girls.*

Saria tells David that in accordance with a prophecy, he must now return to his own land, separating them until the gods bring them together. He goes through the wall into the shrine, where the rhino statue suddenly shatters, the tribesmen joyously declare they are free of the age-old curse and the moon instantly reappears! David is told that he was gone from the present day for only a moment. Back at his camp, David greets a group of newcomers, including an English girl called Sarah, who looks exactly like Saria. They recognize each other.

COMMENTARY. *Slave Girls* is one of the most profoundly, even audaciously, silly films ever made. With its tyrannical queen, African setting and ancient curse, it was probably inspired by *She,* but H. Rider Haggard would have been embarrassed by the association. The story is extremely convoluted and has to be explained two or three times during the film. I'm quite sure that most of the audience at whom the film was aimed would not have bothered to figure it out. (There is no explanation for why the prehistoric people speak English; perhaps the gods who sent David back in time also let him understand a prehistoric language.) *Slave Girls* is the only one of Hammer's four prehistoric films in which people speak English and therefore the only one with intelligible dialogue.

The best thing that can be said about the script is that it was probably intended to be an updating and a more politically acceptable version of the Lost World cliché of a white tribe deep in Africa. Here the white tribe is not more advanced than the blacks and certainly makes a mess of its dominant position. The bad white queen is dependent on blacks to keep her in power. She repays the black tribe for their support by giving them women as "brides," who are never seen again. It is the black tribe which is punished by the gods for thousands of years for allying with Kari; nothing is said about any of the whites, including Kari's supporters, being punished.

In spite of its title *Slave Girls* was not especially exploitative. Kari appears nude once, but this was before Hammer got into real nudity. In her nude scene, Martine Beswick is photographed from behind above her waist and from in front above her breasts. There are two scenes of slave girls dancing and one of Kari dancing. Only Kari's dance is erotic. Fights between girls are not emphasized. When Kari kills a slave girl it's over in a few seconds. In the big brawl at the end, we see only short, quick shots of men fighting women and women fighting women. *Slave Girls* was intended to be exploitative but it is too mild to be offensive. The worst exploitation involves the men, as when the overseer spits on the old man, or when David and the old man both heat their chains over fire and suffer severe pain before they are able to break the chains. The reason the film is universally despised is not because it's excessively exploitative but because it's absurd, talky and, whenever Martine Beswick is not on the screen, not at all exciting.

The moment the Amazon leader punches David is an effective shock and very satisfying. The great white hunter realizes he's in big trouble. However, mostly the Amazons do not seem very tough. They usually just stand around with their whips (which they don't actually use much) and spears, looking mean. They are rather quickly defeated in the finale. Only Kari exudes physical power, just as only she has erotic power.

The slave girls are pretty blonde girls in brown bikini tops and loin cloths. The Amazons are grumpy dark girls in black bikini tops and loin cloths.

Beswick is definitely the only reason to watch *Slave Girls*. No actress could have done more with Kari's obsessive tyranny, incredible arrogance, sexual demands and mad cruelty. When Kari meets David, she is absolutely unconcerned that he is seeing her naked. Her attitude is clearly that if he fails to please her, she can always kill him. Beswick is a little taller than Latimer and effortlessly dominates him. In a review of *Slave Girls* in the online *Images Journal* (www.imagesjournal.com, issue eight), Gary Johnson fully appreciates Beswick's power. "With sharply angular face and a stunning physique, Beswick commands attention every moment she's on screen. Her sensual features are balanced by the haughty, almost evil contours of her face. Given the opportunity, she might have become another Barbara Steele [a British actress famous for her work in Italian horror films].... She's alternately seductive, bratty, childish, and sluttish.... Beswick treats the role seriously, with no trace that the movie should be considered tongue-in-cheek. In interviews, she said, 'I'm going to make this work—no matter what it is.'" Aside from Beswick, Johnson rightly considers the film "a treasure trove for connoisseurs of camp."

It is hard to think of many cases of a very good performance in a leading role in a very bad film. The only one that occurs to me is Sheryl Lee in *Twin Peaks: Fire Walk with Me* (1992). I consider Beswick's Kari the best performances by a woman in a prehistoric film, the best villain in a prehistoric film, and (since Greg Martell's Neanderthal Man in *Dinosaurus!* (1960) and Hirotaro Honda's Peking Man in *Peking Man* (1997) are both stranded in the modern world) one of the two best performances in any film actually set in prehistory, together with Peter Elliott's man-ape in *Missing Link* (1988).

Jamaican-born Beswick was one of the few actresses to appear in three James Bond films, as an uncredited dancer in *Dr. No*, as one of the gypsy girls in *From Russia With Love* and as the agent who kills herself under torture in *Thunderball*. She played Nupondi in *One Million Years B.C.* (1966) and made such a vivid impression Hammer gave her the leads in *Slave Girls* and *Dr. Jekyll and Sister Hyde* (1971).

Beswick went on to play the Queen of Evil in Oliver Stone's debut film *Seizure* (1974); it's not every actress who can play a character called the Queen of Evil, but clearly Beswick qualified. She remained moderately busy into the 1990s, including a stint on the soap opera *Days of Our Lives*. She is a cult figure much in demand at fan conventions.

Michael Carreras, who produced, directed and wrote *Slave Girls*, produced dozens of Hammer films. He directed ten films, of which the only one of any importance was *The Lost Continent* (1968). He wrote seven films, including three of Hammer's four prehistoric movies—*Slave Girls, One Million Years B.C.* and *Creatures the World Forgot* (1971). Fans of caveman movies can forgive him for *Slave Girls* due to his work on *One Million Years B.C.*

Slave Girls was shot at Elstree Studio in Britain in six weeks in January and February 1966. It was the only one of Hammer's four caveman films shot in England rather than on location. (*One Million Years B.C.* and *When Dinosaurs Ruled the Earth* were both filmed in the Canary Islands, while *Creatures the World Forgot* was made in Namibia.) *Slave Girls* was made to get some more value out of the props, sets and costumes used in *One Million Years B.C.* and to exploit the success of that film. In addition to Beswick, Yvonne Horner worked in both *One Million Years B.C.* and *Slave Girls*.

Pouty, kittenish Edina Ronay was in a dozen British films in the 1960s and '70s, including one film each from Britain's two top comedy series, *St. Trinian's* and *Carry On*. She played Mary Kelly, a victim of Jack the Ripper, in *A Study in Terror* (1965), a notable British film in which Sherlock Holmes investigates the Ripper. Michael Latimer also had a minor career. Sydney Bromley, who played Ullo the old man, was a character actor in dozens of films from the 1940s to the '80s. Carol White was the busiest of the *Slave Girls* actresses, with over 40 film parts.

In the U.S. *Variety* reviewed *Slave Girls* Jan. 25, 1967, only a month after their Dec. 28, 1966 review of *One Million Years B.C.* Hammer shelved the film until July 1968 in Britain but they were careful to get it out as soon as possible after the Raquel Welch movie in America. The *Variety* reviewer called *Slave Girls* "a sadistic fantasy" with "a sick premise which gets worse as it goes along" and "unbelievably infantile" dialogue. He praised only the "production values" and Michael Reed's "fine camerawork." Johnson and Del Vecchio (*Hammer Films*) consider *Slave Girls* "a terrible movie." In 1994 Martine Beswick laughingly accepted the award for the worst ever Hammer Film at the FANEX convention in Baltimore. She showed as much class while receiving this "prize" as she had in the film almost thirty years before.

The DVD of *Slave Girls* is 90 minutes long. Johnson and Del Vecchio and the *Variety* review agree that the original U.S. release was 95 minutes. Johnson/Del Vecchio say the British release was only 74 minutes. The DVD includes a short, uncritical documentary on Hammer's prehistoric adventures, *Lands Before Time*; see Part II of this list. Ref: Johnson/Del Vecchio. *Hammer Films*; *Internet Movie Database*; MK 4.

A Special Christmas (1971) *see* **B.C.: A Special Christmas** (1971)

Springtime in the Rock Age (1940) U.S.; dir. Dave Fleischer; Fleischer/ Paramount. Animated short film; 7 min.; b&w. Screenplay, Dan Gordon; music, Sammy Timberg.

Bugs and moths play havoc among the cavemen. The title is a play on *Springtime in the Rockies*, a 1937 Gene Autry Western. Ref. Webb. *Animated Film Encyclopedia*; not viewed.

Stanley and the Dinosaurs (1991) U.S.; dir. John Clark Matthews; Churchill Films. Animated short video; 22 min.; color. Screenplay, John Clark Matthews based on book *Stanley* by Syd Hoff; music, Steven Kohn. VOICES: Corey Burton (*Stanley*).

Schoolboy Stanley, much put-upon by teachers and bullies, dreams of living in the Stone Age. In his dream, caveman Stanley dislikes living in a cave with insects, bats and the other, crude cavemen. He invents the lever, the fork and singing, grows flowers, paints art, is polite and shares with others while the other cavemen grab the best food for themselves, leaving little for old people and children. Annoyed by his constant innovations ("We're tired of you being different"), the cavemen evict Stanley from the cave. With the help of his talking dinosaur friends Stanley builds a stone house with a thatch roof and even a window. The cavemen foolishly try to hunt dinosaurs with only clubs for weapons. When several dinosaurs gang up on the cavemen, Stanley saves the dimwits and shows them his house. Overawed by Stanley's achievements, the cavemen reform and learn to share, plant flowers and paint art, including abstract art.

This short, award-winning children's film, based on Hoff's 1962 book, gave small children a lesson about brains over brawn. Unfortunately it also smugly perpetuated stereotypes about stupid, nasty cavemen, who in this case are reformed by learning to follow the first intellectual. The scene in which cavemen withhold food from children and old people is of course borrowed from *One Million B.C.* (1940) and *One Million Years B.C.* (1966). The talking dinosaurs are smarter than the unreformed cavemen, who cannot figure out that it isn't wise to hunt dinosaurs with clubs. Ref: *OCLC World Cat*; MK 6.

The Stone Age (1931) U.S.; dir. Walter Lantz, Bill Nolan; Universal. Animated short film; 7 min.; b&w. Music, James Dietrich. When he sees Putrid Pete club his girl and drag her off, a prehistoric Oswald the Rabbit decides to be a ladies' man with his own club. Ref: Jones. *Illustrated Dinosaur Movie Guide*; Webb. *Animated Film Encyclopedia*; not viewed.

The Stone Age (1962) *see* **La Edad de Piedra** (1962)

A Stone Age Adventure (1915) U.S.; dir. L.M. Glackens; Bray/Eclectic. Animated short film; b&w; silent.

No information on the story is available. See *Stone Age Roost Robber* (1916) for information on director L.M. Glackens. Ref: Webb. *Animated Film Encyclopedia*; Lenburg. *Encyclopedia of Animated Films*; not viewed.

A Stone Age Error (1932) U.S.; dir. John Foster, Mannie Davis; Van Beuren/ RKO. Animated short film; 7 min.; b&w. Music, Gene Rodemich. (In the series *Aesop's Sound Fables*).

No information on the story of this short cartoon is available. Ref: Webb. *Animated Film Encyclopedia*; not viewed.

A Stone Age Romance (1929) U.S.; dir. Paul Terry; Van Beuren/Pathé. Animated short film; 6 min.; b&w. Music, Josiah Zuro. (In the series *Aesop's Sound Fables*).

A tough caveman frightens the animals but a flapper makes a fool of him. Ref: Jones. *Illustrated Dinosaur Movie Guide*; Webb. *Animated Film Encyclopedia*; not viewed.

Stone Age Roost Robber (1916) U.S.; dir. L.M. Glackens; Bray. Animated short film; b&w.

Information on the story is not available. According to Lenburg, Glackens was a "famed painter-illustrator" who turned to animation and made a series of "beautifully executed humorous drawings comparing modern customs with those of bygone times." Glackens also made *A Stone Age Adventure* (1915). Ref: Lenburg. *Encyclopedia of Animated Films*; not viewed.

Stone Age Stunts (1930) U.S.; dir. John Foster; Van Beuren/Pathé. Animated short film; 6 min.; b&w. Music, Jack Ward, Gene Rodemich.

"A couple of stone age mice travel on their dinosaur to a café where a bear makes a play for the girl and the whole place catches fire." Ref: Webb. *Animated Film Encyclopedia*; Lenburg. *Encyclopedia of Animated Films*; not viewed.

The Story of Mankind (1957) U.S.; dir. Irwin Allen; Warner. 99 min.; color. Screenplay, Irwin Allen, Charles Bennett based on nonfiction book by Hendrik Willem van Loon; photography, Nicholas Musuraca; music, Paul Sawtell. CAST: Ronald Colman (*Spirit of Man*); Vincent Price (*Devil*); Cedric Hardwicke (*High Justice*); Don Megowan (*Early Man*); Nancy Miller (*Early Woman*); Burt Nelson (*Second Early Man*).

A Heavenly Tribunal hears the Devil and the Spirit of Man debate whether mankind should be allowed to destroy itself. Each side reviews man's historical record, including a glance at prehistory.

Van Loon's 1921 book had been extremely popular for decades when Irwin Allen, early in his checkered career, used its title and little else for this misguided comedy, crowded with second-banana stars. *Variety* (Oct. 23, 1957) found it "ponderous and dull." Gary Smith (*Epic Films*) agrees. Maltin is a little less unfavorable. *The Story of Mankind* is so unpopular it still hasn't been released on video. Ref: *Internet Movie Database*; Smith. *Epic Films*; not viewed.

Stubble Trouble (2000) U.S.; dir. Joseph E. Merideth; Calabash Animation. Animated short film; 4 min.; color. Screenplay, Joseph E. Merideth.

This Oscar-nominated animated short told the story of a caveman who is rejected by women because of his heavy beard. He goes to great lengths to shave the beard, which always grows back rapidly. Finally he meets a woman who likes him as he is. Ref: *Internet Movie Database*; not viewed.

Stuck on You (1983) U.S.; dir. Michael Herz, Samuel Weil; Troma. 88 or 97 min.; color. Screenplay, Stuart Strutin, Warren Leight, Don Perman, Darren Kloomok, Melanie Mintz, Anthony Gittleson, Duffy Caesar Magesis, Michael Herz, Lloyd Kaufman; photography, Lloyd Kaufman; music, various artists. CAST: Irwin Corey (*Judge Gabriel*); Virginia Penta (*Carol*); Mark Mikulski (*Bill*); Denise Silbert (*Cavewoman*); Eddie Brill (*Caveman*); Kire Godal (*Cavewoman*); George Kaminsky (*Horny Caveman*); Regan Kennedy (*Gay Caveman*); Dick Warren (*Gay Caveman*); Edith Blume (*Cavewoman*).

In this low-brow sex comedy with nine writers (one of whom was one of the two directors, while another was the photographer), a judge who is really an angel tries to save a couple's relationship by showing them lovers through the ages. These include a cave couple, Adam and Eve, Arthur and Guinevere, Napoleon and Josephine.

The mercifully brief caveman scenes include a girl in a leopard skin bikini, gay prehistoric hairdressers, an axle phallic symbol developed by the inventor of the wheel and one scene of anal intercourse. *Variety* (Oct. 5, 1983) was scornful and said the film was dedicated to the question "just how much fun can be had with bodily functions." Ref: Jones. *Illustrated Dinosaur Movie Guide*; MK 1.

Tagani (1957) Philippines; dir. Wolf Bayer. Feature film; b&w. CAST: Andrés Centenera (*Bahal*); Myrna Mirasol (*Lian*); Bert Olivar (*Sakil*); Bruno Punzalan (*Rakan*); Cesar Ramirez (*Ramir*); Jesus Ramos (*Timor*); Alicia Virgil (*Kiila*).

According to a note by Brian Thomas in *Videohound's Dragon* on the cheap 1970 U.S. SF film *Horror of the Blood Monsters*, *Tagani* was "a Philippines-made caveman fantasy epic.... It had action, monsters, violence and scantily-clad cave girls—everything an exploitation producer could want." *Tagani* was bought by Independent International, which tinted scenes from the Filipino film and edited them into *Horror of the Blood Monsters*, which was set on an alien planet (see Part III of this list). Ref: Thomas. *Videohound's Dragon*; *Internet Movie Database*; not viewed.

Taur, il Re della Forze Bruta (1962) *see* **Taur the Mighty** (1962)

Taur, the King of Brutal Force (1962) *see* **Taur the Mighty** (1962)

Taur the Mighty (1962) [alt. *Taur, il Re della Forze Bruta*; *Taur, the King of Brutal Force*] Italy; dir. Antonio Leonviola; Italia Film/Coronet Film/Galatea. 94 min.; color. Screenplay, Antonio Leonviola, Fabio Piccioni; photography, Memmo Mancori; music, Roberto Nicolosi. CAST: Joe Robinson (*Taur, or Thor*); Harry Baird (*Ubaratutu*); Bella Cortez (*Akhiba*); Janine Hendy; Thea Fleming (*Jia*); Claudia Capone (*Tuja*); Antonio Leonviola (*Elkhab*).

Around 1500 B.C. the peaceful Surupak tribe is attacked by the aggressive Kicsos tribe, led by the Grand Priest Elkhab. The defeated Surupak men are forced to work in the Kicsos' gold mine, while the young women are trained for gladiatorial combat. Ubaratutu, an African slave of the late king of the Surupak, and mighty hero Taur join with Ciros, the true king of the Kicsos, to defeat Elkhab, who rules through his puppet Queen Akhiba. The heroes lead a slave revolt, Taur kills Elkhab and Ciros takes over as king and weds the daughter of the dead Surupak king.

Leonviola made two films, *Taur the Mighty* and *Thor and the Amazon Women* (1963), in the Yugoslav grottoes of Postumia, probably at the same time. The two pepla have very similar plots and the same two heroes, Taur (or Thor) and Ubaratutu. See *Thor and the Amazon Women* for more details. Ref: Smith. *Epic Films*; Lucanio. *With Fire and Sword*; *Internet Movie Database*; not viewed.

Teenage Caveman (1958) [alt. *Out of the Darkness*; *Prehistoric World*] U.S.; dir. Roger Corman; American International. 66 min.; b&w. Screenplay, R. Wright Campbell; photography, Floyd Crosby; music, Albert Glasser. CAST: Robert Vaughn (*The Boy, the Young*

Symbol Maker); Darah Marshall (*The Maiden*); Leslie Bradley (*Symbol Maker*); Frank DeKova (*The Black-Bearded One*); June Jocelyn (*Symbol Maker's Wife*); Jonathan Haze (*Curly-Haired Boy*); Beach Dickerson (*Fair-Haired Boy/Man from Burning Plains/Tom-Tom Player/ Bear*); Robert Shayne (*Keeper of the Small Fire*); Charles Thompson (*Tribesman*).

After a few Biblical lines from a narrator ("and a voice said, let there be light") we see primitive people living in a cave in craggy mountains. The Boy, the son of the Clan's powerful Symbol Maker ("the Symbol Makers are the light of the People!") and soon to become the Young Symbol Maker, doubts the validity of the Clan's ancient and immutable Law, especially the prohibition on going beyond the river. Abundant game can be seen across the river, but the Law says that besides the "great animals" and the "sinking earth" the forbidden territory contains "the God Who Kills with His Touch." The Boy is told that "it is forbidden by the Law to question the signs and gifts and mysteries of the gods.... The Law was given to keep us safe. Unless we live by the Word and the Law death will come to us."

The Symbol Maker is injured while hunting a bear. While he is recovering, the lame, vindictive Black-Bearded One convinces the Symbol Maker's son that he is right to question the Law and go beyond the river. In fact the Black-Bearded One wants to get the Boy into trouble so he can supplant the Symbol Maker himself.

The Boy takes three young men with him across the river. They see giant lizards fight ("the great animals") and one of the Boy's companions dies in quicksand ("the sinking earth"). Since his disobedience brought death to the Clan the Boy knows he will be punished severely. He remains across the river while his two surviving friends flee back to the cave.

Alone, the Boy invents a bow and arrow (even faster than Weakhands in *Brute Force*). He sees the God Who Kills with His Touch, a tall, misshapen creature who walks on two legs. Fleeing, he is attacked by wild dogs but is saved by his father, who has recovered from his wounds and broken the Law to find him. They return to the cave, where the Black-Bearded One persuades the Clan to make him the new Symbol Maker and ostracize the Boy; no one can talk to him until his initiation. The Boy (who has also invented the flute) and the Maiden nevertheless plan to mate.

An injured man on horseback comes across the Burning Plain to the mountain. None of the Clan has ever seen a horse. The Black-Bearded One, now the Symbol Maker, denounces the stranger as an "evil thing" and has the Clan kill him. The Boy argues that the stranger proves that there are other clans in the world and that the Burning Plain is not lifeless as the Law says. At his initiation the Boy promises to obey the Law, but secretly he plans to seek a new way since "the Law is old but age is not always truth.... Someone must break the Law, must find the truth." Otherwise "the ages pass and the Clan remains huddled in the same place."

The Boy and the Maiden are now mated. The Maiden only reluctantly agrees to let the Boy go across the river again. This time he goes alone, with his bow and arrow. His father again follows him. The Black-Bearded One tells the Clan that they must kill both the deposed Symbol Maker and his son, and that they can rightfully cross the river themselves on this sacred mission.

In the forbidden land, the Boy, his father, the Black-Bearded One, the Clan, the wild dogs and the God Who Kills with His Touch (in fact, virtually the entire cast except for the Maiden)

The Maiden (Darah Marshall) and the Young Symbol Maker (Robert Vaughn) in Roger Corman's *Teenage Caveman*.

all meet. The Boy had planned to shoot the God with his arrow, to show the Clan that it can be killed. But before he shoots he sees the God stagger around feebly and decides "this is no evil thing." He tries to speak with the God. As the Clansmen fight off the dogs, the Black-Bearded One crushes the God's skull with a rock. The Boy kills the Black-Bearded One with his arrow, then removes the "God's" helmet and sees an incredibly old man, who quickly dies. Inside the dead man's radiation suit the Boy finds a book—a treasure trove of new "symbols," both words and pictures. The Boy and his father agree that "a new Law will be made. We will seek out men in other places."

As they leave we hear the words of the dead old man, a scientist who had survived the nuclear war which created this world. Radiation had given him extremely long life but made him poisonous to other people. Fallout also turned some animals into giants and forced the few survivors into remote places where their sensible temporary rules against entering radioactive areas had turned into senseless permanent laws. Finally, the narrator tells us, "This happened a long time ago." We are descended from the survivors of a nuclear war! "Will it happen again? And if it does, will there be any survivors—the next time?"

COMMENTARY. Ambitious young director Roger Corman simply wanted to make an exploitable caveman movie for teenagers, to follow AIP's previous juvenile hits *I Was a Teenage Werewolf* and *I Was a Teenage Frankenstein* (both 1957). Being Corman he made something a little smarter and quirkier than anyone else would have done in the same circumstances. Corman and screenwriter R. Wright Campbell devised a tale which rose above teenage angst to consider society's need to examine and change tradition. Many who have seen the little film must share my surprise that the script is actually intelligent. Campbell would later co-write with Charles Beaumont one of Corman's best films, *The Masque of the Red Death* (1964).

The characters speak in serious, almost florid language, as the quotes above show. The dialogue usually does not quite become silly. There are only three major characters: the boy, his father and the villain. (The girl, though listed second in the credits, is given little to do.) Although the theme is youthful rebellion against authority, the father is portrayed as smart, reasonable and brave, just a little slow to change. The tribesmen are not stupid or vicious, but afraid of challenges to the Law which has apparently kept them safe. The film presents these men and their viewpoint fairly, without scoring cheap points at their expense.

The villain has a personal rather than a principled agenda. There are no real ideological conservatives in the film, just people who fear change and a lone villain who exploits that fear for his own ends. The Black-Bearded One, who pretends to be a conservative, is actually a revolutionary. He overthrows the Symbol Maker (what a good name for a filmmaker that would be!) and his son the next Symbol Maker; makes himself boss; kills any outsiders who enter his territory; and even orders people to violate the Law he supposedly upholds by crossing the river to kill whoever flees there.

As quoted by Mark F. Berry (*Dinosaur Filmography*) Corman has said that he was quite happy with the script and cast but felt that the film was badly hurt by the limitations of a very small budget and a tight shooting schedule of only 10 days. He also disliked the title *Teenage Caveman*, which was imposed by AIP. Corman shot the film as *Prehistoric World*.

There are only a few interesting details of primitive life. The hunters use rattles to drive game before them into a trap. A healer sews up the Symbol Maker's wounds with a long bone needle. The Boy hastily makes fire as a big animal prowls nearby, showing the audience that fire was necessary to protect people against animals. The Boy comes up with the string of inventions traditional for caveman films, in this case one oft-seen invention, the bow, and one unusual innovation, the flute. The seriousness with which the people take their religion and their determination to live by it are the film's most important (and probably accurate) comment on early man. The most unsuccessful detail is the absence of names, which leads to tongue twisters like "the Symbol Maker's Mate." Since these people had the intelligence of modern humans, they would have had real names.

The small cast does well but Robert Vaughn, besides being too old for his part at 25, looks silly in a caveman costume. The plot required the Boy to be intelligent and articulate. He is the descendant of intelligent people who had a civilization (and destroyed it) and he is also the ancestor of the people of a second civilization (ours). He is a revolutionary who transforms his world, so it isn't a case of Vaughan looking too smart for his part. But I will always maintain that Vaughn just looks funny wearing an animal skin, unlike the actors who played his father and the villain. Vaughn has always said that he detested the film.

The film concludes with two surprise endings in quick succession. For most of the film, unwary audiences would assume they are seeing a story set in the Stone Age, though there are hints, such as The Burning Plains and The God Who Kills with His Touch, that something else is true. At the end, we are told that the story takes place after a nuclear war which destroyed most of the world; therefore presumably in our grim future. Then we are told that it really did take place "long ago" after all, that we are descended from cavemen who were descendants of an earlier civilization that destroyed itself. But there's a third layer! In the book the Boy takes from the dead "God" we see a picture of the United Nations building and a caption about Hiroshima. This suggests we have just watched a film made by a civilization which will arise after ours is destroyed. Only Corman would put such complications in a teenage caveman movie.

Variety (Sept. 17, 1958) noted with some surprise that "the message is handled with restraint and good taste and gives substance to the production." The screenplay "tends to get a little heavily symbolic at times. But, at least, the symbols are fresh and thoughtful and the ending is provocative." Hardy's *Science Fiction* says "the film is mounted with a seriousness which is compelling." See Appendix B for a list of films set in the future involving primitive humans after the fall of our civilization. Ref: Berry. *Dinosaur Filmography*; Warren. *Keep Watching the Skies!*; Jones. *Illustrated Dinosaur Movie Guide*; MK 7.

The Terrible Thunderlizards (1993) *see* **Eek! and the Terrible Thunderlizards** (1993)

Thor and the Amazon Women (1963) [alt. *Le Gladiatrici*; *The Women Gladiators*] Italy; dir. Antonio Leonviola; Itala Film/Coronet/Galatea. Screenplay, Antonio Leonviola, Maria Sofia Scandurra; photography, Memmo Mancori; music, Roberto Nicolosi. CAST: Joe Robinson (*Thor*); Suzy Andersen (*Tamar*); Harry Baird (*Ubaratutu*); Maria Fiore (*Yamad*); Janine Hendy (*Queen Nera*); Alberto Cevenini (*Hamok*).

[I have not seen this film. This synopsis and commentary are based on a detailed and witty report by Albert Walker, online at *www.agony-booth.com.*] In 16,000 B.C., Queen Neri, a black woman, and her Njala Amazon tribe (who are all white except Neri) have taken the "city" of Babylos (which is really mostly caves). Tamar and Hamok, the adult daughter and small son of the dead king of Babylos, have taken refuge among the simple people led by the Shepherd King in the mountains of Harr. Neri enforces a violent matriarchy. Men are enslaved in the salt mines; captured enemy women and Amazons who fall out of favor with the Queen are forced to fight as gladiatrices. The Sybil, a prophetess, tells Neri that a man of tremendous strength will defeat 101 Amazons and destroy her kingdom. A gladiatrix (whose name sounds like "Galidor," according to Walker) tells Neri that this must be Thor, a mighty hermit.

Neri sends Amazons under Yamad, her chief Captain, with Galidor to capture Thor. Thor refuses to fight women but they attack and wound him. He is saved and hidden by Ubaratutu, an equally strong black man. The Amazons capture Tamar and Hamok and take them to Neri, who fortunately does not know the boy is the true ruler of Babylos. Hamok is enslaved and Tamar is trained for the gladiatorial contests. Any gladiatrix who kills 21 opponents will be set free to join the Amazon army. Galidor has killed 19 women. Her trick is to make friends with naïve new fighters and then betray them in their first fight. Neri has promised her high rank when she kills her last two victims. Galidor quickly makes friends with Tamar.

Hamok escapes with the aid of a little girl who is in a sort of prep school for gladiatrices. They reach the Shepherd King, who has trouble raising allies to fight the fearsome Amazons. Thor and Ubaratutu reach Babylos just as the Amazons execute Neri's latest discarded lover, a black man. Ubaratutu is captured and married to Neri, who tells him he is the King. Thor penetrates the Queen's grotto to rescue Ubaratutu, who is too thick-witted to believe that Neri will soon have him killed too. "But I'm the King!" he protests. Only when Thor is captured does Ubaratutu finally realize his peril and flee.

Meanwhile Yamad tells Tamar that she wants to overthrow Neri and abolish her matriarchal system. Galidor betrays Yamad to Neri, who kills Yamad by torture on a rack and rewards Galidor by allowing her to fight the novice Tamar and another weak opponent in the Triangle of Death, in which three women fight and only one survives. Galidor signals the third woman to join her in attacking Tamar; she then kills the gullible girl from behind. Galidor and Tamar fight, while Neri has Thor in a tug-of-war with 101 Amazons over a pit of fire. Thor holds his ground until the rope burns and breaks. Ubaratutu leads the slaves in revolt and a general brawl breaks out, in which the gladiatrices and the male slaves defeat the Amazons. Tamar with difficulty kills Galidor, then spears Neri, leaving Thor with little to do. (He was probably tired from the tug-of-war.) Little Hamok becomes king.

COMMENTARY. This film and *Taur the Mighty* (1962) were both filmed in the Yugoslav grottoes at Postumia, probably back to back. They have the same director, screenwriters, cinematographer and score composer and largely the same plots. Robinson and Baird play characters with the same names in both films, even though *Taur* takes place in 1500 B.C. and *Thor* in 16,000 B.C. Janine Hendy is in both films; she may have been the same actress listed as Gloria Hendy in Leonviola's *Mole Men Against the Son of Hercules* (1961) and in Fellini's *La Dolce Vita* (1960).

Lucanio (*With Fire and Sword*) reserves judgment but Smith (*Epic Films*) says that *Thor* is "about as bad as they come" and online critic Albert Walker agrees. The clever, treacherous Galidor is an interesting villain and by all accounts Hendy is an outstanding evil tyrant. Walker complains that Hendy sometimes looks bored, even when watching gladiatorial contests while stroking her white cat (like Blofeld in *You Only Live Twice*), but that may have been a good way to convey Neri's cruelty: she is bored even by death. Except for Neri and Galidor, the film had nothing going for it except sleazy exploitation. Neri puts Ubaratutu on a revolving platform and has him flex his muscles as she appraises him as a possible "husband." Most disgusting of all, several women are killed in repeated Triangle of Death contests. Walker says that the actresses were inept fighters. In a bizarre detail, when a fallen gladiatrix is about to be killed, a crowd of little girls cover their eyes and the queen even covers her cat's eyes!

The film expresses an indignant Italian male condemnation of the concept of female domination. The narrator tells us that under Neri "there grew a matriarchal civilization so frightful, the dim echoes of its cruelty and violence have come down to us across the abyss of 18,000 years.... Men were considered inferior beings, destined from birth to a condition of slavery." The narrator also says Neri's gladiatorial contests were "the first time in human history that humans were forced to kill one another in mortal combat." A woman gladiator moans "The only hope is for an early death!" while a male slave complains "The life of a man in here is worth nothing. Much less than that of an animal."

The good people are loud in their denunciation of Neri's system. Thor sniffily informs Neri, "Your throne is shaking, false queen. As free men we are here to restore justice." Yamad says "the rule of women is the most frightful and horrible form of government.... A woman cannot deprive herself of every human sentiment in the name of a superiority that Nature never meant to assign to her." She wants to "build a happy life again, at the side of a man who is stronger than I am." When she kills Neri, Tamar announces, "The reign of terror is over!"

Surprisingly Neri is so confident of her dominance over men that she has a squad of male bodyguards and does not hesitate to give them orders like "Arrest that worm of a man!" She considers women to be more of a threat to her than the men. (I wonder if Hammer's Michael Carreras saw *Thor and the Amazon Women* when he invented cruel Queen Kari of the Amazons for *Slave Girls* (1967)).

The film's treatment of the black characters is even more politically incorrect than its view of women. In his discussion of Leonviola's *Mole Men Against the Son of Hercules* (1961), Lucanio says that the muscular black sidekicks in Leonviola's three pepla, *Mole Men*, *Taur* and *Thor*, each "unfortunately functions occasionally as a comic foil, but for the most part Leonviola has given the character intelligence and dignity; most importantly, he is, at moments of trial, equal in valor and resolve to the white hero." Walker disagrees; he notes that Ubaratutu calls

Thor "Master" for no good reason and is too stupid to detect Queen Neri's evil plans, including her intention to kill him. Besides Ubaratutu, the only black character is Queen Neri, the merciless villain.

The Amazons have uniforms, helmets and a variety of blade weapons, while the simple hill folk have fur costumes and longbows. As in *Colossus of the Stone Age* (1962), the more advanced people are the aggressors and attack more primitive people.

Walker reports that the homoeroticism typical of the pepla is especially blatant in *Thor*. Ubaratutu sucks poison from Thor's ankle, then gives him a massage. The two mighty men arm-wrestle and later wrestle in earnest. Mostly naked male slaves sleep in a heap. Two girl prisoners hold hands. Ref: Lucanio. *With Fire and Sword*; Smith. *Epic Films*; Albert Walker in http://www.agonybooth.com; Internet Movie Database; not viewed.

Those Magnificent Men in Their Flying Machines, or How I Flew from London to Paris in 25 Hours, 11 Minutes (1965) U.S.; dir. Ken Annakin; 20th Century–Fox. 133 min.; color (Neanderthal scene in b&w). Screenplay, Jack Davies, Ken Annakin; photography, Christopher Challis; music, Ron Goodwin. CAST: Red Skelton (*Neanderthal Man*); James Robertson Justice (*Narrator*).

In 1910, bunglers, cheats and comically obsessed nationalists dominate a cross-Channel air race from London to Paris. This big-budget but overlong and too-often silly comedy featured marvelous flying sequences with fascinating old planes, a strong cast, a jaunty song and a hilarious animated credit sequence by Ronald Searle.

Red Skelton appears at the very start of the film as The Neanderthal Man, sporting an idiot grin, who gazes at birds enviously, begins to flap his arms and eagerly jumps off a cliff. We see the imprint of his body in the sand at the bottom of the cliff. As James Robertson Justice sonorously reads the introduction, Skelton, in appropriate costumes and with increasingly elaborate wings, tries to fly in ancient and medieval times and finally in early primitive airplanes. Each attempt ends in disaster, leading into Searle's animated opening.

At the end of the film, we see Skelton again, as a frustrated modern air traveler whose flight has been cancelled. He dreams of flying without an airplane and we see an animated Neanderthal Skelton successfully flying, leading into the end credits.

Variety's favorable review (June 2, 1965) noted Skelton's "very funny prolog." Skelton was then one of the most popular comedians in the world and is listed among the stars of the film, even though he only did a brief cameo. Although he played several characters in quick succession, the credits simply call him "the Neanderthal Man." His Neanderthal is certainly idiotic, but the characters in the 1910 scenes are almost as foolish, so the film seems to be saying that man's capacity for silliness hasn't changed much. Ref: Jones. *Illustrated Dinosaur Movie Guide*; MK 7.

Those Primitive Days (1916) U.S.; Cub/Mutual. Short film; b&w; silent. CAST: Betty Compson; Dave Morris; Neal Burns.

A "burlesque" on cavemen, according to Jones. Ref: Jones. *Illustrated Dinosaur Movie Guide*; not viewed.

The Three Ages (1923) U.S.; dir. Buster Keaton, Edward F. Cline; Keaton/ Metro. 63 min.; b&w; silent. Screenplay, Buster Keaton, Jean Havez, Joseph A. Mitchell, Clyde Bruckman; photography, Elgin Lessley, William C. McGann; music, Robert Israel. CAST: Buster Keaton (*The Boy*); Margeret Leahy (*The Girl*); Wallace Beery (*The Adventurer*); Lillian Lawrence (*The Girl's Mother*); Joe Roberts (*The Girl's Father*); Blanche Payson (*The Amazon*).

The film begins as a book titled *The Three Ages* opens to a page reading, "If you let your mind wander back through history, you will find the one thing that has not changed since the world began is Love." The book explains that the film will show this to be true in three periods—the Stone Age, the Roman period and the modern world.

In the Stone Age, we see the Girl (Leahy) lounging in a leopard skin, as an intertitle announces "Beauty is a part of yesterday, today and forever." Next comes the villain, a burly caveman (Beery), on the back of a mammoth with long, curled tusks. An intertitle warns, "In every age Beauty is sought by the Adventurer." The third intertitle introduces the hero. "For every age there is the faithful worshipper at beauty's shrine." The Boy (Keaton) stands on the back of a giant, docile Brontosaurus, then on its head, which acts like a giant crane.

The rival suitors quarrel and are soon pulling the Girl back and forth between them. An intertitle announces "Youth is eternally protected by the sheltering arms of parents," as the Girl's parents break up the altercation. Her father tests the Adventurer by hitting him in the chest, arm, leg and head with a club. The tough villain never flinches. The father then hits the Boy a single blow and knocks him flat.

Recovering, the Boy sends in his card (a rock with his picture scratched on it) to a Soothsayer, who agrees to see him. The Boy asks if the Girl loves only him. The Soothsayer uses a turtle to read the "weegee" board (spelled thus in the dialogue intertitle). The answer is "yes" but the turtle bites the Boy's finger. The film then switches first to ancient Rome, then to the modern world, and tells the same story of thwarted love, with the same characters.

When the film returns to the Stone Age, the Boy is playing golf with a typical caveman's club as a golf club, a rock as a ball—and a caddy. He interrupts his game when he sees the Adventurer roughly forcing his attentions on the Girl. Still unsure whether the Girl prefers him, the Boy decides to test her. "A man's attempt to arouse jealousy is as old as time" an intertitle informs us. The Boy approaches a girl who is lying prone on a rock, facing the camera. He woos her; she is indifferent. Seeing another caveman dragging a girl by the hair into a cave, the Boy grabs the girl's hair. She indignantly gets to her feet, revealing that she is at least a foot taller than he is. She hits him with her club, knocking him over a cliff into a pond. The film then goes to the Roman and modern stories again.

Back in the Stone Age, the Adventurer finds the Boy wooing the Girl and challenges him. "We will fight this out at sunrise." The discouraged Boy dictates his will to a girl who writes it on a rock with a hammer and chisel, like a modern secretary. At sunrise, the rivals ceremoniously pick clubs and pace off several steps, as in a formal modern duel. The Boy is quickly knocked down. He manages to fit a rock into a hole in his club and uses this improved weapon to clobber his opponent. The trick club is noticed and the Adventurer demands that the referees punish the Boy. They tie him to the tail of a mammoth, which begins dragging him across the countryside. The film returns to the Roman and modern stories.

The Boy finally unties himself from the mammoth and gets back to the Girl's cave, where she is about to be handed over to the Adventurer. The Boy grabs her (so dexterously that the villain mistakenly embraces the Girl's mother), flings her over his shoulder in true caveman style and flees up a steep hill. The angry cavemen attack en masse but the Boy drives them back with a fusillade of rocks. The cavemen begin launching rocks up at the fugitives, using a pair of flexible young trees as catapults. As the Adventurer climbs up the hill, the Boy sneaks down and gets behind the cavemen. He knocks them out one by one, then launches himself by tree-catapult back up to the top of the hill, where the Adventurer is forcing himself on the Girl. The villain is knocked over a cliff, apparently with fatal results, and the Boy drags the Girl away by her hair, as she smiles happily.

After similar triumphs for true love in the Roman and modern stories, an intertitle tells us "And if anything more were needed to show that love had not changed." We then see the prehistoric Boy and Girl with no fewer than 11 children, followed by the Roman couple with only five children, and the modern couple — with a dog. Obviously some things have changed.

The Boy (Buster Keaton) plays a round of prehistoric golf in *The Three Ages*. The caddy had better watch out for the backswing.

COMMENTARY. In 1923, Keaton had worked in only one feature-length comedy, *The Saphead* (1920), which he did not write or direct. Keaton was apparently quite nervous about switching from shorts to features. He waited until Harold Lloyd had made several comedy features and Chaplin had made two before he made *The Three Ages*, directing from his own screenplay.

The three-story structure was of course a spoof of Griffith's *Intolerance* (1916). Audiences had not been kind to *Intolerance*, but the film did prove that movie audiences could understand multiple stories in one film. Keaton put three stories in his feature so that if he lost confidence in the project he could break up the film and release the material as three shorts after all. Each story takes about 20 minutes to tell.

The Brontosaurus on which Keaton rides was created by an unknown animator and resembles Gertie in Winsor McCay's famous early cartoon *Gertie the Dinosaur* (1909).

One of the crosses Keaton had to bear while making *The Three Ages* was Margaret Leahy, an English non-actress who won a beauty contest in which the prize was a contract to work in a Hollywood film. When Leahy unsurprisingly turned out to be incompetent, she was demoted from a dramatic film to Keaton's comedy. Keaton objected strenuously but producer Joseph Schenck airily insisted that comedy actresses didn't need to know how to act. Keaton and co-director Cline wasted a great deal of time trying to get a passable performance out of Leahy, whose best effort at a pleasant smile is a toothy grimace. The camera avoids her as much as possible. Leahy of course never worked in another film, but she was lucky to be in a Keaton comedy which is better-remembered than most dramas of the '20s. Leahy's short-lived Cinderella story may have helped the film when it was released in Britain. The British premiere was attended by the Queen Mother, an honor shared by few other caveman movies.

Wallace Beery was the only star in the film beside Keaton. He played villainous cads in a huge number of silents, menacing practically every actress in 1920s Hollywood, until he graduated to a greater variety of roles in the talkies. In *The Three Ages* he is at his best in the modern story, where he looks like his usual suave cad, wearing a suit and a nasty thin mustache. In the Stone Age story, he is just another big, grubby caveman.

Surprisingly, the Roman and modern stories provide more opportunity for Keaton to show off his fabulous athleticism. I would say that the Roman scenes are the funniest, with the modern tale perhaps a little funnier than the Stone Age story, but the whole film remains entertaining today. It is a vast improvement over Chaplin's *His Prehistoric Past* (1914). Keaton realized that anachronisms, such as the secretary taking dictation on a rock, or the ritualistic duel, are the key to comedy about the past. *The Three Ages* is the major silent caveman comedy and an influence on all subsequent prehistoric comedies, including Laurel and Hardy's *Flying Elephants* (1928), *The Flintstones* (1960–66 on TV; film, 1994) and *Caveman* (1981).

Variety (Oct. 4, 1923) was very pleased and noted the "picture disposes of the argument that a knockabout comedy can't be interesting for over two reels. *The Three Reels* is a continuous laugh for nearly an hour." Klepper (*Silent Films*) and Berry (*Dinosaur Filmography*) were also very favorably impressed. Ref: Jones. *Illustrated Dinosaur Movie Guide*; Berry, *Dinosaur Filmography*; Klepper. *Silent Films, 1877–1996*; *Internet Movie Database*; MK 8.

Through the Ages (1914) U.K.; dir. Dave Aylott; Martin. 965 feet; b&w; silent. CAST: Ernie Westo; Bob Reed; Sid Butler.

"Knocked-out boxer dreams of fighting in Stone Age" in this comedy. Ref: Gifford. *British Film Catalogue*; Jones. *Illustrated Dinosaur Movie Guide*; not viewed.

Tony Sarg's Almanac (1921–23) U.S.; dir. Tony Sarg; Sarg/Dawley/Rialto. Series of animated short films; b&w; silent.

Of this series of 19 silhouette animation shorts, three are definitely prehistoric: *The First Circus* (1921), *The First Dentist* (1921) and *The First Flivver* (1922). A fourth, *Why They Love Cavemen* (1922) is probably prehistoric. *The Original Golfer, The Original Movie, The First Earfull, The First Degree* and *The First Barber* (all 1922) may be prehistoric but this cannot be confirmed. Others in the series are based on Biblical prehistory, such as *Adam Raises Cain* (1921) and *Noah Put the Cat Out* (1922). Ref: Webb. *Animated Film Encyclopedia*; not viewed.

Toot, Whistle, Plunk and Boom (1953) U.S.; dir. Charles A. Nichols, Ward Kimball; Disney. Animated short film; 10 min.; color.

"Ooh-ah-gah-wah!" (From left) *Toot, Whistle, Plunk and Boom.*

Screenplay, Dick Huemer; music, Joseph Dubin, Oliver Wallace; songs, Sonny Burke, Jack Elliott. VOICES: Bill Thompson (*Prof. Owl*); The Mellowmen (*Singers*).

Professor Owl explains the history of musical instruments to his class, beginning with four nameless cavemen. A caveman whistling through a blade of grass led to woodwind instruments; tooting through an animal's horn led to the brass; plunking on a bow was the beginning of the strings; and a man booming on his big stomach evolved into percussion instruments.

The short is a rapid succession of brief, clever scenes involving many periods of history and ethnic groups, but it always comes back to the cavemen, who solemnly chant "Ooh-ah-gah-wah" as they play their primitive instruments while the Owl provides sprightly narration. One scene briefly shows a smiling cavegirl being dragged off by her hair by a huge caveman.

Toot, Whistle, Plunk and Boom was the first cartoon filmed in Cinemascope and was a departure from Disney's usual naturalistic style. The short, which won the Academy Award for Best Animated Short, was clearly influenced by the highly stylized graphics of Disney's rival UPA.

In 1959 the *Walt Disney Presents* TV series had an episode titled *Toot, Whistle, Plunk and Boom* which included this short and other Disney animation about music. *Toot, Whistle, Plunk and Boom* was chosen by a large jury of animators as the 29th best short cartoon ever made, in *The 50 Greatest Cartoons* (1994), edited by Jerry Beck. It is included in the DVD set *The Fantasia Anthology*. Ref: Smith. *Disney A to Z*; Beck. *The 50 Greatest Cartoons*; MK 7.

The Tribe (1974) [alt. *Cro-Magnon*] U.S.; dir. Richard A. Colla; Universal TV/ABC. TV film; 74 min.; color. Screenplay, Lane Slate; music, David Shire. CAST: Victor French (*Mathis*); Warren Vanders (*Gorin*); Henry Wilcoxon (*Cana*); Adriana Shaw (*Jen*); Stewart Moss (*Gato*); Sam Gilman (*Rouse*); Tani Phelps Guthrie (*Sarish*); Mark Gruner (*Perron*); Meg Wylie (*Hertha*); Nancy Elliot (*Ardis*); Jeanine Brown (*Orda*); Dominique Pinassi (*Kiska*); Jack Scalici (*Neanderthal*); Paul Richards (*Narrator*).

Mathis, the leader of a band of Cro-Magnons, is injured and insists his people move on without him. He escapes from two big cats and rejoins the tribe in time to lead them against marauding Neanderthals.

This *Wednesday Movie of the Week* was as quickly forgotten as most TV films, but it seems to have tried to introduce a level of realism into the caveman film just a few years after the all-out fantasy of Hammer's *One Million Years B.C.* (1966). *Variety* (Dec. 11, 1974) complained that the "well-intentioned effort ... barely escaped being a completely still-life portrait of our ancestors.... what was missing was a plot capable of holding interest." Leslie Halliwell in *Halliwell's Television Companion* agreed and called the film "paralysingly boring."

Victor French was a hard-working tough-guy actor. *Variety* reported "Only French succeeded in projecting a character of striking identity and audience rapport." The only other well-known name in the cast was Henry Wilcoxon, almost 70 in 1974 but a star of epics from the 1930s through the 1950s, including Cecil B. DeMille's *Cleopatra* (1934) and *The Crusades* (1935), *The Last of the Mohicans* (1936) and *Scaramouche* (1952). Ref: Jones. *Illustrated Dinosaur Movie Guide*; not viewed.

'Twas Ever Thus (1915) U.S.; Paramount. four reels; b&w; silent. Screenplay, Elsie Janis. CAST: Elsie Janis (*Lithesome/Prudence Alden/Marian Gordon*); Hobart Bosworth (*Hard Muscle/Col. Warren/John Rogers*); Owen Moore (*Long Biceps/Frank Warren/Jack Rogers*); Myrtle Stedman (*Joysome/ Betty Judkins/Chorus Girl*).

Jones says that this film "includes a comedy

sequence set in the Stone Age." Judging by the character names, the leading actors all played three characters, one prehistoric and two modern. The names of the prehistoric characters ("Lithesome," "Joysome," "Hard Muscle," "Long Biceps") are notably silly. Screenwriter-actress Janis worked in only a few films, but Bosworth, Moore and Stedman each were in dozens of early movies. Ref: Jones. *Illustrated Dinosaur Movie Guide*; *Internet Movie Database*; not viewed.

Twist Again (1964) Yugoslavia; dir. Ivo Vrbanic; Zagreb. Animated short film; 12 min.; color.

This cartoon suggested that the sixties dance craze the Twist started in the Stone Age. Ref: Jones. *Illustrated Dinosaur Movie Guide*; not viewed.

Two Arrows: A Crime Story from the Stone Age (1989) USSR; Alla Surikova; Mosfilm. 94 min.; color. Screenplay, Aleksandr Volodin based on his play; photography, Grigori Belenky; music, Gennadi Gladkov. CAST: Armen Dzhigarkhanyan; Alexander Kuznetsov; Nikolai Karachentsov; Leonid Yarmolnik.

Internet Movie Database says this film is a crime comedy set among cavemen. Ref: *Internet Movie Database*; not viewed.

2000 B.C. (1931) U.S.; dir. Frank Moser, Paul Terry; Moser-Terry-Coffman/ Educational/ Fox. Animated short film; 6 min.; b&w. Music, Philip A. Scheib.

This cartoon short showed "life and love in prehistoric times," according to Webb. It was animated by Vladimir Tytla, later a major animator for Disney (*Fantasia*, 1940). Ref: Webb. *Animated Film Encyclopedia*; not viewed.

The 2,000 Year Old Man (1975) U.S.; dir. Dale Case, Leo Salkin; Crossbow Productions/Acre Enterprises/CBS. Animated TV special; 25 min.; color. Screenplay, Carl Reiner, Mel Brooks; music, Mort Garson. VOICES: Mel Brooks (*2000 Year Old Man*); Carl Reiner (*Commentator*).

A short, bearded man with glasses arrives from the Middle East, claiming to be 2000 years old. He is interviewed by a reporter.

Although he tells stories about historical characters ("Joan of Arc—such a cutie!") and although there were no prehistoric people 2000 years ago, the Old Man's memories take place mostly among cavemen. He emphasizes the ignorance of early people. "Nobody kept time. We didn't know, we didn't write. We just sat around and pointed at the sky and said, 'Oh, hot world.' We didn't even know it was the sun." On another subject, "We didn't know anything. We were so dumb. We didn't even know who was the ladies and who was the fellows." "Who was the person who discovered the female?" the reporter asks. "Bernie." "How did that happen?" "One morning he woke up smiling."

"What was the means of transportation?" "Mostly fear. You met something that wanted to eat you, you could do two miles a minute." Fear was also the origin of singing, which was a way of calling for help. The first song was "A lion is eating my foot off!" What was the first national anthem? "It wasn't nations, it was caves. Each cave had an anthem." His cave's anthem was, "Let 'em all go to hell except Cave 76!"

The old man reveals that shaking hands began as a way of finding out if a man had a rock or a knife. (This may actually be true.) Dancing was also born of fear. By dancing a man kept another person's hands and feet busy, so he couldn't get hit or kicked. Marriage began when a man needed a woman to watch out behind him to make sure an animal didn't creep up on him. The first job was hitting a tree with a stick "just to keep busy. There was absolutely nothing to do. Hitting a tree with a stick was a good job. You couldn't get that job. Looking at the sky was a big job, and keeping an eye on each other."

The first primitive comedian was Murray the Nut. When a tiger walked into the cave ("uninvited"), Murray grabbed his tail and the tiger ate him. "We got hysterical. That was the best joke we ever had." The first language was "basic Rock—about 200 years before Hebrew. 'Hey, don't throw that rock at me.' 'Put that rock down.' That was Rock." The Old Man was open to new developments. "When religion came in, I was one of the first in that."

COMMENTARY. The cavemen are simply-drawn figures in loincloths. They look something like the characters in Johnny Hart's *B.C.* comic strip. The women wear either very long hair or bikinis. The backgrounds are as minimalist as the characters. *The 2000 Year Old Man* was

147   2001: A Space Odyssey (I)

A reporter interviews the *2000 Year Old Man.*

developed by Reiner and Brooks as a stand-up comedy routine before coming to TV as an animated special. It is one of a very few animated TV programs aimed at adults rather than children, according to Woolery's *Animated TV Specials.*

The skit is brilliantly funny and has become so famous that a DVD was released containing only the 26 minute program. The DVD blurb says *The 2000 Year Old Man* "is credited with being one of the all-time greatest comedic pieces by comedians such as Whoopi Goldberg, Richard Lewis, Billy Crystal and Bill Cosby" and quotes Crystal as saying "It changed my life." Woolery calls the routine "one of the funniest improvisational schticks aired on television up to its time." *Variety* (Jan. 15, 1975) surprisingly found the short only "mildly amusing."

Despite its hilarity, *The 2000 Year Old Man* is a dark (and very Jewish) comedy which presents a pessimistic, Hobbesian view of man. Fear is responsible for almost everything in the development of man. Primitive people are dumb, ignorant, bored, suspicious and have nothing to do. The anthem of Cave 76 and the hilarity at Murray the Nut's demise highlight the selfish and even sadistic side of the hero. Toward the end of the skit, the Old Man coolly informs the Interviewer that, while he would be very upset if he broke a finger, he would be not at all concerned if the Interviewer suddenly died. Brooks returned to prehistory briefly in a segment of *History of the World, Part I* (1981). Ref: Woolery. *Animated TV Specials*; Lenburg. *Encyclopedia of Animated Cartoons*; *Internet Movie Database*; MK 8.

2001: A Space Odyssey (1968) Segment *The Dawn of Man.* U.K./U.S.; dir. Stanley Kubrick; MGM/Polaris. 15 min. segment in 139, 148 or 160 min. feature; color. Screenplay, Stanley Kubrick, Arthur C. Clarke, based on short story *Expedition to Earth* (alt. *Encounter in the Dawn*) by Clarke (the rest of *2001* was based on Clarke's *The Sentinel*); photography, John Alcott (Geoffrey Unsworth photographed most of *2001*); music, Richard Strauss (*Thus Spake Zarathushtra*), Gyorgy Ligeti (*Requiem*). CAST: Daniel Richter (*Moonwatcher*); Richard Woods (*One-Ear, Man-ape Killed by Moonwatcher*); Terry Duggan (*Man-ape Killed by Leopard*); Jimmy Bell (*Man-ape*); Simon Davis (*Man-ape*); Jonathan Daw (*Man-ape*); Peter Delmar (*Man-ape*); David Fleetwood (*Man-ape*); David Hines (*Man-ape*); Tony Jackson (*Man-ape*); Mike Lovell (*Man-ape*); Scott MacKee (*Man-ape*); Laurence Marchant (*Man-ape*); Darryl Paes (*Man-ape*); Joe Refalo (*Man-ape*); Andy Wallace (*Man-ape*); Bob Wilyman (*Man-ape*); John Ashley (*Female Ape*); David Charkham (*Female Ape*); Danny Grover (*Female Ape*); Brian Hawley (*Female Ape*).

A title announces *The Dawn of Man*, four million years ago in the African desert. We see a series of stunning landscapes, then a troop of man-apes sitting in the dust and eating vegetation. The apes walk on all fours. They interact peacefully with several tapirs. The largest ape (called Moonwatcher in Clarke's novel of *2001*, but unnamed in the film) is the leader. Occasionally conflict breaks out between two apes or between an ape and a tapir. These problems are settled by threat displays without actual violence. A leopard leaps on an ape and kills him. A more serious confrontation occurs when Moonwatcher's troop is driven from a waterhole by a larger troop of man-apes led by One-Ear. Here too the dispute is settled by threat displays without real fighting, but the losers may die from lack of water.

At night Moonwatcher's troop sleeps in a shallow cave under an overhanging rock face. Moonwatcher lives up to his name by gazing curiously at the sky. In the morning, unbelievably, a rectangular, upright monolith, about 12 feet tall with smooth sides and 90-degree corners stands outside the apes' shelter. The terrified apes surround the monolith, screaming and making threat displays. Moonwatcher advances, retreats, advances again and finally touches the inconceivable apparition.

The other apes in turn also touch the monolith.

Later the monolith has disappeared. Moonwatcher sits in the dust, contemplating a pile of tapir bones. He picks up a bone and begins hitting the other bones with it. A bone bounces and flies into the air. Other bones are smashed. Moonwatcher hits more and more powerfully and ecstatically (in slow motion). Finally he smashes the tapir's skull with a two-handed overhead blow. We see a quick cut of a tapir being killed, then a scene of Moonwatcher's troop greedily eating raw meat.

Moonwatcher and his troop approach the water-hole, which is held by One-Ear's larger troop. Moonwatcher and a few other apes in his troop are armed with bones and walk almost erect. Both sides go into threat displays. One-Ear approaches Moonwatcher threateningly. Moonwatcher clubs One-Ear in the head with a bone, knocking him down. He hits One-Ear again and again, killing him. Other apes of Moonwatcher's troop take turns clubbing the corpse. Terrified, the apes of One-Ear's troop flee into the desert, perhaps to die of thirst. Exultantly, Moonwatcher flings the bone into the air. In mid-toss it is replaced by a similarly-shaped spaceship, in the longest (4,000,000 years) and most famous flash-forward in film history.

In 2001, Americans find an alien monolith, apparently identical to the one we saw in the ancient African desert, buried on Earth's moon. The monolith directs a signal at Jupiter. The U.S. keeps the monolith a secret from the Russians and the public and launches a huge spaceship on the long trip to Jupiter. After most of the crew are killed by the onboard computer HAL, surviving astronaut Bowman reaches his destination and the next phase of man's development.

COMMENTARY. Most of the films in this list have poor reputations among critics and audiences. Some of them deserve nothing better. In contrast, *2001* is one of the most prestigious films ever made. It was the sixth highest ranking film in the British Film Institute's 2001 critics' poll and the twelfth highest in the directors' poll. As of mid-2004 *2001* is the 71st best film as rated by users of *Internet Movie Database*. *2001* was made on a $6,000,000 budget, which it overshot by 75 percent. The total cost of $10,500,000 was enormous in 1968. The film was finished 16 months late. In its Jan. 5, 1972 issue, *Variety* reported that *2001* had grossed over $21,500,000 in the U.S.-Canada market. Since about half of a film's gross is returned to the studio as rental and since prints and advertising are major additional costs, MGM did not reach a profit at the domestic box office but certainly did from foreign sales and eventual video revenues.

At first Kubrick and Clarke had planned to have the aliens appear in the *Dawn of Man* sequence. As Clarke put it in his introduction to Daniel Richter's book (published after Kubrick's death), he and Kubrick wanted "to show how ape-men might be trained, with patience, to improve their way of life. It was part of Stanley's genius that he spotted what was missing from this approach. It was too simpleminded; worse than that, it lacked the magic he was seeking."

In 1968 information about australopithecines was still new and controversial. Louis Leakey had found Homo Habilis in Africa only in 1961. Also in 1961, Robert Ardrey's popular book *African Genesis* had postulated that humans evolved from apes when they learned how to kill, a concept which became central to the *Dawn of Man* in *2001*. (Ardrey's book turned up in another 1960s cult media event. In an episode of *I Spy* (1965–68), Bill Cosby's Alexander Scott is seen reading *African Genesis*; Scott was an athlete and spy, an intelligent modern black man interested in the African origins of mankind.)

Some viewers think that

Moonwatcher (Daniel Richter) discovers aggression in the *Dawn of Man* sequence in *2001: A Space Odyssey*.

the aliens' monolith gave the man-apes a physiological brain boost, perhaps when they touched the monolith. I think Kubrick and Clarke intended a different explanation. The aliens want to jump-start human evolution. They do this by setting the hominids a test, by showing them something that could not possibly exist in the natural world. If the man-apes had been hopelessly stupid, they would have learned nothing from this. But Moonwatcher, with his active curiosity, figured out that since the monolith couldn't be part of the natural world it must have been created by someone. That told him that it was possible to create things, to make tools — and weapons. He discovered the bone weapon and began killing animals. Eating meat would provide a source of protein and over a long time increase the size of their brains. Clarke's screenplay presumed that the man-apes were on the way to extinction during a prolonged African drought. The aliens' intervention saved mankind from failure and extinction. (One thing wrong with this scenario is the fact that early hominids got meat by scavenging dead animals, without having to kill them.)

Another question is why the man-apes suddenly began walking erect. This signals the audience that they are becoming human but why did they start walking upright at that exact time? The best explanation I can think of is that the hominids could have walked erect before but they had no reason to. It was more natural and convenient for them to walk on all fours. When they developed weapons, they had a reason to stand erect so they could better use blunt-trauma weapons.

Kubrick would probably have been annoyed to hear this, but his *Dawn of Man* has several similarities with Griffith's *Brute Force* (1914). In the silent film, the hero's band of humans is about to be wiped out by hostile humans who have the same weapons. Both sides have clubs, but the villains are more numerous. Weakhands invents a superior weapon and saves the day. In *The Dawn of Man* both sides are equally armed because neither has any weapons at all. One-Ear's more numerous troop drives Moonwatcher's troop from their water supply until Moonwatcher invents the first weapon and reverses the tide of battle.

The big difference between the two films is that Griffith thinks that the invention of weapons was a good development because it allowed people to defend themselves and establish law and order, thus making it possible for them to advance in other spheres of activity. Kubrick and Clarke see the first weapons as the start of mankind's long history of violence and war. Griffith and Clarke and Kubrick would all agree that weapons were a necessary part of man's advancement. Kubrick's film was based on the Killer Ape Theory of early man, the idea that man was a successful aggressor. This theory has now fallen out of favor. The first hominids are now seen as vegetarians and scavengers rather than hunters. In *Surviving in Africa*, the second part of his PBS documentary *In Search of Human Origins*, Don Johanson shows the Moonwatcher bone-crushing scene (and a big fight scene from *Quest for Fire*) as examples of films that got early man wrong.

We have a detailed account of the preparation and filming of the *Dawn of Man* by an insider, Daniel Richter, who choreographed the man-apes, played Moonwatcher and wrote about it in his book *Moonwatcher's Memoir* (2002). Richter was an impoverished, 28-year-old American mime working in London when Kubrick hired him in October 1966. He worked for ten months before he was ready to shoot the sequence in August 1967. Richter had studied at the American Mime Theatre and had observed many of the world's best mimes in Europe and Japan. He was especially impressed by Japan's Noh theatre. Remarkably, Richter was a heroin addict during the whole period he worked on *2001*. His habit was controlled by drugs provided by Britain's National Health Service, but he was terrified that Kubrick would find out his secret and fire him. A disgruntled employee did tell Kubrick, who kept Richter on the film.

Kubrick was determined that his whole film should be scientifically accurate. Not only must the future sets and costumes resemble real spaceships and astronauts' equipment, but the man-apes (never called "ape-men" by the filmmakers) had to be unprecedentedly realistic hominids. Kubrick, Richter and makeup artist Stuart Freeborn (a veteran of dozens of films, including Kubrick's *Dr. Strangelove*) read books and technical articles on early man. While Freeborn struggled with the difficult technical problems of turning actors into convincing apes, Richter visited the apes at London zoos, studied reconstructions of early hominids by Maurice Wilson of London's Museum of Natural History and viewed films by primatologist

Jane Goodall, her husband Hugo van Lawick and other scientists.

Richter got his best inspirations from gibbons, who spend most of their time in trees but walk erect when on the ground, while chimps and gorillas walk on their knuckles. He was also inspired by Guy, a powerful gorilla who had been kept in a too-small cage at a zoo for 20 years. It was not certain that Richter would perform Moonwatcher but eventually Kubrick decided that in addition to training the other actors Richter would play the lead man-ape. Since Moonwatcher was the leader he had to be the biggest ape, so the actors used for the other apes had to be even smaller than Richter. He discovered that actors could not be taught movement and athletes could not learn acting in the time available. He finally hired young professional dancers from TV variety shows. Women were ineligible because their hips were too wide. The four female apes in the film were played by male actors.

Both the futuristic scenes and the prehistoric sequence in *2001* required major innovations in filmmaking techniques. One of Freeborn's chief problems was that apes' heads and legs are much smaller than human heads and legs. Freeborn built up the ape-suit shoulders to make the actors' heads look smaller. He had to develop new urethane materials for the body suits and masks and create new techniques to permit actors inside the masks to snarl and vocalize realistically. Actors could work the apes' tongues with their own tongues. Freeborn's costumes and masks and Richter's choreography were miracles of realism, more than a decade before the work of makeup master Rick Baker and primate actor Peter Elliott.

Stephanie Schwamm's *The Making of 2001* includes a 7-page chapter by Herb A. Lightman on the front-projection system used for the *Dawn of Man*. Lightman writes "Perhaps the most significant single technique utilized in MGM's *2001: A Space Odyssey*—considered in terms of its potential value to the film industry as a whole—is Stanley Kramer's extensive use of a completely new departure in the application of front-projection for background transparencies." Kubrick's team found the stark desert scenery he needed for the man-apes in Namibia (then Southwest Africa) but the director felt that filming on location would have been difficult and prohibitively expensive. (Nevertheless, a few years later Hammer made *Creatures the World Forgot* (1972) on location in Namibia.) The size of the required backgrounds meant that the standard techniques (use of a painted backdrop, the blue-screen matting system or large-scale rear-projection) would have lacked the realism the director demanded. Kubrick sent a team to Namibia to photograph the backgrounds. His specialists built the biggest front-projection screen used up to that time (40 × 90 feet) on one of the biggest sound stages in the world, Stage Three at London's MGM Studio, and invented a powerful 8 × 10 projector to project the backgrounds on the highly-reflective giant screen.

The *Dawn of Man* was shot after all the futuristic scenes had been completed. Many problems occurred during filming. The actors playing female apes had to befriend the two real baby chimps who played the baby apes. Flies had to be doped with carbon dioxide to make them passive in scenes showing flies on the apes' faces. The twelve tapirs used in the sequence were temperamental and the leopard, which was supposed to "kill" an ape played by its trainer Terry Duggan, instead almost attacked Richter. A tapir was killed in a fall on the set. Richter insists this was an accident, but it was useful for the filmmakers. They stored the dead animal in a refrigerator and later brought him out, suspended him from wires and filmed him falling, to simulate a tapir being killed by the man-apes.

The actors had to wear large, hard contact lenses which could injure their eyes if left in too long. Their suits quickly became extremely hot and it was difficult to breath in the masks. The actors, who had to perform quick, powerful ape movements, soon become exhausted and were unable to work for more than two minutes at a time. Kubrick insisted on using real meat in the meat-eating scene, even though the raw meat nauseated the actors, fat from the meat damaged the ape costumes and Freeborn came up with a substitute material which he said would look exactly like meat on the screen. Always the perfectionist, Kubrick insisted on many retakes. Richter says he "killed" Richard Woods, who played One-Ear, 32 times, as well as smashing several skulls during the bone-smashing scene. The ape scenes were filmed silent, with Kubrick frequently shouting directions. The best ape actors added ape sounds later.

Richter was forced to choose one credit,

either as actor or choreographer. He choose the actor's credit and is listed fourth in the cast, after Keir Dullea, Gary Lockwood and William Sylvester. (Even people who admire the *Dawn of Man* would probably place Richter fifth, after Douglas Rain as the voice of HAL.) Geoffrey Unsworth, one of the most prestigious cinematographers in the world, shot the future scenes and is the sole director of photography credited for *2001*. John Alcott, who photographed the *Dawn of Man*, was credited for "additional photography." Alcott went on to be the principal photographer on three more Kubrick films, *A Clockwork Orange* (1971), *Barry Lyndon* (1975) and *The Shining* (1980). (In 1982 Alcott photographed a much less realistic view of ancient man, the sword-and-sorcery epic *The Beastmaster*.)

The film does not credit Clarke's stories; most secondary sources cite his story *The Sentinel*, about the discovery of a monolith on the moon, but not his story *Encounter in the Dawn* (retitled *Expedition to Earth*), about a meeting between aliens and Earth's man-apes. The cast credits list Richard Wood as the actor who played One-Ear but this is wrong, according to Richter's book and *Internet Movie Database*, both of which say he is Richard Woods.

2001 was nominated for Oscars for Best Screenplay, Direction and Art Direction and won for Best Special Effects. Surprisingly it was not nominated for Best Picture. There was no Oscar for makeup in 1968, but *Planet of the Apes* won a special Oscar for its makeup. Arthur C. Clarke recalls in his introduction to Richter's book that "I wondered, as loudly as possible, whether the judges had passed over *2001* because they thought we used real apes." At least one reviewer made that error. The *Newsweek* review by Joseph Morgenstern, reprinted in Schwamm's *The Making of 2001*, said the *Dawn of Man* was made by "cutting constantly between real apes and actors." (Only the baby chimps were real apes.)

The music in *2001* is as famous as the film's visual splendors and funereal pace. Kubrick hired Alex North, who had composed the score for Kubrick's *Spartacus* (1960), to write music for his science fiction project. In the end, Kubrick replaced North's work with music by several classical composers. Two pieces are heard in the *Dawn of Man*. When the monolith first appears to the man-apes we hear contemporary composer Gyorgy Ligeti's choral *Requiem for Soprano, Mezzo-Soprano, Two Mixed Choirs and Orchestra*, which accompanies the uproar the incomprehensible vision produces among the apes. When Moonwatcher smashes the bones we get Richard Strauss's *Thus Spake Zarathushtra*, which most people think of as "the *2001* music." The majestic Strauss fanfare is heard repeatedly at key moments throughout the film, including during the enigmatic final scene.

Variety (April 3, 1968) was cautious about *2001*, which their reviewer described as "big, beautiful but plodding ... a major achievement in special effects and cinematography" which "lacks dramatic appeal." He concluded "*2001* is not a cinematic landmark." *Variety* especially damned the "surprisingly dull prolog" featuring the man-apes and said "the makeup is amateurish compared to that in *Planet of the Apes*." Other reviewers were similarly standoffish.

In an introduction to Schwamm's *The Making of 2001*, Jay Cocks wrote "The first public screening of *2001: A Space Odyssey* was a catastrophe.... The first laughter began with the appearance of the first apes. This was only a few months after *Planet of the Apes* had been released and become a big hit.... The laughter stopped after a time, but the restiveness increased, turning finally to outright mockery and hostility during the Star Gate sequence." Kubrick was forced to cut the film. The *Variety* review gives the length as 160 minutes but the best-known version is 139 minutes. The DVD is 148 minutes, but that includes 4 minutes of music over a blank screen after the end of the credits.

Frederick J. Ordway was scientific and technical consultant on *2001*. After the film was completed Ordway wrote an alarmed memo to Kubrick (found in Schwamm's *The Making of 2001*), raising several points. The first was "The *Dawn of Man* scene should be shortened, and above all narrated. The importance of this cannot be overemphasized. No one with whom I talked understood the real meaning of this visually beautiful and deeply significant sequence. Its intended impact was lost. Certainly some reviewers, aided by press releases and Arthur Clarke's lucid comments, knew what it was all about, but the audience doesn't." Kubrick apparently did cut the *Dawn of Man* but he resolutely refused to add narration. Michel Chion, in his book *Kubrick's Cinema*

Odyssey (2001), wrote, "I think the wonderful cut, simultaneously in both sound and image, that connects the image of apes eating meat to a savage struggle between two clans could have been the result of one of these cuts."

MGM apparently agreed with Ordway that the ape scenes were a problem. The film's original theatrical trailer (included on the DVD) includes many shots from the futuristic scenes but completely omits *The Dawn of Man*.

Charles Champlin, reviewing for the *Los Angeles Times*, called the sequence "interminable." Kubrick certainly holds shots of apes sitting in the dirt munching vegetation far longer than other directors would have, but there are also many shots in the film's futuristic scenes which are held for an amazingly long time. I think the *Dawn of Man* is crowded with detail and moves fast for a Kubrick film. A lot happens in 15 minutes: introducing the apes and establishing their passivity; the leopard killing an ape; the apes being driven from their water-hole; establishing Moonwatcher as an individual; the apes' reaction to the monolith; Moonwatcher smashing the bones; the first meat-eating; and the final fight at the water-hole.

Since 1968, the position of *2001* as the most prestigious SF film ever made has solidified, as reflected in the long note on Kubrick's film in Hardy's *Science Fiction*. However, even Hardy has some reservations about Kubrick's misanthropic outlook, noting that "for Kubrick, man is little more than the property of the unseen aliens." Misanthropy is at the heart of Kubrick's and Clarke's vision. The apes become human precisely when they learn to kill. As online critic James Berardinelli writes, "Like the Fruit of Knowledge in the Garden of Eden, this leads to a spurt of change and a fall from grace." The famous cut from the bone to the spaceship indicates the Kubrick and Clarke feel that little has changed in 4,000,000 years since the man-apes became the first murderers. Technological change has accelerated but human aggression has remained the same. In the modern scenes, the cold, bureaucratic, ruthless astronauts are totally unlikeable, much less sympathetic than HAL the malfunctioning computer. In his introduction to Richter's book Clarke recalls that when he saw the film at the United Nations with Secretary General U Thant and other diplomats, as he watched *The Dawn of Man*, "this, I suddenly realized, is where all the trouble started and this very building is where we are trying to stop it."

I recognize the greatness of *2001* but I find the film's misanthropy rather distasteful. The famous flash-forward from bone to spaceship dismisses all of human history, both primitive and modern. At the end, the astronaut Bowman has passed through space and time and has nothing to do with Earth. He has left mankind behind. The people on Earth are an irrelevancy, since the only significant legacy of mankind is Bowman's superbeing. Humans are now free to destroy themselves, since they are of no further interest to the aliens. (This reading was undermined by the more cheerful sequel, *2010* (1984).)

The *Dawn of Man* contains scenes that audiences remember permanently. The astounding appearance of the monolith among the apes, Moonwatcher exultantly breaking bones with his new weapon, and the bone suddenly turning into the spaceship are among the most famous scenes in film history. User's comments in *Internet Movie Database* show that many fans are fascinated by the film but admit they do not understand it. For some people, *2001* becomes less fascinating once it is explained to them. The mystery is more interesting than the solution. Kubrick's achievement is not only that he was able to express his challenging ideas on screen but that he did so with visual splendors and a narrative which, however confusing, brought in a huge audience.

Ironically, *The Dawn of Man* may hold up better than the futuristic scenes in *2001*. The vast spaceships full of future technology fascinated audiences in 1968. They had seen nothing like it and believed that perhaps it would soon actually come to pass. Now we have seen many expensive space films and we know that huge spaceships and bases on the moon have not been built and perhaps never will be. But our primitive hominid ancestors did exist and no films except *2001* and the little-known *Missing Link* (1988) have depicted them.

The Dawn of Man was burlesqued in Mel Brooks' *History of the World Part I* (1981). The long-delayed sequel *2010* (1984), made from a Clarke novel with a more famous cast than the original but a less-inspired director, was routine. Ref: Richter. *Moonwatcher's Memoir*; Schwam. *Making of 2001: A Space Odyssey*; Jones. *Illustrated Dinosaur Movie Guide*; Hardy. *Overlook Film Encyclopedia: Science Fiction*; *Internet Movie Database*; MK 10.

An Unearthly Child (1963) *see* Doctor Who (1963–1989)

The Virgin Goddess (1950) *see* Prehistoric Women (1950)

Viva Rock Vegas (2000) *see* The Flintstones in Viva Rock Vegas (2000)

Voláni Radu (1978) Czechoslovakia; dir. Jan Schmidt; Filmové Studio Barrandov. Feature film. Screenplay, Milan Pavlik, based on novel by Eduard Storch; photography, Jirí Macák; music, Zdenek Liska. *CAST:* Ludvik Hradilek; Jirí Bartoska; Milada Janderová; Miroslav Moravec; Gabriela Osvaldová; Bohumil Vávra.
One of three Czech films made by the same director and largely the same cast, all based on Storch's prehistoric novels. See also *Na Veliké Rece* and *Settlement of Crows* (both also 1978). Ref: *Internet Movie Database*; not viewed.

Wanpaku Omukashi Kum-Kum (1975) *see* Kum-Kum (1975)

Wars of the Primal Tribes (1914) *see* Brute Force (1914)

Way Back When a Nag Was Only a Horse (1940) U.S.; dir. Dave Fleischer; Fleischer Studio/Paramount. Animated short film; 7 min.; b&w. Screenplay, Joseph Stultz. (In the *Stone Age Cartoons* series).
Dragged to a store by his wife, a caveman loiters at the music counter with a pretty salesgirl. Paramount's and Fleischer's *Stone Age Cartoon* series featured anachronistic situation comedy apparently somewhat similar to *The Flintstones*. Ref: Webb. *The Animated Film Encyclopedia*; not viewed.

Way Back When a Night Club Was a Stick (1940) U.S.; dir. Dave Fleischer; Fleischer Studio/Paramount. Animated short film; 7 min.; b&w. Screenplay, William Turner. (In the *Stone Age Cartoons* series).
"Mr. Stonebroke forsakes babysitting to sneak off to Lucky's Wreck-reation Club," according to Webb. His wife finds him and "busts up the joint." Ref: Webb. *The Animated Film Encyclopedia*; not viewed.

Way Back When a Raspberry Was a Fruit (1940) U.S.; dir. Dave Fleischer; Fleischer Studio/Paramount. Animated short film; 7 min.; b&w. Screenplay, Dan Gordon. (In the *Stone Age Cartoons* series).
Prehistoric gardening. Ref: Webb. *The Animated Film Encyclopedia*; not viewed.

Way Back When a Triangle Had Its Points (1940) U.S.; dir. Dave Fleischer; Fleischer Studio/Paramount. Animated short film; 7 min.; b&w. Screenplay, William Turner. (In the *Stone Age Cartoons* series).
I.M. Stonebroke, owner of a rock company, takes his pretty stenographer to the Cave Inn Night Club, but his wife finds out. Ref: Webb. *The Animated Film Encyclopedia*; not viewed.

Way Back When Women Had Their Weigh (1940) U.S.; dir. Dave Fleischer; Fleischer Studio/Paramount. Animated short film; 7 min.; b&w. Screenplay, Tedd Pierce. (In the *Stone Age Cartoons* series).
A fat caveman goes on a rigorous weight-loss program to please a girl, then discovers she prefers portly men. Ref: Webb. *The Animated Film Encyclopedia*; not viewed.

The Weathering Continent (1992) Japan; dir. Koichi Mashimo; IG/Kadokawa. Animated film; 60 min.; color. Screenplay, Koichi Mashimo based on novel by Sei Takekawa.
A series of natural disasters destroys Atlantis. In an age of drought and bandits, three heroes face the anger of the dead Atlanteans, who are disturbed by plunderers. Clements and McCarthy say this film, even at only 60 min., was "hypnotically slow." It was, however, one of the few films to place Atlantis in prehistory rather than historical periods; cf. *The Laws of the Sun* (2000). Ref: Clements/McCarthy. *The Anime Encyclopedia*; not viewed.

Wedding Belts (1940) U.S.; dir. Dave Fleischer; Fleischer/Paramount. Animated short film; 7 min.; b&w. Screenplay, George Manuell; music, Sammy Timberg. *VOICES:* Pinto Colvig, Jack Mercer. (In the *Stone Age Cartoons* series).
"Two lovesick swains are shown the hazards of married life by their parents," according to Webb. Ref: Webb. *Animated Film Encyclopedia*; not viewed.

What's New, Mr. Magoo (1977-79) Episode, *Caveman Magoo*. U.S.; DePatie-Freleng. Episode of animated TV series; ca. 12 min.; color. VOICE: Jim Backus (*Mr. Magoo*).

Two episodes were shown in each 25-min. shows in this cartoon series. The episodes were later repackaged as part of *The UPA Cartoon Show* (1990). Ref: Lenburg. *Encyclopedia of Animated Cartoons*; not viewed.

The Wheel (2001) *see* **Rocks** (2001)

When Clubs Were Clubs (1915) U.S.; dir. Dave Aylott; Martin. Short film; b&w; silent. CAST: Ernie Westo; Bob Reed; Johnny Butt.

A caveman comedy. Ref: Jones. *Illustrated Dinosaur Movie Guide*; not viewed.

When Dinosaurs Ruled the Earth (1970) U.K.; dir. Val Guest; Hammer. 96 or 100 min.; color. Screenplay, Val Guest, from treatment by J.G. Ballard; photography, Dick Bush; music, Mario Nascimbene. CAST: Victoria Vetri (*Sanna*); Robin Hawdon (*Tara*); Patrick Allen (*Kingsor*); Drew Hanley (*Khaku*); Sean Caffrey (*Kane*); Magda Konopka (*Ulido*); Imogen Hassall (*Ayak*); Patrick Holt (*Ammon*) Carol-Anne Hawkins (*Yani*); Maria O'Brien (*Omah*).

In a time when there is as yet no moon, Kingsor, tyrannical leader of the Rock Tribe, is disturbed by the obvious instability of the sun. He decides to sacrifice three blonde girls to the sun god. At dawn the three sacrifices stand on the edge of a cliff over the sea while three men wearing animal masks stand behind them swinging bolas. Kingsor waits for the sun to rise fully; then he will signal the men to smash the women's heads and send them over the cliff. As tension rises, one girl panics and runs; a masked man chases her but both fall to their deaths over the cliff. The deadly ceremony resumes. Suddenly a large piece breaks away from the sun and heads for Earth (where it will become the moon). At the same time a tremendous windstorm sweeps down on the crowd. In the panic, Sanna, one of the sacrifices, gets away, climbs partway down the cliff and leaps into the sea.

Sanna struggles in the stormswept sea until she is rescued by Tara, a fisherman of the Sand Tribe, who is on a sea-going raft with his friends. Kane, Kingsor's second-in-command, sees Sanna on the raft and tells Kingsor, who is determined to kill Sanna to appease the sun god. Tara and Sanna land in the Sand Tribe's village just as the Sand People are in the middle of the delicate process of tying down a captured plesiosaurus, a giant, web-footed dinosaur. Ammon, the statesmanlike leader of the Sand People, gives Sanna refuge but Tara's mate Ayak instantly becomes jealous of Sanna, to whom Tara is attracted. The plesiosaurus breaks loose, injures a child and runs amuck until brave Tara sets the beast on fire and kills it.

As the Sand People settle down to a very large meal of plesiosaurus steaks and celebrate with a dance, Ayak notices Tara is preoccupied with Sanna, who is industriously building herself a palm frond hut down the beach. To Ayak's annoyance, Tara visits Sanna and gives her his knife and a necklace. Meanwhile Kingsor leads a large armed party to get Sanna back to be sacrificed. Ayak incites the Sand women against Sanna, telling them the newcomer is responsible for the strange behavior of the sun. Ammon and Ulido, the mate of Tara's friend Khaku, are the only Sand People beside Tara who support Sanna. Ayak attacks Sanna in the surf; Ulido comes to her aid and Ammon breaks up the fight.

When Kingsor reaches the Sand People's village and demands Sanna back, Sanna manages to escape into the jungle, pursued by Kane and other Rock men. As Sanna hides in a tree a giant snake crawls over her body; she saves herself by remaining perfectly still until the snake drops off her and kills a Rock man. A Chasmosaurus, a compact, belligerent dinosaur, kills two more men and injures Kane. Tara, Khaku and other Sand men go after Sanna. They find the same Chasmosaurus's cave; the beast kills Khaku but is killed when it falls over a cliff while chasing Tara. Kane is saved. At the village Khaku's corpse is placed on a small raft which is set afire and sent out to sea. As the sinister moon grows larger Kingsor whips the fearful Sand People into a hysterical frenzy and everyone except Tara, Ammon and Ulido agree to hunt and kill Sanna.

Meanwhile back in the jungle, Sanna, fleeing from a dinosaur, hides in what appears to be a hollow tree stump. Instead it is a carnivorous plant, which swallows her. The plucky girl cuts her way out with her knife but has to cut off much of her long blonde hair to escape. Later Tara finds her hair and assumes that Sanna is dead. Exhausted, Sanna takes shelter in a giant, broken dinosaur egg. A baby dinosaur emerges from another egg. At the village Ulido, stricken with grief for Khaku, tends Kane's wounds and Kane begins to transfer his loyalty from Kingsor to Tara's few friends. Tara tells Kingsor that Sanna is dead, which Tara actually believes. The mother dinosaur finds Sanna in the egg and instantly accepts the girl as one of her own offspring.

Sanna quickly makes friends with the mother dinosaur and her baby, with whom she plays hide and seek. She tries to train the baby by playing on a hollow-bone pipe. She saves two tribesmen from the mother dinosaur, who meekly lets the men go when Sanna insists. Tara finds a woman dying her small daughter's blonde hair black, in case Kingsor decides to sacrifice any more girls. As he wanders sadly, Tara is attacked by a Rhamphorynchus, a flying dinosaur, which carries him to its nest, where he kills it with his spear. Next Tara sees Sanna cheerfully leading the mother dinosaur around. When he tries to "save" her, the mother dinosaur almost attacks him. Tara is astounded when Sanna simply orders the dinosaur to leave.

A man sees Tara and Sanna together and tells Kingsor; when Tara returns to the village after visiting Sanna in her little one-woman cave, Kingsor condemns him for protecting Sanna. Fed up with her former mate, Ayak spits in Tara's face. When Tara refuses to tell where Sanna is, Kingsor ties Tara to a raft like Khaku's funeral raft, sets it afire and pushes it out to sea. Fortunately, a Tylosaur, a sea-going dinosaur, smashes the raft, freeing Tara, who swims to safety although Kingsor and his men believe him dead. Tara staggers to Sanna's cave, where he recovers.

Kingsor leads a combined land and sea operation to finally track down Sanna, with the Sand People's rafts patrolling offshore as the Rock men search every nook and cranny on land. After a long chase (interrupted by a very brief fight between two dinosaurs) dozens of men surround the lovers.

Sanna (Victoria Vetri) in an atypically fierce pose in *When Dinosaurs Ruled the Earth*.

The mother dinosaur comes running up, scatters the men and carries Sanna off in her mouth. Tara is caught and taken to the village, where he is tied to a frame and is about to be burned alive. To everyone's astonishment, the sea suddenly runs away from the beach, in the first lunar tide. The retreating tide uncovers giant crabs, which attack and kill several men. A giant tidal wave threatens the land. The people flee. Sanna races into the village and frees Tara. Ayak drowns in quicksand despite Tara's efforts to save her. Sanna, Tara, Ulido and her

Tara (Robin Hawdon) dives from a sea raft to rescue Sanna in *When Dinosaurs Ruled the Earth*.

new mate Kane launch a raft to ride out the wave. Kingsor, still convinced that killing Sanna will appease the gods, attacks the foursome but they escape out to sea. Kingsor, Ammon and perhaps everyone else are killed by the tidal wave. The four survivors on the raft are cast ashore. They observe the first solar eclipse and kneel to worship the new moon and the restored sun.

COMMENTARY. Among silly, unrealistic caveman movies, *When Dinosaurs Ruled the Earth* is the hardcore stuff. Where else can you see a girl in a tiny bikini leading a giant dinosaur around and telling it what to do? Nevertheless, the film's production values, special effects, humor, music and cast all make it far more entertaining than duds such as *Wild Women of Wongo* (1958). The script is fast-moving and full of incident and the movie repackages all the elements which made *One Million Years B.C.* a success for Hammer: beautiful, tanned, scantily-clad young men and women, monsters, fights, impressive scenery and a love story. If you don't mind the lack of realism you can smile from the beginning to the end of *When Dinosaurs Ruled*.

The silliness starts with the opening scene, which begins the film in the midst of a crisis. We see three blonde girls in bikinis and cloaks lined up at the edge of a cliff over the sea, with a large crowd behind them. Directly behind each sacrificial maiden is a man wearing a crocodile mask and endlessly swinging a bola, while Kingsor closely watches the sunrise which will signal him to give the order to kill. Behind the three executioners, other men bang rhythmically on human skulls with bones.

As if all this weren't enough, the narrator intones (in the only English words heard in the film), "A time of beginnings, of darkness, of light, of the sun, the Earth, the sea, of man. The beginnings of man living with man, by the sea, in the mountains. The beginnings of love, hate and fear. Man's fear of the unknown, man's fear lest the sun should leave him, leave him alone in everlasting darkness. A time when the color of a woman's hair condemned her, a sacrifice to the sun. A time when there was as yet no moon." While the viewer is absorbing all this information, the tireless executioners keep swinging their bolas in a circular motion over their heads, the girls keep hyperventilating and Kingsor keeps studying the sunrise. If a viewer can sit through that scene without laughing, he is ready for the rest of *When Dinosaurs Ruled the Earth*.

Most of the film is less violent than *One Million Years B.C.* The Rock People and the Sand People get along with each other quite well, although unfortunately they agree on the need to kill Sanna. Until almost everyone is apparently killed by the tidal wave in the finale, there aren't many deaths. Instead of being an all-purpose brute like the villains in *One Million Years B.C.* Kingsor is simply obsessed with sacrificing girls to the sun god, a project which almost everyone agrees makes sense because of the ominous changes in the sun. Ayak, the other villain, also is not really evil; she just lets her jealousy get the better of her. It is perhaps no coincidence that her name suggests the word "amok." There are no real villains in *When Dinosaurs Ruled*.

The dinosaurs are all realistic, unlike the giant lizards who were mixed with correct dinosaurs in *One Million Years B.C.*, but the *When Dinosaurs Ruled* dinosaurs are less scary than the *One Million Years B.C.* menagerie and, despite the film's title, even seem a bit wimpy. The Sand People actually tie up a Plesiosaurus with ropes. (Why? How?) When the creature breaks free he only injures one person before the villagers burn him to death. The biggest dinosaur is seen only briefly and its only function is to force Sanna into the carnivorous plant. Two dinosaurs fight each other very briefly during the climatic chase scene. In *One Million Years B.C.* Loana escapes after being snatched by a pterodactyl only when another flying monster attacks the one who has her; in *When Dinosaurs Ruled* when Tara is grabbed by a flying Rhamphorynchus, he kills the creature himself. And of course there is the mother dinosaur who attacks people only when they seem to threaten Sanna and who always lets people go when Sanna tells her to. Only the grumpy Chasmosaurus does much damage to the humans, and even he foolishly runs off the edge of a cliff. Jim Danforth's dinosaurs are excellent; they're just not allowed to do much. The giant crabs are quite dangerous and kill several men but they are seen very briefly. I suspect the crab scene was cut.

The obligatory girl fights are also on the wimpy side. A brief fight between two women we know nothing about breaks out in the Rock Tribe's camp, for reasons which I couldn't figure out. The main catfight is between Sanna and Ayak in the surf, with Ulido joining in. In the fight in *One Million Years B.C.* Marine Beswick's Nupondi looks like a serious fighter. When she and Raquel Welch's Loana knock each other around a cave, there is a desperate quality to the scene lacking in the surf fight in *When Dinosaurs Ruled*. The Loana-Nupondi fight has a real winner and a loser, while the surf fight is just three girls in bikinis struggling in the water until a man breaks up the contest. Ayak has a knife during the surf fight but fails to stab Sanna, which makes Ayak look quite ineffectual. And after Ulido joins in there are two good girls against one bad girl; to produce tension it should have been two villains against one heroine.

There are many audacious inaccuracies and absurdities in *When Dinosaurs Ruled*, besides the presence of humans and dinosaurs in the same story. The moon, of course, was formed long before humans evolved. (And why would the moon splitting away from the sun immediately cause a windstorm on Earth?) Early humans did not tie up large, dangerous animals, as the Sand People do to the Plesiosaurus here. Ancient people either avoided large animals or killed them. The villagers keep large vats of flammable liquid around, apparently solely for dinosaur control and fiery funerals. They even have sleds piled high with flammable materials which can be pulled around on ropes to surround escaping dinosaurs. The tribes' ceremonial life includes several silly details (in addition to the endlessly swinging bolas in the opening execution scene.) In one ceremony, the women kneel in a line and fold their arms in front of their chins. In another, women and children kneel and sway back and forth as they chant. On the other hand when Kingsor whips everyone into a frenzy of fear and the women roll in the sand, shrieking, the scene is effective, scary and far from silly.

When Dinosaurs Ruled was filmed in the Canary Islands, the same location as *One Million Years B.C.*, but Guest's 1971 film has a much darker palette than the 1966 film. *One Million Years B.C.* was set in deserts and mountains, under a blazing sun. *When Dinosaurs Ruled* has twilight beach scenes and many jungle scenes. (In 1972, Hammer returned to deserts and mountains for their final, relatively realistic prehistoric film, *Creatures the World Forgot*.) Guest probably used every bit of interesting Canary Islands scenery which was not in *One Million Years B.C.* but some scenes were filmed in England and the jungles sometimes look like studio sets. In his autobiography *So You Want to Be in Pictures* (2001) Val Guest wrote that the picture was shot from October 14, 1968 to Jan. 8, 1969 (excluding special effects) with only "12 concentrated days" in the Canaries.

It is easy to make fun of *When Dinosaurs Ruled* but the film is an exciting adventure with many assets. Jim Danforth said that the movie is "not serious enough to be taken seriously, nor is it flamboyant enough to be a grand adventure, nor is it intentionally humorous enough to be a comedy." It does succeed as an enchanted fairy-tale, with beautiful, nearly-naked people, scary but not too dangerous monsters, and constant danger but a happy ending for most of the heroes. The special effects brought Hammer the only Oscar nomination in its history (for Jim Danforth and Roger Dicken). The dinosaurs are more consistently excellent than Harryhausen's in *One Million Years B.C.* Nascimbene's score was almost the equal of his work on *One Million Years*. This time his music is surprisingly gentle, wistful and often choral.

The cast is perfectly adequate for the needs of the film. Veteran Patrick Allen gives a slow-burn performance as the frustrated religious maniac Kingsor, who tries and fails throughout the film to kill one lightly-armed girl and twice tries unsuccessfully to kill the somewhat scrawny hero. Val Guest has harshly criticized Victoria Vetri, a *Playboy* pin-up girl with little acting experience. In his 2001 autobiography Guest said Vetri got the part because she had "a big admirer in the American distributor's camp." Nevertheless, her performance, as Mark F. Berry says in *Dinosaur Filmography*, is "natural and appealing" and she keeps her dignity in her ridiculously skimpy costume. Best of all, she's funny, which is more than Raquel Welch was in *One Million Years B.C.* Vetri has a delightful smile during intervals when nothing is trying to kill her.

Imogen Hassall's background was as unpromising as Vetri's. Hassall was known as a party girl, often seen with famous men in "Swinging London." She has the best part in *When Dinosaurs Ruled* and gives the best performance (really the second best performance in any of Hammer's caveman films, after Martine Beswick in *Slave Girls*), conveying Ayak's hurt and rage at Tara's leaving her for Sanna.

In *Tuesday's Child* (2002), his biography of Hassall, Dan Leissner writes that the novice actress "actually does it very well, conveying vividly with her face and body not just the extremes of Ayak's jealous fury but the subtleties of hurt and confusion, making her sympathetic." When Kingsor condemns Tara Ayak spits on Tara, but a few minutes later when Tara has apparently been killed, Ayak breaks down and weeps. It is interesting that the two best performances in Hammer's four prehistoric films, Beswick in *Slave Girls* and Hassall in *When Dinosaurs Ruled*, are women villains.

A chase scene in which Sanna and Tara are hemmed in by dozens of men and find more enemies wherever they turn is suspenseful but too prolonged and abruptly interrupted by brief shots of two dinosaurs fighting. Throughout the film there are surprisingly large crowd scenes, certainly larger than the 20 or 30 people who constituted real prehistoric bands. The giant wave scene at the end is impressive.

The film has a few realistic, or at least convincing, touches. The seagoing raft is unusual in prehistoric films but quite accurate. We see fishing nets, though we don't see them used for fishing. (We do see Sanna fishing successfully with her hands.) There are a few older, toothless women, in addition to the young beauties. Sanna's hollow-bone musical pipe probably existed. In a reversal of the usual practice, the big dance scene has men dancing as women watch (until the irrepressible Ayak joins in). An old man keeps track of the phases of the brand new moon by painting them on a rock, while Sanna makes calendar markings on her cave wall. The language used in the film consists of a few words repeated frequently. Words seem to have multiple meanings. We hear "akita," "akoba," "nikro," "wandi," "adana," "ozo," "yapasha" and "makan" again and again. The repetition of a few simple words does suggest a people just beginning to learn to speak. In an interesting scene, Kane tells Kingsor that he saw Sanna rescued from the sea by the Shell People's raft by drawing a picture of the raft; he evidently has never seen a boat before and has no word for it.

In his autobiography Guest writes that Hammer presented him with a poster full of exotic images, dominated by a dinosaur with a girl in its mouth, and told him to write and direct a film to match the poster. (Guest does not mention J.G. Ballard's contribution.) Guest was able to get the girl in the dinosaur's mouth, without horrific bloodshed, by having the mother dinosaur take Sanna gently in her mouth and carry her to safety. *When Dinosaurs Ruled* received a G rating in the U.S. Acres of near-nudity counted for little so long as there was no real nudity. Vetri and Hawdon did do a nude love scene which was in the version released in European countries. Two stills from the nude scene are found in *The House of Horror*, a book on Hammer by Allen Eyles. Brief shots from the love scene appear in a three-minute Hammer promotional short, *Beauties and Beasts*, which centered on Vetri as the next Hammer sex symbol in the footsteps of Ursula Andress and Raquel Welch. Responding to another censorship issue, Hammer redubbed lines in which Kane's name was spoken, changing it from one syllable to two, to avoid suspicion that they were referring to the Biblical Cain.

Val Guest was one of the busiest British directors, with dozens of films to his credit, including the first two *Quatermass* films (1955, 1957) and *The Day the Earth Caught Fire* (1961). He also wrote over 70 screenplays. "Treatment" writer J.G. Ballard was a major science fiction novelist; Spielberg's *Empire of the Sun* was based on Ballard's experiences as a boy in China during World War II. Jim Danforth has worked in various special effects jobs in dozens of films, including *Caveman* (1981). Old-timers Patrick Holt (who was 56 when he worked in *When Dinosaurs Ruled*) and Patrick Allen have the most credits of anyone in the cast, with dozens of films apiece. Robin Hawdon did more work on stage than in films.

Of the three leading ladies, tall, Polish-born Magda Konopka had the best career, with about two dozen mostly European films. Victoria Vetri and Imogen Hassall were both ambitious actresses who would probably not have agreed to work in *When Dinosaurs Ruled* had it not been for Raquel Welch's spectacular success in *One Million Years B.C.* Both fell victim to the Curse of the Cavegirl, which has consigned to obscurity almost all actresses who have played in prehistoric films with the exceptions of Mae Marsh, Carole Landis, Raquel Welch and Rae Dawn Chong. Vetri was in only 10 films from 1962 to 1973. Party girl Hassall worked in 12 mostly obscure films before she committed suicide in 1980.

Variety (Oct. 14, 1970) considered *When Dinosaurs Ruled* "undemanding escapist nonsense" with "not over many unintended jokes." The reviewer praised the "excellently conceived" special effects and noted "the prehistoric animals steal the show." In an interview in *Memories of Hammer* (edited by Gary and Susan Svehla, 2002) Val Guest gave his verdict. "It was a sort of cobbled together picture. We did the best we could with that. I wasn't all that happy with the final cut. I'd done my final cut and went off on another picture. There was re-editing — and I was not happy with it."

Most critics have been unimpressed by *When Dinosaurs Ruled the Earth* but Leonard Maltin's *Movie & Video Guide* notes the "fact-paced, enjoyable" film's "beautiful locations" and "very good special effects" and gives it a respectable rating of three out of four. *When Dinosaurs Ruled the Earth* took the dinosaurs-and-bikinis subgenre about as far as it could go, plunging deep into completely non-realistic fantasy. For their final prehistoric film, *Creatures the World Forgot* (1972), Hammer would go in the opposite direction, toward more realism than they had ever attempted. Ref: Larson. *Music from the House of Hammer*; Jones. *Illustrated Dinosaur Movie Guide*; Senn/Johnson. *Fantastic Cinema Subject Guide*; Johnson/Del Vecchio. *Hammer Films*; Berry. *Dinosaur Filmography*; Guest. *So You Want to Be in Picture*; Smith. *Epic Films*; Svehla. *Memories of Hammer*; Leissner. *Tuesday's Child*; MK 7.

When Men Carried Clubs and Women Played Ding Dong (1971) [alt. *Quando Gli Uomini Armarono la Clava e con le Donne Fecero Din-Don*; *When Women Played Ding-Dong*] Italy; dir. Bruno Corbucci, Pasquale Festa Campanile; Empire Films. 95 or 100 min.; color. Screenplay, Bruno Corbucci, Massimo Felisatti, Fabio Pittorru, based on *Lysistrata* and *Women at the Feast of Demeter* by Aristophanes; photography, Fausto Zuccoli; music, Giancarlo Chiaramello. CAST: Antonio Sabato (*Ari*); Nadia Cassini (*Listra*); Aldo Giuffrè (*Gott*); Vittorio Caprioli (*Grand Prof*); Elio Pandolfi (*Lonno*); Howard Ross; Lucretia Love; Valeria Fabrizi.

Among the Cave Dwellers and their rivals the Lake Dwellers, women are completely subordinate to men but both men and women are obsessed by "ding-dong" (sex). Handsome Ari wins virgin Listra in a piglet-catching contest, but their attempts to make love are constantly interrupted by outbreaks of foolish fighting between the Cave and Lake Men. Fed up, Listra leads the other Cave Women in a strike; they refuse to have ding-dong until the fighting stops. Soon the Lake Women join the strike. Desperate, the men try to make peace but insults lead to quarrels, which lead to more fighting. Finally, Ari and Listra leave on the only horse to find peace together.

When Men Carried Clubs was Festa Campanile's third caveman comedy in two years, but it was not a sequel to *When Women Had Tails* (1970) and *When Women Lost Their Tails* (1971). Here Festa Campanile shared direction tasks with Corbucci and did without Senta Berger, the popular star of his first two cave comedies. Many of the cast, especially Sabato and Ross, were veterans with dozens of credits in low-budget Italian films.

The film of course is based on Aristophanes' play *Lysistrata*, in which Athenian women go on a make-love-not-war sex strike. In 1971 the old play had fresh relevance during the Cold War but Festa Campanile was not the right man to do an up-to-date version of Aristophanes. *Clubs/Ding Dong* was all too similar to Festa Campanile's two previous silly caveman comedies, featuring nudity, slapstick, low-brow humor, jokey dialogue and really dumb cavemen. The men are foolish-looking, with the same very long hair as in the director's previous cave comedies; this time they also have scraggly beards, pop-eyes and high-pitched voices. They challenge each other with loud burps and farts and engage in mass head-butting, stomach-butting and butt-kicking battles. (The credits say that the Italian Acrobatic Team was employed in the film.) When they see a horse for the first time, they wonder if it lays eggs. A man discovers the boomerang, but keeps hitting himself in the head. When the Lake Dwellers cut the Cave Dwellers off from water, the Cave men drink urine, then try to drill for water and instead strike oil.

The dialogue in the English-language version (which was very hard to understand in the DVD I watched) includes anachronisms like "Screwball!" The boss of the Cave Dwellers says that "Women are not capable of thinking" and that war leads to improvements in civilization. The film is highly episodic and gag-centered. A few scenes are really amusing: the head-butting fights; an episode in which the Cave Men saw through the stilts of the Lake Men's dwellings and collapse them into the water; and a scene in which dozens of nude girls in a giant tree taunt the cavemen.

The feature was reviewed very unfavorably under the title *When Women Played Ding-Dong* in *Video Watchdog* 112. Ref: Jones. *Illustrated Dinosaur Movie Guide*; Internet Movie Database; MK 4.

When Men Were Men (1925) U.S.; dir. Paul Terry; Fables Pictures/Pathé. Animated short film; 10 min.; b&w; silent. "A caveman makes dinosaurs work for him and steals his bride in the approved fashion." Ref: Webb. *Animated Film Encyclopedia*; Jones. *Illustrated Dinosaur Movie Guide*; not viewed.

When Women Had Tails (1970) [alt. *Quando le Donne Avevano la Coda*] Italy; dir. Pasquale Festa Campanile; Clesi Cinematografica. 110 min.; color. Screenplay, Lina Wertmuller, Ottavio Jemma, Marcello Coscia, Pasquale Festa Campanile; photography, Franco Di Giacomo; music, Ennio Morricone. CAST: Senta Berger (*Filli*); Giuliano Gemma (*Ulli*); Lando Buzzanca (*Kao*); Frank Wolff (*Grr*); Lino Toffolo (*Put*); Francesco Mulé (*Uto*); Aldo Giuffrè (*Zog*); Renzo Montagnani (*Maluc*).

When a caveman is killed his seven sons are cast adrift in a basket. They land on an island where they grow up to be rough, club-waving dunces. When they discover fire, they manage to burn the whole island. Escaping on logs to the mainland, they catch Filli, the first woman they have ever seen, who has long blonde hair and a tail. They call her "the animal."

Handsome Ulli keeps Filli in a cage and learns how to make love with her. When Kao is killed while trying to fly, the others casually eat him. Effeminate Maluc is uninterested in Filli, but the other four brothers figure out that playing with Filli is fun and all want their turn. Fed up, Filli persuades Ulli to flee with her. "Bring that back! It's public property!" the brothers protest. The brothers pursue the lovers, but are captured by a whole tribe of amorous Amazons, who use them for "zag-zag" (sex). Ulli is tempted to join the orgy, but instead he and Filli remain a couple.

COMMENTARY: *When Women Had Tails* plays like an eroticized combination of the Three Stooges and *Snow White and the Seven Dwarfs*. The cavemen have comically long hair and are incredibly ignorant and dimwitted. Two of them invent a slingshot but keep firing it backwards and hitting themselves in the face. They fall into their own animal traps. They call fire "him" and manage to burn their own home.

Some of their dialogue is humorously anachronistic; when the brothers tell Kao not to try to fly, he replies "Don't be reactionary" before plunging to his death. When the boys get into a big fight over Filli, bashing each other with clubs, one of them calls a truce with a comically unconvincing "After all, we're not savages. We're civilized human beings." After Filli agrees to pick a man to make love with her, the brothers clean themselves up and decorate themselves ridiculously with huge displays of feathers and flowers, looking like Carmen Miranda singing "The Lady in the Tutti-Frutti Hat."

Senta Berger goes almost naked and is hung from a spit, kept in a cage, led by a rope around her neck, knocked out with a club and called "the animal." Her character eats human flesh, plays a game of mutual face-licking with Ulli and makes love to five different men. Berger, who returned for the

Zany cavemen try to fly in Italy's *When Women Had Tails.*

sequel *When Women Lost Their Tails* (1971), no doubt acquired a reputation among Italian male movie-goers as a really good sport. The male actors were equally enthusiastic, taking pratfalls and going barefoot throughout the film, eschewing the usual fur boots.

The film may have appealed to women as well as men. The men in the movie are stupid, ignorant and crude — little boys in men's bodies. Filli is much more sophisticated than the men and soon has them fighting for her favors. Ulli finally becomes a mature companion for Filli.

Variety (Dec. 23, 1970) praised the work of photographer Di Giacomo, famous composer Morricone, and art director Enrico Yob, but considered the film an "embarrassingly low-class farce" with gags and situations "either vulgar in excess or bordering on unremitting burlesque or both." Berger was an international star and Gemma a busy local star in Italy. Wertmuller had not yet begun her important work as a director and screenwriter. Festa Campanile was a prolific director and writer, who made the sequel *When Women Lost their Tails* and co-directed *When Men Carried Clubs and Women Played Ding-Dong* (1971). *Variety* reported that the farce was "rolling them in the aisles and lining them up at the boxoffice" in Italy. Ref: Jones. *Illustrated Dinosaur Movie Guide*; Senn/Johnson. *Fantastic Cinema Subject Guide*; MK 5.

When Women Lost Their Tails (1971) [alt. *Quando le Donne Persero la Coda*] Italy/West Germany; dir. Pasquale Festa Campanile; Clesi Cinematografica/Terra. 95 min.; color. Screenplay, Lina Wertmuller, Ottavio Jemma, Marcello Coscia, Maria Grazia Fistri; photography, Silvano Ippoliti; music, Ennio Morricone, Bruno Nicolai. CAST: Senta Berger (*Filli*); Frank Wolff (*Grr*); Lando Buzzanca (*Ham*); Lino Toffolo (*Put*); Francesco Mulé (*Uto*); Aldo Puglisi (*Zog*); Renzo Montagnani (*Maluc*); Fiammetta Baralla (*Contortia*); Mario Adorf (*Merchant*).

Cavewoman Filli lives with five cavemen, all of them idiots. Four make love to her — all except gay, effeminate Maluc. Filli muses, "I don't mind doing it. I like it. But I want to do it with affection, with feeling." Into their idyllic lives comes fast-talking conman Ham, who introduces the concept of money to the slow-witted cavemen. He gets them fighting over money and going into debt. They sell him their home and he rents it back to them. They become his wage slaves.

Filli likes Ham because he gives her foreplay instead of the cavemen's quickie technique. Eventually, the cavemen sell Filli to Ham, who rents them his huge girlfriend Contortia. Later, Filli and her child are sold to a merchant who promises to "liberate" her so that she can earn money like a man — as a prostitute.

COMMENTARY. In the second of his three caveman sex comedies, Festa Campanile managed to keep Senta Berger from *When Women Had Tails* (1970) but lost his other major star Giuliano Gemma. The second *Tails* film has a satirical, anti-capitalist approach. Wertmuller and her co-screenwriters seem to be saying that mankind would have been better off staying primitive if civilization means a market economy. They probably even disapprove of Filli's desire for romantic love, which turns out to be another trap to lead her into slavery.

In addition to its political message, the second *Tails* film has some cute caveman gags. The boys have their home inside a dinosaur's skeleton. They climb up ladders, then jump down because they're too stupid to figure out they can climb down. Filli has a few *Flintstones*-style gadgets, including a talking cockatoo she uses like a can-opener to open oysters, and a small volcanic vent over which she heats food. The boys engage in the Three Stooges–like antics typical of Festa Campanile's caveman comedies. Maluc is an outrageously stereotyped effeminate gay character. As in all three of Festa Campanile's cave comedies, the woman is smarter than the men.

Each of Festa Campanile's caveman films has a serious satirical point. *When Women Had Tails* is about the superiority of women over men. *When Women Lost Their Tails* is about economic injustice. *When Men Carried Clubs and Women Played Ding Dong* (1971) is about war and peace. The satire doesn't elevate these simple comedies much, but each of the films has several funny moments. Ref: Jones. *Illustrated Dinosaur Movie Guide*; Senn/Johnson. *Fantastic Cinema Subject Guide*; MK 5.

When Women Played Ding Dong (1971) *see* **When Men Carried Clubs and Women Played Ding Dong** (1971)

Why They Love Cavemen (1921) U.S.; dir. Tony Sarg; Sarg/Dawley/Rialto. Animated short film; b&w; silent. (In the series *Tony Sarg's Almanac*).

A silhouette animation film. Even Webb has no information on the story, but the film was probably about prehistory (instead of using "caveman" as a term for a brutish modern man, as some other films of the period did) since other films in the *Tony Sarg's Almanac* series are definitely about prehistoric men. Ref: Webb. *Animated Film Encyclopedia*; not viewed.

Wild Women of Wongo (1958) U.S.; dir. James L. Wolcott; Wolcott/Tropical Pictures. 71 min.; color. Screenplay, Cedric Rutherford; photography, Harry Walsh. CAST: Jean Hawkshaw (*Omoo*); Johnny Walsh (*Engor*); Ed Fury (*Gahbo*); Mary Ann Webb (*Mona*); Rex Richards (*King of Wongo*); Pat Crowley (*Wongo Man*); Cande Gerrard (*Ahtee*); Adrienne Bourbeau (*Wana*); Zuni Dyer (*Priestess*); Burt Williams (*King of Goona*).

A woman's voice announces "I am Mother Nature.... Father Time and I have worked hand in hand to make a better world." She explains that 10,000 years ago they performed an experiment by making all the women of the prehistoric village of Wongo beautiful, while all the men were homely. At the same time they made all the men of the nearby village of Goona handsome, but all the Goona women plain. She remarks dryly, "It didn't work."

The blue-haired king of Wongo consults the priestess of the temple of the dragon god (actually an alligator) about the upcoming mating of Wongo maidens and young men. Young Ako has bought the king's daughter Omoo for his bride. Engor, son of the king of Goona, visits to ask the Wongo men to join with Goona against raiding apemen. Wongo's women, who have never seen a handsome man, are agog at Engor, while he is amazed by the Wongo women, especially Omoo. The jealous Wongo men decide to have Ako kill Engor, but when Ako attacks Engor the women all tackle him. Engor flees, unchivalrously leaving the women to face the wrath of their men. The king orders the women to go to the temple; every night one woman is to offer herself as a sacrifice to the dragon god, until one is taken.

After several nights no woman has been killed; the priestess tries to solve this problem by leading the women in frenzied dancing. Soon a five-foot alligator attacks several women while they are swimming. Omoo bravely dashes into the water, wrestles the gator and with difficulty kills it. Nasty Ahtee says Omoo should have let the gator kill her, but Omoo points out that women are allowed to resist since if the gator can be killed it must not really be the dragon god.

Two apemen (who look only mildly simian) attack Omoo's friend Mona as she takes her turn waiting for the god. The women attack the apemen with spears, forcing them into the water where an alligator kills them. The women decide that has satisfied their obligation to provide blood for the dragon god and return to the village, which they find deserted. Ahtee refuses to obey Omoo's orders, leading to a catfight between her and Mona.

With no men in Wongo, the women eagerly head for Goona. Meanwhile, the young Goona men are sent into the forest without weapons, where they must stay "for a moon" to show their readiness for marriage to the Goona women. The Wongo women meet the Goona women, who jealously threaten them. In the forest, the Wongo women find Engor, who explains that the men cannot associate with women until their initiation is complete. Annoyed, the women take all the men prisoner, using spears, ropes and nets. The men are resentful ("You forget you are only a woman!") but soon mutual attraction develops. Meanwhile the Wongo men, who had fled from the apemen, discover the homely Goona women, to everyone's mutual delight. The Wongo women take their captives to the temple, where the Wongo men and their new mates also show up. The priestess orders the women to untie the men and blesses the many new unions.

COMMENTARY. In this book I have tried to show that many caveman movies deserve somewhat more respect than they usually get. Such is not the case with

Wild Women of Wongo. It is every bit as bad as its title suggests. It is as bad as many people assume most caveman films are. *Wild Women of Wongo* and *Prehistoric Women* (1950) are both cheap (though made in color), exploitative (though very modest) 1950s films about the battle of the sexes in prehistory. Both show modern white humans living in ancient jungles. Both feature dangerous modern animals but no recreations of extinct animals. Each has a catfight between two women and some tribal dancing. Both end in reconciliation and general happiness and both have villains

Wild Women of Wongo hunt men.

who are only briefly-seen — the apemen in *Wongo* and the memorable Guadi the Giant in *Prehistoric Women*. The heroes of both films are called Engor. I have no doubt that the makers of *Wongo* had seen *Prehistoric Women*.

There the similarities end. *Prehistoric Women* has an endlessly-talking narrator and no dialogue by the characters. In *Wongo* the narration is confined to Mother Nature's short opening, while the characters talk constantly.

The dialogue and acting in *Wongo* make the chattering narrator and taciturn characters of the earlier film seem like a good tactic. All the *Wongo* dialogue is formal and even florid, as when Ako's father remarks "I am made proud by the marriage of my son with the king's daughter." The only exception is a very ill-conceived talking parrot who comments on the action in modern dialogue, such as "Hey, take it easy!" The dialogue is delivered with admirably straight faces but without much conviction. The only exception to the dismal acting is Zuni Dyer, who overacts with delightful enthusiasm as the priestess of the dragon god, fixing her hair and striking a dramatic pose before letting people enter the temple, and throwing herself into lines like "Dance, maidens of Wongo, before the dragon god! Offer yourselves in sacrifice! Dance! Dance! Dance!" The dance wasn't much good, but the priestess was tremendous. Everyone is dressed like characters in an Italian peplum — miniskirts for the women, bare chests and short skirts for the men. Everyone's hair is very modern-looking. Fittingly, *Wongo* was filmed on several beaches in Florida.

While *Prehistoric Women* earnestly tried to present a few facts about early men, *Wongo* doesn't aspire to be anything except a mild romantic farce. There are no interesting details except for "the white bird's wing of peace," which is carried as a flag of truce. The women in the 1950 film sensibly live in treehouses to protect themselves from jungle animals. People in *Wongo* live in tiny huts on the beach, despite the alligators crawling everywhere.

There are four exploitation scenes. The girls' temple dance and the catfight between Mona and Ahtee are silly and prolonged. A few girls swim in the nude; this is filmed underwater — and at a distance. Omoo's fight with the (suspiciously sluggish) alligator is undoubtedly a great exploitation scene and comes the closest to a little feminism as anything in the film. The women are also supposed to be good at using spears and setting ambushes, but they are not very convincing. Any attempt to find real feminism in *Wongo* is defeated by the girls' enthusiastic laughter at the catfight and by the knowing winks that all the men (but not the grinning women) make at the audiences in the final mass wedding scene.

All the characters are interested only in the opposite sex. The Wongo women and Goona men are obsessed with each other. The unattractive Wongo men and Goona women are afraid of losing their potential mates. *Wongo*'s smarmy, very outdated attitudes and deadly attempts at humor (together with an insistently comic soundtrack) make it one of the worst prehistoric films and make *Prehistoric Women* look pretty good by comparison.

Wild Women of Wongo was issued in the DVD *Primitive Triple Feature*, with two equally cheesy 1950s features about modern primitives, *Bowanga Bowanga* (1951) and *Virgin Sacrifice* (1959). Ref: Jones. *Illustrated Dinosaur Movie Guide*; Senn/Johnson. *Fantastic Cinema Subject Guide*; MK 2.

Wind Up Wilma (1981) *see* **The Flintstones: Wind Up Wilma** (1981)

Witch Without a Broom (1967) [alt. *Una Bruja sin Escoba*] Spain/US; dir. Joe Lacy; PRC/Sidney Pink. 88 min.; color. Screenplay, Howard Berk (José Luis Navarro); photography, Alphonso Nieva; music, Fernando Garcia Morcillo. *CAST:* Jeffrey Hunter (*Garver Logan*); Maria Perschy (*Marianna*); Gustavo Roja (*Cayo*); Perla Cristal; Al Mulock (*Wurlitz the Wizard*).

A medieval witch time-switches a modern man to the caveman period, ancient Rome, her own time and the future. Everywhere they go, innumerable people find them irresistibly attractive. *Variety* (April 12, 1967) reported that "production values are fine ... color is good.... The actors do the best they can" but the dialogue is "archly inept." Ref: *Internet Movie Database*; not viewed.

The Women Gladiators (1963) *see* **Thor and the Amazon Women** (1963)

Women of the Prehistoric Planet (1966) U.S.; dir. Arthur C. Pierce; Realart. 91 min.; color. Screenplay, Arthur C. Pierce; photography, Archie Dalzell; music, Hans J. Salter (uncredited stock music). *CAST:* Wendell Corey (*Adm. King*); Keith Larsen (*Cmdr. Scott*); John Agar (*Dr. Farrell*); Irene Tsu (*Linda*); Roberto Ito (*Tang*); Paul Gilbert (*Lt. Bradley*); Merry Anders (*Lt. Lamont*); Stuart Margolin (*Chief*).

A spaceship crewed by both humans and Centaurans lands on an unknown planet, one of the "inner planets" of a "new sun," where they kill one unimpressive dinosaur. Linda, who is half human and half Centauran and who has "never even seen a boy of my own age," meets Tang, a young man, also half–Centauran, the descendant of people who survived when an earlier spaceship crashed on the planet. The two fall in love but are attacked by savage cavemen. They are saved by men from Linda's spaceship. As a volcano erupts, the ship leaves but Linda and Tang remain behind together. The expedition commander names the planet "Earth" and we see North and South America recede as the ship goes into space.

Women of the Prehistoric Planet came out the year *Star Trek* came to TV and is very much like a terrible episode of some routine SF TV series — slow and repetitious with portentous dialogue, cheap sets and silly costumes. And it's twice as long as a TV episode. Nothing happens fast except the two young people falling in love.

The theme is racial tolerance. The Centaurians are played by Asian actors, the humans by whites. Many humans are prejudiced against Centaurans, who once had a high civilization but somehow reduced their planet to a desert waste. Tang, who has been alone since his astronaut parents died, lives in a cave but with all the necessities of life, including abundant food. He plays the flute and speaks the same language as the spacemen. The real primitives, the cavemen, are seen briefly. They are savages with spears and stone axes, who wish to kill Tang even though there is plenty of land to share. They have no dialogue. They may have been all wiped out in the big fight scene or in the volcanic eruption, which would mean that mankind may be descended entirely from the space visitors and not at all from primitive man.

Variety (Nov. 23, 1966) approved of the acting and photography and found that though "strictly in the B category, enough novelty is displayed to maintain interest." Berry, on the other hand, considers the film dreadful in every way and evidence that SF films were still at the *Flash Gordon* level only two years before *Planet of the Apes* and *2001*, both in 1968. *Women of the Prehistoric Planet* shares with the anodyne TV series *Battlestar Galactica* (1978–80) and the superior films *Quatermass and the Pit* (1967) and *Star Wars* (1977) the idea that mankind is descended from space visitors. Ref: Berry. *Dinosaur Filmography*; Hardy. *Overlook Film Encyclopedia: Science Fiction*; MK 2.

X-Files (1998) U.S.; dir. Rob Bowman; 20th Century–Fox. 121 min.; color. Screenplay, Chris Carter; screenplay, Ward Russell; music, Mark Snow. CAST: David Duchovny (*Fox Mulder*); Gillian Anderson (*Dana Scully*); John Neville (*Well-Manicured Man*); William B. Davis (*Cigarette-Smoking Man*); Martin Landau (*Alvin Kurtzweil*); Blythe Danner; Armin Mueller-Stahl; Craig Davis (*First Primitive*); Carrick O'Quinn (*Second Primitive*).

In "North Texas, 35,000 B.C." two fur-clad men caught in a snowstorm take shelter in a huge cave. They make fire, explore the cavern and are killed by violent space aliens. In modern times, the aliens and human conspirators threaten the world.

The prehistoric men look tough and competent. They don't have time in the four minute sequence to do much. The film was based on the popular 1993–2002 TV series. The brief prologue establishes that the creatures who bedeviled the heroes throughout the series arrived on Earth millennia ago. It's hard to prove that there have been no aliens on Earth, but 35,000 B.C. is much earlier than the date anthropologists believe humans reached the Western Hemisphere. Ref: *Internet Movie Database*; MK 6.

Xena: Warrior Princess (1995–2001) episode 106, *Lifeblood* (2000), with excerpts from unused pilot film *Amazon High* [alt. *Amazon Nation*]. U.S.; dir. Paul Grinder, Michael Hurst; Renaissance Pictures. Episode of TV series; 44 min.; color. Screenplay, R.J. Stewart, George Strayton, Tom O'Neill; music, Joseph LoDuca. CAST: Lucy Lawless (*Xena*); Renee O'Connor (*Gabrielle*); Selma Blair (*Utma Cyane*); Danielle Cormack (*Samsara*); Kate Elliott (*Yakut*); Claudia Black (*Karina*); Shelley Edwards (*Cyane*); Karl Urban (*Kor*); Monica McSwain (*Olan*).

In ancient times, grim, Greek warrior woman Xena and her cheerful, idealistic companion Gabrielle visit their friends the Northern Amazons, who live apart from men in the Russian forest. Gabrielle, an Amazon princess, quickly comes into conflict with Cyane, the unwise, bloodthirsty Northern Amazon queen, over two issues. Cyane wants to attack and destroy a male-led tribe which attacked the Amazons and killed many of them, including the shamaness Yakut. Since the men were defeated and no longer pose a threat, Gabrielle counsels peace. Also Xena's infant daughter Eve is to be initiated as an Amazon, but Gabrielle objects to Cyane's insistence on baptizing Eve in blood.

Xena is visited by the spirit of the dead shamaness Yakut, who shows her visions of the prehistoric origins of the Amazons. In the beginning, the proto–Amazons (who did not call themselves Amazons) are simply women whose men had been killed by enemies. They are led by the warlike Samsara, who bids a shaman to summon the Utma, a legendary leader from the future. When the Utma appears, she is a frightened California high school girl called Cyane, who has no idea how she got there! Cyane the Utma is horrified by the Amazon's constant fighting with men but she shows real courage. The proto–Amazons eat horses but do not ride them. When the Utma rides a horse, the other women bow to her, crying "She has mounted a high one!" She begins to teach the Amazons to ride.

Samsara becomes jealous of the Utma and challenges her to a foot race to see who will lead the tribe. During the race Samsara uses dirty tricks and the Utma falls into a river. She is rescued by Kor, a caveman. In his cave, they share a kiss. Samsara arrives, defeats Kor and wants to kill him. The Utma saves Kor, but Samsara accuses her of siding with men.

Kor's male-led tribe captures the Utma and orders Kor to kill her. He refuses. Samsara and the Amazons attack the men, drive them off and rescue the Utma. The male tribe condemns Kor to death, but the Utma and the other Amazons attack again, on horseback for the first time, defeat the men again and save Kor. Samsara wants to pursue and annihilate the men, but the Utma does not permit this. She tells Kor to go to his people and teach them a better way. The Amazons are impressed by the Utma's courage and compassion. Her name Cyane becomes the name of all subsequent Northern Amazon queens.

Xena interrupts the ceremony at which the Amazons and the current Queen Cyane are about to bathe Eve in blood. She tells them all she has learned about the true origins of the Amazon heritage. The Amazons, even Cyane, have a change of heart, baptize Eve in water and call off their war of revenge.

COMMENTARY. *Xena: Warrior Princess* and Renaissance Picture's parallel series *Hercules: The Legendary Journeys* (1994–2000) were far from flawless but became very popular internationally. Both series had charismatic, exciting lead actors, Joseph LoDuca's Emmy-nominated scores, beautiful New Zealand scenery, usually impressive production values, and scripts which reflected considerable knowledge of ancient history and lore (though filtered through highly anachronistic stories and attitudes).

After *Xena* and *Hercules* became hits, Renaissance Pictures decided to produce a third series, to be set in prehistory and titled *Amazon High* (alt. *Amazon Nation*). A pilot film titled *Amazon High* was directed by Michael Hurst, New Zealand's busiest young actor, who played Iolaus, Hercules's sidekick, in the *Hercules* series and directed several episodes of both *Xena* and *Hercules*.

No series was ever made and the pilot was never shown. It is frustrating that a feature-length film set in prehistory was made by a firm with Renaissance Picture's track record but will never be seen, except for the excerpts seen in the *Xena* episode *Lifeblood*. Paul Grinder directed the *Lifeblood* scenes with Xena, Gabrielle and the later Amazons.

The episode is quite disappointing, though Hurst's original film may have been better. The writers simply duplicate the prehistoric story in Xena's time. The quarrel between Gabrielle and bloodthirsty Cyane parallels that between the Utma Cyane and militaristic Samsara. Both stories end when the good Amazon queen prevails, the bad Amazon queen reforms and the Amazons decide not to wipe out a defeated male enemy. The episode cuts back and forth between the old and new stories, which confused many viewers. After a film about 90 minutes long was squeezed into about half of a 44-minute episode, both stories seemed rushed and underdeveloped.

The *Whoosh* site for *Xena* fans (*http://www.whoosh.org*) has a synopsis of the *Amazon High* pilot, contributed by Cheryl Ande, one of the few fans to have seen it. The film has the same plot as the prehistoric segments of *Lifeblood* with some additional details. Kor's caveman tribe are cannibals. The Amazons (who initially call themselves the Tretomlec) have a male shaman until his death. Cyane's sidekick Olan can speak to animals. In a crisis, Olan coolly asks Cyane, "If you get killed, can I have your shoes?"

Selma Blair (*Legally Blonde*; *Hellboy*) is a busy young American actress. Commanding Danielle Cormack is the most prestigious New Zealand actress and very popular among *Xena* fans for playing Ephiny, an ideal Amazon queen, in several episodes. Karl Urban, who played Kor, is a New Zealand actor who played recurring villain Julius Caesar in many *Xena* stories. Urban's Kor is one of the cutest cavemen ever filmed. Ref: Whoosh website episode guide, *http://www.whoosh.org*; MK 4.

II

Documentaries

The Age of Mammals (1981) U.S.; dir. Doug Beswick, Mark Wolf; Charles Cahill & Associates. Animated short; 10 min.; color. Screenplay, Gail Morgan Hickman, Jim Aupperle.

A few shots show the last of the dinosaurs, followed by several prehistoric mammals, including Eohippus, an early horse, and the wooly mammoth. At the end, Neanderthal man appears. The film calls him "small and weak," able to survive only by using his intelligence to make clothes and tools. (Actually, Neanderthal was very strong.) In conclusion, the film asks, "Will man survive? The choice is ours." The animated animals and men in *The Age of Mammals* are mostly static, but still evocative. Ref: Berry. *Dinosaur Filmography*; MK 6.

The Age of Man (1968) U.K.; BBC/Time-Life. 20 min.; b&w. (no. 8 in series *Evolution of Living Things*).

A brief overview of human evolution. Ref: *OCLC WorldCat*; not viewed.

America's Stone Age Explorers (2004) U.K./U.S.; TV6/BBC/WGBH/PBS. 55 min.; color. Producer, Richard Reisz; writer, Nigel Levy; narrator, Peter Thomas. (In the *Nova* TV series)

The Clovis spear point, dating to 13,000 years before the present, was "the greatest technological breakthrough of the Stone Age ... a prehistoric weapon of mass destruction" which helped the Paleo-Indians wipe out the North American mammoths and other megafauna. Clovis points have been found in many different environments in 48 states. Recently, apparently pre–Clovis sites have been found, such as Meadowcroft, Pennsylvania and Monte Verde in Chile. There is evidence that plants and animals lived along the Alaska coast during the height of the Ice Age, suggesting that humans could have moved by boat from Beringia to the American Northwest before the Clovis period. Alaskan natives today can make long sea voyages in small boats built with prehistoric techniques. European-like DNA has been found in modern Ojibwa Indians, but this strain may have come from Siberia. The Solutreans, who disappeared in France around 18,000 B.C., had spear points which resembled Clovis points more than ancient Siberian weapons. The Clovis point may have been invented in America, not imported. A few experts believe that the Solutreans could have migrated across the Atlantic during the Ice Age. The Gault Site (Texas) shows a vast variety of Clovis tools. Clovis points were traded over hundreds of miles. Ancient groups may have exchanged women and technology. Caches of tools such as the Fenn Cache (Idaho) suggest seasonal migrations. Ref: viewed. MK: 8.

Ancient Britains (1996) [alt. *Ancient Britons*] U.K.; producer, Ruth Wood; Cromwell Productions. 47 min.; color. Writer, Les Prince; narrator, Kate Harper. (no. 6 in the series *Ancient Civilizations*)

A study of ancient monuments and settlements in Britain, including Stonehenge. Ref: *OCLC WorldCat*; not viewed.

Ancient Britons (1966) *see* **Ancient Britains** (1996)

Ancient Man (2003) U.S.; Disney Educational Productions/ABC News. ca. 18 min.; color. Producer, Kathleen Ryan; narrators, Johnny Lancaster, Zina Camblin. (In the series *Ancient & Modern Cultures*)

In a program aimed at high school students, archeologists study ancient clothing and knots to develop a new view of Paleolithic life. Ref: *OCLC WorldCat*; not viewed.

The Ancients of North America (1992) U.S.; dir. Tom Naughton; Arkios Productions/Time-Life. ca. 24 min.; color. Writer, Pierre Charboneau; narrator, John Rhys-Davies. (In the *Archaeology* TV series).

An examination of the Paleo-Indians, the

(II) The Animal Within

first inhabitants of the American Southwest. Included in the Time-Life video *Ancient America*, together with *Cannibals!* (about the Anasazi Indians). Ref: *OCLC WorldCat*; not viewed.

The Animal Within (1974) [alt. *Up from the Apes*] U.S.; dir. Mel Stuart, Walton Green; American National Enterprises. Feature film; color. Producer, David L. Wolper; based on books by Robert Ardrey. With: Anthony Zerbe; Janos Prohaska, Anthony Prohaska, Robert Prohaska.

A study of the nature of man, beginning with prehistoric humans. Ref: Jones. *Illustrated Dinosaur Movie Guide*; *Internet Movie Database*; not viewed.

The Animal World (1956) U.S.; dir. Irwin Allen; Warner Bros. 81 min.; color. Writer, Irwin Allen; photography, Harold Wellman; music, Paul Sawtell; animators, Ray Harryhausen, Willis O'Brien; narrators, Theodore van Eltz, John Storm.

This ambitious but mediocre documentary attempts to tell the whole story of animal life on Earth from the beginning to modern man. Dinosaurs and modern animals appear. An early scene shows a model caveman with a sword (!) being gobbled by a Brontosaurus. The voiceover admits the scene was impossible, saying "Man had not yet been created, but if he had been ..." Excerpts from *The Animal World* appeared in *Trog* (1970).

Variety (April 18, 1956) was very enthusiastic about the film, but Berry considers it hopelessly old-fashioned, corny and ill-conceived, except for the dinosaurs, modeled by O'Brien and animated by Harryhausen. Ref: Berry. *Dinosaur Filmography*; Webber. *Dinosaur Films of Ray Harryhausen*; *Internet Movie Database*; not viewed.

Ape Man: Adventures in Human Evolution (2000) *see* **Dawn of Man: The Story of Human Evolution** (2000)

Ape Man: The Story of Human Evolution (1994) U.K.; Granada Television/ A&E. ca. 200 min.; color. Producer, Rod Caird; dir. James Black (Parts 1, 2), Chris Nicholson (Parts 3, 4); based on nonfiction book by Rod Caird; narrator, Walter Cronkite; scientific consultant, Robert Foley.

The whole story of humans from the early primates. Part 1. *The Human Puzzle*. Early bipedalism; the Taung Skull from South Africa; the Lucy skeleton in Ethiopia; Homo Habilis and the first tools; scavenging for meat by early hominids.

Part 2. *Giant Strides*. Examines DNA evidence, including the Mitochondrial Eve theory, which assumes that Asian Homo Erectus (including Peking Man) died out and was not an ancestor of modern man. A recent important insight is that bipedalism developed long before brain growth and toolmaking. A drought may have encouraged bipedalism by replacing trees with savanna, requiring longer walks. Walking erect also permitted hominids to carry food long distances by hand, perhaps to females taking care of infants. Tools permitted scavenging of bone marrow. Homo Erectus left Africa about 1,000,000 years ago. Firemaking was very important but it is hard to date when it began.

Part 3. *All in the Mind*. It is difficult to see how the human brain became different from those of the smarter apes, but language seems to have been central. As people lived in larger groups they had greater need for language for communication and planning. Language seems to go back 2,000,000 years to Homo Habilis, a time of growth in population and the disappearance of australopithecines. Neanderthals had tools and probably a simple language, they were physically strong and tough, yet they eventually failed. Neanderthal specimens have bone damage typical of rodeo cowboys today, caused by hunting large animals. They took care of injured and old people and were the first people to bury their dead. It is hard to say why the Neanderthals disappeared and we are unsure whether they were among the ancestors of modern Europeans. Anatomically-modern humans lived at Klasies in South Africa 100,000 years ago and probably had a complex language. Very early modern humans produced a variety of specialized, difficult-to-make tools and weapons. To make these, they had to plan and to pass on knowledge to their young. They began to make non-utilitarian objects, including beads for personal adornment. Painted caves may have been places of worship.

Part 4. *Science and Fiction*. Neanderthals were long maligned by European scientists, who preferred to believe that modern humans were found in Europe far back in antiquity and that Neanderthals were brutish savages and an evolutionary dead end which left no descendants.

(The documentary includes brief scenes from Griffith's *Man's Genesis* and *Brute Force* as a commentary on Neanderthal. Griffith probably intended Weakhands and his people, the heroes of the two films, as modern humans, but he may have thought of Monkeywalk's band, the villains in *Brute Force*, as Neanderthals. *Ape Man* shows scenes of both groups without distinction.) An arthritic Neanderthal specimen was used to argue that Neanderthal was stooped. The Piltdown Man forgery, "found" in England in 1912, fitted the current theory that big brains preceded other physiological changes; it had a human skull and an apelike jaw (which was actually an ape's jaw). The forgery was planted in a very old strata to support the idea that very early Europeans were modern. The forgery was not exposed until 1953. (This was the year in which *The Neanderthal Man*, a potboiler discussed in Part III, included a reference to Piltdown Man as a genuine fossil.)

The Piltdown Man forgery led to rejection of the Taung Skull, a genuine early hominid found in South Africa in the 1920s, which had a small brain but humanlike teeth and jaws. Peking Man, a group of Homo Erectus fossils found in China in 1929, was embraced; scientists for many years assumed Asia was the home of the earliest humans. The tropics were assumed to be a place for low savages only, so Africa was not viewed as a site for human evolution. Only in the late 1940s did the discovery of more and more African fossils lead to a consideration of Africa as the original home of mankind.

Raymond Dart, discoverer of the Taung Skull, proposed that early humans were innately violent predators. Robert Ardrey popularized this idea in several books (which were sources for the views presented in *2001: A Space Odyssey*, 1968). Later research (accepted by Dart) showed that early Africans were prey to predators, not predators themselves.

Walter Cronkite's remarks are superficial but many experts describe their work in some detail. There are no elaborate reenactments; students in modern clothes demonstrate ancient practices, such as how hominids butchered an animal. *Ape Man* is one of the first of the wave of sophisticated documentaries on early man in the 1990s. Ref: *OCLC WorldCat*; MK 9.

The Ape That Took Over the World (2001) see Our Earliest Ancestors: The Ape That Took Over the World (2001)

The Aquatic Ape: A New Model for Human Evolution? (2000) U.K.; producer, Richard Chambers; BBC/Discovery Channel. 50 min; color. Narrator, Andrew Sachs.

Examines Elaine Morgan's challenge to the Savanna Theory. Morgan proposed that a race of semi-aquatic, bipedal apes once inhabited the Danakil Alps in Ethiopia. Ref: *OCLC WorldCat*; not viewed.

The Ascent of Man (1974) U.K./U.S.; dir., Mike Jackson, Adrian Malone; BBC/Time-Life Films/PBS/WHBH. 13 parts, 676 min.; color. Producer, Adrian Malone; writer-narrator, Jacob Bronowski.

Reviewing the first part of this prestigious series, *Variety* (Jan. 15, 1975) wrote "Once again, the BBC has shown U.S. public television how to make programs that are eminently educational while at the same time being entertaining, dramatic and highly visual." *Variety* noted that *The Ascent of Man* "is virtually the individual creation of the late Dr. Jacob Bronowski ... a passionate and highly effective teacher."

Of the 13 parts, only the first two concern prehistory, while the eighth part covers the development of our understanding of human evolution. The other sections deal with the history of other sciences, arts and skills. Part 1. *Lower Than the Angels* (man's anatomical and intellectual evolution); Part 2. *Harvest of the Seasons* (the Neolithic Era, including early agriculture; domestication of animals; nomadism; warfare; the traditional lifestyle of the Bakhtiari people of Iran). Part 8. *Ladder of Creation* (19th century evolutionary theories). The *Variety* reviewer complained that "much of the material covered by *Lower Than the Angels* has been presented often on television" and "is almost a yawn" but is saved by "the spontaneous narration of Bronowski, whose accent in itself is a marvel, combining Polish and Oxbridge." Ref: *OCLC WorldCat*; not viewed.

Before the Romans (1975) U.S.; dir. Terrence Ladlow; International Film Bureau. 27 min.; color.

Prehistoric sites in Britain, including settlements, ritual centers, flint mines, burial sites, monoliths and trails that may have connected holy sites. Ref: *OCLC WorldCat*; not viewed.

Before We Ruled the Earth (2003) U.S.; dir. Pierre de Lespinois; Evergreen Films/Discovery Channel. 2 49-min. parts; color. Producer, Bill Latka; writers, Brian Fagan, Sandra Gregory, Bill Latka; music, Dean Grinsfelder; narrators, Linda Hunt, John Slattery.

Dramatic reenactments (including computer-generated images of extinct animals) show the lives of Homo Erectus, Neanderthals and early Cro-Magnons, including the use of fire and tools and the development of communications. There are several brief segments titled "How We Know What We Know" which discuss fossils and other evidence on which the program is based.

Part 1. *Hunt or Be Hunted*. In Africa, 1.7 million years ago, at the time of Homo Ergaster, two hominids flee from a huge sabre-tooth cat. They make it to a tree. The cat kills a large animal. When the cat leaves its kill, three hominids scavenge meat from the kill. One hominid is killed when the cat returns. Toolmaking was the first revolution in man's history. A young man creates a sharp hand-ax—and cuts his hand. The better hand-ax permits better scavenging and the breaking of bones to get marrow, increasing humans' protein intake and eventually their intelligence.

In England, 300,000 years ago, a band of Homo Erectus, armed with fire, hunt a herd of Megalocerus (giant elk). Although the humans have no speech, they have a sophisticated organization for the hunt, involving two groups of hunters. With fire, they drive the animals to a cliff edge but some of the torches go out and the elk, more frightened of the cliff than the fires, attack the men, hurting two of them. Close-up hunting is extremely hazardous and few Homo Erectus males live beyond their teens. Quarrels break out as men blame each other for the failure. The people know which plants are edible and which have healing power. As a woman uses pine resin to treat a wound, a man notices that the resin makes fire burn persistently. He finds that a torch coated with resin will stay alight even in rain. At a second hunt, men armed with long-burning resin-coated torches drive the elk over the cliff.

40,000 years ago, in Ice Age Europe, Neanderthals hunt the Giant Steppe Bison at close quarters with spears. Since their spears are too heavy to throw far, stabbing the large, dangerous animals is their only way to make a kill. The stone tip breaks off in the wound, causing profuse bleeding. The Neanderthals live in a cave during the long winter. Most of their diet is meat. They have good knives and scrappers. After killing a bison they find a tip of an antler horn in the meat. They can't figure this out, since they know reindeer would never fight a bison. They do not realize that other humans are making spearheads of antler horn.

In a hard winter, the beasts are scattered and hunters have to go ever farther to find game. With the band starving, three hunters go on a long, terrible journey for food. They can make fire but they do not have bone needles and cannot make well-fitted, weatherproof clothing. After days of hardships, they rest in a rock shelter where they find another mysterious antler tip, which they still do not realize is a spearhead. They also find the image of a bison carved on a stone. They cannot understand this—it looks like a bison but it isn't a bison. One man dies of exposure. The other two press on and finally find bison. Armed only with stone-tipped spears, they try to kill a one-ton animal. One man is hurt. Suddenly the bison is felled by three thrown spears. Two Cro-Magnons, dressed in weatherproof clothes and armed with light throwing spears, finish off the bison. The two Neanderthals retreat, dooming themselves and their band to starvation.

Part 2. *Mastering the Beasts*. 15,000 years ago in Southern France, Tzori, a young hunter, is exploring a cave to see if it is safe for his people. He awakens a huge bear which charges out the cave entrance and kills a man. The shaman blames Tzori for the death and tells him he must redeem himself by leading a ritual hunt to ensure the passage of the dead man to the next world. Tzori and two other hunters use belladonna berries to induce a hallucinatory trance; they visit a cave in which detailed images of animals have been drawn by their ancestors. Their visions tell them they must hunt the giant ox, one of the most dangerous beasts. The men are excellent hunters, who know the habits of animals and can imitate their calls. Their only possible tactic is to make the ox attack them, so they will be close enough to throw their spears. Each man has an atlatl and several spears. The hunters kill the ox and escape without injury.

In the Beringian Land Bridge between Siberia and Alaska about 15,000 years ago, three hunters wound a wooly mammoth which turns on them and kills them. The three women in their band, Irniq, Sila and Una, soon realize that their men will not return. Spring is coming much too early (since the Ice Age is ending). Due to the warm weather, mammoth meat they have buried in the permafrost as a natural refrigerator is rotten when they dig it up. While they are out hunting small game with little success, a violent Arctic wind blows the roof off their home (made of mammoth bones and skins). Wolves steal their stored food. Without men, food or shelter, the three women and Sila's baby face imminent death.

They go to the home of their ancestors but find it deserted. The ancestors' hut, which was once on high ground, is now on the shore of the rapidly rising sea. They have never heard of women hunting mammoths, but now they have no choice. They find the wounded mammoth which killed the men, still with a spear in its side. It is moving slowly but is still far from death and very dangerous. Their spears can kill a mammoth only if they can hit a vulnerable spot from close in. Sila cannot put her baby down because there are predators everywhere. Sila (carrying the baby) and Una distract the mammoth while Irniq rolls under the beast and stabs it in the belly. The mammoth races off but finally collapses. They finish it off. Soon after they join another band of men and women and move East, joining the first humans in the Western Hemisphere.

Among the Clovis Culture Paleo-Indians about 13,000 years ago, Makwa and Tiak are hunters and traders. They often trade for obsidian rocks which make the best spear points. Clovis points break off in a wound, causing massive trauma. Children play at hunting. As two boys chase a rabbit, one of them, Koji, falls down a sinkhole. He awakens a giant sloth. Before the animal can kill him, Koji is pulled to safety by men brought by the other boy, using a rope made of vines.

A few centuries later, all the megafauna of

An incredibly brave Beringian woman must kill a wounded mammoth in *Before We Ruled the Earth*.

North America are gone except the buffalo. Three groups of Paleo-Indians organize a great buffalo drive to kill hundreds of animals. After weeks of patient preparation they spring their trap. Young men disguised as buffalo calves approach the herd. One hunter, Moak, is frightened by a snake and jumps up, causing the buffalo to stampede and ruining the hunt. A council condemns Moak's cowardice and orders him to work with the women and children building the butchering camp. The hunters again drive the buffalo and this time manage to drive hundreds of them over a cliff. Then comes the dangerous work of finishing off wounded animals. One slightly wounded buffalo breaks loose and charges into the women's camp. Moak redeems himself by spearing and killing the beast before it can hurt anyone.

This excellent documentary packs a lot of information into its little dramas. The first part is about humans whose bodies and brains were different from ours. The second part deals with anatomically-modern humans. Humans advance from scavengers to predators. People first speak not at all, then a little, then fluently. The earliest people have no names; anatomically-modern characters are given names. The vital importance of improving tools, weapons, shelter and clothing is stressed. Their speech is not translated but the narrator (mostly Linda Hunt) explains everything that happens.

Of course the reenactments are speculative but they reflect sophisticated, up-to-date information about prehistoric man. They emphasize early man's hardiness, courage, ingenuity, adaptability and growing intelligence, the constant danger in which they lived and their increasing capacity for communication, cooperation and organization. The stories are dramatically effective precisely because they are convincing. The tale of the Neanderthals' failing in their last hunt is perhaps the saddest scene in any prehistoric film or TV show, while the story of the three incredibly brave Beringian women killing the mammoth is probably the most terrifying and awe-inspiring scene involving early humans. There are no films that do as much as this program to encourage respect for our ancient ancestors. Ref: *OCLC WorldCat*; MK 9.

Beginning of History: Stone Age (1950) U.K./U.S.; International Film Bureau. 21 min.; b&w.

Examines both Old Stone Age hunters and New Stone Age farmers in Britain, including early tools and cultivation methods. Also covers glacial movements; the movement of agricultural techniques from the Middle East to Britain; and burial mounds. The Bureau also released *Beginning of History: Bronze Age* and *Beginning of History: Iron Age* and a 46 min. film combining all three short films and covering the whole period from early prehistory to the Roman invasion of Britain. Ref: *OCLC WorldCat*; not viewed.

The Beginnings of Man (1990) U.S.; dir. Jan Horn; Wombat Films/Stewart International. 6 30-min. parts; color. Presented by Andrew Sillen.

In six parts. 1. *The Prophecy and the Bone*. Three men looked for the Missing Link: Arthur Keith believed in the Piltdown Man; Raymond Dart and Robert Broom supported the evidence of Africa's Taung Skull. 2. *The Fire and the Stone*. The fossil record shows how early humans evolved from being mostly vegetarian to mainly carnivorous. 3. *The Men from the North*.

The life and demise of the Neanderthals and their relationship to modern man. 4. *The Men from the South*. The appearance of modern humans in Southern Africa, perhaps as early as 100,000 years ago. 5. *A Matter of Time*. Dating techniques, including radiometric and optical dating. 6. *The People of Origin*. Examines the San people of Southern Africa for clues to the lives of the earliest modern humans. Ref: *OCLC WorldCat*; not viewed.

Between the Whole Numbers (1970) U.S.; National Council of Teachers of Mathematics/General Learning Corp. Animated short film; 12 min.; color.

In this cartoon for elementary students, cavemen learn that numbers exist between the whole numbers when they divide bearskins. Ref: *OCLC WorldCat*; not viewed.

Bharat Ki-cchap: The Identity of India (1988) India; dir. Chandita Mukherjee; National Council for Science and Technology Communication/Comet Project. 13 parts; ca. 686 min.; color.

The first of thirteen parts in this documentary on the history of science and technology in India was a general overview. The second part, *The Stone Age: Till 3500 B.C.*, examines contemporary tribal communities which continue to practice techniques used in the Stone Age, including stone tools, cave paintings and gathering of forest products. The third part, *The Harappan Civilization, 3500 to 2000 B.C.*, dealt with the earliest organized societies. All other parts were set in historical periods. Ref: *OCLC WorldCat*; not viewed.

The Birth of Europe (1991) U.K.; BBC/A&E/Coronet. ca. 385 min.; color. Producer, Michael Andrews; narrator, Nigel Anthony.

The first two of seven parts were set in prehistory. *Out of the Ice* (55 min.) covers the lives and mysterious disappearance of the Neanderthals and the coming of modern humans during the Ice Age. *Colliding Continents and the Age of Bronze* (55 min.) examines the development of modern tools, the shift from agricultural to military societies and the Minoan and Mycenaean civilizations. Ref: *OCLC WorldCat*; not viewed.

The Body in the Bog (1985) U.K.; BBC. 30 min,; color. Producer, Simon Campbell-Jones.

The British Museum's analysis of an Iron Age body found in a peat bog in Cheshire, England. Ref: *OCLC WorldCat*; not viewed.

Bonehead Detectives of the Paleoworld (1997) Segment, *Mystery of the Neanderthal*. U.S.; dir. John McCally; Stone House Productions/Discovery Channel. Segment of TV series; 22 min.; color. Screenplay, David Bock. CAST: Danny Tamberelli (*Sam*); Rebecca Budig (*Allie*).

Bonehead Detectives of the Paleoworld was a juvenile documentary series, hosted by two children, which concentrated on dinosaurs. *Mystery of the Neanderthal* was apparently the only segment devoted to prehistoric humans. A few seconds from Griffith's *Man's Genesis*, showing Bruteforce kidnapping Lilywhite, are used without attribution to show stereotypes of early man which the documentary tries to refute. The two child hosts sneer at the acting in this scene, oblivious to the facts that Wilfrid Lucas was a terrifying villain and went on to work in over 100 films. Information on Neanderthals provided by the show was elementary but reliable.

Mystery of the Neanderthal was included in the video *Awesome Ancestors*, together with another *Bonehead Detectives* segment *Reptile in the Family*, which examined the Dimetrodon, a possible ancestor of all mammals. Ref: MK 5.

Bronze Age Blast Off (1979) U.K.; BBC/ Films Inc. 50 min.; color. Producer-writer, Dominic Flessati.

Argues that ancient Europeans achieved excellence in metalworking. Ref: *OCLC WorldCat*; not viewed.

Calypso's Search for Atlantis (1978) U.S.; Les Requins Associés/David L. Wolper Productions. 2-part TV special; 2 × 50 min.; color. (In TV series *The Cousteau Odyssey*) Host, Jacques-Yves Cousteau.

The Cousteau Odyssey (1977–78), a series of oceanographic documentaries, followed *The Undersea World of Jacques Cousteau* (1966–76). In the two part episode *Calypso's Search for Atlantis*, Jacques Cousteau "searched" the most likely sites in the Aegean while his rather long-suffering son Phillipe Cousteau was sent to examine dubious clues in the Caribbean. The result was at least more responsible than most Atlantis documentaries. Ref: *Internet Movie Database*; MK 6.

Other serious Atlantean documentaries are: *Aegean: Legacy of Atlantis* (1995, Time-Life Video); *Atlantis* (1975, Orpheus Films); *The Atlantis Connection* (1977, Kentucky Educational Television); *Atlantis in the Andes* (2001, Learning Channel); *Atlantis, Mystery of the Minoans* (1995, Discovery Channel); *Atlantis Reborn* and *Atlantis Uncovered* (both 1999, BBC); *Atlantis, the Lost Civilization* (1996, A&E); *Discovery Atlantis* (1997, Discovery Channel School); *The Heart of Atlantis* (1990, RAI, Italy); *Helike: The Real Atlantis* (2000, BBC); *The Hunt for Atlantis* (1993, Discovery Channel); *Lost City of Atlantis* (1997, History Channel); *Lost City of the Aegean* (1993, Learning Channel); *The Search for Atlantis* (1996, Atlantic Productions/ A&E); and *Thera/Santorini* (1999, Studio Zero TV).

More dubious documentaries on the subject are *The A.R.E.'s 2003 Search for Atlantis* (2003, Association for Research and Enlightenment); *Atlantis and the World's Shifting Crust* (1995, Laura Lee Press); *Atlantis: In Search of a Lost Continent* (1997, Questar, Inc.); *English Sacred Sites: The Atlantis Connection* (1999, Lightworks Audio/Video), which claims to connect Atlantis and Stonehenge; *In Search of Atlantis* (1976, Alan Landsburg Productions); *Is Atlantis in the Bible?* (1990, Halo TV/ Film Productions); *The Legend of Atlantis* (2000, dir. Elia the Prophet; Royal Atlantis Film/Terra Entertainment); *Prehistory, Ancient History (5,000 B.C.E.–10,000 B.C.E.)* (1988, Meta Center/Moody Video, in the series *Black History Lectures*), which claims to provide a black perspective on Atlantis; *The Road to Atlantis* (1987, Mako Films); and *World of the Unknown* (1996, UFO Central Video).

Internet Movie Database claims that a 1933 German documentary *The Search for Atlantis* was a record of "of an expedition to South America, organized by the Nazi government, to search for the legendary lost city of Atlantis." I can find no confirmation of this film and I believe it never existed. David Stuart Hull's book *Film in the Third Reich* (1969) says that in the mid–1930s German brothers Franz and Edgar Eichhorn tried to sell "spectacular" footage they had shot on the Amazon. They may have tried to use this material as an Atlantis documentary but they finally sold it to Ufa, a large German film company which was of course under Nazi control. Ufa made a feature film *Kautschuk* (alt. *Die Grüne Holle; The Green Hell*, 1938, dir. Eduard von Borsody) from the Eichorn footage. The feature had nothing to do with Atlantis.

The Cardiff Giant (1999) U.S.; Weller & Grossman Productions/History Channel. 50 min.; color. (In the TV series *In Search of History*). Screenwriter, Sean P. Geary; narrator, David Ackroyd.

In 1868 the Cardiff Giant, a huge stone over ten feet tall, was found in upstate New York and exhibited as the remains of an ancient man. Historians examine one of the most famous archeological hoaxes in history. Ref: *OCLC WorldCat*; MK 7.

Cave Beneath the Sea (1994) Australia/U.S.; dir. Bertrand Morin; New Dominion Pictures/Quai 32/Learning Channel. 28 min.; color. Screenwriter, George Bledsoe; narrator, John Rhys-Davies (In the *Archaeology* TV series)

The 1985 discovery of prehistoric cave paintings in the underwater Cosquer Cave on the Mediterranean cost of France. Both *Cave Beneath the Sea* and *People of the Bog*, an *Archaeology* segment about ancient, not prehistoric Europe, were included in the misleadingly titled 1995 video *Prehistoric Inhabitants*. Ref: *OCLC WorldCat*; MK 7.

Caveman Couture (2001) *see* **Old Fashioned: The Real Caveman Couture** (2001)

The Cavemen (1997) U.S.; FilmRoos/History Channel. ca. 44 min.; color. Producer, Lionel Friedberg; narrator, David Ackroyd (Shown in two History Channel series: *In Search of History* and *Secrets of the Ancient World*).

This short documentary efficiently presents a good deal of information on the Neanderthals. It discusses their wide geographic range and low population density; their skill at surviving the Ice Age; their clothing, appearance and great bodily strength; their life expectancy and burial customs, including grave goods which suggest belief in an afterlife. The narrator explains that the discovery of an elderly, arthritic specimen called the Old Man of LaChapelle caused scientists to wrongly describe Neanderthals as shambling brutes. Evidence of this prejudice is shown by excerpts from two silent Hollywood films, Keaton's comedy *The Three Ages* (1923) and Griffith's *Brute Force* (1914).

Onscreen experts debate the nature of Neanderthal intelligence; whether they had language; possible survival cannibalism; the status of Neanderthal women; their encounter with Cro-Magnons and why they died out; and whether modern humans are descended from them. Includes brief reenactments of simple scenes. The otherwise fine documentary makes a bad error when it intercuts from actors convincingly made up as Neanderthals to modern black people of a simple-technology culture (apparently Africans or Australian aborigines) who look nothing like the ancient Neanderthals. Ref: *OCLC WorldCat*; MK 9.

The Caves of Altamira (1989) Spain; dir. José Antonio Parno; Spanish Ministry of Culture/Films for the Humanities. 26 min.; color. Screenwriter, Manuel Fernandez Miranda. Cave drawings of animals and mysterious symbols in Altamira Cave in Spain. Ref: *OCLC WorldCat*; not viewed.

The Celts: Rich Tradition & Ancient Myths (1986) U.K./France/Austria; dir. David Richardson; BBC/FR3/Osterreichischer Rundfunk. ca. 330 min.; color. Producer, Tony McAuley; writer-narrator, Frank Delaney. The first of six parts, *The Man with the Golden Shoes*, includes reconstruction of a Celtic Iron Age village. Ref: *OCLC WorldCat*; not viewed.

Challenging the Human Evolution Model (1994) *see* **Some Liked It Hot** (1994)

Chariots of the Gods (1970) [orig. *Erinnerungen an die Zukunft*] West Germany; dir. Harald Reinl; Terra Filmkunst. 92 min.; color. Screenplay, Harald Reinl, Wilhelm Roggersdorf based on books by Erich von Daniken.

"Was God an astronaut?" asked the posters for this uncritical presentation of von Daniken's theories of extraterrestrial influence on early man. Incredibly, Reinl's film was nominated for an Oscar for Best Documentary. *The Case of the Ancient Astronauts* (1979, PBS) was a critical examination of von Daniken's assault on history. Ref: *Internet Movie Database*; not viewed.

Claims that aliens visited prehistoric Earth are also made in: *Ancient Aliens* (1997, A&E/

History Channel); *Chariots of the Gods: The Mysteries Continue* (1996); *Chariots of the Gods* (an "update," 1997); *In Quest of Ancient Aliens* (1999, Blair & Associates); *In Search of Ancient Astronauts* (1972, Alan Landsburg Productions); *In Search of Ancient Aviators* (1976, Alan Landsburg Productions); *In Search of Ancient Mysteries* (1989, Alan Landsburg Productions); *In Search of Strange Visitors* (1976, Alan Landsburg Productions); *The Outer Space Connection* (1987, Alan Landsburg Productions), which claims that aliens who visited Earth thousands of years ago will return on Dec. 24, 2011; and *Thinking Allowed: Neil Freer: Who Were the Gods?* (1992, Thinking Allowed Productions);

Other heterodox claims about prehistory have been made in several videos. *The Hidden History of the Human Race* (1996, ITV Productions) claims that humans descended from "a higher realm." *Mysterious Origins of Man* (1995, BC Video) claims that "unexplained mysteries" and "shocking evidence" justify its attacks on accepted theories about human prehistory and was followed by several more BC Video products: *Companion Tape to the Mysterious Origins of Man* (1996); *The Mystery of Jurassic Art* (alt. *Jurassic Art*, claiming that Peruvian and Mexican artifacts prove that humans lived with dinosaurs, 1999); *Rewriting Man's History* (1999); and *Challenging New Theories* (1999). In *Quest for the Lost Civilizations* (1998, Channel Four/Learning Channel, in three parts: *Heaven's Mirror*; *Forgotten Knowledge*; *Ancient Mariners*), producer-writer Graham Hancock presents astronomical and geological evidence, including the supposed underwater structures off the Japanese island of Yonaguni, which he believes proves that an advanced civilization existed about 10,500 B.C. Also note *Technologies of the Gods: The Case for Pre-historic High Technology* (1998, Mystic Fire Video).

Children of Eve (1987) U.K./U.S.; BBC/WGBH-TV/PBS. 58 min.; color. Producer-writer, John Groom; narrator, Don Wescott. (In the *Nova* TV series)

Investigates two new methods of studying early humans—blood protein analysis and mitochondrial DNA—and the theories based on these techniques, including "mitochondrial Eve," a single African woman who may have been the ancestor of all modern humans. Ref: *OCLC WorldCat*; not viewed.

Coincidence in Paradise (1999) U.S.; dir. Matthias von Gunten; First Run/ Icarus Films. 88 min.; color. Writer-producer, Matthias von Gunten. Meave Leakey and other scholars discuss the latest findings on human origins. Ref: *OCLC WorldCat*; not viewed.

Coming Into America (2004) *see* **Scientific American Frontiers: Coming Into America** (2004)

The Coming of Man (1968) U.K.; Halas & Batchelor Cartoon Films. Animated short film; 13 min.; color. Animators: John Halas, Joy Batchelor.

Explains the special adaptations that distinguished early man from other animals. Ref: *OCLC WorldCat*; not viewed.

The Coming of Man (1986) Australia; Opus Films. 67 min.; color. Producer-writer-narrator, Robert Raymond. (In the series *Australian Ark*)

The 50,000 year history of the Australian Aborigines. Explains artifacts including the 30,000-year-old skull of a cremated woman, walls markings and engraved stone faces in the desert. Ref: *OCLC WorldCat*; not viewed.

The Compulsive Communicators (1978) *see* **Life on Earth: The Compulsive Communicators** (1978)

Conquest (2003) U.S.; dir. Louis C. Tarantino; Greystone Communications /History Channel. 22-min. episode of documentary TV series; color. Host-writer-producer, Peter Woodward.

In each short segment of the *Conquest* series on the History Channel, erudite English actor Peter Woodward (son of Edward Woodward, star of *The Equalizer*) leads the enthusiastic amateurs of the *Conquest* Fight Team in learning an historical or modern form of combat. The emphasis is on the specific tactics imposed by weapons technology.

In this untitled segment, Team members (in modern dress) must make and learn to use prehistoric weapons. They produce throwing, stabbing and clubbing weapons; knapp stones with flint to make hand-axes; make fire with an animal-sinew bow-drill; sharpen spear-points, harden them in fire and bind them to spears; and create a blowpipe and dart. They learn to vastly improve spear-throwing with an atlatl. They make animal-hide shields and reed body armor for combat against other humans. Finally, they use their arsenal against a "bear" (Woodward) and learn that with short-range weapons, the ambush is the only feasible tactic. This rapid-fire segment should convince audiences of the ingenuity, skill and courage of early man. MK 8.

Cosmic Africa (2003) South Africa; dir. Craig Foster, Damon Foster; Cosmos Studios. 72 min.; color. Writer, Hugh Brody; photography, Damon Foster; music, Grant McLachlan, Barry Donnelly. Host, Thebe Medupe.

South African astrophysicist Thebe Medupe attempts to "reconcile science and myth" in this documentary on African prehistoric sites, according to a review in *Variety* (Dec. 1, 2003). Traveling "from ancient monoliths in the Egyptian Sahara to prehistoric cave paintings in Namibia to towering cliff dwellings in Mali" the film is "fascinating and studded with sumptuous imagery." At a Namibian stone formation which is older than Stonehenge, Medupe calculates the positions of the stars 7,000 years ago to investigate the astronomical science of the ancient Naptan people. In a reenactment of an ancient myth, a girl throws a handful of ashes into the air and creates the Milky Way. *Variety* praised Damon Foster's photography and McLachlan's and Donnelly's multi-ethnic music. The executive producer was Ann Duryan, widow of Carl Sagan, writer-host of *Cosmos*. Ref: *Variety* (Dec. 1, 2003); not viewed.

Cosmic Highway (1998) Episode, *Mysteries of the Megaliths: Eric Gets a Date, Ken Goes Around in Circles*. Canada; dir. Nick Orchard; Hit the Highway Productions/Canada Television Fund. 24 min. episode in TV series; color. Writers-hosts, Ken Hewitt-White, Eric Dunn.

Examines the megaliths of England and the possibility that they were used as calendars. Ref: *OCLC WorldCat*; not viewed.

[**Cracking the Ice Age** (1996) U.K./U.S.; BBC/PBS. Not about prehistoric man. This climatological study suggests that the rise of the Himalayas caused an early Ice Age, long before man. Ref: *OCLC WorldCat*.]

Cracking the Stone Age Code (1971) U.K.; BBC. 52 min.; color. Producer, Paul Johnstone; host, Alexander Thom.

Surveys theories about Britain's standing stones and stone rings and cites evidence that ancient Britons may have had sophisticated understanding of mathematics, geometry and astronomy earlier than the Greeks. Ref: *OCLC WorldCat*; not viewed.

Cragghunowen (1989) Ireland; dir. Joe O'Donnell; Cragghunowen Project/Films for the Humanities. 25 min.; color. Producer-writer, Joe O'Donnell; narrator, Des Nealson.

The Cragghunowen Project recreated fences, pottery and other artifacts from Bronze Age Ireland and reenacted the daily life of the people. Ref: *OCLC WorldCat*; not viewed.

Dating the Dreamtime (1989) Australia; dir. David Evans; Australian Broadcasting Corp. 60 min.; color. Reporter, Andrew Waterworth.

Anthropologists use new methods to recalculate the date of the arrival of humans in Australia and establish the origin of the Swamp People of Central Australia. Ref: *OCLC WorldCat*; not viewed.

The Dawn of Humankind (1992) U.S.; WQED-TV/National Academy of Sciences. 58 min.; color. Producer-writer, Gail Willumson; narrator, Mark Lenard. (In the TV series *The Infinite Voyage*)

Studies the whole history of prehistoric man, from Australopithecus through Homo Erectus, Homo Habilis, Neanderthals and Cro-Magnons. Includes discoveries by archeologist Hilary Deacon and geneticist Rebecca Cann and the theory of mitochondrial Eve. Ref: *OCLC WorldCat*; not viewed.

Dawn of Man: The Story of Human Evolution (2000) (alt. *Ape Man*) U.K./U.S.; dir. Jeff Morgan; BBC/Tomato Films/Learning Channel. ca. 300 min; color. Producer, Philip Martin; consultant Leslie C. Aiello; narrator, Hugh Quarshie; music, Paul Lawler.

In 6 parts. 1. *First Born* (dir. Jeff Morgan). The Taung Skull, 2,600,000 years old, found in South Africa, represents Australopithecus Africanus, who were bipedal and made the first bone weapons. Lucy, an almost complete 3,000,000 year old skeleton found in Ethiopia, was erect but a tree-dweller. Raymond Dart's Killer Ape theory, which says that man became human through violence, is now doubted. A drought 3,000,00 years ago led to the development of Australopithecus Robustus, with big jaws designed to eat roots. We are descended from smaller Australopithecines who ate meat, breaking bones with stone tools to get the marrow. These early ancestors were scavengers, not hunters. Their toolmaking required intelligence and meat-eating led to growth in brain size.

2. *Body* (dir. Charlie Smith). In the 1890s, when scientists were searching for the "Missing Link" between apes and humans, Eugene Dubois found Homo Erectus in Java. Unexpectedly it had an ape's brain but a largely human leg. Richard Leakey and Paul Walker found the skeleton of a 12-year-old boy, about 1,500,000 years old at Lake Takana in Kenya. His people were tall and very strong but with small brains. It is not clear whether or not they could talk. Hominids walked upright before they acquired large brains. They looked human before they were human. (Primate actor Peter Elliott, the star of *Missing Link*, advised director Charlie Smith in this segment.)

3. *Love* (dir. Harvey Jones) Homo Heidelbergensis were the first humans in Europe, beginning almost 500,000 years ago. Europe then had lions, elephants and cave bears. The brain of Heidelbergensis was almost as large as modern man's. He hunted as well as scavenged. He built huts, wore skins and made specialized tools. The Altamira Skull in Italy, flint fragments found in England, spears made 400,000 years ago in Germany and evidence of organized hunting in Spain, where the humans drove animals into traps in a swamp, all show that Heidelbergensis was highly successful. He may have made art objects and may have had a simple language and an emotional attachment to family.

4. *Exodus* (dir. Jeff Morgan) There is no evidence that modern humans evolved from Neanderthals. The earliest known remains of modern humans, found in coastal South Africa, may be 120,000 years old. These people were expert at making stone points and specialized tools such as awls, with which they made clothing. They caught fish from the sea, which required cooperation. They probably cooked on hearths and decorated themselves with red ochre. Modern humans moved from

Early modern humans migrate from Africa in *The Dawn of Man*.

Africa perhaps 100,000 years ago, migrating along the coast of South Asia until they reached Australia about 60,000 years ago. They invented boats and nets. A second, later migration moved down the Nile to the Mediterranean and beyond.

5. *Contact* (dir. Lisa Silcock) Neanderthal and modern human remains have been found in the same cave in Portugal, but at different periods. Neanderthal DNA differs from modern man's. Neanderthals made fireplaces and specialized tools but their technology varied little in 200,000 years. Modern humans invented a greater variety of tools and used personal ornaments. Some ornaments made by Neanderthals have been found; these objects are simpler than the ornaments of modern humans. Modern people traded over a large area while Neanderthals were stranded in small areas during the last stages of the Ice Age.

6. *Human* (dir. David Wilson) A small, beautiful carving of a woman's head and wall paintings of animals, found in caves in France, are about 25,000 years old. We cannot understand their meaning, but they resemble the cliff art of South Africa's San People, which is only

a few hundred years old. Trance visions induced by modern San shamans of the Kalahari at rituals for healing the sick resemble the results of experiments with modern subjects adept at self-hypnosis. All this suggests that ancient people had a spiritual world. The series is a very sophisticated overview of human evolution, marred somewhat by spooky, showy photography. The video set is about 100 min. longer than the TV series, which was in four parts: *First Born*; *Body Human*; *Contact*; *Out of Africa*. Ref: *OCLC WorldCat*; MK 9.

Dead Men Talk (1991) U.K.; Granada TV/Channel 4. 50 min.; color.

Discusses the use of computers and other new technology in determining the time and place of the origin of humans. Ref: *OCLC WorldCat*; not viewed.

Death of the Iceman (2002) U.S.; Learning Channel. ca. 50 min.; color. Producers-writers, Sue Learoyd, Nathan Williams; narrator, Dilly Barlow. Ten years after 5000-year-old ice mummy Ötzi the Iceman was found in the Alps in 1991, x-rays revealed an arrowhead in his shoulder. This documentary speculates on how Ötzi may have been killed, focusing too much on his death rather than his life. Ref: *OCLC WorldCat*; MK 7.

Dr. Leakey and the Dawn of Man (1966) U.S.; dir. Nicolas Noxon, Guy Blanchard; National Geographic Society/Wolper Productions. 53 min.; color. Producer-writer, Nicholas Noxon.

Dr. Louis Leakey worked for years before finding remains which proved that mankind originated in Africa. Ref: *OCLC WorldCat*; not viewed.

Dogs and More Dogs (2004) WGBH/Documentary Guild. 55 min.; color. Producer, Paula S. Apsell. (In the *Nova* series)

About a third of this study of the relationship between dogs and humans examines how wolves turned into domesticated animals 10,000 to 14,000 years ago. Zoologist Ray Coppinger doubts that early humans deliberately domesticated and trained dogs and rejects the ideas that dogs gave Cro-Magnons an advantage over Neanderthals or that humans developed language in order to communicate with dogs. Coppinger believes that wolves became domesticated when they began to hang around dumps for wasted human food and that dogs hunted small game for humans. Ref: viewed. MK 8.

The Earliest South Carolinians (1990?) U.S.; dir. Albert C. Goodyear; CQ Television Network/University of South Carolina Institute of Archeology and Anthropology. 22 min.; color. Writer, Albert C. Goodyear; narrator, Robert Bailey.

The archeological investigation of a 10,000-year-old Clovis site. Ref: *OCLC WorldCat*; not viewed.

The Early Americans (1975) U.S.; dir. Alan Pendry; Shell Film Unit. 41 min.; color. Producer, Douglas Gordon; narrator, Peter Marinker.

Humans in America from the nomadic hunters of the Ice Age to the complex societies of the 15th century. Archeologists investigate the remains of a mammoth hunt in Arizona, one of the earliest prehistoric sites in America. Ref: *OCLC WorldCat*; not viewed.

Early Indians of South Dakota (1980) U.S.; KUSD-TV/South Dakota Public Television. 14 min.; color. Producers, Cliff Jansen, Richard Muller. (In the series *South Dakota Adventure*)

Explores the theories about early Native Americans and the archeological methods used to investigate them. Ref: *OCLC WorldCat*; not viewed.

Early Man (2001) U.S.; Full Circle Entertainment/Goldhil Home Media. ca. 150 min.; color. Producer-director-writer, Ned Rodgers. (In the *Just the Facts Learning Series*)

Part 1. *The Beginning of Mankind*. The first apes who walked upright; how scientists determine the age of fossils. Part 2. *Ancestors of Modern Man*. The genus Homo. Part 3. *Dawn of Civilization*. The Neanderthals and anatomically-modern humans; the art of early modern humans, including the Lascaux Cave; man's entry into Australia and the Americas; the development of farming and the domestication of animals.

This somewhat dry, academic presentation covers the whole history of man from the first hominids to the beginnings of civilization and the techniques with which we study early humans. There are no reenactments; we see lecturers, charts, fossils, ancient tools, museum displays and artists' conceptions of early humans. The presentation is very fact-filled but sometimes repetitious, with some inappropriate music. A few unusual theories are offered. Experts propose that Neanderthals may have built some shelters instead of relying solely on caves and that Neanderthals may have died out from respiratory diseases caught from modern humans. Ref: *OCLC WorldCat*; MK 8.

Early Man in North America (1972) U.S.; Films Inc. 12 min.; color. With: Louis Leakey.

Louis Leakey, a major authority on African prehistory, makes the unorthodox claim that humans have been in the Western Hemisphere for 100,000 years. The films cites early mounds, evidence of a far-reaching trading system, an advanced building society in the St. Louis area and the cliff-dwelling Pueblo of the Southwest. The OCLC library cataloging record says this is "an edited version of *In Search of the Lost World*, an MGM documentary." Ref: *OCLC WorldCat*; not viewed.

Ellen's Energy Adventure (1996) U.S.; EPCOT Center/Disney. Short film; 20 min.; color. Music, Bruce Broughton. CAST: Ellen DeGeneres; Bill Nye; Alex Trebek; Willard Scott; Jamie Lee Curtis; Michael Richards (*Caveman Discovering Fire*).

Bill Nye (of the educational TV show *Bill Nye, the Science Guy*, 1993–2002) takes Ellen DeGeneres through time to study the history of man's use of energy, beginning with the "discovery" of fire by a caveman. Ref: *Internet Movie Database*; not viewed.

Enchanted Forest (1936) *see* **Der Ewiger Wald** (1936)

The Enduring Mystery of Stonehenge (1998) U.S.; dir. Melissa Jo Peltier; MPH Entertainment/History Channel. 50 min.; color. Writer, Kelly McPherson; narrator, David Ackroyd. (in TV series *In Search of History*)

Aubrey Burl and other experts examine the archeological puzzles of Stonehenge. Ref: *OCLC WorldCat*; MK 7.

Erinnerungen an die Zukunft (1970) *see* **Chariots of the Gods** (1970)

The Eternal Forest (1936) *see* **Der Ewiger Wald** (1936)

Evolution (1923) U.S./Belgium; dir. Max Fleischer, Ovide Decroly; Red Seal Pictures/Inkwell Studios. 42 min. silent; b&w.

This was probably the first documentary film to include footage of prehistoric man. The film begins with the origin of the solar system and the Earth, then depicts the beginning of life on Earth. Dinosaurs are represented by still models and by footage from Willis O'Brien's *The Ghost of Slumber Mountain* (1919).

A few brief shots of Stonehenge and some reproductions of cave art show "the earliest activities of man." The film shows a reconstructed skull of "the walking Ape-Man of Java" and claims it lived 500,000 years ago and was "the first known human being." Embarrassingly, *Evolution* then presents Piltdown Man, an alleged 100,000 year old fossil "discovered" in England in 1915 which had not yet been exposed as a deliberate fraud when the film was made in 1923. At last come brief still shots of Neanderthal and Cro-Magnon Man (described as "the highest type of primitive man" and "the first true man" respectively), then modern "primitive" humans and finally the skyscrapers of a modern city.

Evolution is inevitably superficial, covering the whole history of life in less than an hour. Its subtitles are sometimes overwrought ("Change! Eternal change!") and of course the film's data is now badly out of date. Nevertheless it represents a fascinating, ambitious and, when it was made only two years before the Scopes Monkey Trial, controversial and even courageous early attempt at natural history education for the masses. Ref: Jones. *Illustrated Dinosaur Movie Guide*; Berry. *Dinosaur Filmography*; Webb. *Animated Film Encyclopedia*; MK 5.

Evolution (1940–41) U.S.; animator, Ray Harryhausen. Uncompleted film; b&w.

Young Ray Harryhausen worked on *Evolution* for several months, intending to produce a 60–90 minute documentary film for the educational market showing the evolution of life from the beginning to the arrival of Homo Sapiens. The project was never completed. Most of the footage, which is described in detail in Roy Webber's *The Dinosaur Films of Ray Harryhausen*, involves dinosaurs but the surviving excerpts include two brief shots of a stocky Neanderthal with a club walking past a waterfall and the rapids of a swift-flowing river with, as Webber puts it, "an appropriately shuffling gait." In both cases, the backgrounds are footage of actual scenery, not animation. The waterfall sequence is in *The Harryhausen Chronicles*, a 1998 documentary. The river sequence is among the extras of the *Harryhausen Chronicles* DVD. Harryhausen would never create another realistic prehistoric human, except for a model of Raquel Welch for the pterosaur scene in *One Million Years B.C.* and a troglodyte for *Sinbad and the Eye of the Tiger* (1977). Ref: Webber. *Dinosaur Films of Ray Harryhausen*; Berry. *Dinosaur Filmography*.

Evolution (2001) Segment, *The Mind's Big Bang*. U.S.; WGBH/NOVA Science Unit/Clear Blue Sky Productions. ca. 60 min.; color. Producers, John Heminway, Michelle Nicholasen; writer, John Heminway; narrator, Liam Neeson. (In the *Nova* TV series)

The first five parts of this seven-part PBS series deal with evolution of pre-human species. Part six, *The Mind's Big Bang*, examines the development of intelligence in modern humans, about 100,000 years ago. The seventh part, *What About God?*, examines the objections of religious Christians to evolution. Ref: *OCLC WorldCat*; not viewed.

Evolution and Human Equality (1987) U.S.; dir. Paul Rocklin; K&S Speakers/ Insight Video. 42 min.; color. Speaker, Stephen Jay Gould. Gould explains how racial differences have been misstated by scientists from before Darwin to the present, permitting racists to use pseudo-science. He notes that new genetic research proves the African origins of Homo Sapiens and the biological equality of the races. Ref: *OCLC WorldCat*; not viewed.

Evolution: Human Origins: A Walk Through Time (1992) U.K.; BBC/Open University. 30 min.; color. Producer, David Jackson; narrator, Peter Skelton.

This examination of evolutionary theory includes an overview of fossil hominids and the earliest evidence of bipedalism. Ref: *OCLC WorldCat*; not viewed.

Evolution of Man (1961) U.S.; American Institute of Biological Sciences/ McGraw-Hill Book Co. 30 min.; b&w. Lecturer, Marshall Newman.

The ascent of man, including the Ice Ages. Made for secondary school students. Ref: *OCLC WorldCat*; not viewed.

Evolution of Man (1988) U.K.; Granada Television International/Films for the Humanities. 20 min.; color. Advisor, Michael Deardon; narrator, Jack Smith. Ref: *OCLC WorldCat*; not viewed.

Der Ewiger Wald (1936) [alt. *The Eternal Forest*; *Enchanted Forest*] Germany; dir. Hans Springer. 75 min.; b&w.

This pseudo-documentary extols Nazi nationalism, equating the ancient German forest with the German people. Scenes showing the earliest pagan settlements make *Ewiger Wald* one of the few films to depict barbarian Europe. The film continues through the Roman period, the Middle Ages and modern times, concluding with a triumphant Hitler. Jeffrey Richards, in *Visions of Yesterday* (1973), calls *Ewiger Wald* a "beautifully photographed and scored ... eulogistic film poem" and "the major cinematization" of Nazi doctrine. Ref: *Internet Movie Database*; not viewed.

Extreme History (2003–) Episode, *Surviving Like Primitive Man* (2003). U.S.; dir. Matthew Ginsburg; History Channel. 22 min.; color. Producer-writer, Michael Stiller; host, Roger Daltrey.

The History Channel tried to alter its staid image and attract a younger audience with this mildly irreverent series, hosted by rock star Roger Daltrey. Steve Watts and David Wescott of the Society of Primitive Technology show Daltrey how to make and use early tools and weapons, including hand axes and slingshots. Daltrey learns that firemaking is extremely difficult. The experts also demonstrate tracking of animals, needle-making, sewing, and building a shelter and a raft. Ref: MK 7.

The Fate of Neanderthal Man: Life and Death in the Ice Age (1999) U.S./Austria; dir. Manfred Bauer, Hannes Schuler; Tangram/Bauer Film Productions/ZDF Enterprises/Films for the Humanities and Sciences. 106 min.; color. Writers, Manfred Bauer, Hannes Schuler.

Part One, *The Mammoth Hunters* (53 min.), concludes that Neanderthals had considerable intelligence, a complex social life and language skills and even music. Part Two, *The Death of Neanderthal Man*, asks whether competition from Cro-Magnons or climatic change led to the Neanderthals' demise and whether modern humans are descended from Neanderthals. Ref: *OCLC WorldCat*; MK 8.

Feet on the Ground, Head in the Stars (1996) U.K.; dir. Ian Russell; BBC/Royal Institution of Great Britain/Films for the Humanities. 60 min.; color. Presenter, Simon Conway Morris.

Morris traces human evolution from the beginnings through Homo Habilis, Homo Erectus and Homo Sapiens, arguing that cosmic events sparked the beginnings of life and that future contact with extraterrestrial intelligence may cause further evolution. Ref: *OCLC WorldCat*; not viewed.

Fire Through the Ages (1978) Norway; dir. Sverre Sandberg; Svekon Films. 11 min.; color.

The importance of fire to people of the Stone Age and Iron Age. Ref: *OCLC WorldCat*; not viewed.

The First Americans (1969) U.S.; dir. Craig Fisher; NBC News/National Academy of Sciences/Films Inc. 52 min.; color. Producer-writer, Craig Fisher; reporter, Hugh Downs.

Traces the migration of the Paleo-Indians across the Bering Sea area to North America. Ref: *OCLC WorldCat*; not viewed.

The First Americans (1991) U.K.; BBC. 50 min.; color. Producer-writer, Simon Campbell-Jones.

A study of the first humans in the Western Hemisphere. Ref: *OCLC WorldCat*; not viewed.

The First Americans (1998) U.S.; dir. Sueann Fincke; MPH Entertainment/ History Channel. ca. 42 min.; color. Writer, Steve Muscarella; narrator, David Ackroyd. (In the TV series *In Search of History*)

Studies theories about the origins of the Paleo-Indians, the first humans in the Americas. Ref: *OCLC WorldCat*; MK 8.

The First Family (1981) U.S.; WVIZ-TV/ Cleveland Museum of Natural History. 60 min.; color. Producer-writer, Milton B. Hoffman; with Donald C. Johanson.

Johanson discusses discoveries in east Africa, including the uncovering in 1975 of the remains of thirteen persons believed to be 3,000,000 years old. Ref: *OCLC WorldCat*; not viewed.

The French Way of Looking at It (1967) *see* **Vingt Mille Ans a la Francais** (1967)

From Homo Erectus to Neanderthal (1972) U.S.; MGM/Films, Inc. 18 min.; color.

A study of archeological evidence of man's evolution. Ref: *OCLC WorldCat*; not viewed.

Genesis (1966) Dir. Jana Merglova; CCM Films. 6 min.; color.

"Presents the origin of man through use of a complicated little box machine made out of polished pieces of wood." Ref: *OCLC WorldCat*; not viewed.

Geosophy: Overview of Earth Mysteries (1988) U.S.; dir. Fehmu Gerceker; Trigon Communications. 95 min.; color.

Experts discuss henges, standing stones and "sacred geometry" at ancient sites in Great Britain. "Geosophy" is not in any dictionary I consulted. Ref: *OCLC WorldCat*; not viewed.

Grimes Graves: The Story of a Neolithic Flint Mine (1988) U.K.; dir. Michael Weigall; English Heritage. 13 min.; color. Writer-producer, Philip Sugg.

Investigates how Neolithic miners extracted flint at a site in Grimes Graves, Norfolk, England. Ref: *OCLC WorldCat*; not viewed.

History of Britain (2000) U.K.; BBC. TV series; 15 50-min. parts; color. Producer, Claire Beavan; writer-presenter, Simon Schama.

This remarkable series traces British history from the earliest times to the present. In Part One *Beginnings (ca. 3100 B.C.–1000 A.D.)*, Schama examines the 5000-year-old Skara Brae site in the Orkney Islands, Europe's most complete Neolithic community, an "intimate, domestic and self-sufficient" village of stone houses containing hearths, indoor toilets and even a "spectacular" dresser. The people kept cattle and dogs, fished and produced ivory necklaces. The Orkneys had standing stones and a burial mound with a "stupendous" vaulted burial chamber. Schama concludes that Neolithic Britain had "a civilization, a style."

By 1000 B.C. Schama finds forest clearing, metalwork in iron and gold, and evidence of population pressure leading to the building of hill forts. The population of Britain in 1000 B.C. may have been as large as in A.D. 1500 Ref: *Internet Movie Database*; MK 9.

History's Ancient Legacies (1998) U.K./ U.S.; Cromwell Productions/Ambrose Video. ca. 150 min.; color. Writer, Matt Ford; narrator, Kate Harper.

Six programs, about 25 min. each, discuss ancient antiquities. Part two uses computer animation to depict the original form of Stonehenge and discusses theories about the prehistoric people who built it. The other segments cover Pompeii, the Aztecs and Maya, ancient Rome, Hadrian's Wall and the Pyramids. Ref: *OCLC WorldCat*; not viewed.

Hoax of the Ages: The Piltdown Man (1997) U.S.; Film Roos/History Channel. 45 min.; color. Producer, Tim Evans. (In the TV series *In Search of History*)

A TV documentary on the most famous archeological fraud, the Piltdown Man, "found" in Sussex in 1908. The remains were supposed to be a very early Briton. Ref: *OCLC WorldCat*; MK 7.

Hominid Evolution (1988) [alt. *Human Evolution*] Canada/U.S.; Documentary Education Resources/University of Waterloo (Ontario), Dept. of Anthropology. 90 min.; color. Producer-writer-presenter, Anne Zeller.

Uses skulls, bones and teeth to examine human evolution. Part one, *The Early Years* (38 min.) investigates the earliest hominids. Part two, *Genus Homo*, discusses Homo Habilis, Homo Erectus, archaic Home Sapiens, Homo Neanderthal and modern Homo Sapiens. Ref: *OCLC WorldCat*; not viewed.

Homo Sapiens (1960) Romania; dir. Ion Popescu-Gopo; Romania Films. Animated film; 10 min.; color.

This animated short blends two previous films, *A Short History* (orig. *Scurte Istorie*, 1958) and *Seven Arts* (alt. *Sapte Arte*, 1959) to show the evolution of man. Ref: *Internet Movie Database*; *OCLC WorldCat*; not viewed.

How Scientists Know About Human Evolution (1991) U.S.; dir. Alan Thwaites; Alan West Video Productions/National Center for Science Education. 19 min.; color. Producer, Barry Bogin; narrator, Saul Wineman. A program for high schools shows how scientists study human fossils and draw conclusions about biological and cultural evolution. Ref: *OCLC WorldCat*; not viewed.

How the Beginning Began (1976) U.S.; Whitehill Films. Animated short film; 9 min.; color. Producer, Hermina Tyrlova.

An animated children's film showing the efforts of a family of cave people to find food and shelter. Ref: *OCLC WorldCat*; not viewed.

The Human Animal: A Natural History of the Human Species (1994) U.K./U.S.; BBC/Discovery Channel. 300 min.; color. Writer-presenter, Desmond Morris.

A TV documentary in six 50-min. parts. The second part, *The Hunting Ape*, discusses human evolution. Other segments cover modern culture and human creativity. Ref: *OCLC WorldCat*; not viewed.

Human Evolution (1988) *see* **Hominid Evolution** (1988)

The Human Journey (1999) U.S./Australia; dir. Roger Scholes; Beyond Productions/Learning Channel/Australian Broadcasting Corp. ca. 150 min; color. Writers, Andrew Waterworth, Roger Scholes; narrator, Henry Rollins.

Part 1. *In Search of Human Origins*. From the Australopithecines through Homo Ergaster, the first definite human ancestor, to the modern humans who left Africa via the Nile Valley.

Part 2. *The Tale of Two Species*. Homo Heidelbergensis was probably the first human species in Europe. In a cave in Spain, a Heidelbergensis band threw their dead down a deep pit. Neanderthals probably evolved from Heidelbergensis. Homo Sapiens from Africa and Neanderthals lived near each other in Palestine. The arthritic Old Man of LaChapelle misled scientists into believing that Neanderthals were stooped and deformed. Neanderthals were well adopted to cold. The made tools, took care of injured people and were the first humans to bury their dead. They probably had a simple language. Modern humans in Europe were more mobile than Neanderthals and may have been nomadic, which gave them an advantage over the static Neanderthals, who lived in small, isolated groups. Modern people made better and more specialized tools and weapons than the unchanging technology of the Neanderthals. Modern humans traded materials over as much as 250 miles. Homo Sapiens and Neanderthals probably lived harmoniously when they were in contact with each other. There is some evidence that Sapiens technology influenced Neanderthal tools. Genetic evidence showed that Neanderthals and modern humans were separate species and rarely or never produced mixed children. The last Neanderthals lived in Spain, where the most recent Neanderthal body (27,000 years old) has been found.

Part 3. *The Creative Explosion.* Homo Sapiens left the Middle East about 90,000 years ago and reached Southeast Asia about 15,000 years later. 75,000 years ago the giant Toba volcanic eruption in Southeast Asia almost wiped out mankind. Human populations plummeted as clouds of debris blanketed the whole world. Humans survived, partly because people can eat almost anything. Sea levels were low and many Indonesian islands were joined together. Bamboo was vastly important for making spears, containers and especially ropes, which were needed to make shelters, bridges and later boats. Seacoasts provided a reliable food source, both fish and seaweed. Probably the first sea crossing in history was made 70,000 to 60,000 years ago, from Indonesia to Australia. Mungo Man, a 60,000 year old body found in Australia, has signs that red ochre was used to decorate the corpse at burial. Ancient Australian rock art shows animals which are now extinct. About 40,000 years ago Cro-Magnons moved into Europe. Mammoths supplied many needs of Cro-Magnons, including ivory and bone for art work. Europeans had needles 25,000 years ago and may have been weaving and sewing textiles. People at the Dolni Vestonice site in Moravia had an organized society. About 20,000 years ago people had pottery and may have made maps. They explored caves up to a mile deep and created art there. The spectacular Lascaux cave paintings, 17,000 years old, were created by the Magdalenians, who built timber scaffolding to reach high on the cave walls. Tools and spears were decorated, often with intricate designs. Flutes, the first musical instruments, appeared about 15,000 years ago. Trading networks extended for at least 300 miles. All these changes reflect a revolution in human consciousness.

The Human Journey is rather dry but reliable and detailed. Ref: *OCLC WorldCat*; MK 9.

The Human Odyssey (2001) Germany; dir. Rainer Hartmann, Heinz Albert Staubitz; ZDF. 156 min.; color.

In three parts: *Out of Africa*; *Dragon Bones*; *The New World*. The history of human settlement of the globe, from the first hominids to Home Sapiens, and from Africa to Asia, Europe, Australia and the Americas. Ref: *OCLC WorldCat*; not viewed.

Human Origins: A Walk Through Time (1992) U.K./U.S.; Open University/BBC/ Pennsylvania State University. 30 min.; color. Producer, David Jackson.

Compares bone structure and muscle attachment of Australopithecus, modern man and other primates. Ref: *OCLC WorldCat*; not viewed.

Human Prehistory and the First Civilizations (2003) U.S.; Teaching Company. 6 120-min. videos; color. Lectures by Brian M. Fagan.

The whole story of prehistory and the ancient civilizations. Ref: *OCLC WorldCat*; not viewed.

Ice Age Crossings (1993) U.S.; dir. Mimi Edmunds; Archaeological Institute of America/ Learning Channel/Quai 32/New Dominion Pictures. 28 min.; color. Producers, Tom Naughton, Nicolas Valcour; writer, George Bledsoe; narrator, John Rhys-Davies. (In the TV series *Archaeology*)

Discoveries of early, non–Clovis Culture artifacts in Montana, Alaska and Brazil suggest that the Western Hemisphere may have been populated by sea routes, not solely by migration over the Bering Straits. A 1994 Time-Life video *Primal Man* included both *Search for Neanderthal* (also 1993) and *Ice Age Crossings*. Ref: *OCLC WorldCat*; MK 7.

Ice World (2003) U.S./U.K.; dir. Tim Lambert; Wall to Wall/Discovery Channel/ Channel Four TV. 92 min.; color. *CAST:* Thierry Lawson (*Bron*); Mark Byron (*Aki*); Natasha Estelle Williams (*Mara*).

24,000 years ago a tiny settlement of Ice Age people exists in what is now Southeast England. Bron is their leader, solely because of his physical prowess. The winters are becoming worse every year and the big herds of reindeer they hunt have disappeared. The 30 people in the clan face starvation. Against the advice of several people, Bron decides the clan should stay where it is during the winter and trust to the spirits to protect them, instead of moving south. As the situation becomes more desperate, two hunters are sent out in a snowstorm. They never return. Children begin dying.

By the spring, only Bron, Aki and Aki's mate Mara are still alive. Aki and Mara blame Bron for the deaths of the others and refuse to obey him. His powerful body is no longer enough to make him a leader. The three survivors set off to find another human group to join. By themselves they cannot hunt large animals and cannot survive. They trek 100 miles to the settlement of another clan they have met occasionally, but they find it deserted. They head south. (The North Sea and the English Channel were then dry land, since so much of Earth's water had turned to ice.)

In Germany the wanderers build a raft for the first time in their lives, to travel down a river. They find humans in an aggregation camp, where people from different clans come together to exchange information. They offer gifts and win temporary acceptance, though they do not speak the local language. They must be accepted into one of the clans by the time the aggregation camp breaks up in a few weeks. Women of child-bearing age are more valuable than men. The chief of a clan is willing to take Mara as his mate but Aki and Bron are rejected. Mara chooses to stay with Aki. The three fugitives steal food and flee.

It is August and the weather is turning cold again. Mara is now pregnant. The threesome reach the Alps and turn East into Austria. As the Ice Age worsens, people have become more jealous of their hunting grounds. A clan of hunters with painted faces drives the three from their land. They see mammoths but cannot possibly hunt them. In Moravia, they begin starving. When they find mushrooms, Mara warns that they do not know which plants in this area are edible, but Aki eats them anyway and gets food poisoning.

They are captured by a hunting party and taken to a surprisingly large town of about 100 people, with permanent huts made of mammoth bones instead of the temporary teepees they are used to. The town's woman healer, who also directs the people's religion, saves Aki's life. Unlike the smaller clans, this group is willing to accept outsiders, but the Northerners find that in this town everyone has specialized work to do, while in their old clan everyone did the same tasks as everyone else. Aki and Bron have no skills besides hunting and are relatively useless. Mara is accepted easily, not only as a child-bearer but also as a hunter. Here, grandparents take care of children while women hunt small game with nets.

First Mara, then Aki, are accepted and are tattooed, as is customary for adults of this clan. Bron, who has been a leader all his life, is too proud to accept a subordinate position and decides to leave. The village is raided by the clan of hunters with painted faces, who are low on food. Aki is stabbed defending the stored food and dies. Bron decides to stay and is tattooed. Aki's and Mara's son is born.

This splendid documentary amounts to a dramatized feature film. Other documentaries, such as *Before We Ruled the Earth* (2003) tell several reenacted stories set in various periods, but only *Ice World* follows the same characters through one story at feature length. People speak in their own languages; their words are not translated. The narrator keeps up a running account of what is happening. (This is the same tactic used in *Prehistoric Women* (1950), a much less accurate feature film.)

Several times *Ice World* breaks away from the story to have archeologists and anthropologists tell us more about the effects of ice on mankind. They say that earlier ice ages froze so much water that Africa was afflicted by drought, turning large areas from forest to savanna and forcing people to become more intelligent to survive in the open. They later tell us that Dolni Vestonice in Moravia became perhaps the first permanent human settlement during the last Ice Age. Moravia (now in the Czech Republic) was a center of artistic innovation and specialized labor at the time of the fictional story.

Besides the impact of climatic change, migration, specialization of labor and exchanges of information between groups, the documentary touches on religion, music, tattooing and face painting as signs of group membership, the great value of women and even shaving. Men shaved with sharp flints because beards retained water and could freeze. The film notes that modern students can make spear points as good as those made during the Ice Age only after years of practice.

The thread that runs through the program is the need for humans to be adaptable to survive. *Ice World* (only a year before the irresponsible

New Ice Age "thriller" *The Day After Tomorrow*, 2004) ends with a warning that another Ice Age is inevitable. The documentary tells the same basic story as *One Million B.C.*, *One Million Years B.C.* and *Quest for Fire*: people of a primitive group are forced to learn from a more advanced group. *Ice World* is one of the most fact-filled and dramatic documentaries on anatomically-modern prehistoric humans. Ref: *OCLC WorldCat*; MK 9.

Iceman (1992) U.K./U.S.; BBC/WGBH/PBS. 50 min.; color. Writer-producer, Katherine Everett; narrator, Peter Thomas. (In the TV series Nova)

The body of a 5300-year-old ice mummy found in the Alps in 1991 (dubbed Ötzi or the Iceman) and the artifacts found with him have yielded much new information about Neolithic life. Ref: *OCLC WorldCat*; not viewed.

The Iceman (1998) U.S.; Spiegel TV; Films for the Humanities & Sciences. 97 min.; color.

Scientists analyze the hair, clothing and stomach contents of Ötzi the Iceman, a 5300-year-old ice mummy found in the Alps in 1991. Ref: *OCLC WorldCat*; not viewed.

Iceman: Hunt for a Killer (2003) U.S.; dir. Brando Quilici; Quilici Productions/ Digital Source Pictures/Discovery Communications. 44 min.; color. Writer, Robert Goldberg; narrator, F. Murray Abraham.

This examination of the Neolithic mummy called Ötzi (the "Iceman" found in the Alps in 1991) tries to reconstruct his death from an arrow wound. The program includes good information but goes too far in speculating on how and why Ötzi was killed. Ref: *OCLC WorldCat*; MK 7.

Iceman: Mummy from the Stone Age (2000) U.S./Austria; producer-dir. Kurt Mündl; Power of Earth TV/ZDF/Discovery Channel. ca. 44 min.; color. Writer, Cheryl Pellerin; narrator, Terry MacDonald; CAST: Arthur Bürger (*Ötzi*).

This exciting TV documentary presents the information learned from the ice mummy found in the Alps in 1991. The Iceman (named Ötzi by scientists) lived 5300 years ago. He had diverse tools and a longbow and arrows. Flint in his arrowheads came from 400 kilometers away in Germany, proving the existence of long-distance trade. His paraphernalia was made from 17 different kinds of wood; he used the best wood for each purpose. He had three layers of clothing including a waterproof grass and bark cloak, a magnificent ten inch high bearskin hat and leather shoes with bearskin soles, stuffed with grass to prevent frostbite.

His copper ax amazed scientists; it existed more than 1000 years before copper was believed to be used in Europe. His stomach showed that his last meals included meat, vegetables and bread. His teeth were worn but had no cavities, due to the absence of processed food. He had many tattoos at acupuncture points, probably to relieve joint pain, about 2000 years before acupuncture had been previously confirmed. He carried fungus with antibiotic properties, probably as a medicine, and moss (perhaps for toilet paper). His tinderkit contained moss and tinder for firemaking. Arsenic in his hair indicated he personally worked copper, which would require 2000 degrees of heat, a ceramic pot, a bellows and a clay mold. The program includes reenactments of a bear hunt and a bear attack on a village. *Iceman: Mummy from the Stone Age* is one of the most informative videos on Neolithic life. Ref: *OCLC WorldCat*; MK 9.

The Identity of India (1988) *see* **Bharat Ki-cchap: The Identity of India** (1988)

In Search of Ancient Ireland (2002) U.S.; dir. Leo Eaton; WNET-TV/Café Productions/ Little Bird/PBS. 180 min.; color.

A popular, three-part documentary series about Ireland from 4000 B.C. to the Norman invasion of A.D. 1170 The first part, *Heroes*, covers the story from the earliest years to the Roman period and includes Neolithic farming and monument building. The sea was important in linking Ireland, Britian and France even in the Stone Age. Early farmers raised sheep, wheat and barley and even created soil on the rocky Aran Islands. Stone Age Irish raised large pyramidal mound-tombs, often aligned with the sun, before the Egyptian pyramids. Passages inside the mounds were elaborately decorated. Sacred stone circles and timber circles were common. Copper was mined and bronze was produced.

A period of peace, with no signs of war or fortress-building, lasted from 2400–1200 B.C., followed by a disastrous agricultural collapse about 1150 B.C., which led to human sacrifices and warfare. People used small willow and cowhide boats. Gold ornaments were produced. *In Search of Ancient Ireland*, which includes the playing of music on modern replicas of 3000-year-old bronze horns, is one of the best documentaries on Neolithic Europe. Ref: *OCLC WorldCat*; MK 9.

In Search of Clovis Man (1992) U.S.; Bureau of Land Management Phoenix Training Center. 60 min.; color.

Clovis Culture Paleo-Indian sites and artifacts found in Arizona. Ref: *OCLC WorldCat*; not viewed.

In Search of Human Origins (1994) U.S.; WGBH/PBS. ca. 180 min.; color. Producer, Peter Jones; presenter, Donald Johanson. (In the *Nova* TV series).

Part 1, *The Story of Lucy*, written by Michael Gunton. Johanson describes how his team found and studied the skeleton of Lucy, an early African hominid. He also explains the significance of hominid footprints found by Mary Leakey and a skull from Lucy's people. Lucy had a small brain but walked erect. Bipedalism was useful during droughts. Erect apes could walk to distant food and carry it in their hands.

Part 2, *Surviving in Africa*, written by Lenora Johanson. Don Johanson disputes the Killer Ape Theory, proposed by anthropologist Raymond Dart, which claimed that man's large brain and use of technology resulted from the ability to hunt. Johanson suggests that early African humans lived by scavenging rather than hunting. Hominids are now seen as first vegetarians who used bones as digging tools, not weapons; then as scavengers who used tools for butchering. Homo Erectus probably stole food from caches hidden by predators. Control of fire was a great change, beginning about 1,000,000 years ago. Johanson show scenes from *2001: A Space Odyssey* and *Quest for Fire* and notes that both films perpetuated false ideas of early humans as violent aggressors.

Part 3, *The Creative Revolution*, written by Lauren Seeley Aguirre. Johanson steps outside his specialty, the early hominids, to study much more recent humans. Human life changed little for about 1,000,000 years, the reign of Homo Erectus. Tools remained the same but Erectus spread from Africa into Asia and Europe. 100,000 years ago (or more) modern humans lived in Africa. Johanson presents both sides of the debate over whether all modern humans came from Africa or whether Erectus evolved into modern people independently in several places. In Europe Neanderthals were probably the first people to bury their dead. Homo Sapiens sites in Europe were often on hilltops while Neanderthals lived in valleys. This may have given the modern humans an advantage in spotting game and planning hunts. A creative revolution saw the beginnings of cave paintings, carvings on objects and other forms of art, and probably the beginning of storytelling. Australia, like the Americas, was populated by fully-modern humans. Ref: *OCLC WorldCat*; MK 9.

In Search of Noah's Ark (1977) U.S.; dir. James L. Conway; Schick Sunn Classic Pictures. 95 min.; color. Writer, James L. Conway, Charles E. Sellier; narrator, Brad Crandall. CAST: Vern Adix (*Noah*).

Variety (Feb. 9, 1977) reported that Schick Sunn played this "low-budget, pseudo-scientific pseudo-documentary" in theatres for weeks before showing it to reviewers. A major TV ad campaign insured good audience response. The film claimed to have "proved conclusively" that Noah lived 5,000 years ago and that the Ark had been found in the Turkish mountains. The *Variety* reviewer noted that some of the documentary footage was "grainy" while the reenactment of the Noah story "can only be described as silly." Producer-writer Sellier had also distributed the German "documentary" *Chariots of the Gods* (1970). Ref: *Internet Movie Database*; not viewed.

Dubious claims that the Noah story is true are found in: *Ancient Secrets of the Bible: Noah's Ark: Fact or Fable?* (1994, Sun-PKO); *Noah's Ark: Was There a Worldwide Flood?* (1994, Sun-PKO); *Noah's Ark: What Happened to It?* (1994, Sun-PKO); *Noah and the Ark* (1991, in the *Science and Genesis* video series, Trinity Broadcast Network); *The Search for Noah's Ark: The Adventure Continues* (1990, Institute for Creation Research); *The Discovery of Noah's Ark* (1997, American Media); *In Search of Noah's Flood* (1990, Alan Landsburg Productions); *The Incredible Discovery of Noah's Ark* (1993, Sun-PKO Productions); *Is It Noah's Ark?* [alt. *Noah's Ark on Ararat*] (2000, Grizzly Adams Productions); and *The Quest for Noah's Ark* (1999, Grizzly Adams Productions).

More or less serious examinations of the possible historical reality of the Flood story are: *Ancient Voices* (1998–99), episode 9, *Seeking Noah's Flood*; *Mysteries of Noah and the Flood* [alt. *Noah's Flood in Context — Legend or History*] (2002, Films for the Humanities and Sciences); *Noah* (1996, A&E/FilmRoos); *Noah's Ark: The True Story* (2003, BBC/Discovery Channel); *Noah's Flood* (1996, BBC/A&E), which suggests that an ancient inundation created the Black Sea and led to Deluge stories; *Quest for Noah's Flood* (2001, National Geographic TV), in which Robert Ballard, discoverer of the *Titanic* wreck, supports the Black Sea theory; *The Search for Noah's Ark* (2001, A&E/History Channel); and *Seeking Noah's Flood* [alt. *Noah's Flood*] (1999, BBC/Learning Channel/Time-Life).

The possible historical basis of another Christian legend, the Garden of Eden, is examined in *In Search of Eden* (2002, Wild Planet/Learning Channel).

In Search of the First Americans (1985) U.S.; dir. Henry Nevison; Center for the Study of Ancient Man, University of Maine. Writers, Henry Nevison, Robson Bonnichsen, Carole Bombard. The search for artifacts of early man in North America, including habitat reconstructions, dating techniques and demonstrations of bone and stone toolmaking. Ref: *OCLC WorldCat*; not viewed.

In Search of the First Language (1994) U.K./U.S.; dir. Melanie Wallace; BBC/WBGH/PBS. 54 min.; color. Producer-writer, Melanie Wallace; narrator, Peter Thomas. (In the *Nova* TV series)

Examines research tracing the development of Indo-European and Sino-Tibetan languages. Ref: *OCLC WorldCat*; not viewed.

In Search of the Lost World (1970?) U.S.; dir. Howard Campbell; MGM. ca. 60 min.; color. Narrator, E.G. Marshall.

The history of early man in the Americas, including the Mayas and Incas. Later released as two shorts: *Early Man in North America* (12 min., 1972) and *Civilizations of Ancient America* (22 min.). Ref: *OCLC WorldCat*; not viewed.

India Invented: An Exploration of Culture and Civilization in Historical Outline (1999) India; dir. Arvind N. Das; Asia-Pacific Communication Associates. 13 30-min. parts; color. Producer-writer, Arvind N. Das.

Part two, *Dawn of Civilization*, covers the period from the Old Stone Age to the coming of the Aryans and the early Harappan civilization. Ref: *OCLC WorldCat*; not viewed.

Island of the Pygmy Mammoth (2002) U.S.; Discovery Channel. ca. 45 min.; color.

Pygmy mammoths, half the normal size of the species, developed on the Channel Islands off the coast of California. Their dwarfism resulted from limited local food. This documentary says that the tiny mammoths were exterminated by Paleo-Indians. Ref: MK 7.

Japan's Mysterious Pyramids (2000) U.S.; dir. Richard L. Schmidt; Triage Entertainment/History Channel. ca. 50 min.; color. Writer, Susan Michaels; narrator, David Ackroyd. (in the TV series *History's Mysteries*)

Theorists claim that the remains of giant structures built about 10,000 years ago exist on the ocean floor off the Japanese island of Yonaguni. In documentaries like this, the History Channel has often been too lenient in their coverage of such dubious theories. Ref: *OCLC WorldCat*; MK 5.

Journey of Discovery: Landscape History of the Bering Land Bridge (1997) U.S.; dir. Francine Lastufka-Taylor; Beringian Heritage International Park Program/ National Park Service/Taylor Productions. Writer-narrator, Francine Lastufka-Taylor; writer, Jeanne Schaaf; with David M. Hopkins.

Hopkins explores the history of the Bering Land Bridge using geology, archeology and paleoecology. Ref: *OCLC WorldCat*; not viewed.

Journey of Man (2003) U.S.; dir. Clive Maltby; Tigress Productions/PBS. ca. 120 min.; color. Producer, Jennifer Beamish; presenter-writer, Spencer Wells.

Geneticist Wells traces modern people with a DNA marker which indicates their descent from the Africans who left Africa and went on to populate the whole planet. (Wells misdates the Red Sea migration at 50,000 years ago. It was probably about 80,000 years ago.)

Wells is on camera and talking constantly. Besides Wells, the stars are the people of isolated, tribal groups in whose blood the marker can still be found. The presentation is somewhat breathless, with promises "to build a family tree for the whole world" and remarks like "the odds for survival were close to zero" and "this is an amazing moment."

Wells presents the Namibian San people, Australian Aborigines, people of a remote village in Southern India, Kazakhs in Central Asia, the incredibly hardy Chukchi of Arctic Northeast Siberia and Navaho Indians of the American Southwest, all of whom have the crucial marker. By not mentioning Peking Man, Java Man and the Neanderthals, he implies to the unwary that the ancient anatomically-modern humans he is tracing were the first Europeans and Asians.

Wells' thesis is that the San's clicking language produced "a quantum leap in thinking"; that the Ice Age drought permitted anatomically-modern humans to travel from Africa across the shallow Red Sea to the Middle East, then to South Asia and Australia; that Cro-Magnons entered Europe from Central Asia rather belatedly; and that Siberians entered the Western Hemisphere about 15,000 B.C. There are no reenactments and little detailed information on ancient ways of life, except as seen in the lives of the modern San and Chukchi. Ref: *OCLC WorldCat*; MK 7.

Journey Through Time: The Human Story (1983) [alt. *L'Homme: Un Voyage dans le Temps*; video title *The First Humans*] Canada; dir. George Geersten; National Film Board of Canada. Animated short film; 11 min.; color. Writer, George Geersten.

An animated film on the origins of humans. Ref: *OCLC WorldCat*; not viewed.

Jungfrauen-Report (1971) *see* **Virgin Report** (1971)

The King of Stonehenge (2003) *see* **Meet the Ancestors: The King of Stonehenge** (2003)

L.A. 10,000 B.C. (2004) U.S.; dir. James Younger; Creative Differences Productions/Discovery Channel. ca. 90 min.; color. Narrator, William Hootkins.

Three Hollywood stunt performers (one of them a woman) are trained in the hunting techniques of the Clovis Culture. They hunt a mammoth and deal with a giant short-faced bear, a lion and a terratorn, an enormous predator bird. The mammoth and terratorn are animatronic monsters capable of limited movement (including the mammoth's "tusk toss"), while the bear and lion are pop-up figures. The documentary is padded and repetitious but it does make several valuable points: that it took great skill to make Clovis points, the weapons of early American hunters; that many dangerous animals threatened the earliest Indians; that atlatls greatly improved the effectiveness of spears; that tracking was often a matter of following an animal's dung trail; that humans tended to wipe out the largest prey first when they entered an area; and that since small bands of humans could not eat much of a mammoth, the giant animals may have been killed to win prestige and social standing for the hunters. Includes brief clips from *Before We Ruled the Earth* (2003). Ref: viewed. MK: 6.

Land of Lost Monsters (2004) [alt. *The Monsters We Met*] Great Britain/U.S.; dir. Andy Byatt (Australia segment), Andrew Graham Brown (North America and New Zealand segments); BBC/Animal Planet. ca. 100 min.; color. Writers, Charlie Foley, Jenny Jones; narrator, William Hootkins.

This fine documentary surveys the relationships between early humans and megafauna (large animals). The first few minutes show Australopithecines in Africa millions of years ago fleeing from all large animals. Another few minutes covers the Neanderthals during the Ice Age, making clear that Neanderthals were intelligent, competent and extremely tough. A reenactment shows Neanderthals using fire to drive a mammoth over a cliff. These brief scenes of African Australopithecines and Neanderthals were borrowed from the BBC/ Discovery Channel 2001 documentary *Walking with Prehistoric Beasts*.

The third section is the longest (about 40 minutes) and covers the first humans in Australia. Dramatic reenactments show humans' first dangerous, often tragic encounters with Diprotedon, the largest marsupial who ever lived; salt water crocodiles; kangaroos; and the Megalania, a giant river lizard which was the largest reptile since the dinosaurs. The first Australians had to decide how to deal with each of the terrifying animals they encountered. Their evolving weapons and especially their use of fire led to the disappearance of all these species except the crocodiles and kangaroos. Manmade fires burned large areas and changed much of the continent from bush to grass.

In ancient Alaska Paleo-Indians already had dogs when they entered the Western Hemisphere. Dogs helped to protect humans against Smilodon Fatalis, a sabre-tooth cat which was one of the biggest cats that ever lived. In Montana humans encountered horses, zebras and camels, all of which became extinct in the Western Hemisphere. Grizzly bears and bison survived, but the giant ground sloth, the short-faced bear (which was 10 feet tall), Smilodon and several kinds of mammoths and mastodons disappeared under the onslaught of early man. Reenactments show humans stalking big animals in camouflage made of hides and antlers. The hunting expertise of the Paleo-Indians is emphasized.

The final section is on the peopling of New Zealand by the Maoris about A.D. 1000, an event long after prehistory. The documentary suggests that ancient human encounters with megafauna are reflected in traditional stories about monsters—and the human heroes who kill monsters. *Land of Lost Monsters* benefits from excellent animation of the extinct animals and intelligent reenactments. Compare *What Killed the Mega Beasts?* (2002). Ref: MK 8.

Lands Before Time (1990) U.K.; producer, Roy Skeggs, Robert Sidaway; Hammer Films. 25 min.; color. Writers, Ashley Sidaway, Robert Sidaway; narrator, Oliver Reed. (In the series *The World of Hammer*)

This segment in a series of short, self-adulatory documentaries by and about Hammer Films covers the studio's prehistoric films (*One Million Years B.C.*, *Slave Girls* and *Creatures the World Forgot*; *When Dinosaurs Ruled the Earth* is missing), as well as their ancient history (*The Viking Queen*, the Egyptian prologue scene in *Blood from the Mummy's Tomb*) and Lost World (*She*, *The Vengeance of She* and *The Lost Continent*) movies. Spectacular scenes from each film are shown, while narrator Oliver Reed sings Hammer's praises. *Lands Before Time* is an extra feature on the DVD for *Slave Girls*. MK 6.

The Lascaux Cave: A Look at Our Prehistoric Past (1990) U.S.; dir. Rachel Stevenson; International Film Bureau. 23 min.; color. Writer-narrator, Leslie G. Freeman.

Freeman discusses the materials and techniques used to paint the walls of the Lascaux Cave in Southern France about 17,000 years ago. Includes footage shot in the cave before it was sealed forever in 1963. Ref: *OCLC WorldCat*; not viewed.

Lascaux: Cradle of Man's Art (1950) U.S.; dir. William Chapman; International Film Bureau. 17 min.; color. This documentary recreates the discovery of the Lascaux Cave paintings by two small boys in 1940. Includes photographs of the paintings and an appraisal of their importance. Ref: *OCLC WorldCat*; not viewed.

Lascaux Revisited (1989) France; dir. Jacques Willemont; Caisse National des Monuments Historiques et des Sites. 35 min.; color. Writer, Alan Aber.

This documentary shows almost the entire collection of prehistoric paintings and carvings in the Lascaux Cave. With animated enhancement of hard-to-see paintings and with music by Beethoven. Ref: *OCLC WorldCat*; not viewed.

Lascaux Treasures (1982) U.S.; UPITN Corporation/Journal Films. 23 min.; color.

This film for high school students shows photos of the cave art and the construction of Lascaux II, a recreation of the cave which will be open to the public. Ref: *OCLC WorldCat*; not viewed.

The Last Neanderthals (1999) [alt. *The Last Neanderthal*] U.S.; dir. Steve Garwood; Discovery Communications/Pinball Productions/Big Rock Productions. 26 min.; color. Writers, Steve Garwood, Mark Etkind; narrator, Dennis Elsas. (In the TV series *Discover Magazine*).

Examines the disappearance of the Neanderthals. Ref: *OCLC WorldCat*; not viewed.

The Last Tribes of Mindanao (1971) U.S.; National Geographic Society. 52 min.; color.

In 1971 the Filipino government claimed to have found a Stone Age tribe, the Tasaday, on Mindanao Island. Other films on the Tasaday include *Cave People of the Philippines* (1972, NBC News, 38 min.), *The Tasaday, Stone Age People in a Space Age World* (1975, Pathescope Educational Media, 30 min., written by John Nance, who wrote a book *The Gentle Tasaday*, 1975) and *A Message from the Stone Age* (1982,

New Dimension Films, 16 min., directed by Nance). In 1986, a Swiss journalist claimed that the Tasaday were not cave-dwellers and were actually part of a previously-known tribe. In 1989 the Filipino Congress recognized the Tasaday as a tribe. The BBC produced a 49-min. documentary on the controversy, *Trial in the Jungle* (1989) written and produced by Bettina Lerner. Also in 1989 WGBH in the U.S. broadcast a 60-min. BBC program *The Lost Tribe* (written by Lerner) on *Nova*. Ref: *OCLC WorldCat*; not viewed.

Legends of the Isles (1997) U.S.; Emdee Productions/Learning Channel/RTE. 6 52-min. programs; color. Narrator, Bosco Hogan.

One of the six programs covered both Stonehenge and the Holy Grail. Bill Orton wrote that the segment did a "credible job" of reviewing information on standing stones in Britain and their possible uses as celestial observatories. The other five programs dealt with other British legends from Boudicca and Arthur to Bonnie Prince Charlie. Ref: *OCLC WorldCat*; Orton. *Arthurian Legends on Film and Television*; not viewed.

Life and Death in the Ice Age (1999) *see* **The Fate of Neanderthal Man: Life and Death in the Ice Age** (1999)

A Life in Ice (1997) [alt. *Life on Ice*] U.K./U.S.; BBC/WGBH/PBS. 50 min.; color. Writer-producer, Tim Haines; narrator, Nigel Le Vaillant. (In the series *Ice Mummies* and the anthology series *Horizon*).

The results of research done on Ötzi the Iceman, the Neolithic ice mummy found in the Alps in 1991. Ref: *OCLC WorldCat*; not viewed.

The Life of Mammals (2003) Segment no. 5, *Food for Thought*. U.K./U.S.; BBC/Discovery Channel. Segment of TV series; 50 min.; color. Writer-presenter, David Attenborough.

In the last of this five part series Attenborough studies orangutans, chimpanzees, gorillas, early hominid footprints found in Tanzania, Namibia's San people, the Dogon people of Mali, the Mayan capital Tikal and modern cities, tracing how the hunt for food led to the development of mankind and eventually civilization. Scenes of a San hunter running down a kudu (a large antelope) over several hours illustrate the oldest human hunting technique, "persistence hunting." Perhaps no scene in any film or program in this book does as much as this sequence to make an audience proud of being human, and humble at the prowess of "primitive" people. The Dogons represent early farmers. Attenborough narrates how the Maya civilization outgrew its food source and collapsed and asks whether the much larger modern civilizations will do the same. Ref: *OCLC WorldCat*; MK 8.

Life on Earth: The Compulsive Communicators (1978) U.K./U.S.; BBC/ Warner Bros. 58 min.; color. Presenter, David Attenborough.

The 13th part of Attenborough's series on the evolution of life traces the development of man's ability to communicate, through speech, art and writing. Attenborough argues that co-operative hunting, agriculture and animal domestication all resulted from this unique human ability. Includes a visit to the Biami people of central New Guinea. *Life on Earth* was on TV in 13 parts in 1978 and later was released on video in 27 parts. *The Compulsive Communicators* was split into two 30 min. parts: *Upright Man* and *Compulsive Communicators*. Ref: *OCLC WorldCat*; not viewed.

Life on Ice (1997) *see* **A Life in Ice** (1997)

Life's Really Big Questions (2000) *see* **Scientific American Frontiers: Life's Really Big Questions** (2000)

Looking at Prehistoric Sites (1982) [alt. *Prehistoric Sites*] U.K.; World Wide Pictures/ English Heritage, Historical Buildings and Monuments Commission. 20 min.; color.

Investigates how, why and by whom Stonehenge and other ancient megalithic monuments of Western England were built. Ref: *OCLC WorldCat*; not viewed.

La Lotta dell'Uomo per la Sua Sopravvivenza (1970–71) see **Man's Struggle for Survival** (1970–71)

Lucy in Disguise (1981) U.S.; dir. David Smeltzer, David Price; Ohio University Film Dept./Smeltzer Films. 59 min.; color. Producer-writer, David Smeltzer.

Tells the story of the discovery and analysis

of Lucy, an Australopithecus Afarensis specimen and the most complete skeleton of an early human ancestor ever found. Ref: *OCLC WorldCat*; not viewed.

The Making of Mankind (1981) U.K./U.S.; BBC/Time-Life Films. 385 min.; color. Producer-writer, Peter Spry-Leverton; writer-narrator, Richard Leakey.

In seven parts. 1. *In the Beginning*. Mankind's adaptable nature has made human evolution possible. 2. *One Small Step*. The oldest human footprint, found near Olduvai Gorge in Tanzania; the Lucy skeleton; the controversy over ancient upright creatures. 3. *A Human Way of Life*. Archeologists piece together a picture of life 1,500,000 years ago; Leakey visits modern hunters-gatherers of the Kalahari. 4. *Beyond Africa*. Peking Man, who used fire for heat and light and possibly for cooking; increasing human intelligence; the beginnings of speech. 5. *A New Era*. The emergence of Homo Sapiens; Neanderthals; burials; prehistoric art, including the cave of Lascaux. 6. *Settling Down*. The shift from nomadic hunter-gatherer culture to the settled farmer-villager. 7. *The Survival of the Species*. Crucial human behavior patterns and technology which produced modern humans; the killer ape theory. Ref: *OCLC WorldCat*; not viewed.

Mammoths of the Ice Age (1995) U.K./U.S.; BBC/WGBH-TV/PBS. 56 min.; color. Producer-writer, Kate O'Sullivan; narrator, Peter Thomas. (In the *Nova* TV series)

Investigates whether humans were responsible for the extermination of the mammoths. Ref: *OCLC WorldCat*; not viewed.

The Man Hunters (1970) U.S.; dir. Nicolas L. Noxon; MGM. 52 min.; color. Producer-writer, Nicolas L. Noxon; narrator, E. G. Marshall.

The "man hunters" are paleoanthropologists, shown piecing together the stories of Australopithecus, Homo Erectus and Neanderthal man. A shorter (20 min.) version was released in 1972 as *Apemen of Africa*. Ref: *OCLC WorldCat*; not viewed.

Man on the Rim: The Peopling of the Pacific (1988) Australia; dir. Robert Raymond; Quantum Films/ABC. Color. Producer, Anthony Buckley; presenter, Alan Thorne.

In 11 parts. 1. *First Footsteps* (human evolution); 2. *Hunters and Gatherers* (the first Australians); 3. *Into the Deep Freeze* (the peopling of Siberia from China); 4. *Flaming Arrows* (migration from Siberia into America); 5. *Changing the Menu* (Asians in Indonesia and New Guinea); 6. *The New Cutting Edge* (the evolution of Bronze Age technology in Asia and the Pacific); 7. *The Powerhouse* (China and Japan); 8. *Pure and Simple*; 9. *Road Without Wheels* (South America); 10. *Feathered Serpent* (Mayan, Aztec and Olmec); 11. *Last Horizon* (Polynesia). The first six parts were prehistoric. Ref: *OCLC WorldCat*; not viewed.

Man, the Deadly Predator (1997) U.S.; dir. Robert Dunlap; Robert Dunlap Film Productions. 24 min.; color. Writers, Mark Ogle, Robert Dunlap. (In the series *Mass Extinctions*)

Early men eliminate the mastodons and other large mammals. Ref: *OCLC WorldCat*; not viewed.

Man's Biological Heritage (1987) U.S.; Educational Video. 82 min.; color. Writer, Mary Lee Nolan.

Part 1, *The Search for Our Ancestors*; pt. 2, *Mankind in the Animal Kingdom*; pt. 3, *Early Hominids in the Fossil Record*; pt. 4, *The Emergence of Modern Man*. Ref: *OCLC WorldCat*; not viewed.

Man's Struggle for Survival (1970–71) [alt. *La Lotta dell'Uomo per la Sua Sopravvivenza*] Italy; dir. Renzo Rossellini; Orizzonte/RAI/Logos Film. Screenplay, Roberto Rossellini; photography, Mario Fioretti; music, Mario Nascimbene. TV miniseries; 12 50–60 min. segments; color.

This dramatized and "reconstructed" documentary was made slowly from 1964 to 1970 and used non-professional actors and a surprisingly large budget to show the history of technology and learning from prehistory to modern times. Roberto Rossellini directed some of his best films during the six years his son Renzo was directing this series from Roberto's script.

The first episode, *Prima della Storia, L'Uomo* (*Before History, Man*) begins with the first modern humans and, according to Peter Brunette's book *Roberto Rossellini*, focuses on the agricultural revolution and Rossellini's idea that matriarchy "was a natural consequence of the relation of women to fertility and the cycles of the moon. From there we move to astronomy and the discovery of the solar year, the Bronze Age, the first machines" and the rise of civilizations.

Brunette praises Nascimbene's "understated, electronic" score (written around the same time he wrote the scores for Hammer's prehistoric trilogy, *One Million Years B.C.*, *When Dinosaurs Ruled the Earth* and *Creatures the World Forgot*, 1966–1971) and notes "color is used magnificently in the film." The series of twelve episodes cost "well over a million dollars." Brunette discusses the first, prehistoric episode in detail, since "a polemic has developed most violently around the notion of matriarchy" central to Rossellini's view of ancient society.

The first scene shows cave-dwelling modern humans living in the most recent Ice Age. Rossellini believed that "the sheer brutality of nature has made them move into the mutual protection provided by communal living" and that after this step, fire, cooking, hunting and animal-keeping arrived quickly. The fact that the breasts of the cavewomen are exposed "along with the superb costumes and the lack of makeup for the women ... makes these scenes seem less awkward than the standard depictions of prehistory."

Rossellini emphasizes man's intelligence, especially his learning to hunt by disguising himself as an animal. He also shows the beginnings of cave art. After the Ice Age, we see people beginning to eat roots and berries, washing clothes, leaving caves and building shelters, and then learning to mill grain and make bread. As in all of Rossellini's historical films, "much time is spent on the supposedly insignificant details of everyday life: food preparation, work, and daily chores."

Rossellini believed that early people were matriarchal because "since man's role in reproduction is unknown at this point, the fertility of the woman, the source of all life for an agricultural people, becomes exalted." A queen's consort is shown wearing artificial breasts whenever he has to give orders; he is later ritually killed and his blood used to fertilize the soil. The episode ends when patriarchy replaces matriarchy as a result of two developments. Astronomy emphasizes solar (male) time over lunar (female) time and people begin to understand the importance of the male in reproduction.

Brunette notes "the utterly sweeping nature of Rossellini's generalization about the establishment of the patriarchy," which brought down a hail of controversy on the filmmaker. I hesitate to criticize a TV episode I have never seen, but it would seem that while Rossellini was ahead of his time in his realistic depiction of everyday details of work and costumes, his ambition and self-confidence led him into error. Not only are his ideas on matriarchy highly speculative, he also misdated many important developments. Communal living, hunting, cave art and gathering roots and berries (and, I suspect, washing clothes) all preceded the last Ice Age. (If modern man invented both hunting and gathering, what did Rossellini believe earlier people ate?) Ref: Brunette. *Roberto Rosselini*; not viewed.

Masters of Metal (1981) U.K.; BBC. 58 min.; color. Producer, Dominic Flessati. (In the TV series *Odyssey*)

Examines sites such as Vinca in Serbia to show that Bronze Age metalworking began about 4500 B.C., long before the date previously assumed. Ref: *OCLC WorldCat*; not viewed.

Meet the Ancestors: The King of Stonehenge (2003) U.K.; Indigo Films/BBC. 60 min.; color.

Investigates a man whose Bronze Age burial site was found three miles from Stonehenge. The film claims that the grave is over 4000 years old, that the man was probably alive during the construction of Stonehenge and that he was an immigrant from Europe. Ref: Indigo Films website, *http://www.indigofilm.com*; not viewed.

Megalithic Monuments of Ireland (1970) Ireland; Society for the Preservation of Historic Ireland. 29 min.; color. Writer, Robert W. Reese.

Illustrates early Irish stone art and architecture, including religious symbols carved on graves. Ref: *OCLC WorldCat*; not viewed.

The Men Who Painted Caves (1975) U.S.; Time-Life films. 52 min.; color. A study of the cave paintings of the Dordogne Valley in France. Ref: *OCLC WorldCat*; not viewed.

Mesolithic Society (1976) U.S.; Carmen Educational Associates. 18 min.; color.

Traditional and experimental archeological methods explore life in Northern Europe at the end of the last Ice Age. Ref: *OCLC WorldCat*; not viewed.

Metals (1980?) U.S.; dir. Samuel Damkin; Globe Trotter Network/Barr Films. 22 min.; color. Producer, Stéphane Dykman; writer, Samuel Damkin.

How prehistoric people developed iron and steel and how those metals changed the way people lived. Ref: *OCLC WorldCat*; not viewed.

The Monsters We Met (2004) *see* **Land of Lost Monsters** (2004)

Mummies of Ancient Chile (1996) U.S.; Discovery Communications. 24 min.; color. Producers, Tom Naughton, Nicolas Valcour; narrator, John Rhys-Davies. (In the TV series *Archaeology.*)

The Chinchorro culture in Chile mummified its dead 5000–1500 B.C. This program and the *Archaeology* segment *Voyages of the Vikings* were combined in a Time-Life video, *Rediscovering the Americas*. Ref: *OCLC WorldCat*; MK 8.

Murder at Stonehenge (2001) U.S./U.K.; dir. Jeremy Freeston; YAP/Thirteen-WNET-TV/PBS/Channel 4. ca. 60 min.; color. Producer, Mark McMullen; Narrator, Liev Schreiber (In the TV series *Secrets of the Dead*)

Stonehenge expert Michael Pitts and other archeologists use modern techniques to research possible explanations for a beheaded skeleton found in a grave beneath Stonehenge. Ref: *OCLC WorldCat*; MK 8.

Mysteries of Mankind (1988) U.S.; National Geographic Society/WQED-TV Pittsburgh. 57 min.; color. Producer-writer, Barbara Jampel; narrator, Richard Kiley.

Discusses the whole history of human evolution at breakneck speed, including the Leakeys, the Lucy skeleton, Afarensis footprints, robust australopithecines, Homo Erectus, the first hunting and tools, Neanderthals and early modern humans and their art. Information on tooth analysis and skull reconstruction is also included. The program notes that australopithecines are now seen as vegetarians, not as "killer apes." Ref: *OCLC WorldCat*; MK 7.

Mysteries of Stonehenge (2002) [alt. *Stonehenge in Context: From Modern Myth to Ancient History*] U.S.; dir. John Scheinfeld; Learning Channel/Crew Neck Productions. 51 min.; color. Producer-writer, John Scheinfeld. (In the TV series *History's Artifacts*)

Archeologists review the many theories posited over several centuries about the origins of Stonehenge. Ref: *OCLC WorldCat*; MK 8.

Mystery of Life (1931) U.S.; dir. George Cochrane; Classic Productions/ Universal. 62 min.; b&w. Writer, H.M. Parshley; with H.M. Parshley, Clarence Darrow.

Smith College professor Parshley and Darrow, defense attorney at the 1925 Scopes "Monkey Trial," present the theory of evolution. The documentary included Willis O'Brien's allosaurus footage from *The Ghost of Slumber Mountain* (1919), which included dinosaurs but not early humans. Stephen Jones calls this almost-forgotten film a "documentary recreation of the history of man." Ref: Jones. *Illustrated Dinosaur Movie Guide*; Berry. *Dinosaur Filmography*; Internet Movie Database; not viewed.

The Mystery of Stonehenge (1965) U.S.; dir. Harry Morgan; CBS News. 57 min.; color. Writer, Marianna Harris; reporters, Charles Collingwood, Eugene Cines.

Dr. Gerald Hawkins discusses his theory that Stonehenge was built to predict solar and lunar alignments. Includes tests which appear to support Hawkins, and evidence of how the stones were moved and positioned. Ref: *OCLC WorldCat*; not viewed.

Mystery of the First Americans (2000) U.S.; dir. Mark Davis; MDTV Productions/WGBH-TV/PBS. 60 min.; color. Writer, Mark Davis; narrator, Joe Morton. (In the *Nova* TV series)

Kennewick Man, 9000-year-old human remains found in Washington in 1996, set off a bitter dispute between scientists and American Indians who oppose the study of even the most ancient Americans. Kennewick Man is of Caucasian appearance, suggesting the complexity of ancient human migration from Northeast Asia into the Americas. Ref: *OCLC WorldCat*; MK 8.

The Naked Ape (1973) U.S.; dir. Donald Driver; animation dir. Charles Swenson; Playboy Enterprises/Murakami Wolf Productions/Universal. 85 min.; color. Writer, Donald Driver, based on nonfiction book by Desmond Morris; photography, John Alonzo; music, Jimmy Webb. CAST: Johnny Crawford (*Lee*); Victoria Principal (*Cathy*); Dennis Olivieri (*Arnie*).

This film combines liveaction and animation, and drama and documentary to present an anti-war parable and documentary information on the evolution of man — all executive produced by Hugh Hefner. *Variety* (Aug. 15, 1973) denounced it as "part liveaction, part animation and all banality ... a lifeless, generally laugh-less throwback to late '60s "with-it" theatrics and pubescent polemics." *Variety* did offer mild praise for the "okay" animation by Swenson and Murakami Wolf Productions, but said the liveaction scenes suggested "amateur home-movie filmmaking gaucheries." Crawford was an ex–Mouseketeer; Principal a future TV star. Ref: *Internet Movie Database*; Jones. *Illustrated Dinosaur Movie Guide*; not viewed.

The Native American Series (1976) U.S.; Journal Films. 56 min.; color.

In three parts. 1. *The Origins, The First 50,000 Years.* 2. *Indian Culture, From 2000 B.C. to 1500 A.D.* 3. *The Indian Experience, After 1500 A.D.* Geological and archeological evidence on the history of the American Indians. The date of 50,000 B.C. for the origin of the Indians is not accepted by most authorities. Ref: *OCLC WorldCat*; not viewed.

Natural Mummies (1996) U.S.; Digital Ranch/ History Channel. ca. 50 min.; color. Producer, Darryl Rehr; writer, Susan Michaels. (In the TV series *History's Mysteries*) A documentary on mummies created by natural processes, not by human mummifiers. Includes Ötzi, the Neolithic "Iceman" of the Alps. Ref: *OCLC WorldCat*; MK 7.

Neanderthal (2001) [alt. *A Neanderthal's World*] U.S./U.K.; dir. Tony Mitchell; Wall to Wall/Discovery Channel/Channel 4. 97 min.; color. Producer, Alex Graham; narrator, Terry MacDonald.

Reconstructs the life of a Neanderthal clan in what is now France — clan life, tool and weapon making, firemaking, hunting and gathering, health and healing, childbirth, rituals and contact with Cro-Magnons. Discovery Communications released a 52-min. version for secondary schools in 2002. Ref: *OCLC WorldCat*; MK 8.

Neanderthals on Trial (2001) U.S.; dir. Mark J. Davis; MDTV Productions/ WGBH-TV/PBS. 55 min.; color. Writer, Mark J. Davis; narrator, Joe Morton. (In the *Nova* TV series)

DNA analysis has revived the old debate over whether the Neanderthal behavior resembled that of modern humans. Differences between modern human DNA and Neanderthal DNA suggest the most recent common ancestor of both lived 500,000 years ago and that the two human types were separate species, but a skeleton of a child, found in Portugal and dating 25,000 years ago, exhibits both modern and Neanderthal traits, suggesting interbreeding. Evidence from Neanderthal tools is subject to differing interpretations. Recent discoveries show that Neanderthals took care of injured people and put flowers in graves. The debate over Neanderthal intelligence continues, with much data but little consensus. Ref: *OCLC WorldCat*; MK 9.

A Neanderthal's World (2001) *see* **Neanderthal** (2001)

Neolithic Europe (2001) U.S.; dir. Tom Dunton; Teaching Company. 360 min.; color. Lecturer, Jeremy Adams.

The Neolithic world in the Middle East and Western Europe, including the origins of agriculture, the advanced Windmill Hill Culture of Britain, and Stonehenge. Ref: *OCLC WorldCat*; not viewed.

Old Fashioned: The Real Caveman Couture (2001) [alt. *Caveman Couture*] U.S.; ABC News Productions. 24 min.; color. Host, Chris Bury; reporter, Robert Krulwich. (A segment of the TV program *Nightline*) New archeological evidence suggests that cave men and women wore cloth, not animal skins. Ref: *OCLC WorldCat*; not viewed.

On the Rocks: Prehistoric Art of France & Spain (1989) U.S.; Gallery of Prehistoric Art. 25 min.; color. Writer-producer, Berna Villiers; photographer-narrator, Douglas Mazonowicz.

Using the award-winning photographs of Douglas Mazonowicz, this film focuses on the cave art of Lascaux and Altamira. Ref: *OCLC WorldCat*; not viewed.

The Origins of Art in France (1968) France/ U.S.; dir. Jean L'Hote, Max-Paul Fouchet; Roland Films on Art. 38 min.; color.

Paleolithic cave art and Celtic art of about 1500 B.C., focusing on women as symbols of beauty and fertility. Ref: *OCLC WorldCat*; not viewed.

The Origins of Man (1993) U.S.; Films for the Humanities. 108 min.; color.

This video release confusingly combines two programs: *Retracing Man's Steps* (on human evolution) and *The Big Bang and Beyond* (on the history of the universe). Ref: *OCLC WorldCat*; not viewed.

Origins, the First Nations (1986) Canada; dir. David Stansfield, Denise Boiteau; TVOntario/Journal Films. 28 min.; color. Producers-writers, David Stansfield, Denise Boiteau; narrator, Fred Napoli. (In the series *Origins, a History of North America*)

The Paleo-Indians, Inuit and Canadian Indians. Ref: *OCLC WorldCat*; not viewed.

Our Earliest Ancestors: The Ape That Took Over the World (2001) U.S./U.K.; dir. Jonathan Renouf; Discovery Channel/BBC. 47 min.; color. Narrator, Bernard Hill.

The "Big Brain Theory" assumed that enhanced intelligence preceded all other human advances. Louis Leakey looked for proof of this theory for decades in East Africa. Leakey's son Richard finally found Skull 1470, which had a 700 cc brain and seemed to prove the theory, just before his father's death in 1972. However the discovery of Lucy by Donald Johanson devastated the Big Brain Theory; Lucy had a small brain but was bipedal. A new dating system confirmed that Skull 1470 was a million years more recent than the Leakeys' had thought. Geochemist Jay Quade found that between 6,000,000 and 8,000,000 years ago Earth changed from mostly forests to mainly grasslands, leading to a mass extinction of species and the end of the long "Planet of the Apes" period. Meave Leakey in 1999 found Flat-Faced Man in Kenya. This 3,500,000 year old hominid was different from Lucy in several ways but lived at about the same time, ending the theory that Lucy represented the only hominid species of her time. We will probably never know whether Lucy or Flat-Faced was our ancestor. Ref: *OCLC WorldCat*; MK 9.

Out of Asia (1998) U.K./U.S.; BBC/Discovery Communications. 51 min.; color. Producer-writer, Chris Hale; narrator, Peter Capaldi.

This documentary argues that Homo Erectus was established in Australia simultaneously with its appearance in Africa and disputes the theory that modern man evolved from Africa. Ref: *OCLC WorldCat*; not viewed.

Out of Darkness (1984) Australia; dir. Peter Butt; Independent Productions/ Video Education Australasia. 50 min.; color. Producer-writer, Peter Butt; narrator, Robyn Williams.

The 50,000-year history of Australia's aborigines, the oldest continuous culture on Earth. Ref: *OCLC WorldCat*; not viewed.

Out of the Fiery Furnace (1983) U.S.; dir. Christopher McCullough; Opus Films/ PBS. 7 52-min. parts; color & b&w. Producer-writer, Robert Raymond; writer-narrator, Michael Charlton; based on nonfiction book by Robert Raymond.

The history of metallurgy and its impact on civilization. The first two of seven parts dealt with prehistory. Part 1. *From Stone to Bronze*. Covers 15,000 to 1500 B.C., when men began to use metal tools. 2. *Swords and Plough Shares*. The transition from the Bronze Age to the Iron Age, in Europe, the Near East, Africa and East Asia, including weapons and tools. The metalworkers of modern primitive societies are studied for insights into early processes. Ref: *OCLC WorldCat*; not viewed.

Paleolithic Society (1975) U.S.; Gateway Educational Media. 21 min.; color. Producer, Clement W. Bending.

People of the Paleolithic period. Ref: *OCLC WorldCat*; not viewed.

Paleoworld: Tracing Human Origins (1995) U.S.; New Dominion Pictures/Wall to Wall Television/Learning Channel. 75 min.; color. Producer, Tom Naughton; writer, Georgann Kane; narrator, Ben Gazzara.

In three parts: 1. *Missing Links*. Homo Erectus in Asia (such as Peking Man) made stone tools, used fire, fought large predators and survived for hundreds of thousands of years. Some specialists now argue that modern Asians are descended from Asian Erectus, not from a recent African migration as required by the Mitochondrial Eve theory. 2. *Trail of the Neanderthal*. The program examines robust Neanderthals, who cared for their injured, buried their dead and survived the European Ice Age, and asks whether they disappeared through extinction or assimilation. 3. *Ape Man*. The origins of bipedalism. These three programs were part of the fifteen part *Paleoworld* series; the other parts covered dinosaurs. *Missing Links* was also issued in a Time-Life video *Struggle to Survive*, together with *Mysteries of Extinction*, a program on the extinction of the dinosaurs. The Time-Life video *Prehistoric Man* combined *Ape Man* and *Trail of the Neanderthals*. Ref: *OCLC WorldCat*; viewed 2 parts; *Ape Man* not viewed; MK 8.

The Past Is Not Another Place: Ritual Landscape (1984) U.K.; Unicorn Organization/Channel Four. 50 min.; color. (In the TV series *Blood of the British*)

The Neolithic period and Bronze Age in Britain, including the creation of megalithic monuments. Ref: *OCLC WorldCat*; not viewed.

People of the Hearth: Paleoindians of the Northern Rockies (1993) U.S.; dir. Daniel J. Smith; Earthtalk Productions. 30 min.; color. Producers, Daniel J. Smith, Dennis Seibel; narrator, Chrysti Scoville.

Archeologists at a site at Barton Gulch, Montana, reconstruct the lives of an early (7400 B.C.) hunter-gatherer people, including their use of the atlatl and preparation of winter food supplies. Ref: *OCLC WorldCat*; not viewed.

The People of the Ice Age (1992) Denmark; Historical-Archeological Research Center. 24 min.; color. Writer, Ole Malling; English language narration, Tony Wedgwood.

A simulation of Ice Age life, filmed at a recreated settlement at Lejre Research Centre in Denmark. Ref: *OCLC WorldCat*; not viewed.

The Peopling of the Pacific (1988) *see* **Man on the Rim: The Peopling of the Pacific** (1988)

Petroglyphs: The Art of the Earliest Americans (1993) U.S.; Double Diamond Corporation. ca. 16 min.; color.

Paleoindian petroglyphic art. Ref: *OCLC WorldCat*; not viewed.

Planet of Life: Apes to Man (2002) U.S./Japan; NHK/Discovery Channel. 53 min.; color. Producer/writer, Adrienne Ciuffo; narrator, Stacy Keach. Ref: *OCLC WorldCat*; not viewed.

Pre-Anglo-Saxon England (1973) U.S.; McIntyre Productions. 10 min.; color. Writer, Frederick McLeod.

British history from Stonehenge to the Roman conquest. Ref: *OCLC WorldCat*; not viewed.

Prehistoric America: A Journey Through the Ice Age and Beyond (2003) U.K./U.S.; BBC/Discovery Channel. 293 min.; color. Producers, Miles Barton, Stephen Dunleavy, Nigel Bean, Ian Gray, Adam White; narrator, Jack Fortune.

Most of this long, very fine documentary deals with the animals of North America 14,000 years ago, when humans first reached the continent. Modern specimens of animals that survived, such as wolves and bison, are shown, together with recreations of extinct animals, such as the Beringian lion (25 percent larger than modern lions), created by BBC MediaArc, the special effects team who did the *Walking with Dinosaurs* series. Humans are only briefly depicted but the documentary emphasizes their skill and adaptability and details the environments which they conquered. In six parts.

Part 1, *Land of the Mammoth*. Beringia, consisting of Northeast Siberia, the Bering Land Bridge, Alaska and the Yukon, was ice-free during the Ice Age. The Land Bridge was 1000 miles wide, since much of Earth's water was frozen in ice. Beringia was a cold, dry grassland, unlike the forests of the area today. The first humans in this harsh environment had to be skilled hunters, adept at making tools, weapons and weatherproof clothing. Humans lived on high, windswept ground, in order to have a better view of the animals, such as the wooly mammoth.

Part 2, *Canyonlands*. What is now the American Southwest area was much wetter during the Ice Age. About 13,000 years ago, humans first found the canyons and animals such as the enormous Columbian mammoth. Humans are briefly shown hunting a camel.

Part 3, *Ice Age Oasis*. Humans reached Florida about 13,000 years ago, when the area had mastodons, llamas and sabre-tooth cats. The first Florida humans have left an unusually full archeological record, including atlatls and flint spear points.

Part 4, *Edge of the Ice*. Evidence suggests that islands of the Pacific Northwest were ice-free during the entire Ice Age. Animals and humans may have used the islands to penetrate the Northwest earlier than once thought. A reenactment shows a man killed by a bear. Early Northwesterners could build boats and navigate. Humans scavenged large animals they could not normally kill.

Part 5, *American Serengeti*. The North American plains at the end of the Ice Age had mammoths, camels, horses, bison and lions bigger than any others in the world; all but the bison became extinct. Humans found a hunters' paradise and took only a thousand years to spread from the Northwest to Mexico.

Part 6, *Mammoths to Manhattan*. Within a thousand years of the arrival of humans in North America, two-thirds of American megafauna species were extinct. Mammoths survived on Wrangel Island off Siberia long after they disappeared in North America. The documentary suggests that climatic change as the Ice Age ended, rather than human hunting, may have destroyed some species. The dog was introduced to the Americas by early humans. Ref: *OCLC WorldCat*; MK 9.

Prehistoric Cultures (1974) U.S.; dir. Eric Carlson; University of Iowa. 25 min.; color. Narrator, James Wise.

Demonstrates flint-knapping and representative artifacts of Paleo-Indian, Archaic and later Indian cultures of the American West. Ref: *OCLC WorldCat*; not viewed.

Prehistoric Humans (1981) U.S.; dir. Peter Matulavich; BFA Educational Media. 17 min.; color. Writer, Peter Matulavich. An educational film for high school students. According to the blurb, "Using handsome artwork as well as live-action re-enactments, this film introduces viewers to the several prehistoric relatives of modern humans," including Ramapithecus, Australopithecus Robustus, Australopithecus Africanus, Homo Habilis, Homo Erectus, Neanderthal and Cro-Magnon. Ref: *OCLC WorldCat*; not viewed.

Prehistoric Images: The First Art of Man (1955) U.S./France; dir. Thomas Rowe, Alexandre Arcady; Renaissance Films/Films de Saturne. 17 min.; color. Writer, Thomas Rowe.

Filmed in the prehistoric caves of Lascaux, Altamira and other painted caves in France and Spain. Ref: *OCLC WorldCat*; not viewed.

Prehistoric Magic (1979) U.S.; WSJK-TV, Knoxville/Tennessee Technological University/Agency for Instructional Television. 15 min.; color. Producer-writer, Sally Crain. (In the series *Young at Art*) This film for children describes the ancient cave paintings of Lascaux in France and the techniques used by cave artists. Children are asked to create their own cave paintings. Ref: *OCLC WorldCat*; not viewed.

Prehistoric Man (1970) U.S.; Barbre Productions/State Historical Society of Colorado/Xerox Films. 17 min.; color. (In the series *Exploring the American Past*)

The development of American Indians from the Bering Strait migration until the 16th Century. Also shows how archeologists gain information about the past from ruins, artifacts and art. Ref: *OCLC WorldCat*; not viewed.

Prehistoric Man (1980) U.K.; Thames TV International. 15 min.; color. (In the TV series *Seeing and Doing*)

How we learn about the lives of ancient man through cave art. Ref: *OCLC WorldCat*; not viewed.

Prehistoric Man (1988) U.K./U.S.; BBC/KCET-TV. 56 min.; color. Producer-writer, Derek Towers; narrator, Tim Piggott-Smith; U.S. narrator, Scott Glenn. (In the TV series *Discoveries Underwater*)

Studies three underwater archeological sites in North America, Scotland and Switzerland which shed light on early man. Ref: *OCLC WorldCat*; not viewed.

Prehistoric Man in Europe (1965) U.S.; Boulton-Hawker Films. 23 min.; color. Producer, D.C. Chipperfield.

The tools and culture of the Paleolithic, Mesolithic, Neolithic, Bronze and Iron Ages in Europe. Ref: *OCLC WorldCat*; not viewed.

Prehistoric Monuments (1990) [alt. *Sacred Sites*; *Prehistoric Monuments of Europe*] U.S.; dir. Gottfried Kirchner; Films for the Humanities. 43 min.; color. Narrator, Keith Elshaw. (In the series *Lost Civilizations*)

Megalithic monuments and tombs at Carnac in Britanny and on the islands of Sardinia, Malta and Gozo. Ref: *OCLC WorldCat*; not viewed.

Prehistoric Monuments of Europe (1990) *see* **Prehistoric Monuments** (1990)

Prehistoric Sites (1974) *see* **Looking at Prehistoric Sites** (1982)

Prehistory (1995) France; Muséum National d'Histoire Naturelle/Laboratoire de Paléontologie Humaine et de Préhistoire. 83 min.; color. With: Henry de Lumley. A general survey of human prehistory. Ref: *OCLC WorldCat*; not viewed.

Prehistory of Spain (2002) Spain; dir. José Briz; EFE/Spanish Ministry of Culture. 23 min.; color. Producer, Alfredo B. de Quiros; writer, Eduardo Chamorro.
 The Stone Age and the Agricultural Revolution in Spain and Portugal. Ref: *OCLC WorldCat*; not viewed.

Prehistory of the Texas Coast (1990) U.S.; Texas A&M University. ca. 47 min.; color. Lecturer, Thomas R. Hester. (In the series *Living on the Edge*) Discusses 11,000 years of human prehistory along Texas' Gulf Coast. Ref: *OCLC WorldCat*; not viewed.

Primal Man (1973–74) U.S.; dir. Dennis Azzarella; David L. Wolper Productions/ Jack Kaufman Productions/ABC. 4 55-min. parts; color. Writer, Dennis Azzarella, Arthur Bramble, Theodore Strauss; narrator, Alexander Scourby.
 In four parts: 1. *The Killer Instinct*. Human aggression; includes Neanderthal. 2. *The Battle for Dominance*. The struggle for social supremacy. 3. *The Struggle for Survival*. Fire, domestication of animals, the beginnings of agriculture. 4. *The Human Factor*. This four-part series, shown over six months from December 1973 to June 1974, was one of the first attempts to present a realistic view of prehistory to a mass audience. David L. Wolper was already

Neanderthals from *Primal Man*.

well-known for intelligent TV documentaries. Alexander Scourby was 60 and famous for his arresting voice and many dignified performances.
 Variety (Dec. 5, 1973) found *The Killer Instinct* "fascinating" and praised the "excellent job of makeup" and the show's "ability to carry the viewer back into the distant past." Later *Variety* (June 26, 1974) was less favorable to *The Struggle to Survival*, calling the special "an exercise in pop anthropology" which "never quite manages to match the script with convincing film footage" and noting "it's difficult to make actors in ape costumes look like anything but actors in ape costumes." In a February 1982 *Cinefantastique* article on the film *Quest for Fire*, Jordan R. Fox named Stanley Kubrick's *2001* and David L. Wolper's *Primal Man* as among the few "notable" previous attempts to depict prehistory for a mass audience.
 Director Azzarella and his crew of 30 died in a plane crash in March 1974. Ref: *OCLC WorldCat*; *www.davidlwolper.com*.; not viewed.

The Real Eve (2002) U.S./Great Britain; dir. Andrew Piddington; Granada Productions/Discovery Channel/Libra Films. 87 min.; color. Producers, Paul Ashton, Amanda Theunissen; based on book *The Peopling of the World* by Stephen Oppenheimer; music, Mark Thomas; narrator, Danny Glover.
 This documentary treats ancient humans with realism and dignity, tracing the descendants of "genetic Eve" (also called "mitochondrial Eve"

or "African Eve"), an African woman who lived about 150,000 years ago and was "the mother of all mankind." The first modern humans in Africa developed organized hunting, which required intelligence, communication and cooperation. Around 80,000 years ago an Ice Age produced an African drought, which forced nomads to become fishers and beachcombers. They migrated across the lowered Red Sea to Yemen, then spread along the coast to India and Southeast Asia. About 74,000 years ago Malayans were almost destroyed by the gigantic Toba volcanic eruption, the biggest explosion in the history of modern humans. About 70,000 years ago humans reached Australia from Malaya by boat.

Around 40,000 before the present Cro-Magnons moved from the Middle East into Europe, where they eventually replaced the Neanderthals. Asians reached the Western Hemisphere in several waves beginning 20,000 to 25,000 years ago.

The documentary is more informative than the similar (and much longer) *Journey of Man* (2003). In the latter we hear mostly from only one geneticist, Spencer Wells; in *The Real Eve*, we hear the ideas of several paleoanthropologists, notably Stephen Oppenheimer, author of the book on which the documentary was based. *Journey of Man* concentrates on modern simple-technology people who are believed to be the descendants of ancient nomads. *The Real Eve* has less on modern people but more on their ancient forbears.

Journey of Man has no extensive reenactment scenes; *The Real Eve* has several excellent dramatic reenactments, depicting ancient Africans hunting zebra; a mass migration across the shallow Red Sea by wading; people fleeing the Toba eruption; the sea voyage to Australia; the accidental death of a child in Lebanon about 44,000 years ago; a lethal confrontation between Neanderthals and Cro-Magnons; and the death of a Caucasian man in a fight with Paleo-Indians in early America. The latter three scenes are reconstructions based on actual skeletal remains, including Kennewick Man. Danny Glover's awed narration is an great asset. MK 9.

Retracing Man's Steps, a program in the video *The Origins of Man* (1993, q.v.).

Return of the Iceman (1998) U.S/Great Britain; producer-dir. Tim Haines; BBC/WGBH. 54 min.; color. Writer-producer, Joseph Mc-

The Neolithic Iceman with his bearskin hat and waterproof grass and bark cloak, in *Return of the Iceman*.

Manus; narrator, Stacy Keach. (In the series *Ice Mummies*).

In 1991 a 5200-year-old ice mummy, later called both the Iceman and Ötzi, was found in the Alps. This BBC/PBS documentary is ten minutes longer than the History Channel's *Iceman: Mummy from the Stone Age* (2000) and has more information on the archeological techniques used to investigate the mummy, but less detailed information on what conclusions can be drawn from the body and its paraphernalia. It covers the Iceman's diet, his copper ax, the many tattoos on his body, and rock drawings which portray his period. *Return of the Iceman* was part of the short series *Ice Mummies* (together with documentaries on ancient but not prehistoric Peruvian and Siberian mummies) and the umbrella series *Nova*. Ref: *OCLC WorldCat*; MK 8.

Le Roman de L'Homme (1997) France; dir. Stéphane Bégoin, Philippe Piazza, Bernard Jourdain, Jean Claude Labracque; TVB/VSP. TV series; 15 26-min. episodes; color.

Episodes: 1. *L'Outil, Preuve de l'Homme* (prehistoric tools in France); 2. *Deux Crânes pour un Homme* (prehistoric skulls found in France); 3. *L'Art, Grandeur de l'Homme* (cave paintings, including Lascaux in France and Altamira in

Spain); 4. *Et Si l'Homme Venait d'Asie?* (Pithecanthropus fossils found in Asia and Indonesia; the work of early paleontologist Eugene Dubois); 5. *Afrique, Terre de l'Homme* (early fossils found in Africa, including the Taung skull; the work of Raymond Dart and Pierre Teilhard de Chardin); 6. *Le Grand Voyage de l'Homme* (migration in Africa and Europe); 7. *Le Feu, Lumière de l'Homme* (Fire and early man); 8. *Etre Homme, C'Est se Tenir Debout* (Australopithecine Afarenis fossils in Ethiopia, including Lucy); 9. *L'Homme Enterre ses Morts* (graves and burial customs); 10. *Art, Mystère de l'Homme* (cave paintings in France); 11. *Le Dernier Grand Voyage* (the Bering Strait migration to the Western Hemisphere); 12. *Le Grand Tournant de l'Homme* (the Neolithic change from nomadism to sedentary life in Mesopotamia); 13. *L'Homme Deviant Cité* (Architecture and houses in Mesopotamia); 14. *L'Homme et Les Dieux* (Early religion and megalithic monuments in Europe, including the site at Carnac, France); 15. *L'Ecriture, Mémoire de l'Homme* (the development of writing in Mesopotamia). Ref: *OCLC WorldCat*; not viewed.

Sacred Sites (1990) *see* **Prehistoric Monuments** (1990)

The Sands of Dreamtime: A Brief History (1997) Australian; Australian Broadcast Corp. 51 min.; color. Producer-writer-narrator, Geoffrey Burchfield.

At the Jinmium Site in the Kimberley Mountains of Australia, archeologists work with aborigines to trace the history of human habitation, using cave paintings, artifacts, Dreamtime stories and radio-carbon dating. Ref: *OCLC WorldCat*; not viewed.

Scientific American Frontiers: Coming Into America (2004) U.S.; dir. John Angier; Chedd-Angier/CPTV/PBS. 60 min.; color. Writer, John Angier; host, Alan Alda.

John Angier and Alan Alda examine challenges to the Clovis-first theory of the ancient peopling of the Americas. Evidence includes Arlington Springs Woman, who lived 13,000 years ago on Santa Rosa Island off California; Clovis points found in New Mexico; the Clovis Gault Site in Texas; Monte Verde Site in Chile, about 14,700 years old; Topper Site in South Carolina, more than 15,000 years old; La Sena Site in Colorado, about 18,000 years old; Cactus Hill Site in Virginia, about 18,000 years old; and Broken Mammoth Site in Alaska, about 14,000 years old. Evidence suggests that ancient people had sea-going boats much earlier than was once believed and that Clovis Culture people did not move around as much as was thought. Alda makes a Clovis point and breaks open a large animal bone with a handmade ancient tool. The show concludes with the radical theory that Solutreans migrated from ancient Europe to America in boats along the edge of the ice cap. Ref: MK 8.

Scientific American Frontiers: Life's Really Big Questions (2000) U.S.; dir. Graham Chedd, Andrew Leibman, John Angier. 60 min.; color. Narrator, Alan Alda.

A TV special with five segments, each about 12 min. *Handmade Humans* shows the importance of humans' hands in the development of tools, weapons and intelligence. (The special also has a segment titled *Noah's Snowball*, which covers a planetary deep freeze about 600,000,000 years ago and has nothing to do with the traditional Noah story.) Ref: *OCLC WorldCat*; MK 8.

The Search for Ancient Americans (1988) U.S.; WQED-TV/National Academy of Sciences. 58 min.; color. Producer-writer, Stephen Eder; narrator, Paul Shenar. (In the TV series *The Infinite Voyage*)

Surveys the study of early Western Hemisphere peoples, including the Mayas, the Anasazi and cultures in Florida. Examines new archeological techniques. Ref: *OCLC WorldCat*; not viewed.

Search for Fossil Man (1974) U.S.; National Geographic Society. 24 min.; color.

Explains "dig site" methods, used to find and identify ancient human remains. Ref: *OCLC WorldCat*; not viewed.

Search for Neanderthal (1993) U.S.; dir. Phil Comeau; Arkios Productions/ Archaeological Institute of America/Learning Channel. 23 min.; color. Narrator, John Rhys-Davies. (In the TV series *Archaeology*.)

Considers why Neanderthals died out and modern man survived. *Primal Man*, a 1994 Time-Life video, included both *Search for Neanderthal* and *Ice Age Crossings* (also 1993). Ref: *OCLC WorldCat*; MK 7.

Search for the First Americans (1992) U.K./U.S.; BBC/WGBH-TV. 60 min.; color. Producer-writer, Simon Campbell-Jones; narrator, Peter Thomas. (In the TV series *Nova*)

Investigates whether humans arrived in the Western Hemisphere before the Bering Sea Migration at the end of the Ice Age. Ref: *OCLC WorldCat*; not viewed.

Search for the First Human (2002) U.S./U.K.; dir. Ben Bowie; JWM Productions/Channel 4/WNET-TV/PBS. 56 min.; color. Producers, Lucy McDowell, Noddy Sahota; narrator, Liev Schreiber. (In the TV series *Secrets of the Dead*)

Orrorin Tugenensis, a possibly 6,000,000-year-old fossil found in 2000 in Kenya's Tugen Hills, is one of the most controversial recent finds. Scientists who believe it was a hominid called it Millennium Man. The 6,000,000 year date and the bipedalism of the specimen are both controversial; the documentary claims that both are probable. Orrorin is much older than Lucy (3,200,000 years old) and is near the presumed date for a common ancestor of man and modern apes. Much of the program details the technical methods of dating soil and remains and of determining bipedalism. Orrorin's back teeth are similar to modern man's while its front teeth are apelike. Orrorin is evidence that bipedalism developed in trees, not in open savannah as previously believed. Orangutans, which live in trees but often support their whole weight on two legs, provide a clue. Orrorin discoverers Martin Pickford and Brigitte Senut claim that Orrorin was more like us than Lucy and was among our ancestors. This would imply significant retrogression in the hominid record. Ref: *OCLC WorldCat*; MK 8.

The Secret Mounds of Pre-Historic America (1996) [alt. *Secret Burial Mounds of Pre-Historic America*] U.S./A&E. ca. 50 min.; color. Narrator, Leonard Nimoy. (In the TV series *Ancient Mysteries*)

Huge mounds and flat-top pyramids were build by ancient peoples of North America for about 2000 years. Ref: *OCLC WorldCat*; not viewed.

The Secret of Stonehenge (1998) U.K./U.S.; dir. Jean-Claude Bragard; BBC/ Learning Channel/Time-Life. 51 min.; color. Narrator, Mark Hamill (In the series *Ancient Voices*)

Suggests that Stonehenge may have been used for ancestor worship. Ref: *OCLC WorldCat*; MK 7.

Secrets of Lost Empires: Stonehenge (1997) U.K./U.S.; BBC/WGBH-TV/PBS. 60 min.; color. Producer, Cynthia Page; producer-writer, Julia Cort; narrator, Stacy Keach. (In the TV series *Nova*).

Archeologist Julian Richards, engineer Mark Whitby, stonemason Roger Hopkins and a large group of volunteers attempt to move, raise and cap a Stonehenge-like structure using only prehistoric techniques. Ref: *OCLC WorldCat*; MK 8.

Secrets of the Bog People (2003) U.S.; dir. Johana Gibbon; Brighton Films/Horsebridge Productions/Learning Channel. 50 min.; color. Writer, Johana Gibbon; narrator, Eric Meyers. The exploration of a 7000-year-old cemetery in Florida's Wingover Bog, which has yielded skeletons, ancient DNA, artifacts and fabrics. Includes reenactments of early life. Ref: *OCLC WorldCat*; MK 8.

Secrets of the Stone Age (1999) U.K.; dirs. Bill Lyons, Christopher Salt; Granada/Channel 4. 153 min.; color. Host, Richard Rudgley.

In three parts. 1. *The Wisdom of the Stones: Life in the Neolithic Age*. Anthropologist Richard Rudgley claims that Neolithic man developed engineering skills, religious systems, acupuncture, bookkeeping and an intricate social structure. 2. *Frozen in Time: Life in the Upper Paleolithic Age*. Rudgley argues for a new view of Ice Age culture, claiming that findings such as a bead "factory," a "cave cathedral" and beautifully sculpted female figurines are evidence of a society in which women and children were equal to men and daily tasks required modern intelligence. 3. *The Human Story: Traces of Humankind's Oldest Relatives*. Rudgley defends the Neanderthals. Ref: *OCLC WorldCat*; not viewed.

Seeking Noah's Flood (1998) U.K.; BBC/ Learning Channel/Time-Life. 50-min.; color. Narrator, Mark Hamill. (In the series *Ancient Voices*). Ref: *OCLC WorldCat*; not viewed.

Seeking the First Americans (1979) U.S.; dir. Graham Chedd; Documentary Education

Resources/Corporation for Public Broadcasting. 59 min.; color. Producer- writer, Graham Chedd; narrator, Stacy Keach. (In the TV series *Odyssey*)

Shows how archeologists search for clues about the earliest Paleoindians in Alaska, New Mexico and Texas. Ref: *OCLC WorldCat*; not viewed.

Set in Stone (1994) U.S.; dir. Linda Zimmerman; Stanford University. Length?; color.

Describes Stonehenge and the controversy surrounding the efforts of the English Heritage organization to protect the site from the public. Ref: *OCLC WorldCat*; not viewed.

Skull Wars: The Missing Link (1995) U.S.; dir., Christopher Rowley; CineNova/ Discovery Channel. 50 min.; color. Narrator, Richard Kiley. (In the series *Searching for Other Worlds*).

The discovery in 1924 of the Taung Child Skull in South Africa set off a battle between advocates of the theory that mankind is descended from small-brained African apes and those who pointed to the Piltdown Man skull as evidence that humans came from large-skulled Asian and European forebears. The controversy was tinged with racism and related to the debate over whether the path to modern man began with changes in the brain or the body. Raymond Dart and Robert Broom of South Africa battled Sir Ian Keith of London for two decades. The discovery of Peking Man hurt Dart's case. By the 1940s the discovery of more and more primitive human remains in Africa forced Keith to admit he was wrong. In the 1950s the Piltdown skull was exposed as a forgery. This tape is highly anecdotal, with actors playing Dart, Broom and Keith. Ref: *OCLC WorldCat*; MK 8.

Some Liked It Hot (1994) [alt. *Challenging the Human Evolution Model*] U.K.; BBC. 50 min.; color. Producer-writer, Christopher Hale; narrator, Geraldine James. (In the TV series *Horizon*).

This program proposes that bipedalism preceded the enlargement of hominid brains. The previous theory was that bipedalism and the increase in brain size occurred simultaneously. Ref: *OCLC WorldCat*; not viewed.

Stone Age Americans (1970) U.S.; dir. Daniel Wilson; ABC. 21 min.; color. Producer, Jules Power.

The Indians of the Mesa Verde area in Colorado disappeared after 13 centuries of development. This program examines their cliff dwellings. Ref: *OCLC WorldCat*; not viewed.

Stone Age to Atomic Age (1961) U.S.; dir. Roger Blais. Ref: Goble. *International Film Index*; not viewed.

Stonehenge (1980) U.S.; Lucerne Films. 15 min.; color.

Archeological research into the age, construction and possible use of Stonehenge, Including how the stones may have been brought to the site and erected and the significance of the location of Stonehenge. Ref: *OCLC WorldCat*; not viewed.

Stonehenge (1988) U.S.; Films for the Humanities. 24 min.; color.

No details on contents. Ref: *OCLC WorldCat*; not viewed.

Stonehenge and Its Cousins: Megalithic Observatories? (1979) U.S.; Harvard University Science Center. 90 min.; color.

No details on contents. Ref: *OCLC WorldCat*; not viewed.

Stonehenge and the Ancient Britons (1998) [alt. *Stonehenge*] U.K.; dir. Bob Carruthers; Cromwell Productions. ca. 50 min.; color. Producer, Lara Lowe; writer, Matt Ford; narrator, Robert Whelan. (In the TV series *Lost Treasures of the Ancient World*)

The British Isles in prehistory, including hunting and farming. This program uses animation and computer graphics to show how ancient monuments may have looked when they were first built. Besides Stonehenge, the series deals with Egyptian, Roman, Mayan and Aztec ruins. In 1998, Cromwell Productions also released a 25 min. program *Stonehenge: A Journey Back in Time* (in the series *History's Ancient Legacies*) probably a cutdown version of *Stonehenge and the Ancient Britons*. Ref: *OCLC WorldCat*; not viewed.

[Stonehenge has been a favorite topic of dubious documentaries about "mysterious" places. These include the episode *The Riddle of the Stones* in the series *Arthur C. Clarke's Mysterious World* (1985); *In Search of Stonehenge* (1976, alt. *In Search of the Magic of Stonehenge*,

Alan Landsburg Productions, narrator, Leonard Nimoy); *Mysterious Places of England* (1995), which Bill Olton (*Arthurian Legend on Film and Television*) calls "superficial"; *Mystic Ruins* (1998, FilmRoos/History Channel); *Secrets of the Unknown: Stonehenge* (1988, alt. *Secrets and Mysteries: Stonehenge*, narrated by Edward Mulhare); *These British Isles* (1990?, U.K., episode, *On the Road to Stonehenge*); *Wonders Sacred and Mysterious* (1993) and *The World's Most Mysterious Places: Europe* (1995).]

Stonehenge: If Only the Stones Could Talk (1984) [alt. *Stonehenge: The Human Factor with Sue Jay*] Australia?; dir. Bill Thompson; Television South Pacific. 28 min. color. Host: Sue Jay. Interviews with two experts and Stonehenge fans on why the monument was built. Bill Olton called this tape "entertaining but remarkably superficial." Ref: *OCLC WorldCat*; Orton. *Arthurian Legend on Film and Television*; not viewed.

Stonehenge: Mystery in the Plain (1980) U.S.; dir. Lawrence Moore; Encyclopaedia Britannica Educational Corp./Vortex Films. 24 min.; color. Producer, Alan Coddington; writer-narrator, Lawrence Moore.

The possible age and astronomical significance of Stonehenge. Ref: *OCLC WorldCat*; not viewed.

Stones and Bones: The Birth of Archaeology (1997) U.S.; Films for the Humanities. 50 min.; color. (In the series *Lost Worlds: The Story of Archaeology*)

The discovery of the ruins of Pompeii and Herculaneum in the 18th century marked the beginnings of modern archeology. This program also covers early excavations in Egypt and England; the development of the concepts of the Stone, Bronze and Iron Ages; the discovery of cave paintings in France and Spain; and the Leakeys' discoveries in Africa. Ref: *OCLC WorldCat*; not viewed.

The Story of Human Evolution (1997) U.S.; Films for the Humanities and Sciences. 93 min.; color.

Paleoanthropologist Friedemann Schrenk visits fossil sites in Africa and museums around the world to trace human evolution. In two parts. 1. *History of the Anthropoid: The Search for the Beginning*. Maeve Leakey discusses Lucy, the Australopithecus Afarenis female found in Ethiopia, and other African finds, including Homo Erectus remains. 2. *Origins of Homo Sapiens: East African Roots*. A study of several cave sites and hominid remains found in Africa. Ref: *OCLC WorldCat*; not viewed.

The Story of Prehistoric Man (1953) U.S.; Coronet Instructional Films. 11 min.; color. With: T. Walter Wallbank.

Filmed exhibits from the Chicago Natural History Museum and the Musée de L'Homme in Paris outline our knowledge of the appearance, habitat and achievements of prehistoric man. Ref: *OCLC WorldCat*; not viewed.

The Tabon Caves (1981) U.S.; dir. Hugh Gibb; Academic Hawaii. 25 min.; color. (In the series *The Philippine Story*)

American archeologist Robert B. Fox and Filipino expert Alfredo Evangelista explain finds made at the Tabon Caves site on Palawan Island in the Philippines, a site which was inhabited at least 50,000 years ago. The stone tools, funeral jars and human remains suggest links to Australian aborigines. Ref: *OCLC WorldCat*; not viewed.

Tales of the Human Dawn (1990) U.S.; dir. Sandra W. Bradley; WETA-TV/ Smithsonian Institution 58 min.; color. Writers, R.B. Phillips, Sandra W. Bradley; narrator, Halo Wines. (In the TV series *Smithsonian World*)

Examines cultural factors that have influenced theories of human evolution. Ref: *OCLC WorldCat*; not viewed.

Tassili N'Ajjer: Prehistoric Rock Paintings of the Sahara (1972) France; dir. Jean-Dominique Lajoux. 16 min.; color.

Early man painted cave walls at the Tassili N'Ajjer site in the Sahara. The art depicts men hunting animals in the verdant landscape which existed there thousands of years ago. Ref: *OCLC WorldCat*; not viewed.

Tracing Human Origins (1995) *see* **Paleoworld: Tracing Human Origins** (1995)

Tracking the First Americans (1999) U.K./ U.S.; dir. Jean Claude Bragard; BBC/Learning Channel/Time-Life. 50 min.; color. Narrator, Mark Hamill. (In the *Ancient Voices* series)

"Luzia," a 12,000-year-old female skull, was found in Brazil. This documentary claims that Luzia and other remains from the same period did not belong to any of the races of the Western Hemisphere. Ref: *OCLC WorldCat*; not viewed.

The Treasury: An Introduction to the Gallery of Early Irish Art in the National Museum of Ireland (1986) Ireland; National Museum of Ireland. 20 min.; color. Prehistoric Irish art. Ref: *OCLC WorldCat*; not viewed.

The Tree That Put the Clock Back (1972) U.K./U.S.; BBC/Time-Life Films. 50 min.; color.
Radio-carbon dating forces a reappraisal of the key dates in the development of early man. Ref: *OCLC WorldCat*; not viewed.

20,000 Years of France (1967) *see* **Vingt Mille Ans a la Francais** (1967)

The Ultimate Guide: Ice Man (2001) U.S.; dir. Brando Quilici; Discovery Channel. 52 min.; color. Writer, Robert Goldberg; narrator, Steve Eastin.
Another special on the study of the body and artifacts of Ötzi the Iceman, the 5200- year-old ice mummy found in the Alps in 1991. The mummy was defrosted to extract dental enamel, bone fragments and the contents of the stomach and intestines. Scientists found an arrowhead in the mummy's back and concluded that the wound killed him. An experiment with the Iceman's clothes and equipment showed that his clothes were excellent for mountain climbing but his shoes were poorly designed for rough walking. His dozens of tattoos suggest that he may have been a shaman. There is speculation that the Iceman may have been a human sacrifice. The program is repetitious and rather melodramatic and concentrates too much on the Iceman's death rather than what we can learn about his life. Ref: *OCLC WorldCat*; MK 7.

Up from the Apes (1974) *see* **The Animal Within** (1974)

Valdivia: America's First Civilization (1990) U.S.; dir. Peter Baumann; Films for the Humanities. 43 min.; color. Producer, Gottfried Kirchner. (In the series *Lost Civilizations*) The 5,000-year-old Neolithic Valdivian Culture of Ecuador. Ref: *OCLC WorldCat*; not viewed.

The Video Griots Trilogy (1990) U.S.; dir. Ulysses Jenkins; Electronic Arts Intermix/Othervisions. 25 min.; color.
Two short experimental films, *Divination* (1989, 11 min.) and *Mutual Native Duplex* (1990, 12 min.), claim that Africans migrated to the Americas in prehistoric times. Jenkins notes that sandpaintings of Africa and the Americas are very similar. Ref: *OCLC WorldCat*; not viewed.

Vingt Mille Ans a la Francais (1967) [alt. *20,000 Years of France*; *The French Way of Looking at It*] France; dir. Jacques Forgeot; Cinéastes Associés. Animated film; 80 min.; color. Screenplay, Jacques Forgeot; photography, Guy Durban; music, Avenir de Monfred.
An animated look at French history, from prehistory to modern times, "from the Lascaux cave paintings to the geometrical forms of today's industrial world," according to Bruno Edera. Edera calls *Vingt Mille Ans* "a strange and enthralling film ... different from anything we have seen before" which took four years to make and "abounds in images of a sumptuous beauty." Ref: Edera. *Full Length Animated Feature Films*; *Internet Movie Database*; not viewed.

Virgin Report (1971) [alt. *Jungfrauen-Report*] West Germany; dir. Jesus Franco; CCC Telecine. 66 or 72 min.; color. Screenplay, Paul Alexander. CAST: Howard Vernon.
According to *Video Watchdog* (no. 107), this highly dubious "documentary" is "a mondo movie about how virginity has been regarded by different cultures and generations, ranging from phallus-worshipping prehistoric times to Berlin's beat clubs of the 1970s." The "mondo" films were sensationalized pseudo-documentaries, often about primitive cultures. Franco was a cult director of cheap, eccentric and fleshy European B-films. The *Watchdog* reviewer says that Franco's "veritable tour of filmmaking styles ... is the movie's only saving grace." Ref: *Internet Movie Database*; not viewed.

Walking with Beasts (2001) *see* **Walking with Prehistoric Beasts** (2001)

Walking with Cavemen (2003) U.K./U.S; dir. Richard Dale, Tim Goodchild; BBC/Discovery Channel. 100 or 117 min.; color. Producer, Peter Georgi; writer, Michael Olmert; U.K. host, Nigel Marven; U.S. host, Alec Baldwin; DVD narrator, Andrew Sachs.

3,000,000 years ago in Africa a troop of Australopithecus Afarensis is in a turf war with another Afarensis troop. Among them is the female who will one day be called Lucy by the paleoanthropologists who find her bones. Afarensis is the first ape to stand and walk on two legs but is otherwise very apelike. The leader of the troop is taken by a crocodile at a waterhole. Two rival males compete for leadership, making frenzied threat displays. (The documentary then looks back to 8,000,000 years ago to explain how droughts had deforested much of Africa, forcing apes to leave the trees and learn to walk erect.)

Lucy was the senior mate of the dead leader. The rival candidates for the leadership contend roughly for her favors. A black eagle almost snatches Lucy's baby. The enemy troop attacks. As Lucy tries to protect her baby, she is struck down and killed by an ape wielding a bone. Lucy's eldest daughter adopts her baby.

2,000,000 years ago Africa is the home of many species of big animals and several kinds of hominids, including the gorilla-like Paranthropus Boisei and clever, inquisitive Homo Habilis. With their big, tough teeth, the Boiseis can eat almost any plants. Their future seems assured. The Habilis have no special advantage, but they have learned to eat meat while Boisei are mostly vegetarian. During a famine, a Habilis leader raids a beehive high in a tree for honey. He must find food for his troop in order to remain the leader. A conflict, mostly consisting of threat displays, breaks out between Habilis and Boisei troops over food. The Habilis leader is killed by a lion while scavenging the lion's kill.

Boisei are specialized vegetarians, too big and powerful for most predators. They are well-adapted but not capable of further adaptation. They will die out as climatic conditions change. Habilis is a jack-of-all-trades and has produced the first stone tools, giving them access to many different kinds of food. Meat-eating gives Habilis enough protein to grow their brains. Only Habilis with his tools can get at bone marrow when they scavenge dead animals left by powerful predators. We see a Habilis troop work together to scare off a threatening lion. A young Habilis who is good at food-gathering takes over as the new dominant male.

1,500,000 years ago a Homo Ergaster band is hunting a sick wildebeest. A young man's impatience ruins the hunt and the beast gets away. Ergaster is the first hominid to speak a simple language. They sweat from hairless bodies, making them efficient walkers. Their brains are the biggest yet — two-thirds the size of modern man's. They have a superb understanding of their environment and can make powerful and precise stone axes. They work together to find, stalk, kill and butcher prey. They do more mutual helping than any previous hominids. Ergaster are the first monogamists; among earlier hominids, the dominant male always had a harem. When a solitary, outside male tries to enter the band, a fight to the death breaks out.

A Homo Ergaster displays an animal tooth in Africa about 1,500,000 years ago, in *Walking with Cavemen.*

Homo Ergaster was the first hominid to leave Africa. He spread across South Asia, becoming Homo Erectus. Asian Erectus gave up the old reliable stone ax for tools made from a very useful plant, bamboo. Erectus hunted small deer and pigs in the vast Asian forests and ate insects voraciously. Mankind became stuck in a technological rut. Ergaster and Erectus used the same stone and bamboo tools for about a million years. A big change occurred when men learned how to control fire.

400,000 years ago in Southern England a young man of a Homo Heidelbergensis band is injured while his band is hunting a giant elk with spears. His band uses herbs for medicine. Their brains are almost as big as ours and they help their wounded. However, when the young hunter dies the band simply leaves him. They do not yet bury their dead.

140,000 years ago in Europe a Neanderthal band is hard-pressed by cold and hunger. Their leader must decide whether to move the band, risking the life of his pregnant mate on an arduous march, or stay where they are and risk death for the whole band. He and two other men go on a hunt to try to get enough food to make the migration unnecessary. When they are ready to give up, they find mammoths and manage to injury one of the giants as it passes through a ravine. They finish it off and return to their cave with enough food for the winter. The Neanderthals had incredible physical and mental toughness. They lived stoically with injuries which would seem intolerable to us. Many Neanderthal bodies we have found had multiple broken bones.

140,000 years ago in Africa men have dark skins for the first time. African humans are in imminent danger of extinction from severe drought. Only the most intelligent and imaginative survive. For instance, we see men bury water in an ostrich egg, as a cache for future use.

30,000 years ago modern man is producing cave art, showing that "they're not simply living in caves but in an imagined world of their own making."

This very well-done documentary has a rather convoluted history. The British version, which was 117 minutes long and had the subtitle *Eye-to-Eye with Your Ancestors*, had a breezy, almost frivolous tone, with host Nigel Marven "time-traveling" to "meet the ancestors." Discovery Channel dumped Marven and his jokes, cut the program by 17 minutes, had Michael Olmert write a serious script and hired Alec Baldwin to host its version. The DVD has narration by Andrew Sachs, best known as Manuel the waiter on *Fawlty Towers*. Sachs does a fine job as a serious narrator and does not appear on camera. Baldwin did appear on camera, so even though both the Baldwin and Sachs versions are 100 minutes long, the latter gives us more footage of the prehistoric people and animals. (I have seen only the Baldwin and Sachs versions, not the longer Marven version.)

Walking with Cavemen has beautiful on-location photography, recorded in South Africa and Iceland. All the hominids, even the most primitive, were performed by actors, not computer-generated creatures. The prehistoric animals were created by the same BBC team that did *Walking with Dinosaurs* (1999). The DVD has extensive extras including information on how the makeup and mechanical effects were achieved. Afarenis characters, for instance, had animatronic jaws. Many actors played individuals from several different species. The actors were trained in movement but were not given much information on their species. A good deal was left to their imagination. However, the scripts were based on up-to-date information, making *Walking with Cavemen* one of the most convincing documentaries on early man. Ref: *OCLC WorldCat*; MK 10.

Walking with Prehistoric Beasts (2001) [alt. *Walking with Beasts*] U.K./U.S.; BBC/Discovery Channel/TV Asahi. 170 min.; color. Producer, Jasper James, Nigel Paterson; writers, Kate Bartlett, Jasper James, Michael Olmert, Nigel Patterson; narrator, Kenneth Branagh.

This program covered prehistoric mammals, from the demise of the dinosaurs to about 10,000 B.C. Two of six sections involved early humans. *Next of Kin* is set in Ethiopia 3,200,000 years ago and examines Australopithecines, the first apes to walk erect. A scene depicting conflict between two groups, involving more threats than real fighting, resembles the Dawn of Man segment of *2001: A Space Odyssey*. Two males within the same group compete for leadership. The Australopithecines were scavengers, not hunters, and were themselves hunted by large predators. Toward the end of the segment, the group gangs up on a predator to save a weak individual. Individuals are identified by names like "Grey" and "Blue."

Mammoth Journey is set in Europe about 30,000 B.C. and depicts the winter migration of hundreds of mammoths from the dry land which is now the North Sea to the Alps during the Ice Age, and the interaction of both Cro-Magnons and Neanderthals with mammoths and other giant animals. Humans are both predators of small animals and scavengers when larger animals, including mammoths, die. The Cro-Magnons wear both animal hides and woven cloth. They collect the bones of mammoths to build shelters, burn animal oils for fuel and paint their faces to fend off the omnipresent flies. When humans kill a giant elk, they must get away with as much meat as they can carry quickly, before large predators are attracted to the kill. Cro-Magnons migrate from Belgium to the Alps, where extensive caves provide winter shelter. A Cro-Magnon is killed by white cave lions. Neanderthals, who do not migrate, depend on small local caves for shelter. A Neanderthal is so tough he survives being run down by a giant rhino. A Neanderthal tribe uses fire to drive two mammoths over a cliff.

The DVD contains an additional 50-minute feature (also narrated by Kenneth Branagh) *The Beasts Within*, which covers the whole history of evolution from the earliest primates, through the monkeys, the great apes, bipedal hominids, toolmaking and the development of spears and the atlatl. The Neanderthals disappeared at about the same time as the megafauna. The program concludes that the giant animals were probably exterminated by sudden warming and vegetation change at the end of the Ice Age, not by human hunting.

All the giant animals were created by the expert BBC team who made the *Walking with Dinosaurs* series. The humans' clothing and weapons and the Neanderthals' big-nosed make-up are convincing. Some brief scenes from *Walking with Prehistoric Beasts*, depicting Australopithecines fleeing from megafauna and Neanderthals attacking mammoths with fire, were repeated in the 2004 BBC/Animal Planet documentary *Land of Lost Monsters*. Ref: *OCLC WorldCat*; MK 8.

Water Babies (1985) U.S.; Golden Dolphin Productions. 48 min.; color.

Desmond Morris and other experts examine the theory that humans originated as water animals. Ref: *OCLC WorldCat*; not viewed.

Water Babies (2001) U.S.; dir. Sabine Pusch; Infonation/Films for the Humanities. 28 min.; color. Producer, Deborah Chaterjee; narrator, Suzanne Bonetti.

The Aquatic Ape Theory of human origins, in opposition to Darwin's Savanna Theory, proposes that the ancestors of man went through a crucial semi-aquatic phase. Ref: *OCLC WorldCat*; not viewed.

The Western Tradition: The Dawn of History (1989) U.S.; WGBH-TV/PBS/ Metropolitan Museum of Art. 30 min.; color. Lecturer, Eugen Weber.

A series of 26 lectures covering Western history from the earliest times to the Renaissance. The first lecture, *The Dawn of History*, explores the evolution of man and the beginnings of religion and complex societies necessary for the beginning of civilization. Ref: *OCLC WorldCat*; not viewed.

What Killed the Mega Beasts? (2002) U.S.; dir. Chris Lent; Darlowsmithson Productions/ Discovery Channel. 92 min.; color. Producer, Alice Keene-Soper; narrator, Terry MacDonald.

Giant beasts such as 17-foot-tall sloths, nine-foot flightless birds and predatory marsupial lions dominated the world for millions of years. This documentary offers three possible reasons for their disappearance — climatic change, hunting by man, or disease ("chill, kill or ill"). Ross MacPhee, Curator of Mammals at the American Museum of Natural History, proposes that a virulent disease killed the giant animals. Realistic computer animation helps to tell the story. Compare *Land of Lost Monsters* (2004) Ref: *OCLC WorldCat*; MK 8.

Who Built Stonehenge? (1986) U.K.; BBC. 51 min.; color. Producer-writer, Dominic Flessati; narrator, Paul Vaughan. (In the TV series *Horizon*)

Historians and archeologists work together to learn about the people who built Stonehenge. Ref: *OCLC WorldCat*; not viewed.

Who Killed the Iceman? (2003) U.S.; Discovery Channel. 52 min.; color. (In the TV series *Assignment Discovery: Forensics*)

A forensic investigation of the arrow wound which killed Ötzi, the Neolithic ice mummy found in the Alps. Ref: *OCLC WorldCat*; MK 8.

Wisconsin's First People (1990?) U.S.; Upper Midwest Filmstrips and Video. 21 min.; color.

The daily lives of Wisconsin's prehistoric Indians. Ref: *OCLC WorldCat*; not viewed.

The World, a Television History (1985) U.K.; Network Television/Goldcrest Television/Channel Four. 26 min. segments; color. Producer, Nicholas Barton; narrator, Robert Powell.

Part 1. *Human Origins, 10,000,000 BC–8000 BC*. Human evolution, from early African hominids, through bipedalism, the development of hands and brains and adaptation to environmental changes. Part 2. *The Agricultural Revolution, 8000 BC–5000 BC*. The transformation from hunters and fishers to farmers. Domesticating plants and animals permitted a huge increase in human population. Part 3. *The Birth of Civilization, 6000 BC–2000 BC*. Part 4. *The Age of Iron, 2000 BC-AD 200*. The last two are probably also relevant. Ref: *OCLC WorldCat*; not viewed.

The World of the Goddess (1990) U.S.; dir. Alan Babbitt; Green Earth Foundation. 103 min.; color. Producer, Richard Sybel; presenter, Marija Gimbutas.

Gimbutas discusses goddess worship in ancient Europe. Ref: *OCLC WorldCat*; not viewed.

III

Fictional Works in Historical, Modern and Extraterrestrial Settings

A number of standard plot devices exist to explain the appearance of prehistoric humans in non-prehistoric settings. At the end of each entry in this section is a one-word code for the plot device used. The code words are listed below.

Extraterrestrial—prehistoric people on another planet, comet, etc. (e.g., *Valley of the Dragons*).

Fake—Someone pretends to be a prehistoric person (e.g., *How to Make a Monster*).

Fantasy—prehistoric people in a fantasy world or fantasy situation (e.g., *Land of the Lost*).

Lost World—prehistoric people exist (often together with dinosaurs) in a self-contained area in the modern world; sometimes underground (e.g., *Land That Time Forgot*).

Relics—Only the relics of prehistoric people are involved (e.g., *Horror Express*).

Revived—prehistoric people brought back to life in the modern world (e.g., *Dinosaurus!*).

Survivors—prehistoric people somehow survive in a historic period or the modern world (e.g., *Creature from the Black Lagoon*).

Throwback—a modern person becomes or acts like a prehistoric person (e.g., *Altered States*).

Timeshift—prehistoric people are sent through time to the modern world by a fantastic or science fiction method (e.g., *The Ugly Little Boy*).

Virtual—prehistoric people created by virtual reality (e.g., *Spacejacked*).

Adam's Family Tree (1997–99) U.K.; Yorkshire TV. TV series; 20 25-min. episodes; color. Screenplay, Brian Walsh, Neil Armstrong; music, Chris Norton. CAST: Anthony Lewis (*Adam*); Alex Cooke (*Adam, 3rd season*).

A 12-year-old boy can call up his ancestors for help whenever he needs to. These include a caveman, according to the online *Encyclopedia of Fantastic Film and Television*. Ref: *Internet Movie Database*; *Encyclopedia of Fantastic Film and Television* [website], http://www.eofftv.com ; not viewed. (Timeshift)

Adventure at the Center of the Earth (1964) *see* **Aventura al Centro de la Tierra** (1964)

The Adventures of Stella Star (1979) *see* **Starcrash** (1979)

All at Sea (1957) *see* **Barnacle Bill** (1957)

Altered States (1980) U.S.; dir. Ken Russell; Warner Bros. 102 min.; color. Screenplay, Paddy Chayefsky (as Sidney Aaron) from his novel; photography, Jordan Cronenweth; music, John Corigliano. CAST: William Hurt (*Edward Jessup*); Blair Brown (*Emily Jessup*); Bob Balaban (*Arthur Rosenberg*); Charles Haid (*Mason Parrish*); Miguel Godreau (*Primal Man*); Charles White Eagle (*Brujo*); Drew Barrymore (*Margaret Jessup*).

Brilliant Harvard psychophysiologist Eddie Jessup tires of his Nobel-track career and his apparently ideal marriage to equally bright anthropologist Emily. He experiments with sensory deprivation in an isolation tank. When asked, "What are you looking for?" he can only answer "I don't know." In Mexico he visits a

The Primal Man (Miquel Godreau) fights a dog in *Altered States*.

remote tribe who use mushrooms as a powerful psychedelic. The tribe's brujo (wise man) tells him "Your soul will become the first soul." Eddie has his first hallucinatory trip in an ancient Indian cave.

He brings the Mexican drugs back to Harvard and uses them in conjunction with the isolation tank, where he sees "the birth of man." After describing early hominids he announces "I'm no longer an observer. I'm one of them." He says he has killed and eaten a goat. When he is removed from the tank he has blood on his mouth. X-rays of his skull show that he has "regressed to some semi-simian creature" or, as a radiologist puts it, "This guy's a fucking gorilla."

Eddie returns to normal but has visions of his body changing, becoming massive and brutish. He claims "I entered another consciousness. I become another self. We've got millions of years of data stored away in that computer bank we call our minds. We've got trillions of unused genes, our whole evolutionary state.... Memory is energy! It doesn't disappear — it's still in there. There's a physiological pathway to our earlier consciousnesses."

He goes into the tank again and comes out hairy and agile, an aggressive hominid. He clubs a security guard, escapes, fights dogs in the street, climbs walls and kills a sheep at the zoo. He again reverts to normal and claims "All I can remember is what was comprehensible to that consciousness. I consisted only of the will to survive, to eat, to drink, to sleep. It was the most supremely satisfying experience of my life."

He reenters the tank. This time there is an explosion of light and energy, which knocks out his two colleagues. Emily saves him from a whirlpool. Eddie tells her, "I was in that ultimate moment of terror that is the beginning of life. It is nothing. Simple, hideous nothing. The final truth of all things is that there is no final Truth. Truth is what's transitory. It's human life that is real." Eddie and Emily are overwhelmed by physical phenomena, from which they are saved only when Eddie finally declares his love for Emily.

COMMENTARY. Paddy Chayefsky insisted that his name be removed from the film. Hardy (*Science Fiction*) says he did this because "the contours of his novel began to get swamped in psychedelia" but *Variety* (Dec. 10, 1980) claimed that the screenplay "follows the Chayefsky novel very closely, retaining much of the dialog and crucial incidents." Arthur Penn was replaced by Russell as director and effects artist John Dykstra also left the project.

Ken Russell was already known for films filled with bizarre and erotic imagery and intellectual speculation, including *Women in Love* (1969), for which he was Oscar-nominated. *Altered States* was the first film for both stage actor William Hurt and 5-year-old Drew Barrymore. Hurt went on to win an Oscar in *Kiss of the Spider Woman* (1985). Hurt and Brown are well cast. Both look and sound intelligent as they speak the film's dialogue, which is full of scientific and philosophical jargon, and both look good in the numerous nude scenes. *Altered States* has more nudity than any other non-pornographic film about prehistory I know of. The Hammer caveman films had acres of near-nudity but the American versions of the Hammer movies had no actual nudity and did not get the R rating given to *Altered States*.

Most audiences would not have been able to keep up with the dialogue, which was delivered fast and crowded with medical, scientific and philosophical technical terms. *Variety* felt that

Russell "downplayed much of Chayefsky's heady philosophy by having the actors, especially Hurt, rattle off their jargon-laden speeches at breakneck speed." Often two people talk at once, making the challenging dialogue even harder to understand. The *Variety* reviewer liked the "exciting combo science fiction-horror film" with its "impressive visual hallucinations" but other critics were less pleased. Hardy denounced *Altered States* as "an awesomely idiotic fusion of science fiction, naked-ape horror and hippie trip," a "tenuously justified light show extravaganza ... anchoring the evocative in crushingly-literalistic imagery." Roger Ebert said *Altered States* could be enjoyed "by special effects lovers and drugged philosophy majors only."

The Primal Man scenes stand out as the most interesting section of the film. The Primal Man was played not by Hurt but by Mexican dancer Miguel Godreau. His makeup was by veteran Dick Smith. The Primal Man may not be an aggressor but he feels threatened by everyone and he constantly threatens or attacks anyone he meets. He doesn't kill anyone but he relentlessly clubs the security guard after he has knocked him out; he would have killed the man if he hadn't been interrupted. He sees all animals as either potential food or potential threats and all people as enemies. He is fairly smart; when he touches the fence of the sheep enclosure at the zoo and gets an electric shock, he doesn't understand what has happened but he manages to get over the fence without being hurt again. He is of course tremendously strong and fast. He unhesitatingly grabs anything that can be used as a weapon. He understands nothing but he gets what he wants through immediate, ruthlessly effective, violent action.

The 10-minute Primal Man scenes in *Altered States* offer a unique, exciting vision of early man. Godreau's Primal Man joins Gregg Martell's Neanderthal Man in *Dinosaurus!* (1960) and Hirotaro Honda's Takashi in *Peking Man* (1997) among the most memorable performances depicting prehistoric humans. All three of these performances showed cavemen as fish-out-of-water characters in the modern world and all were more effective than any performance I know of depicting early man in prehistory. The tough but gentle characters in *Dinosaurus!* and *Peking Man* were much less threatening than the fierce Primal Man in Russell's film.

Altered States bears some resemblance to the trivial B-film *The Neanderthal Man* (1953). In both films a scientist regresses to a primeval state and enjoys the experience of freedom, power and unfettered aggression. In both the scientist comes to regret going too far. The 1953 film clearly states that the scientist was an idiot for preferring the primitive state; with 1950s smugness the script punishes and kills him. This at least is internally consistent. In *Altered States* the "now I've gone too far" climax seems a climb-down by a film which had gloried in excess up to that moment. *Altered States* also shares several elements with *An American Werewolf in London* (1981): a hero whose body is drastically and painfully altered, turning him into a beast; horrific visions; the hero waking up in a zoo; and a woman who loves the hero and tries to save him.

Russell's vision is that God and "ultimate truth" do not exist and that in a horrendous world only human life is "real." For early man, the vital struggle for survival was all that mattered. For modern man, survival is not the main issue; love is what can save him. After the riveting Primal Man sequence the film goes downhill as it tries to go "beyond genetics" and Eddie begins blowing things up with psychic energy. The ending is pretty silly as the hero and heroine are overwhelmed by special effects which may threaten them with exile to "an alternate universe."

Corigliano's score was nominated for an Oscar. Russell's film was a cult favorite and was further immortalized by the jokey title of a *Xena: Warrior Princess* episode "Altared States" (1996). Ref: Hardy. *Overlook Film Encyclopedia: Science Fiction*; Jones. *Illustrated Dinosaur Movie Guide*; MK 7. (Throwback)

Ape Man of the Jungle (1962) [alt. *Tarzak contro gli Uomini Leopardo*; *Tarzak Against the Leopard Men*] Italy; dir. Carlo Veo (as Charlie Foster); P.C.F/American International Pictures. Music, Aldo Piga. CAST: Ralph Hudson (*Tarzak*); Rita Klein; Nuccia Cardinale.

An Italian jungle picture in which the Tarzanesque hero battles a tribe of "leopard men" and a missing link apeman. Ref: Jones. *Illustrated Dinosaur Movie Guide*; *Internet Movie Database*; not viewed. (Survivors)

At Long Last Love (1975) U.S.; dir. Peter Bogdanovich; 20th-Century–Fox. 118 min.;

color. Screenplay, Peter Bogdanovich; photography, Laszlo Kovacs; music, Cole Porter. *CAST:* Burt Reynolds; Cybill Shepherd; Madeleine Kahn; Eileen Brennan; John Hillerman; Mildred Natwick.

This musical comedy, set in the 1930s, had too much art deco, too much Cybill Shepherd and (if possible) even too much Cole Porter. Kahn was the only real singer in the cast; her solo performance of a caveman number "Find Me a Primitive Man" was one of the few highlights. *Variety* (March 5, 1975) called *At Long Last Love* "stylish but limp." Compare *On the Town* (1949). Ref: Jones. *Illustrated Dinosaur Movie Guide*; Nash. *Motion Picture Guide*; MK 4. (Fake)

At the Earth's Core (1976) U.K.; dir. Kevin Connor; Amicus/American International Pictures. 89 min.; color. Screenplay, Milton Subotsky based on novel by Edgar Rice Burroughs; photography, Alan Hume; music, Mike Vickers. *CAST:* Doug McClure (*David Innes*); Peter Cushing (*Dr. Abner Perry*); Caroline Munro (*Dia*); Cy Grant (*Ra*); Godfrey James (*Ghak*); Sean Lynch (*Hoojah*); Michael Crane (*Jubal*); Bobby Parr (*Sagoth Chief*).

In Victorian Wales, eccentric English scientist Dr. Perry and American adventurer David Innes prepare to test the doctor's "Iron Mole," designed to dig tunnels. The Mole goes straight down, delivering Perry and Innes to Pellucidar, a underground world where primitive humans are enslaved by the hominid, pig-faced Sagoths and the telepathic, flying Mahars. Two-fisted Innes falls in love with Princess Dia, befriends local hero Ra, rallies the feuding human tribes and leads a revolt of slaves who man machines which control the flow of volcanic lava.

At the Earth's Core was perhaps the least successful of a series of four juvenile fantasy adventures of the late '70s, including *The Land That Time Forgot* (1975), *The People That Time Forgot* (1977) and *Warlords of Atlantis* (1978). All were directed by Kevin Connor and starred Doug McClure; all but *Warlords* were made by Amicus and based on tales by Edgar Rice Burroughs. Peter Cushing was the most popular star and the best actor in any of the four films and Caroline Munro the most luscious girl in the series, but *At the Earth's Core* is best remembered for its unusually weak script and sluggish, unconvincing monsters.

Cushing's prissy scientist points out that the human slaves are "intellectually superior" to

Princess Dia (Caroline Munro) in *At the Earth's Core*. The movie should be so well constructed.

their Sagoth captors who get their power from the mind-reading Mahars. Early in the film, David attempts to rescue Dia from unwanted attentions by a villain. His ignorance of Pellucidarian ways causes him to insult Dia by refusing to take her for himself, thus rendering her unmarriageable. The old man who explains this to David tells him that Dia will never forgive him and for a long time she doesn't. Later in the film, of course, she does forgive him (and a little too easily), but the scene in which David realizes he has turned her into an enemy is atypically mature for this kind of movie and is a rebuke to the arrogant Westerners who usually stride through Lost World films.

Variety (June 23, 1976) praised the film's "nicely stylized visual look" and Vickers' score. The likeable Munro (who succeeded Raquel Welch as one of the top pin-up girls in the world; who was the only actress ever placed under contract by Hammer; and who was in every British fantasy series of her time, including both *Dr. Phibes* films, a Hammer Dracula movie, a Harryhausen Sinbad film and a James Bond film as well as this entry in the Amicus Burroughs series) maintains an admirably straight face while saying lines like "Hoojah the Sly One will bring Jubal the Ugly One." Best of all, Cushing makes the most of his doddering scientist, who carries an umbrella (against underground showers?) throughout the film, chirps "How interesting!" as a monster bears down on him, peevishly dismisses the underground people with "They're so excitable. Like all foreigners" and "Noisy lot, aren't they?" and warns the enemy "You cannot mesmerize me. I'm British!" Ref: Jones. *Illustrated Dinosaur Movie Guide*; Berry. *Dinosaur Filmography*; MK 4. (Lost World)

Ator the Blade Master (1984) [alt. *The Cave Dwellers*; *Ator the Invincible*; *The Blade Master*] Italy; dir. Joe D'Amato (under pseud. David Hills); Metaxa/New Line. 92 min.; color. Screenplay, Joe D'Amato; photography, Joe D'Amato; music, Carlo Rustichelli. CAST: Miles O'Keefe (*Ator*); Lisa Foster (*Mila*); Chen Wong (*Thong*); David Brandon (*Zor*); Charles Borromel (*Akronas*).

The four Italian *Ator* films (1983–90) were rock-bottom sword-and-sorcery movies set in the usual clichéd pseudo-ancient world full of sword-swinging barbarians. The second film in the series was called *The Cave Dwellers* (among other titles) because of two scenes.

First, one group of cavemen is enjoying a disgusting and apparently cannibalistic meal when they are attacked and destroyed in their spacious cave by another group of primitives. In the second scene, the captive heroine watches in horror as the cavemen sacrifice a prisoner and their primitive leader eats the victim's heart (on camera). The hero soon arrives to rescue her and decimate the cave people. The only human accoutrements in the vast cave are a throne and a sacrificial altar. The rest of the film, and apparently the other *Ator* movies, have no other prehistoric content.

I have seen *Ator the Blade Master* only in the version shown on *Mystery Science Theatre 3000*, under the title *Cave Dwellers*. Some of the original dialogue was obscured by the comedians' jeering comments, but I doubt anything of interest was lost. D'Amato was a prolific Italian hack director, who made several *Emanuelle* porn films. Ref: Stanley. *Creature Features*; MK 1. (Survivors)

Ator the Invincible (1984) *see* **Ator the Blade Master** (1984)

Aventura al Centro de la Tierra (1964) [trans. *Adventure at the Center of the Earth*] Mexico; dir. Alfredo B. Crevenna; Producciones Sotomayor. 78 min.; b&w. Screenplay, Jose Maria Fernandez Unsain; photography, Raul Martinez Solares; music, Raul Lavista. CAST: Jose Elias Moreno (*Prof. Diaz*); Kitty de Hoyos (*Hilda Ramirez*); Javier Solos (*Dr. Manuel Rios*); Columba Dominguez (*Laura Ponce*); Carlos Cortes (*Dr. Peña*); David Reynoso (*Rocha*).

In modern Mexico Professor Diaz leads an expedition to explore a cave full of prehistoric monsters, including a Cyclops and several hairy Bat-Men. Several explorers are killed in accidents, by the monsters or by an expedition member who turns greedy when diamonds are discovered. The Cyclops is killed in a fall. A Bat-Man kidnaps Diaz's secretary Hilda. He swims underwater with her to his lair, where he romantically proffers a rat and a snake as food. After Hilda is rescued, the Bat-Man follows her back to the expedition's camp, where he is shot by a hail of bullets and buried by an avalanche.

This ambitious Mexican film begins with a long (five paragraphs!), erudite title crawl discussing the origins of man and the theories of Aristotle and Darwin. The film's dinosaur footage is entirely borrowed from other films, including the much-plundered *One Million B.C.* (1940). *Aventura* also has brief glimpses of prehistoric people, borrowed from Mexico's own *El Bello Durmiente* (1952). This footage is presented when the Professor shows his team a film. I have seen *Aventura* only in Spanish and Mark F. Berry has only a partial translation of the dialogue; neither of us is sure whether the film-within-the-film is supposed to represent real footage of prehistoric people in the modern world or if the Professor tells his team that this is how filmmakers have envisioned prehistory.

The Cyclops and the Bat-Man have rarely been used in films and, as far as I know, never presented as prehistoric relics in any film except this. The Bat-Man has a hairy face and body, big teeth and claws, and large wings. He eats rats, tears a snake apart with his bare hands and survives being shot several times. The film's title and some details (including the heroine spelunking in a dress) are borrowed from Hollywood's *Journey to the Center of the Earth* (1959). As Mark F. Berry points out, the one-sided romance between a monster and a girl was highly reminiscent of both *King Kong* and *The Creature from the Black Lagoon*. The film even has the Bat-Man swim away with the girl underwater, like the Gill-Man in *Black Lagoon*; an underwater Bat-Man seems very odd.

The stark locations in Mexico's huge Cacahuamilpa Grottoes are impressive and Berry rightly praises the director, cast, photographer and score composer. Berry considers *Aventura*'s monsters not "remotely adequate." The creatures are indeed cheap-looking in an otherwise well-made film, but the Bat-Man does manage to look both grotesque and pitiful, in the tradition of sympathetic movie monsters.

The Mexican film industry made at least four prehistoric films, of which this is the most elaborate production. *Isla de los Dinosaurios* (1965) is also in Part III. *El Bello Durmiente* (1951) and *La Edad de Piedra* (1962) are in Part I. Ref: *Internet Movie Database*; Berry. *Dinosaur Filmography*; viewed in Spanish; MK 5. (Lost World)

Aysecik and the Bewitched Dwarfs in Dreamland (1971) [alt. *The Turkish Wizard of Oz*] Turkey; dir. Tunc Basaran; Hisar Film/Oren Film. 100 min.; color. Screenplay, Hamdi Degirmencioglu, based on *The Wizard of Oz* by L. Frank Baum. CAST: Zeynep Degirmencioglu (*Aysecik*); Süleyman Turan (*Iron Woodman*); Metin Serezli (*Scarecrow*); Ali Sen (*Cowardly Lion*); Suna Selen (*Wicked Witch of the South*); Cemâl Konca (*Wizard*).

A tornado carries farmgirl Aysecik and her dog Banju to Dreamland, where they encounter a good witch, a bad witch, an iron woodman, a scarecrow, a cowardly lion, a Wizard, dwarfs, balls of fire, fighting trees, a country of China dolls and "a legion of hammer-throwing cavemen," according to the synopsis in *Internet Movie Database*. A user's comment in *IMDB* says this is "one of the most faithful" film adaptations of Baum's classic. Ref: *Internet Movie Database*; not viewed. (Fantasy)

The Banana Monster (1973) *see* **Schlock!** (1973)

Barnacle Bill (1957) [alt. *All At Sea*] U.K.; dir. Charles Frend; Ealing. 87 min.; b&w. Screenplay, T.E.B. Clarke; photography, Douglas Slocombe; music, John Addison. CAST: Alec Guinness (*William Ambrose/Six Ancestors*); Irene Browne; Maurice Denham. Alec Guinness plays a caveman! William Ambrose is expected to be a hardy seafaring man like his ancestors, but he suffers from seasickness whenever he sets sail. In addition to Ambrose, Guinness plays his six ancestors from different periods who cheer Ambrose on. *Variety* (Dec. 25, 1957) felt this "amiable light entertainment ... promised more than has been actually fulfilled" and that Guinness was inspired only "during the brief opportunities he gets to impersonate his half a dozen ancestors, including a slaphappy Stone Age sailor." Ref: Jones. *Illustrated Dinosaur Movie Guide*; Gifford. *British Film Catalogue*; MK 6. (Timeshift)

BeastMaster (1999–2002) Episode, *Manlinks* (2000). Alliance Atlantis/Tribune Entertainment. 45 min. episode in TV series; color. Based on book by Andre Norton. CAST: Daniel Goddard (*Dar, the Beastmaster*); Jackson Raine (*Tao*).

This routine, talky sword-and-sorcery series came in the wake of the superior *Hercules* (1994–2000) and *Xena* (1995–2001). The hero Dar, who communicates with animals, is an underdressed Tarzanesque figure whose duty is to protect the forest and its animals against various exploiters and villains. In the episode "Manlinks" Dar encounters a race of ancient intelligent apemen who wear clothes and can read but cannot talk. Except for their muteness, the creatures strongly resemble the apes of *Planet of the Apes* (1968). As in the film, they are divided between intellectuals with chimp faces and big gorillas who fight. A character mentions a "wall of ice" advancing in the mountains, suggesting that the *BeastMaster* world is set during the last Ice Age. Ref: *Internet Movie Database*; MK 3. (Survivors)

The Blade Master (1984) *see* **Ator the Blade Master** (1984)

Blood Creatures from the Prehistoric Planet (1970) *see* **Horror of the Blood Monsters** (1970)

Buck Rogers (1939) U.S.; dir. Ford Beebe, Saul A. Goodkind; Universal. Serial film; 12 chapters; b&w. Screenplay, Norman S. Hall, Ray Trampe; photography, Jerome Ash. CAST: Buster Crabbe (*Buck Rogers*); Constance Moore (*Wilma Deering*); Anthony Ward (*Killer Kane*); Henry Brandon (*Capt. Laska*).

This well-known serial film featured the Zuggs of the planet Saturn, whom Kinnard describes as "an outcast race of hideous Saturnian primitives." The Zuggs are easily controlled by the villains since they worship a "human robot" created by the agents of arch-fiend Killer Kane. Kane's men have the Zuggs revolt against Buck Rogers' Saturnian allies. Eventually Rogers returns the human robot to his normal human form. Since the Zuggs still worship him, the liberated ex-robot tells them to lay down their arms.

The eighth episode was "Revolt of the Zuggs." The serial film was edited into a feature film *Planet Outlaws* and later into a film *Destination Saturn* for television distribution. Ref: Kinnard. *Science Fiction Serials*; not viewed. (Extraterrestrial)

Buddy's Lost World (1936) U.S.; dir. Jack King; Warner Bros. Animated short film; 7 min.; b&w. Screenplay, Bob Clampett; music, Norman Spencer. VOICE: Tommy Bond.

Cartoon hero Buddy and his dog Bozo find an island full of dinosaurs and primitive men. Buddy is swallowed by a carnivorous plant whose roots lead to an underground city where cavemen bury bones like dogs and play an odd form of croquet to the tune of "Lullaby of Broadway." A tribe of cavemen (parodies of The Three Stooges) drop Buddy in a cooking pot, but he is rescued by a Brontosaurus. Cannibalism, represented by lip-smacking savages and huge cooking pots, was surprisingly common in old-time Hollywood cartoons, which were intended for both children and adults; usually African natives were the culprits, not cave people. Ref: Webb. *Animated Film Encyclopedia*; Beck/Friedwald. *Looney Tunes and Merrie Melodies*; Jones. *Illustrated Dinosaur Movie World*; not viewed. (Lost World)

Buffy the Vampire Slayer (1997–2003) Episode, *Get It Done* (2003). U.S.; dir. Douglas Petrie; 20th Century–Fox Television/Mutant Enemy Inc. Episode of TV series; 45 min.; color. Screenplay, Douglas Petrie. CAST: Sarah Michelle Gellar (*Buffy Summers*). According to the mythology of this popular and critically respected series, demons and vampires have assaulted mankind since the beginning of time. Humanity has always been saved by the Vampire Slayers, girls with limited super-powers. In the 137th of 144 *Buffy* episodes, Buffy either time travels or has a vision and confronts the men who created the first Slayer — three African men in elegant traditional costumes. Buffy denounces them for exploiting all the Slayers from the first to her. This scene presages the end of the series and is a graceful acknowledgment of the African origins of mankind. Ref: *Internet Movie Database*; MK 6. (Fantasy)

California Man (1992) *see* **Encino Man** (1992)

California Woman (1996) *see* **Encino Woman** (1996)

Captain Caveman and the Teen Angels (1980) U.S.; Hanna-Barbera. Animated TV series; 16 episodes (32 segments); color. Music, Hoyt Curtin. VOICES: Mel Blanc (*Captain Caveman*); Vernee Watson (*Dee Dee*); Marilyn Schreffler (*Brenda*); Laurel Page (*Taffy*).

Captain Caveman began as a component series of *Scooby's All-Star Laff-a-Lympics* (1978–80). The first 16 "Cavey" episodes from the *Scooby* series were repeated in the new series, followed by 16 original episodes. Cavey, awakened in the modern world, is assisted in his adventures by his "club of tricks," his limited superpowers, his wacky sidekick Cave Bird and three teenage girls (spoofing *Charlie's Angels*). Cavey also appeared in *The Flintstone Kids* (1986–88) and *The Flintstones Comedy Show* (1980–82); both are in Part I. *New episodes:* "The Scarifying Seaweed Secret," "The Dummy," "Cavey and the Volcanic Villain," "Prehistoric Panic," "Cavey and the Baffling Buffalo Men," "Dragonhead," "Cavey and the Murky Mississippi Mystery," "Old Cavey in New York," "Cavey and the Albino Rhino," "Kentucky Cavey," "Cavey Goes to College," "The Haunting of Hog's Hollow," "The Legend of Devil's Run," "The Mystery of the Meandering Mummy," "The Old Caveman and the Sea," "Lights ... Camera ... Cavey." Ref: Lenburg. *Encyclopedia of Animated Cartoons*; Erickson. *Television Cartoon Series*; not viewed. (Revived)

Carry on Cleo (1964) U.K.; dir. Gerald Thomas; Anglo-Amalgamated. 92 min; color. Screenplay, Talbot Rothwell based loosely on Shakespeare's plays *Julius Caesar* and *Anthony and Cleopatra*; photography, Alan Hume;

music, Eric Rogers. *CAST:* Sidney James (*Mark Anthony*); Kenneth Williams (*Julius Caesar*); Kenneth Connor (*Hengist Pod*); Charles Hawtrey (*Seneca*); Joan Sims (*Calpurnia*); Jim Dale (*Horsa*); Amanda Barrie (*Cleopatra*); Julie Stevens (*Gloria*); Sheila Hancock (*Senna Pod*); Jon Pertwee (*Soothsayer*).

In 50 B.C. simpering Roman Emperor Julius Caesar and his short-tempered, long-suffering subordinate Mark Anthony invade Britain, whose inhabitants still live in caves, wear animal skins, brandish clubs and drag girls around by the hair. They even still have dinosaurs; diminutive, hen-pecked, good-humored Briton Hengist Pod mentions that his mother-in-law had been eaten by a Brontosaurus "and the Brontosaurus died the next day." Mighty British warrior Horsa is captured by the Romans after a fierce fight. Hengist runs away but is captured anyway through his own stupidity.

In Rome, Horsa and Hengist escape from the slave market and hide in the Temple of the Vestal Virgins (who are fed up with being virgins). Meanwhile Caesar has figured out that almost everyone he knows is plotting to kill him. ("Oh infamy! Infamy! They've all got it in for me.") When Caesar goes to "consult" (nudge, nudge) the Virgins mighty Horsa single-handedly saves him from several assassins, but Hengist gets the credit and is hailed as an invincible warrior. ("You're impregnable!" "No, my wife and I simply decided not to have any children.")

Hengist is made Caesar's personal bodyguard. For a while his fearsome reputation frightens off assassins. Caesar sends Anthony to Egypt, where he is entranced by dimwitted but seductive Cleopatra, who spends almost all her time bathing in ass's milk and travels exclusively in a rolled-up carpet. Cleopatra persuades Anthony to kill Caesar.

Caesar travels to Egypt where Anthony and Cleopatra try to finish him off. This time Hengist by a miracle kills the assassin. Hengist, Horsa and other British slaves steal a galley and return to Britain. Caesar returns to Rome only to be killed after all. Anthony learns to enjoy sharing milk baths with Cleopatra. In Britain, Hengist and Horsa happily go back to cave life. The only useful item Hengist brings back from the civilized world is an aphrodisiac which he stole from Cleopatra's palace and which he uses to impress his hitherto shrewish wife Senna and produce many children.

COMMENTARY. The British made 28 *Carry On* films from 1958 to 1978. Most were written by Rothwell and directed by Thomas. James, Connor, Williams, Sims and Dale were series regulars. All had modest careers outside the series; Dale went on to do several Disney comedies. The *Carry On* films were low-brow comedies which employed puns, one-liners, double entendres and ethnic and gender stereotypes. As a British critic pointed out the series celebrated the lascivious, the lazy and the cowardly over the virtuous, the industrious and the brave. The movies were lewd, rude and crude but, in 1964 when *Carry on Cleo* was made, not yet nude.

Cleo, the first color *Carry On*, is one of the best of the series. The jokes come thick and fast and many are quite funny. Of course the film mocks conventional epics such as *Ben Hur* (1959) and *Cleopatra*, the failed 1963 epic with Elizabeth Taylor. (*Cleo* reused many costumes and props from *Cleopatra*.) Maltin and Halliwell both rate *Carry On Cleo* higher than the Taylor film. *Variety* (Dec. 16, 1964) found *Cleo* "full of yocks" and "all-out healthy vulgarity" which sometimes "suffer from repetition." Smith (*Epic Films*) was amused by the "typically delirious" *Cleo*.

Most of *Cleo* is set in Rome and Egypt, the civilized parts of the ancient world. The primitive Britons easily hold their own against the more advanced Romans and Egyptians. The brief scenes set in "prehistoric" Britain have, if possible, even crazier humor than the rest of the film. The cave people speak in a rapid-fire, joke-strewn patter. Hengist is the proud inventor of the square wheel; he rejects the circular wheel because of its tendency to roll backwards when going uphill. *Cleo* is one of the few caveman films to actually show a girl being dragged by her hair. Horsa drags his happily smiling bride down the aisle at their wedding. Ref: Gifford. *British Film Catalogue*; Lucanio. *With Fire and Sword*; Smith. *Epic Films*; MK 7. (Survivors)

Il Castelo della Pauro (1973) *see* **Frankenstein's Castle of Freaks** (1973)

The Cave Dwellers (1984) *see* **Ator the Blade Master** (1984)

Colonel Bleep (1957) U.S.; Ullman/Soundac. 104 6-min. stories shown in 24-min. episodes; color. Screenplay, Robert D. Buchanan. *VOICE:* Noel Taylor (*Narrator*).

In the future, Col. Bleep, an agent of Planet Futura, fights villainous mastermind Dr. Destructo and pirate Capt. Patch. Among Bleep's sidekick's is Scratch, a super-strong revived caveman. *Colonel Bleep* was one of the first TV cartoon series made in color. Erickson says the U.S. series mimicked the "frenetic pace and severely limited animation" of Japanese TV cartoons. Narrator Noel Taylor was the only voice actor; the characters rarely spoke. Ref: Lenburg. *Encyclopedia of Animated Cartoons*; Erickson. *Television Cartoon Shows*; not viewed. (Revived/Extraterrestrial)

Conan the Destroyer (1984) U.S.; dir. Richard Fleischer; De Laurentiis/Universal. 103 min.; color. Screenplay, Stanley Mann based on stories by Robert E. Howard; photography, Jack Cardiff; music, Basil Poledouris. CAST: Arnold Schwarzenegger (*Conan*); Mako (*Akiro*); Tracey Walter (*Malak*); Pat Roach (*Man Ape*).

On a quest, Conan knows he will face an enemy magician. He decides to collect his friend the wizard Akiro in order to fight magic with magic. (Conan and Akiro are the only characters to return from *Conan the Barbarian* (1982).) Conan arrives just in time to save Akiro, who has been tied to a spit by primitive men who intend to cook and eat him. After rescuing Akiro Conan and his friends ride past a dinosaur skeleton, which they ignore (suggesting that the sight is not unusual). Later Conan fights a creature with the body of a man and the face of a gorilla, called a "Man Ape" in the credits.

Conan's friend Malak calls the primitives "savages." They wear furs and have their faces painted white. They use only primitive weapons, the usual clubs and stone axes. The fight between them and Conan is the shortest in the film, since Conan is so superior a fighter that he wins easily, killing several primitives and putting the rest to flight. Akiro says that the primitives thought they could do magic themselves if they ate him. The primitive men, the dinosaur skeleton and the Man Ape all suggest Conan's world is not far removed from prehistory. Ref: *Internet Movie Database*; MK 6. (Survivors)

The Crater Lake Monster (1977) U.S.; dir. William R. Stromberg; Crown International Pictures. 85 min.; color. Screenplay, William R. Stromberg, Richard Cardella; photography, Paul Gentry. CAST: Richard Cardella (*Steve Hanson*); Glenn Roberts (*Arnie*); Mark Siegel (*Mitch*); Bob Hyman (*Doc Calkins*); Kacey Cobb (*Susan*).

In an "Indian cavern" near remote Crater Lake, paleo-researchers find cave paintings of a man fighting a plesiosaurus. Soon a meteor lands in the lake; a plesiosaurus egg embedded in the meteor hatches and the beast begins eating the local people.

The cave paintings are the only hint of ancient man in this low-budget monster movie. Mark F. Berry reports that the inconsistent script and amateurish cast sank the film, despite fine dinosaur animation by Dave Allen (who worked on *When Dinosaurs Ruled the Earth*), Phil Tippett, Randy Cook and Jim Danforth. Ref: Berry. *Dinosaur Filmography*; not viewed. (Relic)

The Creature from the Black Lagoon (1954) U.S.; dir. Jack Arnold, James C. Havens (underwater scenes); Universal/William Alland Productions. 79 min.; b&w. Screenplay, Harry Essex, Arthur Ross; photography, William E. Snyder; music, Hans Salter, Henry Mancini, Herman Stein. CAST: Richard Carlson (*David Reed*); Julia Adams (*Kay*); Richard Denning (*Mark Williams*); Antonio Moreno (*Carl Maia*); Nestor Paiva (*Capt. Lucas*); Whit Bissell (*Edwin Thompson*); Ricou Browning (*Gillman, in water*); Ben Chapman (*Gillman, on land*).

The narrator intones "In the beginning God created the Heaven and the Earth" and briefly describes the beginnings of life in the sea. We see webbed footprints leaving the prehistoric sea. In modern Brazil, Dr. Maia finds a fossilized giant webbed hand in a Devonian deposit up a tributary of the Amazon. He goes downriver and convinces David Reed, his girlfriend Kay and Dr. Thompson, all responsible scientists, as well as arrogant, publicity-hungry Mark Williams, to accompany him as he searches for more fossils.

When they return to Maia's camp, they find his two Indian guards dead. We see what the scientists do not, the webbed hand of the Creature which killed them. As David and Mark don scuba gear and explore the Black Lagoon at the head of the tributary, we see the whole humanoid Creature for the first time. He is tall with arms and legs, webbed feet and hands, gills around his head and a face midway between a man and a fish. In a famous scene, Kay swims on the surface of the lagoon unaware that the Gillman is swimming beneath her, studying her and mimicking her movements.

Incidents quickly escalate. The Creature is caught in a net and almost breaks the ship's mast before he gets away. Mark shoots the Creature with a speargun, but he quickly recovers. He comes on board, seizes a sailor and takes him overboard to his death. He then tries to grab Kay but is scared off by lanterns. The scientists use drugs to make the Creature groggy and follow him onto land. He kills another sailor and again tries to get the girl. He collapses and is captured, but escapes; Dr. Thompson is seriously burned trying to stop him.

As the scientists try to leave the lagoon they find the Creature has built a barrier at the exit. Mark again shoots him with a speargun, but the Creature kills him. There are now only four humans left. David rigs up a spray gun loaded with sedative and briefly incapacitates the Creature. As the humans try to break the barrier and escape, the Creature appears again and finally succeeds in kidnapping Kay. The heroes follow him into his cave lair and shoot him. He dives into the water and apparently dies.

COMMENTARY. *Creature from the Black Lagoon* was released in the midst of a supposedly poor period for horror (1947–1956) by Universal, the premier studio of the first Golden Age of Hollywood horror (1931–46). It is a pivotal film in horror history. It looks back to the Universal horror classics of the '30s by presenting an interesting, even sympathetic monster. It looks ahead to the slashers, with a monster which kills again and again and survives repeated attempts to destroy it. And of course it foreshadows *Jaws* (1975) by playing on universal fears of what lurks beneath the surface of a body of water.

The Creature, who is supposedly unchanged since the Devonian period (which the film says was 150 million years ago; it was in fact 360 to 410 million years ago), is merely defending his territory against intruders. He wants to kidnap the heroine for amorous reasons, not to hurt her. He proves he is intelligent when he blocks the entrance to the lagoon, trapping the humans. He is strong and kills men quickly and easily. And producer William Alland insisted that he was based on a genuine Amazonian legend of an underwater man. (Like the Creature, the Latin characters are treated with more respect than was usual in U.S. films of the 1950s. Dr. Maia is an intelligent scientist. Riverboat captain Lucas is uneducated and does some comic relief, but he is not ridiculed. He stands up to Mark's bullying. In the end it's the two Brazilians, Maia and Lucas, who kill the Creature while the American hero and heroine are helpless.)

Creature was originally released in 3-D and advertised as the "first underwater 3-D picture" but it works just as well shown flat on TV. It is remembered not for the few 3-D shots of spearguns pointed into the camera, but for its eerie atmosphere, beautiful b&w photography, very clear underwater scenes and evocative monster (created

The Creature from the Black Lagoon (probably Ben Chapman, not Ricou Browning) in all his glory.

by Millicent Patrick); the contrast between the bickering scientists and the silent, clever Creature; and the potent sensuality of the scene in which the Creature swims silently beneath the unsuspecting heroine.

Arnold had already done his first SF film, *It Came from Outer Space* (1953) and would go on to do several more, including his masterpiece *The Incredible Shrinking Man* (1957). Carlson and Denning were each in several 1950s SF films. Ricou Browning went on to play the Creature in two sequels and to direct underwater scenes in the *Sea Hunt* TV series (1958–61) and in *Thunderball* (1965).

The DVD has commentary by expert Tom Weaver and a featurette by David J. Skal on the production of the film, with comments by actors Chapman, Browning and Adams. Hardy (*Science Fiction*) calls *Creature* "an excellent example of how to make a good monster movie." *Variety* (Feb. 10, 1954) was impressed by *Creature*'s "excellent exploitation possibilities" and Arnold's "first-rate job of developing chills and suspense." The *Variety* review also praised almost every actor who played a human, but did not even mention Ricou Browning, who was also not in the film's credits.

Creature from the Black Lagoon was followed by two ordinary sequels, *Revenge of the Creature* (1955) and *The Creature Walks Among Us* (1956). Gillmen also showed up in *City Under the Sea* (1965, U.K., dir. Jacques Tourneur, alt. *War Gods of the Deep*) and *It's Alive!* (1968, U.S.; dir. Larry Buchanan). Also see *Voyage to the Planet of Prehistoric Women* (1966), a film about Venusian gillwomen. Ref: Warren. *Keep Watching the Skies!*; Hardy. *Overlook Film Encyclopedia: Science Fiction*; MK 9. (Survivors)

Creature of Destruction (1967) U.S.; dir. Larry Buchanan; Azalea. 80 min.; color. Screenplay, Tony Huston; photography, Robert C. Jessup. CAST: Les Tremayne (*Dr. John Basso*); Aron Kincaid (*Capt. Dell*); Pat Delaney (*Doreena*); Neil Fletcher (*Sam Crane*).

A hypnotist reverts a woman to her murderous prehistoric self. Jones and Senn/Johnson say this was a remake of *The She-Creature* (1956), one of several uncredited remakes of 1950s AIP films made by Buchanan in the 1960s. Stanley, Jones and Senn/Johnson all agree the 1967 film was terrible. The same monster costume was used in Buchanan's *It's Alive* (1968). Ref: Jones. *Illustrated Dinosaur Movie Guide*; Stanley. *Creature Features Movie Guide Strikes Again*; Senn/Johnson. *Fantastic Cinema Subject Guide*; not viewed. (Throwback)

Creatures from the Prehistoric Planet (1970) *see* **Horror of the Blood Monsters** (1970)

The Creeping Flesh (1972) U.K.; dir. Freddie Francis; Columbia/Tigon. 89 min.; color. Screenplay, Peter Spenceley, Jonathon Rumbelow; photography, Norman Warwick; music, Paul Ferris. CAST: Christopher Lee (*James Hildern*); Peter Cushing (*Emmanuel Hildern*); Lorna Heilbron (*Penelope*); George Benson (*Waterlow*); Kenneth J. Warren (*Lenny*); Duncan Lamont (*Inspector*). In the 1890s an English scientist imprisons his nymphomaniac wife and seeks to "inoculate against evil" his daughter, using serum from the skeleton (found in New Guinea) of a man whose species lived before the Neanderthals. The results are of course disastrous.

Francis was an accomplished director. The film was praised by *Variety* (March 14, 1972) and by Hardy's *Overlook Film Encyclopedia: Horror*. The prehistoric man in *The Creeping Flesh* is said to be more intelligent than the Neanderthals but his blood is contagiously evil. By coincidence Cushing and Lee made another film in 1972, *Horror Express*, also set about 1900, in which prehistoric remains cause an outbreak of horror. Ref: Hardy. *Overlook Film Encyclopedia: Horror*; Jones. *Illustrated Dinosaur Movie Guide*; MK 7. (Relic)

Dino Boy (1966–68) *see* **Space Ghost and Dino Boy** (1966–68)

Dinosaur Island (1993) U.S.; dir. Jim Wynorski, Fred Olen Ray; Pacific Trust. 80 min.; color. Screenplay, Bob Sheridan, Christopher Wooden; photography, Gary Graver; music, Chuck Cirino. CAST: Ross Hagen (*Capt. Jason Briggs*); Richard Gabai (*Private Skeemer*); Antonia Dorian (*April*); Michelle Bauer (*June*); Peter Spellos (*Private Turbowski*); Tom Shell (*Private Kincaid*); Griffen Drew (*May*); Toni Naples (*Queen Morgana*); Becky LeBeau (*Virgin Sacrifice*).

U.S. Army men from a wrecked plane discover a Pacific island crawling with dinosaurs and lightly-clad primitive women. Grumpy Queen Morgana distrusts the newcomers but

(III) Dinosaurus!

three of her girls (whom the troops name April, May and June) are much friendlier. With difficulty the men manage to kill a Tyrannosaurus Rex and win even Morgana's trust. Mark F. Berry reported that "the outlandish plot keeps things moving briskly" and even the cast is mostly adequate, but the dinosaurs vary widely in quality. Ref: Berry. *Dinosaur Filmography*; not viewed. (Lost World)

Dinosaurus! (1960) U.S.; dir. Irvin S. Yeaworth, Jr.; Universal. 84 min.; color. Screenplay, Dan E. Weisburd, Jean Yeaworth; photography, Stanley Cortez; music, Ronald Stein. CAST: Ward Ramsey (*Bart Thompson*); Paul Lukather (*Chuck*); Kristina Hanson (*Betty Piper*); Alan Roberts (*Julio*); Gregg Martell (*The Neanderthal*); Fred Engelberg (*Mike Hacker*); Wayne Tredway (*Dumpy*); Luci Blain (*Chica*); Howard Dayton (*Mousy*); Jack Younger (*Jasper*).

On a Caribbean island, American Bart Thompson and his team are dynamiting underwater to create a deep harbor. While swimming, Bart's girlfriend Betty sees a dinosaur at the bottom of the harbor. Soon the men confirm that two frozen dinosaurs lie in the harbor, dislodged from an underground cold river by the explosions. The two monsters are brought ashore and identified by little boy Julio, a dinosaur enthusiast, as a vegetarian Brontosaurus and a carnivorous Tyrannosaurus Rex.

Hacker, the island's villainous boss and Julio's guardian, wants to exploit the dinosaurs for money. He also finds the frozen corpse of a Neanderthal man, stone knife in hand. Hacker hides the caveman, intending to take him to the U.S. and sell him. At night during a storm, the dinosaurs revive.

The Tyrannosaurus quickly kills the drunken Irishman whom Bart had assigned to guard the dinosaurs. The caveman also comes to life. The Tyrannosaurus attacks a small bus and kills several people. (The audience does not see the carnage but, in a shocking scene, Julio does.) The Neanderthal Man explores Betty's deserted home, having many comic run-ins with modern technology. Julio makes friends first with the peaceful Brontosaurus, then with the caveman. Hacker and his henchmen Mousy and Jasper find the caveman and Julio but the primitive man easily overpowers them and escapes with Julio.

The panicking islanders and the Americans take refuge at an old fort and fill the moat with oil. Julio and his friend the Neanderthal Man are happily riding the Brontosaurus when they see the not over-bright Betty being chased by the Tyrannosaurus. The caveman instantly leaps to her rescue and stabs the monster in the foot with an ax, making it drop Betty. He carries Betty into an old mine, where she is frightened he will attack her.

As the ever-curious Julio watches, the Tyrannosaurus and the Brontosaurus fight each other. The Brontosaurus is injured but escapes. The caveman rescues Julio and brings him into the mine, to which the Tyrannosaurus lays siege. Hacker orders Jasper and Mousy to distract the dinosaur so he can get the caveman. Unsurprisingly they refuse and flee; Hacker shoots Mousy dead. While Bart and his chubby friend Dumpy ineffectively lob Molotov cocktails at the Tyrannosaurus Hacker gets into the mine down a rope through an opening in the roof. When this escape is blocked Hacker, at his most incredibly evil, orders Julio and Betty at gunpoint to distract the dinosaur while he escapes

The Neanderthal Man (Gregg Martell) rescues Betty (Kristina Hanson) in *Dinosaurus!*

with the caveman. The Neanderthal attacks Hacker, who shoots him in the arm, being careful not to kill the valuable specimen.

The Tyrannosaur's efforts to force his way into the mine cause the mine's fragile roof to collapse. Hacker panics, flees and is killed by the Tyrannosaurus. The gallant Neanderthal, despite his wound, holds a roof beam up until the Tyrannosaurus leaves and Bart rescues Betty and Julio. The caveman finally collapses and is killed by the cave-in. The Brontosaurus drowns in quicksand. All the survivors gather at the fort and set the oil in the moat alight to fend off the attacking Tyrannosaurus. The oil will soon burn out and allow the monster to get in and kill everyone. Bart attacks the Tyrannosaurus with a steam shovel and manages to push it over a cliff into the sea.

COMMENTARY. European art filmmakers and critics often admire American B films—sometimes more than is reasonable. Alain Resnais, director of *Hiroshima Mon Amour* (1959) and *Last Year at Marienbad* (1961), was a little too generous when he chose Gregg C. Tallas's charming but minor *Prehistoric Women* (1950) as one of the ten best films released in France in 1955. In France's *Cahiers du Cinéma* (March 1961) Iranian critic Fereydoun Hoveyda called the "Mack Sennett-type gags" in *Dinosaurus!* "brilliant" and gushed "I cannot mention all the good moments in *Dinosaurus!* I would lack space." Here I am going to take enough space to praise *Dinosaurus!* as this gem of a B movie deserves.

Dinosaurus! was filmed in part on St. Croix in the Virgin Islands. The scenery is beautiful and islanders used as extras provide local color. The first 30 minutes or so are a little slow, though they contain an effective shock when Betty comes face to face with the frozen Tyrannosaurus Rex while swimming underwater. The last 50 minutes are fast-paced with an adroit balance of comedy, terror and action.

Dinosaurus! is blessed with an unusually despicable villain. Hacker hits Julio and crushes the boy's beloved dinosaur toys. He demands a bribe for cooperating with the American harbor-dredging team. He tries to blackmail Chica, a girl in love with Bart's friend Chuck, into becoming his girlfriend. He orders his henchmen to make a suicidal attack on the Tyrannosaurus to allow him to get at the caveman; when they refuse he kills one of them. Finally, in a tour de force of evil which is shocking even today, he is ready to sacrifice Betty's and Julio's lives to save himself and the caveman he intends to sell. This kind of villain doesn't grow on trees. Hacker is so detestable the film compromises on his ethnicity. His name Mike Hacker suggests an American but his accent is unidentifiably foreign.

The cast is utterly unknown but does well. Ward Ramsey looks like he can take care of himself in a tight spot and Kristina Hanson is spunky and beautiful. Alan Roberts is a charmingly enthusiastic child actor. Fred Engelberg ably personifies Hacker's outrageous villainy and his two henchmen are appropriately weasely and dimwitted.

When Jasper offers his theory on where a caveman would hide, Hacker sarcastically says, "Your intelligence never ceases to amaze me. I didn't know you were an anthropologist." Jasper replies modestly, "Aw, not a very good one, boss. I ain't been to church in years." Even the badly overdone drunken Irishman has one good line. He says that when he first saw the dinosaurs he didn't report them because he was afraid they were the D.T.s!

I agree with Mark F. Berry (*Dinosaur Filmography*) and Bill Warren (*Keep Watching The Skies!*) that Gregg Martell's work as the Neanderthal Man in *Dinosaurus!* is the finest performance ever by an actor playing a prehistoric person. Martell's Neanderthal is brave, charming, funny, chivalrous and, once seen, never to be forgotten. As Julio puts it, he's "one terrific caveman." The caveman is found frozen with a stone knife clutched in his hand. Clearly he went down fighting, possibly against the Tyrannosaurus Rex which was frozen at the same place. When the Neanderthal thaws out and revives, he threatens the drunken Irishman with his knife, but he doesn't kill him, which he easily could have done. (The Tyrannosaurus gets the Irishman a minute later.)

We next see the Neanderthal peering in through the window of Betty's mother's home. He sees a bowl of fruit on the table but he can't figure out how to get through the window. He can't understand how the transparent glass is able to stop him and he doesn't realize that he could break the glass. As he looks in he comes face-to-face with Betty's mother, who is wearing a facepack and curlers. In a great belly laugh joke, each of them screams in horror at the sight of the other and flees. Betty's mother escapes from the house but the hungry Neanderthal returns to try to get the food.

His adventures in the house are the funniest scenes in any prehistoric film. He stares uncomprehendingly at everything. First he arms himself with a fire ax. He smashes a short-wave radio which emits a sinister whining noise. He tries the fruit in the fruit bowl. It is wax and he spits it out with a disgusted face. Next he sees himself in a mirror; he sneaks up on the mirror and smashes it with his ax. He pulls a book from a bookshelf and tries to eat it. With mounting frustration, he goes off-camera into the bathroom. We hear a thud and the toilet flushing and the caveman flees in terror back into camera-view. Next he tries the bedroom. He almost smashes an 18th-century framed portrait. But he's learning and he smashes neither the portrait nor a second mirror. From the portrait he gets an idea of clothes and unselfconsciously dons Betty's mother's apron over his bare chest and short fur costume.

Fortunately he gets rid of the apron before Julio shows up. The little boy is delighted to meet a real caveman and shows his new friend the food in the refrigerator. The Neanderthal is fascinated by the gas fires on top of the stove and almost sets fire to the house before he learns how to control them. When Julio sits down at the table the caveman studies the chair and how Julio is sitting in it; he tries a chair but can't get comfortable. He ends up sitting on top of the chair back. Julio's attempt to get him to eat with a fork is a dismal failure. The three villains arrive and get tough with the Neanderthal and Julio. The diminutive Neanderthal effortlessly knocks Jasper and Mousy down. When Hacker attacks him, he instantly hits the bully with a pie. A caveman hitting someone with a pie is splendidly surreal but it also shows the Neanderthal's ingenuity. He's the only person in the world who has never seen a pie fight in a movie. It just comes naturally to him.

During the prolonged scenes in the house, we laugh at the Neanderthal's problems, his mistakes and his growing frustration but we never laugh at him. He retains an invincible dignity. He's simply a man out of his element. Once he escapes from the house and returns to the jungle, he is the master of his environment. He ceases to be funny and becomes a great hero, a miniature Tarzan. He smiles mischievously as he easily loses the three villains in the forest. Next we see him and Julio riding on the back of the friendly Brontosaurus. Julio is excited but the Neanderthal looks as calm and confident as an Indian prince atop an elephant. He defends women and children instinctively. He risks his life to rescue first Betty and then Julio from the Tyrannosaurus. When Hacker threatens Betty and Julio the Neanderthal chivalrously rushes to defend them. Even wounded, he sacrifices his life to save them in the cave-in, showing his great strength by holding the roof up until they escape. No other movie caveman does so much to make the audience proud to be human.

Dinosaurus! does not overstate the Neanderthal's intelligence. Like real Neanderthals, Martell's caveman is undoubtedly slower-witted than the modern characters. But that makes him even more appealing. He is an average guy with the twin handicaps of having a slow mind and finding himself in a strange world, but he comes through magnificently. He shows signs of intelligence. Even in the comedy scenes in the house he figures out the gas flames on top of the stove, the mirror, the portrait and the apron, not to mention a found weapon (the pie). Once he gets into the forest no one can outwit him. The film does overrate the Neanderthal's strength when he holds up the roof of the cave, like Hercules in an Italian pepla film. However, Neanderthals did have about three times the upper body strength of modern humans, so perhaps a little exaggeration is pardonable.

Martell's short, stocky body is appropriate for a Neanderthal, though he is nowhere near as powerfully built as a real Neanderthal. Martell's Neanderthal speaks rarely. When he does talk it sounds like inarticulate grunts. This probably underrates Neanderthals, who probably had a language, perhaps more a gesture language than a spoken one. The Neanderthal Man twice almost kills a man, first the Irishman, then Hacker. Both time he relents. His generosity is realistic. Living in small isolated groups, Neanderthals would rarely kill other people.

Betty and her boyfriend Bart are grateful for the Neanderthal's heroics but they are always suspicious of him. Only Julio is truly his friend. After the cavemen saves Betty from the Tyrannosaurus and takes her into the mine, Bart shouts, "He saved her life but there's no telling what he'll do next!" In the mine, Betty is terrified that the Neanderthal will attack her.

She parries his romantic overtures and plays for time. He touches her hair and jewelry; she sings a lullaby in hopes of putting him to sleep. John Lone's Charlie in *Iceman* (1984), Hirotaro Honda's Takashi in *Peking Man* (1997), Richard Kiel's Eegah in *Eegah!* (1962) and Martell's Neanderthal Man in *Dinosaurus!* each assume that any modern girl would be eager to have a sexual relationship with him. In his own world this would be true. A prehistoric woman would naturally prefer to attach herself to the strongest man and all four of the prehistoric men in those films are very competent and strong. He has no idea that she would object and therefore he has no inkling that she would perceive his actions as a threat.

Producer Jack H. Harris and his team aimed the film at children and realized that the Neanderthal Man was going to be such a popular character that they needed to comfort children about his death. Saddened Julio asks Bart, "Why did the caveman have to die?" Bart replies, "He slept all those years, and then he woke up like Rip van Winkle. He found the world so changed he didn't want it any more." He undoubtedly found our world very different from his, but I can't believe that Martell's indomitable Neanderthal Man would ever have wanted to die.

There are some errors in the light-hearted film which must be mentioned even though they don't detract from the audience's enjoyment. There were no Neanderthals or any other pre-modern humans in the Caribbean or anywhere else in the Western Hemisphere. *Dinosaurus!* implies that the Neanderthal Man is familiar with dinosaurs from his previous life, but of course early man and dinosaurs never co-existed. Finally, the Tyrannosaurus Rex ignores being bombarded with Molotov cocktails; even the largest animals retreat from fire.

Director Yeaworth and producer Harris had previously collaborated on the popular youth SF film *The Blob* (1958). The story of *Dinosaurus!* was developed by Harris. SF authors Alfred Bester and Algis Budrys helped with script development but are uncredited.

The director's wife Jean Yeaworth wrote the comedy scenes of the Neanderthal exploring the house. After the slow beginning the film moves along beautifully. All the scenes involving the Neanderthal, both comic and adventurous, are just about perfect, a miracle of inspired writing and performance. The dinosaurs in *Dinosaurus!* were created by Marcel Delgado, who had created the models for *King Kong* almost 30 years before. The animation was done by a team led by veterans Wah Chang and Gene Warren who were advised by the originator of stop-motion, Willis O'Brien. Cinematographer Stanley Cortez had been nominated for an Oscar for photographing *The Magnificent Ambersons*. All these technical workers were veterans of many films, but Harris and Yeaworth made only a few movies, despite the success of *The Blob*. Jean Yeaworth wrote only one film besides *Dinosaurus!* Gregg Martell remained as obscure as the rest of the cast, although he did play another caveman in the inferior *Valley of the Dragons* (1961). Footage from *Dinosaurus!* is shown in a movie theatre in John Landis's caveman comedy *Schlock!* (1973).

Variety (June 15, 1960) appreciated *Dinosaurus!* as a comedy, especially Martell's "richly comic performance" but worried that audiences might not be pleased if they expected an action film and instead saw a light comedy. The *Variety* reviewer felt the dinosaur effects were only good enough for children and disliked all the actors except Martell. Leslie Halliwell (*Halliwell's Film & Video Guide*) called *Dinosaurus!* "risible" but Leonard Maltin (*Maltin's Movie & Video Guide*) found it "interesting and amusing." Ref: Warren. *Keep Watching the Skies!*; Berry. *Dinosaur Filmography*; MK 8. (Revived)

Don't Go Near the Park (1981) U.S.; dir. Lawrence D. Foldes; distributed by Home Video Productions. 80 min.; color. Screenplay, Linwood Chase; photography, William DeDiego. CAST: Aldo Ray (*Taft*); Meeno Peluce (*Nick*); Tamara Taylor (*Bondi*); Crackers Phinn (*Mark/Gar*); Linnea Quigley (*Bondi's Mother*); Shane O'Brien (*Cave Boy*).

In 12,000 B.C., a tribe of superhumans possesses the secret of eternal youth. Their Queen discovers two men who have abused their powers and sentences them to an eternity of deathless old age. In modern Los Angeles the two geriatric villains can recapture eternal youth by sacrificing a teenage virgin.

Quigley was a frequent star of B films. Ray was in some mainstream films before descending to the Bs. The film got a very low rating from users of the *Internet Movie Database*. Ref: *Internet Movie Database*; not viewed. (Survivors)

(III) Eegah!

Eegah! (1962) U.S.; dir. Arch Hall Sr. as Nicholas Merriwether; Fairway International. 90 min.; color. Screenplay, Bob Wehling, Arch Hall Sr.; photography, Vilis Lapenieks; music, Henri Price, Arch Hall Jr. CAST: Arch Hall Jr. (*Tom Nelson*); Marilyn Manning (*Roxy Miller*); Richard Kiel (*Eegah*); Arch Hall Sr., as William Watters (*Robert Miller*).

In the modern West, high school girl Roxy Miller is driving at night in the desert when her car is stopped by an enormous, bearded young caveman. She faints. The giant runs off when Tom, Roxy's baby-faced, rock-singing boyfriend, drives up. Tom and Roxy's father Robert Miller don't know whether to believe her story. Mr. Miller, a writer of "adventure books," goes to unexplored Shadow Mountain (sporting a pith helmet) to investigate the giant. There he is captured by the primitive man, whom he calls Eegah.

Roxy and Tom go to the mountain in Tom's dune buggy to find her father. While Tom is exploring, Eegah kidnaps Roxy and takes her to his cave, where Miller is already a prisoner. Miller keeps his daughter calm and tells her to be friendly to Eegah without encouraging his obvious amorous interest. She even gives Eegah a shave. After a tense night, just as Eegah gets around to undressing Roxy, Tom finds the cave. The three modern people manage to escape, but love-struck Eegah follows them back to town, where he terrifies many people. Eegah finally finds Roxy at a teenage party. He easily defeats the teenage boys who try to defend her, but the police arrive and shoot the caveman dead. Miller calls him "Poor devil!" and quotes from Genesis, "There were giants in the earth in those days."

COMMENTARY. Most of *Eegah* recalls H.L. Mencken's description of Warren G. Harding's prose—"It's so bad a kind of grandeur creeps into it." The writing, the direction and the acting by everyone with intelligible lines are all equally amateurish. The film's status as a guilty-pleasure cult film derives from a few surreal scenes and from the literally towering performance by Richard Kiel as Eegah. Eegah is always curious and eager to please. He is a perfect representative of the ungainly, oversized, powerful, unstoppable, dangerous teenage male libido. He knows he needs a woman to end his loneliness and to give him children, and he woos Roxy as nicely as he knows how.

Eegah's cave has cave paintings which are not faded but clear and bright, as if Eegah had just made them or if he was constantly touching up old art. In addition to the expected pictures of animals, he has a new profile drawing of Roxy in her car! We never learn his real name; Roxy's father calls him Eegah because he frequently says "Eegah." He has a definite language, in which he talks to his dead relatives, whose skulls are mounted on crosses hung with smocks, as if they were alive. In the film's most surreal moment, Eegah introduces Roxy to his dead family, like a well-brought-up young man introducing his date to his parents.

Miller believes that Eegah is the last of his people, that the rest of his tribe died decades before and that Eegah is much older than he looks and is being kept young by constantly drinking the cave's sulfur-laced water. Whatever his age, his interest in Roxy is completely that of a teenager. When the girl, desperate to distract him, gives him her ring, he instantly throws it

Eegah (Richard Kiel) introduces terrified Roxy (Marilyn Manning) to the family in *Eegah!*

away, just like the aborigine in *Walkabout* (1971), who throws away a toy soldier for the same reason — it's of no use to him, and therefore of no interest.

During her imprisonment in the cave, Eegah brings her flowers. When she shaves off his thick beard, she likes what she sees. Even though she fears Eegah and flees from him as soon as she can, she feels sorry for his loneliness. After the three modern humans escape, they agree to keep quiet about Eegah so people won't hunt him. Roxy tries to save Eegah from the police. She mourns his death.

My favorite images from the film are of Eegah striding confidently around the modern town, unselfconsciously carrying Roxy's perfumed scarf, which he smells as he tries to find her. He is puzzled by everything he sees, but he is not afraid of anything or anyone. He has no knowledge of modern weapons and doesn't realize until it is too late that he must fear the little humans who flee before him.

Eegah makes two mistakes about ancient people. There never were "cavemen" like Eegah in the Western Hemisphere, since the earliest Paleo-Indians were already more advanced than the stereotype movie caveman Eegah represents. Second, prehistoric people did not have a better sense of smell than we have, so Roxy's scarf could not have helped Eegah to find her. Despite these errors and the general level of incompetence in *Eegah* (which is rated the seventh worst film ever made by *Internet Movie Database* voters), there's a real movie in there somewhere, struggling to get out. Ref: Jones. *Illustrated Dinosaur Movie Guide*; Senn/Johnson. *Fantastic Cinema Subject Guide*; Warren. *Keep Watching the Skies!*; MK 2. (Survivors)

Encino Man (1992) [alt. *California Man*] U.S.; dir. Les Mayfield; Hollywood Pictures. 88 min.; color. Screenplay, Shawn Schepps; photography, Robert Brinkmann; music, J. Peter Robinson. CAST: Sean Astin (*Dave Morgan*); Brendan Fraser (*Link*); Pauly Shore (*Stoney Brown*); Megan Ward (*Robyn Sweeney*); Robin Tunney (*Ella*); Michael DeLuise (*Matt*); Mariette Hartley (*Mrs. Morgan*); Richard Masur (*Mr. Morgan*); Sandra Hess (*Cavegirl*).

In the Ice Age, a man and woman in heavy furs make fire in a cave but are buried in an earthquake. In modern California, high school geeks Dave and Stoney dig up a frozen caveman in Dave's backyard. When he thaws out, they call him Link (for "Missing Link") and pass him off as an Estonian exchange student. Link becomes popular with girls for his athletic body and enthusiastic dancing. Dave tries to figure out how to use Link to become popular himself, but a school bully targets both of them.

This disappointing comedy starts out badly but improves a little as it goes on. Soon after he revives, Link meets a dog; he scratches himself and howls in imitation of the dog. Later he eats dogfood. He pulls a girl's hair roughly to smell it. However, other scenes give Link a measure of dignity, including a moving sequence in which he realizes that he is alone in a new world. The script makes half-hearted efforts to portray Link as more serious than the shallow high school boys. "He doesn't care about being cool, he only cares about survival," Stoney explains.

Link refuses to fight when the bully hits him, showing that cavemen were not naturally violent. Later Link beats up the same bully when he attacks Dave. A modern girl is attracted to Link, but in the end the cavewoman from the prelude turns up (also thawed out in the backyard). She and Link immediately pair off, suggesting that the film did not dare allow primitive Link to become intimate with a modern woman.

It may seem silly to carp about inaccuracies in a summer teenage film, but it should be pointed out that there never were "cavemen" in the Western Hemisphere, since humans could not reach the Americas until they learned how to survive in the Arctic. Showing Link and his mate wearing warm fur clothing and making fire was correct. Showing them in a cave was wrong. People in the Ice Age had to learn to make their own shelters, rather than rely on convenient caves, of which there were very few. Also, Link is white and the film never mentions that the earliest people in the Western Hemisphere were the ancestors of American Indians.

Variety (May 25, 1992) denounced *Encino Man* as "mindless" and "unfunny" but also called Fraser's Link "winsome." The film has apparently not been completely forgotten. In his book *Generation Kill* (2004) Evan Wright reports that the men of an American unit in the 2003 Iraq War called one of their officers "Encino Man" because they considered him dimwitted. Ref: *Internet Movie Database*; Jones. *Illustrated Dinosaur Movie Guide*; MK 4. (Revived)

Encino Woman (1996) [alt. *California Woman*] U.S.; dir. Shawn Schepps; ZM Productions/Disney Television/ABC. TV film; ca 90 min.; color. Screenplay, Anne Joseph, Shawn Schepps; photography, Russ T. Alsobrook; music, David Lawrence. CAST: Corey Parker (*David Hosenfelt*); Katherine Kousi (*Lucy*); Jay Thomas (*Marvin Reckler*); John Kassir (*Jean Michel*).

A young prehistoric woman is thawed out by a California earthquake and attacks a car, spear in hand. She is taken home by David, a junior executive at a marketing film, who calls her Lucy. She becomes a spokesperson for a cosmetic firm due to her "animal personality."

Variety (April 15, 1996) approved of the acting and the "intriguing costumes" in this TV film, inspired by the 1992 feature film *Encino Man*. Nevertheless, the reviewer dismissed the crude slapstick with which the film presented Lucy's introduction to the modern world. Ref: *Internet Movie Database*; not viewed. (Revived)

Farscape (1999–2003) Episode *The Three Crichtons* (2000). U.S.; dir. Catherine Millar; Hallmark Entertainment/Jim Henson TV/Sci-Fi Channel. Episode of TV series; 45 min.; color. Screenplay, Grant McAloon. CAST: Ben Browder (*John Crichton*); Claudia Black (*Aeryn Sun*); Virginia Hey (*Pa'u Zotoh Zhaan*).

John Crichton, an astronaut, is hurled through space to a distant part of the Universe, among strange aliens. In this episode, an alien research ship tries to kidnap Crichton for study, but instead produces an ape-like "caveman Crichton" and a big-brained "future Crichton," each with almost identical DNA. Ref: *Internet Movie Database*; *www.Farscape.com*; not viewed.(Throwback)

Le Fatiche de Ercole (1958) *see* **Hercules** (1958)

Flesh Creatures (1970) *see* **Horror of the Blood Monsters** (1970)

Flint the Time Detective (1998) Japan; dir. Hiroshi Fukutomi, Koichi Takada, Shinji Okuda; Tac/Pioneer. Animated TV series; 43 25-min. episodes; color. Screenplay, Hideki Sonoda. Petrafina Dagmar, an agent of the Dark Lord, travels to one million B.C. to capture a timeshifter, a creature with magic powers. When caveboy triceratops-hunter Flint Hammerhead (called Genshi in the Japanese version) and his father refuse to give Petra the penguin-like time-shifter, she turns them into stone with her fossilizer ray. In the 25th century, Flint is defossilized by the Bureau of Space and Time Investigations and becomes their agent, fighting Petra in many time periods for possession of many time-shifters. Flint's father remains a talking rock, part of Flint's stone ax, which also has a fossilizer-defossilizer ray. One of Flint's adventures takes place in very ancient Japan, where Petra tries to take the place of legendary queen Himiko. (For several other Japanese anime (animated) productions which either present unorthodox views of prehistory, or have some survivors of prehistory active in the modern world, see the list under *Laws of the Sun* (1990) in Part I.) Ref: Clements/McCarthy. *The Anime Encyclopedia*; not viewed. (Timeshift)

Frankenstein and the Monster from Hell (1974) U.K.; dir. Terence Fisher; Hammer. 99 min.; color. Screenplay, Anthony Hinds (as John Elder); photography, Brian Probyn; music, James Bernard. CAST: Peter Cushing (*Baron Victor Frankenstein*); Shane Briant (*Simon Helder*); Madeline Smith (*Sarah, the Angel*); David Prowse (*Creature*); John Stratton (*Klauss, Asylum Director*); Patrick Troughton (*Graverobber*); Bernard Lee (*Tarmut*); Charles Lloyd Pack (*Prof. Durandel*).

In 19th century Germany, Frankenstein is held in an insane asylum, where he intimidates the corrupt director and does as he pleases. With the assistance of Dr. Helder, a sane doctor convicted of illegal medical experiments, and Sarah, a mute, innocent inmate known as "the Angel," Frankenstein operates on the body of Schneider, a brutish homicidal maniac whom he calls "a throwback, more animal than man, Neolithic." He arranges the suicide of the Professor, a brilliant musician and mathematician, then transplants his brain into Schneider's body. Schneider's personality takes over the genius's mind. The Creature runs amuck and kills the director who had abused Angel. He is shot by guards and torn apart by the inmates. Frankenstein, now completely insane, insists on carrying on with more experiments.

The "throwback" Monster in *Monster from Hell* is one of Hammer's most memorable creatures, with a massive, hairy body, a broad,

The "Neolithic" (actually more Neanderthal) Creature (David Prowse) in *Frankenstein and the Monster from Hell*.

brutish, scarred face and a bald head. He is beautifully ugly, especially in contrast with somewhat effete Briant. A scene in which the Professor wakes up and is horrified to find himself in Schneider's body is very moving, perhaps the best work in Prowse's career. The script errs when it calls the monstrous Creature a "Neolithic" throwback. Neolithic people were anatomically-modern and looked like us. The Creature looks more Neanderthal.

Monster from Hell was Cushing's last film as Frankenstein and therefore the end of perhaps the greatest achievement ever by an actor playing the same character in a series of films. Cushing was at his most gaunt in the film, which was made soon after the death of his wife. It was also the last film made by Terence Fisher, Hammer's most celebrated director. Hammer ceased production in 1976. *Monster from Hell* was their last worthwhile film.

Hammer had emphasized sexuality and nudity in its horror films for several years. For *Monster from Hell* Fisher and Cushing dropped the sex and went back to the Gothic splendors of their early collaborations, though on very constricted sets. Prowse and Cushing worked together once more — on *Star Wars* (1977).

Variety (June 26, 1974) was pleased by the "good tight little dual bill item," which was released in the U.S. in a double bill with *Captain Kronos: Vampire Hunter*. Hardy's *Overlook Film Encyclopedia: Horror* called *Monster from Hell* "a pivotal film in the genre" but a different critic writing in Hardy's *Overlook Film Encyclopedia: Science Fiction* deemed it "routine." Ref: *Internet Movie Database*; Hardy. *Overlook Film Encyclopedia: Horror*; Hardy. *Overlook Film Encyclopedia: Science Fiction*; MK 7. (Throwback)

Frankenstein's Castle of Freaks (1973) [alt. *Il Castelo della Pauro*; *Terror*; *Terror Castle*; *Monsters of Dr. Frankenstein*] Italy; dir. Robert H. Oliver; Classic Films International. 89 min.; color. Screenplay, Robert H. Oliver; photography, Mario Mancini; music, Marcello Gigante. CAST: Rosanno Brazzi (*Count Frankenstein*); Michael Dunn (*Genz*); Edmund Purdom (*Prefect Ewing*); Gordon Mitchell (*Igor*); Loren Ewing (*Goliath*); Boris Lugosi (*Ook*).

In 19th century Italy, Neanderthals (complete with furs, clubs and a cave home) terrorize the country. One is captured and falls into the hands of Frankenstein who transplants a new brain into the caveman whom he calls Goliath. Frankenstein quarrels with his dwarf assistant Genz, who allies with Ook, another Neanderthal, played by "Boris Lugosi" (no relation to Bela). The two cavemen battle each other in the bloody climax. Hardy (*Horror*) called the low-budget horror-erotic film "inept" including "Ook sporting a pair of tennis shorts underneath his hairy disguise." The film marked a nadir for Brazzi's career and perhaps even those of Dunn, Purdom and Mitchell. Ref: Hardy. *The Overlook Film Encyclopedia: Horror*; Jones. *Illustrated Dinosaur Movie Guide*; Senn/Johnson. *Fantastic Cinema Subject Guide*; not viewed. (Survivors)

Galaxy of the Dinosaurs (1992) U.S.; dir. Lance Randas; Suburban Tempe Company. 62 min.; color. Screenplay, John Killough; photography, J.R. Bookwalter, Todd Hone. CAST: James Black (*Capt. Kronik*); Joseph Daw (*Bob the Caveman*); Christine Morrison (*Morda*).

Astronauts land on a planet inhabited by dinosaurs, a galactic criminal and "Bob the Caveman." Mark F. Berry reports that the film is absolutely inept and amateurish, except for borrowed dinosaur footage from *Planet of Dinosaurs* (1978), and is completely mirthless, though intended as a comedy. Ref: Berry. *Dinosaur Filmography*; not viewed. (Extraterrestrial)

Gargoyles (1972) U.S.; dir. B.W.L. Norton; Tomorrow Entertainment. TV film; 74 min.; color. Screenplay, Stephen Karpf, Elinor Karpf; photography, Earl Rath; music, Robert Prince. CAST: Cornel Wilde (*Mercer Boley*); Jennifer Salt (*Diana Boley*); Grayson Hall (*Mrs. Parks*); Bernie Casey (*Head Gargoyle*); Scott Glenn (*James Reeger*).

In Mexico an archeologist and his photographer daughter are attacked by Gargoyles, the descendants of an ancient race, who must recover the skeleton of their monstrous ancestor. Leslie Halliwell called it a "foolish but effective horror piece." Stephen Jones was unimpressed, except for "an atmospheric opening, the eerie desert location and some impressive make-up effects" designed by Ellis Burman and Stan Winston. Ref: Jones. *Illustrated Dinosaur Movie Guide*; Marill. *Movies Made for Television*; Halliwell. *Halliwell's Television Companion*; not viewed. (Survivors)

Gill Women of Venus (1966) *see* **Voyage to the Planet of Prehistoric Women** (1966)

Hercules (1958) [alt. *Le Fatiche de Ercole*; *The Labors of Hercules*] Italy; dir. Pietro Francisci; Galatea/Embassy Pictures. 98 or 107 min.; color. Screenplay, Pietro Francisci, Ennio de Concini, Gaio Frattini based on poem *The Argonauts* by Apollonius of Rhodes; photography, Mario Bava; music, Enzo Masseti. CAST: Steve Reeves (*Hercules*); Sylva Koscina (*Iole*); Fabrizio Mioni (*Jason*); Ivo Garrani (*Pelias, King of Jolco*); Gianna Maria Canale (*Antea*).

Usurper King Pelias sends his rival Jason, together with Hercules and several other heroes, on a quest for the Golden Fleece. After escaping from an island of Amazons, the heroes arrive in the Colchides, the land of the Golden Fleece, where they must fight a horde of ape-men. They finally arrive home with the Fleece and defeat Pelias.

This unassuming but charming film was amazingly successful in America and set off the wave of Italian muscleman films of the late 1950s and early 1960s. *Hercules* is better than most of its imitators, though not to be compared with Ray Harryhausen's *Jason and the Argonauts* (1963), a much more accurate version of the Jason myth. Dark-toned photography by Mario Bava, later a major director of horror films, gives *Hercules* an enchanted, fairy-tale feeling. Nevertheless, *Variety* (May 15, 1959) considered *Hercules* fit for "non-discriminating" audiences only.

The ape-men, who have clubs and short fur costumes, are seen only briefly and in semi-darkness. They are hairy and agile; they make animalistic sounds but do not speak. The faces of only a few of the ape-men are seen clearly, no doubt as a cost-saving measure. They fit in well with the film's fairy-tale atmosphere and are certainly more menacing than the phony-looking, scarcely mobile dragon Jason fights for the Fleece. Ref: Smith. *Epic Films*; *Internet Movie Database*; MK 7. (Survivors)

Horror Express (1972) [alt. *Panico en el Transiberiano*] U.K./Spain; dir. Eugenio Martin; Granada/Benmar. 98 min.; color. Screenplay, Eugenio Martin, Arnaud D'Usseau; photography, Alejandro Ulloa; music, John Cacavas. CAST: Christopher Lee (*Prof. Alexander Saxton*); Peter Cushing (*Dr. Wells*); Telly Savalas (*Capt. Kazan*).

Around 1900, the Trans-Siberian Express travels from China to Russia, carrying arrogant Prof. Saxton (Lee), his rival Wells (Cushing) and a skeleton which Saxton believes is a 2,000,000-year-old missing link. In fact the creature is an ancient extraterrestrial who returns to life and begins to absorb intelligence from people, turning them into possessed zombies. More and more passengers become infected. Matters are not helped by a mad Cossack commander (Savalas).

Hardy (*Horror*) says the film "enthusiastically piles incident upon incident." *Variety* (Oct. 25, 1972) called it "taut and well-paced throughout" with a "topnotch cast." *Horror Express* won the best screenplay award at the Sitges SF Film Festival, partly for flashes of humor, such as when a Russian points out that Cushing and Lee could be possessed monsters and Cushing replies primly "But we're English." The same year, Cushing and Lee faced another prehistoric menace in *The Creeping Flesh*. Ref: Hardy. *Overlook Film Encyclopedia: Horror*; Jones. *Illustrated Dinosaur Movie Guide*; MK 8. (Relic)

Horror of the Blood Monsters (1970) [alt. *Blood Creatures from the Prehistoric Planet*; *Vampire Men of the Lost Planet*; *Creatures of the Red Planet*; *Flesh Creatures*] U.S.; dir. Al Adamson; Independent International. 85 min.; color/tinted. Screenplay, Sue McNair; photography, Vilmos Zsigmond, William G. Troiano; music, Mike Velarde. CAST: John Carradine (*Dr. Rynning*); Robert Dix (*Dr. Manning*); Vicki Volante (*Valerie*); Joey Benson (*Willy*); Jennifer Bishop (*Lian Malian*); Bruce Powers (*Cmdr. Bryce*).

When an epidemic of vampirism breaks out on Earth, an expedition is sent to the planet where the invaders are based. After fighting cat men, snake people and prehistoric reptiles as well as the vampires, the humans are victorious.

Mark F. Berry (*Dinosaur Filmography*) says the planet's denizens included "Neanderthal-like brutes." Berry considers *Horror of the Blood Monsters* "one of the worst excuses for a motion picture ever to be foisted on the public," but Hardy (*Horror*) calls it "one of the better of the numerous exploitation films ... directed by Adamson" and "energetically, if unimaginatively, mounted." The film contained creature footage from frequently-plundered *One Million B.C.* (1940) and at least two low-budget films. According to Brian Thomas (*Videohound's Dragon*) one of these was "a Philippines-made caveman fantasy epic entitled *Tagani*" (see Part I of this list). *Tagani* was in b&w so Adamson tinted it and explained to the audience that the sky on the strange planet changes color frequently. Zsigmond went on to become a major cinematographer of big films, including *Close Encounters of the Third Kind* (1977). Ref: Berry. *Dinosaur Filmography*; Jones. *Illustrated Dinosaur Movie Guide*; Hardy. *Overlook Film Encyclopedia: Horror*; Thomas. *Videohound's Dragon*; not viewed. (Extraterrestrial)

Hound of the Baskervilles (1988) U.K.; dir. Brian Bell; Granada TV/WGBH. TV film; 105 min.; color. Screenplay, T.R. Bowen based on novel by Arthur Conan Doyle; music, Patrick Gowers. CAST: Jeremy Brett (*Sherlock Holmes*); Edward Hardwicke (*Dr. Watson*).

While investigating a murderous conspiracy on the bleak Devonshire moors, Sherlock Holmes hides in a prehistoric stone shelter.

Only Doyle would have thought of having the world's most brilliant detective hide out in a caveman's home. There have been at least seven English-language, feature-length, talking versions of *Hound*. As far as I know this was the only one to feature the prehistoric dwelling. The best version, the 1959 Hammer film starring Peter Cushing, rushed through a cleverly altered script in 87 minutes, leaving no time for such details. Brett is revered for the best impersonation of Holmes in the long history of film and TV versions of the tales, but his reputation rests mainly on the series of 50-minute episodes made by Granada from Doyle's short stories. Granada's and Brett's feature-length Holmes TV films made from the novels were less successful and this funereal-paced *Hound* is no exception. Ref: *Internet Movie Database*; MK 5. (Relic)

House II: The Second Story (1987) U.S.; dir. Ethan Wiley; New World. 85 min.; color. Screenplay, Ethan Wiley; photography, Mac Ahlberg; music, Harry Manfredini. CAST: Arye Gross (*Jesse*); Jonathan Stark (*Charlie*); Royal Dano (*Gramps*); Bill Maher (*John*); Gus Rethwisch (*Arnold the Barbarian*).

Two not overly-bright young men explore a sinister old house, where they find an old zombie and an Aztec skull with magic powers. When the skull opens an "inter-dimensional" door, a Stone Age man comes through, steals the skull and disappears into a prehistoric jungle. The heroes must follow him and retrieve the skull from the dinosaur-infested environment.

Variety (May 20, 1987) and Mark F. Berry (*Dinosaur Filmography*) agree that the film veers ineffectively between horror and comedy, but Berry praises the "marvelously atmospheric" prehistoric scenes. Ref: Jones. *Illustrated Dinosaur Movie Guide*; Berry. *Dinosaur Filmography*; MK 4. (Timeshift)

How to Make a Monster (1958) U.S.; dir. Herbert L. Strock; American International Pictures. 75 min.; b&w/color. Screenplay, Kenneth Langtry, Herman Cohen; photography, Maury Gertzman; music, Paul Dunlap. CAST: Robert H. Harris (*Peter Drummond*); Gary Clarke (*Tony Mantell/Teenage Frankenstein*); Gary

Conway (*Larry Drake/Teenage Werewolf*); Morris Ankrum (*Capt. Hancock*).

A Hollywood makeup man is fired when new studio leaders reject horror films in favor of rock-n-roll movies. He disguises himself as a caveman, puts two young actors under hypnotic suggestion, turns them into a Frankenstein monster and a werewolf, and sends them after the studio executives.

This AIP horror-comedy spoofs the studio's *I Was a Teenage Frankenstein* (1957) and *I Was a Teenage Werewolf* (1958). *Variety* (Sept. 17, 1958) found it serviceable but "rather mild." Hardy calls it "dismally routine" except for the backstage look at AIP's studio. Ref: Jones. *Illustrated Dinosaur Movie Guide*; Senn/Johnson. *Fantastic Cinema Subject Guide*; Hardy. *Overlook Film Encyclopedia: Horror*; not viewed. (Fake)

Ice Woman (1993) U.S.; dir. Michael Zen. Direct-to-video film; 78 min.; color. CAST: Deborah Wells (*Frozen Cavewoman*); Ashlyn Gere.

According to *Internet Movie Database* this is a hardcore pornographic video. It starts in prehistory when "a caveman gets clobbered to death because he sleeps with another caveman's wife." A cavewoman is frozen, then revived in modern times by a scientist and his wife. Followed by a sequel, *Ice Woman 2* (1994). Ref: *Internet Movie Database*; not viewed (Revived).

Ice Woman 2 (1993) U.S.; dir. Michael Zen. Direct-to-video film; color. CAST: Deborah Wells (*Frozen Cavewoman*); Ashlyn Gere.

A hardcore sequel to the previous video, set in modern times and the future. Ref: *Internet Movie Database*; not viewed. (Revived)

Iceman (1984) U.S.; dir. Fred Schepisi; Universal. 100 min.; color. Screenplay, Chip Proser, John Drimmer; photography, Ian Baker; music, Bruce Smeaton. CAST: Timothy Hutton (*Dr. Stanley Shepherd*); Lindsay Crouse (*Dr. Diane Brady*); John Lone ("*Charlie,*" *Charu the Iceman*); Josef Sommer (*Whitman*); David Strathairn (*Dr. Singe*); Philip Akin (*Dr. Vermeil*); Danny Glover (*Loomis*); James Tolkan (*Maynard*).

In the Alaskan Arctic a team working for Polaris Mining and Chemical digs an ice block containing a prehistoric man out of a glacier and flies it, slung under a helicopter, to their research center. Bearded, mildly rebellious anthropologist Shepherd is called in from his work studying Eskimo culture to assist with the spectacular find. Shepherd says the man is a Neanderthal, 20,000 to 40,000 years old. Although freezing destroys cell walls, scientists hope to discover a few intact cells. They cut him out of the ice with lasers and are about to start cutting him up, to send his brain and other organs to various institutes, when they detect cell metastasis, then brain waves, then a heartbeat. The Iceman wakes up screaming.

The panicked researchers sedate him. Polaris executives are immediately interested in discovering the substance, apparently derived from the buttercups in the Iceman's stomach, which prevented cell crystallization during prolonged freezing. This would permit them to sell a kind of immortality to rich and powerful people. The research team debates the ethics of prolonging the lives of geniuses versus immortalizing dictators. Polaris moves the Iceman to their vivarium, evicting several bears to give him the whole place to himself. He eats berries, makes fire by expertly striking two rocks together, makes a spear and kills, cooks and eats a pig. He quickly finds hidden equipment and the wall which separates the vivarium

Charu the Iceman (John Lone) in *Ice Man*.

from the rest of the Center. He now realizes he is in a strange, unnatural world. He makes threat displays at Polaris staff who tranquilize him with a dart gun. Shepherd enters the vivarium alone to make contact. The Iceman makes threat displays, knocks Shepherd down and threatens to kill him with a rock. He spares his life and, having established dominance, roughly examines Shepherd's teeth, hands, shoes and clothes. They exchange names. The Iceman is Charu, whom Shepherd nicknames Charlie. He speaks his own language in very short, quick bursts.

Shepherd brings in a linguist who says Charlie has a large vocabulary but it will take a long time to decipher it. Charlie laughs and sings when Shepherd sings "Heart of Gold" to him.

Over Shephard's objections Polaris sedates Charlie again and performs many experiments, trying to find the "elusive cryoprotectorant." They almost freeze Charlie to death before they give up. When he is revived, Charlie distrusts Shepherd. He gives Shepherd his spear and signals that he wants Shepherd to kill him. Shepherd is horrified.

Charlie draws an elaborate sand drawing. To help Shepherd reestablish contact, Diane Brady, a member of the team, nervously enters the vivarium with Shepherd. Charlie smells and touches her with great interest. He chivalrously offers her an insect to eat; at Shepherd's urging, she reluctantly eats it. When he pushes her legs apart, Shepherd signals that Brady is his. Charlie offers to trade a piece of modern equipment he has found and cached in exchange for the woman. When Shepherd refuses Charlie is very disappointed but accepts the situation. Charlie draws pictures of his woman and children. Suddenly a helicopter flies over the vivarium's sunroof. Charlie becomes tremendously excited and tries to climb to the helicopter. With the aid of the linguist and several elderly Eskimo informants, Shepherd realizes that Charlie has a mythology similar to Eskimo legends. Charlie thinks the helicopter is a trickster bird who is a messenger of the gods, come to take him to heaven or punish him for his sins. Shepherd deduces that when Charlie died he was on a dreamwalk, a journey to offer himself to the gods. Shepherd also speculates that the magnetic pole flipped, causing a rapid change in temperature. Game animals left the area, leaving Charu's tribe to face starvation. They thought they had offended the gods. As leader it was Charu's responsibility to save his people at the cost of his own life.

Charlie chants and paints his body and face. He figures out how to work the door control and escapes from the vivarium. He runs terrified through corridors full of incomprehensible equipment, lights and sounds. After stabbing the first man he meets and getting out of the building, he leaps for a low-flying helicopter and is knocked down and captured. The head of Polaris insists on flying Charlie south, where he will be studied and detained for the rest of his life. Shepherd decides to let Charlie complete his dreamwalk, instead of living a life which would be intolerable to him. He frees Charlie and they flee across the snow, pursued by both the helicopter and men in snowmobiles. This time Charlie manages to grab the landing gear of the helicopter. He joyously lets go at a great height and falls to his death, completing his mission for his tribe.

COMMENTARY. The age Charlie gives for Charlie (20,000 to 40,000 years old) is correct for the last Neanderthals, but Neanderthals lived only in Europe and the Middle East, not in Siberia or Alaska. Neanderthals did not use bone needles and could not make weatherproof clothes, nor did they build shelters. They relied on caves for winter survival. People could not survive in Siberia and Alaska until they could make specialized Arctic clothing and huts. Also, Charlie looks like a modern man, nothing like the Neanderthals, who were short, squat and big-nosed. We believe that Neanderthals did not make art, as Charlie does. Charlie's large vocabulary is also wrong for Neanderthals, who may have had a simple language, or may have spoken mainly with their hands, but probably did not have an elaborate language.

In spite of the misidentification of Charlie, *Iceman* admirably presents a positive picture of ancient man. Charu, to give him his real name, is brave, tough and determined. He makes a spear and can use it with deadly effect. He has a religion and makes art. He is devoted to his family and tribe. He is intelligent, quickly finds the hidden vivarium wall and learns how to work the door controls and get out of his prison. He is much stronger than any of the modern people, but he doesn't kill Shepherd or assault Brady, in whom he is sexually interested. The problem is that the film is mostly told from the point of view of the modern people. We learn about Charu through them, and through a haze of technical and medical jargon and sophomoric philosophical discussions.

Hutton's politically correct anthropologist actually seems a bit insensitive. He no sooner learns Charu's name then he nicknames him Charlie and he spends more time trying to teach Charlie English than attempting to understand his language. Besides calling Charlie a Neanderthal, Shepherd makes another dubious judgment. He remarks "Look at his teeth! He's a hunter!" Huh? One problem is that *Iceman* tries to be too realistic. It assaults the audience with technical chatter which does not really convince us that the fantastic events are possible. The story confines the revived ancient man to the Research Center for almost the whole movie, while the less realistic *Dinosaurus!* (1960) and *Peking Man* (1997) allowed their revived cavemen to get out of the lab and interact with the modern world, giving the actors opportunities for richer explorations of both the comic and serious sides of the situation.

John Lone wears minimal makeup as Charlie, permitting the actor to give a real performance without intelligible dialogue. Charlie registers fear, rage, determination and joy. We sometimes see events from his point of view, as when he wakes up and finds himself surrounded by masked doctors, in an environment he could never imagine. Charlie of course has no idea that an immense period of time has passed since he was with his people. He assumes that his tribe is still out there, depending on him to fulfill his sacred mission, and that he has fallen into the hands of spirits or demons.

Hong Kong actor Lone had done only three films before *Iceman* and has done only a dozen since. He was nominated for Golden Globes for *Year of the Dragon* (1985) and *The Last Emperor* (1987). Hutton and Crouse have been busy stars. When he made *Iceman* Hutton had already won both an Oscar and a Golden Globe for *Ordinary People* (1980). The same year she did *Iceman* Crouse was nominated for an Oscar for *Places in the Heart* (1984). Neither Hutton or Crouse has a chance to really score points in *Iceman*, as Lone did. Schepisi's films have been few but often good, including *The Chant of Jimmie Blacksmith* (1978) and *Barbarossa* (1982). *Iceman*, filmed in beautiful locations in Manitoba and British Columbia, is an ambitious film by an important director with three talented young stars, but it is only a partial success.

Critics have been starkly divided on *Iceman*. *Variety* (April 11, 1984) found the film "preposterous" and felt that Lone's Charlie resembled too much the primitive man in Ken Russell's *Altered States* (1980). The reviewer also worried that there had been too many movies about primitive humans, after *Caveman* (1981), *Quest for Fire* (1981) and the 1984 Tarzan film *Greystoke*. *Variety* liked only Lone's performance, Baker's photography and some "tense" scenes. Leslie Halliwell (*Halliwell's Film & Video Guide*) found the film boring and preachy, while Hardy (*Science Fiction*) felt the conflict among the scientists was effectively "underplayed." Hardy applauded Lone's "inventive performance" and the film's "anthropologically realistic, non-clichéd view of the caveman." Leonard Maltin's *Movie & Video Guide* gave *Iceman* a very high rating of 3½ and especially praised Lone's "remarkable performance."

There are so many similarities between *Iceman* and *Peking Man* that the Japanese filmmakers may have seen the U.S. film. In both films the revived prehistoric man almost brains the modern hero, then relents; in both the primitive people are confined to a vivarium while scientists and businessmen quarrel over the ethical issues they raise; and in both the early humans escape and determine their own fate. Ref: Hardy. *Overlook Film Encyclopedia: Science Fiction*; MK 8. (Revived)

Invasion of the Animal People (1960) [alt. *Terror in the Midnight Sun; Space Invasion from Lapland*] Sweden/U.S.; dir. Virgil W. Vogel, Jerry Warren; Ungar Films/Fortuna. 55 or 73 min.; color. Screenplay, Arthur C. Pierce, Jerry Warren; photography, Hilding Bladh; music, Harry Arnold, Allan Johansson. CAST: Barbara Wilson (*Diane*); John Carradine (*Narrator*); Bengt Blomgren (*Col. Bottinger*); Ake Grönberg (*Dr. Henrik*); Robert Burton (*Frederick Wilson*).

An alien spaceship lands in Lapland and disgorges a giant Stone Age hominid monster who attacks Laplanders and scientists. After the humans, with difficulty, injure the creature, it is recaptured by the more advanced aliens, who depart into space with it.

Vogel made this low-budget SF film in Lapland; Warren added about 20 minutes of chatty dialogue with Carradine and Burton. Unlikely though it may seem that space-faring aliens would bring a huge Stone Age monster along in their spaceship, both Hardy and Jones insist that that's what the creature is. Hardy reports that the Swedish film had an admirably eerie atmosphere, but Warren's scenes were as bad as his usual efforts. Even *Variety* failed to review it. Ref: Hardy. *Overlook Film Encyclopedia: Science Fiction*; Jones. *Illustrated Dinosaur Movie Guide*; Warren. *Keep Watching the Skies!*; not viewed. (Extraterrestrial)

La Isla de los Dinosaurios (1966) [alt. *Island of the Dinosaurs*] Mexico/U.S.; dir. Rafael Portillo; Cinematográfica Calderón/Hal Roach. 76 min.; b&w. Screenplay, Alfredo Salazar; photography, Agustin Jimenez; music, Gustavo Cesar Carrion. *CAST:* Armando Silvestre (*Molo*); Alma Delia Fuentes (*Laura*); Manuel Fabregas (*Prof. Portillo*); Elsa Cardenas (*Esther*); Genaro Morena (*Pablo*); Crox Alvarado (*Caveman*); Cavernario Galindo (*Caveman*); Julie Jantzen (*Cavewoman*); Victorio Blanco (*Old Caveman*).

Professor Portillo and his three students are stranded on a remote island in the Atlantic when their plane is forced down. Laura meets Molo, who has been driven out by his Stone Age tribe. They fall in love and escape giant lizards and a gorilla. Molo regains the leadership of his tribe. After surviving a volcanic eruption, Laura gives up a chance to return to civilization in the explorers' repaired plane and elects to stay with Molo in his primitive world.

As Mark F. Berry (*Dinosaur Filmography*) points out, *Isla de los Dinosaurios* was as much a remake of *One Million B.C.* (1940) as was *One Million Years B.C.* (also 1966). The hero is driven from his tribe and falls in love with a girl from a more civilized community; he regains the leadership of his tribe; the girl teaches civilization to the cavemen; they survive ordeals by giant beasts and volcano; and the girl stays with her primitive lover. In addition *Isla de los Dinosaurios* reused a great deal of stock footage from *One Million B.C.* and was co-produced by Hal Roach Studios, makers of the 1940 film. Once again we see a cave feast during which men take most of the food, leaving little for women, children and the old. Once more an older man drives the young hero from the cave and the tribe in a fight with staffs. The hero and heroine wear costumes that are essentially the same as those in the 1940 film so that stock footage can be inserted. A major difference between the two films is the fact that in the Mexican remake the girl comes from modern civilization rather than relatively civilized cave people. While Tumak in *One Million B.C.* lives with the Shell People and is impressed by their technology, Molo does not encounter any of the explorers except Laura until the end of the film. Surprisingly Laura manages to make Molo a stone-tipped spear and a stone ax, both improvements on his tribe's equipment.

Molo's people have fire and talk a little. Unlike in the 1940 film and the 1966 Hammer remake, the girl and the caveman do not speak the same language. Molo treats Laura roughly when he first meets her. He threatens her with his club and steals her locket. Later he pulls her along by her hair; he doesn't drag her by her hair only because she manages to stay on her feet. In an interesting scene, Laura hugs a child and the child's mother shoves her, afraid that Laura wants to steal her child. Molo shoves the mother aside, increasing her alarm. When Laura gives the woman a gift to make friends the woman thinks that Laura is trying to buy the child. Soon Laura is reforming the cave people, feeding women, children and old people first and teaching cave girls to take care of their hair.

I have seen the film only in Spanish. The cast and photography are adequate but the direction is uninspired. Armando Silvestre is well-cast as a good-hearted, Tarzanesque savage. Ref: Jones. *Illustrated Dinosaur Movie Guide*; Senn/Johnson. *Fantastic Cinema Subject Guide*; Berry. *Dinosaur Filmography*; viewed in Spanish; MK 5.(Lost World)

Island of the Dinosaurs (1966) *see* **La Isla de los Dinosaurios** (1966)

It's About Time (1966–67) [U.S.; United Artists TV/CBS. TV series; 26 25-min. episodes; color. This dismal series was set both in prehistoric times and the modern world. See Part I for details.] (Timeshift)

Jan-Gel, the Beast from the East (1999) U.S.; dir. Conrad Brooks; Quality Film & Video. 53 min.; color. Screenplay, Conrad Brooks; music, Ellsworth Hall. *CAST:* Dale Clukey (*Jan-Gel*); Conrad Brooks; Beth Simmons.

A 50,000-year-old human monster awakes and runs amok in the hills of Maryland and West Virginia, killing and mutilating but also falling in love. Director-screenwriter-actor Brooks was a supporting actor in dozens of low-budget films, including Ed Wood's *Plan 9 from Outer Space* (1959). According to the only user's comment on the film's page on *Internet Movie Database*, *Jan-Gel* is dreadful, almost worthy of Ed Wood himself. And there were no humans in North America 50,000 years ago. Ref: *Internet Movie Database*; not viewed. (Survivors)

Journey to the Center of the Earth (1967–69) U.S.; Filmation. Animated TV series; 17 25-min. episodes; color. Based on novel by Jules Verne. *VOICES:* Ted Knight (*Prof. Lindenbrook/Count Saccnuson*); Jane Webb (*Cindy Lindenbrook*); Pat Harrington Jr. (*Alec McEwen/ Lars/Torg/Gertrude the Duck*).

Prof. Lindenbrook, with his niece, student, guide and duck, are all stranded in an underground world, where they are menaced by villain Count Saccnuson and underworld creatures. According to Jones, the latter include cavemen, winged reptiles, dinosaurs and "fossil men" (whatever they may be). Ted Knight is best known as a regular on *The Mary Tyler Moore Show*. The 1967–69 series was repeated on the Sci-Fi Channel's *Cartoon Quest* in the 1990s. The series was based on the 1959 film version, which had no cavemen but did have Gertrude the Duck. Other film and TV versions of the Verne novel did not feature cavemen, although a 1999 miniseries did have reptile-men. Ref: Jones. *Illustrated Dinosaur Movie Guide*; Lenburg. *Encyclopedia of Animated Cartoons*. 2nd ed.; not viewed. (Lost World)

Journey to the Center of the Earth (1999) U.S.; dir. George Miller; Hallmark Entertainment/USA Network. TV miniseries; 178 min.; color (& video version, 139 min.). Screenplay, Thomas Baum based on novel by Jules Verne; photography, Bruce Phillips, John Stokes; music, Bruce Rowland. *CAST:* Treat Williams (*Prof. Lytton*); Jeremy London (*Jonas*); Tushka Bergen (*Alice Hastings*); Hugh Keays-Byrne (*McNiff*); Petra Yared (*Ralna*); Bryan Brown (*Casper Hastings*).

In late 19th century New Zealand an expedition is stranded underground in a world of dinosaurs, flying reptiles, natives similar to the Maori and the Sauroids, an intelligent reptilian-human species. After many difficulties, the explorers escape to the surface. There are two Australian directors called George Miller. This is the *Man from Snowy River* (1982) Miller, not the *Mad Max/Road Warrior* (1979, 1981) Miller. The miniseries was modestly entertaining but too long, with mediocre but sometimes imaginative special effects. Very oddly, one of the best effects, a swarm of flying pterodactyls, is left out of the shortened video version. Ref: Berry. *Dinosaur Filmography*; *Internet Movie Database*; MK 5. (Lost World)

Jungle Jim in the Forbidden Land (1952) U.S.; dir. Lew Landers; Columbia. 65 min.; b&w. Screenplay, Samuel Newman; photography, Fayte Browne; music, Mischa Bakaleinikoff. *CAST:* Johnny Weissmuller (*Jungle Jim*); Angela Greene (*Linda Roberts*); Jean Willies (*Denise*); William Tannen (*Doc*); Fred Berest (*Zulu*); Clem Erickson (*Giant Man*); Irmgard H. H. Raschke (*Giant Woman*).

In backlot Africa, villains Denise, Doc and Zulu kidnap anthropologist Linda, frame Jungle Jim for murder and capture two of the mysterious Giant People, a male and a female, all as part of an elaborate scheme to poach elephants. The Giant Woman is killed. Jim finally gets the better of the villains by setting off an elephant stampede. The Giant Man saves Linda by grabbing Denise and jumping over a cliff, killing himself and her. In one of the last lines of the film Linda announces helpfully that the Giant People are "missing links."

Aging and overweight, Weissmuller was demoted from Tarzan to Jungle Jim and made 13 of the juvenile adventure quickies from 1948 to 1955. Bill Warren, in *Keep Watching the Skies!*, reports that *Jungle Jim in the Forbidden Land* was as silly and dependent on stock jungle footage as the rest of the series. The Giant People are tall, but not real giants. They are covered with hair; the male's face is hairy, the female's is more human. The male has a mouthful of jagged teeth. The Giant People growl and shriek but do not talk. They are savage but not villainous. Like the elephants, the Giant People are powerful but cannot cope with the human villains without Jungle Jim's help. Warren's book has a rare illustration of the two Giant People.

Variety (March 5, 1952) found *Jungle Jim in the Forbidden Land* "implausible" but "okay" for "moppet [child] ticket-buyers." Jungle Jim again faced pre-humans in *Killer Ape* (1953). Ref: Warren. *Keep Watching the Skies!*; not viewed. (Survivors)

Killer Ape (1953) U.S.; Spencer G. Bennet; Columbia. 68 min.; b&w. Screenplay, Arthur Hoerl, Carroll Young; photography, William Whitley; music, Mischa Bakaleinikoff. CAST: Johnny Weissmuller (*Jungle Jim*); Carol Thurston (*Shari*); Max Palmer (*Man-Ape*); Nestor Pavia (*Andrews*).

Jungle Jim fights a gang led by Pavia, who is drugging jungle animals, and a creature which the credits call a "man-ape." Jones and Senn/Johnson call him a caveman.

Weissmuller made the *Jungle Jim* series, based on a comic strip, after his *Tarzan* series petered out. Palmer was a giant character actor. *Variety* (Nov. 25, 1953) said dismissively that the film was "no worse, but certainly no better, than predecessors in the series" and that the comic chimp Tamba "fares better than the human actors in the story." The same team made the serial *King of the Congo* (1952), featuring cavemen. Jungle Jim also dealt with pre-humans in *Jungle Jim in the Forbidden Land* (1952). Ref: Jones. *Illustrated Dinosaur Movie Guide*; Senn/Johnson. *Fantastic Cinema Subject Guide*; Warren. *Killer Ape*; not viewed. (Survivors)

King of the Congo (1952) [alt. *The Mighty Thunda*] U.S.; dir. Spencer G. Bennet, Wallace Grissell; Columbia. Serial film; 15 chapters; b&w. Screenplay, Royal K. Cole, Arthur Hoerl, George H. Plympton; photography, William Whitley; music, Mischa Bakaleinikoff. CAST: Buster Crabbe (*Thunda/Roger Drum*); Gloria Dee (*Pha*); Leonard Penn (*Boris*); Jack Ingram (*Clark*); Rusty Westcoatt (*Kor*); William Fawcett (*High Priest*).

Thunda, King of the Congo, is actually Capt. Drum of the U.S. Air Corps. His opponent is Boris, a scheming subversive who is seeking a mineral deposit more radioactive than uranium. Thunda allies with Queen Pha of the Rock People and later establishes friendship between the Rock People and the Cave Men.

The serial film, which had persisted for 40 years, was killed off by television in the early 1950s. This was one of the last serials and, according to Rainey, the last of several serials to feature an imitation Tarzan. *King of the Congo* has many similarities to the 1953 feature *Killer Ape*. Both were made by the same studio, director, photographer and score composer; Hoerl worked on both screenplays. Both were based on comic strips and each starred an aging ex–Tarzan actor. The 1952 serial, which has cavemen but no dinosaurs, has little similarity to a 1929 serial, *King of the Kongo*, which had dinosaurs but no cavemen. Chapters: "Mission of Menace," "Red Shadows in the Jungle," "Into the Valley of Mist," "Thunda Meets His Match," "Thunda Turns the Tables," "Thunda's Desperate Chance," "Thunda Trapped," "Mission of Evil," "Menace of the Magnetic Rocks," "Lair of the Leopard," "An Ally from the Sky," "Riding Wild," "Red Raiders," "Savage Vengeance," "Judgment of the Jungle." Ref: Jones. *Illustrated Dinosaur Movie Guide*; Rainey. *Serials and Series*; not viewed. (Survivors)

Kolchak: The Night Stalker (1974) Episode, *Primal Screen*. U.S.; dir. Robert Scheerer; Universal TV/Francy Productions/ABC. Episode of TV series; 50 min.; color. Screenplay, Bill S. Ballinger, David Chase. CAST: Darren McGavin (*Carl Kolchak*); Simon Oakland (*Tony Vincenzo*); John Marley (*Capt. Molnar*); Pat Harrington Jr. (*Thomas Kitzmiller*); Kate Woodville (*Helen Lynch*); Jamie Farr (*Jack Burton*); Gary Buxley (*Humanoid*).

The series dealt with a Chicago reporter who routinely investigates supernatural events. In this, the thirteenth of 20 episodes, million-year-old cells from an Arctic soil sample thaw out and grow into a prehistoric apeman who kills on the city streets at night.

Kolchak lasted only one season but is fondly remembered as one of the best fantastic series on TV. Guest star John Marley was famous for his performance as the studio chief in *The Godfather* (1972). Ref: Jones. *Illustrated Dinosaur Movie Guide*; Morton. *Complete Directory to Science Fiction, Fantasy and Horror Television Series*; not viewed. (Revived)

The Labors of Hercules (1958) *see* **Hercules** (1958)

Land of the Lost (1974–77) U.S.; Krofft Entertainment/NBC. TV series; 43 25-min. episodes; color. Music, Jimmie Haskell, Michael Lloyd. CAST: Spencer Milligan (*Rick Marshall*); Wesley Eure (*Will Marshall*); Kathy Coleman

(*Holly Marshall*); Ron Harper (*Jack Marshall*); Phillip Paley (*Cha-Ka*); Walter Edmiston (*Enik*); Sharon Baird (*Sa*); Joe Giamalva (*Ta*); Scutter McCay (*Ta, season 2*); Joe Locke (*Sleestack Leader*); Richard Kiel (*Malak*).

The Marshalls, a modern family, go through a fissure into a land full of strange creatures, including dinosaurs, dragons, the Pakuni and the Sleestacks. The Pakuni are small, hairy, friendly, mischievous missing links. The Sleestacks are hostile, bipedal, intelligent reptiles. The principle Pakuni are Cha-Ka and his parents Sa and Ta. Enik is an advanced Sleestack time-traveler. The Marshalls have a pet baby brontosaurus, Dopey, who is trained to pull carts and do other work.

Unlike the relatively realistic *Korg: 70,000 B.C.*, *Land of the Lost* had many fantastic story elements, such as crystal-powered pylons which control the physical laws of the land. Towering Richard Kiel played Malak, a primitive man, in two 1976 episodes, fourteen years after playing the caveman in *Eegah!* (1962) and one year before playing Jaws in *The Spy Who Loved Me* (1977). The series' dinosaur puppets were created by veteran special effects artist Wah Chang, who also worked on *Dinosaurus!*, *The Time Machine* (both 1960) and *Planet of the Apes* (1968).

In a Sept. 13, 1974 article on children's TV programming, *Variety* wrote that "most disappointing of the live-action entries is NBC's *Land of the Lost*." Many fans and TV historians disagree. Both George Woolery and Alan Morton consider the original *Land of the Lost* series one of the best children's fantasy series in TV history. David Gerrold, best known as a *Star Trek* writer, was script editor for the first season and wrote several episodes. Other well-known SF writers who wrote for *Land of the Lost* were Ben Bova, Larry Niven, Theodore Sturgeon and D.C. Fontana. *Star Trek* actor Walter Koenig wrote the episode in which Enik was introduced.

In an attempt to add an educational level to the series, producers Sid and Marty Krofft hired a linguistics professor to develop a Pakuni language and invited child viewers to join the Marshall family in trying to decipher the tongue. This was an unsuccessful ploy and Pakuni linguistics were soon forgotten and replaced by straightforward adventure episodes. The menacing Sleestacks were more popular with fans than the adorable Pakuni.

In the 24th episode, "The Longest Day" (written by Joyce Perry, dir. Gordon Wiles), Rick is put on trial by the Sleestacks after time mysteriously stops. In a temple full of strange smoke he has several visions, in one of which he briefly sees himself and the two children Will and Holly as cave people, huddling around a fire in skins.

The 1991 re-make series was a lamentable failure. Episodes: "Cha-Ka," "The Sleestack God," "Dopey," "Downstream," "Tag Team," "The Stranger," "Album," "Skylons," "The Hole," "The Paku Who Came to Dinner," "The Search," "The Possession," "Follow That Dinosaur," "Stone Soup," "Elsewhen," "Hurricane," "Circle," "Tar Pit," "The Zarn," "Fair Trade," "One of Our Pylons Is Missing," "The Test," "Gravity Storm," "The Longest Day," "The Pylon Express," "A Nice Day," "Baby Sitter," "The Musician," "Split Personality," "Blackout," "After-Shock," "Survival Kit," "The Orb," "Repairman," "Medusa," "Cornered," "Flying Dutchman," "Hot-Air Artist," "Abominable Snowman," "Timestop," "Ancient Guardian," "Scarab," "Medicine Man." Ref:

Holly (Kathy Coleman), Cha-Ka the Pakuni (Philip Paley) and a unicorn in TV's *Land of the Lost.*

Woolery. *Children's Television*; Morton. *Complete Directory to Science Fiction, Fantasy and Horror Television Series*; viewed several episodes; MK 7. (Fantasy)

Land of the Lost (1991) U.S.; Krofft Entertainment. TV series; 26 25-min. episodes; color. Music, Kevin Kiner. CAST: Timothy Bottoms (*Tom Porter*); Jennifer Drugan (*Annie Porter*); Robert Guam (*Kevin Porter*); Shannon Day (*Christa*); Bobby Porter (*Stink*); Ed Gale (*Tasha*); Danny Mann (*Tasha Voice*); Tom Allard (*Shung*); Brian Williams (*Keeg*); R.C. Tass (*Nim*).

As in the original 1974–77 series, a modern family accidentally enters a fantastic world with dinosaurs, ape-people and the popular, villainous Sleestacks. The Porters' friends are Christa, a jungle girl; Tasha, a baby dinosaur; and Stink, a juvenile ape-human. The Sleestacks are more advanced than in the original series. This second series is considered insignificant compared to the fondly-remembered 1970s original. Episodes: "Tasha," "Something's Watching," "Shung the Terrible," "Jungle Girl," "The Crystal," "Wild Thing," "Day for Knight," "Kevin vs. the Volcano," "Mind Games," "Flight to Freedom," "Heat Wave," "The Thief," "Power Play," "The Sorceress," "Dreammaker," "Opah," "The Gladiators," "Life's a Beach," "Future Boy," "Siren's Song," "In Dinos We Trust," "Annie in Charge," "Make My Day," "Cheers," "Sorceress's Apprentice," "Misery Loves Company." Ref: Morton. *Complete Directory to Science Fiction, Fantasy and Horror Television Series*; Jones. *Illustrated Dinosaur Movie Guide*; viewed 4 episodes; MK 4. (Fantasy)

The Land That Time Forgot (1975) U.K.; dir. Kevin Connor; American International Pictures/Amicus. 91 min.; color. Screenplay, James Cawthorn, Michael Moorcock based on novel by Edgar Rice Burroughs; photography, Alan Hume; music, Douglas Gamley. CAST: Doug McClure (*Bowen Tyler*); John McEnery (*Capt. Von Schoenvorts*); Susan Penhaligon (*Lisa Clayton*); Anthony Ainley (*Dietz*); Keith Barron (*Bradley*); Godfrey James (*Borg*); Bobby Parr (*Ahm*); Steve James (*First Stolu*).

Tribal women of Caprona bathe in the waters of a mysterious fountain in *The Land That Time Forgot*.

During World War I, survivors of a torpedoed Allied ship are taken aboard a German submarine. In the South Atlantic, the lost U-boat discovers the uncharted volcanic island of Caprona, inhabited by many kinds of dinosaurs and cave people representing several different stages of human development. The German and Allied sailors join forces to survive and try to refine petroleum and refuel the submarine. They meet friendly caveman Ahm, whose people are the Bolu, the most primitive human group on Caprona. The more advanced primitives, the Stolu and the Galu, are both aggressive. Ahm is killed by a pterodactyl. When English girl Lisa is kidnapped by the Stolu, two-fisted American Tyler rescues Lisa and together they meet the Galu, who resemble modern humans. Tyler makes the mistake of announcing "we Galu." This enrages the Galu, who attack Tyler and Lisa. They are saved by a volcanic eruption but stranded when the submarine and its crew are destroyed by volcanic debris.

COMMENTARY. *Variety* (April 9, 1975) dismissed the film and criticized the dinosaur effects especially harshly. Mark F. Berry (*Dinosaur Filmography*) defended the "surprisingly literate" film and felt that the dinosaurs were a mixed bunch, some much better than the others. *The Land That Time Forgot* is a pleasant juvenile adventure, though the first half, aboard the submarine, is padded and the second half, on the island, a little rushed. Ahm, the sailors' friend, is likeable but is treated like a pet by the modern people. The other cavemen are quarrelsome and violent, though not more so than the Germans and British. While people in Hammer's Films caveman movies, beginning with *One Million Years B.C.* (1966), were all anatomically-modern, Hammer's rival Amicus took the trouble to use makeup to differentiate the primitive Bolu and intermediate Stolu from the modern Galu.

The Land That Time Forgot has one of the most bizarre premises of any film about prehistoric humans. Ahm of the backward Bolu joins the Stolu and becomes one of them. He doesn't just change tribes, he changes species. His appearance is different, his intelligence expands and he expects to go up another step and become a Galu. Capronans apparently alter their species by drinking the microbe-infested water, in accordance with "the strange laws of Caprona," as Tyler puts it. This odd concept probably baffled audiences. As Berry notes, "Burroughs' complex concepts of Capronian evolution do not translate easily to the screen, and the whole notion of the 'secret of Caprona' is never satisfactorily explained."

Three men who worked on *The Land That Time Forgot* were nominated for Oscars for other films — production designer Maurice Carter and special effects artists Derek Meddings and Roger Dicken. A less successful sequel, *The People That Time Forgot*, appeared in 1977. Ref: Berry. *Dinosaur Filmography*; Jones. *Illustrated Dinosaur Movie Guide*; Senn/Johnson. *Fantastic Cinema Subject Guide*; MK 6. (Lost World)

The Last Dinosaur (1977) U.S./Japan; dir. Alexander Grasshof, Shusei Kotani; Rankin-Bass/Tsuburaya. 94 min.; color. Screenplay, William Overgard; photography, Shoji Ueda; music, Maury Laws. CAST: Richard Boone (*Masten Thrust*); Steven Keats (*Chuck Wade*); Joan Van Ark (*Francesca Banks*); Luther Rackley (*Bunta*); Tetsu Nakamura (*Dr. Kawamoto*).

Big game hunter Masten Thrust (great name!) leads an expedition to a mysterious verdant valley in the Arctic, where they discover dinosaurs and a Neanderthal-like tribe. As casualties mount, the tribe turns hostile and Thrust becomes obsessed with killing a Tyrannosaurus Rex.

Not much attention is paid to the primitive humans in this odd film, a U.S.-Japanese co-production which was made as a theatrical feature but released as a TV film in the U.S. Boone was 60 when he made it, but his age is fitting for his character, who yearns for glory before it's too late. Mark F. Berry objected to the over-sized, Godzilla-inspired dinosaurs. Ref: Berry. *Dinosaur Filmography*; Jones. *Illustrated Dinosaur Movie Guide*; Senn/Johnson. *Fantastic Cinema Subject Guide*; MK 4. (Lost World)

The Laughter of God (1990) [alt. *Married to Murder*] Great Britain; dir. Tony Bicat. 88 min.; color. Screenplay, Tony Bicat; photography, John Kenway; music, Nick Bicat. CAST: Peter Firth (*Steve Clemant*); Amanda Donohoe (*Jane Clemant*).

Workers on a construction site in rural Britain find the grave of an ancient man. The workers and their boss Steve (Firth) know that the body and its accoutrements would be valuable to scientists, but if they report the find the site will be closed down, Steve's small company will go bankrupt and they will all be out of work. They rebury the body, swear each other to secrecy and get on with their work. Unhappily married Steve decides to kill his bitchy wife Jane and bury her at the same site. Jane survives, Steve is arrested, the authorities discover the ancient body and the men lose their jobs.

This routine but well-cast murder thriller has one moving scene. The workers bury the ancient corpse as respectfully as possible and struggle to find words to express their feelings about a man whose life they cannot imagine but who may have been among their ancestors. Steve suggests that the ancient man would have preferred to be left in peace rather than be studied by scientists. Ref: *Internet Movie Database*; MK 5. (Relic)

Lost in Space (1965–68) Episode no. 64, *The Space Primevals* (1967). U.S.; dir. Nathan Juran; Irwin Allen Productions/20th Century–Fox TV/CBS. Episode of TV series; 50 min.; color. Screenplay, Peter Packer. CAST: Guy Williams (*John Robinson*); June Lockhart (*Maureen Robinson*); Marta Kristen (*Judy*); Angela Cartwright (*Penny*); Billy Mumy (*Will*); Jonathan Harris (*Dr. Smith*); Mark Goddard (*Don West*); Bob May (*Robot*); Arthur Batanides (*Rongah*). An American family, their robot and two friends, including unreliable Dr. Smith, are lost in the universe aboard their spaceship. In the fifth episode of the third season, the Robinsons have to "cap" a volcano before it destroys their ship and rescue Dr. Smith and Don, who are being held underground by people whom Philips/Garcia call "hostile cavemen." Ref: Philips/Garcia. *Science Fiction Television Series*; not viewed. (Extraterrestrial)

The Lost World (1925) U.S.; dir. Harry O. Hoyt; First National Pictures. 63, 93 or 104 min.; b&w; silent. Screenplay, Marion Fairfax, based on novel by Arthur Conan Doyle; photography, Arthur Edeson; music, Arthur Friml. CAST: Bessie Love (*Paula White*); Wallace Beery (*Prof. Challenger*); Lewis Stone (*Sir John Roxton*); Arthur Hoyt (*Prof. Summerlee*); Lloyd Hughes (*Edward Malone*); Alma Bennett (*Gladys Hungerford*); Bull Montana (*Ape-Man*).

Pugnacious Prof. Challenger, skeptical Prof. Summerlee, veteran hunter Roxton, cub reporter Malone and Paula White, daughter and "trained assistant" to missing scientist Maple White, travel to the upper Amazon to explore the plateau where Maple White claimed to have seen dinosaurs. They are stranded on the plateau, with dinosaurs and a hostile Apeman. After much of the Lost World is destroyed by a volcanic eruption and fire, the heroes finally escape and return to London with a Brontosaurus, which escapes and terrifies Londoners before quietly swimming down the Thames.

The Lost World was the most important silent special effects film and introduced audiences to sights they had never seen before. Willis O'Brien's animated dinosaurs were a revelation in 1925 and were O'Brien's best work besides *King Kong* (1933). Model maker Marcel Delgado worked with O'Brien on both *Lost World* and *King Kong*. Wallace Beery, Lewis Stone and Bessie Love were busy actors in dozens of silents and talkies. Love and Stone were each nominated for Oscars in subsequent years. Beery was nominated twice and won once. Beery had already played a caveman in Keaton's *The Three Ages* (1923) and almost looked like one in *The Lost World*, with his wild eyebrows and unkempt beard. Challenger is supposed to be irascible, but the script makes him almost irrational; he hates news reporters so much he attacks them on sight. Stone gives the best performance as an adventurer getting a little past his prime, who loses the girl to the younger and (frankly) lesser Malone.

The Ape-Man (Bull Montana) in *The Lost World* (1925).

The Apeman is very primitive with a simian face, big teeth, a nasty grimace and a powerful, hairy body. He leaps and climbs agilely. He is consistently hostile and drops a large rock on the explorers' camp almost as soon as he sees them. He lives in a cave with a chimpanzee; they seem to get along splendidly. The Apeman has no tools or weapons at all and his cave is completely bare of human accoutrements. There seems to be only one ape-person; nothing is said about how his kind reproduce. The film also has no interest in how the Apeman survives among hordes of dinosaurs; he's just there, an added peril for the heroes. At one point Roxton shoots the Apeman in the arm. He washes the wound with water and seems to ignore it, except possibly as a motive for revenge. As the explorers escape from the plateau down a long rope ladder, the Apeman begins hauling the ladder back up, with Malone still on it. Just as the Apeman is about to kill Malone Roxton shoots him in the chest. Malone escapes and the Apeman apparently dies. Roxton may have killed the last Apeman and destroyed their species, but the scene is intended to show Roxton's nobility, since Malone is his successful rival for Paula's affection. In Doyle's novel there was a whole tribe of apemen, who were wiped out by more advanced tribesmen and the explorers. The Apeman's costume and make-up were created by Cecil Holland. Bull Montana, a busy small-part actor in silents, had previously played an apeman in *Go and Get It* (1920), a comedy in which a gorilla is given a transplanted human brain.

Variety (Feb. 11, 1925) reports the running length of the picture as 104 minutes. The film was brutally cut to 63 minutes when sound came in. Even dinosaur footage was sacrificed. This was the length of all video versions, including the Lumivision DVD, until 2001, when a new, 93-minute DVD was assembled from several sources and released by Image Entertainment. The *Variety* reviewer in 1925 was enthusiastic about the whole film but of course he gave most of his attention to the dinosaurs, writing "no matter what the cost, either in labor or money, the results fully justify the expenditure." The review does not mention the Apeman. In the first major dinosaur movie, the big beasts stole the show from the lone caveman, just as they would in most subsequent dinosaur-caveman collaborations in films. Ref: Jones. *Illustrated Dinosaur Movie Guide*; Senn/Johnson. *Fantastic Cinema Subject Guide*; Berry. *Dinosaur Filmography*; MK 7. (Lost World)

[Two later versions of **The Lost World** (1960, starring Claude Rains; and 1992, starring John Rhys Davies) featured "native tribes" rather than prehistoric humans. Indeed, in the 1960 file the most important primitive character is referred to solely as "Native Girl."]

The Lost World (1998) [alt. *Sir Arthur Conan Doyle's The Lost World*] Canada; dir. Bob Keen; Fries Film Group/Trimark. 98 min.; color. Screenplay, Leopold St. Pierre, Jean Lafleur, based on novel by Arthur Conan Doyle; photography, Barry Gravelle; music, Milan Kymlicka. CAST: Patrick Bergin (*Prof. Challenger*); Jane Heitmeyer (*Amanda White*); Julian Casey (*Arthur Malone*); David Nerman (*John Roxton*); Michael Sinelnikoff (*Prof. Summerlee*); Georgiane Minot Payeur (*Djena*).

In 1934 Prof. Challenger leads an expedition to prove the existence of prehistoric life on a remote plateau in Mongolia. Besides dinosaurs, they find a stone house made by primitive men. Later a Neanderthal drugs Summerlee with a blowgun.

Mark F. Berry considers the 1998 film to be the worst version of *The Lost World* ever made, "plodding, depressing and at times purely silly." It even turned Roxton from a swashbucklering English sportsman to a churlish American villain. Sinelnikoff was in three versions of *The Lost World*, the 1998 and 1999 films and the 1999–2002 TV series. Ref: Berry. *Dinosaur Filmography*; *Internet Movie Database*; not viewed. (Lost World)

The Lost World (1999) Canada/Australia; dir. Richard Franklin; New Line/Village Roadshow. TV film; 93 min.; color. Screenplay, Jim Henshaw, Peter Mohan based on novel by Arthur Conan Doyle. CAST: Peter McCauley (*Prof. Challenger*); Rachel Blakeley (*Marguerite Krux*); William de Vry (*John Malone*); William Snow (*Sir John Roxton*); Jennifer O'Dell (*Veronica*); Michael Sinelnikoff (*Prof. Summerlee*); Laura Vazquez (*Assai*).

Once again Prof. Challenger leads an expedition which becomes stranded in an Amazonian plateau lost in time. Besides dinosaurs, they discover Veronica, the obligatory lightly-clad jungle girl, and two groups of natives—the reasonably friendly Zanga tribe and dangerous apemen. Arrogant Marguerite, a member of the expedition, turns out to be ruthless and treacherous.

Mark F. Berry calls this 1999 version "lightweight and forgettable," qualitatively in the middle of the three turn-of-the-century films of *The Lost World*, better than the 1998 Patrick Bergin film but inferior to the 2001 BBC TV miniseries with Bob Hoskins. Franklin's film led to a 1999–2002 TV series with the same cast. Ref: Berry. *Dinosaur Filmography*; *Internet Movie Database*; not viewed. (Lost World)

The Lost World (1999–2002) Canada/Australia/New Zealand; Coote Hayes Productions/St. Clare Entertainment/Telescene Film Group. TV series; 66 45-min. episodes; color. Based on novel by Arthur Conan Doyle; music, Garry McDonald, Lawrence Stone. CAST: Peter McCauley (*Prof. Challenger*); Rachel Blakeley (*Marguerite Krux*); David Orth (*Ned Malone*); William Snow (*Sir John Roxton*); Jennifer O'Dell (*Veronica*); Michael Sinelnikoff (*Prof. Summerlee*); Lara Cox (*Finn*); Jerome Ehlers (*Tribune*).

This series continues the adventures of the characters in the 1999 TV film by Richard Franklin, with the same cast except for Orth and Cox.

Marguerite remains unscrupulous, but is usually merely cynical and sarcastic rather than treacherous, to make her a viable character for the duration of the series. The series keeps the apemen from the TV film and adds lizard-men, an intelligent species who are half-human, half-dinosaur! The lizard-men and their leader Tribune were introduced in the series' first episode "More Than Human." They have a Roman-style civilization and use humans as slaves and gladiators. Ref: *Internet Movie Database*; *Lost World Official Site* (*www.lostworldtv.net*); not viewed. (Lost World)

The Lost World (2001) U.S.; dir., Stuart Orne; BBC/A&E. TV miniseries; 150 min.; color. Screenplay, Adrian Hodges, Tony Mulholland based on novel by Arthur Conan Doyle; photography, David Odd; music, Rob Lane. CAST: Bob Hoskins (*George Challenger*); James Fox (*Leo Summerlee*); Tom Ward (*Lord John Roxton*); Matthew Rhys (*Edward Malone*); Elaine Cassidy (*Agnes Clooney*); Peter Falk (*Rev. Kerr*); Nathaniel Lees (*Chief*); Robert Hardy (*Prof. Illingworth*); Malcolm Shields (*Lead Apeman*); Paul Joseph (*Apeman*); Jane Howie (*Apeman*); Mason West (*Apeman*); Julia Walshaw (*Apeman*).

Challenger and his expedition are stranded on an Amazonian plateau when a religious maniac (Falk) destroys a bridge which is their only escape route. Besides many dinosaurs, they meet an Indian tribe and savage apemen. When the apemen are captured and caged in the Indian village, they whip themselves into a noisy frenzy. Challenge realizes too late that they are summoning dinosaurs to attack the village! After escaping from the plateau, Challenger and the survivors return to London, where Challenger reluctantly gives up his chance for fame and denies finding anything, thus saving the dinosaurs, Indians and apemen from outsiders.

This miniseries is the longest version of the oft-filmed tale. Hoskins is a splendid, plebian Challenger. There is excellent waspish byplay between Challenger and Fox's stuffy scientist. In the conflict between the explorers and the Indians, the point of view of both sides is made clear. The dinosaurs are exceptionally well-done, by the makers of the *Walking with Dinosaurs* documentary series. Mark F. Berry considers the 2001 version to be not only the best of the three TV versions made 1998–2001, but also the best version ever, even preferable to the famous 1925 silent film. Ref: Berry. *Dinosaur Filmography*; *Internet Movie Database*; MK 7. (Lost World)

Lucille Love, The Girl of Mystery (1914) U.S.; dir. Francis Ford; Universal. Serial film; 15 2-reel chapters; b&w; silent. Screenplay, Grace Cunard, Francis Ford. CAST: Grace Cunard (*Lucille Love*); Francis Ford (*Loubeque/Hugo*); Harry Schumm (*Lt. Gibson*); John Ford.

Lucille Love travels the world, from the Wild West to remote jungles, to fight sinister spy Hugo, who has framed her fiancé for the theft of secret papers. In one adventure, Lucille is captured by tribesmen on a mysterious island. Escaping on an elephant, she plunges through the ground and lands in an underground realm of man-apes. The energetic Lucille rallies the missing links to attack the natives on the surface.

Lucille Love was one of many early, silent serial films to feature a plucky girl heroine; it came out the same year as *The Perils of Pauline*. The only two serial films to involve prehistoric humans were *Lucille Love*, one of the first serials, and *King of the Congo* (1952), one of the last. The leading lady and the leading man of *Lucille Love* co-wrote the serial; he directed it and played the villain. Rainey notes that *Lucille Love* "established Cunard and Ford as serial stars." John Ford, Francis Ford's brother and future director of classic Westerns, played at least one small part in the serial. Ref: Jones. *Illustrated Dinosaur Movie Guide*; Rainey. *Serials and Series*; not viewed. (Lost World)

Luggage of the Gods! (1983) U.S.; dir. David Kendall; General Films/Filmworld. 74 min.; color. Screenplay, David Kendall; photography, Steven Ross; music, Cengiz Yaltkaya. CAST: Mark Stolzenberg (*Yuk*); Gabriel Barre (*Tull*); Gwen Ellison (*Hubba*); Martin Haber (*Zoot*); Rochelle Robins (*Kono*); Lou Leccese (*Flon*); Dog Thomas (*Gum*); John Tarrant (*Whitaker*).

A tribe of cavemen lives quietly in a remote area of America. Clever little Yuk and big, slow-witted Tull are friendly rivals for the affections of shy Hubba. Ruled by stick-in-the-mud leaders, the cavemen bow to the ground whenever a plane flies overhead. One day a plane is forced to jettison its cargo, including a great deal of luggage and a crate of counterfeit artworks being transported by crooks Whitaker and Lionel.

Yuk and Tull find the luggage, which Yuk is sure was sent to them by the gods, but the leaders drive the two friends from the tribe for disturbing people. Living on their own with the luggage, they learn to enjoy modern clothes and even how to use binoculars and a radio. Whitaker and Lionel arrive to reclaim their fake art but Yuk gets hold of their gun and the crooks flee. Yuk and Tull are hailed as heroes for saving the tribe from the outsiders and the leaders allow everyone to use the luggage. The tribe learns "Build Me Up, Buttercup" from the radio and chants the pop song while performing primitive dances. Excited by pictures in a magazine, Yuk learns to read the crooks' map and departs for the outside world with Tull and Hubba.

COMMENTARY. It's nice to see a low-budget but non-exploitative independent film about cavemen, but *Luggage of the Gods!* is padded and does little with its premise. Compared to *Caveman* (1981) and Greg Martell's scences in *Dinosaurus!* (1960), David Kendall's comedy is seriously deficient in belly laughs. *Luggage* presents a compendium of caveman movie conventions, including walking stooped over, cave art, tribal dances, an invented language and a heroine with very clean, attractive hair. Stolzenberg is funny but looks too modern. Barre is much more primitive in appearance and behavior. *Variety* (June 15, 1983) dismissed the "slowly-paced ... uneventful" film, which "lacks the punch or invention" to compete with its better-budgeted rivals. The little-known comedy was clearly inspired by *The Gods Must Be Crazy* (1981), in which a coke bottle dropped from a plane causes concern among Kalahari tribesmen who know nothing of the outside world, and the cargo cults who worship Western cargoes in Papua New Guinea and the Pacific Islands. This was the first film for writer-director Kendall and most of his cast. Kendall has been a busy TV director and writer. A knowledgeable user's note on *Internet Movie Database* says that the performers were New York stage actors and the *Variety* review states that the film was made in New York City parks. Stolzenberg has written books on comedy, clowning and mime. Barre was nominated for a Tony in 1989. Ref: *Internet Movie Database*. MK:5 (Survivors)

Mad as a Mars Hare (1963) U.S.; dir. Chuck Jones, Maurice Noble; Warner Bros. Animated short film; 7 min.; color. Screenplay, John Dunn; music, Bill Lava. *VOICES:* Mel Blanc.

Bugs Bunny and megalomaniac Marvin Martian fight a small war on Mars. After many changes of fortune, Marvin shoots Bugs with an Acme Space-Time gun, which will send him forward into the future where he will be "a useful but harmless slave to me." Instead the blast turns Bugs into a Neanderthal-like cave rabbit. "I had the silly thing in reverse," Marvin muses. Ref: Jones. *Illustrated Dinosaur Movie Guide*; Beck/Friedwald. *Looney Tunes and Merrie Melodies*; not viewed. (Extraterrestrial)

Married to Murder (1990) *see* **The Laughter of God** (1990)

The Mighty Thunda (1952) *see* **King of the Congo** (1952)

The Missing Link (1927) U.S.; dir. Charles F. Reiser; Warner Bros. 71 min.; b&w; silent. Screenplay, Darryl F. Zanuck; photography, Dev Jennings. *CAST:* Syd Chaplin (*Arthur Wells*); Ruth Hiatt (*Beatrice Braden*); Tom Braden (*Col. Braden*); Crawford Kent (*Lord Dryden*); Sam Baker (*Missing Link*); Akka (*Chimpanzee*).

In this comedy, a timid poet (Chaplin) takes the place of a woman-hating big game hunter in an expedition to Africa to find the Missing Link. Although he initially mistakes the harmless chimp Akka for the Missing Link, he finally manages to rescue a girl and capture the real monster. Syd Chaplin was Charlie's brother. *Variety* (May 11, 1927) reported that Chaplin and the chimp were the only highlights in this jungle comedy, which had "plenty of laughs" between "slow moments." Ref: Jones. *Illustrated Dinosaur Movie Guide*; *American Film Institute: Feature Films, 1921–1930*; not viewed. (Survivors)

Mistress of the Apes (1981) U.S.; dir. Larry Buchanan; Cineworld/Buchanan Productions. 84 min.; color. Screenplay, Larry Buchanan; photography, Nicholas von Sternberg; music, Near Man (Group). *CAST:* Jennie Neumann (*Susan Jamison*); Barbara Leigh (*Laura*); Garth Pillsbury (*Paul Cory*); Walt Robin (*David*).

Scientist Susan Jamison detests the chauvinist male members of her expedition in Kenya. When they are killed, she decides to live with a Neanderthal tribe — who respect her! "She found fulfillment in the jungle — with an ape that walked like a man!"

This low-budget exploitation entry from the eccentric Buchanan was photographed by Josef von Sternberg's son. Make-up artists Rick Bottin and Greg Cannom went on to work in dozens of big and small films. In actuality, there never were Neanderthals in Kenya. Ref: Jones. *Illustrated Dinosaur Movie Guide*; *Internet Movie Database*; not viewed. (Survivors)

Monster on the Campus (1958) U.S.; dir. Jack Arnold; Universal International. 77 min.; b&w. Screenplay, David Duncan; photography, Russell Metty; stock music by Henry Mancini, Hans J. Salter and others. CAST: Arthur Franz (*Prof. Donald Blake*); Joanna Moore (*Madeline Howard*); Judson Platt (*Lt. Mark Stevens*); Nancy Walters (*Sylvia Lockwood*); Troy Donahue (*Jimmy Flanders*); Whit Bissell (*Dr. Cole*); Eddie Parker (*Prof. Blake as Monster*).

A scientist brings the preserved remains of a prehistoric fish from Madagascar to an American campus. A dog and a dragonfly who eat some of the fish become monsters and the professor himself becomes a Neanderthal throwback and commits murders.

Variety (Oct. 15, 1958) was pleased by this "pretty fair thriller," including the acting, the "logically developed" script and "constant suspense." Hardy's *Science Fiction*, however, calls it "perhaps the least interesting" of Arnold's SF films, which included *Creature from the Black Lagoon* (1954) and *The Incredible Shrinking Man* (1957). Joanna Moore was the mother of Tatum O'Neal. Ref: Jones. *Illustrated Dinosaur Movie Guide*; Senn/Johnson. *Fantastic Cinema Subject Guide*; Hardy. *Overlook Film Encyclopedia: Science Fiction*; Warren. *Keep Watching the Skies!*; not viewed. (Throwback)

Monsters of Dr. Frankenstein (1973) *see* **Frankenstein's Castle of Freaks** (1973)

My Science Project (1985) U.S.; dir. Jonathan Betuel; Touchstone. 94 min.; color. Screenplay, Jonathan Betuel; photography, David M. Walsh; music, Peter Bernstein, Bill Heller. CAST: John Stockwell (*Michael Harlan*); Danielle von Zerneck (*Ellie Sawyer*); Fisher Stevens (*Vince Latello*); Dennis Hopper (*Bob Roberts*); Raphael Sbarge (*Sherman*); Richard Masur (*Detective Nulty*); Hank Calia (*Neanderthal Man*).

Searching a military junkyard for his high school science project, a student finds a contraption which "breaks the barriers of space and time." The climax at the high school features a Neanderthal man, Cleopatra, Nazis, Godzilla, gladiators and a Tyrannosaurus Rex. One of three teenage SF comedies of 1985, together with *Real Genius* and *Weird Science*. *Variety* (Aug. 14, 1985) called the film "slight" but applauded Betuel's "brisk pace." Hardy (*Science Fiction*) liked the "engaging comedy" and especially Hopper's zany hippie science teacher. However, Mark F. Berry enjoyed little except the excellent dinosaur by effects veterans Doug Beswick and Rick Baker. Ref: Hardy. *Overlook Film Encyclopedia: Science Fiction*; Berry. *Dinosaur Filmography*; Jones. *Illustrated Dinosaur Movie Guide*; not viewed. (Timeshift)

The Neanderthal Man (1953) U.S.; dir. E.A. DuPont; Global Productions. 77 min.; b&w. Screenplay, Aubrey Wisberg, Jack Pollexfen; photography, Stanley Cortez; music, Albert Glasser. CAST: Robert Shayne (*Prof. Clifford Groves*); Richard Crane (*Dr. Ross Harkness*); Doris Merrick (*Ruth Marshall*); Joyce Terry (*Jan Groves*); Beverly Garland (*Nola*).

In the mountains of California, Prof. Groves, stung by his fellow naturalists' rejection of his theories about early man, experiments by injecting his cat and his housekeeper with a serum which causes them to regress to their prehistoric antecedents, a sabre-toothed tiger and an ape-woman. He injects himself, becomes a Neanderthal, goes on a rampage and is killed by the tiger.

Perhaps no film has expressed the horror and contempt too many people feel about primitive man as much as *Neanderthal Man*. Groves, the misguided scientist, takes the view that ancient man was highly advanced. He denounces "modern man's boasting pride in his alleged superiority" and his "artificial culture" and says "Man is not himself. He's part of every ancestor he's ever had.... Man has lost nothing of his emotions from the dawn of history." Groves shows skeptical scientists drawings of the skulls of a chimpanzee and several hominids and claims that even Java Man was much smarter than chimps. (Unfortunately his lineup includes the fraudulent Piltdown Man, a forgery which was exposed in 1953, the year *Neanderthal Man* was made.) Groves claims that Neanderthals with their large brains must have been as intelligent as modern humans. The other scientists say that brain size does not relate to "quality of intelligence."

Of course this touches on a real debate. Brain size does correlate to intelligence and Neanderthal brains were fairly close to ours in size. On the other hand Neanderthal brains were probably wired differently than ours; there must have been a physiological reason why they didn't invent the technology that anatomically-modern prehistoric humans developed. The film insists that Groves' respect for ancient man is an absurd mistake. When Groves becomes a Neanderthal he is a savage killer with a (completely inaccurate) apelike face and long claws. "All my basic animal instincts were enlarged and enflamed.... I gloried in my strength and ferocity. Modern man was completely subordinated, leaving only the hungry urge to kill," Groves writes in his lab notes. A witness describes him as "a gorilla covered with hair, the spittle running from his mouth." Compare *Altered States* (1980), a much more sophisticated film about a scientist who rather enjoys regressing to a savage primitive.

The film gives Neanderthal Man high marks for incredible strength. In his primitive form Groves kills two men and a dog and kidnaps and rapes (offscreen) a girl played by future cult star Beverly Garland. She even says he dragged her by the hair. At the end the reasonable young scientist Harkness concludes "the terrible things he did, all of us are capable of doing when we give way to the baseness which is part of every one of us." Groves with his sympathetic view of early man becomes just another mad scientist who meddles in things best left alone.

DuPont's career went back to German silents but he could do little with this clichéd, *Jekyll/Hyde* rip-off, except highlight the beautiful mountain setting, the colorful rustics and Cortez's sharp b&w photography. The unambitious film never even had a *Variety* review. Ref: Jones. *Illustrated Dinosaur Movie Guide*; Senn/Johnson. *Fantastic Cinema Subject Guide*; Hardy. *Overlook Film Encyclopedia: Science Fiction*; MK 3. (Throwback)

Un Nueva Criatura (1971) Spain; dir. Francisco G. Siurano; Herga Films. 12 min.; color. Screenplay, Francisco G. Siurano; photography, Ricardo Albinana; music, Federico Martinez Tudó. CAST: Alexis; Beatriz Valdés.

In this short film an apeman and a little girl tour a zoo. Ref: Jones. *Illustrated Dinosaur Movie Guide*; *Internet Movie Database*; not viewed. (Fantasy)

Ogu and Mampato in Rapa Nui (2002) Chile; dir. Alejandro Rojas; Cineanimadores. Animated film; 80 min.; color. Screenplay, Daniel Turkieltaub based on comic book by Themo Lobos.

Mampato, a Chilean boy with a time-travel belt, and his caveman friend Ogu visit Rapa Nui (Easter Island) in ancient times and learn about old customs. A children's film with an educational agenda, based on a comic book. Ref: *Internet Movie Database*; not viewed. (Timeshift)

On the Town (1949) U.S.; dir. Gene Kelly, Stanley Donen; MGM. 98 min.; color. Screenplay, Adolph Green, Betty Comden; photography, Harold Rosson; music, Roger Edens, Leonard Bernstein. CAST: Gene Kelly (*Gabey*); Frank Sinatra (*Chip*); Betty Garrett (*Brunhilde Esterhazy*); Ann Miller (*Claire Huddesen*); Jules Munshin (*Ozzie*); Vera-Ellen (*Ivy Smith*).

The Neanderthal Man called itself "Adult Entertainment" in 1953.

Three sailors enjoy shore leave in New York. A lady anthropologist (Miller) falls for a sailor (Munshin) who appears to be a caveman throwback, inspiring the "Prehistoric Man" dance scene. Like the much inferior *At Long Last Love* (1975), this musical is included in this list because of a single number. *On the Town* is one of the most popular and critically respected classic musicals. The vivacious Miller may be unlikely casting for an anthropologist but *Variety* (Dec. 7, 1949) said that the "Prehistoric Man" dance, set among the dinosaur skeletons of a museum, was "a funfest and free-for-all for the leads." Ref: Jones. *Illustrated Dinosaur Movie Guide*; Berry. *Dinosaur Filmography*; MK 8. (Throwback)

One Million Heels B.C. (1993) U.S.; American Independent Producers. Feature film; color. CAST: Michelle Bauer (*Cavegirl*). A modern girl finds a cavegirl in her backyard. They take a lot of showers. Bauer, the star of this exploitation comedy, has had a long career in similar B-films. Ref: *Internet Movie Database*; not viewed. (Timeshift)

Panico en el Transiberiano (1972) *see* **Horror Express** (1972)

Pathfinders to Venus (1961) U.K.; dir. Guy Verney, Reginald Collin; ABC. TV miniseries; 8 30-min. episodes; b&w. Screenplay, Terence Hulke, Eric Paice. CAST: Stewart Guidotti (*Geoffrey Wedgwood*); Gerald Flood (*Conway Henderson*); Pamela Barney (*Prof. Mary Meadows*); George Coulouris (*Harcourt Brown*); Graydon Gould (*Capt. Wilson*).

A British spaceship is sent to Venus to rescue a stranded American astronaut. The explorers encounter primitive apemen, carnivorous plants, pterodactyls and a volcanic eruption. They are rescued by a Russian spaceship.

Pathfinders to Venus was the third of three children's SF miniseries, after *Pathfinders in Space* (1960) and *Pathfinders to Mars* (1960–61). With its low-budget sets and special effects, ABC's *Pathfinders* series was a precursor to the BBC's *Dr. Who* (1963–89). Writers Hulke and Paice went on to write for *The Avengers* (1961–69); Hulke wrote for *Dr. Who*. Ref: Jones. *Illustrated Dinosaur Movie Guide*; Fulton/Betancourt. *Sci-Fi Channel Encyclopedia of TV Science Fiction*; not viewed. (Extraterrestrial)

Pekin Genjin (1997) *see* **Peking Man** (1997)

Peking Man (1997) [alt. *Pekin Genjin*] Japan; dir. Junya Sato; Toei. 114 min.; color. Screenplay, Akira Hayasaka. CAST: Hirotaro Honda (*Takashi*); Naoto Ogata (*Sakura*).

In 1929 the bones of Peking Man are found in Northern China. In 1941 the Japanese raid an American museum in Peking but find the Americans have removed the prized relics. In 1998 (the near future when the film was released) a Japanese salvage ship manages to recover the bones from an American ship sunk during the war. In 2001 Japan launches its first manned space shuttle. Two young biologists (identified in the English language version only as Mr. Sakura and Miss Takei) accompany an astronaut into space with a secret mission.

The biologists prepare three DNA samples from Peking Man, which will be exposed to special nutrients and zero gravity in orbit to "revive the dormant DNA." The mission is commanded from the ground by Osone, imperious head of Japan's Life Science Laboratory, who tells his cringing subordinates that if he can revive an extinct human species "I'll be God." Osone has another team working in Siberia which has already created a full-size mammoth from prehistoric DNA! The cells fed by the Peking Man DNA on the spaceship multiply rapidly, but after a meteor strikes the spaceship the "baby shuttle" containing the culture separates from the main ship and heads for Earth.

Sakura and Miss Takei return to Earth and hurry to the small island near Okinawa where the shuttle landed. They find footprints leading away from the shuttle. Soon they find three stocky, naked, hairy hominids, an adult male, an adult female and a male juvenile, who are almost mute but have great strength and a form of extrasensory perception. The biologists strip almost naked to try to win the trust of the prehistoric people. The adult male hominid attacks the scientists with a huge rock he handles as easily as a baseball, but at the last moment he spares their lives. They are beginning to make friends when Osone orders them by radio to anaesthetize the primitives and bring them to the lab for study.

In the Academy's vivarium the biologists, who name the adult male Takashi, the female Hanako and the boy Kenji, are eager to study the unique specimens. Takashi and Hanako grab red shirts from Osone personnel and pile them around a rock, making a shrine to which they pray. Takashi tries to have sex with Miss Takei. After she is rescued Osone asks the shocked young woman to have intercourse with Takashi, to see if they are the same "genus" and can produce a child. (Actually, individuals must be of the same species to reproduce, and Peking Man was not the same species as modern man.) Miss Takei is horrified and refuses.

Publicity-mad Osone demands that the scientists train the hominids as athletes, for "a Superman show." Meanwhile, a scientist from China's Biotechnology Institute and Meimei, a Chinese woman reporter working in Japan, decide they should return the new Peking Man people to China because "They're Chinese, like us." An American institute tries to bribe Sakura to hand the hominids over to them.

At a track meet, Takashi and Hanako outperform all the modern athletes but fail at their events (the javelin and the high jump) due to their indiscipline and lack of interest. Meimei kidnaps Kenji (keeping him happy with candy) and Takashi races from the stadium and across the city in pursuit. The Chinese make friends with Takashi; when the Japanese police catch up with the fugitives Takashi hurls them all over a theater.

After the Chinese conspirators smuggle Takashi and Kenji to China, Osone puts the inconsolable Hanako in a machine which makes her memories of prehistoric life visible on a screen. They see a red mountain resembling the impromptu shrine the hominids built in the vivarium. The process causes Hanako to fall ill; modern medicine cannot help her because of her different physiology. To save her, Sakura and Miss Takei steal Hanako from the lab and fly her to China.

While visiting the Great Wall of China, Takashi and Kenji sense at a great distance the mammoth at the Osone facility in Siberia. They excitedly doff their clothes and race off across the steppes, leaving behind all their pursuers except the athletic Meimei. At the same time the mammoth senses the hominids, crashes out of his enclosure and races south, pursued by two Osone employees in a van. At the border, Chinese guards are astounded when the mammoth smashes through their barrier. The shaken guards stop the Osone vehicle. "You have no passport!" "Did the mammoth have a passport?"

Even in an airplane, Hanako can sense where Takashi and Kenji are. She directs Sakura and Takei, who land their plane, steal a vehicle and head into the steppes near where the remains of Peking Man were found decades before. Hanako, Takashi and Kenji are joyfully reunited, just as the mammoth arrives. They mount the mammoth and ride off to the red mountain (seen in Osone's memory machine), as Sakura, Miss Takei and Meimei bid them farewell.

COMMENTARY: *Peking Man* is full of the heartfelt, somewhat naive idealism typical of Japanese science fiction. In both 1941 and 2001 China, Japan and America fight over Peking Man as a prize. In the end, even the fervently nationalistic Meimei realizes that "When they were alive, there were no nations" and that the Peking Man belongs to no one. The vainglorious Osone and his American and Chinese counterparts are defeated and the heroes realize that the prehistoric people can "hear the earth's heartbeat" in ways modern humans can

This poster shows Takashi the revived Peking Man (Hirotaro Honda) and his family aboard a mammoth in Japan's *Peking Man*.

never do. *Peking Man*'s anti-nationalistic theme is clearest in the glorious scene when the mammoth storms through the border barrier.

The film is very well-produced and never cheap-looking, except for the obviously computer-generated mammoth. Even the spaceship scenes are excellent, with the three actors floating weightlessly around the shuttle without visible wires. The first third of the film, as the prehistoric people are created, lost and found, is suspenseful; the middle third, is charming and heart-warming. The finale is a bit predictable and overdone ("Run! Run to freedom!") but still moving.

Hanako's breasts are visible throughout much of the film, as are Miss Takei's for a few scenes. This completely casual nudity and the near-rape scene may have hurt the film's chances in America, where distributors may have felt that it was too racy for children but would have little appeal to adults. Both those objections are wrong, but *Peking Man* has had no theatrical or video release in the U.S.

There are several interesting and moving scenes involving the primitive people. When the scientists first see Takashi, he is fishing with his hands, using ESP to find the fish. Sakura watches in wonder as Takashi patiently teaches his son to make stone tools. When a fire breaks out in a theatre, Takashi's first thought is to save the boy Kenji.

By far the best element in the film are the three primitive people. Their bodies look strong enough to make their displays of superstrength believable. All three of them are likeable, but Hirotaro Honda's Takashi is the best. He always maintains his confidence and dignity, no matter what the more intelligent modern humans do. He is often frustrated by the modern world but never frightened by it. He performs his superfeats almost effortlessly; he runs faster than trained athletes, does Tarzan leaps over cars, climbs a building, fights several men at once and opens handcuffs at will. Takashi is strong, brave, compassionate and gentle — an ideal man. Meimei admiringly tells him, "You're so strong you don't know tears." He is never aggressive but he is an overwhelming fighter when he thinks he or his family are being threatened. Honda's Takashi is almost as marvelous a creation as Greg Martell's Neanderthal Man in *Dinosaurus!* (1960).

The most disturbing scene occurs in the vivarium when Takashi casually begins to remove Miss Takei's clothes. Clearly, Takashi has no concept of rape and is surprised when Miss Takei resists and becomes hysterical. Osone says "They don't have sex for love, but to preserve their species." For once, Osone is partly right. Takashi does love his family and does not love Miss Takei, but he assumes that she would be willing to have sex with him, not out of lust but for enjoyment and perhaps procreation. The fact that Takashi knew that his mate Hanako would not object to his making love to Miss Takei shows that the prehistoric people's attitudes toward sex are far different from ours.

A scientist in the film mentions that Peking Man's brain was 1078 cc, while the average modern human brain is 1350 cc. This implies that Peking Man was about 80 percent as intelligent as modern man, and that is how the primitives in *Peking Man* are played. In fact, Peking Man was a specimen of Homo Erectus, and was certainly not almost as smart as modern humans. The filmmakers did not want their hero to be too stupid, so they raised his intelligence to about the level of Greg Martell's Neanderthal in *Dinosaurus!*—or Rocky Balboa in *Rocky* (1976). This makes him just smart enough to be attractive. (As Kathleen Turner said in *Body Heat* (1981), "You're not too bright, are you? I like that in a man.") Takashi's hair even makes him look a little like Moe Howard of the Three Stooges, another of the most popular half-wits in films.

Takashi is always curious about his strange new surroundings, though never very impressed by them. He is always resilient and hopeful. He is intelligent enough to solve some of the challenges the modern humans throw at him. When the scientists use supersonic waves to try to control him, he finds and destroys the speaker boxes from which the waves come. In the end, the modern heroes discover that the prehistoric people have at least one word—"upar" for friend.

Peking Man was the last film by Junya Sato, who made 34 films from 1973 to 1997, including two which became well-known internationally, *The Go Masters* (1982) and *Silk Road* (1988). Hirotaro Honda, a veteran character actor, was 46 when he played Takashi. Ref: *Internet Movie Database*; MK 8. (Revived)

The People That Time Forgot (1977) U.K.; dir. Kevin Connor; Amicus/American International Pictures. 90 min.; color. Screenplay,

(III) The People That Time Forgot

Patrick Tilley, based on novel by Edgar Rice Burroughs; photography, Alan Hume; music, John Scott. CAST: Patrick Wayne (*Ben McBride*); Doug McClure (*Bowen Tyler*); Sarah Douglas (*Charly*); Dana Gillespie (*Ajor*); Thorley Walters (*Norfolk*); Shane Rimmer (*Hogan*); Tony Britton (*Capt. Lawton*); John Hallam (*Chang-Sha*); David Prowse (*Executioner*); Milton Reid (*Sabbala*); Kiran Shah.

In 1919 an expedition goes to Antarctic waters to find the crew missing since the events of *The Land That Time Forgot* (1975). Their plane is attacked by a pterodactyl and forced to land on the island of Caprona, where only Bowen Tyler survives from the first film. Aided by Ajor, a primitive girl befriended by Tyler, the explorers must deal with dinosaurs, aggressive tribesmen and a volcanic eruption.

In *The Land That Time Forgot*, all the primitive people are hostile and dangerous except for one individual, the docile caveman Ahm. During the interval between the stories told in the two films, Tyler and Lisa, the survivors at the end of *Land That Time Forgot*, worked to civilize the most advanced tribe they knew of, the Galu. They advanced the Galu "from the Stone Age to the Iron Age" but their interference only led to catastrophe. The top tribe of Caprona turned out to be the Nagas, who decided that the advances introduced by Tyler might make the Galu a dangerous enemy. The Nagas wiped out most of the Galu, except for Ajor and a pair of Galu men who are killed by the Bandu tribe in *People That Time Forgot*.

Lisa was so disgusted with the Nagas that she refused to cooperate with their plans; they sacrificed her to their volcano god. Interestingly the Nagas didn't get rid of the allegedly stout-hearted Tyler; they kept him a prisoner, apparently hoping to convince him to share his knowledge of advanced technology. The Nagas are civilized, not prehistoric at all. They ride horses, fight with swords, have samurai-style armor, helmets, banners and masks, make their headquarters in a walled fortress complete with dungeons and refer to Ajor as "that creature." Tyler appears to be almost as arrogant; he seems to be more concerned about "two years' work destroyed" by the Nagas than about the slaughter of the Galu, for which he was partly responsible. It's an interesting coincidence that two arrogant Americans who run roughshod over primitive societies, Taylor in *Planet of the Apes* (1968) and Tyler in the two Amicus Burroughs films, share almost the same name.

Caprona's prehistoric people are represented only by Ajor and by a few scenes in which the two doomed Galu men and the Bandu are briefly seen. The Bandu have more realistic fur clothing and hide shields than the tribes in *Land That Time Forgot* and use spears and bows and arrows. They stake out prisoners to be eaten by a large dinosaur — a sensible way to keep the dinosaur happy. Ajor has little to do. When the modern people first meet her, Lady Charlotte ("Charly") mocks the American Ben by calling Ajor "A genuine cavegirl. Should suit you perfectly."

While the ethnology of Caprona in *Land That Time Forgot* was too complicated and confusing, the situation in *People That Time Forgot* is too simple. Ajor and Tyler explain hurriedly what happened in the three years since the first film, then the film settles down to a straight fight between the two civilized groups, the modern outsiders and the medieval Nagas. All the civilized people are pretty rough

Sabbala (character actor Milton Reid) threatens cavegirl Ajor (Dana Gillespie) in *The People That Time Forgot*.

customers in this film. The aristocratic English girl (Douglas) packs a gun and even the comic-relief bumbling professor sidekick, played by loveable Thorley Walters, has a sword hidden in his innocent-looking walking stick. Tyler is killed, along with many of the Nagas, giving a measure of justice to the slaughtered Galu. Caprona is ravaged by a volcanic eruption, making it unclear whether any of the natives survive. Ajor, last of the Galu, escapes but must leave Caprona forever. Her character is further treated with disrespect by an abrupt romantic relationship with American sidekick Hogan, who is twice her age and whom she doesn't even meet until the end of the film. He promises to take her to Nebraska, which the British screenwriter apparently thought was like Caprona without the volcanoes and dinosaurs.

The big scene which Amicus hoped would sell *People That Time Forgot*, the dogfight between a pterodactyl and a World War I-era biplane with a machine gun, occurs early in the film. *Variety* (June 22, 1977) felt the "fast-paced adventure-fantasy" with "clever special effects" was "a natural for juve [juvenile] audiences" but most critics and fans agree with Mark F. Berry (*Dinosaur Filmography*) who found it inferior to *The Land That Time Forgot* in special effects, script and acting (especially by wooden Wayne).

David Prowse was Darth Vader in *Star Wars* the same year he played a tribal executioner in this film. Character actor Milton Reid played menacing ethnic types in dozens of British films; his role as the brutish Naga leader Sabbala was an unusually big part for him. The well-endowed Dana Gillespie, unlike the Hammer cavegirls, was given English dialogue to speak. She was hailed as a new sex symbol for her work in *The People That Time Forgot* but her part as a gloomy cavegirl whose friends were already dead and who muttered about the invincible volcano god did Gillespie no favors and her subsequent career was insignificant.

Amicus made the film in the Canary Islands, on La Palma, a more lush environment than the volcanic islands of Lanzarote and Tenerife where Hammer made *One Million Years B.C.* (1966) and *When Dinosaurs Ruled the Earth* (1970). Amicus planned a third Burroughs/Caprona film, a sequel to be called *Out of Time's Abyss*, but it was never made. Ref: Jones. *Illustrated Dinosaur Movie Guide*; Berry. *Dinosaur Filmography*; MK 4. (Lost World)

The Phantom Empire (1986) U.S.; dir. Fred Olen Ray; American Independent Productions. 83 min.; color. Screenplay, Fred Olen Ray, T.L. Lankford; photography, photography, Gary Graver; music, Robert Garrett. CAST: Ross Hagen (*Cort Eastman*); Jeffrey Combs (*Andrew Paris*); Dawn Wildsmith (*Eddy Colchilde*); Robert Quarry (*Prof. Strock*); Michelle Bauer (*Cave Bunny*); Sybil Danning (*Queen of R'ylia*); Russ Tamblyn (*Bill*).

An underground expedition seeks the lost civilization of R'ylia. The explorers discover an all-female colony of cave people and are menaced by dinosaurs, cannibals, robots and the ruthless Queen of R'ylia, an alien stranded on Earth. The heroes are repeatedly rescued by a girl they call "Cave Bunny."

Incorrigible director Ray made this B-movie in six days on a negligible budget with borrowed dinosaur footage (from *Planet of the Dinosaurs*, 1978). *Video Watchdog* (Feb. 2003) said "For all its abundant flaws, *The Phantom Empire* still manages to be reasonably enjoyable." Mark F. Berry found it tedious but did enjoy some of the film's in-jokes and the cast. Wildsmith, who plays the tough-talking heroine, was Ray's wife. Quarry, Tamblyn, Danning and Bauer were familiar B-movie veterans. The queen's robot was a copy of Robby the Robot from *Forbidden Planet* (1956).

Films about fictitious prehistoric civilizations such as Atlantis are excluded from this list. Hence the absence of the delirious 1935 Gene Autry serial film *The Phantom Empire*, from which Ray's film borrowed its title and premise. The serial film has an Atlantis-style ancient underground civilization, invaded by cowboys, but no primitives. Ray's film is included because "Cave Bunny" is identified as a cavegirl. Ref: Berry. *Dinosaur Filmography*; Jones. *Illustrated Dinosaur Movie Guide*; not viewed. (Lost World)

The Pit (1983) [alt. *Teddy*] Canada; dir. Lew Lehman; New World. 96 min.; color. Screenplay, Ian A. Stuart; photography, Fred Guthe. CAST: Sammy Snyders (*Jamie Benjamin*); Jeannie Elias (*Sandra*); Laura Hollingsworth (*Marg Livingstone*).

Preoccupied by sex, 12-year-old Jamie reads adult girlie magazines and plays Peeping Tom. Schoolmates and neighbors shun him. He discovers four small furry creatures he calls "trogs" in a pit in the forest. At the suggestion of his teddy bear, who can speak to him, Jamie feeds his tormentors to the hungry trogs. The police destroy the creatures but an epilogue provides an ominous ending.

Variety (May 23, 1984) called *The Pit* an "unsuccessful horror film that fails to adequately develop a very interesting (and rarely explored) genre premise: precocious child sexuality." *Variety* reviewer "Lor" felt that the film's horror and supernatural elements undermined the serious theme about a persecuted boy who turns on his community. He concluded, "Monster suits design is unusual, but unconvincing." Senn/Johnson write "Though they are talked of as being primitive humanoids, missing links, etc, the appearance of these troglodytes is a little off the usual caveman look with their large snouts full of big teeth and their big eyes and shaggy bodies." Ref: Senn/Johnson. *Fantastic Cinema Subject Guide*; not viewed. (Survivors)

The Prehistoric Man (1908) U.K.; dir. Walter R. Booth; Urban Trading Co. Part-animated short film; 300 feet; b&w; silent.

Gifford's *British Animated Films* quotes a 1908 periodical which reports that the trick film shows an artist who draws "a conventional prehistoric ogre of forbidding aspect and threatening demeanor, armed with a prehistoric stone hammer." The prehistoric man comes to life and walks off the drawing sheet into the artist's world. He follows the artist around causing "innumerable calamities" (or as many as could be shown in 300 feet of film) until the artist has the bright idea of drawing a "prehistoric animal," which also comes to life and swallows the prehistoric man. The artist destroys the canvas on which the creatures were drawn, getting rid of the animal (presumably a dinosaur) in the process. Ref: Gifford. *British Animated Films*; Gifford. *British Film Catalogue*; Jones. *Illustrated Dinosaur Movie Guide*; Berry. *Dinosaur Filmography*; not viewed. (Revived)

Prehistoric Man (1911) U.K.; H. O. Martinek; British & Colonial. Short film; 370 feet; b&w; silent. In this comedy, a "man dressed as cave man for pageant is mistaken for real one" according to Gifford. (In Britain a "pageant" is a costume play.) Ref: Gifford. *British Film Catalogue*; not viewed. (Fake)

Pre-Hysterical Man (1948) U.S.; dir. Seymour Kneitel; Famous/Paramount. Animated short film; 8 min.; color. Screenplay, Carl Meyer, Jack Mercer; music, Winston Sharples. VOICES: Jack Mercer (*Popeye*); Mae Questel (*Olive Oyl*).

In Yellowstone Park, Olive Oyl falls into a deep hole, where she meets a dinosaur and a caveman. The caveman, who wants a woman, saves Olive from the dinosaur. When Popeye arrives, the caveman defeats him and feeds him to the dinosaur — but Popeye of course has his spinach.

Mercer and Questel were the familiar voices of Popeye and Olive in hundreds of *Popeye* short cartoons. Ref: Webb. *Animated Film Encyclopedia*; *Internet Movie Database*; not viewed. (Lost World)

Prisoners of the Lost Universe (1983) U.S.; dir. Terry Marcel; Marcel-Robertson/Showtime. TV film; 94 min.; color. Screenplay, Terry Marcel, Harry Robertson; photography, Derek V. Browne; music, Harry Robertson. CAST: Richard Hatch (*Dan*); Kay Lenz (*Carrie*); John Saxon (*Kleel*); Ray Charleson (*Greenman*); Philip Van der Byl (*Manbeast*); Myles Robertson (*Waterbeast*).

Three modern people are swept into a parallel universe, where the masses are tyrannized by a warlord. The synopsis in *Internet Movie Database* mentions "tribes of savage cavemen" and a user's comment notes "the pygmies with light-up eyes were definitely original." Ref: *Internet Movie Database*; not viewed. (Extraterestrial)

Quatermass and the Pit (1958–59) UK; dir. Rudolph Cartier; BBC. TV series; 6 35-min. episodes; b&w. Screenplay, Nigel Kneale; music, Trevor Duncan. CAST: André Morell (*Prof. Quatermass*); Christine Finn (*Barbara Judd*); Cec Linder (*Dr. Matthew Roney*); Anthony Bushell (*Col. Breen*); John Stratton (*Capt. Potter*); Michael Ripper (*Sergeant*). The screenplay tells the same story as the film *Quatermass and the Pit* (1967), but at greater length. Nigel Kneale wrote the three legendary *Quatermass* series for the BBC, beginning with *The Quatermass Experiment* (1953) and *Quatermass II* (1955). All three were remade as feature films by Hammer Films, first *The Quatermass Xperiment* (1955) and *Quatermass II: Enemy from Space* (1957), followed by the long-delayed *Quatermass and the Pit* (1967). The production of all three series and all three films were worthy of the intelligence of Kneale's scripts. Fulton and Betancourt believe that, of the several actors who portrayed him, Morell was the "definitive" Quatermass. Episodes: "The Halfman," "The Ghosts," "Imps and Demons," "The Enchanted," "The Wild Hunt," "Hob." Ref: Fulton/Betancourt. *The Sci-Fi Channel Encyclopedia of TV Science Fiction*; not viewed. (Relic)

Quatermass and the Pit (1967) [alt. *Five Million Years to Earth*] U.K.; dir. Roy Ward Baker; Hammer. 97 min.; color. Screenplay, Nigel Kneale; photography, Arthur Grant; music, Tristram Cary. CAST: Andrew Keir (*Prof. Bernard Quatermass*); James Donald (*Dr. Matthew Roney*); Barbara Shelley (*Barbara Judd*); Julian Glover (*Col. Breen*); Duncan Lamont (*Sladden*); Bryan Marshall (*Capt. Potter*).

Dr. Roney (James Donald) exhibits his reconstruction of an unexpectedly advanced prehistoric man in *Quatermass and the Pit* (1967).

Workers digging an Underground (subway) tunnel discover several strange skeletons beneath Hob's Lane (which could mean "Devil's Lane") in London. Scientists Dr. Roney and Barbara Judd determine they are ape-men who lived 5,000,000 years ago and had much bigger skulls than they should have had at that time. Also found is a large, almost impenetrable cylinder, which arrogant Col. Breen insists is a German World War II missile. Eccentric government expert Quatermass studies old records and finds that hauntings and other "devilish" happenings have been reported in the area for centuries.

When the cylinder finally opens, the investigators find the remains of insect-like beings. Quatermass believes that the cylinder is a crashed spaceship and the insects are Martians who kidnapped very early hominids, took them to Mars and through surgery and selective breeding gave them enhanced intelligence and Martian instincts. Barbara is especially sensitive to the influence of the spaceship. She has a "racial memory" of a hideous "race purge" of Martians millions of years ago. Quatermass concludes that the Martians massacred mutated individuals and instilled the same survival instinct in all humans. The Martians have died out but as Barbara says "We're the Martians now."

The government unwisely allows the press into the excavation site. Many people, including Quatermass, become zombie-like and impelled to destroy anyone different from themselves. They use psychokinetic energy to attack people who are less affected. Breen is killed. Chaos spreads across London. A huge white insect figure, which looks like a horned devil, appears, created by transformation of "mass into energy." Roney, who is unaffected, recalls that iron has traditionally been used to fight the Devil, and that iron can ground and dissipate energy. Roney rams a construction crane into the insect-devil figure, destroying it and killing himself. Barbara, Quatermass and other affected people return to normal.

COMMENTARY. "You realize what you're implying. That we owe our human condition to the intervention of insects." Thus does a government official react to Quatermass's theory of Martian control of the evolution of early man. Refusal to believe the shocking idea of insect dominance of Earth leads the government to open the site of the Martian ship to a large crowd, thus creating the conditions for an epidemic spread of revived Martian influence. Kneale seems to be saying that we must face the truth about our possibly unpleasant origins if we wish to avoid falling unnecessarily back into the chaos of the past. At the same time Kneale finds wisdom in the human past. Pre-modern people knew better than we do how to fight evil, even if it took the form of insect-devils from Mars. The clue to defeating the influence of the long-dead Martians comes from records about ghosts and demons dating back to the Middle Ages. Ancient man survived the Martians; medieval and early modern people kept them at bay; only modern man is so arrogant that he has forgotten the danger.

The film's major assets are Kneale's intelligent and audacious script, a fine cast, plenty of suspense and truly unnerving depictions of mass violence (on a modest budget) both in Barbara's televised "memories" of an ancient Martian massacre, and in the chaos among humans at the end of the tale. Despite all this, Hardy (*Science Fiction*) disparages the film and asserts that the much longer 1959 TV version was "definitive version" of Kneale's story. Hardy especially deplores Baker's "limp" direction and the film's "glossy production values," as if something cheaper would have been preferable. I found nothing about the serviceable direction which detracted from the script, the cast or the suspense. No doubt the TV series, which I have not seen, fully deserves its legendary status, but the film was probably the best non-horror movie Hammer ever made and a fitting conclusion to the Quatermass series. *Quatermass and the Pit* influenced the many *Dr. Who* stories about prehistoric aliens who affected the development of mankind. It forms an interesting companion with another British film about alien influence on early man, Kubrick's *2001: A Space Odyssey*. The late 1960s were certainly a boom period for very diverse British cinematic depictions of prehistory, with *One Million Years B.C.* (1966), *Quatermass and the Pit* (1967) and *2001* (1968).

Leonard Maltin and *Variety* (Jan. 31, 1968) were both much more impressed by the 1967 film than Hardy, although *Variety* noted "routine, somewhat distended development." James Donald specialized in upper class and intellectual types and is best known in the U.S. for playing the ineffectual British commander in *The Great Escape* (1963). Andrew Keir frequently played authority figures in British films, often for Hammer. Barbara Shelley, who is convincing both as a smart scientist and a possessed insect-person, was also busy in Hammer and other films. Ref: Hardy. *Overlook Film Encyclopedia: Science Fiction*; *Internet Movie Database*; MK 8. (Relic)

Reason and Emotion (1943) U.S.; dir. Bill Roberts; Disney. Animated short film; 8 min.; color. Inside a child's brain, Emotion (depicted as a caveman) gives the orders and the child hurts himself. Reason (an egghead) arrives and takes over as the child grows up. Inside the adult's brain, Emotion is still a petulant child, while Reason is in charge — most of the time. Emotion says "I want to live dangerously." When the man sees a pretty girl, Emotion takes over ("Aw, they like the rough stuff!") and results in the man getting slapped. In the war, Emotion is panicked by wild war rumors. The film also shows that Hitler uses Emotion rather than Reason to control people. In the mind of a German, Hitler appeals to fear, sympathy and hate and Emotion enslaves Reason. The short concludes that Reason and Emotion are both needed and must work together in life and in the war effort.

Top Disney animators Ward Kimball and Ollie Johnston worked on this wartime short. Director Bill Roberts worked as animator or sequence director on many of Disney's major cartoon features. *Reason and Emotion* was nominated for an Oscar for Best Short Cartoon. Ref: Smith. *Disney A to Z*; *Internet Movie Database*; MK 8. (Fantasy)

Return of the Ape Man (1944) U.S.; dir. Phil Rosen; Monogram. 60 or 68 min.; b&w. Screenplay, Robert Charles; photography, Marcel Le Picard. CAST: Bela Lugosi (*Prof. Dexter*); John Carradine (*Prof. Gilmore*); Frank Moran (*Ape Man*); Judith Gibson (*Anne*); Michael Ames (*Steve*).

Lugosi and Carradine are scientists who find a frozen prehistoric man in the Arctic and revive him. Lugosi decides the creature needs a modern brain. "Some people's brains would never be missed," he muses. With his new brain, the caveman actually learns to play the piano, but of course he soon goes on a rampage. In the climax Lugosi, armed with a blowtorch, fights the apeman. Both die.

Return of the Ape Man was not a sequel to *The Ape Man* (1943), in which Lugosi finds himself turning into a gorilla. Both were from Monogram, one of the humblest of the Poverty Row studios. Veteran horror actor George Zucco is credited as the Ape Man but did not

Dexter (Bela Lugosi) tries cajolery with the Ape Man (Frank Moran) in *Return of the Ape Man*. It doesn't work.

appear in the film. *Variety* (July 26, 1944) considered the film "average" for a double bill. Hardy finds it "delightfully absurd." Ref: Hardy. *The Overlook Film Encyclopedia: Horror*; not viewed. (Revived)

Rocky Jones, Space Ranger (1954) Episode, *Blast-Off*. U.S.; dir. Hollingsworth Morse; Roland Reed productions. 3-part episode of syndicated TV series; 3 × 25 min.; b&w. Screenplay, Arthur Hoerl, Marianne Mosner. CAST: Richard Crane (*Rocky Jones*); Robert Lyden (*Bobby*); Walter Coy (*Toro*); Donna Martell (*Moanna*); Don Megowan (*Poli*); Paul Marion (*Zakar*); Maurice Cass (*Prof. Newton*); Peter Orwitz (*Orak*); Charles Stevens (*Shaman*).

In the 21st Century, Space Ranger Rocky Jones protects the United Planets against evildoers. In the 3-part episode *Blast-Off*, Rocky and cadet Bobby crash-land on a small planetoid in our solar system, shared by two primitive tribes. Toro, the statesmanlike leader of the Valley People, and his daughter Moanna worship Rocky as a god, the "All-High," who landed on the planet centuries before and taught the natives to live in peace. Zakar, leader of the Hill People, believes the All-High never existed and that Rocky is an invader intent on enslaving the planet's inhabitants. To repair his ship, Rocky invents a forge and teaches the natives how to use it. Bobby teaches the giant Poli to play a flute. Zakar unleashes two landslides to destroy first Rocky's ship, then a rescue ship sent to save the stranded men. When Moanna is poisoned by a deadly flower and Zakar is injured, Prof. Newton, a doctor on the rescue ship, saves their lives with modern medicine. Moanna shows the Rangers the ship of the All-High, apparently an alien from an unknown planet. With difficulty, the Rangers repair the ancient spaceship and depart. Zakar and Moanna join in marriage and lead their peoples into peace.

COMMENTARY. The primitive people on this apparently nameless planetoid seem to be very dependent on outsiders for any progress they make. The All-High teaches them to be peaceable and the Rangers teach them medicine, music and metalworking. Ref: Lucanio/Coville. *American Science Fiction Television Series of the 1950s*; Morton. *Complete Directory to Science Fiction, Fantasy and Horror Television Series*; not viewed. (Extraterrestrial)

Rod Brown of the Rocket Rangers (1953–54) Episode *The Stone Men of Venus* (1954). U.S.; CBS TV. Episode of TV series; 25 min.; b&w. CAST: Cliff Robertson (*Ranger Rod Brown*). In episode 38 of this juvenile space opera series, *The Stone Men of Venus*, "a petrified figure of a prehistoric Venusian is stolen from an interplanetary museum and held for ransom." Ref: Morton. *Complete Directory to Science Fiction, Fantasy and Horror Television Series*; not viewed. (Extraterrestrial)

Run for the Hills (1953) U.S.; dir. Lew Landers; Jack Broder Productions. 72 min.; b&w. Screenplay, Richard Straubb, Leonard Neubauer. CAST: Sonny Tufts (*Charley Johnson*); Barbara Payton (*Jane Johnson*); George Sanders (*TV Commentator*); Rosemary Colligan (*Cave Girl*).

An insurance salesman becomes so concerned about nuclear war that he moves his family into a cave. According to the *Variety* (July 8, 1953) review, Payton wears a leopard skin, suggesting a return to the cave people of prehistory. Colligan's "Cave Girl" is a minor character, 15th in the credits, and was probably a modern rustic. *Variety* said the film was "asinine," dull and "overlong at 72 minutes." Ref: Nash. *Motion Picture Guide*; *Internet Movie Database*; not viewed. (Fake)

Schlock! (1973) [alt. *The Banana Monster*] U.S.; dir. John Landis; Harris Enterprises/ Gazotskie Enterprises. 79 min.; color. Screenplay, John Landis; photography, Robert E. Collins; music, David Gibson. CAST: John Landis (*Schlockthropus*); Saul Kahan (*Sgt. Wino*); E.G. Harty (*Prof. Shlibovitz*); Eliza Garrett (*Mindy Binerman*); Eric Allison (*Joe Putzman*); Forrest J. Ackerman (*Man in Cinema*); Donald F. Glut (*Movie Patron*); John Chambers (*National Guard officer*).

At a suburban California playground, an obnoxious reporter covers an incompetent police investigation of the latest massacre by the Banana Killer, who has killed 789 (!) people in three weeks. Four teenagers find a cave full of blood, bones and bananas and idiotically decide to explore it; two survive. A scientist theorizes that a "shlockthropus" has revived after being frozen for 20,000,000 (!) years. Schlock falls in love with blind girl Mindy, who thinks he's a dog! After many incidents Schlock kidnaps Mindy at a high school dance. She is rescued and Schlock is shot by the police and troops. As he dies he reaches out for Mindy.

Landis was 21 and makeup artist Rick Baker was 20 when they made this ultra-low-budget comedy for $61,000 in 1971. It was not released for two years. Much of *Schlock* was inspired by other films, both classic and obscure. Landis was disgusted by the incompetent *Trog* (1970) and decided to use the same premise for a comedy. He quoted one of the few good scenes in *Trog*, in which a photographer takes a picture of Trog and the apeman kills him with a rock. In Landis' film a reporter tries to interview Schlock, who tears his arm off. *Schlock* also borrows from *2001* and *King Kong*. The blind girl is a salute to the blind hermit in *Bride of Frankenstein* and perhaps to the blind white girl who falls in love with Sidney Poitier without knowing he is black in *A Patch of Blue* (1965). A scene with Schlock and a little girl at a duck pond is another quote from *Bride of Frankenstein*. At a theatre Schlock is more terrified than the blasé human audience by scenes from *The Blob* (1958) and *Dinosaurus!* (1960). Schlock tears a car apart, in a scene which recalls *Big Business* (1929), with Laurel and Hardy. Landis may also have seen *Eegah!*, which has much the same story as *Schlock*.

Landis went on to become one of the top comedy directors of the 1970s and '80s. Rick Baker won six of the first eighteen Oscars for makeup. Many of the cast were friends and relatives of Landis and Baker. John Chambers, who plays the National Guard officer, was a makeup artist on *Planet of the Apes* (1968).

Landis had planned on using a deliberately "bad" ape suit until he met Baker, who was already producing excellent work, and decided to use a good character costume and mask. Baker's mask permitted an expressive performance; Schlock could register love, fear, anger, exasperation and confusion. His face is completely apelike and not at all human; the result is an extremely expressive ape. In his comments on the *Schlock* DVD Landis said he considers the suit and mask "subtle" because they look "schlocky" like a real B-movie ape suit but they also work as character makeup. The suit became more ratty as the film went through its 16-day production. The inconsistencies in the condition of the suit from scene to scene form another "schlocky" in-joke. Landis had

The Schlockthropus has only one thing on his mind in *Schlock.*

not intended to play Schlock himself but actors wanted too much money for the job. Landis is probably the only person ever to direct a film while wearing a gorilla suit.

Schlock is smarter than most of the idiotic human characters. In many scenes humans simply ignore Schlock even though he is a gorilla and the town is supposedly being terrorized by the Banana Killer. At the theater, Schlock even takes a little boy to the restroom. As the movie progresses, Schlock becomes more human and more sympathetic.

Variety (March 28, 1973) was amused by this "77 minutes of imaginative fun that probably will intrigue the young." Hardy (*Science Fiction*) calls *Schlock* "the most successful creature-feature spoof of the seventies." Landis' film won the Golden Asteroid prize at the 1973 Trieste Festival of Science Fiction Films. Ref: Hardy. *Overlook Film Encyclopedia: Science Fiction*; MK 7. (Revived)

Scooby's All-Star Laff-a-Lympics (1978–80) Component series *Captain Caveman and the Teen Angels*. [alt. *Scooby's All-Stars*; *Scooby's Laff-a-Lympics*] U.S.; Hanna-Barbera. Segment of animated TV series; 8-min. episodes; color. Music, Hoyt Curtin. *VOICES:* Mel Blanc (*Captain Caveman*); Marilyn Schreffler (*Brenda Chance*); Vernee Watson (*Dee Dee Sykes*); Laurel Page (*Taffy Dare*).

One *Captain Caveman* cartoon was shown in each episode of this anthology series, which had three other component cartoons. Captain Caveman was thawed out in the modern world after millions of years frozen in ice. Armed with a magic "club of tricks" and various superpowers, he teamed up for superhero adventures with three teenage girls, who spoof *Charlie's Angels*. The hero, known to his friends as "Cavey," also received dubious help from Cave Bird, the series' obligatory wacky animal sidekick. The first 16 episodes (through "Playing Footsie with Big Foot") were repeated in the stand-alone series *Captain Caveman and the Teen Angels* (1980), followed by eight original episodes. Cavey also appeared in *The and The Flintstones Comedy Show* (1980–82); see Part I. Episodes: "The Kooky Case of the Cryptic Keys," "The Mixed Up Mystery of Deadman's Reef," "What a Flight for a Fight," "The Creepy Case of the Creaky Charter Boat," "Big Scare in the Big Top," "Double Dribble Riddle," "The Crazy Case of the Tell-Tale Tape," "The Creepy Claw Caper," "Cavey and the Kabula Clue," "Cavey and the Weirdo Wolfman," "The Disappearing Elephant Mystery," "The Fur Freight Fright," "Ride 'Em Caveman," "The Strange Case of the Creature from Space," "The Mystery Mansion Mix-Up," "Playing Footsie with Big Foot," "Disco Cavey," "Muscle-Bound Cavey," "Cavey's Crazy Car Caper," "Cavey's Mexicali 500," "Wild West Cavey," "Cavey's Winter Carnival Caper," "Cavey's Fashion Fiasco," "Cavey's Missing Missile Mystery." Ref: Lenburg. *Encyclopedia of Animated Cartoons*; Erickson. *Television Cartoon Series*; not viewed. (Revived)

The She-Creature (1956) U.S.; dir. Edward L. Cahn; Golden State Productions/American International Pictures. 77 min.; b&w. Screenplay, Lou Rusoff; photography, Frederick E. West; music, Ronald Stein. *CAST:* Chester Morris (*Dr. Carlo Lombardi*); Marla English (*Andrea*); Tom Conway (*Timothy Chappel*); Cathy Downs (*Dorothy Chappel*); Lance Fuller (*Dr. Ted Erickson*); Frieda Inescourt (*Mrs. Chappel*); Paul Blaisdell (*The She-Creature*); Ron Randell (*Lt. James*); El Brendel (*Olaf the Butler*).

A hypnotist can summon up a prehistoric sea monster from the evolutionary past of his lovely assistant. He uses the creature to commit murders (which he predicts, boosting his business as a psychic) but the monster finally turns on him.

The murderous anthropomorphic monster has scales, long blonde hair and huge breasts (though played by a male stuntman). *Variety* (Sept. 5, 1956) gave only a brief review of "this shoddy material" with a "disjointed, haphazard" script. Hardy (*Horror*) is also dismissive, and notes that the (unacknowledged) remake *Creature of Destruction* (1967) was even worse. Ref: Senn/Johnson. *Fantastic Cinema Subject Guide*. Hardy. *Overlook Film Encyclopedia: Horror*; not viewed. (Throwback)

Sinbad and the Eye of the Tiger (1977) U.K.; dir. Sam Wanamaker; Columbia. 112 min.; color. Screenplay, Beverley Cross; photography, Ted Moore; music, Roy Budd. *CAST:* Patrick Wayne (*Sinbad*); Taryn Power (*Dione*); Jane Seymour (*Farah*); Margaret Whiting (*Zenobia*); Patrick Troughton (*Melanthius*); Kurt Christian (*Rafi*); Nadim Sawalha (*Hassan*); Damien Thomas (*Prince Kassim*); Peter Mayhew (*Minoton*).

The evil sorceress Zenobia (a gloriously scenery-chewing performance by Whiting) curses Prince Kassim, turning him into a baboon, so her son Rafi can become Caliph. Sinbad and Kassim's sister Farah (together with Sinbad's long-suffering crew, whose lives Sinbad always seems willing to sacrifice to solve his girlfriend's problems) voyage to find a miraculous cure before the curse becomes permanent. Zenobia and Rafi pursue them, armed with the Minoton, a giant mechanical warrior. Sinbad's party gains the help of wise magician Melanthius and his daughter Dione. Marvels include fighting skeletons, Zenobia turning herself into a seagull, a giant wasp, an Arctic fight with a giant walrus, a giant primitive man ("Trog" the Troglodyte) and a sabre-toothed tiger. In a climactic battle the tiger kills Trog and Sinbad manages to kill the tiger.

Ray Harryhausen's Trog the troglodyte prepares to fight in *Sinbad and the Eye of the Tiger*.

The last and least of Roy Harryhausen's three *Arabian Nights* films, after *The Seventh Voyage of Sinbad* (1958) and *The Golden Voyage of Sinbad* (1974), *Eye of the Tiger* had a limp script but a good cast, except for Patrick (son of John) Wayne and Taryn (daughter of Tyrone) Power. Harryhausen's creatures are as splendid as usual; the most fascinating is the big walrus. Trog is a huge, hairy creature with a fur costume and a horn in his forehead. Melanthius helpfully identifies him as "one of man's ancestors" and adds "they have no idea of language but these primates were known for their gentleness with the female of the species." Sure enough, mute, slow-witted Trog soon becomes devoted to Dione. For a while we expect a fight between the Minoton and Trog but the Minoton is unexpectedly destroyed in an accident. Trog makes himself useful by recognizing an image drawn by Melanthius and leading Sinbad's party to their destination, then opening a giant door and finally by fighting the tiger and dying to save the heroes. The primitive giant was at first supposed to be played by an actor but was finally created as a special effect. In his autobiography *Ray Harryhausen: An Animated Life* (2004), Harryhausen recalled that he decided that "a character based on a real cave dweller would be ideal. However, to enable him to be kinetically suitable for a fantasy adventure, I designed him to be much bigger than a real troglodyte would have been, and as an additional touch gave him a horn in his forehead making him look aggressive, even though he was a bit of a softy."

Harryhausen described in his book how carefully he worked on Trog's reaction shots. "This 'animated passivity' is extremely time-consuming, but the end result, especially in the case of Trog, was well worth the effort. I have always been dismayed that few critics, or indeed fans, ever mention the animation of Trog. To me he represented some of the most detailed character movements I have ever achieved." Trog is the only prehistoric human created by Harryhausen, except for a miniature of Raquel Welch he made for the pterosaur scene in *One Million Years B.C.* and a Neanderthal made for the abortive documentary project *Evolution* (1940–41).

In a largely dismissive review, *Variety* (May 25, 1977) noted "the care taken with the effects shows despite the overall corniness of the film." Ref: Nash. *Motion Picture Guide*; Harryhausen/Dalton. *Ray Harryhausen*; MK 5. (Survivors)

Sir Arthur Conan Doyle's The Lost World (1998) *see* **The Lost World** (1998)

Skullduggery (1970) U.S.; dir. Gordon Douglas; Universal. 105 min.; color. Screenplay, Nelson Gidding, based on novel *Les Animaux*

Denitures by Vercors; photography, Robert Moreno; music, Oliver Nelson. CAST: Burt Reynolds (*Douglas Temple*); Susan Clark (*Dr. Sybil Greame*); Roger C. Carmel (*Otto Kreps*); Paul Hubschmid (*Vancruysen*); Chips Rafferty (*Pop Dillingham*); Alexander Knox (*Buffington*); Edward Fox (*Bruce Spofford*); Wilfrid Hyde-White (*Eaton*); William Marshall (*Attorney General*); Rhys Williams (*Judge Draper*); Pat Suzuki (*Topazia*).

Rogues Reynolds and Carmel join anthropologist Clark's expedition into the interior of New Guinea, hoping to find minerals. Instead they find the Tropis, short, furry, friendly humanoids with nearly human intelligence. The explorers, especially missionary Rafferty, begin to think the Tropis are human. Native Papuans eat Tropis, a sinister mine-owner wants to breed them as submissive laborers, and a Rhodesian racist (Hyde-Whyte in an atypical villainous role) wants to use them as evidence that black people are subhuman. Tropi female Topazia has a baby with Carmel. In the end a trial is held to decide if the Tropis have human rights.

Both *Variety* (March 18, 1970) and critic-turned-director Joe Dante, in a 1970 review reprinted in *Video Watchdog* 98 (August 2003), felt the film went off in too many directions. Dante said *Skullduggery* "at times seems like a spoof of jungle movies, while at others leans toward dramatic satire on the nature of man." The *Variety* reviewer said the production "lacks consistent sense of what it is about, where it is going." In particular, *Variety* complained that the stars played the film too "light-heartedly" for the serious issues about the definition of humanity which it attempted to raise. Dante enjoyed Carmel's and Hyde-Whyte's performances and said the Tropis, played by 24 students from the University of Jakarta, are "the film's one major success." In particular he called Suzuki's performance as Topazia, the principal Tropi character, "nothing short of marvelous." *Variety* on the other hand said that the Tropis were excessively ape-like and should have been more human. However one feels about the acting, the Tropis were perhaps the most adorable primitive humans ever filmed. The film seemed to want to say more about the exploitation of modern third-world peoples than the nature of prehistoric humans. *Skullduggery* was a failure with both audiences and critics. Novelist Vercors had his name removed from the film. Ref: Nash. *Motion Picture Guide*; Jones. *Illustrated Dinosaur Movie Guide*; MK 4 (Survivors).

A typically adorable Tropi in *Skullduggery*.

The Slime People (1963) U.S.; dir. Robert Hutton; Joseph Robertson Productions/Hansen Enterprises. 60 or 76 min.; b&w. Screenplay, Blair Robertson, Vance Skarstedt; photography, William G. Troiano; music, Lou Foman. CAST: Robert Hutton (*Tom Gregory*); Les Tremayne (*Norman Tolliver*); Robert Burton (*Prof. Galvin*); Judee Morton (*Bonnie Galbraith*); Susan Hart (*Lisa Galbraith*); William Boyce (*Cal Johnson*); John Close; Jock Putnam (*Slime Person*).

Nuclear testing awakens underworld prehistoric humanoids in Los Angeles. They form a "fog dome" over the city, raising temperatures. A few humans discover how to defeat them.

1963 was pretty late for a b&w SF B-film about a monstrous invasion. Even *Variety* failed to review *The Slime People*. The fog produced by the invaders was useful in disguising the cheapness of the special effects. Nash (*Motion Picture Guide*), Hardy (*Science Fiction*) and Maltin (*Movie & Video Guide*) all agree the film, the only one directed by actor Hutton, was trivial. Maltin says it "talks itself to death." Ref: Nash. *Motion Picture Guide*; Hardy. *Overlook Film Encyclopedia: Science Fiction*; not viewed. (Revived)

Space Ghost and Dino Boy (1966–68) U.S.; Hanna-Barbera/ CBS. Animated TV series; 18 25-min. episodes; color. *CAST:* Johnny Carson [not the talk show host] (*Tod, the Dino Boy*); Mike Road (*Ugh*); Don Messick (*Bronto*).

Tod, a modern boy, parachutes from a disabled plane and finds himself in a prehistoric world. Riding his pet dinosaur Bronto and aided by his friend the caveman Ugh, Tod becomes Dino Boy and confronts villains such as Treemen, Worm People, Ant Warriors, Wolf People, the Mighty Snow People, the High Priest of the Sun People, the Rock Pygmies and the Bird Riders.

One *Dino Boy* episode and two *Space Ghost* segments were shown in each show. *Space Ghost* continued in a new show in 1976; *Dino Boy* was less successful and was never revived. The series had a remarkable collection of prehistoric humanoid and human groups, mostly villainous. Many were named in the episode titles. Episodes: "The Sacrifice," "The Treemen," "Marooned," "The Worm People," "The Moss Men," "The Rock Pygmies," "Giant Ants," "The Fire God," "Danger River," "The Vampire Men," "The Wolf People," "Valley of the Giants," "The Bird Riders," "The Marksman," "The Terrible Chase," "The Mighty Snow Creature," "The Spear Warriors," "The Ant Warriors." Ref: Lenburg. *Encyclopedia of Animated Cartoons*; Woolery. *Children's Television*; Erickson. *Television Cartoon Shows*; not viewed. (Lost World)

Space Invasion from Lapland (1960) *see* **Invasion of the Animal People** (1960)

Space: 1999 (1975–77) episode *The Full Circle* (1975) U.K.; dir. Bob Kellett; ITC/Group Three/Gerry Anderson Productions. 50 min.; color. Screenplay, Jesse Lasky Jr., Pat Silver; music, Barry Gray. *CAST:* Martin Landau (*John Koenig*); Barbara Bain (*Dr. Helena Russell*); Oliver Cotton (*Spearman*); Zienia Merton (*Sandra*).

In the series, Earth's moon (!) is blown out of orbit and flies through space with the hapless human passengers of Moonbase Alpha. In the episode *The Full Circle* a ship launched from Alpha to explore a misty planet called Retha returns with the crew missing; the only occupant is a dead caveman. An Alphan search party descends to the planet to search for the missing crew. Sandra is kidnapped by cavemen. The leader of the cavemen looks like Koenig, the captain of the Alpha. Eventually it turns out that the Alphans were turned into their Cro-Magnon equivalents. The spacemen reflect that human motivations have changed very little over time.

The expensive series was made by veteran British producer Gerry Anderson for the U.S. market. Every week American stars Landau and Bain were supported by British guest players, such as Cotton in this episode. The series was in syndication in America but lasted only two seasons and 48 episodes, of which *The Full Circle* was the fifteenth. Critics were dismissive but the series has its fan cult, like every other TV SF show. Ref: Morton. *Complete Directory to Science Fiction, Fantasy and Horror Television Series*; Fulton/Betancourt. *Sci-Fi Channel of TV Science Fiction*; not viewed. (Extraterrestrial)

Space: 1999 (1975–77) Episode *Missing Link* (1976) U.K.; dir. Ray Austin; ITC/Group Three/Gerry Anderson Productions. 50 min.; color. Screenplay, Edward di Lorenzo. *CAST:* Martin Landau (*John Koenig*); Peter Cushing (*Raan*); Joanna Dunham (*Vana*).

Koenig is transported through space to the planet Zenno, where he is studied by an anthropologist who believes that humans are the missing links who led to his superior species. Ref: Morton. *Complete Directory to Science Fiction, Fantasy and Horror Television Series*; Fulton/Betancourt. *Sci-Fi Channel of TV Science Fiction*; not viewed. (Extraterrestrial)

Space Patrol (1950–55) Episode, *The Primitive Men of Planet X* (1953) U.S.; dir. Dick Darley; Mike Moser Productions. Episode of TV series; 25 min.; b&w. Screenplay, Norman Jolley. *CAST:* Edward Kemmer (*Commander Buzz Corry*); Bela Kovacs (*Prince Baccarratti*).

Space Patrol was one of the most long-lasting of the juvenile space opera TV series of the early 1950s. When Planet X wanders into our solar system, its ruler, cunning Prince Baccarratti, becomes a persistent nemesis of Space Patrol Commander Buzz Corry. The fourth (1953-54) season introduced multi-episode stories, with each episode ending in a cliffhanger. Episodes 139–153 told of Corry's adventures on Planet X. In episode 142, *The Primitive Men of Planet X*, Buzz flees from the planet's dinosaurs and takes refuge in a cave, where he is menaced by a race of "half-humans."

Ref: Lucanio/Coville. *American Science Fiction Television Series of the 1950s*; Morton. *Complete Directory to Science Fiction, Fantasy and Horror Television Series*; not viewed. (Extraterrestrial)

Spacejacked (1997) U.S.; dir. Jeremiah Cullinane; Concorde-New Horizons. 89 min.; color. Screenplay, Brendan Broderick, Daniella Purcell. CAST: Corbin Bernsen (*Barnes*); Amanda Pays (*Dawn*); Brian Monaghan (*VR Caveman*).

A space cruise ship is hijacked. This low-budget SF film, which received few if any reviews, very few users' comments and a very low user rating on *Internet Movie Database*, included a virtual reality caveman, called "VR Caveman" in the credits. Ref: *Internet Movie Database*; not viewed. (Virtual)

Starcrash (1979) [alt. *The Adventures of Stella Star*] Italy; dir. Luigi Cozzi (as Lewis Coates); Columbia/AIP/Film Enterprise. 91 min.; color. Screenplay, Luigi Cozzi, Nat Wachsberger; photography, Paul Beeson, Robert D'Ettore; music, John Barry. CAST: Marjoe Gartner (*Akton*); Caroline Munro (*Stella Star*); Christopher Plummer (*Emperor of the Galaxy*); Joe Spinnell (*Count Zarth Arn*); David Hasselhoff (*Simon*); Robert Tessier (*Thor*); Nadia Cassini (*Queen of the Amazons*); Judd Hamilton (*Elle*).

Space pilot and smuggler Stella Star (sic!) is recruited by the Emperor of the Galaxy to defeat evil Count Zarth Arn. Her enemies include an army of Amazons, a giant robot and a horde of shambling, grunting cavemen. The cavemen are in the film for only a few minutes, have three fight scenes and destroy a robot with primitive clubs. Their sudden appearance in the midst of a film full of spaceships, robots and ray guns is an effective surprise. The primitive men are aligned with the villains, who have advanced technology. A few minutes after the cavemen appear their planet is blown up by their villainous allies.

Variety (March 28, 1979) berated the film for its script, direction, photography and special effects. Hardy (*Science Fiction*) more accurately called the "lunatic" feature with its scantily-clad heroine and cheap special effects a "blatant" rip-off of both *Barbarella* (1967) and *Star Wars* (1977), but noted its "breakneck direction and serial-like action are surprisingly appealing." Plummer has lines like "I wouldn't be Emperor if I didn't have a few powers. Halt the flow of Time!" Ref: Hardy. *Overlook Film Encyclopedia: Science Fiction*; MK 7. (Extraterrestrial)

Stargate SG-1 (1997–) Episode no. 5, *The Broca Divide* (1997) U.S./Canada; dir. William Gereghty; Gekko Film/Kawoosh Productions/Showtime. episode in TV series; 45 min.; color. Screenplay, Jonathan Glassner. CAST: Richard Dean Anderson (*Col. Jack O'Neill*); Amanda Topping (*Capt. Samantha Carter*); Michael Shanks (*Dr. Daniel Jackson*).

A team of military-scientific explorers go through a time-space portal to new worlds. In the fifth episode of the first season, *The Broca Divide*, they discover a planet divided between a light and dark side. The bright side is populated by the Untouched, a Bronze Age people. The dark side has the Touched, who are animalistic primitives. Most of the Stargate team and men at their Earth base become infected and begin to act like the brutish Touched. Ref: *Internet Movie Database*; not viewed. (Extraterrestrial)

Starlost (1973–74) episode no. 2, *Lazarus from the Mist* (1973). Canada; dir. Leo Orenstein; CTV. Episode of TV series; 50 min.; color. Screenplay, Douglas Hall, Don Wallace. CAST: Keir Dullea (*Devon*); Frank Converse (*Dr. Gerald Aaron*); Alan Bleviss (*Dweller*); Mel Tuck (*Dweller*).

In this unsuccessful, 16-episode SF series, a few people discover that their community is actually inside a dome on board a spaceship, the *Ark*, carrying the only survivors of mankind. The ship will crash into a star unless the few passengers who accept this reality can prevent it. Harlan Ellison created the series but became disenchanted and had his name taken off the credits.

In the second episode, the heroes revive a frozen scientist who may be able to help them but they are "threatened by a tribe of savage cavemen," according to Philips/ Garcia. Morton calls the villains "mutants." Ref: Philips/Garcia. *Science Fiction Television Series*; Morton. *The Complete Directory to Science Fiction, Fantasy and Horror Television Series*; not viewed. (Extraterrestrial)

Stig of the Dump (1981) U.K.; dir. Richard Handford; Thames TV/Independent TV. TV miniseries; 10 25-min. episodes; color. Screenplay, Maggie Wadey, based on novel by Clive

King; music, Paul Lewis. *CAST:* Keith Jayne (*Stig*); Grant Ashley Warnock (*Barney*); Kenneth Gilbert (*Chief*); Nigel Patterson (*Tribesman*).

Young Barney discovers a teenaged caveman living in a garbage dump. The two boys have adventures together. This miniseries was sufficiently well-remembered to inspire a remake in 2002. Ref: *Internet Movie Database*; not viewed. (Survivors)

Stig of the Dump (2002) U.K.; dir. John Hay; Childsplay/BBC. TV miniseries; 5 36-min. episodes; color. Screenplay, Peter Tabern, based on novel by Clive King; photography, Graham Frake; music, Debbie Wiseman. *CAST:* Thomas Sangster (*Barney*); Robert Tannion (*Stig*); Geoffrey Palmer (*Robert Tollworth*); Phyllida Law (*Marjorie Tollworth*); Saskia Wickham (*Caroline*); Julian Curry (*Museum Guide*).

A remake of the popular 1981 miniseries, about a modern boy who finds a teenage caveman. This version had a few famous adult actors and won an International Emmy. Ref: *Internet Movie Database*; not viewed. (Survivors)

Stingray (1963–65) Episode, *The Cool Cave Man* (1965). U.K.; dir. Alan Pattillo; AP Films/ATV/ITC. Episode of puppet TV series; 25 min.; color. Screenplay, Gerry Anderson, Sylvia Anderson; music, Berry Gray. *VOICES:* Don Mason (*Troy Tempest*); Robert Easton (*Phones*); Lois Maxwell (*Atlanta*).

Stingray was the Andersons' third "Supermarionation" puppet TV series and the first in color. The World Aquanaut Security Patrol (WASP) patrols the undersea world in 2065. *The Cool Cave Man* (the 18th of 39 episodes) featured a concept so outrageous even the Andersons did not present it as a "real" story. Capt. Tempest dreams of a battle with "underwater cavemen" (!) who steal a dangerous radioactive isotope from a sunken freighter. Fulton and Betancourt recall the series' "visual invention, imaginative flair, characterization and continuity of detail." Lois Maxwell was Moneypenny in the early, classic James Bond films. Ref: Fulton/Betancourt. *Sci-Fi Channel Encyclopedia of TV Science Fiction*; Jones. *Illustrated Dinosaur Movie Guide*; not viewed.(Fantasy)

Stone Age Romeos (1955) U.S.; dir. Jules White; Columbia. 16 min.; b&w. Screenplay, Felix Adler; photography, Ira Morgan. *CAST:* Moe Howard (*Moe*); Larry Fine (*Larry*); Shemp Howard (*Shemp*); Emil Sitka (*B. Bopper, Curator*); Dee Green (*Baggie*); Nancy Saunders (*Maggie*); Virginia Hunter (*Aggie*); Joe Palma, Cy Schindell, Bill Wallace (*Cavemen*).

A museum offers a reward for proof that cavemen still exist. The Three Stooges fake footage of themselves as cavemen (using footage from *I'm a Monkey's Uncle* (1948), also directed by White). Lenburg, Maurer and Lenburg (*Three Stooges Scrapbook*) rate this short a three on a scale of one to four. 1955 was the year of Shemp Howard's death, but new Stooges shorts starring him were released into 1956. [In *Outer Space Jitters* (1957), one of the last Stooges shorts, the boys go to Venus. Jones (*Illustrated Dinosaur Movie Guide*) says that the Venusian character played by Dan Blocker (later of *Gunsmoke*) was a "prehistoric caveman." *Internet Movie Database* calls him a "prehistoric goon." But Lenburg, Maurer and Lenburg simply call Blocker's character "a brawny-looking zombie called Goon" and say the Venusian villains planned to turn the Stooges into Goons, which seems to disassociate Goons from cavemen.] Ref: Lenburg/Maurer/Lenburg. *The Three Stooges Scrapbook*; Jones. *Illustrated Dinosaur Movie Guide*; *Internet Movie Database*; not viewed. (Fake)

The Stoneman (2004) U.S.; dir. Ewing Miles Brown; Cori Movie Ventures. Feature film; color. Screenplay, J. Neal; photography, Richard Bennett; music, John Hajewski. *CAST:* Pat Morita (*Prof. Stevens*); Christopher Atkins (*Kip Hollings*); Robin Riker (*Dr. Anna Weston*); Ron Masak (*Lt. J.D. Hill*); Bernie Kopell (*Prof. Milano*); Steve Henneberry (*The Stoneman*).

According to *Internet Movie Database*, this B film was made in 2002. It was still being offered for sale in the 2004 American Film Market, when *Variety* (Feb. 23, 2004, AFM supplement, p. 38) said that in the film "a Stone Age man discovered in the jungle terrorizes Los Angeles." Steve Henneberry played the strongman Tower on *American Gladiators* (1991–94). Ref: *Internet Movie Database*; not viewed. (Survivors)

Superbeast (1972) Philippines/U.S.; dir. George Schenk; United Artists/A&S. 90 min.; color. Screenplay, George Schenk; photography, Nonong Rasca; music, Richard LaSalle. *CAST:* Antoinette Bower (*Dr. Alix Pardee*);

Craig Littler (*Dr. Bill Fleming*); Harry Lauter (*Stewart Victor*); Richard Santos (*Benny, Experimental Subject*).

In the Filipino jungle, prisoners are handed over to an American doctor (Lauter) whose experiments change them into Neanderthal-like throwbacks. Expert riflemen hunt the primitive creatures, in scenes reminiscent of *The Most Dangerous Game* (1932). A woman doctor (Bower) is marked for death when she discovers the horrors, but she manages to give the villain a dose of his own serum, turning him into the "Superbeast."

Variety (Oct. 4, 1972) felt that the stars gave only "standard" performances, but Jones (*Illustrated Dinosaur Movie Guide*) liked the villainous performance by Lauter, a veteran of dozens of 1950s B films. Jones also admired makeup effects by John Chambers. *Variety* liked LaSalle's score and the film's "exquisite scenery" and felt Schenk "manages to insert plenty of atmosphere in the proceedings and injects enough suspense to sustain interest." Filmed back-to-back with *Daughters of Satan*; the two films were released as one of the last double features. Ref: Jones. *Illustrated Dinosaur Movie Guide*; not viewed. (Throwback)

The Tale of Tsar Saltan (1966) U.S.S.R.; dir. Aleksandr Ptushko; Ivanov-Vano Animation Studio/Mosfilm. 81 min.; color. Screenplay, Igor Gelein, Aleksandr Ptushko based on poem by Alexander Pushkin; photography, Igor Gelein, Valentin Zakharov; music, Gavril Popov. *CAST:* Vladimir Andreyev (*Tsar Saltan*); Larissa Golubkina (*Tsaritsa*); Oleg Vidov (*Tsarevich Guiron*); Xenia Ryabinkina (*Swan Fairy*).

While foolish Tsar Saltan is off fighting an invasion of troglodytes, his enemies forge an order to kill the Tsar's queen and his newborn but fast-growing son. A swan fairy puts everything right.

Aleksandr Ptushko's liveaction fantasies are among the finest fairy tale films ever made — stylized, lavish, endlessly imaginative, exceptionally beautiful and more true to the spirit of traditional fairy tales than the classic Disney cartoons. In *Tsar Saltan* an army of short but fierce Troglodytes pours across the Russian countryside. They have hairy bodies, grotesque faces and enormous heads. According to an interview in the DVD, many of the actors who played troglodytes had faces painted on their stomachs while their real faces were hidden behind giant hairpieces. The troglodytes are armed only with enormous bones. (One wonders what animal could have provided such gigantic bones.) In victory they jeer and frolic. We see a horde of hundreds of troglodytes charging across a wheat field. This shot probably has more prehistoric people in it than any scene in any other film. Peasants set fires as a scorched earth defense. When the Tsar arrives with his army of medieval knights and big cannon, the troglodytes in defeat show an astounding ability to run backwards. No one seems to be actually killed in these fights. The troglodytes are grotesquely comic secondary villains in one of the world's greatest fairy tale films. Ref: *Internet Movie Database*; MK 9. (Survivors)

Tanya's Island (1980) Canada; dir. Alfred Sole; Baker Films/IFEX. 82 min.; color. Screenplay, Pierre Brousseau; photography, Mark Irwin; music, Jean Musy. *CAST:* D.D. Winters (later known as Vanity) (*Tanya*); Richard Sargent (*Lobo*); Mariette Levesque (*Kelly*); Don McCleod (*Blue the Ape*).

A model (played by real-life model Winters) quarrels with her boyfriend and becomes attracted to an apelike missing link on a remote island.

The realistic ape costume was created by Rick Baker and Rob Bottin. *Variety* (May 13, 1981) approved of nothing except the ape makeup, called the film "crude and laughable ... plodding" and noted the movie's "frequent nudity and violent sex scenes strain the limits of pic's R rating." *Tanya's Island* is known mainly for a scene in which Blue the Ape rapes the heroine. Ref: Jones. *Illustrated Dinosaur Movie Guide*; Senn. *Fantastic Cinema Subject Guide*; not viewed. (Survivors)

Tarzak Against the Leopard Man (1962) see **Ape Man of the Jungle** (1962)

Tarzak contro gli Uomini Leopardo (1962) see **Ape Man of the Jungle** (1962)

Tarzan, the Epic Adventures (1996–97) U.S.; Keller Siegel Entertainment. TV series; 22 45-min. episodes; color. Based on stories by Edgar Rice Burroughs. *CAST:* Joe Lara (*Tarzan*). This short-lived series attempted to remain close to Burroughs' stories, in which

Tarzan often encountered lost worlds. In the first episode, *Tarzan's Return*, Tarzan and a human villain visit Pellucidar, the scene of *At the Earth's Core* (1976), and meet the Mahars, Burroughs' bird-like villains. Tarzan returned to Pellucidar in the 17th episode *Tarzan and the Mahars*. The 19th episode, *Tarzan and the Beast of Dunali*, and the 20th, *Tarzan and the Shadow of Anger*, both featured an ape man, while the 21st, *Tarzan and the Mystery of the Lake*, had a possible Missing Link. Ref: www.tvtome.com; not viewed. (Lost World)

Teddy (1983) *see* **The Pit** (1983)

Teenage Cavegirl (2004) U.S.; dir. Nicholas Medina; Image Entertainment. Direct-to-DVD; 80 min.; color. CAST: Jezebelle Bond (*Tahra*); Evan Stone (*Tiko*).

The blurb proclaimed "Meet the Erotic Cave Bunny" in "this affectionate, racy tribute to monster matinees ... packed with beautiful babes and rampaging dino-beasts" and "hilarious and sexy misadventures." Tattooed cavewoman Tahra and her mate Tiko are time-warped to the modern world in this direct-to-DVD erotic feature. Ref: *Amazon.com*; not viewed. (Timeshift)

Terror Castle (1973) *see* **Frankenstein's Castle of Freaks** (1973)

Terror in the Midnight Sun (1960) *see* **Invasion of the Animal People** (1960)

Themroc (1972) France; dir. Claude Faraldo; Filmantrope/ Productions FDL. 110 min.; color. Screenplay, Claude Faraldo; photography, Jean-Marc Ripert; music, Harald Maury. CAST: Michel Piccoli (*Themroc*); Béatrice Romand (*Sister*); Marilù Tolo (*Secretary*); Francesca Romana Coluzzi (*Neighbor*); Jeanne Herviale (*Mother*); Miou-Miou.

Themroc, a Parisian worker, struggles dispiritedly with malfunctioning kitchen appliances in the dingy apartment he shares with his mother and sister. He smells and touches his nude, sleeping sister. His stern mother sends him off to work. The workers quarrel with each other over trifles. People are regimented and passive and have little contact with each other.

Themroc is sent to the boss's office for discipline; he has sex with the boss's secretary. He becomes more and more animalistic, speaking only in grunts and animal cries. He returns home and immediately has sex (offscreen) with his sister, who is willing. He walls up the door to his third-floor room and knocks out the outer wall, making a cliff-face cave in the apartment building, accessible only by a rope ladder. He throws out all the furniture. His sister joins him and several of the neighbors begin to mimic his wild behavior.

The police attack Themroc ineffectually with tear gas. He throws the gas bombs back at them. At night, he goes out and kills two policemen. By this time he has unusual strength. He hauls the two corpses back to the apartment, where he and the other wild people have a joyous cannibal feast. The police send a worker to wall Themroc and his friends up alive, but Themroc brings out the worker's wild side. More and more people are effected as a wave of primitivism seems about to sweep across Paris.

COMMENTARY. *Themroc* goes far beyond mere bashing of the bourgeoisie to a horrifying but exhilarating full-scale assault on civilization. The gap between the people who join Themroc and those who remain normal is as wide as the difference between the white girl and the aborigine in Nicolas Roeg's *Walkabout*, made only one year earlier in 1971. Perhaps Faraldo was influenced by *Walkabout* but he can't be accused of copying it. His vision of urban primitivism is completely original.

While *Walkabout* showed off the beauty of the Australian Outback, *Themroc* makes Paris look awful. Everything is either grimy or phony and absurd. The normal people often interrupt each other, making them almost as unintelligible as the new primitives, who speak only in cries. The primitives touch and clasp each other like apes. I suspect the actors studied zoo animals to prepare for the film. Piccoli's performance is perfect in a unique, difficult role.

Variety (Feb. 21, 1973) called the anarchic (but "technically assured") movie "a loud film, in ideas as well as decibels," "a social comedy of the absurd in filmic form," which "has a liberating drive and taste despite its subject." Jones (*Illustrated Dinosaur Movie Guide*) calls it "often amusing." Ref: *Internet Movie Database*; Jones. *Illustrated Dinosaur Movie Guide*; Bergan/Karney. *Holt Foreign Film Guide*; MK 8. (Throwback)

The 13th Warrior (1999) U.S.; dir. John McTiernan, Michael Crichton (uncredited); Touchstone/Disney. 102 min.; color. Screenplay,

William Wisher, Warren Lewis, based on novel *The Eaters of the Dead* by Michael Crichton; photography, Peter Menzies; music, Jerry Goldsmith. CAST: Antonio Banderas (*Ahmed Ibn Fahdlan*); Vladimir Kulich (*Buliwyf*); Omar Sharif (*Malchisidek*); Dennis Storhoi (*Herger the Joyous*); Sven Wollter (*King Hrothgar*); Diane Venora (*Queen Weilew*); Maria Bonnevie (*Olga*); Turid Balke (*Old Woman Oracle*); Susan Willis (*Wendol Mother*).

In 922 Ahmed Ibn Fahdlan of Baghdad ("I was a poet in the greatest city in the world") is exiled to the barbarous far north because of his interest in the wife of a powerful man. In Russia he is captured by Vikings, who receive word of "a terror that must not be named," a monstrous, apparently supernatural enemy which is ravaging Viking settlements in Scandinavia. A old woman soothsayer says the evil can be defeated only by a team of twelve Vikings and one foreigner. Ibn Fahdlan is forced to accompany the twelve warriors, led by Buliwyf, who volunteer to face this enemy. At first the crude Vikings despise the Arab for his short stature, his refusal to drink alcohol and even his small horse, but he soon becomes a good warrior. (His horse does well too.)

The 13 champions reach the village of King Hrothgar. At a Viking farm they find victims of an enemy attack, who have been partially eaten. The enemy attack the village. They appear to be huge bears with human intelligence. Some are killed but they take away their dead. They attack again on horseback. This time the Vikings get to examine some of the enemy dead and find they are stocky, broadfaced men wearing war paint and animal headdresses and claws. An old forest crone tells the Vikings the enemy are the Wendol and that they must kill both the revered Mother of the Wendol and the Wendol army leader to defeat them. The Vikings find and penetrate the giant cave which is the Wendol lair. They kill the Mother and escape by swimming an underground river. The Wendol attack the fortified village again. In a big fight Buliwyf kills the Wendol war leader. The Wendol disappear into the night. Buliwyf dies of his wounds. Ibn Fahdlan returns to his own country.

Neanderthals on horseback! In medieval Norway! Fighting Vikings and an Arab! In a *Seven Samurai* homage! In John McTierman's *The 13th Warrior*.

COMMENTARY. Russia really was dominated by the Vikings in the 10th century. Ibn Fahdlan was an Arab diplomat sent to the Vikings of the Volga. He wrote an account of his experiences among the barbarous Northmen, in which he mentioned "mist monsters" or "wendol," whom he describes as hairy and brutish. Michael Crichton believes that Ibn Fahdlan's description of these creatures strongly suggests Neanderthal anatomy. In the appendix to his novel *The Eaters of the Dead*, Crichton quotes two scholars with opposing views of the question. Geoffrey Wrightwood of Oxford believes that Ibn Fahdlan may actually have encountered Neanderthals who survived in a remote area of Northern Europe to the 10th century. E. D. Goodrich of the University of Philadelphia sees little evidence to support such a fantastic possibility.

In his novel Crichton considered the Wendol to be Neanderthals in medieval Scandinavia. The film itself never clearly states that the Wendol are prehistoric. Despite being cannibals the film's Wendol are not unsophisticated. They have swords and spears and ride horses. They control their army with signal horns. They are deceptive; the Vikings consider them clever. In addition to wearing animal disguises and carrying off their dead to convince their enemies they are demons, the Wendol disguise their entire army as a "fireworm," an object of superstitious dread among the Vikings. They fight only at night; the Vikings think they can see in the dark. At their lair, they have a long wooden bridge to their otherwise inaccessible cave door. We see a little of their religion. They are holding a sacred ceremony deep in their cave when the Vikings attack. The sacred Mother of the Wendol apparently has spent her whole life at the bottom of the great cave.

The 13th Warrior is full of details of Viking life, some convincing, some much less convincing but very cool. Buliwyf is the correct Viking name for Beowulf and this is one of the few films about the legendary hero. The climatic battle, in which the enemy on horseback attacks a fortified village in a rainstorm, is a fairly close copy of the final battle in Kurosawa's *Seven Samurai* (1954). McTiernan was best known for directing *Die Hard* (1988). Banderas had just become a star for *The Mask of Zorro* (1998). The film has plenty of action and some dry wit. Despite all these assets, *Variety* (Aug. 30, 1999) was scathing about this "bloody but anemic story of he-men with broadswords." On the other hand, Leonard Maltin gives the film a 3-star rating. *The 13th Warrior* sat on the shelf for two years after its production in 1997. It took in only $33,000,000 against its budget of $65,000,000. However, comments on the film's *Internet Movie Database* page show that it has a body of enthusiastic fans. It's hard not to admire a film which presents relatively positive images of three of the more maligned groups in history—Arabs, Vikings and prehistoric man. Ref: *Internet Movie Database*; Crichton. *Eaters of the Dead*; MK 7. (Survivors)

Trog (1970) U.K.; dir. Freddie Francis; Warner Bros. 93 min.; color. Screenplay, Aben Kandel; photography, Desmond Dickinson; music, John Scott. CAST: Joan Crawford (*Dr. Brockton*); Michael Gough (*Sam Murdock*); Bernard Kay (*Insp. Greenham*); Kim Braden (*Anne Brockton*); Joe Cornelius (*Trog*); David Griffin (*Malcolm Travers*); Thorley Walters (*Magistrate*); Chloe Franks (*Little Girl*).

In the English moors, three spelunkers explore a deep cave. As they venture past an underwater pool, one of them is killed by a short, hairy hominid with a massive apelike face. Malcolm, one of the survivors, is a science student who brings Dr. Brockton, from the conveniently nearby Brockton Research Institute, to the site. She photographs the creature and pronounces him a "troglodyte ... half-man, half-ape" and "the greatest scientific find of modern time" who probably survived being frozen "in icy hibernation" from a distant age. When the police try to capture the creature he kills a member of the "Sub-Aqua Team" and an inquisitive photographer. Brockton anesthetizes him with tranquilizer darts.

Brockton, Malcolm and other scientists study Trog, while vindictive local bully Murdock demands that the "monster" be destroyed. As the local judge slowly deliberates the case, Brockton tames Trog, who plays with a doll and learns simple tasks. He responds to soft music and certain colors but becomes angry at flash photography, loud music and a luckless dog. The scientists perform surgery on Trog to permit him to talk. They show him films of dinosaur skeletons and he recalls seeing dinosaurs fight during his prehistoric life.

Murdock breaks into the lab and frees Trog

Trog the Troglodyte (Joe Cornelius) in *Trog*.

in hopes he will go on a rampage and discredit Brockton. He does, killing first Murdock and then other people who panic at his approach. He steals a little girl, whom he mistakes for his doll, from a schoolyard and takes her deep into his cave. Brockton gets the child away from Trog and the police kill him.

COMMENTARY. *Trog* is a silly, unambitious late entry in the tradition of films about misunderstood monsters, with a very inaccurate view of early man. Joan Crawford's character at various times says that Trog is 10,000,000 or 1,000,000 or "thousands" of years old, that he is "a missing link" or has "some resemblance to the Neanderthal man." In addition to these rapid-fire contradictions, he co-existed with dinosaurs. Trog's huge ape face on a relatively small body looks like no known hominid. Trog has only two moods: pathetic or enraged. The debate over his fate is expressed in the most simplistic terms. Brockton simply argues for the study of early man, while Murdock spews errant bigotry. These discussions drone on endlessly. Much of Trog's cave is too spacious and well-lit, as usual in caveman films, but the first few minutes of the movie, in which the spelunkers penetrate narrow, claustrophobic, winding passages, is convincing and suspenseful. The only other inspired moment comes when an eager photographer sticks a camera in Trog's face and Trog promptly flattens him with a giant rock.

Trog was the last film in superstar Crawford's distinguished, 46-year-long career. She soldiers gallantly on through the film, but shows no real interest in the material. Crawford was not the only great star to do a prehistoric movie toward the end of her career; Elizabeth Taylor had better luck as a cavewoman in *The Flintstones* (1994). Gough, a skilled character actor whose haggard face caused him to languish in B-horror films between playing villains in Disney 1950s swashbucklers and Alfred the Butler in the first few *Batman* films, is required to overact severely. He is far less effective than Jeff Corey as a very similar character, small-town bigot Luke Benson in *Superman and the Mole Men* (1951). Freddie Francis was one of the best cinematographers in the world until he turned to directing and got stuck in horror films which he deplored but to which he often gave some visual flair. *Trog* was one of his failures. Besides the spelunking scenes and the photographer's demise the only asset in *Trog* was four minutes of footage from the documentary *The Animal World* (1956), created by Ray Harryhausen. The borrowed footage is poorly tinted and poorly matched to the new film. *Variety* (Sept. 30, 1970) was kind to *Trog* which it felt "carries enough exploitable elements to score nicely in its intended market, where contrivance, a bit of corn and an imaginative premise spell b.o. [boxoffice] coin" and offers "chilling entertainment ... provided nobody delves too deeply into logic and reality." The *Variety* reviewer also credited Francis with maintaining "a fast and often suspenseful pace." Other critics were harsher. Stephen Jones called it "trash," Mark F. Berry deemed it "a dreadful picture, a disaster on every front" and Leonard Maltin rates it a "bomb." Ref: Jones. *Illustrated Dinosaur Movie Guide*; Senn/Johnson. *Fantastic Cinema Subject Guide*; Berry. *Dinosaur Filmography*; MK 2. (Revived)

The Turkish Wizard of Oz (1971) *see* **Aysecik and the Bewitched Dwarfs in Dreamland** (1971)

TV Funhouse (2000–2001) U.S.; Comedy Central/Poochie Doochie Productions. Animated TV series; 25-min. episodes; color. *VOICES:* Doug Dale (*Doug the Host*); Robert Smigel (*Various Voices*).

In this adult animated series, host Doug leads his "Anipals" in wacky adventures. He sets a theme for each show, such as "Western Day," "Spaceman Day," "Mexican Day"— and "Caveman Day." Ref: *Internet Movie Database*; not viewed. (Fantasy)

The Twilight Zone (1985–1988) Episode, *The Hunters* (1988). U.S.; dir. Paul Lynch; Persistence of Vision/CBS. Episode of TV series; ca. 50 min.; color. Screenplay, Paul Chitlik, Jeremy Bertrand Finch. Music, Merle Saunders, The Grateful Dead. *CAST:* Louise Fletcher (*Dr. Cline*); Michael Hogan (*Sheriff*); Steven Andrade (*Steve*); Les Carlson (*Jim Hilsen*); Bob Warner (*Farmer Jacobs*).

An archeologist (Fletcher) explores a newly-discovered cave, finding wall paintings of hunting scenes. Animals in the area are mysteriously killed and dragged into the cave; the images on the walls move and change shape. The original inhabitants of the cave have been revived.

The 1980s *Twilight Zone* revival series was considered trivial compared with the original series (1959–65) but it had some good stories. Marc Scott Zicree's book *The Twilight Zone Companion* (1989) does not list *The Hunters* among the best episodes. Ref: Jones. *Illustrated Dinosaur Movie Guide*; Morton. *Complete Directory to Science Fiction, Fantasy and Horror Television Series*; *Internet Movie Database*; not viewed. (Revived)

The Ugly Little Boy (1979) Canada, Highgate Films; dir. Barry Morse, Don Thompson. 25 min.; TV film; color. Screenplay based on story by Isaac Asimov. CAST: Kate Reid (*Nurse Fellows*); Barry Morse (*Dr. Hospkins*); Guy Big (*Neanderthal Boy*).

Researchers use a time machine to bring people from the past to the present for study. They capture a small Neanderthal boy, who plays by himself in a containment unit. The time machine acts on the principle of a rubber band; everything brought forward in time has to be sent back in a few months or the system will break down. A nurse (Reid) objects to the head researcher's (Morse) callous treatment of the boy. She learns that when the boy is sent back in time he will go back exactly as far as he came forward and will therefore reappear several weeks after he disappeared, since he has spent that much time in the modern world. She asks what will happen if his tribe has moved on and he is deposited alone in the wilderness. When the boy must be sent back, she suddenly dashes into the containment unit and, in front of the stunned research team, vanishes with him into the distant past.

This short Canadian film was shown on HBO in the U.S. as part an anthology film titled *Three Tales Dark and Dangerous*. The Neanderthal boy's makeup is credible, but the film ignores the fact that Neanderthals were much stronger than modern humans. The Neanderthal is also made to appear more primitive than his kind really were. When a bowl of water is placed before him he kneels and laps the water without picking up the bowl. Reid is moving as a woman who discovers her humanity through contact with a boy whom others consider barely human. Dwarf actor Guy Big died in 1978, the year before the release of *The Ugly Little Boy*. Ref: *Internet Movie Database*; MK 7. (Timeshift)

Uncle Crock's Block (1975–76) Component series *Wacky and Packy*. U.S.; Filmation. Segment of animated TV series; 16 ca. 15-min. episodes; color. VOICES: Charles Nelson Reilly (*Uncle Crock*); Allan Melvin (*Wacky/Packy*).

Reilly was the liveaction host for this animated series, which spoofed local children's shows. Each 50-min. episode presented stories from three component series, including a *Wacky and Packy* story. Wacky is a caveman and Packy is his pet mastodon. Through a timewarp they are stranded in the concrete jungles of New York. Hal Erickson said the series was "not bad at all" and "good for a laugh or two."

Episodes: "The New York Sweats," "In the Zoo," "Wacky's Featured Romance," "Packy Come Home," "Let's Make a Bundle." "All in a Day's Work," "The Party Crushers," "Magic Mayhem," "The Bad News Cruise," "The Fender Benders," "Uncle Sam Wants You?" "No Place Like Home," "One of Your Missing Links Is Missing," "The Shopping Spree," "Getting a Piece of the Rock," "Is This Any Way to Run an Airplane." Ref: Lenburg. *Encyclopedia of Animated Cartoons*; Erickson. *Television Cartoon Series*; not viewed. (Timeshift)

Untamed Women (1952) U.S.; dir. W. Merle Connell; Jewell Productions/Embassy Pictures. 70 min.; b&w. Screenplay, George Wallace Sayre; photography, Glen Gano; music, Raoul Kraushaar. CAST: Mikel Conrad (*Steve*); Doris Merrick (*Sandra*); Richard Monahan (*Benny*); Mark Lowell (*Ed*); Morgan Jones (*Andy*); Midge Ware (*Myra*); Lyle Talbot (*Col. Loring*).

Four U.S. Air Corps men are cast ashore on a Pacific island after their bomber is shot down in World War II. They are taken prisoner by a tribe of miniskirted lovelies described variously as "descendants of the Druids" or "barbaric women raiders." As in *Dinosaur Island* (1993) the women's queen, Sandra the Priestess, is anti-man, associating the newcomers with the island's brutish "Hairy Men." The airmen help fight dinosaurs and Hairy Men, winning Sandra's approval, but almost everyone is killed in a volcanic eruption.

Mark F. Berry considers *Untamed Women* one of the most ridiculous films in the dinosaur genre (which is saying a lot). The primitive women wear "mascara, lipstick and male-fantasy costumes," speak dialogue full of "yea," "thou" and "thine" and perform crude dance numbers. Berry notes the "leering, sensationalistic quality" of Sayre's script. *Variety* (Aug. 13, 1952) reported "the story is ludicrous, acting amateurish and production values meager."

The Hairy Men, rather than the tribal girls, make *Untamed Women* relevant to this list. Ref: Jones. *Illustrated Dinosaur Movie Guide*; Senn/Johnson. *Fantastic Cinema Subject Guide*; Berry. *Dinosaur Filmography*; not viewed. (Lost World)

Valley of the Dinosaurs (1974) U.S.; Hanna-Barbera. Animated TV series; 15 25-min. episodes; color. *VOICES:* Mike Road (*John Butler*); Shannon Farnon (*Kim Butler*); Margene Fudenna (*Katie Butler*); Jackie Earle Haley (*Greg Butler*); Alan Oppenheimer (*Gorak*); Joan Gardner (*Gera*); Melanie Baker (*Tana*); Stacey Bertheau (*Lok*).

While exploring the Amazon the Butler family is stranded in a lost world of cavemen and dinosaurs, where they befriend a primitive family (who speak English). Each family has exactly the same composition—father (John and Gorak), mother (Kim and Gera), a teenager (Katie and Lok), a child (Greg and Tana) and a pet (Digger the Butlers' dog and Clomb, the cave people's pet stegosaurus.)

The series stressed educational lessons on the scientific principles used by the modern family to find food, water and shelter. Even better, the fast-paced episodes treated the primitive people with real respect. Gorak is intelligent and supremely knowledgeable about his environment. When crimes are committed, the tribal people conduct fair trials and either forgive penitent wrong-doers or sentence them to exile, not death. Some of the cave people's "superstitions" prove valid; others they discard. Gera produces a traditional medicine which cures Kim of a dangerous illness. The tribal family uses rollers and a block and tackle to move heavy objects; the modern family shows them how to use the wheel and a sailboat and how to build a small dam. The series emphasized mutual respect and cooperation between different cultures, while telling exciting stories in the adventurous spirit of *Jonny Quest* (1964–65) and Edgar Rice Burroughs.

Valley of the Dinosaurs came out the same year as *Korg: 70,000 B.C.*, an inferior attempt at a realistic liveaction children's program on prehistoric humans. Hal Erickson (*Television Cartoon Shows*) approved of *Valley*'s "well-knit storylines" and the "downpedalled, non-strident fashion" in which it made its points about how divergent cultures could learn from each other. Episodes: "Forbidden Fruit," "What Goes Up," "A Turned Turtle," "The Volcano," "Smoke Screen," "Pteranodon," "The Saber-Tooth Kids," "After Shock," "Top Cave, Please," "S.O.S.," "Fire," "Rain of Meteors," "To Fly a Kite," "Test Flight," "The Big Toothache," "Torch." Ref: Lenburg. *Encyclopedia of Animated Cartoons*; Woolery. *Children's Television*; Erickson. *Television Cartoon Shows*; Jones. *Illustrated Dinosaur Movie Guide*; 4 episodes viewed; MK 8. (Lost World)

Valley of the Dragons (1961) U.S.; dir. Edward Bernds; Columbia. 79 min.; b&w. Screenplay, Edward Bernds based on novel *Career of a Comet* by Jules Verne; photography, Brydon Baker; music, Rudy Raksin. *CAST:* Cesare Danova (*Capt. Hector Servadac*); Sean McClory (*Michael Denning*); Joan Staley (*Deena*); Danielle DeMetz (*Nateeta*); Gregg Martell (*Od-Loo*); Gil Perkins (*Tarn*); I. Stanford Jolley (*Patoo*); Michael Lane (*Anoka*).

In Algeria in 1881, a duel between French Army officer Hector Servadac and Irish adventurer Michael Denning is interrupted when part of Earth is pulled aboard a passing comet. They discover that the comet had previously picked up passengers from the prehistoric age—dinosaurs, mastodons, giant lizards, giant spiders, "subhuman" Neanderthals, mole-men and two feuding tribes of cavepeople. Hector and Michael become separated and each joins a different tribe and acquires a local girlfriend.

In one tribe, Deena wants Hector for herself and saves him from both the spears of the men and the attentions of the other women. Meanwhile Michael saves an old man who was wounded by a wild ox. In the old man's tribe Michael and Nateeta become attracted to each other. When hulking Anoka, who wants Nateeta, threatens Michael, the Irishman defeats the caveman twice, first with his fists, then with a sling he hastily invents. Nateeta's tribe captures Deena. The two-fisted Irishman frees her (punching out another obdurate caveman) and she leads Nateeta's people to Deena's tribe.

The two tribes are about to come to blows when a volcano erupts, unleashing an earthquake. People are killed or scattered. The eruption also brings giant lizards out of their lairs. They besiege Nateeta and many of her people in a cave. Michael, Hector and many cavemen attack the giants with spears, then bury them under a landslide set off by gunpowder invented by Hector. The tribes make friends and Hector and Michael settle down with their girlfriends to await the comet's return to Earth.

COMMENTARY. *Valley of the Dragons* is unambitious and ridiculous but enjoyable. Danova and McClory are likeable, Staley and De Metz are delightful and the cheap film has something of the jaunty, tongue-in-cheek air of the better Verne and Wells adaptations. *Valley* was practically built around footage from *One Million B.C.* (1940). Scenes from Hal Roach's 1940 epic have appeared in more than a dozen films but Mark F. Berry (*Dinosaur Filmography*) believes that *Valley* probably borrows more *One Million B.C.* footage than any other film. In addition to dinosaurs, giant lizards, the volcanic eruption (including a shocking shot of a girl being engulfed by lava) and the earthquake, *Valley* has 1940 scenes showing the hero (Victor Mature in 1940, Danova here) floating unconscious down a river while being menaced by monsters; a caveman (Lon Chaney Jr. in 1940) attacked by an ox; and a cave besieged by a giant lizard until the monster is killed by a landslide.

The Neanderthals in *Valley* have huge noses, bulging eyes, prominent teeth, long hair and claw-like hands; all but the big nose and maybe the hair are far different from real Neanderthals. (Berry reproduces a close-up of a *Valley of the Dragons* Neanderthal.) Servadac calls the Neanderthals "subhuman" and when Denning meets the anatomically-modern humans, he says, "At least they're human — not like those Neanderthals." The mole men look much the same as the faux Neanderthals but are afraid of the light, a fact which comes in handy when they are chasing Hector and Deena. The anatomically-modern cavemen are familiar stereotypes: amorous cavegirls, a hulking bully, and a statesmanlike old man.

The concept of the comet visiting Earth repeatedly and picking up new life forms each time could have been a logical (for once) way to put cavemen and dinosaurs together, but the film throws away that possibility by insisting that the dinosaurs and cavemen did live together "more than a thousand centuries ago." 100,000 years ago is about right for anatomically-modern humans and much too recent for dinosaurs. Servadac, who is for some reason an expert astronomer and an authority on ancient life, announces that in prehistory "the tribes were very small, scarcely larger than families. And they fought constant wars with each other." The first statement is quite accurate; the second is not true at all. The two modern visitors quite effortlessly take command of the two caveman tribes, impressing the prehistoric people with their clever inventions and ready fists. The two tribes cannot make friends until the two outsiders show them how.

Ed Bernds was director of about 90 B-level features and shorts, including about 30 Three Stooges shorts. He wrote about 50 screenplays. Danova was a star in Italian swashbucklers who in Hollywood usually played secondary parts, from *Cleopatra* (1963) to *Animal House* (1978). Affable Irish character actor Sean McClory had smaller parts in dozens of films, including *The Quiet Man* (1952). Joan Staley, a 1958 *Playboy* centerfold, had a brief but busy career in TV and small film parts from 1957 to 1972. Danielle De Metz had a similarly modest career

"Subhuman" Neanderthals, cavegirls and modern heroes vie for space in this crowded Mexican lobby card for *Valley of the Dragons*.

covering exactly the same years. Gregg Martell's small part in *Valley* was his only caveman role besides his Neanderthal Man in *Dinosaurus!* (1960). In *Dinosaurus!* Martell gave the greatest performance as a caveman of any actor in any film but in *Valley of the Dragons* he had nothing distinctive to do. *Variety* (Nov. 22, 1961) sniffed at "a corny caveman saga that is shopworn even by 20-year-old cinema standards" with "maidens more indigenous to Schwab's than the Stone Age." Mark F. Berry (*Dinosaur Filmography*) felt the light byplay between the two heroes and Joan Staley's sexy performance made the film "diverting" though "utterly preposterous ... an amusing and affable dose of mindless hooey." Verne's novel was also made into Karel Zeman's *On the Comet* (1970), a much superior film which includes dinosaurs but no cavemen. Ref: Jones. *Illustrated Dinosaur Movie Guide*; Berry. *Dinosaur Filmography*; MK 5. (Extraterrestrial)

Vampire Man of the Lost Planet (1970) see **Horror of the Blood Monsters** (1970)

Virtual Encounters (1996) U.S.; dir. Cybil Richards; Surrender Cinema. 84 min.; color. Screenplay, Lucas Riley. CAST: Elizabeth Kaitan (*Amy*); Rob Lee (*Michael*); Jill Kelly (*Cave Girl*); Vince Voyeur (*Cave Boy*).

A softcore film in which a woman has sexual encounters via virtual reality. The credits include "Cave Girl" and "Cave Boy." Ref: *Internet Movie Database*; not viewed. (Virtual)

Voyage to the Bottom of the Sea (1964–68) U.S.; 20th Century Fox TV/ABC. TV series; 110 50-min. episodes; color. Music, Paul Sawtell. CAST: Richard Basehart (*Adm. Nelson*); David Hedison (*Cmdr. Lee Crane*).

The advanced naval submarine *Seaview* constantly encounters monsters and other SF and horror situations. Three episodes in this Irwin Allen series are relevant to this list.

Episode 7. *Turn Back the Clock* (1964) Dir., Felix Feist; screenplay, Sheldon Stark. CAST: Nick Adams (*Jason Kemp*); Yvonne Craig (*Carol Denning*); Les Tremayne (*Dr. Denning*); Vitina Marcus (*Native Girl*); Robert Cornthwaite (*Zeigler*).

The *Seaview* discovers a verdant, prehistoric land in the Antarctic, with dinosaurs and natives. Series regular Hedison and guest star Marcus were in the 1960 film *The Lost World*, which had no cavemen. Footage from that film was used in this episode. Craig played Batgirl on the *Batman* series (1966–68). Cornthwaite played Dr. Carrington, the scientist who prefers the alien to people, in *The Thing from Another World* (1951).

Episode 20. *The Invaders* (1964) Dir., Sobey Martin; screenplay, William Read Woodfield. CAST: Robert Duvall (*Zar*); Michael McDonald.

A metal coffin, revealed by an earthquake and brought aboard the *Seaview*, contains Zar (an early role for unknown Duvall), a humanoid from a previous evolutionary cycle, who has been in suspended animation for 20,000,000 years.

Episode 76. *The Fossil Men* (1966) Dir., Justus Addiss; screenplay, John N. Whitton. CAST: Brendan Dillon; Jerry Catron.

Prehistoric rock men who want to use the *Seaview* to conquer the world capture Adm. Nelson. Ref: Philips/Garcia. *Science Fiction Television Series*; Morton. *Complete Directory to Science Fiction, Fantasy and Horror Television Series*; not viewed. (Survivors)

Voyage to the Planet of Prehistoric Women (1966) [alt. *Gill Women of Venus*] U.S.; dir. Peter Bogdanovich (as Derek Thomas); Filmgroup/ AIP. 79 min.; color. Screenplay, Henry Ney; photography, Fleming Olsen; music, Keith Benjamin. CAST: Mamie Van Doren (*Moana*); Mary Marr (*Gill Woman*); Paige Lee (*Gill Women*); Peter Bogdanovich (*Narrator*).

Astronauts land on Venus and discover dinosaurs and pterodactyls. A young astronaut thinks he hears a girl's far-off voice; his colleagues ridicule him. The Earthmen never meet the people of Venus—blonde, telepathic gillwomen who wander around the beach in trousers and clamshell bras. The gillwomen worship a pterodactyl (apparently the only one on the planet) as their god and ask him to destroy the invaders. The pterodactyl does attack the astronauts and is killed.

The gillwomen then call on a volcano to erupt in order to eliminate the Earthmen. When the volcano duly erupts, two astronauts, trapped by lava, save themselves by ordering John, their giant robot, to carry them to safety. After reaching safety they abandon John, who has been wrecked by wading through lava. The gillwomen discover the dead pterodactyl and the burned-out remains of John. The young astronaut finds a stone with a face carved on it but the other Earthmen ignore his argument that the stone proves the existence of Venusians; he must join them as they take off for Earth. The gillwomen decide the pterodactyl was a false god and begin to worship what's left of John.

COMMENTARY. This was the second reworking of special effects footage from *Planeta Burg* (Soviet, 1962) produced by Roger Corman, after *Voyage to the Prehistoric Planet* (1965), which had dinosaurs but not primitive people. *Voyage to the Planet of Prehistoric Women* was also the first film directed by Peter Bogdanovich (who was probably glad later that he used a pseudonym while making this monstrosity). The Soviet material was interesting and often impressive. Most of the footage added by Bogdanovich is fatuous, but the sight of the disillusioned gillwomen stoning a statue of the pterodactyl god is weirdly surreal.

Corman's and Bogdanovich's goal was simply to find a way to use the purchased footage while showing off a minor celebrity (Van Doren) and several attractive women. Nevertheless they came up with a fairly interesting concept. Since neither the pterodactyl nor John the robot have supernatural powers, it is the gillwomen who must have some kind of mental power. It is presumably they who cause the pterodactyl to attack the astronauts and then cause the volcano to erupt. But they are unaware of their own special powers and ascribe everything they do to their god.

When the astronauts explore the bottom of the Venusian sea they find an underwater city. They assume it was once aboveground and was submerged in a cataclysm. In fact the gillwomen can breathe underwater and presumably live in the city under the sea. However, we also see the gillwomen sleeping on rocks near the sea, until Moana starts their day with a telepathic "Sisters, awake." The women apparently do not understand that they use telepathy. They have always done it so they don't realize that it is in any way extraordinary. The sensitive astronaut mentally overhears one of the women, but none of the women worry about being overheard. The women may be immortal, since it is hard to see how they would reproduce.

When the astronauts land one of them announces that Venus is "truly a prehistoric planet." It was necessary to reassure the audience of this since nothing looks especially prehistoric except for the pterodactyl and other dinosaurs. The gillwomen are among the oddest "prehistoric" people in films. *Voyage* gives audiences a vision of a unisex planet, possibly populated by immortals. The women have telepathy but are unaware of it. They have power over nature, but ascribe that power successively to two male gods, both of them false. The film seems to be saying that women should be more conscious of their own abilities, but this is probably reading too much into the humble project.

Variety didn't bother to review the film, which had little or no theatrical release before going into syndication on TV. Mark F. Berry found it campy and "laughable." Ref: Berry. *Dinosaur Filmography*; Hardy. *Overlook Film Encyclopedia: Science Fiction*; Senn/Johnson. *Fantastic Cinema Subject Guide*; Jones. *Illustrated Dinosaur Movie Guide*; MK 4. (Extraterrestrial)

Wacky and Packy *see* **Uncle Crock's Block** (1975–76).

White Pongo (1945) U.S.; dir. Sam Newfield; PRC. 77 min.; b&w. Screenplay, Raymond I. Schrock; photography, Jack Greenhalgh. CAST: Richard Fraser (*Geoffrey Bishop*); Maris Wrixon (*Pamela*); Lionel Royce (*Van Dorn*); Al Eben (*Kroegert*); Ray Corrigan (*White Pongo*).

An expedition in Africa seeks an albino gorilla which is presumed to be the missing link. The ape kills a mutinous safari guide, kidnaps the heroine and defeats a rival black gorilla before being captured by the safari.

Variety (Dec. 5, 1945) found the film a "drawn-out affair" which "strains credulity all the way" and moves at "a snail's pace." Even the fight between the two gorillas was "poorly-staged." Ref: Jones. *Illustrated Dinosaur Movie Guide*; not viewed. (Survivors)

Xena: Warrior Princess (1995–2001) Episode 44, *The Price* (1997). U.S.; dir. Oley Sassone; Renaissance Pictures. Episode of TV series; 44-min.; color. Producer, Rob Tapert; screenplay, Steven L. Sears; music, Joseph LoDuca. CAST: Lucy Lawless (*Xena*); Renee O'Connor (*Gabrielle*); Paul Glover (*Menticles*); Charles Mesure (*Mercer*); Tamati Rice (*Garel*); Mark Perry (*Galipan*); Justin Curry (*G'Kug*).

In northern Greece, woman warrior Xena

and her friend Gabrielle are attacked by the Horde, savage fighters who are among the few enemies who frighten even Xena, a former warlord. Years before her army was decimated by the brutish Horde, who skin their victims alive. The Hordemen fight with a variety of club and blade weapons, including axes which they throw with unnerving accuracy. Barely escaping from a river ambush, Xena and Gabrielle end up inside the stockade of a besieged Athenian outpost, where the thoroughly demoralized garrison awaits its doom.

Xena rallies the Athenians with her fearsome reputation and a ferocious war speech ending with "We're gonna kill 'em all!" With her new army, Xena defeats a Horde attack. She brutalizes a Horde prisoner, withholds scarce water from seriously wounded men, forces wounded men to fight and refuses to consider negotiating with the Horde, whom she regards as animals. Gabrielle is appalled that Xena is reverting to her old, ruthless warlord habits.

Wounded Hordemen lying between the two armies cry out "Kaltaka!" The Athenians believe Kaltaka is the Horde's war god. Gabrielle discovers from the Horde prisoner that "Kaltaka" actually means "water." She goes alone to the battlefield, bringing water to the wounded. Xena is horrified that Gabrielle, the only person she loves, is in a hopeless position, but instead of killing her, the Hordemen decide that her gesture means that a truce is in force and go out to collect their wounded. Xena finally realizes that the Hordemen are capable of intelligence and have a warrior's code of honor. To settle the battle, Xena challenges the towering Horde leader to a personal duel. She beats him with difficulty, then deliberately turns her back on him, forcing him to either acknowledge her victory or violate his own code. The leader tries to kill Xena, but several of his own warriors throw axes into his back, killing the giant. The Hordemen lift the siege and leave. Xena thanks Gabrielle for saving everyone with her compassion and courage.

COMMENTARY. *Xena* stories were based on history and myth from the Trojan War to the early Roman Empire. One episode, *Lifeblood* (2000), has flashback scenes showing the prehistoric origins of the Amazons, complete with cavemen. See Part I for general information on *Xena* and for *Lifeblood*. Three other episodes (*The Price, Daughter of Pomira* and *The Abyss*) deal with primitive, uncivilized Europeans who co-existed with ancient civilizations. These episodes reflect the fact that early in the first millennium B.C. Greece was the only civilized corner of Europe. The three stories depict European primitives in a series full of civilized non-Europeans, from Egyptians to Indians and Chinese. In *The Price*, the first episode about primitive Europeans, the Horde dress in warpaint, skins and headdresses which exaggerate their height. They look somewhat like North American Plains Indians and the episode resembles many Western films about besieged frontier forts. The Horde became one of the fans' favorite villains. The opening scenes, in which Hordemen attack without warning from underwater or from trees, are truly terrifying. However, the Hordemen are seen mainly as a group, rarely as individuals. They are first shown as a fearsome enemy, then humanized. The episode is mainly about Gabrielle's efforts to once again save Xena from herself. MK 7. Ref for all *Xena* episodes: *Whoosh* website (www.whoosh.org). (Survivors)

Xena: Warrior Princess (1995–2001) Episode 64, *Fins, Femmes and Gems* (1998). U.S.; dir. Josh Becker; Renaissance Pictures. Screenplay, Adam Armus, Nora Kay Fisher; music, Joseph LoDuca. CAST: Lucy Lawless (*Xena*); Renee O'Connor (*Gabrielle*); Ted Raimi (*Joxer*); Alexandra Tydings (*Aphrodite*).

The goddess Aphrodite casts a spell over Xena's and Gabrielle's dim-witted friend Joxer, making him believe he is Attis the Apeman, the subject of a legend in which he falls in love with a human girl. As Attis, Joxer envisions Gabrielle as an ape-girl, giving both Ted Raimi and Renee O'Connor a chance to chimp out. MK 6. (Fake)

Xena: Warrior Princess (1995–2001) Episode 79, *Daughter of Pomira* (1999). Dir., Patrick Norris. 44 min.; color. Screenplay, Linda McGibney; music, Joseph LoDuca. CAST: Lucy Lawless (*Xena*); Renee O'Connor (*Gabrielle*); Beth Allen (*Vanessa/Pilee*); Craig Ancell (*Milo*); Bruce Hopkins (*Rahl*); Mandy McMullin (*Adiah*).

In a remote area, Greek settlers fear the nearby Horde. They hire Milo, a ruthless mercenary, to kill Horde people, including women and children. Xena agrees to rescue Vanessa, a Greek child kidnapped by the Horde years before. The Horde lives in a cave (naturally!), which Xena enters in disguise. She kidnaps Vanessa, but is surprised when the girl resists. At the Greek settlement, Vanessa insists on calling herself Pilee, her Horde name, and rejects her Greek parents. The Horde (who call themselves Pomira) come to rescue Pilee. War almost breaks out, but Xena uses Pilee to mediate between the Greeks and her statesmanlike Pomira foster father. When Milo objects to the prospect of peace, Xena reluctantly has to fight and kill him. Pilee returns to the Pomira but will act as an intermediary between the two peoples.

COMMENTARY. Like *The Price*, the other *Xena* Horde episode, *Daughter of Pomira* relocates the conventions of the Western to the ancient world. The episode recalls many Western films such as *Two Rode Together* (1961) and of course *The Searchers* (1956), which in turn were based on real captivity narratives. The Horde/Pomira once again take the role of the Indians. *Daughter of Pomira* is one of the weaker *Xena* episodes and was a disappointment for fans who had eagerly awaited the return of the Horde ever since *The Price*. After being humanized in this episode, the Horde made no more appearances in *Xena*. MK 4. (Survivors)

Xena: Warrior Princess (1995–2001) Episode 118, *The Abyss* (2001). Dir., Rick Jacobson. 44 min.; color. Screenplay, James Kahn; music, Joseph LoDuca. CAST: Lucy Lawless (*Xena*); Renee O'Connor (*Gabrielle*); William Gregory Lee (*Virgil*); Ian Harcourt (*Rubio*); John Wielemaker (*Alpha Male*); Mark Williams (*Fire Maker*).

Somewhere in a remote area of Europe, an apparently all-male cannibal tribe captures two of Xena's friends and kills and consumes one of them. The survivor, Virgil, is confined with Rubio, a prisoner who confounds the cannibals by refusing to eat and remaining incredibly skinny. Xena and Gabrielle fight the cannibals, but Gabrielle, who had mistakenly killed an innocent man in the previous episode, hesitates to kill her opponent. She is wounded and thrown into a river. Xena rescues her but Gabrielle becomes dangerously ill and Xena has no alternative except to hand her over to the cannibals.

As Xena anticipated, they nurse Gabrielle back to health in order to eat her. At the last minute, Xena attacks the cannibal camp and frees Gabrielle, Virgil and Rubio. Xena lures the main force of cannibals into an abyss where she has single-handedly built a huge log dam! Gabrielle must cut a rope to collapse the dam and drown the cannibals. However, a small group of cannibals attack Gabrielle and Virgil. While Xena tries to hold off the whole cannibal army, Gabrielle must overcome her reluctance to kill. She finally dispatches several enemies and cuts the rope. The cannibals drown as Xena leaps to safety.

COMMENTARY: In comparison with the Horde/Pomira, the cannibals are more disgusting and completely unsympathetic. They have no women and children. We are not told any of the cannibals' names. Their leaders are called "Alpha Male" and "Fire Maker." The cannibals, who don't seem very bright, coat their victims in mud and put a tube in their mouths prior to roasting them, a horrifying scene borrowed from the 1966 adventure film *The Naked Prey*. MK 5. (Survivors)

Yesterday's World (1952) U.S.; dir. Richard Irving; Revue Productions. TV special; 25 min.; b&w. Screenplay, Howard Irving Young; photography, Philip Tannura. CAST: Bonita Granville (*Kay*); Robert Boon; Robert Rockwell. (In the series *Chevron Theatre*)

American Kay, her fiancé Jeff and their guide Claude (who is attracted to Kay) are flying through the Dordogne in France, a region which has a mysterious reputation. Claude says that whole areas have never been surveyed and local people "never go into the deep valleys." The trio make an emergency landing in a valley and find the place amazingly cold. We see a giant spider. They hear big animals and soon see giant lizards. They flee and find a cave with an opening hidden by brush. Inside are a small fire, a spear, a stone ax, a flint knife, a bearskin and a huge footprint. Claude says, "We weren't meant to be here, to see what we have seen, things that have been hidden away for thousands and thousands of years." Suddenly they are accosted not by a caveman but by a giant gorilla, who knocks the two men down and threatens Kay. Jeff shoots the beast. Finally, we see Kay tell her story to people who suspect she is insane; Jeff and Claude have vanished completely.

This is certainly the only Lost World story set in France. The accoutrements in the cave are clearly human, but the animal we see is definitely an ape, not an ape-man; he wears a standard, cheap Hollywood gorilla suit. Did the gorilla kill the human inhabitant of the cave? Is the human merely absent and is the gorilla his companion? These questions seem rather pointless, since the story is an arbitrary exercise in weirdness and suspense. The giant lizards are from *One Million B.C.* (1940). Scenes in the mysterious valley are tinted green, while scenes set in normal places are in ordinary b&w. *Daily Variety* (Feb. 11 1952) said that while the TV special "builds in suspense, its climax is disappointing." Ref: viewing; MK 4. (Lost World)

Zingo, Son of the Sea (1914) Italy; Ambrosia. Serial film; 4 episodes; b&w; silent.

A caveman is discovered on a remote jungle island and has many adventures. Episodes: *Zingo, Son of the Sea*; *Zingo's War in the Clouds*; *Zingo and the White Elephant*; *Zingo in Africa*. Ref: Jones. *Illustrated Dinosaur Movie Guide*; not viewed. (Survivors)

Appendix A: Misleading Titles, Unknown Contents, Aborted and Proposed Projects

Beach Babes 2: Cave Girl Island (1995) U.S.; dir. David DeCoteau (as Ellen Cabot); Torchlight.

A porn film set on an apparently prehistoric island which is really a theme park. Ref: *Internet Movie Database*; Berry. *Dinosaur Filmography*; not viewed.

Beyond the Horizon (1937) [alt. *Wahan*] India; dir. K. Narayan Kale.

Jones (*Illustrated Dinosaur Movie Guide*) says this is a "prehistoric" tale, but an annotation by Ashish Rajadhyaksha and Paul Willemen in their *Encyclopedia of Indian Cinema* (1994) indicate it was set in ancient civilized India. Not viewed.

The Cave Dwellers (1914) U.S.; dir. Tefft Johnson; Vitagraph. Screenplay, Elaine Sterne. CAST: Bobby Connelly.

Both *Internet Movie Database* and Alan Goble's *International Film Index* say that this film is different from the 1913 *Cave Dwellers* by Bison Studio (see Part I) but information of the content of the Vitagraph film is elusive. It is not in Jones's *Illustrated Dinosaur Movie Guide*. Johnson was an actor in Vitagraph's *The Caveman* (1912). Connelly was a child actor, only five years old in 1914. Ref: *Internet Movie Database*; Goble. *International Film Index*; not viewed.

The Cave Girl (1921) U.S.; dir. Joseph Franz; Inspiration Pictures. Screenplay based on play by Guy Bolton. CAST: Teddie Gerard (*Margot*).

A modern story about a girl who works for a professor "who wants to revert to primitive modes of living." Ref: *American Film Institute Catalog: Feature Films, 1921–1930*; not viewed.

[For the next several entries, note that in silent films, the term "caveman" was often used to describe a brutish modern man, not a prehistoric man.]

The Cave Man (1915) U.S.; dir. Theodore Marston; Vitagraph. Screenplay, Marguerite Bertsch based on play by Gelett Burgess. CAST: Robert Edeson; Fay Wallace.

A modern story about a society girl who befriends a rough coal heaver, based on the same play as *The Caveman* (1926). Jones says this version may have included a prehistoric flashback scene. The brief *Variety* review (Dec. 3, 1915) sheds no light on the question of prehistoric content. Ref: Jones. *Illustrated Dinosaur Movie Guide*; *Internet Movie Database*; not viewed.

Cave Man Stuff (1918) U.S.; dir. Allen Curtis; Nestor/Universal. Short film; b&w; silent. Screenplay, Tom Gibson. CAST: Gale Henry; Milton Sims.

Contents unknown. Ref: *Internet Movie Database*; not viewed.

A Cave Man Wooing (1912) U.S.; dir. Otis Turner; Independent Moving Pictures. Feature film; b&w; silent. Screenplay, B.M. Connors. CAST: King Baggott.

Character names are modern. Ref: *Internet Movie Database*; not viewed.

The Cave Man's Bride (1919) U.S.; dir. Charles Brown; Celebrated Players. Animated short film; b&w; silent.

In the *Mutt and Jeff* cartoon series (1913, 1916–23, 1925–29). Contents unknown. Ref: Webb. *Animated Film Encyclopedia*; Lenburg. *Encyclopedia of Animated Cartoons*; not viewed.

Cavedweller (2004) U.S.; dir. Lisa Cholodenko. *CAST:* Kyra Sedgwick; Aidan Quinn.

A modern drama. Ref: *Internet Movie Database*; not viewed.

The Caveman (1926) U.S.; dir. Lewis Milestone; Warner Bros. 75 min.; b&w; silent. Screenplay, Daryl Zanuck based on play by Gelett Burgess. *CAST:* Matt Moore; Marie Prevost; Myrna Loy.

Set in the modern world; see *Cave Man* (1915) for a synopsis. Ref: *Variety* review (March 3, 1926); *American Film Institute Catalog: Feature Films, 1921–1930*; not viewed.

Caveman Rainbow (1993) Canada; dir. Jeremy Podeswa.

Contents unknown. Ref: *Internet Movie Database*; not viewed.

Caveman's Bluff (1917) [possibly titled *Caveman's Buff*] U.S.; dir. Sidney Drew; Metro Pictures. Short film; b&w; silent. *CAST:* Sidney Drew.

Contents unknown. *Internet Movie Database* gives the title, probably incorrectly, as *Caveman's Buff*. Ref: Goble. *International Film Index*; *Internet Movie Database*; not viewed.

The Caveman's Valentine (1993) U.S.; dir. Kasi Lemmons; MCA/Universal. 105 min.; color. Screenplay, George Dawes Green, based on his novel. *CAST:* Samuel L. Jackson (*Romulus Ledbetter*).

Set in modern times. A schizophrenic pianist lives in a cave in an urban park. Ref: *Internet Movie Database*; not viewed.

Dinosaur Girl (1970s) U.K.; Hammer Films. Proposed feature film.

Berry reports that Hammer planned this film as either a prequel or a sequel to *When Dinosaurs Ruled the Earth* (1971). *Dinosaur Girl* was to star Victoria Vetri, the leading lady of *When Dinosaurs Ruled*. Ref: Berry. *Dinosaur Filmography*.

Domestic Affairs (1999) U.S.; dir. Pierre Woodman. Made-for-video film. *CAST:* includes Alain Deloine (*Cave Boy*); Michaella May (*Cave Girl*).

An erotic video. Contents unknown. Ref: *Internet Movie Database*; not viewed.

La Edad de la Piedra (1965) Spain; dir. Gabriel Blanco. Animated short film; 12 min.; color.

The title means "The Stone Age." The contents of this animated short are not known. Ref: Jones. *Illustrated Dinosaur Movie Guide*; Lee. *Reference Guide to Fantastic Films*; not viewed.

The First Barber (1922) U.S.; dir. Tony Sarg; Sarg/Darley/Rialto. Animated short film; b&w; silent. (In the *Tony Sarg's Almanac* series).

Webb says a skunk attacks a barber shop in this silhouette animation short. It is not clear whether this is set in prehistoric times, but other shorts in Sarg's cartoon *Almanac* series were prehistoric, such as *The First Flivver* (1922). Ref: Webb. *Animated Film Encyclopedia*; not viewed.

The First Degree (1922) U.S.; dir. Tony Sarg; Sarg/Darley/Rialto. Animated short film; b&w; silent. (In the *Tony Sarg's Almanac* series).

Even Webb has no information on the story of this silhouette animation short. Other shorts Sarg's animated *Almanac* series were prehistoric, such as *The First Flivver* (1922). Ref: Webb. *Animated Film Encyclopedia*; not viewed.

The First Earfull (1922) U.S.; dir. Tony Sarg; Sarg/Darley/Rialto. Animated short film; b&w; silent. (In the *Tony Sarg's Almanac* series).

Even Webb has no information on the story of this silhouette animation short. Other shorts Sarg's animated *Almanac* series were prehistoric, such as *The First Flivver* (1922). Ref: Webb. *Animated Film Encyclopedia*; not viewed.

Fred the Caveman (2002) Canada; Rudi Bloss; Tube Productions. Animated short film; color. Screenplay, Rudi Bloss.

Contents unknown. Ref: *Internet Movie Database*; not viewed.

The Gorilla Story (1951?) U.S.; dir. Arthur Hilton; Crown Pictures. TV film; ca. 30 min.; b&w. *CAST:* Buster Keaton.

It is unclear whether this film ever existed. The above information is from Stephen Jones' *Illustrated Dinosaur Movie Guide*. Jones says the short film was "apparently made for TV and released theatrically in the UK." *Internet Movie Database* says that the only film made by Hilton and starring Keaton was *The Misadventures of Buster Keaton* (1951), a compilation of episodes from a TV series called *Life with Buster*. There is no record of *The Gorilla Story* in Gifford's *British Film Catalogue*. Jones says that in *The Gorilla Story* Keaton "is a member of an expedition searching for the missing link. He dreams he meets a talking gorilla." Ref: Jones. *Illustrated Dinosaur Movie Guide*; not viewed.

His Prehistoric Blunder (1922) U.S.; dir. Craig Hutchinson; Universal. Short film; silent; b&w. *CAST:* Roy Atwell.

Minimal information on this film, with no indication of content, is found in *Internet Movie Database* and Goble's *International Film Index*. Not viewed.

The Incredible Petrified World (1960) U.S.; dir. Jerry Warren.

One source claims the lost world in this ultra-low-budget quickie included a caveman, but other sources say the denizen of the underground world is a modern man who was stranded there. Not viewed.

The March of Time (1930) U.S.; MGM. Uncompleted film project. *CAST:* Buster Keaton (*Caveman*); Marie Dressler; Ann Dvorak; Bing Crosby.

A user's note on *Internet Movie Database* says this was a never-completed musical film and that only a sound recording of a Bing Crosby number survives. It was probably going to be a series of comedy episodes set through history. Keaton was cast to repeat his caveman part seven years after *The Three Ages* (1923). Ref: *Internet Movie Database*; not viewed.

The Mighty Peking Man (1977) [alt. *Goliathon*] Hong Kong; dir. Ho Meng-Hau (as Homer Gaugh); Shaw Bros./World Northal. 100 min.; color.

An earthquake awakens a giant (70-foot tall!) hairy biped in an ice cave in Tibet. He is captured, escapes and runs amok in Hong Kong. Nothing except the English language title ties this Hong Kong clone of *King Kong* to the prehistoric Peking Man, a group of Homo Erectus specimens. Ref: Jones. *Illustrated Dinosaur Movie Guide*; Thomas. *Videohound's Dragon*; not viewed.

Minotaur (2005?) U.K.; dir. Jonathan English; Lion's Gate. Proposed feature film; color. *CAST:* Steven Berkoff; Tony Todd.

In the 14th century B.C. villagers must give up young men and women for sacrifice to a god. Variety (Aug. 23, 2004, p. 10) said in this new treatment of the Theseus myth director English "is going for a darker, dirtier Iron Age version that he believes is closer to historical reality." Ref: *Internet Movie Database*.

The Original Golfer (1922) U.S.; dir. Tony Sarg; Sarg/Darley/Rialto. Animated short film; b&w; silent. (In the *Tony Sarg's Almanac* series).

Even Webb has no information on the story of this silhouette animation short. Other shorts in Sarg's animated *Almanac* series were prehistoric, such as *The First Flivver* (1922). Ref: Webb. *Animated Film Encyclopedia*; not viewed.

The Original Movie (1922). U.S.; dir. Tony Sarg; Sarg/Darley/Rialto. Animated short film; b&w; silent. (In the *Tony Sarg's Almanac* series).

Even Webb has no information on the story of this silhouette animation short. Other shorts Sarg's animated *Almanac* series were prehistoric, such as *The First Flivver* (1922). Ref: Webb. *Animated Film Encyclopedia*; not viewed.

Out of Time's Abyss (1970s) Proposed film. U.K.; Amicus.

Amicus planned a third film based on Edgar Rice Burroughs' Caprona stories, after *The Land That Time Forgot* (1975) and *The People That Time Forgot* (1977) but it was never made. Ref: Berry. *Dinosaur Filmography*.

Pedagogical Institution (College to You) (1940) U.S.; dir. Dave Fleischer; Fleischer/ Paramount. Animated short film; b&w. Screenplay, Joseph Stultz; music, Sammy Timberg.

This animated short was in Fleischer's *Stone Age* series, but Webb's synopsis does not sound prehistoric. "Joe Goof tries for a degree so he can get a job." Ref: Webb. *Animated Film Encyclopedia*; not viewed.

Prehistoric Hayseeds (1923) Australia; dir. Beaumont Smith; Beaumont Smith Productions. Screenplay, Beaumont Smith; photography, Lacey Percival. *CAST:* Hector St. Clair (*Wup*); Lotus Thompson (*Golden Girl*); Gordon Collingridge (*Owen Osborne*); Nina Dacre (*Tessie Worth*); Kathleen Mack (*Mrs. Wup*); J.P. O'Neill (*Dad Hayseed*); Pinky Weatherlee (*Mum Hayseed*); Roy Wilson (*Beetle Brows*); Dunstan Webb (*Terry*).

Information of the content of this early Australian film is elusive. Most character names are modern. Ref: *Internet Movie Database*; Goble. *International Film Index*; not viewed.

The Prehistoric Man (1917) [alt. *Az Ösember*] Hungary; dir. Alfred Deésy, or Cornelius Hintner; Star. Feature film; silent; b&w. Screenplay, Zoltán Somlyó, Ernö Györi.

Goble (*International Film Index*) and *Internet Movie Database* say this silent was directed by Hintner; Lee (*Reference Guide to Fantastic Films*) says it was made by Deésy. Lee gives this synopsis: "Rays make monkey as smart as a man; monkey then lusts after a woman and gains political power; returned to original state at end." Not viewed.

Prelude to Taurus (1972) U.S. Feature film; color. *CAST:* Pamela Tiffin; Robert Walker, Jr.

Jones (*Illustrated Dinosaur Movies Guide*) gives the above minimal information and says "Arctic scientists thaw out bodies frozen for a million years." The existence of the film is confirmed by Goble's *International Film Index*, but confirmation of the contents is elusive.

The Primevals (1978–?) U.S.; dir. Charles Band, David Allen; Empire Pictures. Proposed film.

This legendary proposed film was never made. Explorers in the Himalayas discover a lost world with a Yeti, lizard men, Neanderthal-like hominids and other creatures. Effects experts Jim Danforth and Phil Tippett were involved in the abortive project. *Cinefantastique* (Feb. 1999) reported that special effects veteran Allen, who had worked on *When Dinosaurs Ruled the Earth* (1970) and *Caveman* (1981), was at work on the project, using the stop-motion technique which many believed had been rendered obsolete by computer-generated effects. *Cinefantastique* said the film would involve a fight in an arena involving "lizard-men, a Yeti and prehistoric humans." However, Allen died later in 1999 and the film has not been completed. Ref: Jones. *Illustrated Dinosaur Movie Guide*; Berry. *Dinosaur Filmography*; not viewed.

Rahan (2006?) France; dir. Christopher Gans; Les Films du Gorak. Proposed film; color. Screenplay, Christopher Gans, Jean-Francois Henry based on comic books by André Chéret and Roger Lecureux; photography, Dan Laustsen.

An ad in *Variety* (May 3, 2004) said that production of *Rahan* would begin in the fall of 2004. In the foreground of the ad is a brawny fist holding a stone knife and a forearm wearing a bracelet of animal teeth. A herd of mammoths stampedes from an erupting volcano. Gans directed the wildly extravagant costume action movie *Brotherhood of the Wolf* (2001). *Internet Movie Database* says the film will appear in 2006. Chéret's and Lecureux's comic book hero Rahan is a Tarzanesque wanderer in prehistory. Ref: *Internet Movie Database*.

The Stone Age (1917) [alt. *Her Cave Man*] U.S.; dir. Ferris Hartman. Short film; b&w; silent. *CAST:* Al St. John; Mary Thurman.

Contents unknown. Ref: *Internet Movie Database*; Goble. *International Film Index*; not viewed.

The Stone Age (1922) U.S.; dir. Charley Chase (as Charles Parrott). Short film; b&w; silent. *CAST:* Charley Chase.

Contents unknown. *Internet Movie Database*, Goble's *International Film Index* and an online filmography of Charley Chase's career at www.goldensilents.com all say Chase made this film but other online Chase filmographies omit it. Not viewed.

The Stone Age (1940) U.S.; dir. Dave Fleischer; Paramount. Animated short film.

Jones (*Illustrated Dinosaur Movie Guide*) and Goble (*International Film Index*) lists this Fleischer film but it is not in Webb (*Animated Film Encyclopedia*) or *Internet Movie Database*. Not viewed.

Stone Age Warriors (1990) Hong Kong; dir. Stanley Tong. Feature film; color.

Set among modern jungle tribesmen. Ref: *Internet Movie Database*; not viewed.

Three Missing Links (1938) U.S.; dir. Jules White; Columbia.

The Three Stooges are studio janitors hired to play natives and an ape in a jungle movie. Ref: Lenburg. *Three Stooges Scrapbook*; not viewed.

The Ugly Dino (1940) U.S.; dir. Dave Fleischer; Fleischer/Paramount. Animated short film; 7 min.; b&w. Screenplay, George Manuell.

Webb reports that this animated short in Fleischer's *Stone Age* series tells the Ugly Duckling story with dinosaurs. Probably without cavemen. Ref: Webb. *Animated Film Encyclopedia*; not viewed.

Voyage to the Prehistoric Planet (1965) U.S.; dir. Curtis Harrington (as John Sebastian); Filmgroup/AIP. 74 min.; color. Screenplay, Curtis Harrington (as John Sebastian). CAST: Basil Rathbone (*Prof. Hartman*); Faith Domergue (*Marcia Evans*).

The first of two films assembled by producer Roger Corman around footage from the 1962 Soviet film *Planeta Burg*. *Voyage to the Prehistoric Planet* has dinosaurs but no primitive people. *Voyage to the Planet of Prehistoric Women* (1966) has "gill women" and is in Part 3. Ref: Berry. *Dinosaur Filmography*; Hardy. Hardy. *Overlook Film Encyclopedia: Science Fiction*; not viewed.

Xena Warrior Princess (1995–2001) Proposed episode *Sticks and Stones*.

During the sixth and final season of *Xena* (2000–2001) Renaissance Pictures announced they were planning to make a prehistoric episode starring Lucy Lawless and Renee O'Connor, about Xena's and Gabrielle's early ancestors. They had already established in previous episodes that Xena and Gabrielle were "soulmates" who met in several different lifetimes. Unhappily, the cave–Xena episode was never made.

After the series ended in 2001, the screenplay for the proposed prehistoric episode, *Sticks and Stones* by Joel Metzger, appeared on Soulmates fan website (www.cousinliz.com). The screenplay has Cro-Magnons and Neanderthals living near each other. They are not friends but neither do they fight. The Cro-Magnons "have no language, only a series of complicated grunts and gestures," according to Metzger. They do have cave paintings. The Neanderthals are more primitive and "fight like rabid dogs" over food. Xena, of course, is a Neanderthal, while Gabrielle is a Cro-Magnon.

Alti, a malignant female shaman with great powers, goes back to the time of these primitives in order to control the future of mankind. She incites the Neanderthals' jealousy of the Cro-Magnons, who have "more food, more hides, more everything!" Alti gives the Neanderthals brain boosts, which instantly give them the power of speech and various technical skills. Metzger says the Neanderthals are "overwhelmed" by their sudden understanding of new concepts. Alti shows them how to make spears, with which they defeat the Cro-Magnons, who only have clubs. Alti even shows the Neanderthals how to create art so they can make statues of her. She plans to create a civilization of intelligent but brutish Neanderthals, with the Cro-Magnons permanently enslaved — and herself as sole goddess.

A benevolent spirit sends the ancient Greek incarnations of Xena and Gabrielle back in time to defeat Alti. Gabrielle finds that the Cro-Magnons do not permit women to use weapons, while Xena of course is top dog of the Neanderthals. Metzger seems to be suggesting that the inferior position of women was an innovation of more advanced societies, and that among the truly primitive, such as his Neanderthals, women can be independent and even dominant, based on individual prowess.

With difficulty the Greek Xena and Gabrielle get the better of Alti. After Alti and the "modern" Xena and Gabrielle return to their own time, the Neanderthals are actually more advanced than the Cro-Magnons, due to Alti's brain boosts. Neanderthal Xena and Cro-Magnon Gabrielle become friends and begin to lead their peoples into cooperation with each other.

Metzger's screenplay underrates the Cro-Magnons by saying they did not have real speech, and underrates the Neanderthals by showing them fighting each other over food. Those errors are of course borrowed from *One Million B.C.* (1940) and *One Million Years B.C.* (1966). Gabrielle gets to quote Charlton Heston's famous line from *Planet of the Apes* (1968), "Get your hands off me, you damned dirty ape!"

Since the screenplay makes clear that the familiar Greek Xena and Gabrielle are descended from their prehistoric counterparts, and since the prehistoric Xena is Neanderthal, the screenplay assumes that the Neanderthals did not die out completely, but that some modern humans are descended from them.

See Part III for *Xena* episodes about primitive people (the "Horde" and cannibals) in the ancient historical period in which most *Xena* stories were set. Ref: *Whoosh* website (www.whoosh.org); Soulmates website (http://cousinliz.com).

Appendix B. Post-Apocalypse Primitives in Film and Television

This appendix lists films and television shows in which, after an apocalyptic collapse of civilization, people have a primitive lifestyle reminiscent of prehistory. Films in which survivors live in the remnants of the ruined civilization, such as *The Omega Man* (1971), are omitted.

America 3000 (1986) U.S.; dir. David Engelbach; Cannon. 92 min. *CAST:* Chuck Wagner (*Korvis*); Laurene Landon (*Vena*).

In the post–Apocalypse American Southwest, men revolt against an Amazon dictatorship. This entertaining, minor *Mad Max* copy features an invented future English, with words like "weaps" for weapons and "regs" for laws. MK 5.

Battlefield Earth: A Saga of the Year 3000 (2000) U.S.; dir. Roger Christian; Morgan Creek. 119 min. *CAST:* John Travolta (*Terl*); Barry Pepper (*Jonnie Tyler*).

Primitive humans in a devastated Earth occupied by arrogant aliens learn than mankind was once civilized and revolt against their oppressors. A catastrophic critical and box-office flop. MK 2.

Beneath the Planet of the Apes (1970) U.S.; dir. Ted Post; 20th Century–Fox. 95 min. *CAST:* James Franciscus (*Brent*); Linda Harrison (*Nova*).

Time-traveling astronauts, dominant apes, primitive humans and atom-bomb–worshipping underground humans struggle in this sequel to *Planet of the Apes* (1968), which repeats the Vietnam-era, anti-military, pro-intellectual and misanthropic views of the first film. MK 7.

Captive Women (1952) [alt. *1,000 Years from Now*; *3000 A.D.*] U.S.; dir. Stuart Gilmore; RKO. 64 min.; b&w. *CAST:* Robert Clarke (*Rob*); Margaret Field (*Ruth*).

Primitive tribes battle in post–Apocalypse New York and New Jersey. Not viewed.

Lord of the Flies (1963) U.K.; dir. Peter Brook; Two Arts. 90 min.; b&w. Screenplay, Peter Brook based on novel by William Golding. *CAST:* James Aubrey (*Ralph*); Tom Chapin (*Jack*).

During a nuclear war, English schoolboys are stranded on an island where they revert to savagery. MK 8. [An inferior 1990 remake stranded the boys (Americans, this time) but did not involve a war. The 1990 film was therefore not post–Apocalypse but merely a juvenile–Robinson-Crusoes-go-bad movie.]

Mad Max Beyond Thunderdome (1985) Australia; dir. George Miller, George Ogilvie; Kennedy-Miller/Warner Bros. 106 min. *CAST:* Mel Gibson (*Max*); Tina Turner (*Aunty Entity*).

Set in Australia, this third film in the series (after *Mad Max* (1979) and *The Road Warrior* (1981)) features the same kind of leather-clad, violent adult post–Apocalypse society seen in the first two films but also a fur-clad, non-violent children's society which represents a primitive but hopeful future. MK 6.

Planet of the Apes (1968) U.S.; dir. Franklin J. Schaffner; 20th Century–Fox. 112 min. *CAST:*

Charlton Heston (*Taylor*); Linda Harrison (*Nova*).

Astronauts go forward to the future and find an Earth where intelligent apes rule primitive, mute, dim-witted humans. The classic is a great SF thriller but its strong misanthropy is distasteful. MK 8. Only the first of five sequels, *Beneath the Planet of the Apes* (1970), featured primitive humans. The 2001 remake had oppressed but not primitive humans on another planet.

Prehistoric Bimbos in Armageddon City (1991) U.S.; dir. Todd Sheets. 80 min.; color.

Apparently nothing about the film is prehistoric except the title. Ref: *Internet Movie Database*; *Amazon.com*; not viewed.

Rocketship X-M (1950) U.S.; dir. Kurt Neumann; Lippert. 78 min.; b&w with tinted sequences. *CAST*: Lloyd Bridges; Osa Massen.

Astronauts find deformed, handicapped, primitive survivors of a nuclear war on Mars. Co-written by uncredited, blacklisted leftist Dalton Trumbo, *Rocketship X-M* is one of the first post–Apocalypse films. Some sources say wrongly that all the Martians are blind. The astronauts find one blind Martian girl; other Martians are sighted but have other disabilities and deformities. MK 7.

Teenage Caveman (2001) U.S.; dir. Larry Clark; Creature Features Productions. Cable TV film; 90 min.; color. *CAST*: Andrew Keegan (*David*).

Teenagers revolt against repressive adults in a post–Apocalypse cave tribe. This remake of Roger Corman's *Teenage Caveman* (1958) was set in the future, while Corman's film was set in the past; see Part I. Clark's remake is merely a teenage sex film. Not viewed.

Thundarr the Barbarian (1980–81) U.S.; Ruby/Spears Enterprises/ABC. Animated TV series.

A barbarians-vs.-wizards story set 2000 years in the future. Ref: Woolery. *Children's Television*; not viewed.

The Time Machine (1960) U.S.; dir. George Pal; MGM/Loew's. 103 min. Based on novel by H.G. Wells. *CAST*: Rod Taylor (*George*); Yvette Mimieux (*Weena*).

In the distant future, a time traveler finds the Morlocks, humans who have regressed to intelligent but brutish underground-dwellers. MK 8. [Also made in 1949 (BBC TV film), 1978 (a U.S. TV film) and 2002 (a U.S. feature film), as well as an episode of the 1995 *Wishbone* children's anthology series.]

World Without End (1956) U.S.; dir. Edward Bernds; Allied Artists. 80 min.. *CAST*: Hugh Marlowe (*John Borden*).

Astronauts from the 20th century land on 26th century Earth and find primitive mutant humans. MK 4.

Yor, the Hunter from the Future (1982) Italy; dir. Antonio Margheriti (as Anthony Dawson); Diamant/Columbia. 88 min. *CAST*: Reb Brown (*Yor*); Corinne Clery (*Ka-Laa*).

Until two-thirds of the way through the film, audiences would assume they are seeing a story set in prehistory. The movie even has a dinosaur. Then the heroes discover that both their own people and the inhabitants of an island full of modern technology are descended from survivors of a nuclear war. This entertaining B-film is notable for the homoerotic display of the hero's body and for a scene in which the good people's tribe offer to sacrifice their children to the gods but do not go through with it. Apparently the offer is enough. MK 6.

Zardoz (1974) U.K.; dir. John Boorman; 20th Century–Fox. 105 min.; color. *CAST*: Sean Connery; Charlotte Rampling.

In postatomic 2293, the Outlands are inhabited only by the Brutals, who fight constantly, while the Vortex is the seat of decadent immortals, some of whom say they wish to die. This ambitious SF film confused audiences. "Zardoz," the name of a fake god, turns out to be a play on *The Wizard of Oz*. Ref: Hardy. *Overlook Film Encyclopedia: Science Fiction*; MK 5.

Appendix C: Outstanding Performances as Prehistoric Characters

In realistic prehistoric settings:

Wilfred Lucas (*Bruteforce*) in *Man's Genesis* (1912)

Dan Richter (*Moonwatcher*) in *2001: A Space Odyssey* (1968)

Peter Elliott (*Man-Ape*) in *Missing Link* (1988)

In non-realistic prehistoric settings:

Alan Reed (*voice of Fred Flintstone*) in *The Flintstones* (TV, 1960–66)

Martine Beswick (*Queen Kari*) in *Slave Girls* (1967)

John Goodman (*Fred Flintstone*) in *The Flintstones* (1994)

In modern settings:

Gregg Martell (*Neanderthal Man*) in *Dinosaurus!* (1960)

Michell Piccoli (*Themroc*) in *Themroc* (1972)

Miguel Godreau (*Primal Man*) in *Altered States* (1980)

John Lone (*Charu/Charlie*) in *Iceman* (1984)

Hirotaro Honda (*Takashi*) in *Peking Man* (1997)

Appendix D: The Creationist Challenge: Productions That Question the Existence of Prehistoric Humans

"Young-earth" creationists object to Darwin's theory of evolution, which they feel conflicts with the creation story in Genesis. They dispute the existence of any hominids before the appearance of modern humans. Movies featuring cavemen would be antithetical to creationist thought.

Instead, creationists have produced films and television programs questioning evolution. These films include *Ape-Men: Fact or Fiction?* (1986, Institute for Creation Research); *The Bible and Science* (1990?, Sound Words); *The Origin of Man* (1980?, Institute for Creation Research); *The Origin of Mankind* (1982, Standard Media International/Eden Films); and *Who Was Adam? A Testable Christian Approach to Human Origins* (2002, Reasons to Believe). In *Science and Genesis* (1991, Trinity Broadcast Network/Reasons to Believe), a set of 7 videocassettes (*Resolving Conflicts between Science and Genesis*; *Comparing Creation Accounts*; *Cavemen, Dinosaurs and the Fossil Record*; *Creation Days*; *Noah and the Ark*; *The Universal Flood*; *Round Table on Genesis One*), Hugh Ross ingeniously attempts to reconcile the fossil record and Biblical literalism by proposing that God first created hominids, then allowed them to die out, then created Adam and Eve.

A pro-science view is presented by *In the Beginning: The Creationist Controversy* (1994, PBS), which examines the roots of the Creationist movement, recent court decisions and textbook selection issues. Another secular discussion of Creationism is found in *What About God*, the last part of the series *Evolution* (2001; see Part II).

The major Hollywood fiction film about the Creationist dispute is *Inherit the Wind* (1960), directed by Stanley Kramer and based on the play by Jerome Lawrence and Robert E. Lee. In the 1920s Tennessee schoolteacher Bertram Cates is charged with teaching evolution in defiance of state law. He is prosecuted by famous fundamentalist Matthew Harrison Brady (Fredric March), a presidential candidate, and defended by shrewd crusading attorney Henry Drummond (Spencer Tracy) in a case which attracts national attention and a visit by scornful big-city journalist E.K. Hornbeck (Gene Kelly), who makes fun of the frenzied locals. Brady wins a guilty verdict but loses the propaganda war; he collapses and dies soon after the verdict. Drummond admires the honestly mistaken Brady more than the cynical Hornbeck.

The play by Lawrence and Lee is of course based on the 1925 trial of John T. Scopes, who was prosecuted by presidential candidate William Jennings Bryan (who died five days after the trial) and defended by Clarence Darrow. Hornbeck is based on acid-tongued H.L. Mencken. The religious anti-evolutionists in the film are obsessed with the question of man's descent from apes. They carry signs with slogans like "You can't make a monkey out of me!" One showman even displays a chimpanzee dressed as a man and chewing a cigar, which somehow illustrates his claim that the apes were created by "devolution" from man.

Variety (July 7, 1960) was very impressed by this "outstanding screen achievement ... a rousing and fascinating motion picture" and praised the entire cast and the "florid, witty, penetrating, compassionate, and sardonic" dialogue. The screenplay, Ernest Laszlo's cinematography, the editing, and Spencer Tracy's acting were nominated for Oscars. March won Best Actor at the Berlin Film Festival. The witty film is probably the best courtroom drama which does not involve a murder.

The biggest reason the film still amazes after forty years is the work of Tracy and March, two of the greatest actors in the history of Hollywood. Tracy is impeccable (and very funny) but March steals scenes even from him. Few films tell such a story — in which two brilliant men who like and admire each other must fight over principles they cannot compromise — and even fewer tell it so well. It's hard to think of another film with a character like March's Brady, a highly intelligent and once-great man who has descended into bigotry and fanaticism, and who sometimes realizes that he has betrayed his potential.

Inherit the Wind was remade three times, each time with important actors in the lead roles. *Inherit the Wind* (1965, U.S.; dir. George Schaefer), a TV film for NBC in the *Hallmark Hall of Fame* series, starred Melvyn Douglas as Drummond, Ed Begley as Brady and Murray Hamilton as Hornbeck (*Variety*, Nov. 11, 1965). *Inherit the Wind* (1988, U.S., dir. David Greene), a TV film, starred Kirk Douglas as Brady, Jason Robards as Drummond and Darren McGavin as Hornbeck (*Variety*, March 30, 1988). *Inherit the Wind* (1999, U.S., dir. Daniel Petrie) was a cable TV film for Showtime with George C. Scott as Brady, Jack Lemmon as Drummond and Beau Bridges as Hornbeck. Still, critics agree that Kramer's original surpassed all the remakes.

Documentaries on the 1925 Scopes Trial include *The Monkey Trial* (1997, A&E/History Channel); *Monkey Trial* (2002, Nebraska ETV/PBS); *Of Monkeys and Men* (1960?, National Educational TV); *The Scopes "Monkey Trial"* (1998, Cinetel Productions/Court Television), a reconstruction in the video series *Landmark American Trials*, with Ed Asner as William Jennings Bryan and Charles Durning as Clarence Darrow); and *12 Days in Dayton: The Scopes Monkey Trial* (2001, Greater Chattanooga Public Television).

Bibliography

Adams, T. R. *The Flintstones: A Modern Stone Age Phenomenon.* Turner Publishing, 1994.

Archer, Steve. *Willis O'Brien: Special Effects Genius.* McFarland, 1993.

Auel, Jean M. *The Clan of the Cave Bear.* Crown, 1980.

Beck, Jerry, ed. *The 50 Greatest Cartoons.* Turner Publishing, 1994.

Beck, Jerry, and Will Friedwald. *Looney Tunes and Merrie Melodies: A Complete Illustrated Guide to the Warner Bros. Cartoons.* Holt, 1989.

Bendazzi, Giannalberto. *Cartoons: One Hundred Years of Cinema Animation.* Indiana University Press, 1994.

Bergan, Ronald, and Robyn Karney. *The Holt Foreign Film Guide.* Henry Holt, 1988.

Berry, Mark F. *The Dinosaur Filmography.* McFarland, 2002.

Bissette, Stephen R. "One Million Years B.C." [Review], *Video Watchdog* no. 40, 1997.

_____. *We Are Going to Eat You!: Third World Cannibal Movies and the Inside Story of Gonna-Goona Films.* SpiderBaby Grafix, 2003. [author's publication of 1990 manuscript]

Bleiler, David., ed. *TLA Video & DVD Guide 2004.* St. Martin's Griffin, 2003.

Blum, Daniel. *A Pictorial History of the Silent Screen.* Putnam, 1953.

Brach, Gérard. *Quest for Fire* [screenplay]. 1980.

Brunette, Peter. *Roberto Rossellini.* Oxford University Press, 1987.

Castleman, Harry, and Walter J. Podrazik. *Harry and Wally's Favorite TV Shows.* Prentice Hall, 1989.

Cecchi Usai, Paolo. *The Griffith Project: Vol. 6, Films Produced in 1912.* British Film Institute, 2002.

Chion, Michel. *Kubrick's Cinema Odyssey.* British Film Institute, 2001.

Connelly, Robert B. *The Motion Picture Guide: Silent Film 1910–1936.* CineBooks, 1985.

Edera, Bruno. *Full Length Animated Feature Films.* Hastings House, 1977.

Encyclopedia of Fantastic Film and Television. http://www.eofftv.com.

Erickson, Hal. *Television Cartoon Shows: An Illustrated Encyclopedia, 1949 through 1993.* McFarland, 1995.

Fox, Jordan R. "Quest for Fire," *Cinefantastique,* Feb. 1982.

Fraser, George MacDonald. *The Hollywood History of the World: From One Million Years B.C. to Apocalypse Now.* Beech Tree Books, 1988.

Fulton, Roger, and John Betancourt. *The Sci-Fi Channel Encyclopedia of TV Science Fiction.* Warner, 1998.

Gifford, Denis. *British Animated Films, 1895–1985.* McFarland, 1987.

_____. *British Film Catalogue 1895–1985.* Facts on File, 1986.

Glut, Donald F. *Dinosaur Valley Girls: The Book.* McFarland, 1998.

Goble. Alan. *The International Film Index, 1895–1990.* Bowker-Saur, 1991.

Halliwell, Leslie, and Philip Purser. *Halliwell's Television Companion.* 2nd ed. Granada, 1982.

Hardy, Phil, ed. *The Overlook Film Encyclopedia: Horror.* Overlook, 1993.

Hardy, Phil, ed. *The Overlook Film Encyclopedia: Science Fiction.* Overlook, 1991.

Harryhausen, Ray. *Film Fantasy Scrapbook.* 2nd ed. Barnes, 1974.

_____, and Tony Dalton. *Ray Harryhausen: An Animated Life.* Billboard Books, 2004.

Henderson, C.J. *The Encyclopedia of Science Fiction Movies.* Checkmark, 2001.

The Internet Movie Database. http://us.imdb.com.

Johnson, Tom, and Deborah Del Vecchio. *Hammer Films: An Exhaustive Filmography.* McFarland, 1996.

Jones, Stephen. *The Illustrated Dinosaur Movie Guide.* Titan Books, 1993.

Kempen, Bernhard. *Abenteuer in Gondwanaland und Neandertal: Prähisotrische Motive in der Literatur und anderen Medien.* Corian, 1994.

_____, and Thomas Deist. *Das Dinosaurier-Filmbuch: von "Gertie the Dinosaur" bis "Jurassic Park."* Tilsner, 1993.

Kinnard, Roy. *Beasts and Behemoths: Prehistoric Creatures in the Movies.* Scarecrow, 1988.
_____. *Science Fiction Serials.* McFarland, 1998.
Klepper, Robert K. *Silent Films, 1877–1996.* McFarland, 1999.
Kline, Jim. *The Complete Films of Buster Keaton.* Citadel, 1993.
Larson, Randall D. *Music from the House of Hammer: Music in the Hammer Horror Films, 1950–1980.* Scarecrow, 1996.
Lee, Walt. *Reference Guide to Fantastic Films.* Hollywood Film Archive, 1974.
Leissner, Dan. *Tuesday's Child: The Life and Death of Imogen Hassall.* Luminary Press, 2002.
Lenburg, Jeff. *The Encyclopedia of Animated Cartoons.* Facts on File, 1991. [with information on TV series episodes omitted from the 1999 2nd ed.]
_____. *The Encyclopedia of Animated Cartoons.* 2nd ed. Checkmark, 1999.
_____, Joan Howard Maurer and Greg Lenburg. *The Three Stooges Scrapbook.* Citadel, 1995.
L'Officier, Jean-Marc. *The Doctor Who Programme Guide.* Target, 1989.
Lucanio, Patrick. *With Fire and Sword: Italian Spectacles on American Screens* Scarecrow, 1994.
_____, and Gary Coville. *American Science Fiction Television Series of the 1950s: Episode Guides and Casts and Credits for Twenty Shows.* McFarland, 1998.
Marill, Alvin H. *Movies Made for Television: The Telefeature and the Mini-series.* New York Zoetrope, 1987.
Morton, Alan. *The Complete Directory to Science Fiction, Fantasy and Horror Television Series: A Comprehensive Guide to the First 50 Years 1946 to 1996.* Other World, 1997.
Nash, Jay Robert, and Stanley Ralph Ross. *The Motion Picture Guide.* CineBooks, 1985 (and updates).
OCLC WorldCat. [subscription database] OCLC, 1969– .
Olton, Bert. *Arthurian Legends on Film and Television.* McFarland, 2000.
Perlman, Martin. "Clan of the Cave Bear," *Cinefantastique*, Oct. 1985.
Philips, Mark, and Frank Garcia. *Science Fiction Television Series: Episode Guides, Histories, and Casts and Credits for 62 Prime Time Shows, 1959 Through 1989.* McFarland, 1996.
Prehistoric Fiction. http://www.trussel.com/f_pre his.htm.
Rainey, Buck. *Serials and Series: A World Filmography 1912–1956.* McFarland, 1999.
Richter, Don. *Moonwatcher's Memoir: A Diary of 2001: A Space Odyssey.* Carroll and Graf, 2002.
Ringgold, Gene, and DeWitt Bodeen. *The Complete Films of Cecil B. DeMille.* Citadel, 1969.
Rosny, J.H. *Quest for Fire.* 1909; trans., 1967; reprint, Ballantine, 1982.
Sanello, Frank. *Reel v. Real: How Hollywood Turns Fact into Fiction.* Taylor, 2003.
Schwam, Stephanie, ed. *The Making of 2001: A Space Odyssey.* Modern Library, 2000.
Scott, Keith. *The Moose That Roared: The Story of Jay Ward, Bill Scott, a Flying Squirrel and a Talking Moose.* St. Martin's, 2000.
Senn, Bryan, and John Johnson. *Fantastic Cinema Subject Guide.* McFarland, 1992.
Shapiro, Marc. *When Dinosaurs Ruled the Screen.* Image Publications, 1992.
Sinyard, Neil. *Silent Movies.* Gallery Books, 1990.
Smith, Dave. *Disney A to Z: The Official Encyclopedia.* Hyperion, 1996.
Smith, Gary Allen. *Epic Films: Casts, Credits and Commentary on Over 350 Historical Spectacle Movies.* 2nd ed. McFarland, 2004.
Stanley, John. *Creature Features: The Science Fiction, Fantasy and Horror Guide.* Updated ed. Berkeley, 2000.
Svehla, Gary, and Susan Svehla, eds. *Memories of Hammer.* Luminary, 2002.
Thomas, Brian. *Videohound's Dragon: Asian Action & Cult Flicks.* Visible Ink, 2003.
Van Hise, James. *Hot-Blooded Dinosaur Movies.* Pioneer, 1993.
Variety. New York, 1907– .
Variety Film Reviews. Bowker, 1985– .
Variety Television Reviews. Garland, 1989– .
Wagenknecht, Edward, and Anthony Slide. *The Films of D.W. Griffith.* Crown, 1975.
Wakabayashi, H. Clark. *Brother Bear: A Transformation Tale.* Disney Editions, 2003.
Warren, Bill. *Keep Watching the Skies! American Science Fiction Movies of the Fifties.* McFarland, 1982 (Vol. 1) and 1986 (Vol. 2).
Webb, Graham. *The Animated Film Encyclopedia: A Complete Guide to American Shorts, Features and Sequences, 1900–1979.* McFarland, 2000.
Webber, Roy P. *The Dinosaur Films of Ray Harryhausen.* McFarland, 2004.
Weldon, Michael. *The Psychotronic Encyclopedia of Film.* Ballantine, 1983.
Woolery, George W. *Animated TV Specials: The Complete Directory to the First Twenty-Five Years, 1962–1987.* Scarecrow, 1989.
_____. *Children's Television: The First Thirty-Five Years, 1946–1981.* Scarecrow, 1983.
World of Hammer. Lands Before Time [videocassette documentary]. Anchor Bay, 1990.

Index

A Spasso nel Tempo 9–10
Aaron, Sidney 213
Abarbanel, Sam X. 117
ABC Weekend Specials 60
Aber, Alan 191
Abominable Snowman 125, 27, 113, 282
Abraham, F. Murray 187
The Abyss (*Xena* episode) 276
Ackerman, Forrest 49, 258
Ackerman, Peter 80
Acupuncture, Prehistoric 187, 203
Adam and Eve 1, 9, 16, 55–56, 72, 137, 288
Adam and Eve, the First Love Story 16
Adam Raises Cain 9, 144
Adamo ed Eva, la Prima Storia d'Amore 16
Adams, Douglas 79
Adams, Jeremy 196
Adams, Julia 221, 223
Adams, Nick 273
Adams, T. R. 61
Adam's Family Tree 213
Adam's Rib 9
Adamson, Al 233
Addis, Justus 273
Addison, John 218
Addy, Mark 68–69
Adix, Vern 188
Adler, Charles 45, 59
Adler, Felix 264
Adorf, Mario 161
Adrift in Time 9–10
Adventure at the Center of the Earth 217–218
Adventure-fantasy films 3
Adventures in Woollyville 46
The Adventures of Sir Lancelot 52
The Adventures of Stella Star 263
The Adventures of Superman 10
Aegean: Legacy of Atlantis 175
Aegean Sea 175
Aesop's Film Fables (series) 16, 53, 136
Africa 94–95, 132–133, 147–148, 179, 172, 178, 180, 182–186, 188, 197, 201–202, 204–205, 207–208, 210, 219

Africa and Atlantis 175
African Atlantic Migration Theory 206
"African Eve" *see* Mitochondrial Eve Theory
Afrique, Terre de l'Homme 202
After School 10
Agar, John 164
The Age of Iron, 2000 B.C.-A.D. 200 210
The Age of Mammals 169
The Age of Man 169
Age of the Great Dinosaurs 10
Aggregation camps (meetings of different tribes) 30, 186
Agostino, Claude 120, 127
The Agricultural Revolution, 8000 B.C.-5000 B.C. 210
Agriculture, Prehistoric 88, 171, 174, 180, 187, 192, 193–194, 196, 200, 204, 210
Aguirre, Laurie Seeley 188
Ahlberg, Mac 233
Aiello, Leslie C. 178
Ainley, Anthony 241
Ainu People (Japan) 89–90
Airplane 28
Akin, Philip 234
Akka (Chimpanzee) 246
Alaska 16–18, 169, 185, 202, 204, 234
Albertini, Adalberto 132
Albinana, Ricardo 248
Alcazar, Angel 16
Alcott, John 147, 151
Alda, Alan 202
Aletter, Frank 85
Alexander, Paul 206
Alexis 248
Alien 26, 28
Alien from L.A. 74
Alien vs. Predator 74
Aliens *see* Extraterrestrials on Earth
All at Sea 218
All in the Family 114
All in the Mind 170
Alland, William 222
Allard, Tom 241
Allen, Beth 275

Allen, David 28, 221, 282
Allen, Heck 58
Allen, Irwin 136, 170, 273
Allen, Patrick 154, 157–158
Allen, R.S. 90
Alley Oop 11, 54
Allison, Eric 258
Alonzo, John 196
Alsberg, Arthur 86
Alsobrook, Russ T. 230
Altamira Cave (Spain) 176, 196, 199, 201–202
Altamira Skull 179
Altered States 3, 5–6, 213–215, 236, 248, 287
Alvarado, Crox 237
Amazon High (pilot for proposed series) 165–166
Amazon Nation (pilot for proposed series) 165–166
Amazons 10, 12, 48–49, 53, 117–118, 132–134, 140–142, 160, 165–166, 232, 263, 270, 285
America 3000 285
American Gladiators 264
American Mime Theater 149
American Museum of Natural History 88, 209
American Serengeti 199
An American Werewolf in London 215
America's Stone Age Explorers 169
Ames, Denise 49
Ames, Michael 256
Aminel, Georges 12
The Anals of History 10
The Anals of History 2 10–11
Ancell, Craig 275
Ancestor worship 203
Ancestors of Modern Man 180
Ancient Aliens 176
Ancient America 170
Ancient & Modern Cultures (series) 169
Ancient Britains 169
Ancient Britons 169
Ancient Civilizations 169
Ancient Man 169
Ancient Mariners 177

Index

Ancient Mysteries (series) 203
Ancient Secrets of the Bible 188
Ancient Voices (series) 189, 203, 205
The Ancients of North America 169–170
Ande, Cheryl 166
Anders, Merry 164
Andersen, Suzy 140
Anderson, Broncho Billy 77
Anderson, Gerry 262, 264
Anderson, Gillian 165
Anderson, Jamie 68
Anderson, Pamela 69
Anderson, Richard Dean 263
Anderson, Sylvia 264
Andrade, Steven 269
Andres, Ursula 158
Andrews, Michael 174
Andreyev, Vladimir 265
Angier, John 202
Animal House 28, 272
The Animal Within 170
The Animal World 4, 48, 170, 269
Ankrum, Morris 234
Ann, Melissa 48
Ann-Margret 60, 68
Annakin, Ken 142
Annaud, Jean-Jacques 1, 5, 120, 123, 125–126
Anno, Takashi 89
Anthony, Nigel 174
Anthony and Cleopatra 219
The Ape Man (1944) 256
Ape Man (1995) 198
Ape Man (2000) 178–180
Ape Man of the Jungle 215
Ape Man: The Story of Human Evolution 5, 170–171
Ape-Men: Fact or Fiction? 288
The Ape That Took Over the World 197
"Apemen" 1, 4, 56–57, 83–84, 94–95, 105–106, 109, 111, 115, 162, 215, 218, 221, 232, 239, 243–245, 248–249, 254–256, 258–259, 266, 275
Apemen of Africa 193
Apes to Man 198
Apollonius of Rhodes 232
Appleigh, Christine 11
Apsell, Paula S. 180
Aquaman 74
The Aquatic Ape: A New Model for Human Evolution? 171
Aquatic Ape Theory 171, 209
Arabian Nights setting 259–260
Arabs 267–268
Aran Islands 187
Ararat, Mount 188
Arcady, Alexandre 199
Archaeology (series) 169, 176, 185, 195, 202
Archeological/paleoanthropological techniques 177, 180, 184, 193–195, 199, 201–203, 205–206
Archie's TV Funnies 11, 54
Arctic Regions 12, 260

Ardrey, Robert 148, 170–171
The A.R.E's 2003 Search for Atlantis 175
Arioli, Don 79
Aristophanes 159
Aristotle 217
Arizona 180, 188
Arkeni 49
Arling, Charles 128
Arlington Springs Woman (Calif.) 202
Armstrong, Curtis 29, 53
Armstrong, Neil 213
Armus, Adam 275
Arnold, Cecile 76
Arnold, Harry 236
Arnold, Jack 86, 221, 223, 247
L'Art, Grandeur de l'Homme 201–202
Art, Mystère de l'Homme 202
The Art of Self-Defense 11
The Art of the Earliest American 198
Art, Prehistoric 17, 34, 36–37, 41–42, 47, 53, 78, 81, 84, 86–88, 99, 101–102, 106, 135–136, 172, 174, 176–177, 179–181, 185–186, 188, 191–199, 201–203, 205–206, 208, 221, 228, 235, 246, 269, 283
Arthur, King 115, 192
Arthur C. Clarke's Mysterious World (series) 204
As in Days of Yore 11
The Ascent of Man 171
Ash, Jerome 218
Ashley, John 147
Ashton, Paul 200
Asia 185, 193, 202
Asian Origin Theory 171, 197, 202, 204
Asimov, Isaac 270
Asner, Edward 289
Assignment Discovery: Forensics (series) 209
Asterix et Obelix: Mission Cleopatra 130
Astin, Sean 229
Astronomy, Prehistoric 158, 178, 194–195, 204–205
At Long Last Love 215–216, 249
At the Earth's Core 3, 216–217, 265
Atkins, Christopher 264
L'Atlantide (1921) 74
L'Atlantide (1972) 74
L'Atlantide (1992) 74
Atlantis 1, 73–74, 89–90, 113, 153, 175
Atlantis (1975) 175
Atlantis and the World's Shifting Crust 175
The Atlantis Connection 175
Atlantis: In Search of a Lost Continent 175
Atlantis in the Andes 175
Atlantis: Milo's Return 74
Atlantis: Mystery of the Minoans 175
Atlantis Reborn 175

Atlantis, the Lost Civilization 175
Atlantis, the Lost Continent (1961) 74
Atlantis: The Lost Empire 74
Atlantis Uncovered 175
Atlatls 121–122, 125, 172, 178, 190, 198, 209
Ator the Blade Master 1, 217
Ator the Invincible 217
Atragon 74, 89
Attenborough, David 192
Atwell, Roy 281
Aubrey, James 285
Audray, Cecile 82, 85
Auel, Jean M. 29, 31–34, 124
August, Edwin 19
August, Joseph H. 55
Aupperle, Jim 28, 169
Aureli, Andrea 16, 35, 37
Austin, Roy 262
Australian Aborigines 123, 177–180, 185, 188, 190–191, 193, 197, 201–202, 205
Australian Ark (series) 177
Australopithecines 148, 158, 184, 190, 193, 195, 208
Australopithecus afarensis 178, 192, 195, 202, 205, 207
Australopithecus africanus 178, 193, 199
Australopithecus robustus 95–96, 179, 195, 199
Austria 186
Autry, Gene 74, 135
Autterson, Gay 67–68, 69–70, 72, 98,
The Avengers 249
Aventura al Centro de la Tierra 15, 217–218
Avery, Tex 58, 62
Awesome Ancestors 175
Aykroyd, David 176, 181, 183, 189
Aylott, Dave 144, 154
Aysecik and the Bewitched Dwarfs in Dreamland 218
Az Ösember 282
Azzarella, Thomas 200

Babbitt, Alan 210
Babel II 89
Bach, Barbara 25, 28, 113
Backus, Jim 75, 154
Baggott, King 279
Baide, Doon 40
Bailey, Robert 180
Bain, Barbara 262
Baird, Harry 137, 140–141
Baird, Sharon 240
Bakaleinikoff, Mischa 238–239
Bakalyan, Richard 86
Baker, Brydon 271
Baker, Buddy 52
Baker, George 99, 104
Baker, Ian 234, 236
Baker, Melanie 271
Baker, Rick 96, 150, 247, 258, 265
Baker, Roy Ward 255
Baker, Sam 246

Bakhtiari People 171
Bakshi, Ralph 13, 36, 56–58, 128
Balaban, Bob 213
Baldwin, Alec 207–208
Baldwin, Stephen 68
Baleson, Tanya 24
Balke, Turid 267
Ballard, J.G. 154, 158
Ballard, Robert 189
Ballinger, Bill 239
Bamboo 185, 208
The Banana Monster 258–259
Band, Charles 282
Banderas, Antonio 267–268
Bantock, Leedham 114
Baralla, Fiammetta 161
Barbarella 263
Barbarossa 236
Barbera, Joseph 60, 62, 64, 68, 90
Barillé, Albert 98–99
Barlow, Dilly 180
Barnacle Bill 218
Barney, Pamela 249
Barre, Gabriel 245–246
Barretta, Bill 50
Barrie, Amanda 220
Barron, Keith 242
Barry, Dave 119
Barry, J.J. 78
Barry, John 263
Barry Lyndon 151
Barrymore, Drew 213–214
Barrymore, Lionel 19, 22
Bart the Bear 29
Barthélémy, Maurice 130
Bartlett, Kate 208
Barton, Milca 198
Barton, Nicholas 210
Barton Gulch Site (Montana) 198
Bartoska, Jirí 97, 132, 153
Basaran, Tunc 218
Basedow, Rainer 130
Basehart, Richard 273
Basket making 17
Bass, Eli 69
Batanides, Arthur 242
Batchelor, Joy 177
Batman (1966–68) 273
Batman films 269
Batmen 217–218
Battaglia, Gianlorenzo 9
The Battery 55
The Battle at Elderbrush Gulch 21
The Battle for Dominance 200
Battle of the Giants 99–104
Battle of the Sexes 49, 53, 70–71, 82, 117–118, 159, 162
Battlefield Earth: A Saga of the Year 3000 285
Battlestar Galactica 165
Bauer, Manfred 182
Bauer, Michelle 23, 223, 249, 253
Baum, L. Frank 218
Baum, Thomas 238
Baumann, Peter 206
Bava, Mario 40, 232
Bayer, Wolf 137
Baywatch 34

BBC MediaArc 198
B.C. 46
B.C.: A Special Christmas 11
B.C. (comic strip) 11, 13, 146
B.C. Rock 3, 5, 11–13
B.C.: The First Thanksgiving 11, 13
Bea, Lauren 49
Beach Babes 2: Cave Girl Island 279
Beamish, Jennifer 189
Bean, Nigel 198
The Bear 126
Beastmaster (1982) 40, 151
BeastMaster (1999–2002) 218
The Beasts Within 209
Beaumont, Charles 139
Beauties and Beasts 158
Beauties of the Night 14
Beauty and the Beast 126
Beavan, Claire 183
Becker, Josh 275
The Bedrock Cops 67
Beebe, Ford 218
Beery, Wallace 142, 144, 243
Beeson, Paul 263
Beethoven, Ludwig van 191
Before a Book Was Written 29
Before History, Man 193–194
Before the Romans 171
Before We Ruled the Earth 5, 81, 172–174, 186, 190
Beginning of History: Stone Age 174
The Beginning of Mankind 180
Beginnings (ca. 3100 B.C.–1000 A.D.) 183
The Beginnings of Man 174
Begley, Ed 289
Bégoin, Stéphane 201
Being Human 3, 13–14
Beirute, Jorge 53
Bejval, Vladimir 86–87
Belenky, Grigori 146
Bell, Alan J.W. 79
Bell, Brian 233
Bell, Jimmy 147
Bell, John 128
Les Belles de Nuit 14
El Bello Durmiente 4, 15, 17, 217
Ben-Hur 220
Benadaret, Bea 60, 70
Benard, Christian 120
Bencich, Steve 16
Bending, Clement W. 197
Beneath the Planet of the Apes 285
Benedict, Ed 62
Benjamin, Keith 273
Bennet, Spencer G. 239
Bennett, Alma 243
Bennett, Brian 129
Bennett, Charles 136
Bennett, Richard 264
Bennicke, Rune Brandt 19
Benny, Jack 46–47
Benoit, Pierre 74
Benson, George 223
Benson, Joey 233
Bentley, Thomas 50
Beowulf 267–268
Berardinelli, James 18, 152

Berest, Fred 238
Berg, Bill 52
Berg, Michael 80
Bergen, Birgit 35
Bergen, Tushka 238
Berger, Gregg 72
Berger, Senta 159–161
Berger, William 82, 85
Bergin, Patrick 244
Bergman, Jeff 70
Beringia 172–174, 189, 198
Beringian Migration 169, 173, 183, 190, 193, 198–199, 202–203
Berk, Howard 164
Berkely, Susan 99
Berkoff, Steven 281
Berman, Matt 120
Berman, Ted 86
Bernard, James 230
Bernds, Edward 271–272, 286
Berner, Sara 116
Bernsen, Corbin 263
Bernstein, Leonard 248
Bernstein, Peter 247
Berry, Halle 64, 66
Berry, Mark F. 4, 6, 15, 28, 66, 69, 99, 103, 112, 115–116, 139, 144, 157, 165, 170, 217, 225, 232–233, 237, 241–242, 244–245, 247, 253, 269–270, 272–274, 280
Bertheau, Stacey 271
Bertsch, Marguerite 279
Besser, Vilém 97, 132
Besstette, Leo 10
Bester, Alfred 227
Beswick, Doug 169, 247
Beswick, Martine 43, 104, 113, 132–135, 157–158, 287
Betuel, Jonathan 247
Between the Whole Numbers 174
The Beverley Hillbillies 69
Beyond Africa 193
Beyond Atlantis 74
Beyond the Horizon 279
Bharat Ki-cchap: The Identity of India 174
Biami People (New Guinea) 192
The Bible and Science 288
Biblical prehistory 1, 9, 16, 55–56, 72, 144, 158, 188–189, 288
Bicat, Nick 242
Bicat, Tony 242
Big, Guy 270
Big Brain Theory 197
Big Business 258
Big Wars 15, 90
Bigfoot 1, 96
Bill and Ted's Excellent Adventure 15
Bilson, Bruce 50
Binns, Edward 10
Bipedalism 12, 25–26, 124, 148–149, 170, 178, 180, 182, 188, 193, 197–198, 203–204, 207, 210
The Birth of a Flivver 15, 48
Birth of a Nation 21, 93
The Birth of Civilization 6000 B.C.–2000 B.C. 210

The Birth of Europe 174
Birth of Japan 89
Bishop, Jennifer 233
Bison and Buffalo 172–173, 191, 199
Bissell, Whit 221, 247
Bissette, Stephen R. 94, 109–110
Bitzer, G.W. 19, 90
Black, Claudia 165, 230
Black, Jack 80
Black, James 170, 231
Black, Karen 49–50
Black and White in Color 126
Black History Lectures (series) 175
The Black Knight 115
Black Sea Flood Theory 189
Blacula 49
The Blade Master 217
Blade Runner 31
Bladh, Hilding 236
Blain, Luci 224
Blair, Selma 165–166
Blair, William 49
Blais, Roger 204
Blaisdell, Paul 259
Blaise, Aaron 16, 18
Blake, Beverley 40
Blakeley, Rachel 244
Blanc, Mel 46, 59–60, 62, 64, 67–70, 72, 86, 90, 98, 116, 119, 219, 246, 259
Blanchard, Guy 180
Blanche, Marie 114
Blanco, Gabriel 280
Blanco, Victorio 237
Blast-Off (*Rocky Jones* episode) 257
Bledsoe, George 176, 185
Bleviss, Alan 263
Blinding of Captives 43–44, 83
Bliss, Lucille 59
The Blob 227, 258
Blocker, Dan 264
Blomgren, Bengt 236
Blood Creatures from the Prehistoric Planet 233
Blood from the Mummy's Tomb 191
Blood of the British (series) 198
Bloss, Rudi 280
Blue Paradise 1, 16
Blume, Edith 137
Boats, Prehistoric 14, 17, 36, 38, 47, 88, 154, 158, 169, 182, 185–186, 188, 199, 202, 218
Bock, David 175
Bodker, Tod 99
Body 179
Body Heat 251
Body Human 179
The Body in the Bog 174–175
Body language 120, 126
Bodypainting 4, 19, 33, 38, 40, 43, 120–121, 208, 235
Bogdanovich, Peter 215–216, 273–274
Bogin, Barry 184
Boiteau, Denise 197

Boldi, Massimo 10
Bolton, Guy 279
Bombard, Carole 189
Bond, Jezebelle 266
Bond, Tommy 219
The Bone Age 55
The Bonehead Age 16
Bonehead Detectives of the Paleoworld 175
Bonetti, Suzanne 209
Bonnaire, Jean-Paul 130
Bonner, Tony 40–41, 45
Bonnet, Franck-Olivier 120
Bonnevie, Maria 267
Bonnichsen, Robson 189
Bonthuys, Gerard 40
Bookwalter, J.R. 231
Boon, Robert 276
Boone, Richard 242
Boorman, John 286
Booth, Walter R. 254
Borden, Olive 55
Borne, Hal 98
Borromel, Charles 217
Bosworth, Hobart 145–146
Bothered by a Beard 16
Bottin, Rick 247, 265
Bottoms, Sam 10
Bottoms, Timothy 241
Bourbeau, Adrienne 162
Bova, Ben 240
Bowen, T.R. 233
Bower, Antoinette 264–265
Bowie, Ben 203
Bowman, Rob 165
Bows and arrows 20, 29, 38–39, 47, 56, 83, 116, 125, 138, 187, 206, 252
Boyce, William 261
Brach, Gérard 120, 125–126
Braden, Kim 268
Braden, Tom 246
Bradley, Leslie 138
Bradley, Sandra W. 205
Bradley, Scott 58
The Brady Bunch 86
Bragard, Jean-Claude 203, 205
Bramble, Arthur 200
Branagh, Kenneth 208–209
Brandon, David 217
Brandon, Henry 218
Brave Raideen 89
Brazil 185, 206
Brazzi, Rosanno 231
Brennan, Eileen 216
Brescia, Alfonso 74
Bresslaw, Bernard 22
Brett, Jeremy 233
Brewer, Alan 12
Brewer, Jameson 69
Briant, Shane 230–231
Bride of Frankenstein 258
The Bridge on the River Kwai 28
Bridges, Beau 289
Bridges, Jimmy 56
Bridges, Lloyd 286
Bright, Laren 60
Brightman, Homer 116

Brill, Eddie 137
Brinkman, Robert 229
Britton, Tony 252
Briz, José 200
The Broca Divide (*Stargate SG-1* episode) 263
Broderick, Brendan 263
Brodine, Norbert 99, 102
Brody, Hugh 178
Broken Mammoth Site (Alaska) 202
Bromley, Sydney 132, 135
Bronowski, Jacob 171
Bronze Age 16, 174–175, 178, 187, 193–194, 197–199, 205, 263
Bronze Age Blast Off 175
Brook, Peter 285
Brooks, Bill 79
Brooks, Conrad 237–238
Brooks, Mel 28, 77, 79, 127, 146–147, 152
Broom, Robert 174, 204
Brother Bear 3–5, 16–19, 80
Brotherhood of the Wolf 282
Broughton, Bruce 181
Brousseau, Pierre 265
Browder, Ben 230
Brown, Blair 213–214
Brown, Bryan 238
Brown, Charles 280
Brown, Ewing Miles 264
Brown, Jeanine 145
Brown, John 119
Brown, Melleny 11
Brown, Reb 286
Brown, Robert 104, 112–113
Brown, William Lyon 104
Browne, Derek V. 254
Browne, Fayte 238
Browne, Irene 218
Brownell, Cara 22
Browning, Ricou 221, 223
Browning, Tod 28
Bruckman, Clyde 142
Una Bruja sin Escoba 164
Bruns, George 86
Brute Force 2–3, 5, 19–22, 92–93, 129, 149, 171, 176
Bryan, Marvin 55
Bryan, William Jennings 288
Buchanan, Larry 223, 246
Buchanan, Robert D. 220
Buck Rogers 218–219
Buckley, Anthony 193
Budd, Roy 12, 259
Buddy's Lost World 219
Budig, Rebecca 175
Budner, Gerald 79
Budrys, Algis 227
Buffy the Vampire Slayer 1, 219
Bugs Bunny 119, 246
Bullock, Harvey 90
The Bullwinkle Show 130
Burchfield, Geoffrey 202
Bureau, Rick 48
Bürger, Arthur 187
Burgess, Anthony 120, 125–127
Burgess, Gelett 279–280

Burian, E.F. 86
Burke, Michelle 34, 126–127
Burke, Sonny 145
Burl, Aubrey 181
Burman, Ellis 232
Burns, Neal 142
Burroughs, Edgar Rice 124, 216, 241–242, 252, 265–266, 271, 281
Burton, Clarence 9
Burton, Corey 135
Burton, Robert 236–237, 261
Bury, Chris 196
Bush, Dick 154
Bushell, Anthony 254
Butler, Daws 13, 60, 116
Butler, Frank 70
Butler, Sid 144
Butt, Johnny 114, 154
Butt, Peter 197
Butterworth, Peter 22
Buxley, Gary 239
Buzzanca, Lando 160–161
Buzzi, Ruth 45, 79, 86
Byatt, Andy 190
Byron, Mark 185

Cabot, Ellen 279
Cacahuamilpa Grottoes (Mexico) 218
Cacavas, John 232
Cactus Hill Site (Va.) 202
Cadman, Stacey 24–25
Caesar, Julius 115, 166, 219
Caesar, Sid 5, 77–79
Caffrey, Sean 154
Cahiers du Cinéma 225
Cahn, Edward L. 259
Caird, Rod 170
Calia, Hank 247
California Man 229
California Woman 230
Callan, Shane 56
Calypso's Search for Atlantis 1, 175–176
Camblin, Zina 169
Cameron, Lorne 16
Camp, Hamilton 59–60
Campanile, Pasquale Festa *see* Festa Campanile, Pasquale
Campbell, Audrey 55
Campbell, Howard 189
Campbell, R. Wright 137, 139
Campbell-Jones, Simon 174, 183, 203
Campos, Marco Antonio 53
Canale, Gianna Maria 232
Canary Islands 108, 135, 157, 253
Canfield, Mary Grace 85
Cann, Rebecca 178
Cannibal Holocaust 94
Cannibalism 10, 12, 15, 23, 35, 38, 55, 73, 76, 94, 110, 120, 124, 160, 166, 176, 217, 219, 221, 254, 266–267, 276
Cannom, Greg 247
Canyonlands 198
Capaldi, Peter 197
Capehorn, Harry 24

Capitalism, Prehistoric 161
Caplan, David A. 50
Capone, Claudia 137
Capone, Gino 37
Caprio, Jack 13
Caprioli, Vittorio 159
Captain Caveman 67
Captain Caveman and Son 59
Captain Caveman and the Teen Angels 219, 259
Captain Kronos, Vampire Hunter 231
Captive Women 285
Car 54, Where Are You? 85
Carafotes, Paul 29
Cardella, Richard 221
Cardenas, Elsa 237
Cardi, Pat 85
Cardiff, Jack 221
The Cardiff Giant 176
Cardinale, Nuccia 215
Cardona, René 53
Caree 49
Carel, Roger 12
Carey, Harry 19, 22
Cargo cults 246
Carlin, George 15
Carlson, Eric 199
Carlson, Les 269
Carlson, Richard 221, 223
Carlyle, Robert 13–14
Carmel, Eddie 55
Carmel, Roger C. 261
Carmichael, Hoagy 60
Carnac Site (Britanny) 200, 202
Carney, Art 61
Carol, Martine 14
Carradine, John 233, 236–237, 256
Carreras, Michael 40, 45, 104, 111, 132, 135, 141
Carrere, Tia 128
Carrion, Gustavo Cesar 237
Carroll, Susette 78
Carruthers, Bob 204
Carry On Christmas 22
Carry On Cleo 3, 5, 219–220
Carry On films 135, 220
Carson, Johnny 262
Carter, Chris 165
Carter, Maurice 242
Cartier, Rudolph 254
Cartoon Quest 238
Cartwright, Angela 242
Cary, Tristram 255
Case, Dale 146
The Case of the Ancient Astronauts 176
Casella, Max 45
Casey, Bernie 15, 232
Casey, Julian 244
Cash, Jim 68
Caspari, Bibi 120
Cass, Maurice 257
Cassidy 10
Cassidy, Elaine 245
Cassidy, Ted 69
Cassini, Nadia 159, 263

Castellaneta, Dan 53
Il Castelo della Pauro 231
Catron, Jerry 273
Cavallone, Alberto 82, 84, 93
Cavanaugh, Christine 23
Cave Beneath the Sea 176
Cave Cat (*Garfield* segment) 72
Cave Dwellers (1913) 22
The Cave Dwellers (1914) 279
The Cave Dwellers (1940) 99–104
The Cave Dwellers (1984) 217
The Cave Dweller's Romance 22
The Cave Girl (1921) 279
Cave Girl (1985) 23–24
Cave Girl Island 279
Cave Girls 22
Cave Kids Adventures 22–23
The Cave-Man (1914) 76–77
The Cave Man (1915) 279
The Cave Man (1933) 23
Cave Man Stuff 279
A Cave Man Wooing 279
The Cave Man's Bride 280
Cave People of the Philippines 191
Cavedweller 280
Cavegirl (1985) 3, 23–24
Cavegirl (2002) 3, 5, 24–25
Cavegirl Rocks! 25
The Caveman (1926) 280
Caveman (1981) 3, 5, 25–28, 43, 60, 109, 113, 127, 144, 158, 236, 246, 282
Caveman Couture 196
Caveman Inki 28–29
Caveman Magoo (*What's New, Mr. Magoo* episode) 154
The Caveman, or Before a Book Was Written 29, 279
Caveman Rainbow 280
Caveman's Bluff 280
Caveman's Buff 280
The Caveman's Valentine 280
The Caveman's War 29
The Cavemen 5, 22, 176
Cavemen, Dinosaurs and the Fossil Record 288
The Caves of Altamira 176
Cavett, Dick 10
Cavewoman 55
Cawthorn, James 241
Cayton, William 86–87
Cedric the Entertainer 80
Cela, Violeta 38
The Celts: Rich Tradition & Ancient Myths 176
Centenera, Andrés 137
Cesta do Praveku 86–87
Cevenini, Alberto 140
Chaban, Michael 72
Chabat, Alain 130
Chaffey, Don 40, 45, 104, 109, 112
Le Chaînon Manquant 11–13
Challenging New Theories 177
Challenging the Human Evolution Model 204
Challis, Christopher 142
Chambers, John 258, 265
Chambers, Richard 171

Chamorro, Eduardo 200
Champion, Michael 78
Chaney, Lon 103
Chaney, Lon, Jr. 99, 103, 112, 272
Chang, Wah 227, 240
Changing Nature (*Dinosaurs* episode) 50
Changing the Menu 193
Channel Islands (Calif.) 189
The Chant of Jimmie Blacksmith 236
Chantler, David 10
Chapin, Tom 285
Chaplin, Charlie 3, 5, 26, 60, 70, 76–77, 144, 246
Chaplin, Syd 246
Chapman, Ben 221–222
Chapman, Michael 29, 31, 34
Chapman, William 191
Charboneau, Pierre 169
Chariots of the Gods (1970) 176–177, 188
Chariots of the Gods (1997) 177
Chariots of the Gods: The Mysteries Continue 177
Charkham, David 147
Charles, John 40, 99
Charles, Robert 256
Charleson, Ray 254
Charlie's Angels 219, 259
Charlotte and Her Amazing Humans (*Dinosaurs* episode) 50
Charlton, Alethea 50
Charlton, Michael 197
Chase, Charlie 282
Chase, David 239
Chase, Linwood 227
Chaterjee, Deborah 209
Chayefsky, Paddy 213–215
Chayette, Jeff 23
Chedd, Graham 202–204
Cheers 28
Chéret, André 128, 282
Chevron Theatre 276
Chiaramello, Giancarlo 159
Chicago Natural History Museum 205
Children, Killing of 20, 39, 128
Children of Eve 177
Children's Television Workshop 46
Chile 195, 202
China 193
Chinchorro Culture 195
Chipperfield, D.C. 199
Chitlik, Paul 269
Cholodenko, Lisa 280
Chong, Rae Dawn 4, 40, 120, 126
Chong, Tommy 126
Christian, Kurt 259
Christian, Roger 285
Chukchi People 190
Cines, Eugene 195
Cirino, Chuck 223
City of Death (*Dr. Who* episode) 52
City Under the Sea 223
Ciuffino, Sabatino 73

Ciuffo, Adrienne 198
Civilizations, Prehistoric (fictional) 1, 56–58, 73–75, 128, 139–140, 177, 189, 227, 253; *see also* Atlantis; Mu/Murania
Clair, René 14
Clampett, Bob 116, 219
Clan of the Cave Bear 3, 5–6, 29–35, 80, 107, 123–124, 126
Clark, Larry 286
Clark, Mamo 99
Clark, Susan 261
Clarke, Arthur C. 147–148, 151–152
Clarke, Robert 285
Clarke, Gary 233
Clarke, T.E.B. 218
Clarke, Warren 12
Clash, Kevin 50
Clash of the Titans 28, 39
Cleopatra (1934) 145
Cleopatra (1963) 220, 272
Clery, Corinne 286
Clifford, Marie 75
Cline, Edward F. 142, 144
A Clockwork Orange 127, 151
Close, John 261
Close Encounters of the Third Kind 233
Clothing, Prehistoric 4, 13, 21, 33–34, 36, 44, 51, 55–56, 73, 75, 77, 81, 85, 88, 91–92, 100, 111, 119, 126, 163, 169, 172, 174, 176, 179, 182, 185, 187, 194, 196, 198, 206, 208, 252
Clovis Culture 169, 173, 180, 188, 190, 202
Club Life in the Stone Age 35
Clukey, Dale 237
Coates, Lewis 263
Cobb, Kacey 221
Coburn, Anthony 50
Coburn, Dorothy 70
Coca, Imogene 85–86
Cochrane, George 195
Coddington, Alan 205
Cohen, Herman 233
Coincidence in Paradise 177
Cokei, Mohammad Siad 120
Cole, Royal K. 239
Coleby, A.E. 114
Coleman, Kathy 239–240
Coleman, Renée 10
Colla, Richard A. 145
Colliding Continents and the Age of Bronze 174
Colligan, Rosemary 257
Collin, Reginald 249
Collingridge, Gordon 282
Collingwood, Charles 195
Collins, Geoffrey 70
Collins, Joan 68
Collins, Phil 16
Collins, Robert E. 258
Colman, Ronald 136
Colonel Bleep 220–221
Col. Heeza Liar, Cave Man 35
Colonna, Jerry 116

Colossus of the Stone Age 2, 35–37, 142
Coluzzi, Francesca Romana 266
Colvig, Pinto 153
Comas Gil, Jaime 16
Combs, Jeffrey 253
Comden, Betty 248
Comeau, Phil 202
Comedy 3, 26, 60–61, 91, 144
Coming Into America 202
The Coming of Man (1968) 177
The Coming of Man (1986) 177
Companion Tape to the Mysterious Origins of Man 177
Comparing Creation Accounts 288
Compson, Betty 142
The Compulsive Communicators 192
Conan Doyle, Arthur 233, 243–245
Conan the Barbarian 1, 39, 56, 221
Conan the Destroyer 1, 221
Confucius' Dark Myth 89
Congo 96
Connell, W. Merle 98, 270
Connelly, Bobby 279
Connery, Sean 286
Connor, Kenneth 22, 220
Connor, Kevin 216, 241, 251
Connors, B.M. 279
Conqueror of Atlantis 74
Conqueror of the World 93–94
Conquest (1983) 37–40
Conquest (2003) 177–178
La Conquista 37–40
La Conquista de la Tierra Perdida 37–40
Conrad, Mikel 270
Contact 179
Converse, Frank 263
Conway, Gary 234
Conway, Gerry 56
Conway, James L. 188
Conway, Tim 53, 70
Conway, Tom 259
Cook, Randy 221
Cooke, Alex 213
The Cool Cave Man (*Stingray* episode) 264
Cooper, Ellen 22
Cooper, Wilkie 104, 109
Copeland, Joan 16
Copper 187, 201
Coppinger, Ray 180
Corbucci, Bruno 159
Corden, Henry 59, 61, 66–67, 69–70, 72, 79–80, 86, 98
Corey, Irwin 137
Corey, Jeff 269
Corey, Wendell 164
Corigliano, John 213, 215
Cormack, Danielle 165–166
Corman, Roger 2, 5, 73, 137, 139–140, 274, 283, 286
Cornelius, Joe 268
Cornello, Jeff 48
Cornthwaite, Robert 273
Corrigan, Ray 274

Cort, Julia 203
Cortes, Carlos 217
Cortez, Bella 73, 137
Cortez, Stanley 224, 227, 247–248
Cosby, Bill 148
Coscia, Marcello 160–161
Cosmic Africa 178
Cosmic Highway 178
Cosquer Cave (France) 176
Costumes *see* Clothing
Cottafavi, Vittorio 74
Cotton, Oliver 262
Coulouris, George 249
Coulter, Michael 13
Cousteau, Jacques-Yves 175
Cousteau, Phillipe 175
The Cousteau Odyssey (TV series) 175
Cox, Lara 244
Cox, Michael J. 119
Cox, Rex 11
Cox, Vincent 40
Coy, Walter 257
Cozzi, Luigi 263
Crabbe, Buster 218, 239
Cracking the Stone Age Code 178
Cragghunowen 178
Craig, Yvonne 273
Crain, Sally 199
Crandall, Brad 188
Crane, Michael 216
Crane, Richard 247, 257
The Crater Lake Monster 221
Cravenna, Alfredo B. 217
Crawford, Joan 66, 268–269
Crawford, Johnny 196
Creation Days 288
Creationism 1, 182, 288–289
The Creationist Controversy 288
The Creative Explosion 185
The Creative Revolution 188
The Creature from the Black Lagoon 5, 86, 218, 221–223, 247
Creature of Destruction 223, 259
The Creature Walks Among Us 223
Creatures of the Red Planet 233
Creatures the World Forgot 2–3, 40–45, 107, 109, 112–113, 135, 150, 157, 159, 191, 194
The Creeping Flesh 223, 233
Crichton, Michael 266–268
Cristal, Perla 164
Cro 45–46
Cro-Magnon 145
Cro-Magnons 10, 29–31, 33–34, 46, 81, 93, 145, 172, 174, 176, 178, 180–181, 183, 185, 188, 190, 196, 199, 201, 209, 262, 283
Cronenweth, Jordan 213
Cronkite, Walter 170–171
Crosby, Bing 281
Crosby, Floyd 137
Cross, Beverley 259
Crouse, Lindsay 14, 234, 236
Crowley, Pat 162
Crowley, Rory L. 29
The Crusades 145
Crutchley, Rosalie 40–41, 45

Crystal, Billy 147
Cuarez, Giovanni 49
Cucci, Tony 10
Cuddington, Chris 69
Cullinane, Jeremiah 263
Cumming, Alan 68
Cummings, Brian 66
Cummings, Jim 45
Cunard, Grace 245
Cundey, Dean 64, 66
Curiosity Shop 11, 46
Curious Pets of Our Ancestors 46, 48
Curry, Julian 264
Curry, Justin 274
Curtin, Hoyt 59–60, 62, 67, 69–70, 80, 88, 219, 259
Curtis, Allen 279
Curtis, Jamie Lee 181
Curtis, Tony 60
Curzon, Aria Noelle 22
Cushing, Peter 216–217, 223, 230–233, 262
Cyclops 217

Dacqmine, Jacques 12
Dacre, Nina 282
The Daemons (*Dr. Who* episode) 52
Daffy Duck and the Dinosaur 46–47
Dailland, Laurent 130
Dale, Doug 269
Dale, Jim 220
Dale, Richard 207
Dalton, Timothy 113
Daltrey, Roger 182
Dalya, Jacqueline 99
Dalzell, Archie 164
D'Amato, Joe 217
Damkin, Samuel 195
Dancing, Prehistoric 15, 37, 42, 106, 117, 119, 132–134, 146, 154, 158, 162, 246, 270
Danakil Alps (Ethiopia) 171
Danforth, Jim 28, 49, 156–158, 221, 282
Danner, Blythe 165
Danning, Sybil 253
Dano, Royal 233
Danova, Cesare 271–272
Dante, Joe 113, 261
Darbois, Richard 12
D'Arc, Sasha 93
Dari, Sam 11
Dark Myth 89
Darlene, Gigi 55
Darley, Dick 262
Darling, Get Me a Crocodile 47
Darpino, Mario 13
Darrow, Clarence 195, 288
Dart, Raymond 171, 174, 179, 188, 202, 204
Darwinism 16, 29, 92–93, 182, 209, 217, 288
Das, Arvind N. 189
Dating techniques 174, 189, 197, 206

Dating the Dreamtime 178
Daughter of Pomira (*Xena* episode) 275–276
Daughters of Satan 265
David, Gilles 130
David and Goliath 28
Davies, Arwyn 75
Davies, Jack 142
Davis, Craig 165
Davis, Jim 72
Davis, Mannie 35, 136
Davis, Mark J. 195–196
Davis, Simon 147
Davis, William B. 165
Daw, Jonathan 147
Daw, Joseph 231
Dawn of Civilization (1999) 189
Dawn of Civilization (2001) 180
The Dawn of History 209
The Dawn of Humankind 178
Dawn of Man (segment) *see 2001: A Space Odyssey*
Dawn of Man: The Story of Human Evolution 5, 178–180
Dawson, Anthony 286
Day, Shannon 241
The Day After Tomorrow 187
The Day the Earth Caught Fire 158
Days of Our Lives 135
Dayton, Howard 224
Deacon, Hilary 178
Dead Men Talk 180
De Angelis, Guido 16, 82
De Angelis, Maurizio 16, 82
Dearden, Michael 182
Dearsley, Joyce 50
Death and burial customs 33, 41, 44, 78, 83, 106, 154, 170, 174, 176–177, 184–185, 188, 193, 196–197, 202, 205, 208, 228
The Death of Neanderthal Man 183
Death of the Iceman 180
Debney, John 80
De Bont, Jon 29, 31, 34–35
De Brulier, Nigel 99, 103
De Concini, Ennio 232
DeCoteau, David 279
Decroly, Ovide 181
DeDiego, William 227
Dee, Gloria 239
Dees, Julie 59, 86
Deésy, Alfred 282
DeGeneres, Ellen 181
Degirmencioglu, Hamdi 218
Degirmencioglu, Zeynep 218
De Hoyos, Kitty 217
DeKorte, Paul 59, 67, 69–70
DeKova, Frank 138
De La Loma, José Antonio 37
Delaney, Frank 176
Delaney, Pat 223
De Lespinois, Pierre 172
Delgado, Marcel 227, 243
DeLisle, Grey 70
The Deliverer (*Xena* episode) 115
Delmar, Peter 147

Deloine, Alain 280
De Luca, Rudy 25, 28
DeLuise, Matt 229
De Lumley, Henry 200
Del Valle, Lilia 15
DeMetz, Danielle 271–272
DeMille, Cecil B. 5, 9, 145
De Monfred, Avenir 206
Dench, Judi 113
Dengate, Dennis 117
Denham, Maurice 218
Denning, Richard 221, 223
Dennis the Menace 114
Dennison, Jo Carroll 117
Dental health, Prehistoric 30, 32, 58, 70–71, 187
Denver, Bob 75
Depardieu, Gerard 5, 130
De Priest, Ed 99
De Quiros, Alfredo B. 200
DeRiso, Arpad 35
Le Dernier Grand Voyage 202
De Sica, Christian 10
De Sica, Manual 10
De Souza, Steven E. 64
Destination Saturn 219
D'Ettore, Robert 263
Deux Crânes pour un Homme 201
DeVito, Danny 64
Devlin, Tony 117
De Vry, William 244
Dexter, Elliott 9
Diamond, Bobby 97
Dick, Leonard 128
Dicken, Roger 157, 242
Dickens, Charles 66
Dickens, Thomas 49
Dickerson, Beach 138
Dickinson, Desmond 268
Die Hard 268
Dietrich, James 136
Di Giacomo, Franco 160–161
Dillon, Brendan 273
Di Lorenzo, Edward 262
Dino and the Cavemouse 67
Dino Boy 262
Dino's Dilemmas 59
Dinosaur 80
The Dinosaur and the Baboon 47–48
The Dinosaur and the Missing Link 47–48, 129
Dinosaur Babes 48–49
Dinosaur Girl (proposed film) 280
Dinosaur Island 223–224
Dinosaur Valley Girls 49–50
Dinosaurs 2–3, 9–10, 12, 14–15, 20–21, 23, 25–27, 29, 35–37, 46–50, 53–54, 56–58, 60, 64–68, 70, 75–76, 78, 85, 87–89, 97–100, 105–106, 108–110, 115–116, 128–129, 135–136, 142, 144, 154–158, 160–161, 164, 169–170, 177, 181, 217–221, 223–227, 230, 232–233, 237–245, 247, 249, 252–254, 262, 266, 268–271, 273–274, 283, 286

Dinosaurs (1991–94) 50
Dinosaurus! 3, 5–6, 31, 46, 129, 134, 215, 224–227, 236, 240, 246, 251, 258, 273, 287
Dippé, Mark 66
Discover Magazine (series) 191
Discoveries Underwater 199
The Discovery (*Dinosaurs* episode) 50
Discovery Atlantis 175
The Discovery of Noah's Ark 188
Disney Company. Florida Animation Studio 18–19
Dittmars, Raymond 128
Divination 206
The Divine Gift 50
Dix, Robert 233
Dixon, David 79
DNA analysis 170, 177, 189–190, 196
Dobberstein, Lothar 69
Dr. Jekyll and Sister Hyde 113, 134
Dr. Leakey and the Dawn of Man 180
Dr. No 113, 134
Dr. Phibes 216
Dr. Strangelove 149
Doctor Who 50–52, 74, 249, 256
Documentaries 1, 4–5, 169–210
Dogon People 192
Dogs 81, 102, 180, 183, 191, 199
Dogs and More Dogs 180
La Dolce Vita 141
Dolni Vestonice Site (Moravia) 185–186
Domergue, Faith 283
Domestic Affairs 280
Domestication of animals 171, 180, 192, 194, 200, 210
Dominguez, Columba 217
Donahue, Troy 247
Donald, James 255–256
Donald and the Wheel 52–53
Donald Duck 53
Donen, Stanley 248
Donnelly, Barry 178
Donner, Richard 86
D'Onofrio, Vincent 14
Donohue, Amanda 242
Don't Go Near the Park 227
Doolittle, John 29
Dordogne Valley (France) 194, 276
Dorf Goes Fishing 53
Doria, Enzo 16
Dorian, Antonia 223
Dougherty, Lee 92
Douglas, Gordon 260
Douglas, Jack 22
Douglas, Kirk 289
Douglas, Melvin 289
Douglas, Sarah 252–253
Downey, Gabrielle 24
Downs, Cathy 259
Downs, Hugh 183
Doyle, Martin 29
Dracula 109, 119
Dragon Bones 185

Dragonslayer 39
Drake, Arnold 55
Dramatized documentaries 5, 172–174, 185–187, 193–194, 201, 207–209
A Dream 76–77
Dressler, Marie 281
Drew, Griffen 49, 223
Drew, Sidney 280
Drimmer, John 234
Driver, Donald 195
Driver, Teri 119
Drop, Mark 50
Drug use, Prehistoric 30, 38, 172
Drugan, Jennifer 241
Dubin, Jay 50
Dubin, Joseph 145
Dubois, Eugene 179, 202
Duchovny, David 165
Dufau, Oscar 67
Dugan, Tom 15
Duggan, Terry 147, 150
Dullea, Keir 151, 263
Duncan, David 247
Duncan, Sandy 72
Duncan, Trevor 254
Dunham, Joanna 262
Dunlap, Paul 233
Dunlap, Robert 193
Dunleavy, Stephen 198
Dunn, Eric 178
Dunn, John W. 53, 115, 246
Dunn, Michael 231
Dunton, Tom 196
DuPont, E.A. 247–248
Durban, Guy 206
Durning, Charles 289
Duryan, Ann 178
D'Usseau, Arnaud 232
Duvall, Robert 273
Dvorak, Ann 281
Dyer, Zuni 162–163
Dykman, Stéphane 195
Dykstra, John 214
Dzhigarkhanyan, Armen 146

The Earliest South Carolinians 180
The Early Americans 180
Early Hominids in the Fossil Record 193
Early Indians of South Dakota 180
Early Man 5, 180–181
Early Man in North America 181, 189
The Early Years 184
Easter Island 12, 248
Eastin, Steve 206
Eastman, George 82, 85
Easton, Robert 264
Eaton, Leo 187
Eben, Al 274
Ebert, Roger 18, 32, 215
L'Ecriture, Mémoire de l'Homme 202
Ecuador 206
La Edad de la Piedra 280
La Edad de Piedra 53
Edens, Roger 248

Eder, Stephen 202
Edeson, Arthur 243
Edeson, Robert 279
Edge of the Ice 199
Edmiston, Walter 240
Edmunds, Mimi 185
Edwards, Edgar 99
Edwards, Shelley 165
Eegah! 3, 32, 113, 227–229, 240, 258
Eek! and the Terrible Thunderlizards 53
Eek! the Cat 53
Effeminate cavemen 70–71, 76–77, 137, 160–161
Ege, Julie 40, 44–45
Eggert, Nicole 29, 32, 34
Ehlers, Jerome 244
Eichorn, Edgar 175
Eichorn, Franz 175
Eisner, Michael 18
El Brendel 259
Elder, John 230
The Electric Company 46
Elfman, Jenna 113
Elfont, Harry 68
Elia the Prophet 175
Elias, Jeannie 253
Elisa, Gillian 75
El Kadi, Nameer 120, 126
El Kadi, Naseer 120 , 126
Ellen's Energy Adventure 181
Elliott, Bob 11
Elliott, Jack 145
Elliott, Kate 165
Elliott, Nancy 145
Elliott, Peter 94–96, 120, 126, 134, 150, 179, 287
Ellison, Gwen 245
Ellison, Harlan 263
Ellison, S.G. 49
Elmer Fudd 119
Elrington, Big Bruno 98
Elsas, Dennis 191
Elshaw, Keith 199
Elsom, Isabel 114
Emanuelle films 217
The Emergence of Modern Man 193
Emishi *see* Ainu People
Emmett, E.V.H. 16
The Emperor's New Groove 17
Empire of the Sun 158
Emyr, Dafydd 75
Enchanted Forest 182
Encino Man 3, 229–230
Encino Woman 230
Endangered Species (*Dinosaurs* episode) 50
The Enduring Mystery of Stonehenge 181
Enemy at the Gate 126
Engelbach, David 285
Engelberg, Fred 224–225
England 172, 175, 177, 179, 181, 183–186, 192, 194–195, 198, 204–205, 208
English, Jonathan 281

English, Marla 259
English Heritage (Organization) 204
English Sacred Sites: The Atlantis Connection 175
Epps, Jack, Jr. 68
Erickson, Clem 238
Erinnerungen an die Zukunft 176
Escape from Atlantis 74
Escola, Maria 38
Esperón, Manual 15, 53
Espiga, Fernando 16
Esser, Carl 114
Essex, Harry 221
Et Si l'Homme Venait d'Asie? 202
The Eternal Feminine 53
The Eternal Forest 182
Ethiopia 202, 208
Etkind, Mark 191
Etre Homme, C'est se Tenir Debout 202
Eure, Wesley 239
Europe 88, 174, 179, 184–185, 196, 199, 201–202, 209
Evangelista, Alfredo 205
Evans, David 178
Evans, Tim 184
Everett, Katherine 187
Evolution (1923) 4, 181
Evolution (uncompleted film, 1940–41) 181–182, 260
Evolution (2001) 182, 288
Evolution and Human Equality 182
Evolution, Human 169, 171, 177–184, 193, 195–198, 202, 204–205, 209 210, 17
Evolution: Human Origins: A Walk Through Time 182
Evolution of Living Things (series) 169
Evolution of Man (1961) 182
Evolution of Man (1988) 182
Der Ewiger Wald 182
Ewing, Bill 88
Ewing, Loren 231
Excalibur 39
Exodus 179
Exploding Campus Guardress 90
Les Exploits Erotique de Maciste dans l'Atlantide 74
Exploring the American Past 199
Extinct Pink 53
Extraterrestrial events and Earth's history 76, 154–156, 183, 254–256
Extraterrestrial settings 218–221, 231–233, 236–237, 242–243, 246, 249, 254, 257, 262–263, 271–274, 286
Extraterrestrials on Earth 10, 15, 48, 52, 68–69, 76, 79, 81, 87, 89, 164–165, 176–177, 232, 236–237, 253, 254–256
Extreme History 182
The Fable of a Stoneage Romeo 54

Fabregas, Manuel 237

Fabrizi, Valeria 159
The Fabulous Funnies: Alley Oop 11, 54
Fagan, Brian 172, 185
Fairbanks, Douglas 71
Fairfax, Marion 243
Fairy tale setting 265
Fake prehistoric people 215–216, 233–234, 254, 257–258, 264, 275
Falk, Peter 245
Fantasia 146
Fantastic Journey 74
Fantastic Voyage 112
Fantasy settings and situations 218–219, 239–241, 248, 256, 264, 269
Faraldo, Claude 266
Farkas, James 10
Farmer Al Falfa (Cartoon character) 16
Farnon, Shannon 271
Farr, Jamie 239
Farscape 230
The Fast Runner 17
The Fate of Neanderthal Man 5, 182–183
Le Fatiche di Ercole 232
Fawcett, William 239
Fawlty Towers 208
The Fearless Vampire Killers 126
Feet on the Ground, Head in the Stars 183
Feist, Felix 273
Felisatti, Massimo 159
Felix in the Bone Age 54–55
Felix in the Stone Age 54–55
Felix the Cat in the Bone Age 54–55
Fellini, Federico 141
Fenn Cache (Idaho) 169
Fernandez Miranda, Manuel 176
Fernandez Unsain, Jose Maria 217
Ferrando, Giancarlo 82
Ferris, Paul 223
Festa Campanile, Pasquale 159–161
Le Feu Lumière di l'Homme 202
Le Feu! Pas Pour les Homes! 79
Feyder, Jacques 74
Field, Margaret 285
Field, Pamela 82, 85
50,000 B.C. (Before Clothing) 47, 55
Fig Leaves 55–56
Tight! Opsa 89
Fights Between Women 42, 44, 49, 106, 117–119, 133, 140–141, 154, 156–157, 162
Finch, Jeremy Bertrand 269
Fincke, Sueann 183
Find Me a Primitive Man (Song) 216
Finding Nemo 19
Fine, Bud 70
Fine, Daniel Scott 72
Fine, Larry 82, 264
Finlayson, James 70–71

Finn, Christine 254
Finn, Earl 78
Fins, Femmes and Gems (*Xena* episode) 275
Fiore, Maria 140
Fioretti, Mario 193
Fire and Ice 3, 5, 13, 36, 56–58, 128
The Fire and the Stone 174
Fire Maidens from Outer Space 74
Fire Monsters Against the Son of Hercules 35–37
Fire Through the Ages 183
Firemaking 12–13, 25, 35, 37, 42, 51–52, 78–79, 81, 84, 87, 94, 116–118, 120–125, 127–128, 139, 160, 165, 170, 172, 177, 181–183, 187–188, 190–191, 193–194, 196–197, 200, 202, 208–209, 229, 234, 237, 276
The First Americans (1969) 183
The First Americans (1991) 183
The First Americans (1998) 5, 183
The First Bad Man 58, 62
The First Barber 144, 280
First Born 178–179
The First Caveman (*Rocky and Bullwinkle* episode) 130
The First Circus 58, 144
The First Degree 144, 280
The First Dentist 58, 144
The First Earfull 144, 280
The First Family 183
The First Flivver 58, 144
First Footsteps 193
The First Humans 190
Firth, Peter 242
Fisher, Craig 183
Fisher, Mary Gale 99
Fisher, Nora Kay 275
Fisher, Terence 230–231
Fishing, Prehistoric 26, 33, 47, 53, 88, 100, 106, 157, 183, 201
Fistful of Dollars 83
Fistri, Maria Grazia 161
Fitt, Terry 120
Fitzhamon, Lewin 115
The Five Ages 59
Five Million Miles to Earth 255–256
Flaiano, Ennio 98
Flaming Arrows 193
Flash Gordon 73, 165
Flat-Faced Man (Hominid) 197
Fleetwood, David 147
Fleischer, Dave 71–72, 76, 135, 153, 281–283
Fleischer, Max 62, 181
Fleischer, Richard 221
Fleming, Thea 137
Flesh Creatures 233
Flessati, Dominic 175, 194, 209
Fletcher, Louise 269
Fletcher, Neil 223
Flint the Time Detective 90, 230
A Flintstone Christmas 59
The Flintstone Family Adventures 67

A Flintstone Family Christmas 59
Flintstone Funnies 59–60, 67
The Flintstone Kids 59, 72, 219, 259
The Flintstone Kids' "Just Say No" Special 60
The Flintstones (1960–66) 3, 5–6, 25, 50, 53, 56, 60–64, 66, 68, 72, 76, 88, 107, 144, 153, 161, 287
The Flintstones (1994) 3, 5, 18, 61, 64–66, 90, 144, 269, 287
A Flintstones Christmas Carol 66
The Flintstones Comedy Hour 66–67, 114
The Flintstones Comedy Show 67, 219, 259
Flintstones franchise 22–23, 26, 59–70, 72, 79–80, 86, 90, 97–98, 114
The Flintstones: Fred's Final Fling 67–68
The Flintstones in Viva Rock Vegas 3, 61, 66, 68–70
The Flintstones: Jogging Fever 69
The Flintstones' Little Big League 69
The Flintstones Meet Rockula and Frankenstone 69
The Flintstones' New Neighbors 69
The Flintstones on Ice 69
The Flintstones: On the Rocks 70
The Flintstones Show 66–67
The Flintstones' 25th Anniversary Celebration 70
Flintstones Vitamins 61
The Flintstones: Wind Up Wilma 70
Flood, Gerald 249
Flood, Staci 49
Floods 188–189, 203, 288
Florek, Dann 64
Floria, Emma 29
Florida 198, 202–203
Flying Elephants 3–5, 26, 60, 70–71, 76–77
Flying Attempts in Prehistory 142, 160
Fogel, Rich 80
Foïs, Marina 130
Foldes, Lawrence D. 227
Foley, Charlie 190
Foley, Robert 170
Foman, Lou 261
Fontana, D.C. 240
Food for Thought 192
Footwear 11, 206
Foray, June 11, 54, 80, 90
Forbidden Planet 253
Ford, Carole Ann 50
Ford, Francis 245
Ford, John 245
Ford, Matt 184, 204
Forgeot, Jacques 206
Forgotten Knowledge 177
Fornari, Vito 16
Forsyth, Bill 13–14
Fortier, Herbert 128
Fortune, Jack 198

Foss, Kenelm 50
The Fossil Men (*Voyage to the Bottom of the Sea* episode) 273
Foster, Charlie 215
Foster, Craig 178
Foster, Damon 178
Foster, John 35, 136
Foster, Lisa 217
Foster, Warren 62
Fouchet, Jean-Paul 196
The Foul Ball Player 71
Four Weddings and a Funeral 45
Fox, Edward 261
Fox, James 245
Fox, Marcia 40
Fox, Robert B. 205
Fox, Scotty 10
Foy, Bryan 115
Frake, Graham 264
France 172, 176, 194, 196–197, 199, 201–202, 205–206
Francis, Freddie 223, 268–269
Francisci, Pietro 232
Franciscus, James 285
Franco, Jesus 74, 206
Frankenstein 109
Frankenstein and the Monster from Hell 5, 230–231
Frankenstein's Castle of Freaks 231
The Frankenstones 67
Franklin, Richard 244
Franklyn, Milt 29
Franks, Chloe 268
Franz, Arthur 247
Franz, Joseph 279
Fraser, Brendan 229
Fraser, Elizabeth Lyn 59–60
Fraser, George MacDonald 109, 111–112
Fraser, Richard 274
Frattini, Gaio 232
Frazetta, Frank 3, 56, 58
Frazetta, Holly 56
Freaks 28
Fred and Barney Meet the Shmoo 72, 98
Fred and Barney Meet the Thing 72, 98
Fred Flintstone and Friends 72, 114
Fred the Caveman 280
Fred's Final Fling 67–68
Freeborn, Stuart 149–150
Freeman, Kathleen 85
Freeman, Leslie G. 191
Freer, Neil 177
Frees, Paul 90, 130
Freeston, Jeremy 195
Freiberger, Fred 88
French, Leigh 77
French, Victor 145
The French Way of Looking at It 206
Frend, Charles 218
Frickert, Joseph 99
Fried, Gerald 85
Friedberg, Lionel 176
Friedman, Ron J. 16
Friml, Arthur 243

Fritz the Cat 56
From Homo Erectus to Neanderthal 183
From Russia with Love 113, 134
From Stone to Bronze 197
Front-projection system 150
Frozen in Time: Life in the Upper Paleolithic Age 203
Fudenna, Margene 271
Fuentes, Alma Delia 237
Fujikawa, Keisuke 88
Fukutomi, Hiroshi 230
Fulci, Lucio 37, 39
The Full Circle (*Space: 1999* episode) 262
The Full Monty 68
The Fulla Bluff Man 71
Fuller, Lance 259
Funakoshi, Mitsuko 69
The Funtastic World of Hanna-Barbera 72
Fury, Ed 49, 162
Future settings *see* Post-apocalyptic settings

G Spots? 72
Gabai, Richard 223
Galaxy of the Dinosaurs 231–232
Gale, Ed 241
Galindo, Cavernario 237
Gambon, Michael 94
Gamley, Douglas 241
Ganger, Ben 50
Gano, Glen 270
Gans, Christopher 282
Garcia, Alonso 37
García, Juan 15
Garcia Morcillo, Fernando 164
Garden of Eden 12, 16, 56, 76, 189
The Gardles 72, 76
Gardner, Helen 131
Gardner, Joan 271
Garfield: His Nine Lives 72–73
Gargoyles 232
Garland, Beverly 247–248
Garlanda, Maria Vittoria 93
Garon, Pauline 9
Garrani, Ivo 232
Garrett, Betty 248
Garrett, Eliza 258
Garrett, Patsy 97
Garrett, Robert 253
Garson, Mort 146
Gartner, Marjoe 263
Garwood, Steve 191
Gaskill, Charles L. 29, 131
Gaugh, Homer 281
Gault Site (Texas) 169, 202
Gazzara, Ben 197
Geary, Sean P. 176
Geersten, George 190
Gelein, Igor 265
Gellar, Sarah Michelle 219
Gemma, Giuliano 160–161
Genesis 183
"Genetic Eve" *see* Mitochondrial Eve Theory

Genius Man 73
The Gentle Tasaday 191
Gentry, Paul 221
Genus Homo 184
George, Gilbert 49
Georgi, Peter 207
Geosophy 183
Gerace, Liliana 16
Gerard, Teddie 279
Gerceker, Fehmu 183
Gere, Ashlyn 234
Gereghty, William 263
Germany 179, 182, 186
Gerrard, Cande 162
Gerrold, David 240
Gerstad, Harry 10
Gertie the Dinosaur 144
Gertzman, Maury 233
Get It Done (*Buffy* episode) 219
Ghost Light (*Dr. Who* episode) 52
The Ghost of Slumber Mountain 48, 181, 195
Giamalva, Joe 240
Giant of Metropolis 1, 36, 73–75
Giant Strides 170
Gibb, Hugh 205
Gibbon, Johana 203
Gibbons 150
Gibbs, Michael 13
Gibson, David 258
Gibson, Judith 256
Gibson, Mel 285
Gibson, Thomas 68
Gibson, Tom 279
Gidding, Nelson 260
Gigante, Marcello 231
Il Gigante di Metropolis 73–75
Gilbert, Kenneth 264
Gilbert, Paul 164
Gilbert, Willie 69
Gilford, Jack 25
Gill, Brian 120
Gill Women of Venus 273–274
Gillespie, Dana 252–253
Gilligan's Island 75, 86
"Gillmen and Gillwomen" 221–223, 273–274
Gilman, Sam 145
Gilmore, Stuart 285
Gimbutas, Marija 210
Ginsburg, Matthew 182
Gittleson, Anthony 137
Giuffrè, Aldo 159–160
Givry, Edgar 128
Glackens, L.M. 136
Le Gladiatrici 140–142
Gladkov, Gennadi 146
Glasser, Albert 137, 247
Glassner, Jonathan 263
Gleason, Jackie 62
Glenn, Scott 199, 232
Glover, Danny 200–201, 234
Glover, Julian 255
Glover, Paul 274
Glut, Donald F. 49–50, 103, 258
Go and Get It 244
The Go Masters 251
Goblin (Musical group) 40

Godal, Kire 137
Goddard, Daniel 218
Goddard, Mark 242
The Godfather 239
Godreau, Miguel 213–215, 287
The Gods Must Be Crazy 45, 246
Goelz, Dave 50
Gogs 3, 5, 25, 75–76
Gogwana (*Gogs* episode) 76
Goldberg, Robert 187, 206
Goldberg, Whoopi 147
Golden Bat 90
The Golden Voyage of Sinbad 260
Golding, William 285
Goldman, Andrea 16
Goldsmith, Jerry 267
Goliathon 281
Golubkina, Larissa 265
Gon the First Man 72, 76, 90
Gone with the Wind 34
Goodall, Jane 150
Goodchild, Tim 207
Goodkind, Saul A. 218
Goodman, Andy 50
Goodman, John 64–66, 68, 287
Goodrich, E.D. 267
Goodwin, Doug 53
Goodwin, Ron 142
Goodyear, Albert C. 180
Goofy (cartoon character) 11
Gordon, Dan 62, 135, 153
Gordon, Douglas 180
Gordon, Leo 56
Gori, Coriolano 132
The Gorilla Story 280–281
Gorillas in the Mist 96
Gottlieb, Carl 25, 28
Gough, Michael 268–269
Gould, Graydon 249
Gould, Stephen Jay 182
Goulding, Ray 11
Gowers, Patrick 233
Gozo Island 200
Grace, Mary 85
Graham, Alex 196
Graham, John 12
Graham Brown, Andrew 190
Grainer, Ron 50
Le Grand Tournant de l'Homme 202
Le Grand Voyage de l'Homme 202
Granite Hotel 76
Grant, Arthur 255
Grant, Cy 216
Granville, Bonita 276
Gras Palau, José 38
Grasshof, Alexander 242
Grateful Dead (music group) 269
Gravelle, Barry 244
Graver, Gary 223, 253
Gray, Barry 262, 264
Gray, Charles 98
Gray, Ian 198
Graybe, Valerie 23
Great Britain 22, 114, 129, 169, 171, 174, 178, 183–184, 197–198, 204, 220

The Great Escape 256
Green, Adolph 248
Green, Dee 82, 264
Green, George Dawes 280
Green, Walton 170
The Green Hell 176
Greene, Angela 238
Greene, David 289
Greene, Kempton 128
Greene, Walter 115–116
Greenhalgh, Jack 274
Gregg, Virginia 59
Gregory, Mark 16
Gregory, Sandra 172
Gregory's Girl 14
Greystoke 96, 236
Grgic, Zlatko 79
Griffin, David 268
Griffith, D.W. 2–3, 5, 19, 21–22, 77, 90, 104, 128–129, 144, 149, 171, 175–176
Grimes Graves: The Story of a Neolithic Flint Mine 183
Grinder, Paul 165–166
Grinsfelder, Dean 172
Grissell, Wallace 239
Grönberg, Ake 236
Groom, John 177
Gross, Arye 233
Grover, Danny 147
Groves, Phil 23
Die Grüne Hole 176
Gruner, Mark 145
Gruskoff, Michael 126
Guam, Robert 241
Guenette, Robert 70
La Guerra del Ferro 82–85
La Guerre du Feu 120–128
Guest, Christopher 12
Guest, Val 154, 158–159
Guidotti, Stewart 249
Guinness, Alec 5, 218
Gunsmoke 264
Gunton, Michael 188
Guthe, Fred 253
Guthrie, Tani Phelps 145
Guy (Gorilla) 150
Guy, Jennifer 24
Guyver 90
Györi, Ernö 282

Habeck, Michael 130
Haber, Martin 245
Hackl, Roland 130
Hagen, Ross 223, 253
Haggard, H. Rider 133
Haid, Charles 213
Haines, Tim 192, 201
Hair-dragging Scenes 15, 49, 85, 128, 143, 145, 220, 237, 248
Hajewski, John 264
Hajime Ningen Gon 76
Halas, John 177
Hale, Alan, Jr. 75
Hale, Christopher 197, 204
Hale, Creighton 99, 103
Haley, Jackie Earle 271
Hall, Arch, Jr. 228

Hall, Arch, Sr. 228
Hall, Douglas 263
Hall, Ellsworth 237
Hall, Grayson 232
Hall, Norman S. 218
Hall, Sinclair 114
Hallam, John 252
Halliwell, Leslie 127
Hallmark Hall of Fame 289
Hamill, Mark 79, 203, 205
Hamilton, Archie 56
Hamilton, Barbara 11
Hamilton, John 10
Hamilton, Judd 263
Hamilton, Murray 289
Hamlin, V.T. 11, 54
Hammer Films 3, 5, 24, 40, 43–44, 76, 109, 112, 125, 191, 214, 242
Hampshire, Keith 11
Hancock, Graham 177
Hancock, Sheila 220
Handford, Richard 263
Handmade Humans 202
Hands and human evolution 202
Handshaking 146
The Handsome Sleeper 15
Handworth, Octavia 128
Hanley, Drew 154
Hanna, William 60, 62, 64, 68, 79, 90
Hannah, Daryl 29, 31–32, 34
Hannah, Page 10
Hanna-Barbera's 50th: A Yabba Dabba Doo Celebration 64
Hannon, Shaun 56
Hanson, Kristina 224–225
The Happy Hooker Goes Hollywood 113
The Harappan Civilization: 3500 to 2000 B.C. 174
Harcourt, Ian 276
Hardwicke, Cedric 136
Hardwicke, Edward 233
Hardy, Oliver 3, 5, 17, 26, 60, 70–71, 76, 258
Hardy, Robert 245
Hare, Ken 40
Harems 76–77, 207
Harper, Kate 169, 184
Harper, Ron 240
Harrington, Curtis 283
Harrington, Pat, Jr. 238–239
Harris, Jack H. 227
Harris, Jonathan 242
Harris, Marianna 195
Harris, Robert H. 233
Harrison, Linda 285–286
Harrison, Wordsworth 115
Harron, Robert 19, 21, 90, 92–93
Harry and the Hendersons 96
Harryhausen, Ray 3, 28, 108–113, 157, 170, 181–182, 216, 232, 260, 269
Harryhausen Chronicles 182
Hart, Johnny 11, 13, 46
Hart, Susan 261
Hartley, Mariette 229

Hartman, Ferris 282
Hartmann, Reiner 185
Hartnell, William 50–51
Hartwig, Gay 59, 69, 114
Harty, E.G. 258
Harvest of the Seasons 171
Haskell, Jimmie 239
Hassall, Imogen 154, 157–158
Hasselhoff, David 263
Hatch, Richard 254
Have Mammoth, Will Travel 46
Havens, James C. 221
Havez, Jean 142
Hawdon, Robin 154, 158
Hawkins, Carol-Anne 154
Hawkins, Gerald 195
Hawks, Howard 55–56
Hawkshaw, Jean 162
Hawley, Brian 147
Hawley, Ormi 128
Hawtrey, Charles 220
Hay, John 264
Hayasaka, Akira 249
Hayashi, Shigeyuki 88
Hayden, Frank 40, 104, 113, 132
Haze, Jonathan 138
The Heart of Atlantis 175
Heaven's Mirror 177
Heavy Traffic 56
Hedison, David 273
Hefner, Hugh 196
Heiderich, Bob 98
Heilbron, Lorna 223
Heitmeyer, Jane 244
Helike: The Real Atlantis 175
Heller, Bill 247
Hellboy 126
Helm, Brigitte 74
Heminway, John 182
Henaine, Gaspar 53
Hendra, Tony 12
Hendy, Gloria 141
Hendy, Janine 137, 140–141
Henneberry, John 264
Henry, Gale 279
Henry, Hank 98
Henry, Jean-Francois 282
Henshaw, Jim 244
Henson, Brian 50
Henson, Jim 65
Her Cave Man 282
Herbert, Percy 104, 112–113
Hercules 35, 232
Hercules and the Captive Women 74
Hercules at the Conquest of Atlantis 74
Hercules in the Haunted World 40
Hercules: The Legendary Journeys 74, 166, 218
Herek, Stephen 15
Herlin, Jacques 82
Heroes 187
Die Herrin von Atlantis 74
Herrman, Petr 86–87
Herviale, Jeanne 266
Herz, Michael 137
Herzog, Werner 126

Hess, Sandra 229
Hester, Thomas R. 200
Heston, Charlton 283, 286
Hewitt-White, Ken 178
Hey, Virginia 230
Heymann, Werner R. 99, 102, 110
Hiatt, Ruth 246
Hiawatha 17
Hickman, Gail Morgan 169
Hicks, Seymour 114
The Hidden History of the Human Race 177
Hill, Bernard 197
Hill, Jacqueline 50
Hillerman, John 216
Hills, David 217
Hilton, Arthur 280–281
Hinds, Anthony 230
Hindu mythological films 1, 279
Hines, David 147
Hines, Margie 76
Hintner, Cornelius 282
Hinton, Ed 10
Hiroshima Mon Amour 119, 225
His Prehistoric Blunder 281
His Prehistoric Past 3, 26, 60, 70, 76–77, 92, 144
Histeria! 77
History of Britain 183–184
History of the Anthropoid: The Search for the Beginning 205
History of the World, Part I 77–79, 127, 147, 152
History's Ancient Legacies 184, 204
History's Artifacts 195
History's Mysteries (series) 189, 196
The Hitch-Hiker's Guide to the Galaxy 79
Hitler, Adolf 182, 256
Ho, Meng-Hau 281
Hoax of the Ages: The Piltdown Man 184
Hodges, Adrian 245
Hoerl, Arthur 239, 257
Hoff, Syd 135–136
Hoffman, Milton B. 183
Hogan, Bosco 192
Hogan, Michael 269
Holland, Cecil 244
Holland, Savage Steve 53
Hollingsworth, Laura 253
Holloway, Sterling 10
Hollyrock-a-Bye-Baby 79, 112
Holt, Bob 11, 13, 54
Holt, Patrick 154, 158
Home on the Range 19
Hominid Evolution 184
Hominids 3–4, 94–96, 147–152, 170, 172, 179–180, 183–185, 188, 192–193, 197, 203, 205, 207, 209–210, 214–215, 247
L'Homme Deviant Cité 202
L'Homme et les Dieux 202
L'Homme Enterre ses Morts 202
L'Homme: Un Voyage dans le Temps 190
Homo Erectus 23, 123, 170–172, 178–179, 183–184, 188, 193, 195, 197, 199, 205, 208, 214, 249–251
Homo Ergaster 96, 172, 184, 207–208
Homo Habilis 148, 170, 178, 183–184, 199, 207
Homo Heidelbergensis 179, 184, 208
Homo Neanderthal *see* Neanderthals
Homo Sapiens 179, 182–185, 188, 193, 201, 205, 208
Homo Sapiens (1960) 184
Homosexuality 57, 78, 137, 142, 160–161
Honda, Hirotaro 134, 215, 227, 249, 251, 287
Hone, Todd 231
The Honeymooners 50, 61–62
Hootkins, William 190
Hopkins, Bruce 275
Hopkins, David M. 189
Hopkins, Roger 203
Hopper, Dennis 247
Horák, Antonin 86
Horizon (series) 192, 204, 209
Horn, Jan 174
Horner, Mike 119
Horner, Yvonne 104, 113, 132, 135
Horror Express 223, 232–233
Horror of the Blood Monsters 137, 233
Horses 159, 165, 169
Hoselton, David 16
Hoskins, Bob 245
Hot Stuff 79
Hound of the Baskervilles 233
House II: The Second Story 233
Houser, Jerry 79–80
Hoveyda, Fereydoun 225
How Scientists Know About Human Evolution 184
How the Beginning Began 184
How to Make a Monster 233–234
Howard, Bruce 75
Howard, Byron 19
Howard, Curly 82
Howard, Moe 68, 82, 251, 264
Howard, Robert E. 221
Howard, Shemp 82, 264
Howe, John 79
Howie, Jane 245
Hoyt, Arthur 243
Hoyt, Harry O. 243
Hradilek, Ludvik 97, 132, 153
Hubbard, Hazel 128
Hubbard, John 99
Hubschmid, Paul 261
Huckleberry Hound 61
Hudson, Ralph 215
Huemer, Dick 145
Hughes, Carol 94–96
Hughes, David 94–96
Hughes, Lloyd 243
The Hula-Hula Dance 76–77
Hulke, Terrence 249
Hull, David Stuart 175
Human 179
The Human Animal: A Natural History of the Human Species 184
Human Evolution 184
The Human Factor 200
The Human Journey 5, 184–185
The Human Odyssey 185
Human Origins: A Walk Through Time 182, 185
Human Origins: 10,000,000 B.C. to 8000 B.C. 210
Human Prehistory and the First Civilizations 185
The Human Puzzle 170
Human sacrifice 35, 48, 73, 108–109, 128, 133, 154, 156, 162, 188, 194, 206, 217, 281, 286
The Human Story: Traces of Humankind's Oldest Relatives 203
A Human Way of Life 193
Hume, Alan 25, 216, 219, 241, 252,
The Hunt for Atlantis 175
Hunt, Linda 172
Hunt or Be Hunted 172
Hunter, Jeffrey 164
Hunter, Kelly 13
Hunter, Virginia 82, 264
The Hunters (*Twilight Zone* [1985–88] episode) 269–270
Hunters and Gatherers 193
The Hunting Ape 184
Hunting, Prehistoric 33, 41–43, 82–83, 100, 102, 104, 110, 117–118, 139, 172–174, 178–180, 183, 186–187, 190–196, 198–199, 201, 204 205, 208 209, 269
Hurden, Sammy 94
Hurst, Michael 165–166
Hurt, William 213–215
Husiatowicz, E. 47
Hussein, Waris 50, 52
Hustak, Zdenek 86
Huston, Tony 223
Hutchinson, Craig 281
Hutton, Robert 261
Hutton, Timothy 234, 236
Hyde-White, Wilfrid 261
Hyland, Jim 10
Hyman, Bob 221
Hysterical History series 115

I Spy 148
I Was a Teenage Frankenstein 139, 234
I Was a Teenage Werewolf 139, 234
I Yabba-Dabba-Do! 79–80
Ibn Fahdlan, Ahmed 267
Ice Age (2002) 3, 5, 66, 80–81
Ice Age Crossings 185, 202
Ice Age Oasis 198
Ice Ages 16, 35–36, 46, 50, 56, 80–81, 130, 169, 173–174, 176, 179–180, 182, 185–187, 190, 193–195, 197–200, 203, 209, 218, 229
Ice Mummies (series) 192, 201

Ice Woman 234
Ice Woman 2 234
Ice World 5, 96, 185–187
Iceman (Ice Mummy) 5, 92, 180, 187, 192, 196, 201, 206, 209
Iceman (1984) 2–3, 6, 34, 109, 126, 227, 234–236, 287
Iceman (1992) 5, 32, 187
The Iceman (1998) 187
Iceman: Hunt for a Killer 187
Iceman: Mummy from the Stone Age 187, 201
If Only the Stones Could Talk 205
Il Etait une Fois l'Homme 98–99
I'm a Monkey's Uncle 3, 82
The Improbable History of Mr. Peabody (Rocky and Bullwinkle segment) 130
In Prehistoric Days 19–22
In Quest of Ancient Aliens 177
In Search of Ancient Astronauts 177
In Search of Ancient Aviators 177
In Search of Ancient Ireland 187–188
In Search of Ancient Mysteries 177
In Search of Atlantis 175
In Search of Clovis Man 188
In Search of Eden 189
In Search of History (series) 176, 181, 183–184
In Search of Human Origins (1994) 4, 127, 149, 188
In Search of Human Origins (1999) 184
In Search of Noah's Ark 188
In Search of Noah's Flood 188
In Search of Stonehenge 204
In Search of Strange Visitors 177
In Search of the First Americans 189
In Search of the First Language 189
In Search of the Lost World 181, 189
In Search of the Magic of Stonehenge 204
In the Beginning 193
In the Beginning: The Creationist Controversy 288
Ince, Ralph 29, 131
The Incredible Discovery of Noah's Ark 188
The Incredible Petrified World 281
The Incredible Shrinking Man 86, 223, 247
India 174, 189–190
India Invented 189
Indian Culture, From 2000 B.C. to 1500 A.D. 196
Indian mythological films 1, 279
Indiana Jones films 128
Indians (America) see Paleo-Indians
Indo-European languages 189
Indonesia 193, 202
Indovina, Franco 98
Inescourt, Frieda 259
Infante, Sonia 53

The Infinite Voyage (series) 178, 202
Ingley, Milton 10
Ingram, Jack 239
Inherit the Wind (1960) 288–289
Inherit the Wind (1965) 289
Inherit the Wind (1988) 289
Inherit the Wind (1999) 289
The Inhumanoids 74
Institute for Research in Human Happiness 89
Into the Deep Freeze 193
Intolerance 21–22, 91, 93, 128, 144
Inuit 16–17, 197, 234–235
The Invaders (Voyage to the Bottom of the Sea episode) 273
Invasion of the Animal People 236–237
Inventions, Prehistoric 11–12, 15, 20, 25, 28–29, 46, 53, 55, 64–65, 73, 75–76, 78, 83, 87–88, 91, 115–119, 135, 137–139, 159–160, 220, 237, 257, 271–272
Ippoliti, Silvano 161
Ireland 178, 187–188, 194, 206
Iron Age 82–85, 89, 176, 183, 195, 197, 199, 205, 210, 281
Ironmaster 3, 82–85, 93
Irving, Richard 276
Irwin, Mark 265
Is Atlantis in the Bible? 175
Is It Noah's Ark 188
Ishiguro, Noburo 88
Ishinomori, Shotaro 10
Ishiyama, Takaaki 89
La Isla de los Dinosaurios 237
Island of Dr. Moreau 2, 96, 113
Island of Lost Souls 2
Island of the Dinosaurs 237
Island of the Pygmy Mammoth 189
Israel, Robert 142
It Came from Outer Space 223
Italian Acrobatic Team 159
Italy 179
Ito, Roberto 164
It's About Time 3, 75, 85–86, 237
It's Alive 223
It's Tough to Be a Bird 86
Iwerks, Ub 23
Izzo, Markanthony 72

Jackson, David 182, 185
Jackson, Michael 60
Jackson, Mike 171
Jackson, Samuel 280
Jackson, Tony 147
Jacobs, Michael 50
Jacobson, Rick 276
James, Geraldine 204
James, Godfrey 216, 242
James, Jasper 208
James, Richard 104
James, Sid 22, 220
James, Steve 242
James Bond films 14, 28, 113, 134, 216, 223, 240, 264
Jampel, Barbara 195
Janderová, Milada 132, 153

Jan-Gel, the Beast from the East 237–238
Janis, Elise 145–146
Jansen, Cliff 180
Jantzen, Julie 237
Japan 88–90, 177, 189, 193, 230
Japanese History 89
Japan's Mysterious Pyramids 189
Jason and the Argonauts 45, 112, 232
Java Man 179, 181, 202, 247
Jaws 222
Jay, Sue 205
Jaylin 119
Jayne, Keith 264
Jemma, Ottavio 160–161
Jenkins, Ulysses 206
Jennewein, Jim 64
Jennings, Dev 246
Jens, Salome 29
Jenson, Len 70
Jessup, Robert C. 223
The Jetsons Meet the Flintstones 86
Jimenez, Agustin 237
Jinmium Site (Australia) 202
Jocelyn, June 138
The Joe Piscopo Show 64
Jogging Fever 69
Johanson, Donald C. 127, 149, 183, 188, 197
Johanson, Lenora 188
Johansson, Allan 236
John, Robert 40–41
Johnson, Gary 134
Johnson, Gerry 60, 90
Johnson, Kristen 68
Johnson, Maudie 13
Johnson, Max 13
Johnson, Russell 75
Johnson, Tefft 29, 131, 279
Johnston, Ollie 256
Johnstone, Paul 178
Jolley, I. Stanford 271
Jolley, Norman 262
Jomon Culture (Japan) 89–90
Jonah story 12
Jones, Chuck 28, 46–47, 246
Jones, Grover 99
Jones, Harvey 179
Jones, Jenny 190
Jones, Morgan 270
Jones, Peter 188
Jones, Simon 79
Jonny Quest 271
Joseph, Anne 230
Joseph, Paul 245
Jourdain, Bernard 201
Journey Beneath the Desert 74
Journey of Discovery 189
Journey of Man 5, 189–190, 201
Journey Through Time: The Human Story 190
Journey to Prehistory 86–87
Journey to the Beginning of Time 1, 5, 86–87
Journey to the Center of the Earth (1959) 74, 217, 238

Journey to the Center of the Earth (1967–69) 238
Journey to the Center of the Earth (1989) 74
Journey to the Center of the Earth (1999) 238
Judith of Bethulia 21
Jungfrauen-Report 206
Jungle Jim in the Forbidden Land 238–239
Juran, Nathan 242
Jurassic Art 176
Jurassic Park 66
Just the Facts Learning Series 180
Justice, James Robertson 142

Kablam! 87–88
Kael, Pauline 28, 127
Kagawa, Yutaka 76
Kahan, Saul 258
Kahn, James 276
Kahn, Madeleine 216
Kaitan, Elizabeth 273
Kalahari Desert 193
Kale, K. Narayan 279
Kaliban, Bob 12
Kaminsky, George 137
Kandel, Aden 268
Kane, Georgann 197
Kapisisi, Lalomal 120
Kaplan, Deborah 68
Karachentsov, Nikolai 146
Karpf, Elinor 232
Karpf, Stephen 232
Karron, Richard 78
Kassir, John 230
Kaufman, Lloyd 137
Kautschuk 176
Kay, Bernard 268
Kazakhs 190
Keach, Stacy 198, 201, 203–204
Keaton, Buster 3, 5, 26, 60, 70, 76, 142–144, 176, 243, 280–281
Keats, Steven 242
Keays-Byrne, Hugh 238
Keegan, Andrew 286
Keen, Bob 244
Keene-Soper, Alice 209
Keir, Andrew 255–256
Keith, Arthur 174
Keith, Ian 204
Keliiliki, Nina 49
Kellett, Bob 262
Kelley, George F. 82
Kelly, Gene 248, 288
Kelly, Jill 273
Kemmer, Edward 262
Kendall, David 245–246
Kennedy, Regan 137
Kennedy Assassination 51
Kennewick Man 195, 201
Kent, Crawford 246
Kent, Gary 99
Kent, Suzanne 78
Kenway, John 242
Kidnapping of women and children 14, 20, 25, 35–36, 42, 48, 55, 71, 78, 91–92, 113

Kiel, Richard 113, 227–228, 240
Kiesouw, Hans 40
Kiesouw, Josje 40
Kiley, Richard 195, 204
Killer Ape 239
Killer Ape Theory 148–149, 152, 171, 179, 188, 193, 195
The Killer Instinct 200
Killough, John 231
Kim, Evan 25
Kimball, Kelly 34
Kimball, Ward 86, 144, 256
Kincaid, Aron 223
Kindt, Jean-Michel 120
Kiner, Kevin 241
King, Clive 263–264
King, Jack 219
King Charlie 76–77
King Kong 3, 48, 58, 102–103, 218, 227, 243, 258, 281
King Kong Lives 96
The King of Stonehenge 194
King of the Congo (1952) 239, 245
King of the Kongo (1929) 239
Kings of the Sun 17
Kingsland, Paddie 79
Kinney, Jack 11
Kirchner, Gottfried 199, 206
Kiss of the Spider Woman 214
Klasies Site (South Africa) 170
Klein, Rita 215
Kleinow, Peter 28
Kloomok, Darren 137
Kneale, Nigel 254–256
Kneitel, Seymour 254
Knight, Ted 238
Knights of the Round Table 115
Knots, Prehistoric 169
Knox, Alexander 261
Koenig, Walter 240
Kohn, Steven 135
Koide, Kazumi 15
Kolchak: The Night Stalker 239
Konca, Cemâl 218
Konopka, Magda 154, 158
Kopell, Bernie 264
Kopp, Bill 53
Korg: 70,000 B.C. 2, 88, 240, 271
Korman, Harvey 64, 68, 70, 90
Koscina, Sylva 232
Kosloff, Theodore 9
Kotani, Shusei 242
Kousi, Katherine 230
Kovacs, Bela 262
Kovacs, Laszlo 216
Kraft, William 56, 58
Krakowski, Jane 68
Kramer, Stanley 288–289
Kraushaar, Raoul 117, 270
Kristen, Marta 242
Krofft, Marty 240
Krofft, Sid 240
Kruger, Sven 93
Krulwich, Robert 196
Kubrick, Stanley 5, 93, 147–152, 200
Kulich, Vladimir 267
Kull the Conqueror 74

Kum-Kum 88, 90
Kum-Kum the Caveman 88
Kurosawa, Akira 83, 268
Kuznetsov, Alexander 146
Kymlicka, Milan 244

L.A. 10,000 B.C. 190
La Palma Island (Canary Islands) 253
The Labors of Hercules 232
Labracque, Jean Claude 201
Lacets 89
Lacy, Joe 164
Ladd, Fred 86
Ladder of Creation 171
Ladlow, Terrence 171
Lafleur, Jean 244
Lajoux, Jean-Dominique 205
Lake, Florence 10
Lambert, Tim 185
Lamont, Duncan 223, 255
Lancaster, Johnny 169
Land of Lost Monsters 5, 190–191, 209
Land of the Lost (1974–77) 5, 113, 239–241
Land of the Lost (1991) 240–241
Land of the Mammoth 198
Land of the Monsters 35–37
The Land That Time Forgot 3, 216, 241–242, 252–253, 281
Landau, Martin 165, 262
Landen, Berry 53
Landers, Lew 238, 257
Landis, Carole 5, 93, 99, 101, 103–104, 107
Landis, John 227, 258 259
Landmark American Trials 289
Landon, Judy 117
Landon, Laurene 285
Lands Before Time 135, 191
Landsburg, Alan 175, 177, 188, 205
Lane, Michael 271
Lane, Rob 245
Langtry, Kenneth 233
Language, Prehistoric 12, 27, 31, 40, 43, 49, 52, 57, 75, 79, 81, 92, 94, 102, 120, 125–126, 134, 139, 146, 158, 163, 170, 173, 176, 179, 180, 182, 184, 186, 189, 190, 192–193, 207, 228, 235, 237, 240, 246, 251, 260, 283
Lankford, T.L. 253
Lansing, Robert 10
Lanteri, Arturo 114
Lantieri, Michael 66
Lantz, Walter 136
Lanzarote Island (Canary Islands) 253
Lapan, Brian 50
Lapenieks, Vilis 228
Lara, Joe 265
Larnicol, Eloise 130
Larsen, Keith 164
Larson, Jack 10
Larson, Randall 110
LaSalle, Richard 264–265

The Lascaux Cave: A Look at Our Prehistoric Past 191
Lascaux Cave (France) 180, 185, 191, 193, 196, 199, 201, 206
Lascaux: Cradle of Man's Art 191
Lascaux Revisited 191
Lascaux Treasures 191
Lascaux II 191
La Sena Site (Colo.) 202
Lasky, Jesse, Jr. 262
The Last Dinosaur 242
The Last Emperor 236
The Last Neanderthal 191
The Last Neanderthals 191
The Last of the Mohicans 145
The Last Tribes of Mindanao 191–192
Last Year at Marienbad 119, 223
Lastufka-Taylor, Francine 189
Laszlo, Ernest 289
Latimer, Michael 132, 134–135
Latka, Bill 172
La Torre, Giuseppe 35
Laughter 33, 78–79, 100, 106, 121–122, 146
The Laughter of God 242
Laurel, Stan 3, 5, 17, 26, 60, 70–71, 76–77, 144, 258
Laustsen, Dan 282
Lauter, Harry 265
Lava, Bill 246
Lavista, Raul 217
Lavoie, Robert 120
Law, Phyllida 264
Lawler, Paul 178
Lawless, Lucy 165, 274–276, 283
Lawrence, David 230
Lawrence, Jerome 288
Lawrence, Lillian 142
Laws, Maury 242
The Laws of the Sun 10, 74, 89
Lawson, Thierry 185
Lazarus from the Mist (*Starlost* episode) 263
Leahy, Margaret 142, 144
Leake, Cynthia 56
Leakey, Louis 148, 180–181, 195, 197, 205
Leakey, Maeve 177, 195, 197, 205
Leakey, Mary 188
Leakey, Richard 179, 193, 195, 197, 205
Learoyd, Sue 180
Leary, Dennis 80
Lease, Maria 99
Lebanon 201
LeBeau, Becky 223
Leccese, Lou 245
Lecureux, Roger 128, 282
Leduc, Michelle 120
Lee, Belinda 37
Lee, Bernard 113, 230
Lee, Christopher 223, 232
Lee, Jennie 19, 22
Lee, Margaret 35, 37
Lee, Paige 273
Lee, Rob 273
Lee, Robert E. 288

Lee, Ruta 67
Lee, Sheryl 134
Lee, William Gregory 276
Lees, Nathaniel 245
The Legend of Atlantis 175
The Legend of the Lost (*Relic Hunter* episode) 128
The Legend of Walks Far Woman 112–113
Legends of the Isles 192
Legrand, Michel 98
Leguizamo, John 80
Lehman, Lew 253
Leibman, Andrew 202
Leigh, Barbara 246
Leight, Warren 137
Leissner, Dan 158
Lejre Research Center 198
Lemerdy, Edith 130
Lemmon, Jack 289
Lemmons, Kasi 280
Lenard, Mark 178
Lennon, Kip 60
Leno, Jay 64
Lent, Chris 209
Lenz, Kay 254
Lenzi, Umberto 82, 84
Leonard, Don 40
Leone, Sergio 83, 110
Leonviola, Antonio 137, 140–141
Le Picard, Marcel 256
Lerner, Bettina 192
Lescoulie, Jack 46
Leslie, Laurie 114
Lessley, Elgin 142
Le Vaillant, Nigel 192
Levant, Brian 64–66, 68
Leven, Mel 86
Levers 117
Levesque, Mariette 265
Levitow, Abe 13
Levy, Nigel 169
Lewis, Anthony 213
Lewis, Paul 264
Lewis, Reg 35, 37
Lewis, Richard 147
Lewis, Warren 267
Leyshon, Paul 24
Lhomme, Pierre 98
L'Hote, Jean 197
Licence to Kill 113
Life and Death in the Ice Age 182
A Life in Ice 192
The Life of Mammals 192
Life on Earth: The Compulsive Communicators 192
Life on Ice 192
Life with Buster 281
Lifeblood (*Xena* episode) 165, 275
Life's Really Big Questions 202
Ligeti, Gyorgy 147, 151
Lightman, Herb A. 150
Lighton, Louis D. 55
Lime, Harold 98
Limited animation 62
Lincoln, Elmo 19, 22
Linde, John 10
Linder, Cec 254

Lindon, Lionel 117
The Link 94–96
The Lion King 18
Lions of the African Night 96
Lisa, Mona 11
Liska, Zdenek 97, 132, 153
Little Boy Boo (*Dinosaurs* episode) 50
Littler, Craig 265
Livesey, Jack 50
The Living Daylights 113
Living on the Edge (series) 200
The Living Sands of Namib 96
Lloyd, Harold 144
Lloyd, Michael 239
Lobos, Themo 248
Local Hero 14
Loch Ness Monster 52, 65
Locke, Joe 240
Lockhart, June 242
Lockwood, Gary 151
LoDuca, Joseph 165–166, 274–276
Lollobrigida, Gina 14
London, Jeremy 238
Lone, John 227, 234, 236, 287
Lone Ranger 28
Long, Shelley 25, 28
The Longest Day (*Land of the Lost* [1974–77] episode) 240
Looking at Prehistoric Sites 192
Looney Tunes: Back in Action 113
Lord of the Flies (1963) 285
Lord of the Flies (1990) 285
Lord of the Rings (1978) 56
Loring, Hope 55
Los Angeles County Museum of Natural History 88
Lost City of Atlantis 175
Lost City of the Aegean 175
Lost Civilizations (series) 199, 206
The Lost Continent 135, 191
Lost in Space 242–243
Lost Treasures of the Ancient World (series) 204
Lost Tribe 191
The Lost World (1925) 2, 5, 48, 116, 129, 243–245
The Lost World (1960) 244, 273
The Lost World (1992) 244
The Lost World (1998) 244
The Lost World (1999) 244
The Lost World (1999–2002) 244–245
The Lost World (2001) 5, 245
Lost world settings (prehistoric people exist in a self-contained area in the modern world) 216–219, 223–224, 237–238, 241–245, 251–254, 262, 265–266, 270–271, 276–277
Lost Worlds: The Story of Archaeology (series) 205
La Lotta dell'Uomo per la Sua Sopravvivenza 193–194
Louise, Tina 75
Love 179
Love, Bessie 243
Love, Lucretia 159

Lovejoy 128
Lovell, Mike 147
The Lover 126
Lowe, Lara 204
Lowell, Mark 270
Lower That The Angels 171
Loy, Myrna 280
Lucas, George 65
Lucas, Tim 127
Lucas, Wilfred 90–93, 175, 287
Lucille Love, the Girl of Mystery 245
Lucy (Australopithecine remains) 170, 178–179, 188, 192–193, 195, 197, 202–203, 205, 207
Lucy in Disguise 192–193
Luez, Laurette 117–118
Luggage of the Gods! 245–246
Lugosi, Bela 256
Lugosi, Boris 231
Luigi, Pierre 111
Lukas, Josef 86–87
Lukather, Paul 224
Lumbly, Carl 25
Lupi, Roldano 73
Lusk, Don 86
Luske, Hamilton S. 52
Lutansky, Ivan 97, 132
Luzia Skull (Brazil) 206
Lyden, Robert 257
Lynch, Paul 269
Lynch, Sean 216
Lynn, Kelly 48
Lynn, Mara 117
Lynne, Iris 48
Lyons, Bill 203
Lyons, H. Agar 114
Lysistrata 159

Macák, Jirí 97, 132, 153
Macaulay, David 45–46
MacDonald, Terry 187, 196, 209
MacGuyver: Lost Treasure of Atlantis 74
Maciste Contro I Mostri 35–37
Mack, Kathleen 282
MacKee, Scott 147
MacLachlan, Kyle 64
MacLeod, Don 265
MacMillan, Norma 97
MacNeille, Tress 45, 70
MacPhee, Ross 209
MacPherson, Jeannie 9
Mad as a Mars Hare 246
Mad Max 238, 285
Mad Max Beyond Thunderdome 2, 285
Maddomen 89
Magdalenian Culture 185
Magesis, Duffy Caesar 137
The Magnificent Ambersons 227
Maher, Bob 233
Mailes, Charles H. 19, 90
Makeup 34, 96, 126, 149–151, 200, 208–209, 215, 232, 234, 242, 244, 247, 258, 265, 270
The Making of Mankind 193
Mako 221

Malatesta, Guido 35, 37
Male and Female 9
Malinda, Jim 88
Malling, Ole 198
Malone, Andrew 171
Malta 200
Maltby, Clive 189
Maltese, Charles 29
Maltin, Leonard 127
Mammoth Journey 209
Mammoths and Mastodons 16–18, 46, 60, 65, 76, 80–82, 84, 86, 88, 97, 100, 103, 117, 121, 124–126, 142–143, 169, 173–174, 180, 182, 185–186, 189–191, 193, 198–199, 208–209, 249–251, 270–271, 282
Mammoths of the Ice Age 193
Man, Christopher 88
Man and His Mate 99–104
A Man Called Flintstone 13, 61, 90
The Man from Atlantis 74
The Man from Snowy River 238
The Man Hunters 193
The Man in the Iron Mask 103
Man on the Rim: The Peopling of the Pacific 193
Man, the Deadly Predator 193
The Man with the Golden Shoes 176
Mancina, Mark 16
Mancini, Henry 53, 115–116, 221, 247
Mancini, Mario 231
Mancori, Memmo 137, 140
Manfredini, Harry 233
Mankind in the Animal Kingdom 193
Manlinks (*BeastMaster* episode) 218
Mann, Danny 241
Mann, Stanley 221
Manning, Marilyn 228
Manuell, George 76, 153, 283
Manzoni, Sarah 126
Marcel, Terry 254
March, Frederic 288–289
The March of Time 281
Marchant, Laurence 147
Marcus, Stephen 24
Marcus, Vitina 273
Margheriti, Antonio 286
Margolin, Stuart 164
Marietto 73
Marin, Luciano 35
Marinker, Peter 180
Marion, Edna 70–71
Marion, Paul 257
Mark Anthony 220
Marks, George Harrison 98
Marley, John 239

Marlowe, Hugh 286
Marr, Mary 273
Marriage, Prehistoric 35–37, 118, 146, 153, 162, 216
Married to Murder 242
Marriott-Wilson, Elsie 114
Mars, Ken 59
Marsh, Gene 76
Marsh, Mae 4, 19, 21, 77, 90–93, 108
Marshall, Bryan 255
Marshall, Darah 138
Marshall, E.G. 189, 193
Marshall, William 49, 261
Marston, Theodore 279
Martell, Donna 257
Martell, Gregg 134, 215, 224–227, 246, 251, 271, 273, 287
Martello, Carlo 132
Martin, Eugenio 232
Martin, Philip 178
Martin, Sobey 273
Martinek, H.O. 254
Martinelli, Marcello 132
Martinez Solares, Gilberto 15
Martinez Solares, Raul 15, 53, 217
Martinez-Tudó, Federico 248
Martin-Laval, Pef 130
Martino, Lea 82
Marven, Nigel 207–208
Marvin, Hank B. 129
Marvin Martian 246
The Mary Tyler Moore Show 238
Masai, Walter 120
Masai People 126
Masak, Ron 264
Mashimo, Koichi 153
The Mask of Zorro 268
Mason, Don 264
Masque of the Red Death 139
Mass Extinctions 193
Masseti, Enzo 232
Masson, Osa 286
Master of the World 84, 93–94
Mastering the Beasts 172–173
Masterpiece Theatre 52
Masters, Rick 119
Masters of Metal 194
Masur, Richard 229, 247
Mathematics, Prehistoric 30, 53, 174, 178
Matheson, Chris 15
Matriarchy 75, 140–142, 193–194
Matt, Just 49
A Matter of Time 174
Matthews, John Clark 135
Matulavich, Peter 199
Mature, Victor 5, 99, 101, 103–104, 108, 272
Matuszak, John 25
Maury, Harald 266
Maxwell, Lois 264
May, Bob 242
May, Michaella 280
Mayas 189, 192
Mayfield, Les 229
Mayhew, Peter 259
Mazonowicz, Douglas 196

Index

Mazurki, Mike 85
McAloon, Grant 230
McAuley, Tony 176
McBride, Rob 10
McCall, Mitzi 114
McCally, John 175
McCarthy, Eoin 13
McCauley, Peter 244
McCay, Scutter 240
McCay, Winsor 144
McCleod, Don 265
McClory, Sean 271–272
McClure, Doug 216, 241, 252
McCracken, Jeff 50
McCullough, Christopher 197
McDonald, Garry 244
McDonald, Michael 273
McDonnell, Babe 98
McDowell, Lucy 203
McEnery, John 241
McGann, William C. 142
McGavin, Darren 239, 289
McGibney, Linda 275
McGill, Everett 120, 126
McGraw, Alyssa 50
McKenzie, Nicolette 111
McKimson, Robert 119
McKinney, Austin 10
McLachlan, Grant 178
McLeish, John 11
McLeod, Frederick 198
McManus, Joseph 201
McMullen, Mark 195
McMullin, Mandy 275
McNair, Sue 233
McPherson, Kelly 181
McSwain, Monica 165
McTiernan, John 266, 268
McWhirter, Julie 70
Meadowcroft Site (Penn.) 169
Meddings, Derek 242
Medicine, Prehistoric 30, 33, 39, 54, 84, 93, 118, 120, 139, 172, 186–187, 196–197, 208, 257, 271
Medina, Nicholas 266
Medupe, Thebe 178
Meekah 11
Meet the Ancestors: The King of Stonehenge 194
Megafauna 169, 173, 190–191, 198–199, 209
Megalithic monuments 169, 171, 178, 181, 183–184, 187, 191–192, 194–196, 198, 200, 202–205
Megalithic Monuments of Ireland 194
Megalocerus 172
Megowan, Don 136, 257
Melford, George 119
The Mellowmen 145
Melvin, Allan 114, 270
The Men from the North 174
The Men from the South 174
The Men Who Painted Caves 194
Mencken, H.L. 288
Mendel, Stephen 56
Meneses, Alex 68
Meniconi, Furio 73

Menville, Scott 59–60
Menzies, Peter 267
Mercer, Jack 76, 114, 153, 254
Mercier, Michelle 98
Meredith, Burgess 88
Merglova, Jana 183
Merideth, Joseph E. 136
Merlin and the Sword 115
Merrick, Doris 247, 270
Merrick, John 117
Merriwether, Nicholas 228
Merton, Zienia 262
Mesa Verde Site (Colo.) 204
Mesolithic Period 194–195, 199
Mesolithic Society 194–195
Mesopotamia 202
A Message from the Stone Age 191
Messick, Don 13, 59–60, 66, 68–70, 72, 79–80, 90, 98, 262
Messmer, Otto 54
Mesure, Charles 274
Metals 195
Metalworking, Prehistoric 83–84, 175, 184, 187, 194–195, 197, 257
Metcalfe, Earl 128
Metty, Russell 247
Metzger, Joel 283
Mexico 15, 177
Meyer, Karl 254
Meyers, Eric 203
Michaels, Susan 189, 196
Middle East 196
The Mighty Gorga 98–99
Mighty Joe Young 48
The Mighty Mightor 97
Mighty Mouse in Prehistoric Peril 115
The Mighty Peking Man 281
The Mighty Thunda 239
Migrations 35, 41–42, 76, 169, 179, 189, 202, 208
Miko, Jim 11
Mikulski, Mark 137
Miles, Christopher 129
Milestone, Lewis 280
Millar, Catherine 230
Millar, Marvin 116
Millennium Man (Kenya) 203
Miller, Ann 248–249
Miller, George (film director) 238, 285
Miller, George (film/TV director) 238
Miller, Nancy 136
Miller, W. Christy 90, 93
Miller, Walter C. 69
Milligan, Spencer 239
Milo, Candy 45
Mimieux, Yvette 286
Mindanao Island 191
The Mind's Big Bang 182
Mining, Prehistoric 171, 183
Minoan Civilization 174
Minotaur 281
Mintz, Melanie 137
Mioni, Fabrizio 232
Miou-Miou 266
Miranda, Carmen 160

Mirasol, Myrna 137
The Misadventures of Buster Keaton 281
Misanthropy 5, 13, 44, 108–109, 152
The Miser's Reversion 94
The Missing Link (1927) 246
The Missing Link (1979) 11–13
Missing Link (1988) 3–5, 94–96, 126, 134, 152, 179, 287
Missing Link (*Space: 1999* episode) 262
"Missing links" 1, 47, 113, 179, 215, 238, 240, 246, 265–266, 274, 281
Missing Links (1995) 197
The Mistress of Atlantis 74
Mistress of the Apes 246–247
Mitchell, Charles 23
Mitchell, Gordon 73, 231
Mitchell, Joseph A. 142
Mitchell, Margaret 34
Mitchell, Tony 196
Mitochondrial Eve Theory 170, 177–178, 197, 200–201
Miyazaki, Hayao 89
Mizusawa, Wataru 88
Moby Dick and the Mighty Mightor 97
Modern settings 2, 4–5, 213–277
Mohan, Peter 244
"Mole Men" 75, 271–272
Mole Men Against the Son of Hercules 75, 141
The Mole People 75
Moll, Richard 25, 64
Molteni, Ambrodio 73
Monaghan, Brian 263
Monahan, Dave 46
Monahan, Richard 270
The Monkey Trial (1997) 289
Monkey Trial (2002) 289
Monster on the Campus 247
Monsters of Dr. Frankenstein 231
The Monsters We Met 190–191
Montagnani, Renzo 160–161
Montana 185, 191
Montana, Bull 243–244
Montanaro, Tony 29
Monte Verde Site (Chile) 169, 202
Montez, Maria 74
Montgomery, Elizabeth 60
Moon in prehistoric religion 154, 156–157
Moorcock, Michael 241
Moonraker 113
Moore, Constance 218
Moore, Joanna 247
Moore, Lawrence 205
Moore, Matt 280
Moore, Michael 4
Moore, Owen 145–146
Moore, Roger 113
Moore, Ted 259
Moran, Frank 256
Moranis, Rick 16, 18, 64
Moravec, Miroslav 132, 153
Moravia 185–186

More, Saba 23
More Than Human (*Lost World* episode) 245
Morell, André 254
Moreno, Antonio 221
Moreno, Genaro 237
Moreno, Jose Elias 217
Moreno, Robert 261
Morgan, Elaine 171
Morgan, Harry 195
Morgan, Ira 264
Morgan, Jeff 178–179
Morin, Bertrand 176
Morita, Pat 264
Morley, Robert 129
Morpheus Mike 48, 97
Morricone, Ennio 160–161
Morris, Chester 259
Morris, Dave 142
Morris, Deiniol 75
Morris, Desmond 120, 127, 184, 196, 209
Morris, Dick 93
Morris, John 77
Morris, Simon Conway 183
Morrison, Christine 231
Morrison, James 131
Morrison, Tom 115
Morrow, Cindy 70
Morrow, Clay 70
Morse, Barry 270
Morse, Hollingsworth 257
Morse, Thomas 49
Mort, Michael 75
Morteo, Charles 88
Morton, Joe 195–196
Morton, Judee 261
Moser, Frank 146
Mosner, Marianne 257
Moss, Stewart 145
The Most Dangerous Game 3, 102, 265
Moulin, Rosita 40
Mounds 187, 203
Mu/Murania 1, 74, 89
Mueller-Stahl, Armin 165
Mukherjee, Chandita 174
Mulan 18
Mulé, Francesco 160–161
Mulhare, Edward 205
Mulholland, Tony 245
Mullahy, Megan 80
Mullaney, Jack 85
Muller, Richard 180
Mulock, Al 164
Mummies 195–196; *see also* Iceman (Ice Mummy)
Mummies of Ancient Chile 195
Mumy, Billy 242
Mündl, Kurt 187
Mungo Man 185
Munro, Caroline 216–217, 263
Munshin, Jules 248–249
Murder at Stonehenge 195
Murphy, Tab 16
Muscarella, Steve 183
Muscat, Mike 29
Musée de L'Homme (Paris) 205

Museum of Natural History (London) 149
Music, Lorenzo 72 116, 130, 151, 157, 161, 194, 215–216, 218, 265
Music in films/TV 13, 15, 18, 28, 34, 45, 58, 62, 76, 79, 86, 94, 102, 108, 110, 112
Music, Prehistoric 25, 42, 46, 50, 78, 87, 100, 138, 144–146, 158, 183, 185, 188, 257
Musical comedies 215–216, 248–249
Musuraca, Nicholas 136
Musy, Jean 265
Mutt and Jeff (series) 280
Mutual Native Duplex 206
My Favorite Year 126
My Science Project 247
Mycenaean Civilization 174
Myers, Zion 82
Mysteries of Mankind 195
Mysteries of Noah and the Flood 189
Mysteries of Stonehenge 195
Mysteries of the Megaliths 178
Mysterious Island 74
Mysterious Origins of Man 177
Mysterious Places of England 205
Mystery in the Plain 205
The Mystery of Jurassic Art 177
Mystery of Life 4, 195
The Mystery of Stonehenge 195
Mystery of the First Americans 5, 195
Mystery of the Neanderthal 175
Mystery Science Theater 3000 217
Mystic Ruins 205

Na Veliké Rece 97
Naff, Lycia 29
Nagel, Conrad 99, 103
Naito, Makato 10
Nakamura, Tetsu 242
The Naked Ape (book) 127
The Naked Ape (film) 195–196
The Naked Prey 276
The Name of the Rose 126
Namibia 43, 96, 135, 150, 178, 190, 192
Nance, John 191–192
Naples, Toni 223
Napoli, Fred 197
Naptan People 178
Nascimbene, Mario 40, 45, 104, 108, 110, 112, 154, 157, 193–194
Nash, Clarence 53
National Museum of Ireland 206
National Science Foundation 46
The Native American Series 196
Natural Mummies 196
Natwick, Mildred 216
Naughton, Tom 169, 185, 195, 197
Naughty Ancient Kum-Kum 88
Navahos 190
Navarro, José Luis 164
Navrátil, Borivoj 94, 132
Nazi propaganda films 182
Neal, J. 264

Nealson, Des 178
Neanderthal 5, 196
The Neanderthal Man 5, 171, 215, 247–248
Neanderthals 2–4, 6, 15, 29–35, 46, 52, 65, 80–81, 88, 93, 120–125, 142, 145, 169–172, 174–176, 178–185, 188, 190–191, 193, 195–197, 199–203, 208–209, 223–227, 231, 233–235, 242, 244, 246–248, 265, 267–272, 282–284
Neanderthals on Trial 5, 196
A Neanderthal's World 196
Near Man (Musical group) 246
Neeson, Liam 182
Neill, Noel 10
Nelson, Burt 136
Nelson, Don 86
Nelson, Gary 75
Nelson, Oliver 261
Nemo, Nancy 119
Neolithic Europe 196
Neolithic Period 4, 89, 171, 174, 182–183, 187–188, 192, 196, 198–199, 202–203, 206, 231
Neptune's Children 74
Nerman, David 244
Neubauer, Leonard 257
Neubaur, Christine 12
Neumann, Jennie 246
Neumann, Kurt 286
Neville, John 165
Nevison, Henry 189
The New Cutting Edge 193
A New Era 193
The New Fred and Barney Show 71, 97–98
New Guinea 126, 192
New Mexico 202, 204
The New World 185
Newark, Derek 50, 52
Newfield, Sam 274
Newman, David 15, 64, 68, 80
Newman, Marshall 182
Newman, Samuel 238
Next of Kin 208
Ney, Henry 273
Nicholasen, Michelle 182
Nicholls, George O. 53
Nicholls, Ted 90
Nichols, Charles A. 59, 144
Nicholson, Chris 170
Nicolai, Bruno 161
Nicoletta, John 74
Nicolosi, Roberto 137, 140
Nieva, Alphonso 164
Night Beauties 14
Nightline (series) 196
Nilsson, Anna Q. 9
Nimoy, Leonard 203, 205
The Nine Ages of Nakedness 98
Niven, Larry 240
Nixon, Allan 117–118
Noah 189
Noah and the Ark 188, 288
Noah Put the Cat Out 144
Noah's Ark 1, 188–189, 203

Noah's Ark on Ararat 188
Noah's Ark: The True Story 189
Noah's Ark: Was There a Worldwide Flood? 188
Noah's Ark: What Happened to It? 188
Noah's Flood 189
Noah's Flood in Context: Legend or History 189
Noble, Maurice 246
Noh Theater 149
Nolan, Bill 136
Nolan, Mary Lee 193
Nomadism 171, 184
Non-human intelligent species (fictional) 52
Norris, Patrick 275
North, Alex 151
North, Jay 114
Northrup, Harry 29
Norton, Andre 218
Norton, B.W.L. 232
Norton, Chris 213
Norton, Cliff 85
Norton, Randy 56
Norway 267
Nose rubbing 15, 17
Nosferatu 126
Not Tonite, Henry 98–99
Nova (Series) 169, 177, 180, 182, 187–189, 192–193, 195–196, 203
Novak, Mickell 99
Novotny, J.A. 86
Noxon, Nicholas 180, 193
Nuba People 126
Nudes on the Rocks 55
Un Nueva Criatura 248
Nye, Bill 181

Oakland, Simon 239
O'Brien, George 55
O'Brien, Laurie 45
O'Brien, Maria 154
O'Brien, Shane 227
O'Brien, Willis 3, 5, 15, 46–48, 97, 116, 129, 170, 181, 195, 227, 243
Occhipinti, Andrea 38
O'Connor, Renée 165, 274–276, 283
O'Connor, Richard L. 88
Octopussy 113
O'Daine, Diane 119
Odd, David 245
O'Dell, Jennifer 244
O'Donnell, Joe 178
O'Donnell, Rosie 64, 66, 68
Odyssey (series) 194, 204
Of Mice and Men 103
Of Monkeys and Men 289
Ogata, Naoto 249
Ogden, Mark 15
Ogilvie, George 285
Ogle, Bob 67, 69
Ogle, Mark 193
Ogu and Mampato in Rapa Nui 248

O'Hanlon, George 86
Ojibwa Indians 169
Okawa, Ryuho 89
O'Keefe, Miles 217
Okuda, Shinji 230
Old Fashioned: The Real Caveman Couture 196
Old Man of LaChapelle (Neanderthal remains) 170, 176, 184
The Oldest Profession: The Prehistoric Era 98
Olduvai Gorge (Tanzania) 193
Olivar, Bert 137
Olive Oyl 114, 254
Oliver, David 23–24
Oliver, Robert H. 231
Olivieri, Dennis 196
Olmecs 193
Olmert, Michael 207–208
Olsen, Fleming 273
Olsen, William 10
Olton, Bill 205
The Omega Man 285
Omens, Woody 77
On the Comet 273
On the Road to Stonehenge 205
On the Rocks 70
On the Rocks: Prehistoric Art of France & Spain 196
On the Town 248–249
Once Upon a Time: Man 98–99
Once Upon a Time: The Americas 99
100,000 B.C. (*Dr. Who* episode) 50–52
One Million AC/DC 98–99
One Million B.C. 2–5, 28, 44, 93, 99–104, 108–109, 136, 187, 217, 233, 237, 272, 277, 283
One Million Heels B.C. 249
One Million Years B.C. 3–5, 15, 16, 28, 37, 40, 41, 43–45, 49, 79, 93, 98, 103–113, 134–136, 145, 157, 182, 187, 191, 194, 237, 242, 253, 256, 260, 283
One Small Step 193
1,000 Years from Now 285
O'Neal, Tatum 247
O'Neill, Eileen 56
O'Neill, J.P. 282
O'Neill, Tom 165
Oppenheimer, Alan 11, 54, 271
Oppenheimer, Stephen 200–201
O'Quinn, Carrick 165
Orangutans 203
Orchard, Nick 178
Ordinary People 236,
Ordway, Frederick J. 151–152
Orenstein, Leo 263
Orfei, Liana 73
The Origin of Man 288
The Origin of Mankind 288
The Original Golfer 144, 281
The Original Movie 144, 281
Origins, a History of North America 197
The Origins of Art in France 196–197

Origins of Homo Sapiens: East African Roots 205
The Origins of Man 197
The Origins, the First 50,000 Years 196
Origins, the First Nations 197
Ornaments and Personal Adornment 11, 41, 43–44, 170, 179, 183
Orne, Stuart 245
Orrorin Tugenensis 203
Orth, David 244
Ortiz, April 45
Orton, Bill 192
Orwitz, Peter 257
Osada Havranu 131
O'Shaughnessy, Brian 40, 45
Ostrander, William 56–57
O'Sullivan, Kate 193
Osvaldová, Gabriela 97, 132, 153
Oswald the Rabbit (Cartoon character) 136
Ötzi *see* Iceman (Ice Mummy)
Our Earliest Ancestors 5, 197
Out of Africa 185
Out of Asia 197
Out of Darkness 197
Out of the Darkness 137–140
Out of the Fiery Furnace 197
Out of the Ice 174
Out of the Past (Relic Hunter episode) 128
Out of Time's Abyss (Proposed film) 253, 281
The Outer Space Connection 177
Outer Space Jitters 264
L'Outil, Preuve de l'Homme 201
Outlaws 117–118
Overgard, William 242

Pabst, G.W. 74
Pacific Area 193
Pacific Northwest (U.S.-Canada) 199
Pacifism 83
Pack, Charles Lloyd 230
Packer, Peter 242
I Padroni del Mondo 93–94
Paes, Darryl 147
Page, Cynthia 203
Page, Laurel 219, 259
Paget, Alfred 19, 22
Paice, Eric 249
Paich, Marty 90
Pal, George 74, 286
Palange, Inez 99
Palella, Oreste 73
Paleo-Indians 15, 17, 99, 169–170, 173, 180–181, 183, 185, 188–189, 190–191, 193, 195–206, 210, 221, 229
Paleoindians of the Northern Rockies 198
Paleolithic Period 197, 199
Paleolithic Society 197
Paleoworld: Tracing Human Origins 5, 197–198
Palestine 184

Palethrope, Joan 129
Paley, Philip 240
Palma, Joe 82, 264
Palmer, Geoffrey 264
Palmer, June 98
Palmer, Max 239
Pancho Talero en la Prehistoria 114
Pandolfi, Elio 159
Panico en el Transiberiano 232–233
Pankin, Stuart 50
Paranthropus Boisei 207
Parker, Corey 230
Parker, Eddie 247
Parker, Tom S. 64
Parks, Hugh 10
Parno, José Antonio 176
Parr, Bobby 216, 242
Parrott, Charles 282
Parshley, H.M. 195
Pasco, Sam 82, 85
The Past Is Not Another Place: Ritual Landscape 198
A Patch of Blue 258
Paterson, Nigel 208
Pathfinders in Space 249
Pathfinders to Mars 249
Pathfinders to Venus 249
Paths of Discovery 18
Patrick, Millicent 223
Patterson, Nigel 264
Patterson, Ray 67, 69, 79, 86
Pattillo, Alan 264
Pavia, Nestor 221, 239
Pavlik, Milan 97, 131, 153
Payeur, Georgiane Minot 244
Pays, Amanda 263
Payson, Blanche 142
Payton, Barbara 257
Pazdernik, Vaclav 86
Pazzafini, Nello 35
Peacock, Daniel 24
The Pebbles and Bamm-Bamm Show 23, 66–67, 72, 114
Pebbles, Dino and Bamm-Bamm 67
Pedagogical Institution (College to You) 281
Pekin Genjin 249–251
Peking Man 170–171, 193, 197, 204, 249–251, 281
Peking Man (1997) 3, 5–6, 32, 134, 215, 227, 236, 249–251, 287
Pellerin, Cheryl 187
Peltier, Melissa Jo 181
Peluce, Meeno 227
Pendry, Alan 180
Pengow, Ivan 35
Penhaligon, Susan 241
Penn, Arthur 214
Penn, Leonard 239
Penn, M.O. 128
Penta, Virginia 137
The People of Origin 174
People of the Hearth: Paleoindians of the Northern Rockies 198
The People of the Ice Age 198

People of the Mist (proposed film) 113
The People That Time Forgot 3, 216, 242, 251–253, 281
The Peopling of the Pacific 193
Pepla films 35–37, 73–74, 137, 140–142, 232
Pepper, Barry 285
Percival, Lacey 282
The Perils of Pauline 245
Perkins, Elizabeth 64–65
Perkins, Gil 271
Perlman, Martin 34
Perlman, Ron 120, 126
Perman, Don 137
Perry, Joyce 240
Perry, Mark 274
Perschy, Maria 164
Pertwee, Jon 220
Peters, Jason 49
Petray, Pepito 114
Petrie, Daniel 289
Petrie, Douglas 219
Petroglyphs: The Art of the Earliest American 198
Petursson, Johan 117
Phantom Empire (1935) 74, 253
The Phantom Empire (1986) 253
Phantom Monkey's Journey to the West 89
Philipe, Gerard 14
The Philippine Story (series) 205
Philippines 191–192, 205
Phillips, Bruce 238
Phillips, R. B. 205
Phinn, Crackers 227
Phoenix, Joaquin 16, 18
Piazza, Phillipe 201
Piccioni, Fabio 137
Piccoli, Michel 266, 287
Picha 11–13
Pickford, Martin 203
Pickford, Mary 93
Piddington, Andrew 200
Pierce, Arthur C. 165, 236
Pierce, Tedd 72, 119, 153
Piga, Aldo 215
Piggott-Smith, Tim 199
Pillsbury, Garth 246
Piltdown Man Forgery 171, 174, 181, 184, 204, 247
Pinassi, Dominique 145
Pink Panther 53, 115
Piper, Brett 48–49
Piscopo, Joe 64
The Pit 253–254
Pittorru, Fabio 159
Pitts, Michael 195
Places in the Heart 236
Plains (U.S.) 199
Plan 9 from Outer Space 238
Planet of Dinosaurs 232
Planet of Life: Apes to Man 198
Planet of the Apes 6, 151, 165, 218, 240, 252, 258, 283, 285–286
"Planet of the Apes" Biological Period 197
Planet of the Dinosaurs 253

Planet Outlaws 219
Planeta Burg 274, 283
Platt, Judson 247
Plewa, Joseph 12
Plummer, Christopher 263
La Plus Vieux Métier du Monde: L'Ere Préhistorique 98
Plympton, George H. 239
Pocahontas 18
Podeswa, Jeremy 280
Poissonnier, Juliette 130
Poitier, Sidney 258
Polanski, Roman 126
Poledouris, Basil 221
Pollack, Naomi 88
Pollexfen, Jack 247
Ponicanová, Beta 97
Poole, Duane 59
Popescu-Gopo, Ion 184
Pope-Stamper, F. 50
Popeye 114, 254
The Popeye and Olive Show 114
Popov, Gavril 265
Porky Pig 116
Pornography 3, 10–11, 55, 98–99, 119, 132, 137, 234, 249, 266, 273, 279–280
Porter, Bobby 241
Porter, Cole 216
Portillo, Rafael 237
Portugal 179, 196, 200
Post, Ted 285
Post-Apocalypse settings 2, 138–140, 285–286
Postumia Grottoes (Yugoslavia) 137, 141
Poteus, Micheline 50
Powell, Robert 210
Power, Jules 204
Power, Taryn 259–260
Power, Tyrone 260
Powers, Bruce 233
Powers, John 2
Pozzato, Pierangelo 16
Pransky, Janelle 88
Prati, Pamela 82, 85
Pratt, Hawley 53, 115
Pre-Anglo-Saxon England 198
Pre-Clovis Cultures 169, 181, 185, 202–203
I Predatori di Atlantide 74
Prehistoric America 5, 198–199
Prehistoric Art of France & Spain 196
Prehistoric Bimbos in Armageddon City 286
Prehistoric Cultures 199
Prehistoric Daze 98–99
Prehistoric Hayseeds 282
Prehistoric Humans 199
Prehistoric Images: The First Art of Man 199
Prehistoric Inhabitants 176
A Prehistoric Love Story 114
Prehistoric Magic 199
The Prehistoric Man (1908) 254
Prehistoric Man (1911) 254
The Prehistoric Man (1917) 282

The Prehistoric Man (1924, Great Britain) 114–115
Prehistoric Man (1924, U.S.) 115
Prehistoric Man (1970) 199
Prehistoric Man (1980) 199
Prehistoric Man (1988) 199
Prehistoric Man (1995) 198
Prehistoric Man in Europe 199
Prehistoric Monuments 199–200
Prehistoric Monuments of Europe 199–200
Prehistoric Peeps 115
Prehistoric Perils 115
Prehistoric Pink 115–116
Prehistoric Popeye 114
Prehistoric Porky 116
Prehistoric Poultry 48, 116, 129
Prehistoric Sites 192
Prehistoric Strip 55
Prehistoric Super Salesman 116
Prehistoric Women (1950) 2, 5, 34, 43–44, 95, 117–119, 162–163, 186, 225
Prehistoric Women (1967) 132–135
Prehistoric World 137–140
Prehistory 200
Prehistory, Ancient History (5,000 B.C.E.-10,000 B.C.E.) 175
Prehistory of Spain 200
Prehistory of the Texas Coast 200
Pre-Hysterical Hare 119
Pre-Hysterical Man 254
Prelude to Taurus 282
Presley, Elvis 68
Prevost, Marie 280
Price, David 192
Price, Henry 228
Price, Vincent 136
The Price (Xena episode) 274–275
Prima della Storia, L'Uomo 193–194
Primal Desires 119
Primal Man (1973–74) 5, 200
Primal Man (1993) 185, 202
Primal Screen (Kolchak episode) 239
The Primevals (proposed film) 282
Primitive Instinct 119
The Primitive Man (1914) 19, 21, 22, 90, 93
The Primitive Men of Planet X (Space Patrol episode) 262–263
Primitive Triple Feature 164
Prince, Les 169
Prince, Robert 232
Princess Mononoke 89
Principal, Victoria 196
Prisoners of the Lost Universe 254
Probyn, Brian 230
Prohaska, Anthony 170
Prohaska, Janos 170
Prohaska, Robert 170
Prometheus and Bob 87–88
The Prophecy and the Bone 174
Proser, Chip 234
Prostitution, Prehistoric 98, 161
Prowse, David 230–231, 252–253

Psychic Wars 90
Pterosaurs 12, 16, 56–57, 65, 69, 76, 106, 110, 116–117, 155–156, 238, 242, 249, 252–253, 273–274
Ptushko, Aleksandr 265
Pueblo Indians 181
Puglisi, Aldo 161
Punzalan, Bruno 137
Purcell, Daniella 263
Purdom, Edmond 231
Pusch, Sabine 209
Pushkin, Alexander 265
Putnam, Jock 261
Putting the Pants on Philip 71
Pyrenees Mountains 123

Quade, Jay 197
Quaid, Dennis 25–26
Quando Gli Uomini Armarono la Clava e con le Donne Fecero Din-Don 159–160
Quando le Donne Avevano la Coda 160–161
Quando le Donne Persero la Coda 161
Quarry, Robert 253
Quarshie, Hugh 178
Quatermass and the Pit (1958–59) 254–255
Quatermass and the Pit (1967) 5, 165, 255–256
Quatermass Experiment (1953) 254
Quatermass Xperiment (1955) 158, 254
Quatermass II (1955) 158, 254
Quatermass II: Enemy from Space (1957) 254
Quest for Camelot 115
Quest for Fire 1–2, 4–6, 31, 34–35, 40, 78, 94, 96, 109, 120–128, 149, 187–188, 200, 236
The Quest for Fire Adventure 127
The Quest for Noah's Ark 188
Quest for Noah's Flood 189
Quest for the Lost Civilizations 177
Questel, Mae 254
The Quiet Man 272
Quigley, Linnea 227
Quilici, Brando 187, 206
Quinn, Aidan 280
Quo Vadis 45

Race Memories 128
Race Suicide 128
Racism in anthropology 170–171, 182, 204
Racism in films 4, 21, 32, 57, 92–93, 127, 141–142
Rackley, Luther 242
Rackstraw, Rob 75
Das Rad 129–130
Rafele, Domenico 16
Rafferty, Chips 261
Ragging Bull 31
Raguse, Elmer 102
Rahan 282

Rahan Fils des Ages Farouches 128
Raichert, Lane 60
Raiders of the Lost Ark 16
Raimi, Sam 64
Raimi, Ted 275
Rain, Douglas 151
Rain Forest 96
Raine, Jackson 218
Rains, Claude 244
Raize, Jason 16
Raksin, Rudy 271
Ramapithecus 199
Ramer, Henry 11
Ramirez, Cesar 137
Ramos, Jesus 137
Rampling, Charlotte 286
Ramsey, Ward 224–225
Randall, Ron 259
Randall, Stephanie 132
Randas, Vance 231
Ranous, William V. 131
Rape 30–32, 35, 42–43, 99, 106, 109, 248, 250–251, 265
Rasca, Nonong 264
Raschke, Irmgard H.H. 238
Rasinski, Connie 115
Rath, Earl 232
Rathbone, Basil 283
Ravenscroft, Thurl 53
Ravera, Lidia 16
Ray, Aldo 227
Ray, Fred Olen 223, 253
Ray, Harrison 49
Ray, Mickey 119
Raymond, Robert 177, 193, 197
Reagan, Nancy 60
The Real Caveman Couture 196
The Real Eve 5, 200–201
Real Genius 247
Realistic tendency in prehistory films/TV 2–3, 21, 43, 88, 95, 124, 145,
Reason and Emotion 256
Rector, Jeff 49
Red Sea Migration 189–190, 201
Redford, Brian 82
Redford, Wanda 50
Rediscovering the Americas 194
Reed, Alan 60–62, 70, 90, 287
Reed, Bob 11, 144, 154
Reed, Michael 132
Reed, Oliver 191
Reed, Pamela 29, 34
Reenacted documentaries *see* Dramatized documentaries
Reese, Robert W. 194
Reeves, George 10
Reeves, Keanu 15
Reeves, Steve 35, 232
Refalo, Joe 147
Rehr, Darryl 196
Reid, Kate 270
Reid, Mary 29
Reid, Milton 252–253
Reilly, Charles Nelson 67, 270
Reiner, Carl 146–147
Reinl, Harald 176
Reiser, Charles F. 246

Reisz, Richard 169
Relic Hunter 128
Relics (of prehistoric humans in the modern world) 221, 223, 232–233, 242, 254–256
Religion, Prehistoric 16–19, 29–31, 33, 35, 37–39, 41–44, 51, 73, 83–84, 89, 131–133, 138–139, 146, 154–156, 162, 170, 172, 178, 180, 183, 186–187, 194, 196, 202–203, 206, 209–210, 235, 250, 257, 268
Remar, James 29, 34
Renouf, Jonathan 197
Repulsion 126
Resnais, Alain 119, 225
Resolving Conflicts between Science and Genesis 288
Rethwisch, Gus 233
Retracing Man's Footsteps 197
Return of the Ape Man 256–257
Return of the Iceman 201
Return to Eden 10
Revenge of the Creature 223
Revived (prehistoric people brought to life in modern times) 219–221, 224–227, 229–230, 234–236, 239, 249–251, 254, 256–259, 261, 268–270
Revolt of the Zuggs (Buck Rogers episode) 219
Rewriting Man's History 177
Reynolds, Burt 216, 261
Reynoso, David 217
R.F.D. 10,000 B.C. 47–48, 129
Rhodes-Flaherty, Lucinda 24
Rhys, Matthew 245
Rhys-Davies, John 169, 176, 185, 195, 202, 244
Rhythm 'n' Greens 129
Rice, Tamati 274
Richard, Viola 70–71
Richards, Cybil 273
Richards, Jeffrey 182
Richards, Julian 203
Richards, Michael 181
Richards, Paul 145
Richards, Rex 162
Richardson, Bob 45
Richardson, David 176
Richardson, John 104, 112–113
Richardson, Kevin 70
Richter, Daniel 147–151, 287
The Riddle of the Stones 204
Riefensthal, Leni 126
Riker, Robin 264
Riley, Lucas 273
Riley, Patrick 10–11
Rimmer, Shane 252
Rintaro 88
Rio, Alicia 11
Ripert, Jean-Marc 266
Ripper, Michael 254
Rispoli, Viviana Maria 93
Ritter, Tex 58
Ritual Landscape 198
Rivero, Jorge 38, 40
Roach, Hal 70, 99, 103–104, 109, 272

Roach, Hal, Jr. 99, 104
Roach, Pat 221
Road, Mike 262, 271
The Road to Atlantis 175
The Road Warrior 238, 285
Robards, Jason 289
Robbins, Dick 59
Roberts, Alan 224–225
Roberts, Bill 256
Roberts, Glenn 221
Roberts, Joe 142
Robertson, Blair 261
Robertson, Cliff 257
Robertson, Harry 254
Robertson, Myles 254
Robey, George 114
Robin Hood 115
Robin Hood (1922) 71
Robin of Sherwood 115
Robin, Walt 246
Robins, Rochelle 245
Les Robins des Bois (Comedy troupe) 130
Robinson, Bumper 60
Robinson, Charlie 55
Robinson, J. Peter 229
Robinson, Joe 137, 140–141
Robinson, W.C. 90
Robuschi, Guido 35
Rochefort, Jean 130
Rock, Joe 59
Rocketship X-M 5, 286
Rocklin, Paul 182
Rocks 129–130
Rockwell, Robert 276
Rocky 69, 251
Rocky and Bullwinkle 130
Rocky Jones, Space Ranger 257
Rod Brown of the Rocket Rangers 257
Rodemich, Gene 136
Rodgers, Ned 180
Rodriguez, Jacqueline 10
Roebuck, Daniel 23–24
Roeg, Nicolas 266
Rogers, Eric 220
Roggersdorf, Wilhelm 176
Roja, Gustavo 164
Rojas, Alejandro 248
Rollins, Henry 184
Roman, Martin 55
Roman, Phil 72
Le Roman de L'Homme 201–202
Romand, Béatrice 266
Romano, Ray 80
Romersa, Joanna 66
Ronay, Edina 132, 135
Rose, Sherrie 10
Rose, Warner 55
Rosen, Phil 256
Rosny, J.H. 34, 120, 124–125
Ross, Arthur 221
Ross, Howard 159
Ross, Hugh 288
Ross, Joe E. 85
Ross, Steven 245
Rossellini, Renzo 193
Rossellini, Roberto 4, 193–194

Rosson, Harold 248
Rossi, Constantino 16
Rostill, John 129
Roswell, Maggie 56
Rothwell, Talbott 219–220
Rotoscoping 57–58
Roundtable on Genesis One 288
Rouve, Jean-Paul 130
Rowe, Thomas 199
Rowland, Bruce 238
Rowley, Christopher 204
Royce, Lionel 274
RRRrrrr!!! 130–131
Rubinstein, Zelda 67
Rudgley, Richard 203
Ruff and Ready 61
Rullo, Cynthia 23
Rumbelow, Jonathan 223
Run for the Hills 257–258
Ruppel, Robh 19
Rusoff, Lou 259
Russell, Ian 183
Russell, Ken 213–215
Russell, Theresa 13
Russell, Ward 165
Russell, William 50, 52
Russia 165, 265, 267
Russo, Luigi 16
Rustichelli, Carlo 217
Rutherford, Cedric 162
Ruvinskis, Wolf 15
Ryabinkina, Xenia 265
Ryan, Kathleen 169

Sabata, Antonio 159
Sabre-tooth cats 29, 45, 65, 76, 80–81, 120, 130, 145, 191, 198, 247, 260
Sachs, Andrew 171, 207–208
Sacred Sites 199
Sagan, Carl 178
Sahara 205
Sahota, Noddy 203
St. Clair, Hector 282
St. Croix (Virgin Islands) 225
St. James, Jon 23
St. John, Al 76–77, 282
St. Pierre, Leopold 244
St. Trinian's films 135
Sais, Marin 119
Saki 10
Salazar, Alfredo 237
Saldanha, Carlos 80
Salerno, Enrico Maria 98
Salkin, Leo 146
Salome, Jens 29
Salt, Christopher 203
Salt, Jennifer 232
Salter, Hans J. 164, 221, 247
Salvi, Emimmo 73
San Martin, Conrado 38, 40
San People 174, 179–180, 190, 192
Sandberg, Sverre 183
Sanders, George 257
Sandford, Tiny 70–71
Sandground, Maurice 11
Sandor, Steve 56
The Sands of Dee 93

The Sands of Dreamtime 202
Sanello, Frank 123–124
Sangster, Thomas 264
Santa Rosa Island (Calif.) 202
Santo Contro Blue Demon en la Atlantida 74
Santorini Island (Greece) 175
Santos, Richard 265
The Saphead 144
Sapte Arte 184
Sarde, Phillipe 120
Sardinia 200
Sarg, Tony 9, 58, 161, 280–281
Sargent, Richard 265
Sassone, Oley 274
Sato, Junya 249, 251
Saunders, Merle 269
Saunders, Nancy 82, 264
Saunders, W.G. 114
Savalas, Telly 232
Savannah Theory 171, 203, 209
Savel, Dava 50
Savino, Chris 70
Sawalha, Nadim 259
Sawtell, Paul 136, 170, 273
Saxon, David 96
Saxon, John 254
Sayles, John 29, 31, 33–34
Sayre, George Wallace 270
Sbarge, Raphael 247
Scalici, Jack 145
Scandurra, Maria Sofia 140
Scaramouche 145
Scarpelli, Umberto 73
Scavenging 149, 170, 172, 179, 188, 208
Schaaf, Jeanne 189
Schade, Fritz 76
Schaefer, George 289
Schafer, Natalie 75
Schaffner, Franklin J. 285
Schama, Simon 183
Scheerer, Robert 239
Scheib, Philip A. 35, 115, 146
Scheinfeld, John 195
Schenck, Joseph 144
Schenk, George 264–265
Schepisi, Fred 234–236
Schepps, Shawn 229–230
Schiegl, Kurt 120
Schifrin, Lalo 25, 28
Schindell, Cy 82, 264
Schlock! 5, 227, 258–259
Schmidt, Jan 97, 131, 153
Schmidt, Richard L. 189
Schmock, Jonathan 12
Scholes, Roger 184
Schreffler, Marilyn 114, 219, 259
Schreiber, Avery 25
Schreiber, Liev 195, 203
Schrenk, Friedemann 205
Schrock, Raymond I. 274
Schuler, Hannes 182
Schumm, Harry 245
Schwartz, Gary 120, 126
Schwartz, Sherwood 75, 85–86
Schwarzenegger, Arnold 221
Science and Fiction 170–171

Science and Genesis 188, 288
Scientific American Frontiers: Coming Into America 202
Scientific American Frontiers: Life's Really Big Questions 202
Scooby's All-Star Laff-a-Lympics 219, 259
Scooby's All-Stars 259
Scooby's Laff-a-Lympics 259
Scopes Monkey Trial 181, 195, 288–289
The Scopes "Monkey Trial" (1998) 289
Scorsese, Martin 31
Scotland 199
Scott, Bill 130
Scott, George C. 289
Scott, Janet 117
Scott, John 252, 268
Scott, Willard 181
Scourby, Alexander 200
Scoville, Chrysti 198
Screamers 74
Scrooge 114
Scurte Istorie 184
The Sea Devils (*Dr. Who* episode) 52
Sea Hunt 223
The Search for Ancient Americans 202
The Search for Atlantis (1933 purported film) 175
The Search for Atlantis (1996) 175
Search for Fossil Man 202
Search for Neanderthal 202
The Search for Noah's Ark 189
The Search for Noah's Ark: The Adventure Continues 188
The Search for Our Ancestors 193
Search for the First Americans 203
Search for the First Human 203
The Searchers 276
Searching for Other Worlds (series) 204
Searle, Ronald 142
Sears, Steven L. 274
Seawright, Roy 102–103
Sebastian, John 283
Second Kiss, First Love (*Cavegirl* episode) 24
Secret Burial Mounds of Pre-Historic America 203
The Secret Mounds of Pre-Historic America 203
The Secret of Gilligan's Island (*Gilligan's Island* episode) 75
The Secret of Stonehenge 203
Secrets and Mysteries: Stonehenge 205
Secrets of Lost Empires: Stonehenge 203
Secrets of the Ancient World (series) 176
Secrets of the Bog People 203
Secrets of the Dead (series) 195, 203
Secrets of the Stone Age 203
Secrets of the Unknown: Stonehenge 205

Sedgwick, Kyra 280
Seeing and Doing 199
Seeking Noah's Flood 189, 203
Seeking the First Americans 203–204
Seibel, Dennis 198
Seidenberg, Mark 80
Seizure 113, 135
Selen, Suna 218
Sellers, Sabrina 38
Sellier, Charles E. 188
Sen, Ali 218
Sensi, Mario 73
Senut, Brigitte 203
Serezli, Metin 218
Sgt. Bilko 85
The Serpents 131
Sesame Street 46
Set in Stone 204
Settlement of Crows 131–132
Settling Down 193
Seva, Tarlok Sing 120
Seven Arts 184
Seven Samurai 108, 267–268
The Seventh Voyage of Sinbad 260
Sexy Proibitissimo 132
Seymour, Jane 259
Shah, Kiran 252
Shakespeare, William 49, 130, 219
Shamanism *see* Religion, Prehistoric
Shanghai Knights 115
Shanks, Michael 263
Shape-shifting 16–18, 22
Sharad of Atlantis 74
Sharif, Omar 267
Sharples, Winston 254
Shaving, Prehistoric 16, 118, 136–137, 186
Shaw, Adriana 145
Shaw, Elizabeth Lloyd 56
Shawlee, Joan 117–118
Shayne, Robert 138, 247
Shazam! 88
She 113, 133, 191
The She-Creature 223, 259
Sheehan, Michael 67
Sheets, Todd 286
Shell, Tom 223
Shelley, Barbara 255–256
Shenar, Paul 202
Shepherd, Cybill 216
Sheridan, Bob 223
Shields, Malcolm 245
The Shining 151
Shire, David 145
Shore, Pauly 229
Shore, Sammy 78
A Short History 184
Siani, Sabrina 38, 40
Siberia 169, 190, 193
Sidaway, Ashley 191
Sidaway, Robert 191
Siegel, Mark 221
Sigmund and the Sea Monster 88
Sigurdsson, Hlynur 64
Silbert, Denise 137
Silcock, Lisa 179

The Silent Enemy 17
Silent Running 126
Silk Road 251
Sillen, Andrew 174
Sills, Milton 9
The Silurians (*Dr. Who* episode) 52
Silver, Elaine 64
Silver, Melanie 64
Silver, Pat 262
Silvestre, Armando 237
Silvestre, Eduardo 53
Silvestri, Alan 29, 31, 34
Simmons, Beth 237
Simon, John 127
Simonetti, Claudio 38, 40
Sims, Joan 22, 220
Sims, Milton 279
Sinatra, Frank 248
Sinbad and the Eye of the Tiger 3, 113, 182, 259–260
Sinelnikoff, Michael 244
Singer, Jane 45
Sino-Tibetan language 189
Sir Arthur Conan Doyle's The Lost World 244
Siren of Atlantis 74
Sisti, Michelin 50
Sitka, Emil 264
Siurano, Francisco G. 248
Skal, David J. 223
Skara Brae (Orkney Islands) 183
Skarstedt, Vance 261
Skeggs, Roy 191
Skelton, Peter 182
Skelton, Red 5, 142
Skull 1470 (Australopithecine remains) 197
Skull Wars: The Missing Link 204
Skullduggery 260–261
Slate, Lane 145
Slattery, John 172
Slaughter, Tod 16
Slave Girls 43, 45, 107–108, 113, 132–135, 141, 157–158, 191, 287
Slavery 117, 132–133
The Slime People 261
Slocombe, Douglas 218
Smeaton, Bruce 234
Smell, Sense of 120, 123, 229
Smeltzer, David 192
Smigel, Robert 269
Smith, Beaumont 282
Smith, Charlie 179
Smith, Daniel J. 198
Smith, David 70
Smith, Dick 215
Smith, Gary Allen 16, 220
Smith, Hal 59
Smith, Jack 182
Smith, Kate 116
Smith, Kiki 22
Smith, Kurtwood 53
Smith, Madeline 230
Smith, Malcolm 69
Smith, Paul J. 116
Smith, Sebastian 115
Smithsonian World 205

Smollett, Jussie 46
Snow, Mark 165
Snow, William 244
Snyder, William E. 221
Snyders, Sammy 253
Society of Primitive Technology 182
Sole, Alfred 265
Solomon, Ed 15
Solos, Javier 217
Solutrean Atlantic Migration Theory 169, 202
Some Liked It Hot 204
Somlyó, Zoltán 282
Sommer, Josef 234
Sommers, Joannie 13
Sonoda, Hideki 230
Sonoyama, Shunji 72, 76
Sorel, Jeanne 117
Sorrell, T.J. 24
Soucie, Kath 79
South Africa 24
South Carolina 180
South Dakota 180
South Dakota Adventure 180
Southwest (U.S.) 170, 198
Space Ghost and Dino Boy 262
Space Invasion from Lapland 236–237
Space: 1999 262
Space Patrol 262–263
The Space Primevals (*Lost in Space* episode) 242–243
Spacejacked 263
Spain 123, 176, 179, 185, 196, 199–200, 202, 205
Spam, Chips 60
Spangler, Donna 49
Spargo, Nicholas 73
Spartacus 151
Spartakus and the Sun Beneath the Sea 74
Sparxx, P.J. 119
Spataro, Rocco 35
Specialization of labor 186
Speech *see* Language
Speed 34
Spellos, Peter 223
Spenceley, Peter 223
Spencer, Norman 219
Spielberg, Steven 65, 158
Spinnell, Joe 263
Splash 31
Sportsman Quartet 116
Springer, Hans 182
Springtime in the Rock Age 135
Springtime in the Rockies 135
Spry-Leverton, Peter 193
The Spy Who Loved Me 28, 113, 240
Stafford, Gino 73
Stafford, Grace 116
Stahr, Monroe 119
Staley, Joan 271–272
Stalling, Carl 29, 46, 116
Stallings, Vernon 35
Stanger, Michelle 49
Stanley and the Dinosaurs 135–136

Stansfield, David 197
Star Trek 86, 164, 240
Star Wars 165, 231, 253, 263
Starcrash 263
Stargate Atlantis 74
Stargate SG-1 263
Stark, Jonathan 233
Stark, Sheldon 273
Starlost 263
Starr, Ringo 5, 25–26, 28
Staubitz, Heinz Albert 185
Stedman, Myrtle 145–146
Steele, Barbara 134
Stefanelli, Benito 82
Stein, Herman 221
Stein, Ronald 224, 259
Stellari, Gian 35
Stenner, Chris 129
Stephenson, John 59–60, 66–70, 72, 80, 86, 90, 97–98
Sterne, Elaine 279
Stevens, Charles 257
Stevens, Fisher 247
Stevens, Julie 220
Stevens, Mickey 114
Stevenson, Alexandra 132
Stevenson, Rachel 191
Stewart, Paul 97
Stewart, R.J. 165
Sticks and Stones (proposed *Xena* episode) 283–284
Stig of the Dump (1981) 263–264
Stig of the Dump (2002) 264
Stiller, Michael 182
Stingray 264
Stocker, John 11
Stockton, Carla 72
Stockwell, John 247
Stokes, John 238
Stolzenberg, Mark 245–246
Stone, Evan 266
Stone, Lawrence 244
Stone, Lewis 243
Stone, Oliver 4, 113, 135
Stone, Sharon 66
The Stone Age (1917) 282
The Stone Age (1922) 282
The Stone Age (1931) 136
Stone Age (1940) 282
The Stone Age (1962) 53
A Stone Age Adventure 136
Stone Age Americans 204
Stone Age Cartoons (series) 62, 71–72, 76, 153, 281, 283
A Stone Age Error 136
A Stone Age Romance 136
Stone Age Romeos 82, 264
Stone Age Roost Robber 136
Stone Age Stunts 136
The Stone Age: Till 3500 B.C. 174
Stone Age to Atomic Age 204
Stone Age Warriors 282–283
The Stone Men of Venus (*Rod Brown* episode) 257
Stonehenge 65, 76, 81, 115, 169, 175, 181, 184, 192, 194–196, 198, 203–205, 209
Stonehenge (1980) 204

Index

Stonehenge (1988) 204
Stonehenge (1998) 204–205
Stonehenge: A Journey Back in Time 204
Stonehenge and Its Cousins: Megalithic Observatories? 204
Stonehenge and the Ancient Britons 204–205
Stonehenge: If Only the Stones Could Talk 205
Stonehenge in Context 195
Stonehenge: Mystery in the Plain 205
Stonehenge: The Human Factor with Sue Jay 205
The Stoneman 264
Stones and Bones: The Birth of Archaeology 205
Storch, Eduard 97, 132, 153
Storey, Edith 29, 131
Storhoi, Dennis 267
Storm, John 170
The Story of Human Evolution 205
The Story of Lucy 188
The Story of Mankind 136
The Story of Prehistoric Man 205
Strathairn, David 234
Strangmüller, Frantisek 86
Stratton, John 230, 254
Straubb, Richard 257
Strauss, Richard 147, 151
Strauss, Theodore 200
Strayton, George 165
Strock, Herbert L. 233
Stromberg, William R. 221
Strong, Tara 80
The Struggle for Survival 200
Struggle to Survive 198
Struthers, Sally 50, 114
Strutin, Stuart 137
Stuart, Ian A. 253
Stuart, Mel 170
Stubble Trouble 136–137
Stuck on You 137
A Study in Terror 135
Stultz, Joseph 153, 181
Sturgeon, Theodore 240
Suarez, Jeremy 16, 18–19
The Sub-Mariner 74
Subotsky, Milton 216
Sugg, Philip 183
Sugiwara, Megumi 76
Suhrstedt, Timothy 15
Sullivan, Pat 54
Sultan, Arne 75
Summers, James 117
Sun worship 38, 154
Sundials 11, 46
Super Atragon 89
Superbeast 264–265
Superhumans, Prehistoric 227
Superman 86
Superman and the Mole Men 75, 269
The Superman/Aquaman Hour of Adventure 74
Surikova, Alla 146

Survival of the Species 193
Surviving in Africa 127, 149, 188
Surviving Like Primitive Man 182
Survivor (TV series) 2
Survivors (prehistoric people survive in an historical or modern period) 215, 217–223, 227–229, 231–232, 237–239, 245–247, 253–254, 259–261, 263–265, 267–268, 273–277
Suspiria 40
Suzuki, Pat 261
Swain, Mack 76–77
Swamp Music (*Dinosaurs* episode) 50
Swamp People (Australia) 178
Swart, Fred 40
Sweeney, D. B. 16
Sweet, Blanche 19, 93
Swenson, Charles 195
Switzerland 199
Sword and Sorcery settings 1, 39, 56, 217, 221
Swords and Plough Shares 197
Sybel, Richard 210
Sykorová, Marie 97, 132
Sylvester, William 151

Tabern, Peter 264
The Tabon Caves 205
Tabon Caves Site (Philippines) 205
Tachi, Eiichi 88
Tagani 137, 233
Takada, Koichi 230
Takana, Lake (Kenya) 179
Takayama, Hideki 10
Takekawa, Sei 153
Takizawa, Toshifumi 15
Talbot, Lyle 270
Talbott, Harold 124
The Tale of Tsar Saltan 5, 265
The Tale of Two Species 184–185
Tales of the Human Dawn 205
Talgorn, Frederic 130
Tallas, Gregg C. 74, 117–118, 225
Tamba (Chimpanzee) 239
Tamberelli, Danny 175
Tamblyn, Russ 253
Tankersley, Joseph 10
Tannen, William 238
Tannion, Robert 264
Tannura, Philip 276
Tanya's Island 265
Tapert, Rob 274
Tapley, Rose 29
Tappi, Malya 104
Tarantino, Louis C. 177
Tarrant, John 245
Tarzak Against the Leopard Men 215
Tarzak contro gli Uomini Leopardo 215
Tarzan 2, 102–103, 124, 236, 238–239, 265–266
Tarzan, the Epic Adventures 265–266
The Tasaday, Stone Age People in a Space Age World 191

Tasaday Tribe 191–192
Tasmanians 123
Tass, R.C. 241
Tassili N'Ajjer: Prehistoric Rock Paintings of the Sahara 205
Tattooing, Prehistoric 186–187, 201, 206
Taubman, Tiffany 50
Taung Child Skull 170–171, 174, 178, 202, 204
Taur, il Re della Forze Bruta 137
Taur the King of Brutal Force 137
Taur the Mighty 36, 137, 141
Taxi Driver 31
Taylor, Elizabeth 5, 64–66, 68, 220, 269
Taylor, Noel 220
Taylor, Rod 286
Taylor, Russi 66–67, 114
Taylor, Tamara 227
Technologies of the Gods: The Case for Pre-Historic High Technology 177
Teddy 253–254
Teegarden, Jim 66
Teenage Cavegirl 266
Teenage Caveman (1958) 2, 5, 73, 137–140
Teenage Caveman (2001) 286
Teeth *see* Dental Health, Prehistoric
Teilhard de Chardin, Pierre 202
Telmig, Akdon 99
The Tempest 49
10 (1979) 28
Tenerife Island (Canary Islands) 253
The Terrible Thunderlizards 53
Terror Castle 231
Terror in the Midnight Sun 236–237
Terror of the Zygons (*Dr. Who* episode) 52
Terry, Joyce 247
Terry, Paul 16, 54, 136, 146, 160
Terwilliger, George W. 128
Tess 126
Tessier, Robert 263
Tetley, Walter 130
Texas 58, 165, 200, 204
Thant, U 152
Thatcher, Kirk R. 50
That's Life (*Fabulous Funnies: Alley Oop* episode) 54
That's My Wife 71
Their First Mistake 71
Themroc 5–6, 266, 287
Thera/Santorini 175
These British Isles (series) 205
Theseus myth 281
Theunissen, Amanda 200
Thiele, Leo 11
Thierry, Sebastian 130
The Thing from Another World 81, 273
Thinking Allowed: Neil Freer: Who Were the Gods? 177
Thiraud, Armand 14

The 13th Warrior 5, 266–268
Thom, Alexander 178
Thomas, Brian 137, 233
Thomas, Damien 259
Thomas, Dave 16, 18
Thomas, Derek 273
Thomas, Dog 245
Thomas, Gerald 219–220
Thomas, Jay 230
Thomas, Lisa 104
Thomas, Mark 200
Thomas, Peter 169, 187, 189, 193, 203
Thomas, Roy 56
Thompson, Bill (actor) 145
Thompson, Bill (director) 205
Thompson, Charles 138
Thompson, Cindy Ann 23–24
Thompson, Don 270
Thompson, Lotus 282
Thor and the Amazon Women 36–37, 137, 140–142
Thorne, Alan 193
Thorne, Dianne 48
Those Magnificent Men in Their Flying Machines 142
Those Primitive Days 142
Three Ages 3, 5, 26, 60, 70, 76, 142–144, 176, 243, 281
3 × 3 Eyes 90
The Three Crichtons (*Farscape* episode) 230
Three-Eyed Prince 90
Three Missing Links 283
The Three Musketeers 103
Three Stooges 3, 49, 53, 60, 68–69, 76, 82, 160–161, 219, 251, 264, 272, 283
3000 A.D. 285
Three Tales Dark and Dangerous 270
Through the Ages 144
Through the Time Barrier (*Superman* episode) 10
Throwbacks (a modern person becomes or acts like a prehistoric person) 213–215, 223, 230–231, 247–249, 259, 264–266
Thundarr the Barbarian 286
Thunderball 113, 134, 223
Thurman, Mary 282
Thurston, Carol 239
Thwaites, Alan 184
Tiffin, Pamela 282
Tilley, Patrick 252
Timberg, Sammy 71–72, 76, 135, 153, 281
The Time Machine (1960) 240, 286
The Time Monster (*Dr. Who* story) 74
The Time Tunnel 86
Timeshift (prehistoric people in the modern world by fantasy or SF means) 85–86, 213, 218, 230, 233, 237, 247–249, 266, 270
Tin-Tan 15
Tinti, Mario 98

Tippett, Phil 221, 282
Toba Volcanic Eruption 185, 201
Todd, Tony 281
Toffolo, Lino 160–161
Tolkan, James 234
Tolo, Marilú 266
Tom and Jerry films 61
Tom Jones 40
Toms, Carl 111
Tong, Stanley 282
Tony Sarg's Almanac 9, 58, 144, 162, 280–281
Tools and Toolmaking, Prehistoric 36, 46, 86, 170, 172, 174, 179, 182, 184–185, 187–189, 195–199, 201–202, 205, 207–209, 237, 251, 271
Toot, Whistle, Plunk and Boom 5, 144–145
Toothache *see* Dental health, Prehistoric
Topper Site (S.C.) 202
Topping, Amanda 263
Torgesson, Eric 99
Torture 42, 44, 48, 109, 141
Tourneur, Jacques 223
Tower of Babel 1
Towers, Derek 199
Tracing Human Origins 197–198
Tracking the First Americans 205–206
Tracy, Spencer 288–289
Trading, Prehistoric 169, 173, 179, 185, 187
Trail of the Neanderthal 197–198
Trampe, Ray 218
Travolta, John 285
Trbovich, Tom 50
The Treasury 206
Trebek, Alex 181
Tredway, Wayne 224
The Tree That Put the Clock Back 206
Treehouses 117
Tremayne, Les 223, 261, 273
Trial in the Jungle 192
Tribal warfare *see* Warfare, Prehistoric
The Tribe 2, 145
The Tribe of Gum (*Dr. Who* episode) 50–52
Trim, Mike 94
Trixie 10
Trog 66, 170, 258, 268–269
"Troglodytes" 3, 253–254, 260, 265, 268–269
Troiano, William G. 233, 261
Trotter, Kathi 48
Troughton, Patrick 230, 259
Trovajoli, Armando 73
Trumbo, Dalton 286
Tsu, Irene 164
Tuck, Mel 263
Tucker, Teri 69
Tufts, Sonny 257
Tugen Hills (Kenya) 203
Tunney, Robin 229
Turan, Süleyman 218

Turkieltaub, Daniel 248
The Turkish Wizard of Oz 218
Turkisher, Art 23
Turn Back the Clock (*Voyage to the Bottom of the Sea* episode) 273
Turner, Kathleen 251
Turner, Otis 279
Turner, Tina 16, 285
Turner, William 153
Turturro, John 14
TV Funhouse 269
Tvaroh, Vaclav 132
'Twas Ever Thus 145–146
12 Days in Dayton: The Scopes Monkey Trial 289
20,000 Years of France 206
Twilight of the Dark Master 90
The Twilight Zone (1959–64) 34, 270
The Twilight Zone (1985–88) 269–270
Twin Peaks: Fire Walk with Me 134
Twist Again 146
Twister 34
Two Arrows 146
Two Rode Together 276
2,000 B.C. 146
2001: A Space Odyssey 2, 4–6, 28, 78, 93, 95–96, 107–108, 111, 125, 127, 147–152, 165, 171, 188, 200, 208, 256, 258, 287
2010 152
The 2,000 Year Old Man 3, 79, 146–147
Tydings, Alexandra 275
Tyrell, Susan 56
Tyrlova, Hermina 184
Tytla, Vladimir 146

Ueda, Shoji 242
Ugala (Proposed film) 113
The Ugly Dino 283
The Ugly Little Boy 5, 270
Uibel, Arvid 129
Ulloa, Alejandro 37, 232
Ulmer, Edgar G. 74
The Ultimate Guide: Ice Man 206
Uncle Crock's Block 270
Undersea Kingdom 74
Underwater archeology 176, 199
Underwater Menace (*Dr. Who* story) 74
An Unearthly Child (*Dr. Who* episode) 50–52
The Universal Flood 288
University of Jakarta 261
Unsworth, Geoffrey 147, 151
Untamed Women 270–271
Up from the Apes 170
UPA Studio 145
The UPA Cartoon Show 154
Upright Man 192
Upton, Nick 75
Urasawa, Yoshio 76
Urban, Karl 165–166
Urbano, Carl 69–70
The Usual Suspects 68

Vaille, David 117
Valcour, Nicolas 185, 195
Valdés, Beatriz 248
Valdés, Germán 15
Valdivia: America's First Civilization 206
Valdivian Culture 206
Vallely, James 12
Valley of Gwangi 113
The Valley of Horses 31
Valley of the Dinosaurs 4–5, 46, 271
Valley of the Dragons 227, 271–273
Vampire Men of the Lost Planet 233
Van Ark, Joan 242
Van der Byl, Philip 254
VanderPyl, Jean 59–60, 64, 66–70, 72, 79–80, 86, 90, 98
Vanders, Warren 145
Van Doren, Mamie 273–274
Van Eltz, Theodore 170
Vanity 265
Van Loon, Hendrik Willem 136
Van Parys, Georges 14
Vanuata Islands 128
Vanzini, Carlo 9
Vanzini, Enrico 9
Vasallo, Carlos 37
Vasquez Rocks 65
Vaughan, Paul 209
Vaughn, Kerry 117
Vaughn, Robert 137–140
Vávra, Bohumil 97, 132, 153
Vazquez, Laura 244
Velarde, Mike 233
Velasquez, Lorena 53
Venable, Ron 12
The Vengeance of She 113, 191
Venora, Diane 267
Veo, Carla 215
Vera-Ellen 248
Vercors 261
Veritas: The Quest 74
Verne, Jules 238, 271–273
Verney, Guy 249
Verno, Jerry 16
Vernon, Howard 206
Vetri, Victoria 44–45, 154, 157–158, 280
Vickers, Mike 216
The Video Griots Trilogy 206
Vidov, Oleg 265
A View to a Kill 113
The Viking Queen 191
Vikings 267–268
Villiers, Berna 196
Vinca Site (Serbia) 194
Vincent, Pascal 130
Vingt Mille Ans a la Francais 206
Virgil, Alicia 137
The Virgin Goddess 117–119
Virgin Report 206
Virtual Encounters 273
Virtual reality (prehistoric people created by virtual reality) 263, 273
Visnjic, Goran 80

Viva Los Vegas! 68
Vogel, Virgil W. 236
Voláni Radu 153
Volante, Vicki 233
Volodin, Aleksandr 146
Von Borsody, Eduard 176
Von Daniken, Erich 176
Von Gunten, Matthias 177
Von Lawick, Hugo 150
Von Sternberg, Josef 246
Von Sternberg, Nicholas 246–247
Von Zerneck, Danielle 247
Voyage to the Bottom of the Sea 273
Voyage to the Planet of Prehistoric Women 223, 273–274, 283
Voyage to the Prehistoric Planet 274, 283
Voyeur, Vince 273
Vrbanic, Ivo 146

Wachsberger, Nat 263
Wacky and Packy 270
Wadey, Maggie 263
Wagner, Chuck 285
Wahan 279
Waites, Thomas G. 29
Wakabayashi, H. Clark 18
Waldo, Janet 90
A Walk Through Time 182, 185
Walkabout 229, 266
Walker, Albert 140–142
Walker, H.M. 70
Walker, Paul 179
Walker, Robert 16, 18
Walker, Robert, Jr. 282
Walking upright *see* Bipedalism
Walking with Beasts 208–209
Walking with Cavemen 5, 207–208
Walking with Dinosaurs 198, 208–209, 245
Walking with Prehistoric Beasts 190, 208–209
Wallace, Andy 147
Wallace, Bill 82, 264
Wallace, Don 263
Wallace, Fay 279
Wallace, Melanie 189
Wallace, Oliver 145
Wallbank, T. Walter 205
Walravens, Jean-Paul 11–13
Walsh, Brian 213
Walsh, David M. 247
Walsh, Harry 162
Walsh, Johnny 162
Walshaw, Julia 245
Walt Disney Presents 145
Walter, Jessica 50
Walter, Tracey 221
Walters, Nancy 247
Walters, Thorley 252–253, 268
Wanamaker, Sam 259
Wanpaku Omukashi Kum-Kum 88
War Gods of the Deep 223
Ward, Anthony 218
Ward, B.J. 59–60, 66, 80

Ward, Jack 71, 136
Ward, Jay 130
Ward, Megan 229
Ward, Tom 245
Ware, Midge 270
Warfare, Prehistoric 3, 12, 19–21, 35, 37, 42–43, 45, 82–85, 107, 124, 127, 147–149, 159, 171, 178, 188, 272
Warlords of Atlantis 74, 216
Warner, Bob 269
Warnock, Grant Ashley 264
Warren, Bill 225, 238
Warren, Dick 137
Warren, Gene 227
Warren, Jerry 49, 236–238, 281
Warren, Kenneth J. 223
Warriors of the Deep (Dr. Who episode) 52
Wars of the Primal Tribes 19–22
Warwick, Norman 223
Water Babies (1985) 209
Water Babies (2001) 209
Water carrying and caching 41, 208
Waterworth, Andrew 178, 184
Watson, Vernee 219, 259
Watters, William 228
Watts, Steve 182
Way, Eileen 50, 52
Way Back When a Nag Was Only a Horse 153
Way Back When a Night Club Was a Stick 153
Way Back When a Raspberry Was a Fruit 153
Way Back When a Triangle Had Its Points 153
Way Back When Women Had Their Weigh 153
Wayne, John 4, 260
Wayne, Patrick 252–253, 259–260
Weapons, Prehistoric 20, 25, 29–30, 36, 43, 51, 57, 73, 78, 82–84, 91, 93–96, 100, 102, 106, 118, 121–122, 148–149, 169–170, 172–174, 177–178, 182, 185–186, 190, 196–198, 202, 209, 237, 252, 275, 283
The Weathering Continent 74, 89, 153
Weatherlee, Pinky 282
Weaver, Tom 223
Webb, Dunstan 282
Webb, Jane 238
Webb, Jimmie 196
Webb, Mary Ann 162
Webber, Roy 181
Weber, Eugen 209
Wedding Belts 153
Wedge, Chris 80–81
Wedgwood, Tony 198
Wehling, Bob 228
Weigall, Michael 183
Weil, Samuel 137
Weinrib, Lenny 59, 114
Weird Science 247
Weisburd, Dan E. 224

Weissmuller, Johnny 238–239
Welch, Bruce 129
Welch, Raquel 4–5, 28, 44–45, 49, 79, 93, 98, 104–105, 108, 111–113, 157–158, 182, 216, 260
Weldon, Michael 99
Welker, Frank 23, 46, 59–60, 66–67, 69–70, 79–80
Welles, Orson 77–78, 127
Wellman, Harold 170
Wells, Dawn 75
Wells, Deborah 234
Wells, H.G. 272, 286
Wells, Sharon 99
Wells, Spencer 189–190, 201
Wertmuller, Lina 160–161
Wescott, David 182
Wescott, Don 177
West, Frederick E. 259
West, Mason 245
Westcoatt, Rusty 239
Western Hemisphere 3–4, 17; *see also* Clovis Culture; Inuit; Paleoindians; Pre-Clovis Cultures
The Western Tradition 209
Westmore, Michael 34
Westo, Ernie 144, 154
What About God? 182, 288
What Killed the Mega-Beasts? 5, 209
What's New, Mr. Magoo 154
Whedon, Joss 1
The Wheel 129–130
Wheels 11–12, 15, 28, 46, 53, 64, 75, 88, 115–116, 130, 137, 220, 271
Whelan, Robert 204
When Clubs Were Clubs 154
When Dinosaurs Ruled the Earth 3–5, 28, 43–44, 107–109, 111–112, 135, 154–159, 194, 221, 253, 280, 282
When Men Carried Clubs and Women played Ding Dong 26, 47, 55, 159–160
When Men Were Men 160
When the Earth Cracked Open (proposed film) 113
When Women Had Tails 3, 26, 160–161
When Women Lost Their Tails 26, 159, 161
When Women Played Ding Dong 159–160
Whitby, Mark 203
White, Adam 198
White, Carol 132, 135
White, Jules 82, 264, 283
White, Vanna 70
White Eagle, Charles 213
White Pongo 274
The White Whale of Mu 89
Whitehead, Mike 48
Whiting, Margaret 259–260
Whitley, William 239
Whitton, John H. 273
Who Built Stonehenge? 209
Who Killed the Iceman? 209

Who Was Adam? 288
Who Were the Gods? 177
Why They Love Cavemen 144, 161–162
Wickham, Saskia 264
Wielemaker, John 276
Wiggins, Lillian 128
Wilcoxon, Henry 145
Wild Women of Wongo 23, 111, 119, 156, 162–164
Wilde, Cornel 232
Wildsmith, Dawn 253
Wiles, Gordon 240
Wiley, Ethan 233
Wilky, L. Guy 9
Willemont, Jacques 191
Williams, Brian 241
Williams, Burt 162
Williams, Catherine 10
Williams, David C. 10
Williams, Frank D. 76
Williams, Guy 242
Williams, John-Michael 49
Williams, Kenneth 220
Williams, Mark 276
Williams, Natasha Estelle 185
Williams, Nathan 180
Williams, Rhys 261
Williams, Robin 5, 13–14
Williams, Robyn 197
Williams, Treat 238
Willies, Jean 238
Willinger, Jason 50
Willis, Susan 267
Willumson, Gail 178
Wilson, Barbara 236
Wilson, Daniel 204
Wilson, David 179
Wilson, Maurice 149
Wilson, Michael J. 80
Wilson, Roy 282
Wilson, Sue 40
Wilson, Ted 10–11
Wilyman, Bob 147
Wind Up Wilma 70
Windmill Hill Culture 196
Windsor, Barbara 22
Wineman, Saul 184
Wines, Halo 205
Wingover Bog Site (Florida) 203
Winston, Stan 232
Winter, Alex 15
Winters, D.D. 265
Winters, Jonathan 64
Wisberg, Aubrey 247
Wisconsin's First People 210
The Wisdom of the Stones: Life in the Neolithic Age 203
Wise, James 199
Wiseman, Debbie 264
Wishbone 286
Wisher, William 267
Witch Without a Broom 164
Wittlinger, Heidi 129–130
The Wizard of Oz 18, 218, 286
Wizards 56
Wladon, Jean 104, 113
Wolbert, Jason 19

Wolcott, James L. 162
Wolf, Mark 169
Wolff, Frank 160–161
Wollter, Sven 267
Wolmark, Nina 128
Wolper, David L. 170, 175, 200
Women *see* Amazons; Battle of the Sexes; Fights between Women; Hair-dragging Scenes; Harems; Kidnapping of Women; Marriage, Prehistoric; Matriarchy; Prostitution; Rape; Women hunters; Women in Prehistoric Art; Women Inventors and Transmitters of Innovations; Women, Status of; Women, Trading and Selling of
Women at the Feast of Demeter 159
The Women Gladiators 140–142
Women hunters 30, 173, 186
Women in Love 214
Women in Prehistoric Art 197
Women Inventors and Transmitters of Innovations 55, 100, 106, 125
Women of the Prehistoric Planet 164–165
Women, Status of 22, 30, 32, 37, 77, 119, 125, 129, 141, 159–162, 176, 186, 193–194, 197, 203, 216, 273–274, 283
Women, Trading and Selling of 42, 45, 114, 161–162, 235
Wonders Sacred and Mysterious 205
Wong, Chen 217
Wood, Ed 99, 238
Wood, Ruth 169
Wooden, Christopher 223
Woodfield, William Read 273
Woodman, Pierre 280
Woods, Frank E. 90
Woods, Richard 147, 150–151
Woodville, Kate 239
Woodward, Alison 10
Woodward, Peter 177–178
Woody Woodpecker 116
The World, a Television History 210
The World Is Not Enough 14
The World of Hammer 191
The World of the Goddess 210
World of the Unknown 175
World Without End 286
The World's Most Mysterious Places: Europe 205
The Worlds of Hammer Lands Before Time doc
Wrangel Island (Siberia) 199
Wright, Evan 229
Wright, Ralph 11
Wrightwood, Geoffrey 267
Wrixon, Maris 274
Wyckoff, Alvin 9
Wyle, George 85
Wylie, Meg 145
Wynn, Tracie 10
Wynorski, Jim 223

X-Files (1998) 165
Xena: Warrior Princess 115, 165–166, 215, 218, 274–276, 283–284

A Yabba Dabba Doo Celebration 64
Yabba Dabba 2 64
Yaltkaya, Cengiz 245
Yamato Culture (Japan) 89–90
Yamazaki, Takashi 76
Yanomana Indians 123
Yared, Petra 238
Yarmolnik, Leonid 146
Year of the Dragon 236
Yeaworth, Irwin S., Jr. 224, 227
Yeaworth, Jean 224, 227
Yesterday's World 276–277
Yob, Enrico 161

Yogi Bear's All-Star Comedy Caper 64
Yojimbo 83
Yokoyama, Hiroyuki 76
Yonaguni Site (Japan) 177, 189
Yor, the Hunter from the Future 286
Yoshida, Yoshiaki 88
You Only Live Twice 141
Young, Carroll 239
Young, Darren 23
Young, Howard 50
Young, Howard Irving 276
Young, Jeremy 50
Young, W. 115
Young at Art (series) 199
Young Frankenstein 126
Younger, Henry 132
Younger, Jack 224

Younger, James 190
Your Show of Shows 85

Zakharov, Valentin 265
Zanuck, Darryl F. 246, 280
Zardoz 286
Zeller, Anne 184
Zeman, Karel 86–87, 273
Zen, Michael 234
Zerbe, Anthony 170
Zimmerman, Linda 204
Zingo, Son of the Sea 277
Zombie 39
Zsigmond, Vilmos 233
Zucco, George 256
Zuccoli, Fausto 159
Zuro, Josiah 136

www.ingramcontent.com/pod-product-compliance
Lightning Source LLC
Chambersburg PA
CBHW081538300426
44116CB00015B/2675